Victory Was Beyond Their Grasp

Victory Was Beyond Their Grasp

With the 272nd Volks-Grenadier Division from the Hürtgen Forest to the Heart of the Reich

by Douglas E. Nash

THE ABERJONA PRESS
Bedford, Pennsylvania

Editor: *Patricia K. Bonn*
Technical Editor: *Edward Miller*
Cartographer: *Tom Houlihan*
Printer: *Mercersburg Printing, Mercersburg, Pennsylvania*

ISBN 10: 0-9777563-2-7
ISBN 13: 978-0-9777563-2-2

On the front cover: Newly-outfitted men of the 272nd Volks-Grenadier Division sing as they march through a German town near the training area at Döberitz, early October 1944. Non-commissioned officers are positioned at the head of the column, followed by each squad's machine gunner shouldering his MG-42.

Except as noted (see below), photos are from the author's collection. Thanks to those who graciously offered the use of their photos.

(Adrario): Fritz Adrario
(Aretz): Helmut Aretz
(CMH): US Army Center of Military History
(eifelmaler.info):
    www.eifelmaler.info/Wollseifen_
    das_tote_Dorf/Bau_der_Urfttalsperre/
    body_bau_der_urfttalsperre.html
(Frey): Erwin Frey
(Fosselmann): Fritz Fosselmann
(Fuhrmeister): Ernst Fuhrmeister
(Gehle): Hermann Gehle
(Gunkel): Otto Gunkel
(Hake): Thomas Hake
(Haslob): Gevert Haslob
(Heckner): Hans Heckner
(Heiermann): Hermann Heiermann
(Hohenstein/Schulz): Adolf Hohenstein,
    courtesy of Klaus Schulz

(Ips): Rudolf Ips
(Johns): Fritz Johns
(Klein): Else Klein
(Klodt): Ralf Klodt
(Moog): Peter Moog
(NA): US National Archives
(Sandmann): Courtesy of Hans-Gerhard
    Sandmann and the 216th/272nd
    Infantry Division Veteran's Association
(Scherzer): Scherzer's Militär Verlag, with
    permission by Herr Scherzer
(Schmidt): Günther Schmidt
(Schulz): Klaus Schulz
(Signal Corps): US Army Signal Corps
(Stefan): Josef Stefan
(Trees): Wolfgang Trees
(Wolfram): Annegret Wolfram
(Zacharuk): Eduard Zacharuk

Contents

Illustrations

Foreword

This book is an attempt by an American historian to describe the experiences of one German Army combat unit during the Second World War and how they fought and died.

As a former commander of *Füsilier Company 272*, although only for a short period of time, I can say that these soldiers, despite the overwhelming odds against them and the technical superiority of the enemy, did as much as humanly possible to carry out their duty.

Like their brothers who served on the Eastern Front, they fought and died for their comrades and to protect their loved ones back home, and not for Hitler and National Socialism.

And like generations of Germans soldiers before them, they served their country honorably and bravely.

May they never be forgotten by younger generations.

May this book serve as a reminder of the horror of war and the suffering that both sides endured as they fought each other in that forest of death—the Hürtgenwald.

Helmut Aretz
Oberleutnant and former commander, *Füsilier Company 272*

Prologue

"Midway upon the journey of our life I found myself within a forest dark, for the straightforward pathway had been lost. Ah me! How hard a thing it is to say what was this forest savage, rough and stern, which in the very thought renews the fear. So bitter is it, death is little more."

Dante Alighieri
Inferno, Cando I
(Longfellow translation)

The Battle of the Hürtgen Forest—known by German veterans as *die Hölle im Hürtgenwald* (the Hell in the Hürtgen Forest), lasted from 12 September 1944, when a costly reconnaissance in force was carried out by the US 3rd Armored Division near the Siegfried Line at Roetgen, until 10 February 1945, when the US 78th Infantry Division secured the Schwammenauel Dam and reached the Roer River.[1] During this five-month period, the German armies defending the Siegfried Line (known to German troops as the *Westwall*), were practically destroyed as an effective fighting force and ended with Allied troops poised to cross the Rhine, the last natural barrier to the heart of Germany.

The fighting was slow and enormously costly in lives and materiel. Losses in the two Allied armies participating in the fighting along the Siegfried Line, the US First and Ninth Armies, were substantial (this does not include the Battle of the Bulge, a separate battle that delayed the outcome in the Hürtgen Forest for nearly two months). All told, during the fighting for the German frontier, First and Ninth Armies lost a combined total of 68,000 men killed, wounded, and missing.

Additionally, the Americans lost another 71,654 men as non-battle casualties, from diverse causes like trench foot, sickness, and battle fatigue, bringing the total number of US casualties in the campaign to nearly 140,000 men.[2] Exact numbers of Germans killed, wounded, and missing during the Siegfried Line campaign are unknown due to the loss of key records, though they were at least as high as those of the Allies. The US First and Ninth Armies reported capturing over 95,000 Germans during this period alone.

American battle casualties within the ten divisions (seven infantry, one airborne, two armored, plus elements of another) and supporting units that took part at one time or another in the Hürtgen Forest portion of the Siegfried Line campaign totaled 33,000 men, more than twenty-five percent of the troops engaged, an extremely high figure by US Army standards at the time. The U.S. suffered some 24,000 killed, wounded and missing. In addition, another 9,000 were classified as being evacuated under the Disease, Non-battle Injury (DNBI) category. German losses were at least equally as great. Since German units were fighting at reduced strengths to begin with, their percentage of casualties was correspondingly higher. Many German divisions were virtually wiped out, only to be hastily rebuilt and committed to battle in the forest and destroyed again.

In all, during this five-month period, some 140,000 U.S. troops faced off against 80,000 Germans in the Hürtgen Forest, on some of the most brutal battlefields ever faced by soldiers of any nation during that war. It was a struggle that measured ground gained in yards, not miles.[3] Unlike the rapid Allied advance across France and the Low Countries in the late summer and fall of 1944, the Battle of the Hürtgen Forest became a slugfest. The fighting there had much more in common with trench warfare in World War I than the "modern" mechanized war, or *Blitzkrieg,* that evolved during World War II.

The Battle of the Hürtgen Forest witnessed dogged defensive fighting by the Germans and equally determined Allied assaults. It was characterized by battles for key towns such as Schmidt and Kesternich, and for objectives hidden in the seemingly endless forest, such as Dead Man's Moor (the *Todtenbruch*) and the Raffelsbrand hunter's lodge. Interrupted by Germany's last-ditch offensive in the Ardennes, WACHT AM RHEIN, that became better known as the Battle of the Bulge, the large-scale fighting in the Hürtgen resumed again with added ferocity on 30 January 1945, when the US First and Ninth Armies were finally able to begin the long-delayed operation to capture the Roer River Dams, which finally fell on 10 February 1945.

During the course of this final phase of the Siegfried Line campaign, the Allies, operating from a position of strategic advantage and employing numerical superiority combined with overwhelming firepower, steadily ground down the weary German defenders. By March 1945, the entire portion of the *Wehrmacht* that fought on the Western Front had become reduced to nothing more than an enormous *Alarmeinheit* (emergency unit), composed of a polyglot of various Army, Air Force, Navy, Labor Service, *Volkssturm,* and *Waffen-SS* units, all invariably hastily thrown together, poorly trained, unfit, and increasingly unmotivated to fight to the last for their *Führer.*

The Allied success in the Hürtgen Forest and along the length of the Siegfried Line paved the way for the even more successful Rhineland campaign, which began at the end of February 1945. In the space of less than two weeks, both the 12th and 21st Army Groups were able to overwhelm the German defenses along the Roer and had closed up to the western bank of the Rhine by 10 March. Seizure of the bridge at Remagen by First Army on 7 March marked the beginning of the end of the *Wehrmacht's* attempts to defend in the west. By the third week of April, the German war effort had almost entirely collapsed and American troops would shake hands with their Red Army counterparts on the bank of the Elbe.

Even the bravest efforts of the individual German soldier came to naught as it only served to prolong a war that Germany had already lost in a strategic sense by 1943. Thousands upon thousands of these men were senselessly sacrificed to hold meaningless towns, bunkers, and fortresses, dying alone or by the hundreds. While the steadfast defense of the *Westwall* initially slowed the Allies during the fall and winter of 1944/45, this temporary success ironically paved the way for the great Soviet advances in the East from January to April 1945.

Hitler gambled and lost when he diverted Germany's dwindling military strength to the West, first to stop the Allies' Normandy invasion, then to launch the ill-fated Ardennes Offensive. His focus on the Western Front made him squander his remaining reserves just when they were needed the most in the east. As a result, the *Ostfront* (Eastern Front) was thinly manned and unprepared to hold back the Soviet juggernaut that relentlessly swept into Berlin by the end of April 1945 and ended a war that Hitler had started five and a half years earlier.

Today, few people understand why the average German soldier did not simply quit and go home. Fewer still can understand what kept him in the line, facing catastrophic losses that reduced companies, battalions, and even regiments to burned-out remnants in the space of a few days. Was the German soldier merely a benumbed robot by this stage of the war or a die-hard fanatic driven by desperation? Was it blind loyalty to Hitler that made them willingly sacrifice themselves in order to prolong a war that they had no hope of winning?

While answering "yes" to these questions provides a convenient explanation that many military historians frequently use today to highlight the moral and martial superiority of Allied troops to those of the Third Reich, it simply does not stand up to close scrutiny. More useful to this debate is to just state that the average German soldier was far more complex and the reasons why he fought—and fought so well—still defy easy categorization.

Increasingly, historians, and students of World War II want to know more details and pose more questions about the German soldier and why he fought. They want to know more about his daily existence, such as what was it like to live and to fight under these clearly hopeless circumstances and how he felt about it. In this vein, it is also worth asking the question: what was it like for the ordinary *Landser* (German slang for an ordinary infantryman) to fight in the hell of the Hürtgen Forest, or survive in the whirlwind battles in the Rhineland? The Hürtgen Forest was a battle, after all, where soldiers of both sides fought over trench lines and bunkers like their fathers had in the First World War. That such curiosity exists today belies the fact that military historians, both young and old alike, do not have a good appreciation for what it was like for the average German soldier who fought there, or for his American opponent, for that matter.

The American experience in the Battle of the Hürtgen Forest and in the Rhineland is well documented by such works as the US Army's Office of Military History's *The Siegfried Line Campaign*, by Charles B. MacDonald, who was an actual participant in the fighting, having fought with the 2nd Infantry Division, and his follow-up study, *The Last Offensive*.[4] Another seminal work, also by MacDonald, was *Three Battles: Arnaville, Altuzzo, and Schmidt*, which was commissioned by the US Army to determine why each of these particular World War Two battles was a success or failure and what timeless lessons could be drawn for tomorrow's leaders.[5] Added to these superb US Army official accounts are other recent works, quite detailed and informative, that are replete with first-hand accounts and situation reports from the archives. Works such as Edward G. Miller's *A Dark and Bloody Ground*, Gerald Astor's *The Bloody Forest,* and Cecil B. Currey's *Follow Me and Die* contributed immensely to the body of literature about the fighting, relying heavily on memoirs and interviews with American participants.

In contrast, there have been few contemporary official German accounts to provide balance, with the notable exception of Wolfgang Trees and Adolf Hohenstein's *Die Hölle in Hürtgenwald* and Gevert Haslob's *Ein Blick zurück in der Eifel.*[6] Kurt Kaeres, another eminent German author and participant in the battle, also published a fictional work describing some of his own experiences that received wide acclaim in Germany, *Das Verstummte Hurra* (The Muted Cheer). German popular accounts of the Rhineland campaign are even sparser, limited to Helmuth Euler's *Entscheidung an Rhein und Ruhr 1945* and Edgar Christoffel's *Krieg am Westwall 1944/45.* A serious study of that campaign from a military perspective has yet to appear, though Heinz Günther Guderian's *Das Letzte Kriegsjahr im Western* admirably covers that phase of the war from the perspective of the *116th Panzer Division.*

Contributing to the lack of detailed knowledge of the German situation at the tactical level, many official German reports and unit daily journals were lost, destroyed, or misplaced after the war. The *Bundeswehr*, modern Germany's successor to the *Wehrmacht*, has also yet to write the definitive official account of the Siegfried Line campaign, though it did commission a comprehensive study in the mid-1970s that was quietly shelved before it was scheduled to go to print.[7] Perhaps the scars, even 60 years later, are still too fresh for most German veterans, whose generation is passing away without sharing its experiences with children or grandchildren. Accounts from those who took part in the fighting can still be found, but most of what they wrote has remained unpublished or was captured briefly in post-war veteran's association newsletters. Most of these stories are not available to the general public and few have been translated. Locating these survivors' accounts requires diligence akin to finding a needle in a haystack.

And while these few personnel accounts are useful, without official German studies or documents to guide their work, they are insufficient for historical purposes. They lack detail from a tactical or operational perspective, though do succeed in bringing to light the experiences of the average soldier. Thus, no study yet has attempted, from the German perspective, to marry the *Alltagsgeschichte* (the history of everyday life) of the battle with official records. Now, for the first time, such records have been uncovered that show the impact of the fighting on a certain German company-sized unit that fought for nearly five months in the Hürtgen Forest and the Rhineland, from both a human and tactical perspective. This book, then, in the story of that company.

Acknowledgments

When I first began work on this book in the summer of 2000 while stationed in Heidelberg, I thought it would practically write itself. The wealth of original company documents I obtained from Emilie C. Stewart in 1993 seemed like more than enough material for a book. That was true, up to a point. I thought that the records provided everything needed to tell the story of *Füsilier Company 272*, but the more work progressed, the more it became apparent that I could not write about this one company without writing the history of its parent division, the *272nd Volks-Grenadier Division.* Once the decision was made to broaden the scope of the book, things began to get complicated. At first glance there was very little to work with except the division's history put together after the war by one of its former artillery battalion commanders, the inestimable Martin Jenner. His book focused primarily the division's predecessor, the *216th Infantry Division* until it was disbanded in December 1943. Less than one twentieth of Jenner's book dealt with the *272nd Volks-Grenadier Division* and the last six months of the war. Therefore, I enlisted the voluntary cooperation of a number of historians, many of them recognized authorities on the Battle of the Hürtgen Forest and the German Army of WWII, to help fill in the gaps. The Internet, only now beginning to realize its full potential, also proved to be a boon, directing me to reliable sources that I would never have considered even ten years ago. Despite a break in work brought about by a tour of duty in Afghanistan from 2001 to 2002, I was able to resume work in earnest in 2004. So here, after many twists and turns, is the final product.

I would first like to acknowledge the contributions of Edward G. Miller and Klaus Schulz, who first convinced me to write the book and directed me towards a wealth of source materials or at least where I could find them. Following their advice, while still stationed in Heidelberg I contacted French MacLean, Colonel, US Army (Retired), Dr. Stephen L. Bowman, and Hans-Gerhard Sandmann, the President of the 216th/272nd Infantry/Volks-Grenadier Division Veterans' Association. Their advice led to further contacts, and this put me in touch with the 78th Infantry Division Veterans' Association, the 8th Infantry Division Association, and Ray Fleig of the 707th Tank Battalion Association.

The 78th Infantry Division Veterans' Association proved to be a gold mine, not only because it publicized my search for survivor interviews, but also provided me with more original source material than I could profitably use. To the following members of these Associations I am extremely grateful: from the 78th Infantry Division Veterans' Association Edward Malouf, John "Robbie" Robinson, Hermann "Red" Gonzalez, William "Bill" Parsons (Editor of *The Flash*), Stan Polny, Frank Camm (Lieutenant General, US Army Retired), James L. Cooper, Melvie Gilbert, Robert L. Greivell, the late Gus E. Hank, B. C. Henderson, W. Merle Hill, Robert A. McChord, John K. Rains; from the 8th Infantry

Division Association, Albert H. Clayton, Merrill B. "Westy" Westhoff, and Walt Landry; and Don Lavender from the 9th Infantry Division Association.

In the United States I would like to acknowledge the help and advice of a number of historians and researchers, including Richard Anderson; Robert Applegate; Jon Bocek; Robert D. Burgess; Greg Canellis; Frederick L. Clemens; Stephen Ehlers; Hugh Foster; Jeff Gowen; Mike Hamidy; Brad Hubbard; David P. Hunter, Jason Long; Michael Miller; Alex Moore, John Mulholland; George Petersen; Jason Pipes; Justin Smith; Major Charles Smith, US Army; Barry Smith; Christian Stock; William A. Stofft, Major General, USA (Ret.); Eric Tobey; Richard L. Baker and the staff of the US Army Military History Institute, Carlisle, PA; the US National Archives; and the dedicated members of the re-enacted 11th Panzer Division.

Special thanks are due to Thomas McKnight, whose forthcoming book about his father's experience at Kesternich as a member of the 78th Infantry Division and the captivity that followed stimulated both of our research efforts. His hard work in translating documents, making maps, and chasing down leads has been a boon and I hope that my assistance to him has been of equal value. I would also like to thank Mrs. Marilee P. Meyer of the Association of Graduates, United States Military Academy, who performed research on several graduates of that noble institution whose paths crossed with that of the 272nd Volks-Grenadier Division.

In Europe, I would like to thank the following historians and researchers for their gracious assistance: Christoph Awender of Sweden; Piet Duits of Oudenbosch, The Netherlands; Veit Scherzer and Manfred von Freiesleben of Scherzer's Militaire-Verlag of Ranis, Germany; Hubert Gees of the Veterans Association, *275th Infanterie-Division;* Timm Haasler of Germany; Gevert Haslob of the *89th Infantry Division Veterans Association;* Heinrich Heckner of Falkensee, Germany; Ralf Klodt of Germany; Volker Lossner of Aachen, Germany; Alex Moore of Leicestershire, UK; Dr. Leo Niehorster; Hans Peulen, Germany; Ron van Rijt of The Netherlands; Ingrid Roux of Heidelberg, Germany; Ralf Anton Schäfer of Germany; Christian Schwinghammer of Stockholm, Sweden; Brigitte Sebald of Heidelberg, Germany; Wolfgang Trees of Triangle Verlag, Germany; Andries Verspeeten of Ghent, Belgium; Hans H. Weber of Switzerland; Jakob Weiler of Hönningen, Germany; Marcus Wendel of Sweden; Annegret Wolfram of Wildbad in Schwartzwald, Germany; and Niklas Zetterling of Germany.

I also wish to acknowledge of the help of this men whom this book is about— the veterans of the *272nd Volks-Grenadier Division*, most especially Friedrich Adrario of Vienna, Austria; Helmut Aretz of Krefeld; Erich Bernutz, of Wernigerode; Helmut Beyer of Göttingen; Erwin Buchwalder of Storkow; Günter Ecker of Herschweiler; Friedrich Fosselmann of Berg; Adolf Fuhrmeister, brother of Hermann Fuhrmeister of Süpplingen; Ernst Fuhrmeister, son of Hermann Fuhrmeister of Bremen; Hermann Gehle of Heilbronn; Erwin Gläsig of Berlin; Otto Gunkel of Bad Sooden; the late Kurt Hake of Düsseldorf; Hermann Heiermann of Dinslaken; Gerd Hörner, of Wuppertal; Frau Maria Horstkotte, widow of Heinrich Horstkotte of Kirchlengern; Rudolf Ips of Gifhorn; the late Fritz Johns of Stendahl; Herbert Kaiser of Schwanebeck; Frau Else Klein, widow of Kurt Klein of Solingen; Heinrich Misskampf of Nauheim; Erich Möckel of Mannichswalde; Peter Moog of Bonn; Frau Erna Ortloff, widow of Harald Ortloff of Rudolstadt; Günther Peukert of Gera; Ferdinand Post of Hamm; Günther Schmidt of Hameln; Josef Stefan of Baden, Austria; Frau Irene Thiele, widow of Friedrich Thiele of Zeimendorf; the late Adolf Thomae of München; Hans Wegener of Hilden, Frau Anna Winkler, widow of Karl Winkler of Trippstadt; Wilfried Wilts of Emden; and last, but certainly not least, Eduard Zacharuk of Taufkirchen.

No acknowledgment would be complete without mentioning the help and forbearance of my wife, Jill, and children, Douglas Jr., Drew, and Deanna. Their tolerance of the seemingly endless days and nights I spent in researching and writing this book is a constant source of wonder and for which I am extremely grateful. While they showed these same admirable qualities during the writing of my first book, *Hell's Gate: The Battle of the Cherkassy Pocket*, the demands of this book took them "above and beyond the call of duty." A move from Europe to the United States, a war, a move to Virginia, and another war all added to the normal stresses and strains a family goes through and they have once again proven that a military family can put up with almost anything! My love and thanks to you all.

Lastly, I would like to thank the late Keith E. "Kit" Bonn of The Aberjona Press. It was he who saw the value of my manuscript and urged me beyond my original goal of covering just *Füsilier Company 272* and elevating it to a study of the *Volks-Grenadier* divisions as a tactical and historical concept. Kit, this one's for you.

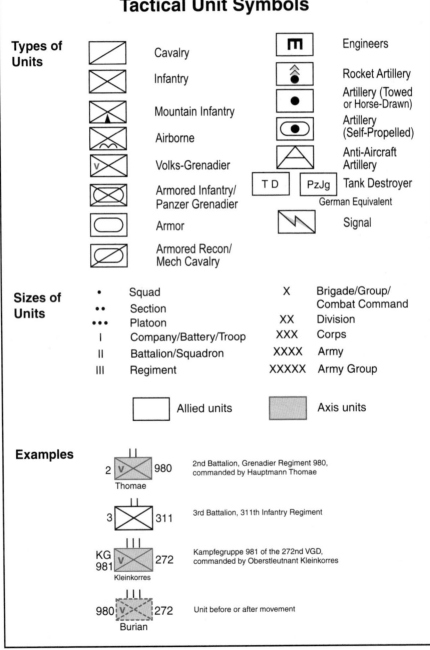

Tactical Unit Symbols

Types of Units

- Cavalry
- Infantry
- Mountain Infantry
- Airborne
- Volks-Grenadier
- Armored Infantry/ Panzer Grenadier
- Armor
- Armored Recon/ Mech Cavalry

- Engineers
- Rocket Artillery
- Artillery (Towed or Horse-Drawn)
- Artillery (Self-Propelled)
- Anti-Aircraft Artillery
- Tank Destroyer — T D | PzJg | German Equivalent
- Signal

Sizes of Units

•	Squad	X	Brigade/Group/ Combat Command
••	Section	XX	Division
•••	Platoon	XXX	Corps
I	Company/Battery/Troop	XXXX	Army
II	Battalion/Squadron	XXXXX	Army Group
III	Regiment		

- Allied units
- Axis units

Examples

2 [V] 980 — Thomae
2nd Battalion, Grenadier Regiment 980, commanded by Hauptmann Thomae

3 [X] 311
3rd Battalion, 311th Infantry Regiment

KG 981 [V] 272 — Kleinkorres
Kampfegruppe 981 of the 272nd VGD, commanded by Oberstleutnant Kleinkorres

980 [V] 272 — Burian
Unit before or after movement

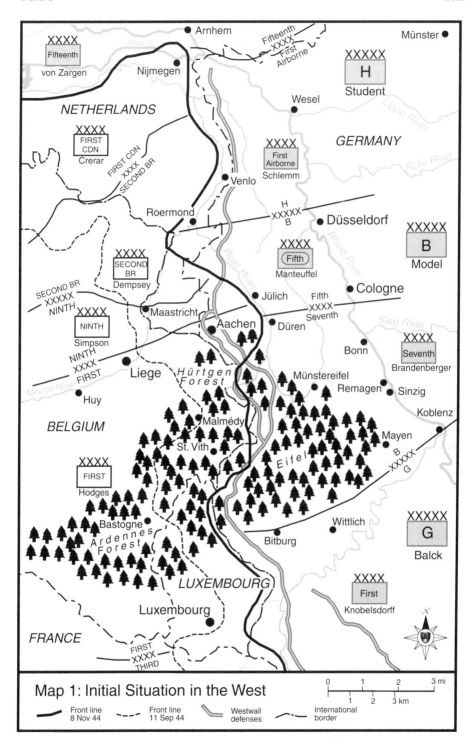

Map 1: Initial Situation in the West

Front line 8 Nov 44	Front line 11 Sep 44	Westwall defenses	International border

0   1   2   3 mi
1   2   3 km

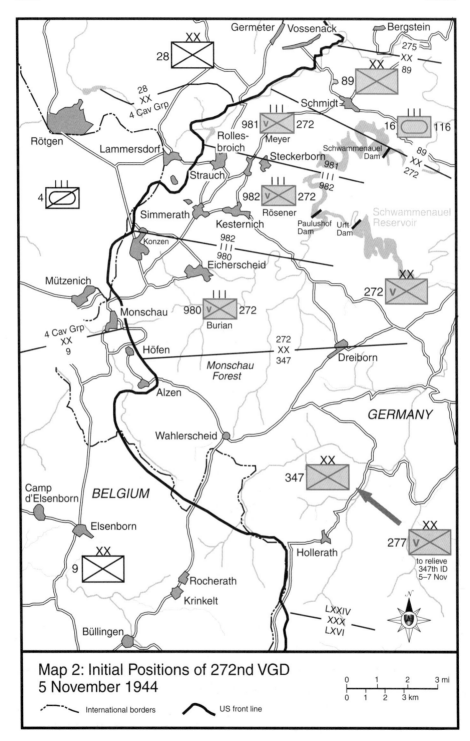

Map 2: Initial Positions of 272nd VGD
5 November 1944

- · - · - International borders   ━━━ US front line

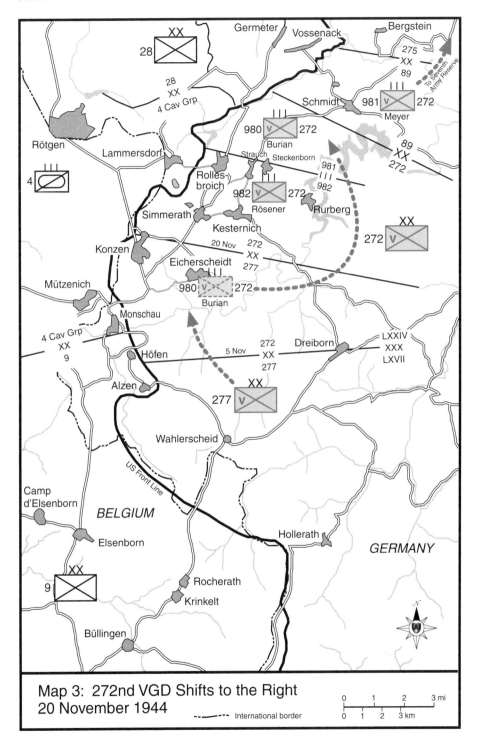

Map 3: 272nd VGD Shifts to the Right
20 November 1944

- - - · - - - International border

0   1   2   3 mi
0   1   2   3 km

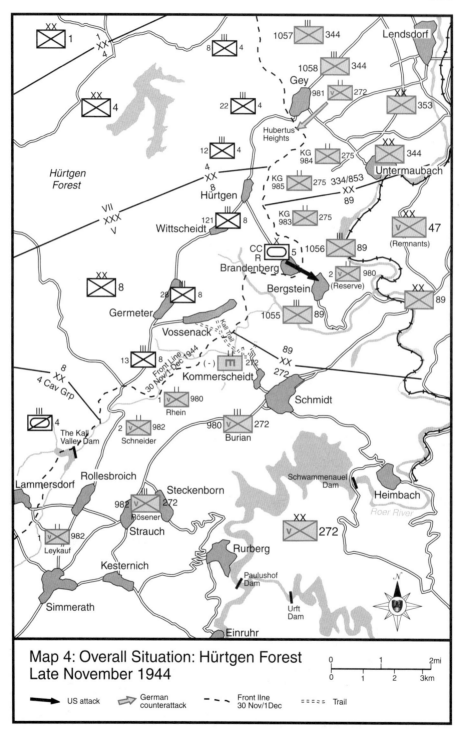

Map 4: Overall Situation: Hürtgen Forest
Late November 1944

0		1		2mi
0	1	2		3km

➡ US attack   ⇨ German counterattack   - - - Front line 30 Nov/1 Dec   ===== Trail

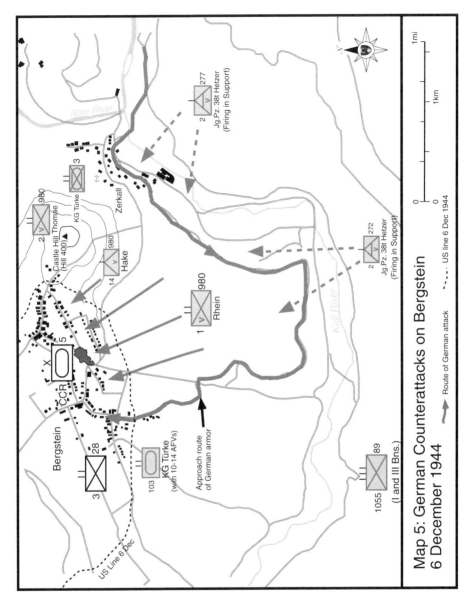

Map 5: German Counterattacks on Bergstein
6 December 1944

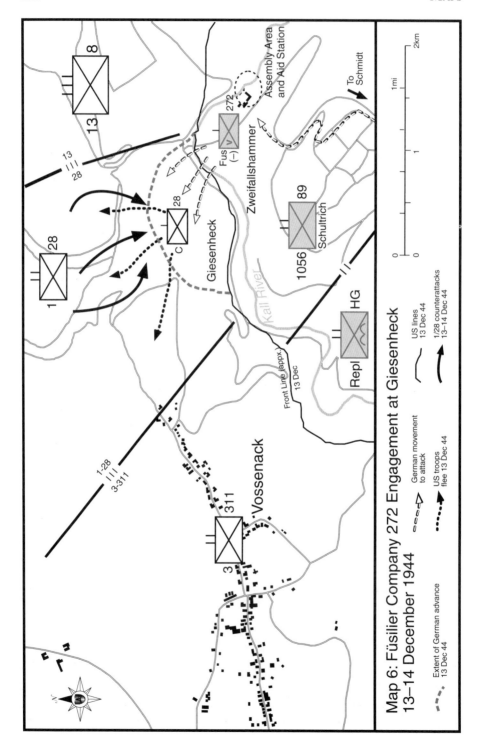

Map 6: Füsilier Company 272 Engagement at Giesenheck
13–14 December 1944

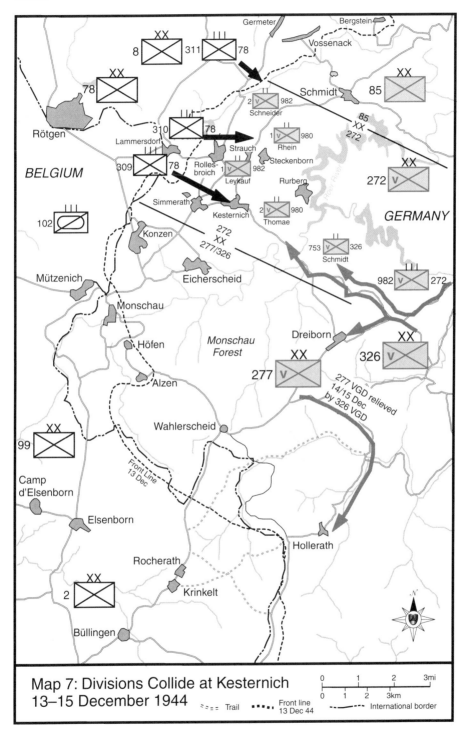

Map 7: Divisions Collide at Kesternich
13–15 December 1944

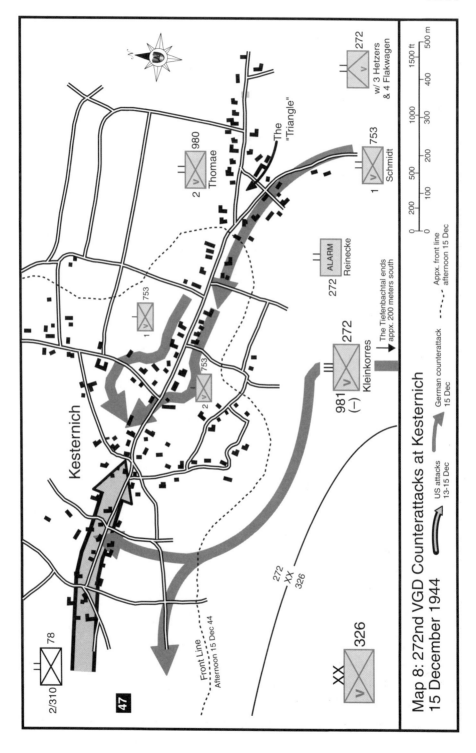

Map 8: 272nd VGD Counterattacks at Kesternich
15 December 1944

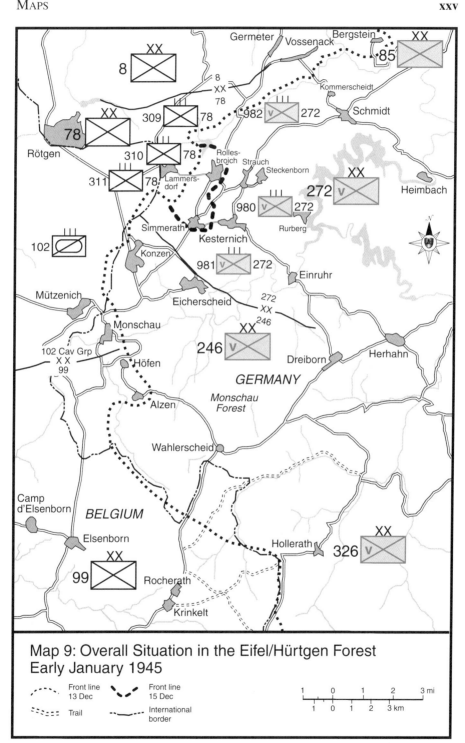

Map 9: Overall Situation in the Eifel/Hürtgen Forest
Early January 1945

Front line 13 Dec	Front line 15 Dec	
Trail	International border	

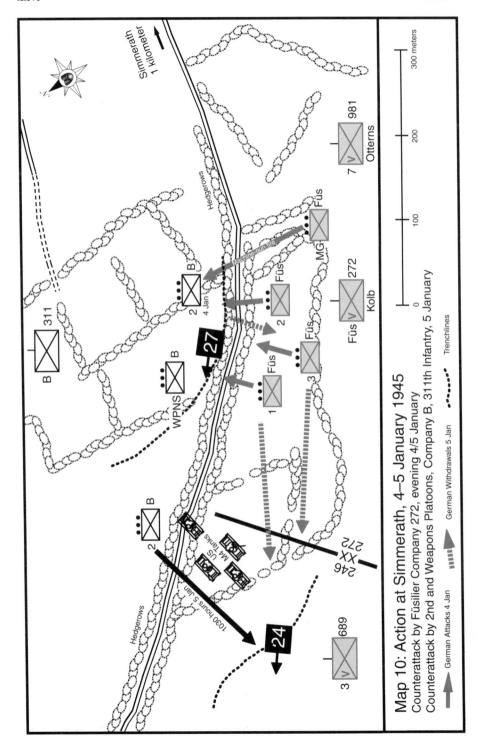

Map 10: Action at Simmerath, 4–5 January 1945

Counterattack by Füsilier Company 272, evening 4/5 January
Counterattack by 2nd and Weapons Platoons, Company B, 311th Infantry, 5 January

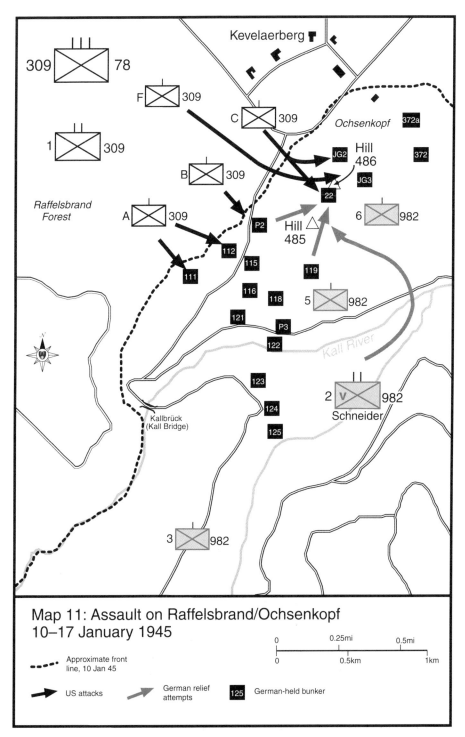

Map 11: Assault on Raffelsbrand/Ochsenkopf
10–17 January 1945

0   0.25mi   0.5mi

0   0.5km   1km

- - - - -   Approximate front
            line, 10 Jan 45

➤   US attacks   ➤   German relief
                          attempts   [125]   German-held bunker

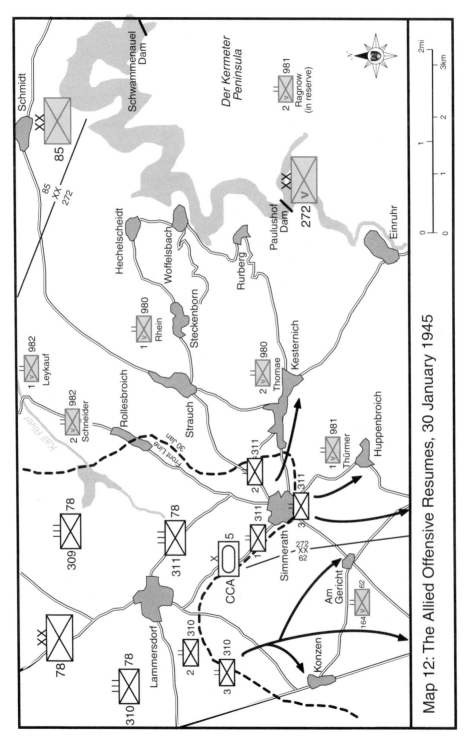

Map 12: The Allied Offensive Resumes, 30 January 1945

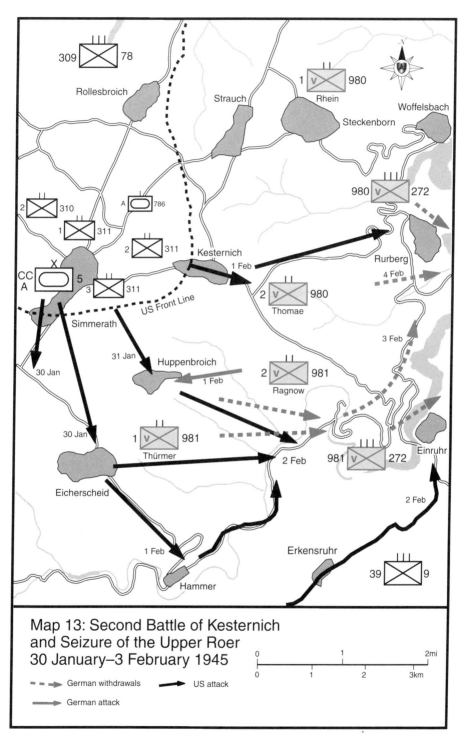

Map 13: Second Battle of Kesternich
and Seizure of the Upper Roer
30 January–3 February 1945

German withdrawals   US attack

German attack

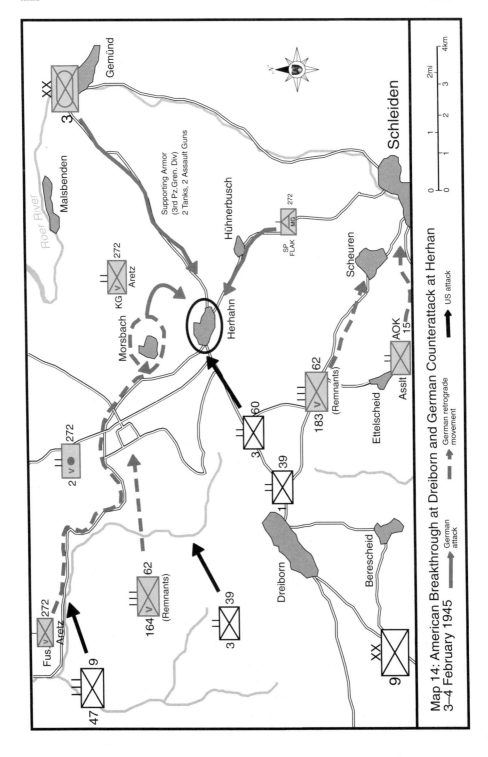

Map 14: American Breakthrough at Dreiborn and German Counterattack at Herhan
3–4 February 1945

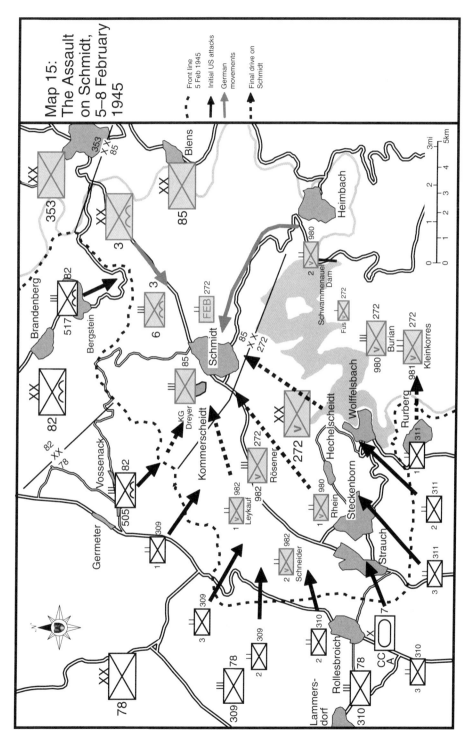

Map 15:
The Assault
on Schmidt,
5–8 February
1945

Front line
5 Feb 1945

Initial US attacks

German
movements

Final drive on
Schmidt

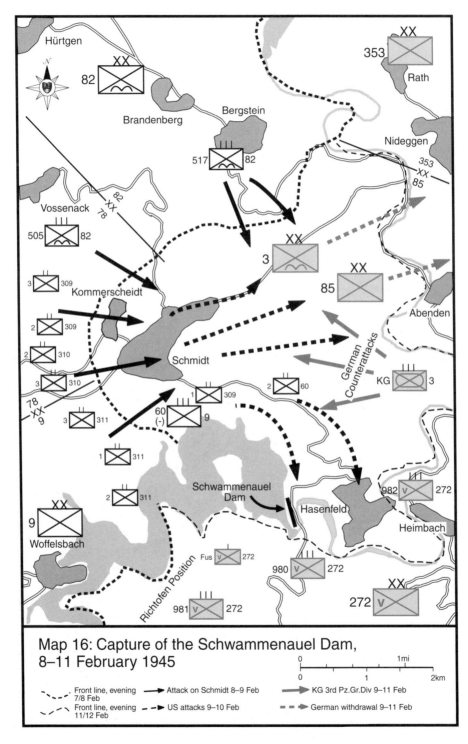

Map 16: Capture of the Schwammenauel Dam,
8–11 February 1945

0   1mi

0   1   2km

········ Front line, evening   ⟶ Attack on Schmidt 8–9 Feb   ⟹ KG 3rd Pz.Gr.Div 9–11 Feb
          7/8 Feb

＿ ＿ ＿ Front line, evening   ⇢⇢ US attacks 9–10 Feb   ⇒ ⇒ German withdrawal 9–11 Feb
          11/12 Feb

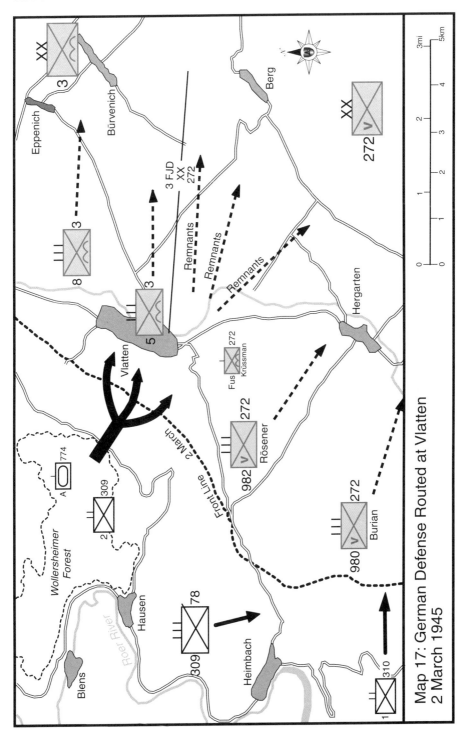

Map 17: German Defense Routed at Vlatten
2 March 1945

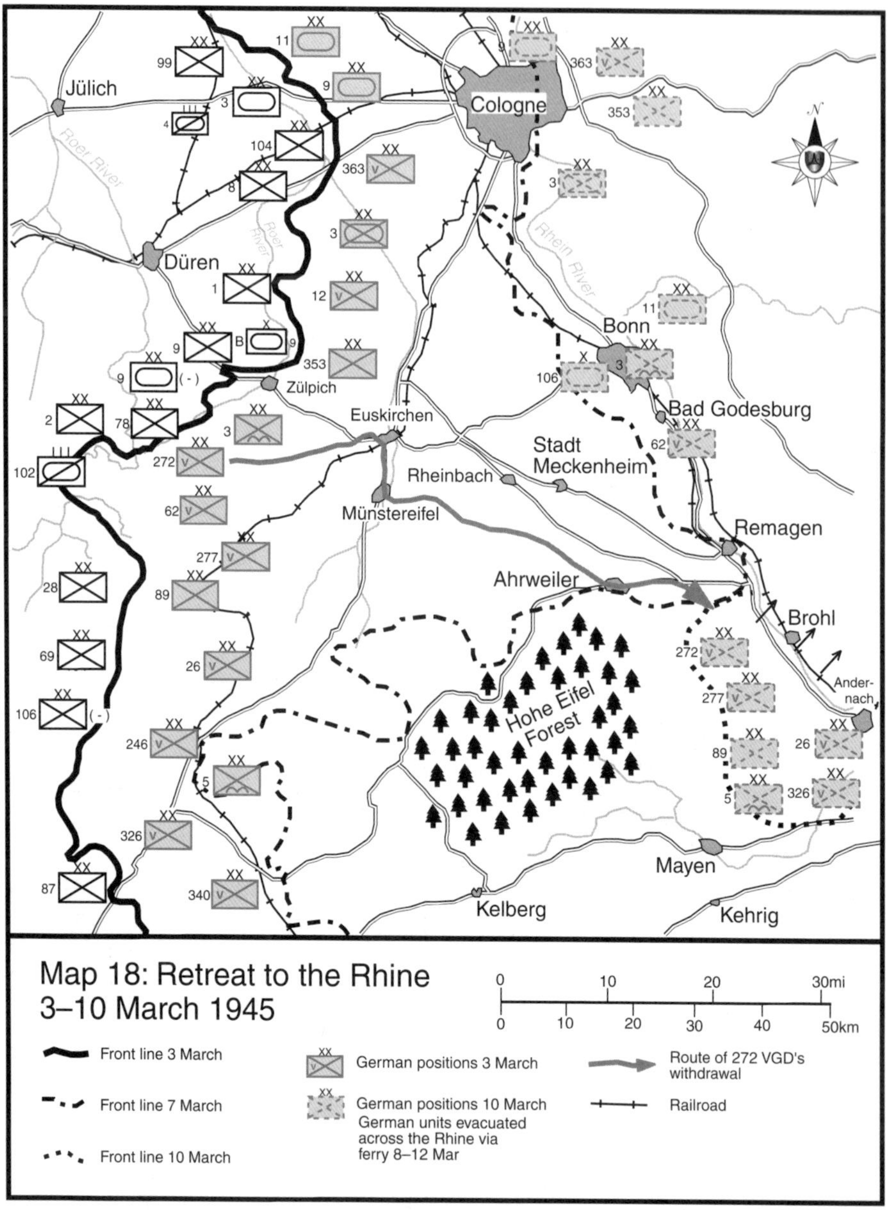
Jülich
Roer River
Düren
Roer River
Zülpich
Cologne
Rhein River
Bonn
Bad Godesburg
Euskirchen
Stadt Meckenheim
Rheinbach
Münstereifel
Remagen
Ahrweiler
Brohl
Andernach
Hohe Eifel Forest
Mayen
Kelberg
Kehrig
N
0 10 20 30mi
0 10 20 30 40 50km
Front line 3 March
Front line 7 March
Front line 10 March
German positions 3 March
German positions 10 March
German units evacuated across the Rhine via ferry 8–12 Mar
Route of 272 VGD's withdrawal
Railroad

Map 18: Retreat to the Rhine 3–10 March 1945

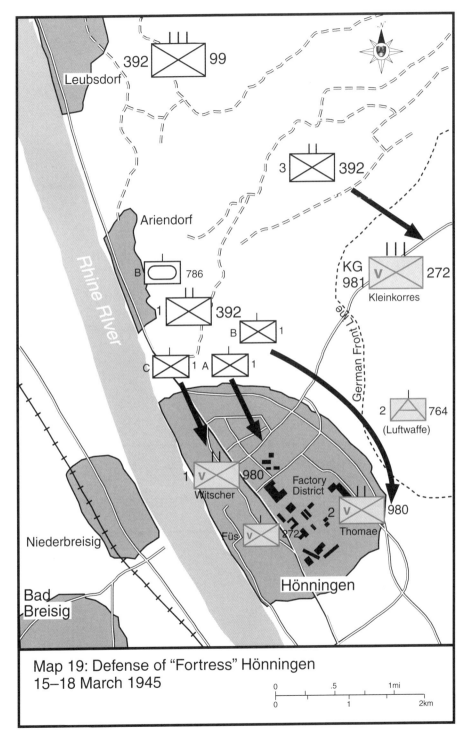

Map 19: Defense of "Fortress" Hönningen
15–18 March 1945

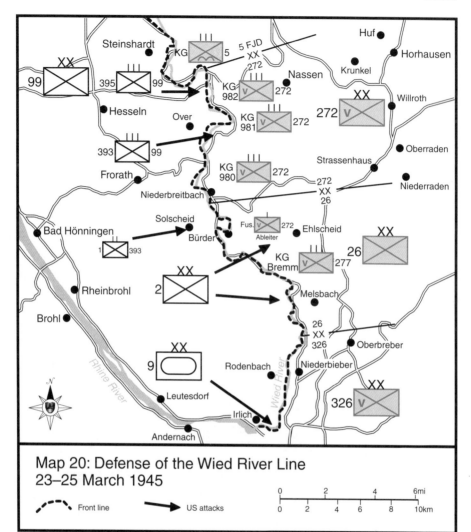

Map 20: Defense of the Wied River Line
23–25 March 1945

- – – – – – Front line
- ➤ US attacks

0   2   4   6mi
0   2   4   6   8   10km

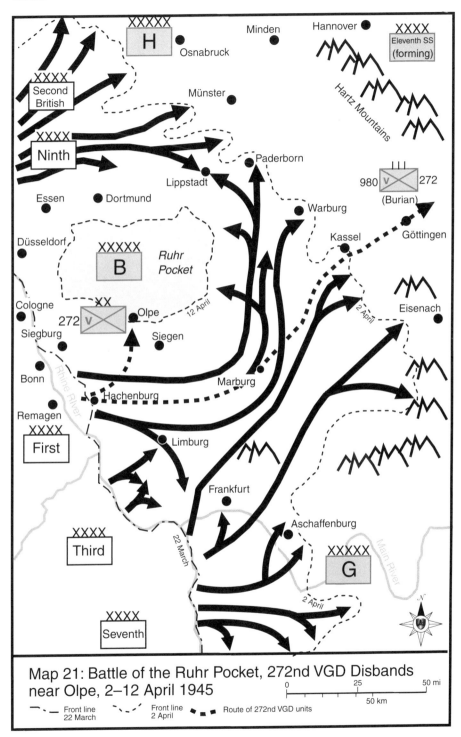

Map 21: Battle of the Ruhr Pocket, 272nd VGD Disbands
near Olpe, 2–12 April 1945

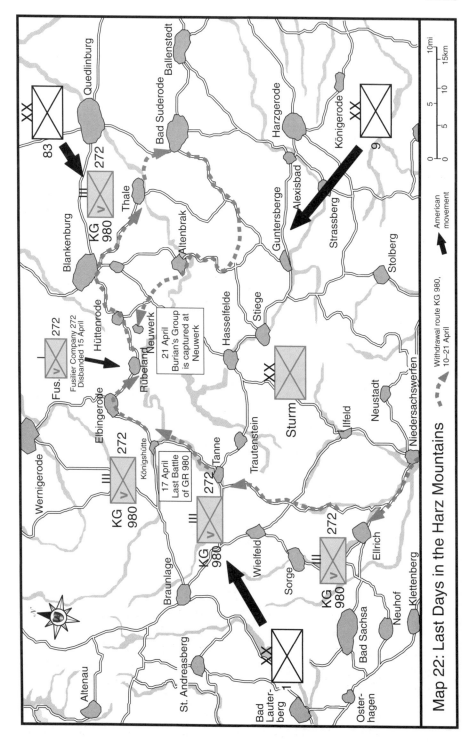

Map 22: Last Days in the Harz Mountains

1

The Story of a Suitcase

The origins of this book can be traced to the acquisition of a remarkable set of documents that illustrate, from a German perspective, what happened to the lowest tactical building block in any army—the infantry company—from the Battle of the Hürtgen Forest, through the Rhineland and into the heart of the Third Reich. From such building blocks, like the infantry company that serves as the focus of this book, battalions, then regiments, and finally entire divisions are made.

While operational records from hundreds of American companies, battalions, regiments, and even individual soldier post-combat interviews are still kept on file in the US National Archives and at the US Army Military History Institute at Carlisle, Pennsylvania, few comparable German records survived the war. Many were deliberately destroyed on orders, while many other documents were abandoned during the *Wehrmacht's* long retreat or claimed by the elements. Locating any group of German company-level documents, therefore, is a rare find indeed.

The document grouping used in the writing of this book came into the author's hands through a roundabout way. In late 1992, Emilie Caldwell Stewart, an American military relics dealer who specialized in German World War II identity documents, ran an advertisement to buy *Wehrpässe* (military identity books) and *Soldbücher* (paybooks) in *Sammler Journal,* a well-known German collectors publication.

Shortly thereafter, she received a letter from a gentleman living in what was the former communist German Democratic Republic, which had reunited with West Germany in 1989 at the end of the Cold War. He wrote that he lived in the village of Tanne, located to the south of the town of Wernigerode in the Harz Mountains of Thuringia. He stated that he had 163 identity documents as well as thousands of other related papers for sale. She immediately accepted and worked out the terms with the seller, agreeing to travel to Germany to complete the transaction.

In early February 1993, Miss Stewart arrived at the seller's tiny village consisting of about twenty houses with unpaved streets that was perched on the side of the mountain. A more rural setting in the former East Germany could not be imagined. The seller lived in a communal house with five other families, sharing the kitchen and living room with the others. The house had once been the home of the champion skier of that area, who had retired and moved away some years before.

The skier had apparently been a *Gebirgsjäger,* or mountain trooper. Miss Stewart bought one of his beautifully carved chairs adorned with *Edelweiss,* his

1

skis, and his photo album. The seller had apparently been using the dirt-floored basement of the house to store antiques he had bought at local auctions. When the original owner of the suitcase died (apparently he was a fellow resident of the same communal home), the seller discovered it in the basement and took ownership. The seller named his price for the suitcase and Miss Stewart bought it.

The moldering suitcase, which had apparently contained the complete *Kompanie Schreibstube,* or company orderly room files and documents for a German infantry company, had been left behind in the farmhouse near the war's end and forgotten when the company moved on. Mrs. Stewart was amazed to discover the variety of its contents—identity papers, pay books, binders filled with casualty reports, mail logs, various correspondence, and even the reporting book or infamous *Kohlenkasten* ("coalbox") of the company *Spiess* (first sergeant). In short, nearly every scrap of official paper this company had carried along with it since its creation in September 1944 until the middle of April 1945 was contained therein. While the suitcase itself was quickly discarded due to its rotten condition, she realized that its contents were of great historical significance.

For some obscure reason, the *Kompanie Schreiber* (company clerk) continued to carry the suitcase full of documents and office supplies to the war's end, perhaps out of loyalty or a sense of duty, long past the point when it no longer mattered. As such, this was not only a great historical find, but an archeological find as well. In this moldy suitcase, figuratively frozen in amber, one could trace a single German infantry company's path through virtually the entire Siegfried Line Campaign and beyond—from the Battle of the Hürtgen Forest to the crossing of the Rhine River to the surrender of the encircled German forces in the Harz Pocket—from early November 1944 to mid-April 1945.

By studying the suitcase's contents, one could easily glean details such as daily losses, after-action reports, letters to next of kin, letters from hospitals describing the disposition of evacuated wounded, letters from anxious loved ones or next of kin inquiring about the fates of their sons, fathers, brothers, husbands, . . . it was all there. Unfortunately, the original owner of the suitcase was never named, though he undoubtedly had some connection with *Füsilier Company 272.*

The papers and documents she discovered all related to *Füsilier Company 272,* a special unit assigned to the *272nd Volks-Grenadier Division (VGD).* Created in September 1944 from the remnants of *Füsilier Battalion 272,* which had been all but destroyed in Normandy the previous month, *Füsilier Company 272* was to function as the division's *Aufklärungs* (reconnaissance company). It actually served as the division's *Feuerwehr* (fire brigade, or quick reaction force), used for emergency situations that demanded hard-hitting, mobile, and well-led units.

Füsilier Company 272 fought in the Battle of the Hürtgen Forest, the northern shoulder during the Battle of the Bulge, around the Roer River dams, the retreat across the Rhine, and was nearly trapped in the Ruhr Pocket. There, the bulk of the *272nd VGD* was finally forced to capitulate, along with the rest of *Generalfeldmarschall* Walter Model's *Army Group B* on 18 April 1945, but a small remnant was able to fight its way to the transitory safety of the Harz Mountains. All that lay in the uncertain future, however, when the cadre of *Füsilier Company 272*, survivors of the retreat across France and the Low Countries, boarded trains along the German-Dutch border in September 1944, bound for the interior of Germany.

As primary source documents, those found in the farmhouse were unsurpassed. Despite years of storage in a dank cellar in Northern Germany, all of the documents were completely undamaged and easily legible. Most of the papers were assembled in binders or folders, making it easy to catalog and sort their contents. While nearly a third of the individual soldier service records and pay books were quickly sold to collectors, the remainder, as well as thousands of pages of other documents relating to the *Füsilier Company 272* were kept together as a set and acquired by the author in 1994.

In all, the document grouping included 163 individual service records and pay books, as well as partial documents for 319 other men, enough material to fill twelve large binders, in addition to eight bound volumes of records. Collating and recording this material required hundreds of hours, but were necessary in order to piece the unit history together again. Once organized, the documents began to paint a clear picture of the life and death of this company from its inception in September 1944 until the end of March 1945, when the official record ends.

The records were maintained by the company clerk, who was responsible for the various files and for processing various administrative actions, such as requests for furloughs, promotions, punishments, and awards. *Füsilier Company 272* was fortunate in that its company clerk, *Obergefreiter* (senior corporal) Ulrich Lorenz, was not only efficient, but also able to write clearly and legibly, an advantage when studying documents written in a different language than one's own. Additionally, Lorenz was assigned to the company from its inception until it was finally disbanded in April 1945.

The orderly room was the repository of all the relevant documents required for the efficient administration of a company-sized unit. The functions of the orderly room were replicated on a larger scale at the battalion, regiment, and division levels, with more personnel with greater specialization being found the further "up the chain" one went. At the company level, however, one clerk (sometimes a mail clerk was assigned as well) was sufficient to handle the workload. The clerk was directly supervised by the company's *Spiess* (first sergeant), *Hauptfeldwebel* Hermann Fuhrmeister, though in practice, these duties were often delegated to the first sergeant's assistant.

The company orderly room with its clerks normally was set up in the company *Tross* ("trains" or administrative-logistics area), usually six to ten kilometers from the front line, where the unit's combat troops were occupying defensive positions. The company trains also consisted of the supply section with its horse-drawn carts; several *Hiwis* (*Hilfwilliger*—Russian prisoners of war who volunteered to serve the Germans) to care for the horses and perform manual labor; the

senior medical NCO and his *Sanitäter* (assistant aid men); and the unit cook
along with his kitchen assistants. One of these kitchen assistants, *Grenadier*
Herbert Pitsch from Berlin, had owned a butcher shop in his hometown before the
war. Lorenz, the company clerk, and his other compatriots in the company's
administrative and logistics area were relatively safe from harm, with only the
occasional air raid or American artillery interdiction barrage to worry about.

The documents that Lorenz used to track administrative actions in the company and the personnel records he maintained consisted of individual service
records, pay books, identification disks, unit roster sheet, and the punishment
book. In addition, he kept up the casualty reporting book, hospital report book,
and the correspondence file for the company commander, *Oberleutnant* Heinz
Kolb. Lorenz, equipped with his trusty typewriter, also prepared hundreds of letters to casualties' next of kin for the commander's signature, wrote letters for the
Hauptfeldwebel to sergeants major of other units in the division, and compiled
the unit daily strength report for the division *IIb*, the enlisted personnel manage-
ment section of the division staff. All of these documents were essential for proper administration of the unit, and Lorenz appears to have done his job well.

In addition, the unit mail clerk, *Füsilier* Johann Anderka, maintained the
record books for both incoming and outgoing mail, as well as official orders and
administrative announcements from division headquarters. While there were no
doubt interruptions at various times due to attacks on the German transportation
network and the bombing of cities, mail appears to have been delivered to the
company with a fair degree of regularity, with packages and mail reaching the
company as late as 16 March 1945. For soldiers who had no writing paper or
envelopes of their own, the mail clerk had a limited supply of writing materials
and postcards to be distributed upon request. In all, enough writing paper; carbon
paper; pencils; pens; blank casualty reports; postcards; and blank paybooks and
identity tags remained on hand to serve the company's needs for several more
weeks, had the war not ended for *Füsilier Company 272* when it did.

Equally as important was the discovery among the documents, of a fragment
of the company's *Kriegstagebuch* (daily combat journal, or *KTB*). This was an
extremely important find, since it provided insight into the more mundane daily
occurrences as well as combat. Apparently, *Hauptfeldwebel* Fuhrmeister dictated
the bulk of the *KTB* to the company clerk, since the various papers are all in
Obergefreiter Lorenz's script throughout. Transcribing and deciphering the journal was a challenge, however, since the journal was written in pencil in old
German shorthand script on scraps of notebook paper. While the translated combat journal proved to be a font of valuable information, it only covered the period from 28 December 1944 to 17 March 1945. Because the official records of the
company began to deteriorate in quality beginning in early February 1945, however, this journal fills in many of the gaps and provides much information not
available through the other documents.

While these documents provide insight as to what was occurring within the
miniature world of *Füsilier Company 272,* they shed little light on the overall

military situation developing around it. This is a common occurrence in any company- or battalion-sized unit whose perspective was limited to its own comparatively short range of action. All too often, information rarely filters down to the small unit level and this failing was even more pronounced in the German Army of 1944–45, whose leaders had good reasons not to reveal the true situation to the combat troops, lest they become demoralized. Consequently, one must resort to other primary source documents or official records in order to place the history of *Füsilier Company 272* into its proper historical context.

Most of all, this grouping of documents also sheds light on a little-known and poorly understood type of combat division that the *Wehrmacht* created during the last year of the war—the *Volks-Grenadier Division,* or "People's Grenadier Division." Long confused with the *Volkssturm,* or "People's Assault Force," an organization created by the Nazi Party at roughly the same time, the *VGD* represented an attempt by the German Army to wring the last ounce of manpower and military capability out of Germany's nearly spent military resources.

Though nearly all American and British combat divisions fought *VGDs* at one time or another during the last eight months of the war, there has been little effort until recently to understand how these divisions were organized, how they were equipped, and how they fought. What made them unique? Did they represent a departure from German military tradition? Were they part of the *SS*? Could they have affected the outcome of the war in Europe? These and other questions have been asked frequently, but little attempt has been made to answer them to the satisfaction of military scholars.

This, then, is the purpose of this book. Using the document grouping as a point of departure, *Füsilier Company 272* will be seen as a microcosm of its larger parent organization, the *272nd VGD.* In many ways, this division was typical of the rest of those created in September and October 1944, at a time when German victory was a forlorn hope and when the best that Germany could expect was a negotiated truce. Fighting exclusively on the Western Front from November 1944 until April 1945, this division experienced brief glimpses of success in battle against American and British troops before it finally succumbed during the Battle of the Ruhr Pocket, the largest battle of encirclement in the west during World War Two.

Designed to secure final victory, these divisions instead found it to be an everelusive goal that continued to recede before them. Despite the extraordinary exertions required to man and equip them, they never lived up to expectations and the men of these divisions were sacrificed senselessly in a vain attempt to overcome Allied supremacy. Hastily assembled and trained, *Volks-Grenadier* divisions were forced to use the bodies of their men as a substitute for firepower and mobility. The result was an enormous bloodletting that drained the German people, *das Volk,* of the last ounce of available manpower—the husbands, sons, and fathers who had so far been spared from the clutches of a total war. They now found that they had become little more than cannon fodder for a *Führer* who, in the end, thought them not worthy of his leadership.

2

The Volks-Grenadier Division

Volks-Grenadier Divisions sprang into being in the aftermath of the 20 July 1944 attempt on Hitler's life, when fanatical loyalty to the Nazi regime rather than skill or leadership ability increasingly became the paramount criteria for service and advancement in the *Wehrmacht*. Adolf Hitler, ever attuned to the latent nationalistic character of the German people, selected the *Volks-Grenadier* honorific "to appeal to the national and military pride of *Das Volk*."[1] It was to be the *Wehrmacht*'s last concerted effort to mobilize Germany's remaining potential manpower to turn the tide of war.

Using the pretext of the assassination attempt to guarantee the *Führer* the Army's future ideological loyalty, Heinrich Himmler, *Reichsführer* (national leader) of the *SS,* convinced Hitler to appoint him commander-in-chief of the *Ersatzheer* (the replacement army). Approved only hours after the attempt on his life, this appointment merely masked Himmler's ambition to increase his own share of power at the Army's expense. His path to this new command was made easier by the fact that many of the key conspirators, such as *Generaloberst* Erich Fromm and *Oberst* Claus *Graf* Schenk von Stauffenberg, had held senior positions in the *Ersatzheer*.[2] Their elimination removed any remaining obstacle to the realization of Himmler's goal.

With this new authority, the *Reichsführer SS* lost no time in creating the groundwork for what he envisioned as a "revolutionary" army answerable to the Nazi Party alone, shorn of its ties to what he considered the old *Heer*'s "reactionary" past.[3] An article appeared shortly thereafter in the 3 August 1944 issue of the official Party newspaper, *Völkischer Beobachter* (The People's Observer), proclaiming that "True marriage between Party and *Wehrmacht* has today become a living reality. . . . The Army that must win this war *must* be the National Socialist People's Army."[4]

Another reason advanced for use of the *"Volks"* designation was the belief that this title would distinguish such units from other infantry divisions of the German Army, perhaps in conscious imitation of the term "Guards Division" as used by the British and Soviet armies. The title "Guards Division" had been bestowed since the middle of the war upon Soviet divisions that had distinguished themselves in battle.[5] Of course, the title *"Volks"* was bestowed on many divisions that had not even seen any fighting at all, much less having distinguished themselves. Left unspoken, of course, must have been the hope that they would do so at the first opportunity so that they might live up to their lofty title.

Nineteen *Volks-Grenadier Divisions*, which constituted the 32nd *Welle* (Mobilization Wave), were to be created on 31 August 1944 to serve as an operational reserve.[6] The orders authorizing their creation, issued by the *Oberkommando des Heeres* (German Army High Command, or *OKH*) on 26 and 28 August 1944, stated that they were to be raised, trained, equipped, and ready for employment on either the Western or Eastern Fronts between 16 September and 26 November 1944. As it turned out, most of these new divisions were initially committed on the Western Front.[7] This order did not affect other types of divisions, such as *Panzer*, *Panzer-Grenadier*, Mountain, or Light Infantry divisions. Nor did it apply to any *Luftwaffe* Parachute or Field divisions, though many airmen were eventually transferred into *VGDs*. In addition to creating *VGDs*, Himmler also authorized the creation of *Volks-Artillerie Corps* (for the command and control of corps-level artillery) and *Volks-Werfer (Mortar) Brigades*. Six more *VGDs* were formed on 16 September 1944.

Seventeen additional *Grenadier Divisions* (initially known as *Sperr Divisions*), which had been formed as part of the 29th Mobilization Wave between 13 and 31 July 1944, were also renamed *Volks-Grenadier Divisions* on 9 October 1944. Seven other divisions in formation during this time, though not initially intended to be *Volks-Grenadier Divisions*, were also converted to the new structure before their establishment was completed. Thus, by mid-October, a total of forty-nine new divisions were created in less than two months, a phenomenal achievement by any standard. [For a more detailed description of how *Volks-Grenadier* divisions were numbered, refer to Appendix D.] In addition, five other veteran divisions were officially re-designated *Volks-Grenadier* divisions by the end of the war.[8]

The nineteen new *Volks-Grenadier* divisions being formed mentioned above, which had divisional numbers from 564 to 582, were merged with the remnants of older divisions that had been shattered during the summer and fall campaigns of 1944.[9] So it came to be that new divisions, like the *575th Volks-Grenadier Division*, were merged with veteran divisions like the *272nd Infantry Division* before their establishment was ever completed. Many older *Kriegsetat* (Wartime Establishment, also known as *Infantry Division 44 neuer Art*) 1944 infantry divisions, whose pre-war organizational structures had been modified during late 1943 and early 1944, were never re-designated as *VGDs* and retained their old titles and structure until the end of the war. This was a function of insufficient time or opportunity to pull them out of the front line to undergo reorganization rather than a deliberate oversight.

Officer assignments to *Volks-Grenadier* divisions were originally intended to be centrally managed by a special office within the *Heerespersonalamt* (Army Personnel Office). Officers could not be moved to non-*Volks-Grenadier* units without the permission of Heinrich Himmler himself, since each assignment had to be vetted to ensure their ideological (that is, National-Socialist) commitment.[10]

This requirement, however, soon proved to be impractical, as it was nearly impossible to micro-manage officer assignments by this late stage of the war. In theory, officers assigned to the new *Volks-Grenadier* divisions were supposed to be the best available and were to be handpicked not only for their leadership and skill, but also for their loyalty to the Nazi Party. According to one authoritative source, officers selected by the Army Personnel Office as regimental and battalion commanders in *Volks-Grenadier* divisions were to be "young, combat-tried . . . officers who had been decorated with the Knight's Cross of the Iron Cross or at least with the German Cross in Gold."[11]

In the case of the *272nd VGD*, nearly all of the officers that had escaped from Normandy with the old division were retained in the same key leadership positions (for the names and positions of key leaders at this time, refer to Appendix A). Many of them met or exceeded the above-stated specifications for the desired types of individual decorations. A noteworthy omission from the officer positions authorized by the new structure, however, was that of divisional chaplain, which had been eliminated by order of Himmler himself.

Volks-Grenadier divisions could hardly be considered to have been politicized or integral components of the National Socialist Political movement like those of the *Waffen-SS,* however. For the most part, these new or rebuilt divisions could not be classified as elite formations by modern or even contemporary standards. Due to severe losses in manpower on the Eastern and Western Fronts during the summer of 1944, Germany was now forced to scrape the bottom on the manpower barrel. Despite this harsh reality, the *Wehrmacht* did initially consider them, in concept at least, to be elite formations, chiefly due to the fact that they were to receive the best armament available, the highest quality of replacement personnel, and that they were to be administratively subordinated to the *Reichsführer-SS.* The *Volks-Grenadier* divisions, as conceived, would receive seasoned cadres of officers and NCOs, and the ranks filled out by young men from the youngest age groups, chiefly those born in 1926 and 1927.[12]

That was the idea, at least in theory. Actually rounding up the manpower was another matter, although Himmler had ultimate control over the *Wehrmacht* and *Waffen-SS* replacement pools. The bitter reality was that experienced manpower had become a scarce commodity by the early autumn of 1944. To fill the ranks of these new divisions, Himmler, as commander in chief of the *Ersatzheer* initiated a series of imaginative and ruthless measures. One such measure was his resort to the use of mobile drafting units, the so-called *Heldenklaukommandos* ("hero-snatcher units").

Comparable to press gangs during the days of Frederick the Great, these roving teams, consisting of Nazi Party officials, military police, and Army recruitment personnel, scoured Germany and the remaining occupied areas for manpower. They resorted to re-activating convalescent soldiers discharged from hospitals as no longer fit for frontline service; culling the now-underemployed *Luftwaffe* for suitable personnel; converting *Kriegsmarine* personnel from sailors to infantrymen; conscripting boys of sixteen and seventeen years of age; and snatching able-bodied workers from German industry or the railways and replacing them with women and forced laborers who were from conquered territories.

Further guidelines were issued to generate additional manpower from the hospitals by shortening a soldier's recuperation. On 21 September 1944, the *Oberkommando der Wehrmacht* (German Armed Forces High Command, or *OKW*) issued an order that specified that the terms "'Limited Fitness for Field Service' and 'Limited Fitness for Duty in the Replacement Army' have been so routinely abused that they are no longer meaningful. They are henceforth no longer to be used."[13] What then followed was a list of requirements that effectively forced military hospitals to discharge patients much earlier than in peacetime and to reclassify soldiers with infirmities or disabilities for front line service. It is doubtful whether these men contributed anything meaningful to a unit's combat effectiveness, but at least it had the immediate effect of freeing up more manpower for the new *Volks-Grenadier* divisions

Many of the new recruits, especially those from the *Luftwaffe* or *Kriegsmarine,* felt a keen loss of status by being forced into the infantry. Certainly, the prospect of being transferred from a relatively safe and secure duty position in the rear area to one fraught with privation and the possibility physical injury, or even death, was enough to dismay many an aspiring airman or sailor. If they were lucky, they received a few weeks of infantry training before being committed directly to battle. Other men who had been previously exempted from service, such as older married men with large numbers of children, no doubt felt resentment and bitterness at being forced to leave their families so late in the war, when final victory was a doubtful proposition.[14]

In addition, many new recruits were obtained by conscripting large numbers of *Volksdeutsche* (ethnic Germans) from the so-called *Volksliste 3* (one of several Nazi-created racial categories that classified ethnic groups by the relative amount of "Germanic" genetic qualities they shared).[15] Although considered less racially "pure" than native Germans, these ethnic Germans were certainly adequate to serve as cannon fodder for the shrinking Reich. Many of these men came from occupied areas of Poland, Ukraine, Rumania, and Yugoslavia. Some spoke little or no German at all. Many of these so-called *Beutedeutscher* or "booty Germans" found their way into *Füsilier Company 272*, such as Eduard Zacharuk, a Rumanian of German descent who hailed from Czernowitz in an area that used to be known as Galicia, now part of modern-day Poland. If they survived, such men were granted conditional citizenship in the Reich after the war.

Due to this heterogeneous makeup and hasty training, many *Volks-Grenadier* divisions, even though well equipped, fared poorly during their initial exposure to combat and failed to justify the high hopes that Hitler had held for them. According to an analysis of such units done shortly after the war by Edward A. Shils and Morris Janowitz:

It was clear that groups so diverse in age composition and background, and especially so mixed in their reactions to becoming infantrymen, could not very quickly become effective fighting units. They had no time to become used to one another and to develop the type of friendliness, which is possible only when loyalties to outside groups have been renounced, or at least put into the background.[16]

Despite having many of the above-described characteristics of a late-war *Volks-Grenadier* divisions, however, the *272nd VGD* fought very well indeed when initially committed to the Hürtgen Forest area in November 1944, and soon gave the US Army a bloody nose at a little-known German village called Kesternich.

Responsibility for the political and ideological indoctrination of these new formations was also assigned to Heinrich Himmler's *SS*, although the *Volks-Grenadier* divisions were not actually part of his *Waffen-SS* organization. To ensure that the ideological training was carried out and that the rank and file displayed "proper" National-Socialist attitudes, a political officer, the *National-sozialistischer Führungsoffizier (NSFO*, or National Socialist Guidance Officer), usually in the grade of first lieutenant or captain, was assigned to each division. (NSFOs were added later to the other divisions, but the *VGD*s were the first ones to include them in their basic *Kriegsstärkenachweisung* (wartime organization and equipment code, or *KStN*, a term similar to the US Army's Table of Organization of Equipment, or TO&E). Independent of the rest of staff, the *NSFO* reported directly upward through his own reporting channels, bypassing the division's chain of command entirely. Many *NSFO*s were combat veterans themselves, but most were recent graduates of officer commissioning mills and Nazi Party leadership schools with little or no front-line experience.

The idea of having *NSFO*s assigned to units had been suggested by Himmler some months before, but had not been implemented due to the Army's reluctance to adopt his proposal. By Hitler's order, however, the National Socialist Leadership Staff of the *OKH* was established on 1 February 1944, primarily for the purpose of ensuring the ideological commitment of the Army's senior leadership. Initially headed by *General der Gebirgstruppe* Ferdinand Schörner, from 14 May 1944 until the war's end, the position was held by *General der Gebirgstruppe* Georg Ritter von Hengl, like Schörner a committed Nazi.[17]

In many units, *NSFO*s were regarded with contempt or suspicion, partly because of their status as "outsiders" and partly because of their Nazi affiliation. Additionally, as Germany's prospects for victory decreased and the dedication of senior and middle-grade officers began increasingly to be called into question by the Nazi hierarchy, *NSFO*s were given the additional duty of monitoring the efficiency of these officers and making recommendations through their independent reporting channel for the replacement of men of "faltering faith." After the war, many senior officers reported being intimidated by their *NSFO*s, even to the point where their own orders were overruled or questioned by someone with the rank of lieutenant or captain!

When the position of *NSFO* was first established, many of the committed Nazis assigned to divisions fighting on the Eastern Front tried to send their reports directly to Martin Bormann, Hitler's personal secretary. When *Generaloberst* Heinz Guderian, then the Army's Chief of the General Staff, learned that Bormann had shown the reports to Hitler, Guderian became furious that they had bypassed the chain of command entirely, even their own, and demanded that they be punished. Although these men were disciplined at Guderian's request, it did not bode well for the kind of reception other *NSFO*s received in their new units.[18]

In this respect, the *NSFO*'s duties paralleled those of the commissars employed by the Red Army, though they were never granted the power to carry out summary executions, as had their Red brethren. They were required to conduct frequent indoctrination briefings to the troops and soldiers were required to sign statements attesting to the fact that they had received such mandatory training.[19] For example, in the *Füsilier Company 272* document grouping there are several such rosters, signed *en masse* immediately after each monthly class, stating that they had been trained on the evils of desertion, the threat of espionage, the crime of self-mutilation in order to evade duty, the dangers of mingling with "inferior" races, and so forth.

In hopes of raising their morale and instilling an *esprit de corps*, *NSFO*s fed the troops a continuous diet of propaganda that depicted Germany as fighting against "Bolshevist Hordes" in the East and "Capitalist Jewry" in the West. They attempted to fill their heads with inspiring reports about the many new wonder weapons, such as the V-1 and V-2 that were being rushed off the assembly lines and would soon turn the tide of the war in Germany's favor. While the men always mouthed the proper response of *Sieg Heil!* and gave the Nazi raised arm salute, this false enthusiasm seldom held up past the gates of the training area, at least according to veterans of the *272nd VGD*. Although the name of the division's *NSFO* is lost to history, veterans claimed to have had little to fear from him, since he apparently had no enthusiasm or talent for his assignment. Certainly, the record does not seem to show any senior officers being relieved of command in the *272nd* by their *NSFO* for "faltering faith."

It was also difficult for any *NSFO* to maintain credibility, especially when the wonder weapons seemed to have little or no effect on the course of the war and when Germany was suffering defeat on all fronts. Shortly after arriving into their new positions in the Hürtgen Forest, on 16 November 1944 a V-1 "Buzz Bomb," which had been officially labeled by Hitler as the *Vergeltungswaffe-1* (Revenge Weapon Number 1) fell short of its target in Belgium and detonated near one of *Artillery Regiment 272*'s firing batteries, causing only minor damage. When word got around of the weapon's seeming ineffectiveness, the stock of the *NSFO* in the division sank even lower. Because of this demonstrated failure of this much-touted wonder weapon, veterans reported hearing hardly a peep from him thereafter.

As a result, the V-1 became sarcastically referred to by the troops as the *Versager-1*, or "Failure Number 1."[20]

<hr/>

By the fall of 1944, the Third Reich's industrial base had reached the highest rate of armaments production that it ever achieved. Despite the Allies' strategic bombing campaign that succeeded mainly in reducing German cities to rubble, it failed to break the population's will to resist or the nation's ability to produce the tools of war. Although levels of weapons production had risen dramatically during this period under the capable administration of Albert Speer, Germany could not sustain them indefinitely. The necessary amounts of raw materials were becoming increasingly hard to procure because of the loss the previous summer of the occupied territories that produced strategic minerals and other items such as copper, aluminum, oil, iron ore, and nickel. Other materials needed for the manufacture of clothing, boots, and equipment, such as cotton, leather, and wool, had also become scarce.

Shortages of these materials forced the German clothing industry to resort to a variety of synthetic materials to make up for the shortfall. Wool and cotton were increasingly replaced as a percentage of uniform cloth by rayon or other petroleum-based fibers. Though these synthetic materials were as strong as the organic ones they replaced, the outward appearance of nearly all types of German uniforms showed a marked decrease in quality and even looked shoddy. While the *Volksgrenadiers* of September 1944 bore little outward resemblance to the well-dressed soldiers who had marched into Poland in September 1939, at least they appeared no different from their infantry brethren marching in the regular infantry, *Panzer*, or *Panzer-Grenadier* divisions.

In the place of the prewar *Feldgrau* (field gray, a color more akin to light forest green) Model 1936 woolen uniform with the dark green collar, pleated pockets, and dark green facings on rank insignia and shoulder boards that the German soldier had worn as he marched to war in September 1939, the *Volksgrenadier* now wore either the Model 1942 or Model 1943 uniforms. Both of these uniforms' jackets dispensed with the pleats and dark green facings, and the cloth itself increasingly assumed more of an olive-brown hue. The percentage of wool to synthetics declined to the point where later war uniforms had a wool content of only fifteen percent, with the remainder consisting of rayon and recycled fibers. When wet, such uniforms quickly lost their shape and heat-retaining quality, unlike uniforms made earlier in the war that had a wool content of eighty-five percent or greater. The evolution of the German Army combat uniform, characterized by increased simplification and economical use of materials, reached its logical conclusion with the introduction of the Model 1944 uniform. This uniform, with its short-cut waist (reminiscent of the famous Eisenhower Jacket) and baggy trousers, was issued beginning in late 1944.[21] Veterans of the *272nd VGD* stated that few of them were issued or even saw this model of uniform, most continuing to wear the older models until the end of the war.

In addition to the plainer cut of their uniforms, they wore no special insignia or badges that marked them as a *Volksgrenadiers* because their status in regards to clothing and accoutrements was truly no different than that of their comrades in the other branches of the *Heer*. Like their comrades in other combat divisions, *Volksgrenadiers* frequently wore camouflaged outer garments that made it difficult for them to be seen in the forest and in the snow. Jackboots, which had come to epitomize the German Army since World War I, had been replaced by the less expensive hobnailed ankle boot with canvas leggings. Subdued rank and national insignia had become commonplace, making it difficult for Allied snipers to pick out German officers. The slouchy but practical M-43 field cap had replaced the snappy side cap of 1939. The trademark *Stahlhelm* (steel helmet) had lost its colorful decals and had acquired a dull, rough surfaced camouflaged coating. The German soldier was now harder to see and correspondingly harder to kill.

Despite all the obstacles faced by an economic system under enormous strain in its fifth year of war, Germany was still able to provide nearly all of what the soldier needed in the field. Filling the new units with soldiers, however, proved to be a greater challenge than equipping them. One method used to reduce the requirement for manpower was by decreasing units' authorized strengths by making companies smaller and by dispensing with or amalgamating supply elements, the so-called *Freie Gliederung* (Unconfined Organization) concept.[22] This also had the added effects of making them easier to command, to control, and to relieve commanders of most of the responsibility for mundane logistics planning.

Though there were fewer men in the infantry battalion in September 1944 as compared to September 1939 (642 versus 838), the average *Volks-Grenadier* unit possessed vastly more firepower. While food had become bland and adulterated by artificial, or replacement (*Ersatz*), materials, the soldier still received sufficient caloric intake to enable him to operate efficiently. Shorn of the niceties prevalent in 1939, the *Volksgrenadier* of the autumn of 1944 presented a leaner, more practical appearance that belied his prowess as a formidable opponent, especially when occupying defensive positions such as those of the Siegfried Line. Stalwart in defense, the *Volksgrenadier* could also, on occasion, demonstrate the élan of his predecessors in the attack.

In this storm of steel that characterized the last few months of World War II in Europe, what was life like for the average soldier on the Western Front in the fall of 1944? To gain this understanding and to have a better feel for what the *Volksgrenadiers* of the *272nd VGD* experienced, it is important for today's reader to know what weapons he carried, how he fought, what he ate, and how he lived. Discipline was also a constant factor that maintained unit cohesion in extreme circumstances, a factor little understood today.

The Weapons of the Volksgrenadier

Not only had the *Volksgrenadier's* uniform evolved, with its greatly simplified construction and disappearance of the fancier dress of his 1939 predecessor, but his weapons had also evolved and had become considerably more lethal. The *Sturmgewehr* 44 (more commonly known as the *Maschinepistole* 44, or MP-44) was to become the trademark weapon of the new *Volks-Grenadier* divisions and many of the newly formed units appear to have been sufficiently equipped with it. According to the divisional history, the *272nd VGD* received only fifty percent of the required number of MP-44s, but surviving members of *Füsilier Company 272* state that their company was fully equipped with the authorized number of weapons, as befitting their status as the division's elite assault company.[23]

The MP-44 traced its origins to a prototype developed in 1941 by the C. G. Haenel Company. Initially designated as a "machine carbine" (*Maschinekarabiner 42 or* Mkb 42), it was the first truly select-fire assault rifle ever manufactured, allowing the firer to choose between single shot and rapid fire with the flick of a lever.[24] The Mkb 42 was a gas-operated weapon that fired a shortened 7.92mm cartridge that retained the hitting power of the longer infantry cartridge at close range, but lacked the stability and accuracy at ranges of 500 meters and beyond, though this was seldom a factor since most infantry fighting took place at ranges of 100 meters or less, especially in the conditions like those that existed in the Hürtgen Forest.

This assault rife, constructed mostly out of metal stampings except for its wooden stock, was noteworthy in that it was easy to manufacture compared to standard rifles, which relied on time-consuming machining and woodcarving. After some early teething problems were overcome, the new weapon was then designated MP-43, then MP-44. Its thirty-round magazine provided an enormous firepower advantage over its predecessor as the standard infantry arm, the venerable Mauser 98K rifle, with a magazine capacity of only five rounds. The MP-44 had a maximum effective range of 400 meters in the single-shot mode and 150 meters in the full-automatic mode.[25] Initial production was delayed because Hitler, when shown the weapon in 1943, expressly forbade its manufacture, believing that its adoption would lead to a wasteful expenditure of ammunition by the infantry that would place too much strain on the manufacturing base and supply channels.

Despite Hitler's opposition, the *Wehrmacht's* infantry weapon testing and development branch, which recognized the superiority of the weapon, began to produce it surreptitiously in collusion with the manufacturing industry. To avoid scrutiny, it was labeled as a machine carbine or machine pistol and not an assault rifle. Initial manufacture and testing was rushed through and most of the initial design flaws, mainly involving proper placement and dimensions of the gas cylinder, were rectified. Initial field trials proved highly successful and troops expressed great enthusiasm for the new weapon, which virtually gave each individual infantryman the firepower of a machine gun. Occurring under Hitler's nose, so to speak, MP-43/44 production in 1943 totaled 30,000 and by August its 1944 production level had topped 59,500.

When Hitler belatedly discovered during an inspection in the fall of 1944 that the weapon was already in wide use, he was so impressed that he immediately approved the weapon's continued production and in December 1944 directed that its name be changed one last time to *Sturmgewehr* (Assault Rifle) 44 or Stg. 44, a far more accurate description (but for the remainder of this book, it will be referred to by the more familiar term MP-44). By March 1945, some 414,000 had been produced and had been widely issued to *Volks-Grenadier* units, panzer divisions, parachute divisions, and the *Waffen-SS*.[26]

The basis of issue for the weapon was twenty-six MP-44s in each of the two thirty-two-man machine-pistol platoons in an infantry company in a *Volks-Grenadier* regiment. The third platoon in each company was equipped with Mauser 98Ks and designated as the infantry platoon. Because of the increased firepower offered by the new weapon, only one squad in each machine-pistol platoon fielded a light MG-42 machine gun. Three *Volksgrenadiers* armed with grenade launchers mounted on Mauser 98Ks rounded out the machine-pistol platoon's firepower. *Volksgrenadiers* armed with an MP-44 were issued two magazine pouches, each one holding three thirty-round magazines. Thus, each soldier going into battle with this weapon could carry as many as 210 rounds of ammunition, including the magazine inserted in the weapon. Though weighing in at eleven pounds, two pounds heavier than the standard Mauser 98K, it had twenty times the firepower.

Supply of the short 7.92mm round, however, never met the demand and there were reports of abandoned or buried weapons being found by American troops when German units retreated. For example, it was reported that abandoned weapons were found in the town of Kesternich in February 1945.[27] In recognition of the high ammunition consumption rate of the weapon and the need to account for that in logistics planning, Albert Speer, the Third Reich's Armaments Minister, issued an edict on 26 October 1944 that stated:

> It appears that the Machine Pistol Model 44 is being issued to Volks-Grenadier divisions in great quantities without insuring that the requisite ammunition is available. It is wrong to give out this machine pistol to units about to enter into battle without first guaranteeing that sufficient ammunition is on hand.[28]

The most advanced infantry weapon in the world at the time, the MP-44 was derided by US Army's Ordnance Corps evaluators as being cheaply made, having poor firing characteristics and was "very easily damaged."[29] There are several photos in existence, however, showing American troops using the weapon and it was widely sought after by US souvenir hunters.[30] The world's first modern assault rifle, the MP-44 was to serve as an inspiration for future weapons such as the AK-47 and the M-16.

Since the supply of MP-44s never met the enormous demand, other weapons were issued in lieu of it. One such weapon was the MP-40 machine pistol, which had been in use since 1939. Firing a 9mm pistol round, this recoil-operated automatic weapon was a favorite with the troops and had proven to be an ideal weapon at close range. With its thirty-round magazine, it was light and compact, making it a favorite with front-line troops. Its poor accuracy at ranges over 100 meters, however, made it unsuited for use on the open battlefield. Obsolete by 1944, thousands of them continued to be used until the end of the war.

In cases when neither MP-44s nor MP-40s were available for issue, many *Volksgrenadiers* were issued the venerable Mauser-designed *Karabiner* model 98 (*Kurz,* or short) or 98K bolt-action 7.92mm rifle. Based on a fifty-year-old design, it had been the standard German infantry weapon since World War I. Rugged, simple, and reliable, it was obsolete before the war began although it continued in use in many countries around the world until the 1980s. Accurate up to 800 meters, it enjoyed a new lease on life with the development of a spigot-type launcher that fit on the end of the barrel that fired a 30mm fragmentation, antitank, or smoke grenade.[31]

Another weapon that saw widespread use in *Volks-Grenadier* divisions was another groundbreaking weapon, the *Karabiner,* or *Gewehr* 43 *Selbstladegewehr* (semi-automatic) rifle. Firing a full-sized 7.92mm cartridge, this gas-operated weapon with a ten-round magazine was superior to the Mauser 98K, but was never manufactured in sufficient quantities, some 405,000 being made in all from 1943 to 1945.[32] Considered a specialist weapon, it was primarily used by snipers. Fitted with a telescopic sight, a sniper could engage and kill targets at ranges exceeding 1,000 meters. Six of these weapons were issued to each infantry company's sniper section in a *Volks-Grenadier* division.

Perhaps the most feared of all German infantry weapons was the *Machinegewehr* Model 1942 or MG-42, the standard machine gun of all *Volks-Grenadier* divisions. Known as the *Hitlersäge* or "Hitler saw" by Soviet soldiers, this multipurpose weapon could serve in the light mode (with bipod), heavy mode (with tripod), or in the antiaircraft mode with a special mount. It became the standard machine gun in 1943, when it began to appear in sufficient quantities to begin replacing the older MG-34. Using the standard 7.92mm cartridge, it had a phenomenal cyclic rate of fire of 1,500 rounds per minute (making a sound reminiscent of a chain saw) though a rate of 150 rounds per minute using a bipod was more practical. Each *Volks-Grenadier* company was issued eleven of these 23.7-pound weapons, two of which were equipped with the standard tripod, which permitted a more accurate sustained rate of fire.[33]

Its chief drawback was its also greatest strength—its high rate of fire. When properly trained, an MG-42 gunner could effectively place a controlled burst of fire on a target (six to nine rounds) with a one-second pull of the trigger. If he fired much longer than that, the barrel would begin to rise up and affect accuracy. The high rate of fire was actually seen as an improvement, since the German

Army had learned that a target usually presented itself for only a few seconds at a time before it moved to cover. Thus, the ability to place a high number of rounds on a target in the shortest amount of time was deemed by the field to be the most important feature in the design of such a weapon.

This worked very well as long as the MG-42 gunner kept his bursts of fire short. *Tactical and Technical Trends*, a US Army combat lessons-learned publication printed throughout the war, discounted the weapon's effectiveness, stating in its March 1943 issue that there was little to fear after the first burst of fire because the typical German machine gunner tended to hold his finger on the trigger far too long. With his rounds flying off harmlessly into the air above their heads, so the document went, the remaining GIs could deal with the machine gun at their leisure after incapacitating its supporting riflemen.[34] This was all well and good, as long as they were not the first man who stumbled upon the enemy and took the brunt of the first burst of accurate fire squarely in the chest!

Ammunition consumption was also a problem. Like the MP-44, unless usage rates were taken into account during logistics planning for a battle. *Volksgrenadiers* (or any other member of the *Wehrmacht*, for that matter) ran the risk of running out of ammunition for their MG-42s if they did not pay careful attention to how much they were firing. Thus, photographs that show nearly every member of an infantry squad festooned with belts of machine-gun ammunition or toting ammunition boxes for the MG-42 are commonplace. When properly trained, supplied, and led, however, *Volksgrenadiers* equipped with this weapon were an often-lethal combination.

Volks-Grenadier regiments, unlike their counterparts in regular infantry divisions, were equipped with a larger complement of infantry support weapons, particularly the 80mm and 120mm mortars, and 75mm infantry howitzers. Besides this, the average *Volksgrenadier* still enjoyed an advantage over his British, French, or Soviet contemporaries because, unlike them, he was trained in the use and control of all of these weapons. Pre-war and early-war training stressed this capability, and it was drilled into soldiers' heads to the point where use of these weapons and the ability to integrate their fires into an overall tactical plan became second nature even for the lowly *Gefreiter* (corporal) in an infantry or *Volks-Grenadier* division.

A serious shortcoming of the *Volks-Grenadier* division structure that was revealed shortly after their introduction to combat was the lack of adequate antitank weapons at regimental level and below. The division's antitank battalion had been beefed up considerably by the addition of a tank destroyer company, and the 1st Battalion of each artillery regiment had been issued eighteen dual-purpose *Feld-Kanone* (field cannon) FK 40 75mm antitank guns/field cannon. *Volks-Grenadier* regiments, however, were authorized nothing larger than the 88mm antitank rocket launcher, the heavy and ungainly *Raketenpanzerbüschse* 54, officially nicknamed the *Panzerschreck* ("tank terror"), but called more commonly *Ofenrohr* ("stovepipe") by the troops. In the place of the three 75mm

Panzerabwehr Kanone 40 PaK 40) antitank guns in the *14th Company* of the earlier *Kriegsetat 44* infantry regiment, the new *14th Company* of the *Volks-
Grenadier* regiment had no cannon at all. Instead, it was lavishly equipped with
seventy-two *Panzerschreck* rocket launchers, organized into three platoons.

When properly trained and firing from cover, a two-man *Panzerschreck* team
could destroy nearly any tank employed by the Allies. Though the weapon's
88mm hollow-charge projectile could easily penetrate 160mm of rolled homoge-
nous steel angled at forty degrees, its maximum effective range of only 120
meters and conspicuous back blast made its use suicidal in open terrain.[35] After
their initial deadly encounter with this weapon, American and British commanders learned to thoroughly prepare their objectives with artillery fire prior to
launching an armored attack. Vulnerable to indirect fire, *Panzerschreck* teams
could do little but huddle in their foxhole until tanks approached within firing
distance.

Much the same applied to the other infantry antitank weapon issued in large
numbers to *Volks-Grenadier* divisions, the famous *Panzerfaust* ("armored fist").
Conceived as a one-shot, disposable weapon, the *Panzerfaust* could be fired by
one man standing, kneeling, or lying prone after receiving a few minutes of rudi-
mentary training. By the fall of 1944, the earlier version of this weapon had
evolved to the *Panzerfaust 100* version, which had a range of 100 meters and
could penetrate over 200mm of armor plate angled at thirty degrees.[36] A truly revolutionary weapon, in the right conditions it could and did result in a number of
tanks being destroyed far out of proportion to the number of men using the
weapon.[37]

The amount of discipline, not to say courage, required by a young *Volksgrenadier* as he lay in wait for an M4 Sherman or T-34 to approach within firing range
must have been phenomenal. Hundreds if not thousands of young soldiers did just
that, however, often at the cost of their lives. In addition to its antitank use, the
Panzerfaust could be used as an indirect fire weapon and as a booby trap. That
Allied troops used thousands of captured *Panzerfausts* against German bunkers
and fighting positions is testimony to its effectiveness.

Volksgrenadier Tactics

Although the introduction of the *Volks-Grenadier* division marked a discernible
evolution of the German infantry division in organization and equipment, their
infantry doctrine appears to have not changed or evolved to take into account the
capabilities of this new type of division. According to one leading authority on
Volks-Grenadier divisions, no new doctrine or training regulations were developed specifically for them at all.[38] Existing doctrinal manuals and training direc-
tives, such as Army Service Training Regulations for Infantry 130/1 continued in
use, though naturally more emphasis was placed on defensive tactics than on the

offense. This manual covered many subjects, including close-order drill, employment of light infantry weapons, and minor tactics. It was designed specifically for the training of the infantry squad, platoon, and company and was probably still the most heavily studied of all infantry regulations in 1944. Older individual privately-purchased manuals, such as Reibert's *Der Dienst Unterricht im Heer* series (Army Service Instruction Handbook), which first appeared in 1929 and covered such diverse subjects as infantry, machine-gun, infantry howitzer, and combat engineer techniques, tactics and procedures—continued in popularity.

These soldier's handbooks, as well as tactical manuals, stressed the importance of the offense and individual initiative. The defense was considered to be a temporary measure, a necessary evil to be endured until proper conditions could be created to resume offensive operations. Individual initiative was inculcated into soldiers of all ranks, who learned that action—even if not completely appropriate for every situation—was preferable to passively awaiting developments. Even a treatise on defensive operations written by a senior officer in 1943 stated "The attack suits the soldier better than defense. All warlike and fighting virtues such as daring, decision, courage, offensive spirit, destructive will, and self-confidence are awakened by, and take their full value from, offensive action."[39]

In terms of its emphasis on the offensive spirit, German tactical doctrine had much in common with contemporary US Army tactical doctrine. Both emphasized fire and maneuver, with perhaps a greater premium being placed on the use of overwhelming firepower by the Americans. This accorded with their nation's method of industrialized warfare that placed a high value on the lives of its soldiers backed up by a system of logistics that was able to deliver vast amounts of ordnance where it was needed. No doubt, Germany would have done the same had its industries been able to match American production capabilities, but the *Wehrmacht* never was a "rich man's army" and consequently placed greater emphasis on the human element.

Another advantage enjoyed by the average US Army infantry unit by the fall of 1944 was the technical means to call for and coordinate the use of artillery and close air support. American radios and fire-control systems were far superior to and issued in greater numbers than anything the Germans possessed. Although German artillery was roughly equivalent gun tube for gun tube to what the Americans had, the US Army artillery's ability to respond, coordinate, and mass fires rapidly gave the average US infantry company, battalion, or regiment the upper hand compared to their opponent. On the German side, shortage of radios resulted in *Volks-Grenadier* units being issued far fewer sets than they required. Each German company, for example, was authorized only one radio set to communicate with battalion headquarters. These sets often failed or were inoperable due to shortages of batteries, forcing company commanders to resort to landline field telephones or the use of messengers to relay important orders or reports. Subordinate platoons relied exclusively on the use of individual messengers.

Though the small arms issued to *Volks-Grenadier* units were generally superior to those of their opponents, this advantage was often largely offset by vastly greater American firepower available on call at the divisional level. Due to a concept known as pooling, designed to reduce the amount of overhead in a division, a number of independent tank, tank destroyer, combat engineer, chemical mortar, and artillery battalions could be attached or placed under the operational control of infantry, armored, or airborne divisions as long as the situation required. Thus, a standard American infantry division of 14,000 men could be augmented for certain operations by a tank battalion, a tank destroyer battalion, and three or four additional artillery battalions, not to mention transportation battalions needed to carry its regiments from one place to another. This made any American infantry division (or British, for that matter) a de facto "mechanized" unit. If a *Volks-Grenadier* division of 10,000 men was fortunate, it might be allocated an additional assault gun battery of twelve guns, one or two additional horse-drawn artillery battalions, and perhaps a heavy tank battalion if the division was designated the *Schwerpunkt* (point of main effort) for a particular operation.

The one advantage a German infantry company might have over that of its American or British counterpart was the care given to the training of its officers. The *Wehrmacht* placed great emphasis in the selection and training of company and field grade officers, stressing the need for mental flexibility, small-unit leadership skills, and something called *Auftragstaktik,* or the use of mission-type orders. This leadership philosophy stressed the importance of allowing each officer assigned a mission the freedom to determine the best method to be used in his particular situation to achieve success. When coupled with a sound military education and experience gained by training and service in the field, it resulted in an officer corps that was second to none, and had a great deal to do with Germany's battlefield victories from 1939 to 1942. In contrast, the American style of leadership during the early stages of the war can best be described as top-down leadership, with officers placed under far greater control at the regimental and battalion level. As the war progressed, this changed as American officers gained experience and as the *Wehrmacht* suffered huge officer casualties that slowly watered down the high quality of the average captain or lieutenant. By November 1944, German officers nonetheless remained a leadership force to be reckoned with at the company and battalion level. Underestimating the ability of the German officer corps, even when leading *Volks-Grenadier* units, often proved to be a fatal mistake.

Though Germany was on the defensive everywhere by the early autumn of 1944, the infantry training establishment still placed strong emphasis on retaining an offensive mindset even if attacking meant only retaking positions just given up. This point was drilled home repeatedly. *Volksgrenadiers*, as the inheritors of this tradition, were drilled in offensive tactics as much as defensive ones, doubly so for the men of the *Füsilier Company 272*, since their unit was designed to serve as the division's reconnaissance and assault force. According to the infantry regulations to which the German Army adhered:

The offensive implies a feeling of superiority. The attacker has the initiative; he determines when and where the battle will be fought. Superiority in numbers is not always the decisive factor. Superiority in leadership, in the training of the troops, in surprise effect, and in quick, active seizure and exploitation of favorable opportunities may lead to complete success against a numerically superior enemy.[40]

Thus, at every level, the German soldier was taught that the defense, whether tactical, operational or strategic, was only a temporary measure until the offense could be resumed, in spite of the fact that the *Wehrmacht* had been fighting defensively on all fronts since the summer of 1943.

Despite the gloomy outlook for the continued survival of the Third Reich, German tactical doctrine, when properly applied and combined with invaluable experience gained during five years of combat on all fronts, every *Volks-Grenadier* division had the potential to become a formidable opponent for their Allied counterparts. The fact that not all *Volks-Grenadier* divisions fought effectively can be traced to a number of factors, many of which were beyond the control of the divisions themselves.

The aforementioned quality and quantity of equipment heavily influenced the effectiveness of newly raised *Volks-Grenadier* divisions. What types of equipment each individual division received upon activation was determined to a certain extent by what was rolling off the assembly lines, themselves subject to Allied bombing and shortages of essential raw materials. Instead of receiving, for example, its allocation of *Jagdpanzer* (Jg.Pz.) 38(t) *"Hetzer"* tank destroyers due to bombing at the Skoda Works in Czechoslovakia, a *Volks-Grenadier* division's antitank battalion might receive instead an equal number of *Sturmgeschütz* Model III (StuG III) assault guns.

For the most part, however, *Volks-Grenadier* divisions formed in the late summer and early autumn of 1944 appeared to have benefited from a concerted effort by the German arms industry's and the *Wehrmacht* ordnance staff's decision to devote considerable attention to the standardization of their equipment and armament. This was a tall order given the disruptions in industry caused by the Allied strategic bombing campaign and its increasingly effective attacks against Germany's transportation infrastructure. Still, most of the new divisions, as well as those rebuilt during this period, were remarkably similar, even though spot shortages of weapons (particularly the MP-44) and vehicles were common.

Whether a *Volks-Grenadier* division was effective when first committed to battle was determined by a number of factors. Whether these factors were all or partially met largely determined whether its baptism of fire was successful or not. These included the size and quality of the cadre; allocation of the new weapons on time and in sufficient quantity; and the source of the majority of the new enlisted personnel. Though these were all important, the most crucial factor of all was the time available to assemble and train the division.

The *Ersatzheer* (the German Replacement Army) considered a training period of three months sufficient to establish and train a combat-ready infantry division that had been "fused into a closely-knit unit." This period included time to form and equip the units and lead them through a training program that began at the squad or gun section level and progressed through the platoon, company or battery, battalion, and regimental levels, culminating with division-level field training exercises. Due to the Germany's deteriorating military and political situation, three months of training in the Zone of the Interior was a luxury that the *Wehrmacht* could no longer afford. Training was therefore accelerated, so that *Volks-Grenadier* divisions were formed and sent out to the front in many cases in six weeks or less.[41]

With such a truncated training program, instruction rarely progressed beyond the company or battalion level, leaving commanders and staffs at regimental level and above few opportunities to improve or practice their skills. They had no other alternative but to learn in the "classroom of the battlefield," with decidedly mixed results. In addition to learning basic small-unit tactics, the rest of the available training time for these divisions was dedicated to antitank defense, marksmanship and gunnery training, as well as small unit level combined-arms live firing exercises, if there was sufficient time available. Some training was set aside for familiarizing leaders with the conditions existing within the intended theater of operations for which a division was earmarked, if that was known in advance. If the tactical situation permitted, training continued upon arrival in the front line in order to further the professional development of small unit leaders.

Even with the increased emphasis on training, results were mixed. An assessment of the state of training of the *Volks-Grenadier* divisions that were then being committed to the Western Front was sent on 1 December 1944 to *Generaloberst* Alfred Jodl at *OKW* Headquarters by Chief of *Oberbefehlshaber (*Commander in Chief) *West* or *OB West, Generalfeldmarschall* Gerd von Rundstedt, who had been reinstated to this position on 3 September 1944. Among other deficiencies, von Rundstedt noted that:

> The state of training of the existing troop units and the newly arrived VGDs is poor due to insufficient time dedicated to [their] instruction. The cessation of training was not anticipated, because of the situation [at the front] that demanded that these units be immediately committed to combat. Greater in-depth training has been disrupted and constrained by the constant commitment of field replacement battalions and army-level leadership and weapons schools to the fighting.[42]

The future combat performance of *Volks-Grenadier* divisions could be predicted by the *Ersatzheer* based upon the factors of available training time, cadre, and equipment. For the new Volks-Grenadier divisions to perform as intended, that is, better than the older organizations, all three factors were required in abundance; in practice, however, there never was enough training time; skilled and experienced leaders; or first-rate equipment available to meet the needs. A few of the more fortunate divisions were assigned to quiet sectors of the front, where they could gain battlefield experience and continue with their training without suffering undue losses. A few others were thrown directly into battle with disastrous results.

Though the autumn of 1944 witnessed a noticeable slacking off of the Allied effort compared with the tremendous success of that summer, the fact that the *Wehrmacht* was overcommitted nearly everywhere meant that most *Volks-Grenadier* divisions were sent to the front before they were truly ready and suffered heavily because of it. Since it possessed the means to satisfy the minimum needs of all three of these factors, the *272nd VGD* was one of the few that was able to achieve all of its training objectives. Even then, it would have benefited from more training time, since two of the three infantry regiments were still considered too inexperienced.

The greatest shortcoming of all of these divisions was due to the lack of experienced junior officers and NCOs. While the manpower allotted to the *Volks-Grenadier* divisions may have been the best still available, the fact that insufficient time to train them as individuals was a deficiency that could never be made up. While the officer candidate schools were churning out large numbers of newly minted second lieutenants, the fact that they were highly motivated and dedicated to Hitler meant little when facing veteran Allied soldiers. That six to eight weeks of NCO training led to the promotions of thousands of corporals to *Unteroffizier*, did not necessarily mean that they had the battlefield wisdom of the old *Fronthasen* (German Army slang for "front hare," or veteran NCO). A few weeks of training did not necessarily mean that a former *Luftwaffe* anti-aircraft NCO, no matter how outstanding he was as an individual, could effectively lead an infantry squad or platoon. This took time and experience in combat.

Yet thousands of men who fit these profiles were poured into the new divisions to assume these critical leadership positions with pitifully little preparation. There was little alternative, since the older existing non-*Volks-Grenadier* divisions still needed a constant stream of replacement personnel, too. So the combat-experienced cadres of the *Volks-Grenadier* divisions tried as best they could to not only train their companies, battalions, and regiments and get the division ready for its first combat assignment, but to train the newly-minted small unit leaders as well. Unfortunately for the *Volksgrenadiers,* the time to do so was far too short and many of these men did not survive their first encounter with the enemy. Those who did, however, often gave a good account of themselves.

Fortunately for the *Volks-Grenadier Divisions*, each division had a mechanism with which to promote the professionalization of its small unit leadership, namely the *Feldersatz* or field replacement battalion. This battalion, an entity unique to the *Wehrmacht,* was not only a trained manpower replacement pool consisting of four line companies (which were often used in direct combat as a stopgap organization), but it also had the divisional leadership *Kampfschule* (combat school) as part of its structure. This combat school focused specifically on training squad and platoon leaders. It taught tactical field craft, small-unit leadership, patrolling, and other vital skills that increased a leader's, and hence the unit's, effectiveness.

Staffed by the best officers and NCOs in the division, the combat school functioned as a miniature NCO academy, achieving noteworthy results with the small time allotted for each individual (2 to 3 weeks being the average amount of time spent in training). Thus, even when a unit was engaged in combat, the average infantry company had several of its corporals or NCO candidates enrolled in the course, so that despite a high rate of casualties, German divisions with such combat schools could still quickly regenerate small unit leadership. There was a limit to what these units could do, of course, and conditions at the front often meant that instruction was shortened or cancelled altogether. Sometimes the combat schools themselves were sent directly to the front when no other reserve was available. When this happened, both elite instructors and students were often killed, wounded, or captured.

To compensate for the lack of sufficient training time, pocket leader's guides were issued that were to be carried inside one's pay book. One of these guides, printed in April 1944 and found in the pay book of a soldier from *Füsilier Company 272,* essentially consisted of a checklist to be memorized along with tactical tips that, if followed, would help him successfully carry out his duties. It included exhortations to the squad leader in order to boost his morale and remind him of how the survival of the nation depended upon how well he performed his duty. Its introduction states:

> My Dear Young Comrade! Much is now expected of you. You know that you have little battle experience. That is why I [that is, the pocket guide] am here as your helper! Refer to me in critical situations and during periods of rest; ponder me well, so you will know what to do the next time. . . . Handle one situation and prepare to deal with the next. You must always be prepared to act decisively. Communicate with your Grenadiers like you would write a telegram—short and energetically![43]

Such learning aids were no doubt welcomed by a young man who only weeks before had been a *U*-boat crewman or an aircraft mechanic, but they could only go so far. Though well intentioned, these kinds of training aids were no adequate substitute for years of experience gained by progressing through the rank structure, with the added leavening of combat experience. Time was simply not on the side of the average *Volksgrenadier.*

Hitler and his subordinates, however, believed that these deficiencies in training and equipment could still be overcome by soldiers who possessed the proper political attitude. He believed that the German Army's traditional program for training and inculcating young leaders was no longer sufficient because it focused too much on the technical aspects of professional education and not enough on the "inner" aspects of leadership. According to one order given on 5 March 1944 by *General der Infanterie* Wilhelm Burgdorf, head of the Army Personnel Office,

> A brave heart is the prerequisite for troop leadership. One must bring this [talent] with him. It cannot be given him through training or professional development. Rather, character and common sense can often be generally weakened by professional development and training. . . . The *Führer* wants soldiers who distinguish themselves by their courage, their willingness to assume responsibility, and whose worthiness as leaders has been tested and further developed [by combat], . . . but the most decisive factors of all in the choosing of leaders is his ability to command; his social origins or where he was educated should not even be taken into consideration. . . .[44]

While accelerated commissioning programs for junior officers and condensed leadership training programs for NCOs could fill the gaps in small-unit leadership, it came at a price. Though zeal and bravery were good things in and of themselves, without sufficient training, combat experience, or maturity, these recently-minted leaders were to suffer inordinate casualties, along with their men, when bad tactical decisions made in the heat of combat led to their squads or platoons being killed or captured.

The lack of tactical finesse and chronic inability to take advantage of the terrain at the battalion level and below can almost be considered a hallmark of late-war *Volks-Grenadier* divisions, as the shortage of effective small unit leadership, inadequate training and combat experience worked against them. When prescribed methods of leadership, doctrine and field craft failed to work or insufficient time was available to acquire the necessary combat savvy, many company and even battalion commanders resorted to desperate tactics that were more akin to that of the Soviet Army than of the *Wehrmacht* of the early war years.

Reports of German leaders resorting to human-wave attacks in the Hürtgen Forest and during the Battle of the Bulge are common, and are convincing evidence of the erosion of German tactical proficiency. One such human-wave attack in the Ardennes is compellingly described by Charles B. MacDonald, who commanded an infantry company in the 2nd Infantry Division that found itself confronted by "waves of fanatical screaming German infantry" from the *277th Volks-Grenadier Division*.[45] The *272nd VGD* was by no means exempt from this tendency, as will be seen. In the final analysis, enthusiasm and dedication to the *Führer* could not compensate for lack skill and experience.

Even if every *Volks-Grenadier* division had had the best leadership available, adequate training time and all its authorized equipment, it still could not obscure the fundamental fact that these divisions were best suited for defensive operations. Lacking any meaningful tactical mobility or means to form a significant commander's reserve (with only six maneuver battalions as compared to nine in US infantry divisions), every battalion was needed in the front line. Nor did they have sufficient combat power, as expressed by the number of available infantry-men, to maintain the momentum of an attack once they had penetrated the enemy's front line positions. Historical evidence demonstrates that when a typi-cal *Volks-Grenadier Divisions* was able to punch a hole through the first defen-sive belt, it were usually so depleted by losses and its men so exhausted, that the momentum so necessary to sustain successful offensive operations often dimin-ished. Even if a *Volks-Grenadier* division should break through the opposing line, its inability to rapidly exploit any penetration, bring up its horse-drawn artillery, and continue the momentum of the attack by committing a powerful reserve meant that these divisions were particularly *unsuited* for offensive operations.

All of these shortcomings meant that commanders at the regimental and divi-sion level had to exert even more leadership influence if any success, whether offensive or defensive, was to be had at all. It was upon the shoulders of the *Volks-Grenadier* division's experienced captains, majors, and colonels that this hard responsibility fell. In practical terms, it meant that they were to be found closer to the front lines than their Allied counterparts. Regimental commanders were often found at the front, close to where the action was, and consequently many of them were killed and wounded. Their personal presence at the focal point of many engagements and the ability of these officers to make on-the-spot decisions retrieved many desperate situations that would have been lost had they sat in their battalion or regimental command posts "leading" by telephone or radio.

Not only did the situation often demand that its company and field grade offi-cers lead by example, but the German Army's *Führungsprinzip* (culture of lead-ership) had been inculcated into them since their days as officer candidates. German officers seldom needed any urging to lead by example. Even so, this cul-ture of leadership was often reinforced by official orders in the event of "falter-ing faith." For example, the *Fifth Panzer Army*, under which the *272nd VGD* was briefly subordinated, issued a standing directive on tactics to division comman-ders on 20 November 1944. As if these men needed any additional urging, the directive stated that:

> Commanders up to and including divisional commanders should be where they can obtain the best overall view of the battlefield, where they can inter-vene personally at a moment's notice. They must not only *lead* their men (emphasis in the original), but they must direct the extensive and varied fire of supporting weapons. We still attack too much with our legs and not enough with our weapons.[46]

That any *Volks-Grenadier* divisions at all achieved offensive successes worth mentioning (and there were a few) can be attributed mainly to the fact that their field officers and senior commanders were often physically present at the point of main effort, practicing hands-on leadership. While this approach was occasionally successful and helped to temporarily overcome their opponents technical and numerical superiority, the costs in terms of commanders killed, wounded, and captured was too high to be indefinitely sustained.

Since each grenadier battalion of a *Volks-Grenadier* regiment was authorized only four officers for its command and staff element [a commander, an *Adjutant* (also known as the operations officer), an orderly officer who functioned as an assistant operations officer, and the battalion medical officer], the loss of a battalion commander or one of his assistants deprived a battalion of its few experienced and skilled leaders when they were needed the most Although battalions were authorized an *Oberstleutnant* as commander in 1939, by 1944 the shortage of field officers usually meant that experienced *Hauptleute* (captains) were assigned instead. These men, though junior in grade for such a position by US standards, overwhelmingly gave a good account of themselves. Unlike the US Army, the *Wehrmacht* did not normally award "battlefield commissions" or rapidly promote its junior officers. The shortage of German officers remained chronic throughout the war, despite efforts to speed up the commissioning process. Other battalion staff functions, such as supply, signal, medical, intelligence, maintenance, and administrative, were filled by noncommissioned officers who had attended special schools to qualify them for these assignments. A surgeon was also authorized, but was not technically considered part of the battalion's leadership staff, although he held officer's rank.

There are numerous examples that depict how rapidly these battalions lost their combat effectiveness when key leaders were killed or wounded at the initial stages of an attack. Although each battalion still had several officers distributed throughout the line companies who could technically fill the shoes of their fallen commanders, these men often lacked tactical acumen or the necessary experience required to handle large units. Unless the division concerned could quickly assign a *Hauptmann* or *Major* from its *Führerreserve* (leader's reserve) to take over such a leaderless battalion, the record shows that these units tended to disintegrate rapidly, often resulting in mass surrenders even when only lightly attacked by Allied units. This tendency only worsened as the war drew toward its end.

Discipline

The maintenance of discipline was to prove to be a constant challenge for commanders at all levels within the new *Volks-Grenadier* divisions, and the *272nd VGD* was no exception. They were not alone in this regard, however, because by the fall of 1944, nearly every German division was beginning to experience disciplinary problems. Most of the instances reported were not of a serious or collective nature, though. Few mutinies or cases of men turning their weapons against their own officers ever took place, in part because the strong obedience to authority that had been inculcated into every German since childhood. Rather, most of the problems seem to have arisen from poor morale and manifested themselves most commonly through individual acts of desertion or malingering.

Considering the heterogeneous makeup of most *Volks-Grenadier* divisions, it is a wonder they held together as long as they did. Part of the reason for this cohesion was due to the aforementioned German respect for authority; another reason was the personal nature of relationships within each squad, where strong bonds of loyalty tied the men together in small primary groups resembling families. While these aspects have been frequently commented on by Shils and Janowitz and other observers, another reason why *Volks-Grenadier* and other divisions held together as long as they did was the draconian methods employed to keep the men in the ranks.[47]

Himmler, as the head of the *Ersatzheer,* tried to instill in the officers of at least one *Volks-Grenadier* division some his own attitudes toward desertion, which he hoped they would carry away with them when they departed for the front. As he stated to the assembled commander and staff:

> I give you the authority to seize every man who turns back, if necessary to tie him up and throw him on a supply wagon . . . put the best, the most energetic, and the most brutal officers of the Division in charge. They will soon round up such a rabble. They will put anyone who answers back up against a wall.[48]

While they are few reports of men being executed for desertion or cowardice while they were still in front line areas, in the communications zone and in the zone of the interior, the situation was far different.

Away from the front lines, the *Heeresstreifendienst* (Army Movement Control Service) and *Feldjäger* (specially empowered military police) kept a lookout for men absent from their units without authority, stragglers, and deserters. Those without papers were taken into custody and sorted out by the *Gestapo* (*Geheime Staatspolezi,* or Secret State Police). Many of these men were forcibly returned to their units, where they often were placed in close arrest or were assigned to the division's own field punishment company. Those unfortunates caught without their weapons behind the front lines were often subjected to drumhead courts martial and executed out of hand or simply hung by the roadside with a placard around their neck inscribed, "I am a traitor who betrayed my Fatherland." In all, as many as 15,000 German soldiers were executed for desertion by the end of the war.[49]

The fear of these roving "head hunters" was often sufficient to keep the men in the ranks should their ideological motivation or love of Fatherland wane. Several veterans of the *272nd VGD* stated that they felt resigned to their fate, since it was commonly believed that anyone caught while absent from their unit without proper authorization would be summarily executed. Two veterans interviewed by the author stated that they had heard that *SS* units existed in the division's rear area just for purpose, though the evidence does not support their assertion. Just the rumor that there were *SS* operating with a free hand was enough to keep many men in their places.

Virtually the only way for a soldier to practically remove himself from his unit was while he was in the front line. At great risk to himself, a *Volksgrenadier* could slip away while on patrol and hide until he judged it was safe enough to approach the American or British front lines. He then could take off his equipment, throw away his rifle, take out a previously secreted surrender leaflet, if he had one, and wave it in the air. More often than not, the Allies took such men prisoner, especially if his information was judged important. There was a danger, though, that the deserter might be shot out of hand by Allied troops or inadvertently step on a mine.

If his comrades detected him in the act of surrendering, he also risked being shot by his own side. Regardless, crossing the lines with the intent of surrendering was always fraught with danger. To help discourage desertion, a policy was promulgated that punished the family left behind by holding them up as an object of scorn and derision. In some cases, such as with senior officers, an entire family would be held hostage (the practice known as *Sippenhaft*) if he surrendered or went over to the other side. In one documented case, the *272nd VGD* distributed leaflets concerning two men from *Grenadier Regiment 980* who had deserted and divulged important information to the Americans. It went on to state that their families had been imprisoned, their property and ration cards confiscated, and that the soldiers themselves would suffer additional punishment after the war.[50]

For non-capital disciplinary offenses, the division's judge advocate could sentence a *Volksgrenadier* to serve in the division's *Strafkompanie* (punishment company), where he was assigned hazardous duties such as clearing minefields or retrieving and burying the dead in the front lines. Should the miscreant survive this arduous punishment and serve out the full term of his sentence, he was then sent back to his unit. Capital offenses or those of a political nature could be dealt with at division level by firing squads. Alternatively, if the judge advocate felt so inclined based on the nature of the offense and the record of the individual's previous service, he could order the convicted man be assigned to one of the harsh *Feld-Straf Gefangen* (field punishment prisoner) or *Bewährungs* (probationary) battalions or even to one of the dreaded 999-series *Fortress Punishment Battalions,* which were even worse.

Whether he stood and fought because of love of Fatherland, a sense of duty, or fear of what might happen to his family, most *Volksgrenadiers* remained with their squads and platoons to the end of the war. It was not until the German front line (and German morale) collapsed in late March and early April 1945 that desertions or straggling assumed catastrophic proportions, but by then it no longer mattered. In this sense, the *Volks-Grenadier* division was no better and no worse than other kinds of divisions. Even the stalwart *Waffen-SS* was plagued by desertions and straggling by the end of the war, especially after Hitler's death relieved them of their oath of loyalty. Considering the patchwork nature of their creation, most *Volks-Grenadier* divisions gave a creditable account of themselves. Provided that a *Volksgrenadier* was properly led, sheltered, and given sufficient ammunition and enough food to eat, he more often than not stayed with the colors until the bitter end.

The Soldier's Repast circa Fall 1944

In terms of morale, Napoleon's adage that an army "marches on its stomach" had not been revoked by 1944 when the *272nd VGD* was first committed to battle in the Hürtgen Forest. Just as it had been true in 1812, a military unit's effectiveness could be (and still is) directly traced to how well and how regularly it was fed, particularly when engaged in battle. For example, the men of *Füsilier Company 272* seem to have been well fed until the retreat to the Rhine River began, when their division's supply system began to fail. All of the surviving veterans interviewed for this book were unanimous in stating that they received plenty to eat at their quarters while training in Falkensee and even in the Hürtgen Forest, though at times the quality or flavor may have been lacking.

Germany's armies have always had a reputation for providing sufficient, if starchy, food for their soldiers. The German Army ration of World War II was built on a tried and true foundation established for the Prussian Army during the time of Bismarck, with additions being made as science demonstrated the benefits of a balanced, nutritive diet to a soldier's health and well being. The size of individual rations were centrally dictated by the *OKH,* based upon the soldier's duty classification and the component class of the food item being issued.

According to the regulations, each soldier was entitled to three meals a day: a breakfast meal, a noon meal, and an evening meal. The noon meal was the largest, constituting half of the caloric consumption for that day, followed by the evening meal, which made up another one-third of the total amount. The smallest meal of the day for the hungry *Soldat* was breakfast, making up only one sixth of the total. The expense of feeding a soldier averaged out to cost between 1.35 and 1.50 *Reichsmarks* a day.[51]

Because *Füsilier Company 272* was a combat unit, it was entitled to the best type of ration, known as *Verpflegungsatz 1* (Ration Basis 1). The farther away from the fighting a soldier went, the smaller and less nutritious rations were served. Ration Basis 1 apportioned 1.698 kilograms, or 3.74 pounds of food per day per man. The ration scales broke this amount down further into amount of bread in the ration (750 grams), fresh meat (136 grams), potatoes and vegetables (570 grams combined) and so on. Ration Basis 1 also authorized the issue of coffee and sugar, as well as seven cigarettes per man per day. Substitutes were issued in lieu of the other foods if they were unavailable.[52] This worked out to be a total about 4,500 calories per day per man, in theory.[53]

Füsilier Company 272 was fortunate in that it had its own *Feldküche* (field kitchen), thus it was able to have its own food cooked and delivered to front-line positions fairly regularly. (*Gulaschkanone* was the *Landser*'s nickname for his beloved field kitchen. It means "goulash cannon," a name derived from the fact that it was a wagon with two wheels and sported a tall stovepipe). This is in contrast to the infantry companies of the *Volks-Grenadier* regiments, where mess facilities were consolidated at the battalion level or higher as part of the *Freie Gliederung* concept, leaving them with little control over their field feeding. While from an organizational standpoint it made sense to reduce overhead by centralization, this system was less flexible than it had been at the beginning of the war.

As for the men of *Füsilier Company 272*, they had their own private company mess hall in the field, so to speak, with all the benefits that this entailed. The company's *Feldkochunteroffizier* (mess sergeant) was *Unteroffizier* Otto Jagielski, who had been a cook in Cologne before the war. Aided by *Grenadier* Herbert Pitsch who served as his assistant, Jagielski was provided a truck-mounted field kitchen, food supplies, and all of the equipment he needed to feed a company of 200 men. If a unit's cook and sergeant major were any good at their job (and Jagielski and Fuhrmeister apparently were), different or scarce foods could be "organized," that is to say, pilfered, traded for, or scrounged in order to add even more variety to the daily ration.

The large noon-day meal usually consisted of a dish called *Eintopf* (one pot), which was a stew or pottage-like dish in which everything—meat, potatoes, beans, peas, and so on—was cooked together in the large central cauldron of the field kitchen and served hot into soldier's mess kits. With a couple of hunks of *Kriegsbrot* (war bread—the Army issue ration loaf of bread sometimes extended with sawdust, or so it seemed to many men), the noontime meal could be very filling indeed. Once a unit was serving in the forward positions in the field, however, this meal often could not be brought up until darkness and on many occasions arrived cold at the fighting positions. Even so, soldiers could at least warm it up in their mess kits if a heat source was available.

Breakfast usually consisted of a slice or two of bread from the previous day, plus some jam or *Schmalz* (pork or goose fat spread with onions and cracklings cooked in with it) and a cup of hot coffee or *Kaffee Ersatz* (coffee substitute). This low-grade coffee, known as *Muckefug*, was usually made of roasted chicory, wheat grain, and other bitter-tasting ingredients.

The evening meal usually consisted of bread; some sausage or other preserved meat; cheese or milk; and pudding, if available. Rations in the field were noticeably deficient in fresh fruits and vegetables, though, and undoubtedly contributed to digestive problems, especially if troops could not be rotated out after prolonged periods in the front lines.

The company mess section, with its field kitchen trailer, normally set up shop in the company trains area under the watchful eye of the first sergeant. When troops were in a rest area or in reserve, they were normally able to line up with their mess kits and eat as in peacetime. As was more often the case, however, food had to be brought up at night by work details to frontline positions in large *Speisenträger* (Food carriers—insulated metal food containers) along with mail, ammunition, and other supplies. To prevent the metal food containers from rattling together and drawing unwanted attention when placed in the horse-drawn wagon or infantry carts (a small two-wheeled wagon authorized for each platoon), straw was usually packed around them to deaden the sound.

Beer or wine was also issued from time to time. *Füsilier Company 272*'s records, for example, show that the company supply sergeant used unit funds and took receipt of 200 liters of beer from *Oberfeldwebel* Klemund of *Supply Regiment 272* on 23 November 1944 from a brewery in the town of Henningerdorf. The cost of the beer was 136 *Reichsmarks*, including an eighteen *Pfennig* (penny) deposit per bottle, which, with the unit at more or less full strength, worked out to be one bottle per man. This was hardly enough to make one inebriated, but one can certainly assume that through clever trading for cigarettes or other sundry items, a soldier if he wished could easily drink more than his prescribed allocation. The empty bottles were returned to Klemund sixteen days later and the supply sergeant collected his deposit of thirty-six *Reichsmarks*, which amounted to three months of an average *Volksgrenadier*'s salary.

While the American soldier got better food the farther to the rear he went, in the *Wehrmacht* the case was just the opposite. In frontline positions, American GIs had to subsist on cold K- or C-rations for weeks on end, while their German counterparts ate warm pork and mashed potato stew several hundred yards away. One American observer of the situation, Sergeant Bill Mauldin, creator of the famous "Up Front" comic strip for *Yank* magazine, earlier remarked:

> Maybe [the Germans] didn't know much about vitamins, but their stuff was filling. It was always a great day when our patrols found caches of Jerry food . . . their sausage is good, and they have a marmalade that comes packed in a big wooden box and isn't bad at all. . . . The Germans have a pretty good chow system. . . . [They] send all their best stuff to the front. One prisoner told me that he had transferred from a cushy job in the rear echelon to the infantry so he could get something to eat.[54]

It wasn't always the case, of course. American interdiction artillery fire often caught and destroyed the food-carrying detail en route to the frontline positions, depriving the Germans of hot food for several days, forcing their officers to order them to open their own equally unappetizing canned rations, or *Eiserne Portionen* (full iron rations).

The *Eiserne Portionen* was a pre-packaged combat ration somewhat like the US Army's K-ration, designed to feed one man for one day. This ration consisted of 250 grams of *Zwieback* (hard biscuits or crackers) packed in waxed paper,

200 grams of canned *Fleischkonserve* (potted meat, beef, ham, or a similar product), and 150 grams of canned *Suppenkonserve* (either condensed canned soup or *Erbswurst* split pea sausage that could be reconstituted as a stew). It was carried in the kitchen trailer situated in the unit's field trains. Another full ration was required to be carried in the battalion or regimental trains.[55] This ration was called the full iron ration because it also included twenty-five grams of *Kaffee Ersatz* (coffee substitute), twenty-five grams of salt, and twenty-five grams of sugar, depending on availability

The *Fleischkonserve* had acquired a poor reputation dating back to the North African campaign and had become a notorious grim joke among both Germans and Italians troops. In North Africa, they had to rely much more on canned goods than the Allies, since fresh foods were scarce due to the climate and shipping problems. To make up this shortfall, the men of Rommel's *Afrikakorps* were frequently issued cans of meat stamped "A.M." issued from Italian food stocks. Like the German *Eiserne Portion*, the Italian canned meat lacked taste and texture, but apparently tasted even worse than the German variety. With their characteristic sense of gallows humor, Rommel's veterans soon nicknamed the canned meat *alter Mann* (old man), *anisus Mussolini* (Mussolini's ass), or *alter Maulesel* (old mule). Actually, AM stood for *Administrazione Militare,* the Italian equivalent for War Department. The various nicknames stuck long after Italy's surrender and the dissolution of the Italian Army's *Administrazione Militare.*[56]

An abbreviated version of the ration, the *Halbeiserne Portion* (half iron ration), consisted of just the meat and hardtack. It was carried by the soldier as specified by the regulation in the small bag attached to his assault pack. The mess sergeant issued this ration to each soldier in a small paper sack containing both the meat and Zwieback with a label attached indicating its contents. The *Halbeiserne Portion* was supposed to be opened only upon receipt of a direct order from a unit's commanding officer and was saved for emergencies, such as when a unit had been separated from its field kitchen for more than two days. Opening it without permission was a serious offense, though as the supply situation became more tenuous, veterans of *Füsilier Company 272* admitted to frequently eating them without permission.

To prepare their iron rations, soldiers heated them with their folding *Esbit* field stoves using trioxane heating tablets. Then, using can openers and eating utensils, they ate their contents straight from the can, as any GI would have done, or spread the meat on the Zwieback.

When on the move from the replacement depot to the front, soldiers were normally issued *Marschverpflegung* (march rations). Issued cold, this ration normally consisted of three or four days' worth of food designed to sustain him until he reached his final destination where normal field kitchens awaited. The *Marschverpflegung* usually consisted of 700 grams of bread, 200 grams of cold meat such as sausage, sardines or smoked bacon, cheese or cheese spread, coffee, sugar and six cigarettes, giving the ration a total weight of 980 grams.[57]

Of course, hungry soldiers could and did eat their way through this ration in a day or less; a decidedly irresponsible act when they could not predict when they would see a field kitchen again, since marches or rail movements often lasted a week or longer. This often forced German soldiers, like soldiers from other armies, of course, to scrounge what they could from the countryside, just as their American, British, and Soviet counterparts did. Rabbit, wild boar, deer, and anything else with four legs or feathers were fair game for a hungry soldier. German troops also were able to trade their rations with local civilians if the latter had not yet been evacuated to the hinterland. Occasionally, a soldier's day was brightened by a food package from his family back home, but as the war dragged on, they discouraged this since the food situation on the home front was far more austere than at the fighting front!

To both promote morale and to provide additional high-energy food for soldiers in combat, the *Heeresverpflegungsamt* (Army Subsistence Department) developed several special ration components beginning in 1940. These included special rations for paratroopers, tank crews, flight crews, and troops involved in front-line combat. These special supplemental rations for infantry, combat engineers and other supporting troops were known as *Grosskampfpäcken* (extended combat package) and *Nahkampfpäcken* (close-combat package).

The contents of these small boxes, eagerly sought after by front-line soldiers, were high in calories and included enriched biscuits (such as *XOX Kraft Keks*), fruit drops, caramel candies, chocolate bars and fruit bars. Weighing ten and a half ounces, these packages provided the hungry soldier a total of 1,086 calories, most of which consisted of high-energy dextrose or sugars. To round out the appeal of this rather innovative item, a package containing six cigarettes was included. Evidence indicates that these special rations were issued up to the end of the war.[58]

Despite the best efforts of the German food industry and the supply sergeant, food sometimes did not make it up to the front for several days and when it did, it was often cold. When this occurred, especially toward the end of the war when supply lines were in doubt, the lack of food and warm beverages contributed to a decline in troop morale and undoubtedly led many *Volksgrenadiers* to surrender at the first opportunity or even desert.

German veterans of the Hürtgen Forest assert that the ones who were the first to surrender or "go over to the other side" were more often than not former *Kriegsmarine* sailors or *Luftwaffe* personnel who were used to far better food and living accommodations. Certainly, the prospect of spending weeks in a sodden hole in the ground; enduring pouring rain or snow; constant Allied artillery fire; and cold, monotonous rations was enough to break all but the strongest man's will to resist.

Though they had been hurriedly assembled, the *Volks-Grenadier* divisions that were formed during September and October 1944 were a welcome addition to the order of battle of the various field armies that received them. The manpower allocated to them was above average, they were relatively well armed, supplied, and equipped, and had been provided the best officers and NCOs that could still be provided by Himmler's *Replacement Army*. Fired up with Nazi propaganda and belief in the wonder weapons then coming off the assembly lines, many men in the ranks of these divisions, whether they were grizzled veterans, *Luftwaffe* or *Kriegsmarine* transfers, or gullible ethnic Germans, honestly believed that they could help turn the tide in Germany's favor. While a few of these divisions were created virtually from whole cloth, the majority that had been formed around the nucleus of burned-out veteran divisions and given a month or two of training seemed to offer great promise. Certainly Hitler placed great stock in them. Though *Volks-Grenadier* divisions had been constructed primarily for conducting defensive operations along the ever-shrinking borders of the Third Reich, it was thought that, when given the right kind of leadership, they also would acquit themselves admirably in the offense. Whether that would prove to be the case remained to be seen. Regardless, the new *Volks-Grenadier* divisions were soon put to the test on the Western Front, where many of them, including the *272nd*, received their baptism of fire.

3

Origins and Lineage of
Füsilier Company 272

Füsilier Company 272's military career, like that of its immediate higher head-quarters, the *272nd VGD*, lasted exactly seven months. During this brief period, the company was almost continuously engaged from the moment it was commit-ted to fighting in the Hürtgen Forest in early November 1944 until the final retreat to the Harz Mountains in April 1945.

Throughout this final chapter in the Third Reich's history, victory remained beyond their grasp. The *Volksgrenadiers* of *Füsilier Company 272* experienced few victories and saw Germany's fortunes decline steadily despite their best efforts. Except for the initial heady days following the announcement of the beginning of the Ardennes Offensive, the company was to experience a steady diet of defeats and withdrawals until its own demise.

The German Army knew that hastily thrown-together units suffered from a lack of cohesion and tactical proficiency, which usually resulted in failure, so it took steps to correct this deficiency by thorough planning and training, but the results did not always live up to expectations. Consequently, rightly or wrongly, *Volks-Grenadier* divisions have often been characterized as being substandard in performance and have come to be regarded by some military historians as being little better than the *Volkssturm*, the Nazi Party's last gasp attempt to mobilize the general population to fight to the last ditch. Unlike many other *Volks-Grenadier* units, the *272nd VGD* was not created from scratch from whatever manpower was available at the time, but was built on the foundation of an older unit that had fought extensively on the Eastern Front and in Normandy and still retained many veterans of this earlier period.

Füsilier Company 272, like its parent division, was different from many of the other units being formed at the same time. The company's genealogy can be traced from its inception at the beginning of the war, where it had roots in the pre-war *Wehrmacht*. Indeed, its lineage derived from the traditions and history of the *2nd Battalion, Infantry Regiment 396* of the *216th Infantry Division*. This her-itage stood the future *Füsilier Company 272* in good stead. To understand how *Füsilier Company 272* evolved into the elite strike force of the *272nd VGD*, it is necessary to start at the beginning.

Infantry Regiment 396 was formed and activated on 26 August 1939, when the German Army High Command or *Oberkommando des Heeres (OKH)* ordered the transfer of several thousand *Landwehr* (home guard) troops from the Hannover area into the German Armed Forces, or *Wehrmacht*. Many of these home guards-men were veterans of the First World War and recently discharged veterans of the Army of the Weimar Republic (the *Reichswehr*), sprinkled with a few younger draftees. The various *Landwehr* companies and battalions were then quickly organized into a standard three-battalion infantry regiment with accompanying regimental antitank and infantry howitzer companies. While still undergoing organization, it was assigned to the Hannover-based *216th Infantry Division*, a unit that was almost wholly composed of men from Lower Saxony. *Infantry Regiment 396* saw limited action on the Western Front (primarily in the Ardennes) in 1939 and 1940. When Hitler launched his campaign in the West on 10 May 1940, the regiment fought along with the rest of the *216th Infantry Division* through Belgium, at Dunkirk, and during the Battle of France from 5 to 25 June 1940.

Following the successful conclusion of Germany's Western Campaign, the regiment settled into occupation duties along the Channel Coast until December 1941. It was then hurriedly transferred along with the rest of the division by rail to the Eastern Front to serve as a *Korsettenstange* (corset stay—a series of wide-ly-spaced strongpoints that help to keep a weak front line from rupturing under enemy pressure, much like the way corset stays helped keep a corset from stretch-ing out of shape) for *Army Group Center,* whose front line was rapidly being ripped apart in the face of the Soviet's massive winter counteroffensive. From 29 December 1941 until 28 January 1942, the bulk of the *216th Infantry Division* and its regiments fought while encircled at Suchinitshsi, until it and the rest of the town's garrison was freed by a relief force.

By now a veteran unit, *Grenadier Regiment 396* (it was renamed with this hon-orary title on 15 October 1942 like most of the remaining infantry regiments in the German Army) fought in the Rzhev salient from 1942 to early 1943 and at Orel during the epic Battle of Kursk. Along with the rest of the German forces in the south of Russia, it took part in many delaying actions that occurred during the long retreat to the Dnieper River defensive line. Here it, as well as the rest of the *216th Infantry Division,* suffered heavy casualties as it struggled against its numerically superior opponent in large-scale defensive battles such as those that took place in and around the city of Gomel in August 1943.

By 12 November 1943, *Grenadier Regiment 396* and its parent division had lost so many men that the entire organization was no longer judged suitable for combat and was officially disbanded by the *OKH*. The regimental staff of *Grenadier Regiment 396* was used to form the staff of *Divisional Group 216,* along with its *1st* and *3rd Battalions,* and continued to fight on the Eastern Front as part of the *102nd Infantry Division,* where it remained until its surrender to the Red Army in May 1945.

Fortunately for the rank and file of *2nd Battalion, Grenadier Regiment 396,* they were spared this fate when the remnant of their battalion was transferred to the West on 17 November, along with the staff of *216th Infantry Division* and other divisional units. Upon arrival in Belgium, these units were to form the newly reactivated *272nd Infantry Division* (the original *272nd Infantry Division* had existed for two months in 1940 before being inactivated after the French campaign).[1]

The entire *2nd Battalion, Grenadier Regiment 396* was used to form the Division's *Füsilier Battalion 272* in Antwerp, Belgium on 15 December 1943. After absorbing a few replacements and undergoing several months of training in Belgium and in the south of France, it was declared ready for combat in March 1944, ahead of the rest of the division's combat elements. That it was ready more quickly can be explained by the fact that it was composed largely of veterans of the Eastern Front, as opposed to the infantry regiments, which had for the most part been created by banding together several reserve or training battalions with little or no combat experience. The exception was *Grenadier Regiment 980*, which, like *Füsilier Battalion 272*, had been created by simply renaming one of the existing units that had been withdrawn from Russia.

Grenadier Regiment 980 was created by re-designating *Grenadier Regiment 348* of the old *216th Infantry Division*. Both of its infantry battalions had been transferred intact from the East and were assigned new numbers to correspond with their new designations. Though the cadre was intact, the regiment still had to absorb nearly a thousand replacements before it reached its authorized strength. Its training program, unlike that of *Füsilier Battalion 272*'s, was seriously hampered by the lack of equipment, for it had been directed to leave all of its heavy weapons and most of its transport in the East with *Division Group 216*. Perhaps the biggest advantage that *Grenadier Regiment 980* had over its sister regiments was that almost its entire leadership cadre had remained with the colors, including its wily and cunning commander, *Oberstleutnant* Ewald Burian.

When the Allied landings in Normandy began on 6 June 1944, the *272nd Infantry Division* was located in the south of France along the Mediterranean Coast, where it was carrying out local security duties while it continued its training program. When the shortage of infantry divisions at the Normandy front had reached a critical stage, *Füsilier Battalion 272* and the rest the division, some 13,000 men in all, were sent there. After enduring a harrowing series of air attacks upon troop trains during movement through southern France to the front, they were committed to the fighting on 7 July

While attached to the *I SS-Panzer Corps,* the division suffered heavy casualties during a defensive campaign against the Allies in the Caen area. Like the infantry regiments, *Füsilier Battalion 272* had suffered likewise. It had sustained such heavy casualties that by 23 July, only 376 men remained out of the 708-man full-strength unit that entered the battle on 7 July.[2] Its commander during this period was *Major* Gerhard Thürmer, himself a veteran of *216th Infantry Division* and the Eastern Front, who was to lead the battalion until it was deactivated and re-designated a *Füsilier* company at Falkensee the following September 1944.

Nearly destroyed in the fighting to save the entrapped elements of *Seventh Army* in the Falaise Pocket, the *272nd Infantry Division* gave ground grudgingly and fought pitched battles against the British and Canadian forces at Caen, Troarn, and Lisieux. When the German front in Normandy finally collapsed between 19 and 29 August, the division was forced to withdraw to the Seine River near Jumierges. From 27 to 29 August, the division, now reduced in size to only 4,000 men, crossed the river virtually intact, improvising a system of ferries to convey its men and remaining material across the river, despite incessant Allied air attacks.[3]

This task completed, the *272nd Infantry Division* was ordered to move to La Bocage, where it was tasked by its higher headquarters with operating the Seine ferries at Duclair so other retreating units could make their way safely across this great river barrier before they were cut off by the Allies. While engaged in this operation, the division received the order, issued on 29 August, from the acting commander of *Army Group B, Generalfeldmarschall* Model, that directed it to assemble behind the Somme River in preparation for its planned reconstitution and replenishment near Brussels. Events quickly overcame this order, however, as the Allies' pressure upon the retreating German forces became overpowering.

Assembling on the northern bank of the Seine near Duclair, the remnant of *Füsilier Battalion 272,* by now less than a hundred men, and the rest of *272nd Infantry Division* managed to cross the Somme and escape through Belgium from 29 August to 9 September. With British forces on its heels, the division established several hastily constructed blocking positions to delay the Allied advance. The division was ordered to blow the bridges at Maastricht as it retreated to further slow the pursuit by the British XXX Corps, a task it was able to successfully perform even although its combat engineer battalion had shrunk in size to less than a company. Despite incessant Allied fighter-bomber attacks and ambushes by Belgian partisans, most of the several thousand survivors of *272nd Infantry Division* were gathered on German soil in an assembly area near the village of Straelen by 12 September 1944.

Not everyone who tried to link up with their retreating division made it. Despite their best efforts, many veterans were taken prisoner either by the Allies or by French, Belgian, or Dutch partisans. One such man, *Oberfeldwebel* Gerhard Sandmann, a veteran of *Grenadier Regiment 398* on the Eastern Front and who had fought with the division in France, was captured on 30 August 1944 near Chalon-sur-Marne by American troops. He had been separated from his company the week before during the chaotic Seine crossing and had taken off on foot with several comrades in order to reach his regiment in Belgium. Unable to outrun the motorized Allied Forces, he spent the rest of the war in various French and American prison camps.[4]

In Straelen, the division carried out a hasty reorganization and was ordered shortly thereafter to proceed to the town of Sterkrade, where the troops boarded awaiting trains from 16 to 18 September. While in Straelen, hundreds of stragglers arrived and were reunited with their companies and some form of order was restored. The men and their remaining equipment were quickly transported in several troop trains to the pre-war infantry school at the Döberitz training area, located approximately 40 kilometers west of Berlin, where they began reorganization as a *Volks-Grenadier* division. While thus engaged, on 17 September 1944, the *272nd Infantry Division* was formally renamed as the *272nd Volks-Grenadier Division*. The remnants of *Füsilier Battalion 272*, still under Thürmer's command, were also scheduled to undergo reorganization into the new *Volks-Grenadier* structure, but no one at the time knew what that signified.

Once it arrived at its new administrative area with the rest of the division, the battalion's remnants were informed that they would be combined to serve as the cadre for a new type of *Füsilier* unit. Using *Oberleutnant* Heinz Kolb's *2nd Company* as the foundation (it was the most intact of all the battalion's three line companies), a single *Füsilier* Company would be organized and thoroughly trained during the next six weeks before it being committed once again to battle. This came as a surprise to Thürmer and the remaining leadership of the old battalion, since they had expected that the battalion would only be reconstituted under its old structure.

In all, only forty-six veterans of the old battalion were kept on to form this new *Füsilier* Company. The rest of the 708 men who had been with the battalion on 7 July had been declared killed, wounded, or missing in action in Normandy and the retreat across France. A few dozen non-combat personnel, mostly from the now-superfluous battalion headquarters and battalion trains, were transferred to other units in *272nd VGD* shortly after arriving in Germany to make up personnel shortfalls elsewhere in the division.

According to the orders that directed the formation of the *272nd VGD*, *Füsilier Company 272* superceded *Füsilier Company 1575*, an entirely new unit that was to have been created at the same location. Though *Füsilier Company 1575* was supposed to have served as the authorized *Füsilier Company* for the newly authorized *575th Volks-Grenadier Division*, apparently neither were personnel ever assigned to this company nor was it ever activated.

Instead, the 126 replacements who had been earmarked to fill the ranks of *Füsilier Company 1575* were assigned to *Füsilier Company 272* beginning on 2 October, even before their former unit's designation could be entered into their pay books. The *575th Volks-Grenadier Division*, which itself had only been forming at Döberitz since 25 August 1944, was also absorbed in its entirety on 17 September 1944 by the now-renamed *272nd VGD*, after being in existence for three short weeks. (For information on the systems used for numbering the new *Volks-Grenadier Divisions*, refer to Appendix D.) Rather than allow the new *Volks-Grenadier* divisions to be formed under their original titles, Hitler decided instead for both propaganda purposes and for continuity sake to keep the old divisions' number in the German Army's order of battle.

Conversion to *Volks-Grenadier* Structure

By the end of the third week of September 1944, the troop trains carrying the depleted and exhausted *272nd Infantry Division* across Germany from Sterkrade to Döberitz were forced to move mainly at night, in order to avoid daylight fighter-bomber attacks, even within the heart of Germany. According to one veteran of the division, *Unteroffizier* Helmut Braun,

> *Jabos* (fighter bombers) took every opportunity of attacking trains during the day . . . they didn't even shy away from shooting at farmers working in the fields. There was no longer any differentiation between the combat troops and the civilian population. The German people were very uneasy due to the constant air attacks and the feeling that in spite of everything, it no longer seemed that this war could be won. . . .[5]

Upon arrival at Döberitz, the individual elements of the division were again reorganized into battalions and regiments. After being fed and issued instructions, the units fanned out to occupy their quarters, where the men remained during the six-week long transformation into a *Volks-Grenadier* division. The troops of the various units were billeted in barracks and, since space was lacking, in a large number private homes between Döberitz and Brandenburg as well, where the local population received them warmly.

Due to lack of living accommodations or barracks at Döberitz, *Füsilier Company 272* was billeted elsewhere. When it arrived at the training area on 18 September 1944, the company was ordered to proceed immediately by truck to Falkensee, a suburb of Berlin approximately fifty kilometers east of Döberitz. There, the company was billeted in the *Falkenhagener Schule,* a local high school next to a lake on the outskirts of town, where it remained for the next six weeks.

Since the company had an accelerated training schedule to follow, and local training areas were inadequate, the company was required to commute daily in coal-gas powered trucks to the immense training area at Döberitz. Here, the *Volksgrenadiers* were able to carry out individual weapons training and conduct live-fire exercises with machine guns, mortars, and infantry howitzers. It was usually late in the evening when the men returned to the school in Falkensee, leaving them barely enough time to clean their gear and sleep before they had to stumble out of bed again to repeat the process the next morning.[6]

Reorganization into a *Volks-Grenadier* division, which began immediately upon arrival at the Döberitz Training Area, proved to be an arduous process, although the division's command and staff were relatively intact. In this regard, the *272nd VGD* appears to have been more fortunate than most of its sister *Volks-Grenadier* divisions. Not only had the bulk of its leadership, staff, and headquarters personnel managed to escape from northern France, but personnel from all of the divisional units and sizeable amounts of its combat troops had made it out as well. Augmented by additional cadre and replacements from the now-defunct *575th Volks-Grenadier Division*, as well by the addition of equipment and horses to replace what had been lost in Normandy, the division's combat engineer, signal, and anti-tank battalions were quickly able to achieve a level of operational capability.

The same went for the division's support elements, which were now consolidated into *Nachschub (Supply) Regiment 272* under the command of *Major* Ritter. This consolidation freed up several hundred manpower positions by reducing the amount of excess personnel in now-superfluous administrative positions. The division's supply, transportation, maintenance, ordnance, field post office, and veterinary battalions and companies were simply renamed, but the medical company was inexplicably disbanded. Due to an administrative oversight, the newly-raised *Medical Company 1545* became instead the division's new casualty clearing station and medical evacuation unit after taking over the numerical designator of the other company. The old *Medical Company 272* was broken up and its personnel distributed to other units.[7]

The "new" *272nd VGD* fielded three infantry regiments and an artillery regiment, along with divisional units, just as it had under the previous *Kriegsetat 44* table of organization and equipment (an older structure officially designated as an *Infanterie Division 44 neuer Art (Inf.Div.n.A. 44)* or Infantry Division 1944 New Type) when it had fought in Normandy as the *272nd Infantry Division* As previously mentioned, the artillery regiment was in the best shape of all four of the division's regiments. Under the stalwart leadership of *Oberstleutnant* August Wilbrandt, the regiment had managed to extricate 752 of its men, 300 horses and enough guns to equip two battalions. Additional batteries and men returned to the regiment several weeks later, after being temporarily attached to the *346th Infantry Division* in Holland.[8]

The orderly withdrawal of *Artillery Regiment 272* and its subsequent equipage with additional cannon made it even more effective when it was recommitted to the battle two months later. Wilbrandt and his officers did not care much for the new unit structure as required by the *Volks-Grenadier* table of organization and equipment, because it authorized each battalion fewer radio sets, ancillary equipment, vehicles, and forward observer personnel than the previous *KStN*. Though firing batteries were now larger (six guns as opposed to four), it made fire direction control more difficult when the tactical situation required that the new six-gun batteries be divided into two- or four-gun sections that could operate independently, as was the accepted practice. At least Wilbrandt and his commanders received all of the guns and equipment they were authorized to quickly bring the regiment up to a high state of readiness.[9]

Though the regiment was still authorized four battalions in its new *Volks-Artillery* regiment structure, *2nd* through *4th Battalions* were reduced from three batteries of four guns each to two batteries of six guns each. While each battery had two additional guns, the removal of the fire-direction control and communications equipment from the two eliminated batteries was not well received by the cadre. Not only were larger batteries more difficult to employ, but this step eliminated a degree of flexibility they had previously enjoyed. The extra equipment available in the old division structure had allowed the battalions to detach two gun elements with fire-direction control equipment to conduct "roving gun" or *Wanderbatterie* operations, a diversionary tactic that had proven enormously successful in Normandy and Italy. The roving gun procedure involved the use of a single gun, located at a different firing position from the rest of the battery, to range a target. Once the target was positively identified and ranged, the roving gun ceased firing and transmitted its firing data (range, elevation, and deflection) to the rest of the battery or battalion, which then conducted a rapid *Feuerüberfall* (ambush by fire) that reduced the chances of being hit by Allied counterbattery fire. The roving gun in the meantime moved to a different firing position and began the process all over again.[10]

The Regiment's *1st Battalion* was equipped with eighteen 75mm dual-purpose Model FK 40 infantry field cannon, organized into three batteries of six guns each. This weapon was virtually identical to the PaK 40 antitank gun, but its carriage had been modified to allow the gun to be elevated to the greater firing angles required for high explosive ammunition. Special firing tables had been developed to allow for indirect fire at ranges up to 13,300 meters. It could also be used in the antitank mode, firing normal PaK 40 75mm armor piercing ammunition as required.[11] The *2nd* and *3rd Battalions* were each equipped with twelve 105mm Model 18 light field howitzers, with two batteries of six guns each, as mentioned above. Only *4th Battalion, Volks-Artillery Regiment 272* was authorized tracked vehicles to tow its twelve 150mm Model 18/40 field howitzers; the other battalions had to rely on teams of horses to pull their guns.

Unlike the artillery regiment, which had survived the Battle of Normandy relatively intact, the situation was quite the opposite with respect to the infantry regiments. Of the three, only one, *Grenadier Regiment 980,* survived the retreat across the Seine with any vestige of combat power and unit cohesion. Even then, *Oberstleutnant* Ewald Burian's regiment had suffered grievously defending against the Canadian's attempt to cut off the bulk of the division before it could reach the ferries at Duclair. Most of its equipment had been lost as well.

When the regiment reached the German frontier, Burian was able to count only 345 officers and men, out of the nearly 2,008 men he had led into Normandy in early July.[12] The rest were either in hospitals, buried in shallow graves, or in Allied POW camps. Those who had survived, however, were the hardened core, mostly NCOs and the experienced corporals who were indispensable for the effective functioning of any combat organization. With the infusion of sufficient recruits and equipment, Burian's regiment could quickly be brought back to a full state of readiness.

In contrast to *Grenadier Regiment 980,* which had been able to escape with its organizational framework if not the bulk of its troops, the division's other two infantry regiments were even more decimated. *Grenadier Regiment 981* had been virtually wiped out during the third week of August and reduced in strength to less than 100 men. Its first commander, *Major* Bodsch, narrowly escaped capture on 19 August when the British surrounded his regimental headquarters and his temporary successor, *Oberstleutnant* Meyer (Bodsch had been wounded), just barely succeeded in getting the remnants across the Seine. *Grenadier Regiment 982* fared little better, though its commander, *Oberstleutnant* Paul Rösener, was at least able to extricate himself and his staff. Consequently, both of these regiments had to be rebuilt from the ground up and were to consist principally of the cadre and recruits of the now-renamed *Grenadier Regiments 1184* and *1185*, respectively.

Thus, the new *Grenadier Regiments 981* and *982* were virtually formed from scratch. The shortage of experienced cadre caused these regiments to conform much more closely to the *Volks-Grenadier* archetype, despite their commanders' best efforts. Consequently, these two regiments faced considerably more challenges in achieving a combat ready status than did Burian's regiment. In this sense, they performed like many of the other *Volks-Grenadier* regiments that were created without the benefit of having enough experienced junior leaders to see them through their formative stages and during their introduction to combat. While Rösener remained in regimental command, Bodsch was officially replaced in mid-September by *Oberstleutnant* Meyer, who had twice previously commanded the regiment in Normandy in mid-July and again at the end of August.

Like the regiments of the older *Kriegsetat 44* table of organization, each *Volks-Grenadier* regiment was composed of two battalions each (*1st Battalion* companies were numbered 1 to 4 with *2nd Battalion* companies being numbered 5 to 8), with a regimental infantry howitzer (the 13th) company and an antitank (14th) company. Because the new VGD structure did not authorize a third battalion for each regiment, the company numerical designations 9 through 12 were omitted, though the designations for the 13th and 14th companies were retained for traditional purposes. If Germany had won the war, the *3rd Battalion* would have been reinstated in each regiment. Each battalion was smaller, however, having been reduced from 708 to 642 men. In turn, each infantry company had been reduced by twenty-three men, from 142 to 119. The regimental headquarters company, in addition to the regimental staff, was authorized a communications platoon, an engineer platoon, a bicycle-mounted reconnaissance platoon, and regimental trains, 187 men in all. Total authorized strength for a *Volks-Grenadier Regiment* was 1,854 men, 154 men fewer than its predecessor.[13] In addition, each regiment, including its constituent battalions and companies, was authorized a total of only nine motor vehicles of all types (including four cargo trucks), ten motorcycles, and 219 horse-drawn vehicles pulled by 430 horses.

Despite the fact that each *Volks-Grenadier* regiment's infantry battalion had sixty-six fewer men than the *Kriegsetat 44* table of organization, it had significantly more firepower. Though it had seventeen fewer machine guns than its predecessor (38 versus 55), each battalion was authorized twice as many machine pistols and assault rifles (253 versus 127). In the case of the heavy weapons company, the *Volks-Grenadier* regiments had even more firepower. Each of the battalion's heavy weapons companies (*4th* and *8th Companies*) consisted of two heavy machine-gun platoons with four MG-42s each, one platoon of 80mm medium mortars with six tubes, and one light infantry gun platoon with four short-barreled 75mm Model 18 infantry howitzers. These replaced the four 120mm mortars in the *Kriegsetat 44* structure, a change that provided the battalion an organic direct-fire capability. When firing a specially designed hollow-charge projectile (that worked similarly to the warhead of the *Panzerfaust*), the 75mm infantry howitzer also had a limited short-range antitank capability.[14]

The division was authorized the same number of signal, engineer, and antitank battalions as under the previous organizational structure, but in the case of the *272nd VGD*, these were created simply by renaming the existing battalions that had survived the retreat from Normandy. After absorbing replacements and new equipment, they were quickly brought back to full operational capacity. *Signal Battalion 272*, authorized a field telephone company, a radio company, and a support platoon, continued under the leadership of its old battalion commander, *Major* Schossig. *Pionier Battalion 272*, led by *Hauptmann* Schlanstein, consisted of two combat engineer, or sapper, companies and a headquarters support company, though records indicate that a third sapper company was unofficially retained, even though it was not authorized by the *Volks-Grenadier* table of organization.

The division's mobile reserve, *Antitank Battalion 272*, was led by *Hauptmann* Friedrich Adrario, who had distinguished himself in Normandy by his steady and resourceful leadership. The table of organization for this type of unit had been modified significantly from that of its predecessor, however, providing it much more capability that it had previously enjoyed. The older organization had been authorized only one towed antitank gun company with twelve 75mm guns, and one self-propelled antiaircraft company with twelve 20mm cannon. The new organization was authorized an antitank gun company with nine 75mm PaK (*1st Company*) and a new tank destroyer (or *Panzerjäger*) company (*2nd Company*) made up of fourteen *Jagdpanzer* Jg.Pz. 38(t) *Hetzer* tank destroyers, equipped with the powerful Model 39 L/48 75mm antitank gun. In addition, the antiaircraft company (*3rd Company*) traded in its twelve 20mm automatic cannon for nine 37mm self-propelled automatic cannon, a marked increase in defensive firepower against low-flying fighter bombers.

All of the administrative and logistical troops would be combined into one regiment, *Supply Regiment 272*, led by the able *Major* Ritter. This unit was authorized 1,075 men and contained a supply battalion, an administrative company, an ammunition supply company, a maintenance company, a medical company, a veterinary company (to care for the division's 3,002 horses) and a field post office. Grouping all of these disparate elements into one regiment simplified and streamlined the task of providing the wherewithal for the combat elements to continue operating at peak efficiency and eliminated several hundred excess positions from the previous table of organization. Much of the responsibility for the logistics operation had also been shifted to the next higher echelon (the corps), which had a much larger number of specialty units able to provide tailored support to its subordinate divisions as required.

Under the new *Volks-Grenadier* establishment, the division was authorized 10,070 men, 2,500 fewer than the comparable *Kriegsetat 44* organizational structure that it replaced, but in general possessed more firepower than before The exact number of troops that were assigned to *272nd VGD* when it returned to the Western Front in early November 1944 is unknown, though the division history states that it was close to its authorized strength. It was, however, now more dependent upon horses in its reduced support regiment than ever before. According to an order issued by the *OKH*, the total number of cargo trucks authorized in the battalion and regimental trains of a *Volks-Grenadier Division* had been reduced to 171, excluding combat and command and control vehicles.[15] Compared to an American infantry division, which possessed as many as 1,440 motor vehicles, this number was very low and is a reflection of why a *Volks-Grenadier* division had such a relatively low degree of logistical capability, especially when conducting offensive operations. In all, three-fourths of the division's transport literally relied upon horsepower to move its stocks of food, ammunition, and other supplies To move everything, each *Volks-Grenadier Division* was authorized a total of 426 motor vehicles of all types, 119 motorcycles, and 1,142 horse-drawn wagons and trailers.

Most unit's of the division subordinate elements retained their former *KStN*, only *"Volks-"* was added to their official titles. For example, *Grenadier Regiment 980* now became *Volks-Grenadier Regiment 980* (though for the remainder of this book, the more familiar term, grenadier regiment, will be used, since there is little evidence that any of the old personnel from the *272nd Infantry Division* took notice of their new regimental designations). For the most part, under the new table of organization the division received more artillery, more machine guns, and the new assault rifle, the *Sturmgewehr* 44 (or MP-44).

As previously mentioned, *Füsilier Battalion 272* was not to be reformed under its old organization—in fact, a battalion was not authorized at all under the new table of organization for a *Volks-Grenadier division*. Under the new structure, the *Füsilier Battalion* was done away with entirely, replaced by the much smaller *Divisions-Füsilier Company* (*KStN* 149V, dated 1 September 1944).[16] Authorized two hundred men, *Füsilier Company 272* was intended to be a powerful, highly mobile unit mounted on bicycles that could carry out reconnaissance missions or serve as an elite force that could be rapidly employed across the divisional front as a commander's reserve.

According to the *KStN*, a *Divisions-Füsilier Company* of a *Volks-Grenadier* division was organized as follows: a company headquarters, two bicycle-mounted machine-pistol platoons of thirty-five men, equipped with MP-44 assault rifles, one thirty-five-man bicycle-mounted rifle platoon, a heavy weapons platoon, an infantry howitzer section, and company trains.

Three officers were authorized for the company—a company commander, an executive officer who doubled as a platoon leader, and the heavy weapons platoon leader. The company commander was intended to be a captain, with the other two officers being first or second lieutenants. It was authorized twenty-eight non-commissioned officers (NCOs) as well as 169 corporals and privates.[17]

The *1st Maschinepistole (*machine pistol*) Platoon* was led by the aforementioned *Leutnant,* who had thirty-four enlisted men, including three NCOs, under his command. The second platoon was organized identically, except its platoon leader was a *Feldwebel* or senior sergeant. Each platoon consisted of three *Gruppen* (squads) of nine men each, eight of whom were armed with MP-44s. The ninth man in each squad was a sniper who was equipped with a G-43 semi-automatic rifle with scope. In addition, the platoon had a light-machine-gun section, consisting of four men with one MG-42 machine gun. In all, each machine-pistol platoon had twenty-six MP-44s, seven rifles, and one machine gun, making each platoon much more lethal than a standard rifle platoon.

The company's bicycle-mounted third platoon was organized somewhat differently than the first and second platoons. Similarly to the older infantry platoon *KStN*, its men were primarily equipped with nineteen Mauser 98Ks instead of MP-44s, nine 9mm machine pistols (MP-40), and three MG-42s. Instead of being grouped into a platoon machine-gun section, an MG-42 was assigned to each squad, the same practice as in the older-model infantry squads from *Kriegsetat 44* infantry divisions. Although the manner in which this platoon was employed can no longer be determined, it was likely intended to be used for defensive operations, since it lacked the hard-hitting firepower of the first two platoons. In the one operation where the platoon's tactical employment is described, it was used as a company reserve force, following closely behind one of the other two platoons carrying out an assault. When well led, this platoon could prove to be as effective as the other two.

The *4th Schwere* (heavy weapons) *Platoon* consisted of one section armed with two tripod-mounted MG-42s and two 80mm medium mortars. This platoon was authorized five NCOs and thirty-four enlisted men.

The *5th Infantry-Geschütz* (infantry howitzer) *Platoon* was equipped with two infantry howitzers and was authorized one officer, four NCOs, and twenty-four enlisted men, including the platoon's ammunition section and drivers.

The company headquarters section and the company trains consisted of one officer (the company commander), eighteen NCOs and eighteen other enlisted men. Included in the company roster but not counted as soldiers were four *Hiwis*, ex-Soviet prisoners of war who had opted to serve the German Army either from a desire to escape slow death in a POW camp, to extract revenge against Stalin's Soviet regime, or other reasons. (For organizational diagram, see Appendix C.)

In all, the company was authorized eighty-nine Mauser 98Ks, eighty-four sub-machine guns or assault rifles, seven light MG-42 machine guns, two heavy machine guns (tripod-mounted MG-42s), two 80mm mortars, and two 75mm Model 18 light infantry howitzers. It was a small, yet hard-hitting force, possessing four times the amount of firepower as the average German Infantry Company of 1941 According to Fleischer, a *Füsilier Company* at its authorized *KStN* strength could fire 570.3 kg weight of shot per minute, compared to the 135.1 kg of shot per minute of a 1941 German infantry company.[18] Shortages of MP-44s, however, resulted in many *Volksgrenadiers* in the *272nd VGD* being issued MP-40 submachine guns or Mauser 98Ks rifles instead. According to veteran's interviews, though, *Füsilier Company 272* received the authorized quantities of this weapon, perhaps as a nod to its elite status within the division.

To provide the mobility required by its reconnaissance mission, *Füsilier Company 272* was authorized one motorcycle, one truck for the field kitchen, nineteen horse-drawn vehicles, ten trailers, fifty-six horses, and 166 bicycles.[19] The company was also authorized three *Raupenschlepper Ost* (Tracked Prime Mover "East") or *RSOs*. These were fully-tracked truck-like vehicles that doubled as prime movers and cargo haulers. Designed by the truck firm of Steyr in Austria, the 4.9 ton *RSO* was slow and noisy, traveling at only twelve miles per hour, but was far superior to horses, especially when used to pull the company's 75mm infantry howitzers or to carry up to three tons of cargo.[20] Most of these horses and vehicles were probably inherited from the now-defunct *Füsilier Battalion 272*, whose equipment, like its manpower, had been parceled out to make up for shortages or new requirements elsewhere.

Taken together, the company had far greater mobility and firepower than an ordinary German infantry company of comparable size, a fact that the division commander took advantage of several times during the company's brief existence. This mobility made it the ideal unit to quickly shift from one place to another across the division's defensive sector, to counterattack and to hold proportionally larger portions of the front line. When compared to a US infantry company, however, which enjoyed access to the divisional pool of 2½-ton cargo trucks, horses, and bicycles had become an anachronism in a war that was becoming increasingly mechanized.

A great deal of work awaited the divisional and regimental staffs before they could begin the task of reorganizing their old division. First, they had to quickly study the new structure and become familiar with its different capabilities. Then they had to train the division and instill a level of tactical proficiency that allowed it to be committed to combat in short order. Despite five years of war, it seemed that there was still a lot to learn. The training manuals and other printed reference material required to educate the commanders and staffs and to facilitate the transition of the division into a new *Volks-Grenadier* division filled an entire truck— in fact, 140 heavy packages of documents, considered a rather extravagant waste of paper by this late stage of the war, according to the opinion of several division veterans.[21]

Sadly for the Division, *Generalleutnant* Friedrich-August Schack, who had led the *216th* and *272nd Infantry Divisions* since May 1943, would not be present to guide the transformation. He had been selected on 3 September 1944 by the *OKH* to assume command of *LXXXI Corps*, and was instructed to hand over temporary command of his division to *Oberst* Friedrich Kittel until another officer could be appointed.[22] Division veterans recall Schack's departure as being a sad moment, for they had fought under him for eighteen months, including the Battles of Kursk and Gomel in Russia, throughout the Normandy Campaign, and the retreat to the *Westwall*.[23]

Kittel was in command for a brief period, replaced by the more senior *Oberst* Georg Kossmala on 16 October 1944. Though he was one grade below the rank required to command a division (that of *Generalmajor*), Kossmala enjoyed a solid reputation in the *Wehrmacht*. Born 20 October 1896 in the Bohemian town of Myslowitz, Kossmala enlisted in the Prussian Army on 13 September 1914, fought in World War I, and was promoted to *Leutnant der Reserve* in 1917. Following the war, he continued his military service in the *Reichswehr*. By April 1938, he was a *Major* commanding the *3rd Battalion* of the *38th Infantry Regiment, 8th Infantry Division* in the garrison town of Schweidnitz.[24]

After leading his battalion during the invasion of Poland in September 1939 and the Invasion of France in May 1940, now-*Oberstleutnant* Kossmala was transferred in September 1940 to command the *1st Battalion, 222nd Infantry Regiment, 75th Infantry Division*. Shortly thereafter, he was transferred to the newly activated *302nd Infantry Division*, where he helped form and lead *1st Battalion, Infantry Regiment 570*. In March 1941, he was transferred yet again to command another newly activated unit, *Security Regiment 3*, which was slated to conduct rear-area security operations for the upcoming invasion of the Soviet Union.

For that first year in Russia, he led his regiment, composed primarily of middle-aged home guardsmen, against bypassed elements of the Red Army and Soviet partisans while attached to the *18th Army* of *Army Group North*. It was while leading this regiment that he was recognized for his leadership by the award of the Knight's Cross on 13 March 1942, two months after being promoted to *Oberst*. Four months later he was transferred to command the *6th Infantry Regiment* of the *30th Infantry Division*, a first-line unit, and fought in and around the Demyansk and Staraya Russa areas. On 26 March 1944 he was awarded the

Oak Leaves to the Knight's Cross while leading the regiment during fighting near the town of Ostrov. His talents as a future division commander were demonstrated for the first time from August to early October 1944, when he assumed temporary command of the *32nd Infantry Division* during the initial stages of the Battle for Courland.

Oberst Kossmala was transferred back to the Western Front for the first time since 1940 when he was ordered to assume command of the *272nd VGD* effective 30 September, but did not actually take command until 16 October 1944, after he had taken two weeks of well-earned leave. Arriving at the temporary headquarters near Döberitz, Kossmala took over command from *Oberst* Kittel, who was immediately thereafter promoted to *Generalmajor* and given command of the *62nd Volks-Grenadier Division.*[25]

Kossmala was assisted in his duties by his new Operations Officer or *Ia*, *Major im Generalstabsdienst (i.G.)* Gerhard Höptner, who had been assigned to the division on 10 September and who had replaced *Major i.G.* Hubert Werner.[26] Höptner was a qualified general staff officer and proved to be Kossmala's strong right arm in the days to come. It was expected that at some point in the future, Kossmala would be promoted and named to permanently command another division, but for the next several months, the *272nd Volks-Grenadier* was his to lead.

Oberst Kossmala was forty-eight years old at the time and brought energy and enthusiasm to his new assignment. He quickly directed his energy toward the organization and training of his command. Since the division had only six weeks to prepare for combat, it needed every ounce of his talents. Normally the task of creating a new division required at least three months, but in the fall of 1944 with the enemy literally at Germany's doorstep, that was a luxury that neither Kossmala nor his soldiers could be allowed.

The *Ia* served as the First General Staff Officer in the division, a position similar to the US Army's G-3. As the *Ia*, Höptner dealt with all areas of the command and control of the units of the division as well as areas of plans, leadership, training, transport, housing, air-raid protection, evaluation, and presentation of combat options to the divisional commander. He also stood in for the divisional commander when the commander himself was not available and was empowered to make decisions in his absence.[27]

Höptner, born 3 June 1917, had been groomed for the General Staff since his entry in the service. On 1 September 1939, he served as Adjutant of *1st Battalion, Artillery Regiment 254, 254th Infantry Division.* During the next two years, he progressed through a variety of command and staff positions within the division, laying the groundwork for his entry into the General Staff. On 8 February 1940, he began his first tour as a battery commander; on 16 April 1941 he was named as the *O1* (1st Orderly Officer, similar to aide-de-camp) to the division commander, *Generalleutnant* Walter Behschnitt.

In recognition of his proven abilities, on 1 May 1942 he was moved up to become an *O1* on the General Staff of *I Corps*, then fighting in the Soviet Union.

After two months in this position, he was transferred to Germany on 30 June 1942 and assigned to *Artillery Replacement Battalion 26* for training, following by his assignment as a liaison officer 26 October 1942 to *Army Artillery Command 303*, commanded by *Generalleutnant* Hans Kratzert. After only a month in this position, Höptner was sent back to the homeland to attend the Artillery Officer Gunnery School for horse-drawn artillery in Thorn.

Having completed this course (similar to the artillery officer advanced course of the US Army), he assumed duties on 26 July 1943 as a battalion commander in *Artillery Regiment 347, 347th Infantry Division*, then stationed in Holland carrying out defensive operations along the Channel Coast. Having completed this qualifying assignment, on 15 October 1943 he was posted to the *Führer Reserve* and temporarily assigned to the staff of the *233rd Reserve Panzer Division*. Finally, having got his branch qualifying assignments out of the way, Höptner was posted on 1 February 1944 to the *Kriegsakademie* (War College) as a student candidate for the General Staff.

While pursuing his studies, he was promoted to *Major* on 1 May 1944, though he not become a fully qualified General Staff Officer until he graduated from the course on 1 August 1944. He was initially ordered to assume duties as the *Ia* of the *134th Infantry Division* beginning on 10 August 1944, but since this division was destroyed in Minsk the month before, this young officer was assigned instead on 10 September 1944 to be the *Ia* of the *272nd VGD*. Thus, by fortunate circumstances, Kossmala was to inherit a talented and experienced operations officer who proved to be an enormous asset to the Division during the months to come.[28]

Under the guiding hands of Kossmala and Höptner, as well as those of the other experienced commanders and NCOs, training and reorganization went forward at a breakneck pace throughout the last week of September and the month of October, with long days spent in the training area firing weapons and conducting field training exercises. After the survivors of the Normandy Campaign returned from their well-earned furloughs at the end of September, there was little free time again until the division was ready for combat.

4

Of Mortal Coil—The Men of *Füsilier Company 272*

Military organizations, even those with the latest equipment and following modern doctrine, are only as effective as the soldiers in their ranks. In this regard, *Füsilier Company 272* was fortunate to have seasoned and effective leadership at its inception. Despite its small size, its excellent initial combat performance can be attributed to the fact its cadre were no strangers to combat. Many had served with *das deutsche Heer* (the German Army) since the beginning of the war.

The new division's command and staff had been informed by the *Ersatzheer* (Replacement Army) headquarters that they had only two months at the most in which to prepare for its next assignment (rumored to be on the Eastern Front). Because of this, the division's cadre, including the veterans of the old *Füsilier Battalion 272,* had to work quickly in order to transform the new *Ersatz* (replacements), many of whom had only recently been transferred from the *Luftwaffe* and *Kriegsmarine*, into well-trained *Volksgrenadiers* During the initial establishment of the company in late September/early October 1944, forty-four of its personnel were transferred from the *Kriegsmarine* and six came from the *Luftwaffe*; the remainder all came from the *Heer*, including thirteen recruits born between 1926 and 1927. The fact that 150 of its men came from the *Heer* represents a relatively high proportion compared to the *Volks-Grenadier* regiments, which were formed with between thirty-five and fifty percent non-*Heer* personnel. The time available at Falkensee to achieve a modicum of tactical efficiency at the squad, platoon, and company level was very limited indeed, so they quickly got to work. The veterans knew that lessons learned in combat were usually costly ones, so they struggled to ensure that the men in the new unit absorbed these lessons as quickly as possible.

The responsibility for training the *Füsilier Company 272*'s new troops fell mainly on its commanding officer and his senior non-commissioned officers. These veterans not only had the responsibility of whipping the new recruits into some semblance of a proficient military organization, but had the standards and proud traditions of the old *Grenadier Regiment 396* to uphold as well. The task was made more difficult since they were not stationed at a normal training area with an array of weapons firing ranges. This forced the commander and NCOs to improvise in order to get the most out of what the area around Falkensee offered.

The new company commander, *Oberleutnant* Heinz Kolb, had commanded the old *2nd Company*, *Füsilier Battalion 272* in Normandy and he had proven himself in some of the most difficult tactical situations imaginable. A tall and slender man, every inch of him personified the professional German officer. Born in the Cologne suburb of Kalk on 25 August 1916, he was the only child of a working class family. Kolb had been working with the city inspector's office in Cologne when he enlisted in the *Heer* in November 1936. Apparently dissatisfied with pursuing a civilian career, he began active duty as a private in *Infantry Regiment 77* of the *26th Infantry Division*. Shortly thereafter, he volunteered for officer training and was commissioned as a *Leutnant der Reserve* (reserve lieutenant) on 1 February 1940 and posted to *Infantry Regiment 306, 211th Infantry Division* as a platoon leader.

Kolb took part in the Western Campaign in 1940 and apparently proved himself a good leader, for he was soon appointed as an acting company commander. During the invasion of the Soviet Union, Kolb initially served on the staff of *Infantry Regiment 306* as the aide-de-camp to his regimental commander. By August 1942, he was leading troops again as a platoon leader and was a full-fledged company commander by November 1942, a position he held until 12 August 1943. While serving in Russia, he began a friendship with *Gefreiter* Kurt Klein, whose life he had saved during a Soviet attack.

When Kolb's battalion had suffered such heavy losses that it could no longer be reconstituted, it was disbanded and its men used to fill out other units. He was then transferred to Germany, where he was briefly posted to a training unit. Kolb was then assigned to the re-activated *272nd Infantry Division* on 18 January 1944, after leading *March Company 328* from its base to Belgium to join the then-forming *Füsilier Battalion 272*. Upon joining the battalion, he was assigned to serve as the commander of *2nd Company*. Here, he again met up with his old friend from the Eastern Front, Kurt Klein, who had somehow managed to get assigned to the same company as Kolb when he heard that his former commander would be leading it.

No stranger to combat, Kolb had received numerous awards for valor while fighting on the Eastern and Western Fronts. On 3 April 1942, he was award the Iron Cross 2nd Class for bravery, followed on 22 July 1943 by the award of the more prestigious Iron Cross 1st Class. His service on the Eastern Front during the terrible winter of 1941/42 was recognized by the awarding of the Russian Front Medal on 20 August 1942, known sarcastically by survivors of the fighting as the *Gefrierfleischordnung*, or the "Order of the Frozen Meat."

Kolb participated in numerous infantry assaults while in the East, recognized by the presentation of the Infantry Assault Badge in Silver on 25 April 1944.[1] Kolb had also been wounded twice. He suffered his first wound on the Eastern Front, where he was awarded the Wound Badge in Black on 7 March 1942, and his second in Normandy, where he earned the Wound Badge in Silver, awarded on 20 September 1944. His frequent participation in close combat during the Normandy Campaign was recognized on 20 September by the award of the Close Combat Badge in Bronze.[2]

An old lung disorder that had developed on the Eastern Front flared up while he was fighting in Normandy, requiring medical evacuation to a field hospital for treatment. Thus, he was not present to see his old company decimated north of the Falaise Pocket and nearly destroyed during the retreat from Normandy. On 22 September 1944, having recuperated from his lung condition, *Oberleutnant* Kolb was chosen from among several other officers from *Füsilier Battalion 272,* who had also survived the debacle in France, to command the reformed division's new *Füsilier* company. At the time, this was considered to be a highly sought-after position.

In addition to his proven leadership, tactical skill, and indisputable bravery, Kolb was also considered, on paper at least, to be politically reliable—an important attribute when one takes into account the degree of attention that Heinrich Himmler was devoting to the newly-raised *Volks-Grenadier* divisions—for Kolb was not only a member of the National Socialist German Workers' Party or NSDAP, but was also a member in good standing of the *Allgemeine-SS,* or General *SS.*

Unlike the *Waffen-SS* or the *SS*-Death's Head formations, the *Allgemeine-SS* served not only as the foundation of the *SS* empire's bureaucratic structure, but also as a sort of a social club or fraternity for those wishing to achieve higher standing in German society, often barred to those of humble origins. In some ways, it was akin to a reserve organization for the *SS,* enabling its members to serve in the Army or other branches of the *Wehrmacht* while still holding honorary rank in the *Allgemeine-SS.* Whether or not Kolb genuinely professed Nazi beliefs can no longer be judged, but according to the remaining records, he possessed all of the traits that the Third Reich was desperately seeking in its junior officers by this stage of the war, when political zeal was adjudged to be just as important as military ability, if not more so.

Still unmarried in 1944, Kolb was engaged to a girl from Berlin who he hoped to marry sometime in the spring of 1945. Described as "very correct, the model of a German officer," by one former soldier and a "fantastic officer" by another, Kolb's leadership skills were soon put to the test.[3] After the change of command ceremony on 22 September 1944, Kolb's predecessor, *Major* Thürmer, departed the company and assumed command of *1st Battalion, Grenadier Regiment 981,* leaving Kolb with the assignment of training and preparing his new command for combat.

While Heinz Kolb, as company commander, was considered the "Father" of *Füsilier Company 272* (at twenty-eight, he was considered the "old man" of the company), the *Spiess,* or first sergeant, was considered to be its "Mother." The company's *Spiess* was *Hauptfeldwebel* Hermann Fuhrmeister. Even older than Kolb, Fuhrmeister had been born in Lower Saxony on 4 December 1902 in the small town of Süpplingen. Fuhrmeister had been working as a salesman in the town of Hildesheim when he volunteered for the service in *Infantry Regiment 396* in January 1937.

A veteran of the Battle of France and the Eastern Front, Fuhrmeister had been transferred along with the other survivors of *2nd Battalion, Grenadier Regiment 396* to Belgium when that unit was converted into *Füsilier Battalion 272*. There, he participated in the Normandy Campaign and was one of the few survivors of the unit that stepped off the train at Döberitz. By September 1944, Fuhrmeister was a decorated combat veteran, having been awarded the Iron Cross 2nd Class, Infantry Assault Badge in Silver, the Wound Badge in Black, and the Russian Front Medal. A large and somewhat forceful man, Fuhrmeister possessed all the traits that made him the epitome of the German NCO—authoritative, blunt-spoken, harsh when necessary, and ever ready to assume responsibility.

The company was authorized two lieutenants—an executive officer and a weapons platoon leader. The unit's executive officer, or second in command, was *Leutnant* Helmut Beyer. Although a relatively young officer and new to the company, Beyer was already a veteran of the Eastern Front. Born in Göttingen on 15 September 1923, Beyer had been attending the city's famous university on a deferment from the draft when he was finally called up for service on 23 July 1942. After a year of training in Göttingen, Belgium, and in Boulogne, France, he was transferred as an officer candidate in October 1943 to the Eastern Front to join his field unit, *Grenadier Regiment 82* of *31st Infantry Division,* then serving in the Gomel area.[4]

Here Beyer fought for several months, gaining the kind of experience and troop leading skills that a young officer can only gain by leading men in battle. After a hospital stay due to wounds suffered in Russia that winter near Bobruisk, Beyer attended an officer's commissioning course in Haguenau, France in early 1944 and was promoted to *Leutnant* that spring. His officer training complete, Beyer was then transferred to *Füsilier Company 272* on 5 October 1944 while it was training in Falkensee. His awards included the Wound Badge in Gold, Iron Cross 2nd Class for his leadership and bravery in Russia the previous winter and the Infantry Assault Badge in Silver

The company's infantry howitzer platoon leader, *Leutnant* Ernst Wegner, was another veteran of the Eastern Front. Wegner was much older than Beyer, having been born 14 October 1909 in Berlin. Married with two children, Wegner had begun his career as a private, volunteering for service in *Infantry Regiment 8* on 1 November 1929. Though he started out as an infantryman, by 1933 he had been qualified to serve as a master farrier. Wegner's first campaign was the invasion of Poland in 1939. As a farrier assigned to the headquarters of *2nd Battalion, Infantry Regiment 82, 31st Infantry Division* (the same division to which Beyer had been assigned), Wegner probably experienced little, if any, combat. He rose to the rank of *Fahnenjunker-Stabsbeschlagmeister*, or officer candidate staff farrier by October 1943. (Farriers repaired and replaced horseshoes and insured that the horses' hooves were properly cared for. In an army that relied chiefly upon horses for transport, a farrier, or *Beschlagmeister*, was a key component of any infantry company or battalion.) Before being admitted to officer candidate school on 8 December 1943, Wegner had served for nearly three years as a farrier instructor at the Army Technical School for specialists.

Wegner's first exposure to the perils of the Eastern Front took place during the summer and fall of 1943, when he served as a staff farrier with *Division Transport Column 150* of the *50th Infantry Division* as it withdrew through the Kuban's Taman Peninsula across the straits of Kerch to the Crimea. While it is no longer possible to determine whether Wegner was involved in the actual fighting, the constant retreat along rutted roads in the Kuban and Crimea must have placed an immense strain on the division's horses and on the men whose job it was to keep them properly shod. In recognition of his achievement during this campaign, he was awarded the War Service Cross with Swords, 2nd Class on 30 November 1943.

Ordered out of the Crimea in October 1943, Wegner reported to the Warthelager Training Area near Posen where he was assigned to Officer-Candidate Course, Class 15, which ran from 8 December 1943 to 15 March 1944. This basic course was followed immediately by the Infantry Platoon Leaders' Course in Döberitz, from which he graduated on 4 July 1944. While a student at Döberitz, he was officially commissioned as a *Leutnant* on 1 May 1944, fifteen years after his initial enlistment. While the fighting in Normandy and on the Eastern Front raged that long, hot summer, Wegner and his classmates continued their officer training as if it were peacetime.

Wegner next attended the Infantry Howitzer Platoon Leader's Course where he gained proficiency in the use of the 75mm and 150mm infantry howitzers. Finally, after nearly one year in training to become an officer, Wegner was assigned to *Füsilier Company 272* on 3 October 1944. His political reliability, at least according to his officer candidate course's senior commander, was secure. He was, according to his course evaluation, "a believer in martial National Socialist thought, which manifested itself in an impressive and convincing manner to his fellow classmates." Whether this spirit would sustain him through the fighting to come remained to be seen, though he had certainly undergone more training than the average American infantry lieutenant.

One man who knew Wegner, *Gefreiter* Peter Moog, stated that, while Wegner was a likeable enough fellow, he lacked confidence in his ability as a leader, since the bulk of his previous service had been spent as a farrier, and not as a true front-line soldier. Understandably, he relied heavily upon his non-commissioned officers to help get the job done. To his credit, Wegner not only sought out the advice of the more experienced NCOs, but he acted upon it as well, to the benefit of everyone in the company. Had a younger, less mature officer been assigned in his place, especially one from one of the *Junker* officer commissioning schools, that might not have been the case and morale would have suffered.[5]

The *Kompanietruppführer* (company headquarters platoon leader) was *Unteroffizier* Kurt Klein. Born 11 July 1915 in the steel-making city of Solingen in the Ruhr industrial area, Klein enlisted in the *Wehrmacht* in February 1939 after fulfilling his mandatory labor service in the *Reichsarbeitsdienst (RAD).* He completed basic training with *5th Company*, *Infantry Replacement Regiment 39* and was shortly thereafter transferred to *10th Company*, *Infantry Regiment 113* of the *39th Infantry Division.* Although his first troop assignment was limited to occupation duty in Holland and Belgium, he was sent with a draft of replacements to join Infantry Regiment 306 in April 1943 to fight in Russia when it was committed to the Kharkov sector. There he met Heinz Kolb and thus began a friendship that lasted until Kolb's death. In October 1943, Klein was transferred to the west to join the *272nd Infantry Division.*

While fighting in Russia, Klein had earned the Infantry Assault Badge in Silver for fighting near Bolya Babka, Selyanin, Stary Ssaltov, and Martovaja in the spring and summer of 1943, though it was not awarded until April 1944, when he was then serving with *2nd Company, Füsilier Battalion 272.* In Normandy, Klein earned the Close Combat Clasp in Bronze for his participation in close-quarters fighting against British and Canadian troops at Troarn, St. Sylvain, Hill 79, Glatigny, St. Pierre sur Dive, Mont Jakob, and Lessard.

Klein was one of only sixteen surviving members of the original *2nd Company* and one of the most experienced. As headquarters platoon leader, Klein was responsible for the portion of the headquarters platoon that accompanied the company commander into battle, minus the company trains that remained in the rear under the supervision of the *Spiess.* As such, Klein served as Kolb's right-hand man in battle, insuring that the radiomen, snipers, medics, and messengers kept up with the commander whether in the attack or defense. He often was called upon to lead counterattacks using headquarters personnel when the other platoons were already committed in a fight.

No stranger to combat, he had already been awarded the Iron Cross 2nd Class and Wound Badge in Black during Normandy. Despite his proven military abilities, however, Klein was not a soldier at heart or a Nazi. Due to his height, muscular build, and blond hair, the *Waffen-SS* had tried to induce him into joining their corps while he was in the *RAD,* but to no avail. All he wanted was to pursue a career as a metal worker in his hometown of Solingen. A good-natured man, Kurt Klein was an avid hiker and lover of the outdoors, always willing to help out his friends and fellow soldiers.

Reliable, experienced, and trustworthy, Klein was a godsend to a busy company commander who needed someone to insure that the company headquarters section kept up with the commander in battle and to take immediate charge of the headquarters in his absence. All the better that Klein was an old friend of Kolb's. While on leave in Cologne before being committed to the Hürtgen Forest, Kolb invited Klein to his house to meet his parents and they welcomed him into the family as one of their own, all the more so since Kolb was an only child. Their friendship would be put to severe tests in the days to come.

Each of the five platoons was in the hands of an experienced veteran NCO as well. The senior sergeant of the *1st Maschinepistole* (machine pistol) *Platoon,*

Oberfeldwebel Herbert Gomm, born 14 March 1910 in Berlin, joined the company on 2 October when he and the rest of the *March Company*, consisting of replacements from *Reconnaissance Replacement and Training Squadron 9*, arrived in Falkensee. Although his service record is not available, the company's personnel roster shows that he joined the *Heer* in November 1935 and had already been awarded the Iron Cross 2nd Class and Wound Badge in Black. After being assigned to the company, Gomm volunteered to become an officer and was sent to an officer's candidate school before the company departed for the Western Front. By mid-January 1945, he was back with the company as a *Leutnant*. Married with children, at thirty-four he was a bit old to be a front-line infantryman in an elite reconnaissance unit, but he was still a rare commodity by that stage of the war—a mature, experienced officer who had been veteran NCO.

Gomm was replaced as the Platoon Sergeant of *1st Platoon* on 7 November by *Feldwebel* Ludwig Hellmonds, born 5 February 1916 in Walsund. A sergeant since 5 January 1937, Hellmonds was the most senior of the five platoon sergeants. He had fought in France and Russia with *Infantry Regiment 462* of the *262nd Infantry Division,* earning the Iron Cross 2nd Class, Infantry Assault Badge in Silver, and Russian Front Medal with that division. Assigned to the *272nd Infantry Division* when his old division was broken up, he fought in Normandy with 2nd *Company, Füsilier Battalion 272* during the summer of 1944. Severely wounded in Normandy, he spent nearly three months recovering from his injuries, for which he had been awarded the Wound Badge in Silver shortly after he rejoined the company near Rollesbroich in the Eifel on 7 November 1944.

The *2nd Maschinepistole* (machine pistol) *Platoon* leader, *Feldwebel* Heinrich Reiners, had been serving in the *Wehrmacht* since 2 November 1937, the year he enlisted in *6th (Bicycle) Squadron, Cavalry Regiment 9,* with whom he had fought in Poland. Born 30 September 1915 in the village of Busch near the town of Erkelenz, Reiners was next assigned to *Reconnaissance Squadron 1* of the *1st Infantry Division,* with which he fought in Holland, Belgium, and France in May 1940. He went with the division into Russia in 1941, where he fought in the battle of Lake Ladoga. He had then been posted to Denmark with the German occupation forces before being assigned to *Reconnaissance Replacement Squadron 9* and then to *Füsilier Company 272* on 30 September 1944. His decorations included the War Service Cross, 2nd Class with Swords and the Russian Front Medal. Although he had not been engaged in frontline combat since 1942, he soon proved himself to be an effective platoon leader.

Reiners's assistant was *Unteroffizier* Franz Matthies, born 7 March 1921 in the town of Bludenz, Austria, who enlisted in November 1939. Matthies, though only an *Unteroffizier,* had been decorated with the Iron Cross 2nd Class for bravery in Normandy while serving with *1st Company, Füsilier Battalion 272*. He was singled out in his award citation for "demonstrating the qualities of a bold fighter," participating in every engagement the battalion took part in that summer. A ski instructor in civilian life, Matthies enlisted while working at a ski resort in his hometown. A veteran of the Balkans Campaign of 1941, he briefly fought in Russia, where he was severely wounded during the early phase of Operation BARBAROSSA, for which he was awarded the Wound Badge in Black.

Feldwebel Kurt Belder, the leader of the *3rd Platoon,* had fought in Normandy with *2nd Company, Füsilier Battalion 272.* Belder, born 24 February 1917 in Berlin-Spandau, began his service with *Grenadier Regiment 376* of the *225th Infantry Division* in November 1938. He, too, had fought in Russia, where he had been awarded the Russian Front Medal, Iron Cross 1st and 2nd Classes, the Infantry Assault Badge in Silver, and the Wound Badge in Black. His platoon, since it was not authorized the new MP-44 assault rifle, was issued Mauser 98 bolt-action rifles instead, making it the most lightly armed platoon in the company. It drew its replacements not from reconnaissance replacement units, but from the infantry.

The *4th Schwere* (heavy weapons) *Platoon* was led by *Feldwebel* Kurt Dirksen, born 11 November 1911 in Berlin. He had fought in Russia with *Infantry Regiment 203* of *76th Infantry Division*, and narrowly evaded capture or death when that division capitulated at Stalingrad with the rest of *Generalfeldmarschall* Friedrich Paulus' *Sixth Army*. For his valor, he had also been awarded the Iron Cross 1st and 2nd Classes, Infantry Assault Badge in Silver, Wound Badge in Black, and Rumanian Campaign medal in Silver with Dniester Clasp. His job was be to whip his new machine gunners and mortar crews into some semblance of military efficiency before being committed to battle.

The *5th Infantry-Geschütz* (infantry howitzer) *Platoon*, armed with two infantry howitzers, had *Feldwebel* Karl Etzmannsdorfer, born 21 October 1914 in Oberthern, assigned as its platoon sergeant. He had originally enlisted in the army in 1935, but completed just two and a half years of service before he transferred to the *Luftwaffe* in June 1938. He served in several antiaircraft or *Fliegerabwehr* units until September 1944, when he was transferred to the infantry as part of Dr. Goebbels's "Total War" declaration that lent its impetus toward the manning of the *Volks-Grenadier* divisions. On 4 October, he was assigned to *Grenadier Regiment 980* of the *272nd VGD*.

Due to his experience with heavy weapons, he was assigned shortly thereafter on 15 October 1944 to *Füsilier Company 272* to serve as the *Richtkriesunteroffizier* (fire direction control NCO) under *Leutnant* Wegner, making him the de facto platoon sergeant. A veteran *Flak* gunner of the air war over Germany, Etzmannsdorfer had been awarded the Czechoslovakian Annexation Medal, the Four Year Service Medal, and the *Luftwaffe Flak* Badge. A professional soldier, he had signed up for twelve years of service and had completed the infantry howitzer platoon leader's course before being assigned to the company. In addition to serving as platoon sergeant, he directed the fire control center, which coordinated and adjusted the fire of the platoon's two howitzers.

The chief of Wegner's gun section was *Unteroffizier* Leonhard Kienberger, born 8 February 1919 in Ansbach. Compared to the others, Kienberger, was a relative newcomer, though he too had done his share of fighting. Enlisting September 1939, he served in a variety of infantry howitzer units before joining *Füsilier Company 272, including* Infantry *Regiment 9* of *23rd Infantry Division, Grenadier Regiment 203* of the *76th Infantry Division* (the same as Dirksen), and *Grenadier Regiment 122* of the *50th Infantry Division,* before that unit was destroyed in the spring of 1944 in the Crimea. Kienberger had fought in France in 1940 as well as in Normandy in the summer of 1944. Like the most of his peers, he had been awarded the Wound Badge in Black, the Russian Front Medal, and the Iron Cross 2nd Class. In addition to these five senior sergeants, there were two other *Feldwebeln*—the company's armorer, *Feldwebel* Heinrich Dietz, and the maintenance NCO, Hermann Otte. The supply NCO position, normally authorized a *Feldwebel*, was filled by the veteran *Unteroffizier* Fritz Johns.

Assisting these men were twenty other NCOs, such as Heinrich Misskampf, Fritz Fosselmann, and Otto Jagielski, who served as squad leaders, assistant platoon leaders, mortar and machine gun section leaders, assistant supply sergeants, cooks, drivers, medical NCOs, armorers, radio section leaders and other headquarters specialists. One detail which stands out as one reviews the original records is how quickly NCOs cycled through the company, so that after January 1945, with a few exceptions, it is impossible to determine who served in which duty position. Suffice to say, as the end approached, experienced NCOs grew scarce as they were killed and wounded, replaced in their turn by NCOs recently transferred from the *Luftwaffe* or *Kriegsmarine*. Try as they might, the replacement NCOs would demonstrate that they had neither the skill nor experience of men such as Hellmonds, Matthies, Dirksen, Belder, and Reiners, and they and their men suffered accordingly.

Rounding out the company's cadre were the few remaining *Gefreiten* (corporals) and *Obergefreiten* (senior corporals), some of whom had been together with the unit throughout its various permutations since France in 1940, Russia, and Normandy. Veteran corporals such as Peter Moog, Hermann Heiermann, Gerhard Ehret, Heinrich Geradts, and Friedrich Felmer not only served as role models and teachers for the new recruits, but also provided the backbone that could be utterly relied upon whenever the tactical situation demanded the utmost steadiness.

Building and Training the Company

Like the other companies of the various battalions and regiments of the *272nd VGD, Füsilier Company 272* had about six weeks to absorb new replacements, complete a rigorous training program, and prepare to ship out to the combat zone somewhere along the *Reich's* crumbling frontier. Even in the best of circumstances, this was a daunting assignment, but it was made all the more challenging by the fact that men and equipment trickled in to the units almost to the last day before they departed the training areas for the front.

The available training time was further reduced when the acting division commander, *Oberst* Kittel, granted two-week furloughs to most of the men who had survived the retreat to northern France. Leaving behind skeleton cadres to receive newly arriving replacements, most of the veterans scattered across the various German states and provinces to visit their families, whom many had not seen for months or even years. Others who could not go home, either owing to their essential duty position or to the fact that their homes were now occupied by the Allies, opted to have their families visit them in the Döberitz area instead. *Unteroffizier* Kurt Klein's wife, Elisabeth, and his daughter, Inge, made the hazardous rail journey from Solingen to Falkensee on 8 October so they could be together for a few days before he shipped out.[6] Other soldiers were sent to abbreviated training courses at specialist schools. Though Kittel's decision to furlough the veterans was a welcome one, it did cut into the limited amount of time available to train the newly assigned replacements.

Once the forty-three veterans of the old *Füsilier Battalion 272* began returning from their furloughs, *Füsilier Company 272* and the other elements of the *272nd VGD* began the business of preparing their troops for war. Beginning on 1 October, new replacements and equipment began to arrive just as the veterans had begun to unpack from their furloughs. On that day, eighteen personnel were assigned to the company from *Infantry Replacement Battalion 338* and *Signal Replacement Company 208*, as well as several returning convalescing veterans from the old *Füsilier Battalion 272*. The following day, 107 new personnel arrived, including thirty-nine men from *Reconnaissance Replacement Squadron 9*, thirty-two from a variety of other units, and thirty-six sailors from the *Kriegsmarine*. These men were assigned to the company directly from *Naval Replacement Battalion 6/12* in Wilhelmshaven.

Between 3 and 19 October, twenty-five more men were assigned to the company from replacement units or convalescent hospitals, bringing it close to its authorized strength of 200 men. By 23 October, the company had reported three officers, twenty-three NCOs, and 171 men assigned, for a total of 197 men. The average age in the company at that time was twenty-four years, a figure that compares favorably with infantry companies at the beginning of the war. The average age of the eighty-one new replacements was twenty years, while that of the twenty-six NCOs was twenty-nine. The veteran *Obergefreiten* and *Gefreiten* demonstrated an average age of twenty-six years. Clearly, *Füsilier Company 272* did not consist of old men and boys, despite the Allied stereotype of *Volks-Grenadier* units generated for propaganda purposes.

Also with the company were four Russian *Hiwis* who had been transferred along with the other veterans of the old *2nd Company*. Although they were not authorized by the company's table of organization, these men were kept on as cooks or wagon drivers. These men, Chermad Chasanow, a Volga Tartar born in 1903; Imangalie Bachtibajew, a Kazakh born in 1892; Gaganscha Alimbetow, a Bashkir tribesman born in 1916; and Kulpeden Eschimow, born in 1925, performed menial duties that allowed qualified soldiers to be freed up for use elsewhere in the company. While many of their fellow *Hiwis* took advantage of the chaos during the German retreat from France and deserted to the Allies, these four stayed on and continued to serve with the company until the end of the war. Needless to say, none of them were granted leave to visit their families, since by September 1944 more than 1,000 kilometers separated them from their homes, now liberated by the Red Army.

By 29 October, the company had achieved its full authorization of 200 personnel. On that date, not counting the four *Hiwis*, four men were attending various courses of instruction at specialists schools, six were recovering from illness in the hospital, one man was on emergency leave, and twenty-one men were serving with the company trains. One officer (*Leutnant* Beyer) and eighteen personnel (three NCOs and fifteen enlisted men) had been temporarily assigned to *Field Replacement Battalion 272*, where they were attending various weapons and leadership courses. They would not link up again with the company until it had arrived in its new defensive positions in the Hürtgen Forest. Therefore, the company's available combat strength or *Kampfstärke* was two officers, twenty-six NCOs and 142 men, for a total of 170.

The replacements, as noted above, came from a variety of sources. Several of them had already completed training with *Aufklärung Ersatz Abteilung 9* and comprised the group of men originally intended for to *Füsilier Company 1575*. Many had been transferred directly to the company from the *Kriegsmarine*, like Eduard Zacharuk, while others were transferred from the *Luftwaffe*. A few, such as *Gefreiter* Albert Trotsky, had fulfilled their initial military obligation and had been demobilized shortly after the end of the Western Campaign in July 1940, returning to their previous occupations. In the case of Albert Trotsky, that meant taking up his old position with the *Reichsbahn* (German National Railway). Once the drive for manpower to flesh out the new *Volks-Grenadier* divisions began in earnest during August and September 1944, these men were again called up for active service and began to pour by the thousands into the various training and replacement units all over the *Reich*.

Each field unit, or *Feldeinheit*, was affiliated by this stage of the war with a dedicated replacement unit. *Füsilier Company 272* was no different. Its replacement unit by this stage of the war was *Reconnaissance Replacement and Training Squadron 5*, located at Stolp, Pomerania. From time to time, depending on availability, the company also received replacements from other reconnaissance replacement units, such as *Reconnaissance Replacement and Training Squadron 14* at Ludwigslust, approximately fifty kilometers south of Schwerin or *Reconnaissance Replacement and Training Squadron 9,* based at Fürstenwalde-Spree, some thirty kilometers east of Berlin. Although *Füsilier Battalion 272* had been affiliated with the squadron in Ludwigslust, for some reason the decision was made to change replacement units for *Füsilier Company 272*.

Toward the end of February 1945, this system began to come apart. Dozens of replacements were assigned to the company from a wide variety of units, which made any distinction about their unit affiliation pointless. Losses were simply occurring at a faster rate than they could be replaced and a unit could count itself lucky to be allocated any replacements at all. From time to time, when no recruits were immediately available from its affiliated replacement and training unit or when combat losses were too heavy to be replaced by one unit alone, replacement units affiliated with other elements the *272nd VGD* were called upon to furnish men.

As the Allies advanced from both the east and the west in the spring of 1945, many training bases were simply overrun. This befell the company's replacement unit late in February 1945, when the Soviet advance toward Berlin engulfed the German forces defending the area surrounding Stolp, including *Reconnaissance Replacement and Training Squadron 5*, which had been mobilized for field service in an effort to stop the Soviet offensive. The few remaining replacements were subsequently forwarded from any still-functioning training depot to whichever unit in the field needed them most, irrespective of required skills, specialty, or unit affiliation. In some cases, replacements were assigned directly from units that supported infantry regiments, such as the large draft of replacements that was assigned to the company in March 1945 from a *March Battalion* originating from *Grenadier Replacement and Training Battalion 398* in Goslar.

Specialists, such as mortar crewmen and infantry howitzer gunners, were normally assigned to the company from Goslar, which had a special training and replacement company providing men with these skills. This unit, *Infantry Howitzer Replacement and Training Company 216,* specialized in training gunners and mortar crewmen. Signal troops generally came from *Signals Replacement and Training Company 208* located at Tiborlager/Schwiebus in Poland. *Sanitäter* (medics) were home based at *Medical Replacement and Training Company 11* located at the Bückeberg training area.

While the bulk of the original members of the old *Füsilier Battalion 272* came from the Hannover area, as had the original *Infantry Regiment 396*, the new replacements that filled the ranks of *Füsilier Company 272* came from all over Germany. Most of them, however, came from the east—from Brandenburg, Pomerania, Mecklenburg, and Thuringia. As previously mentioned, at least a dozen *Volksdeutsche* or ethnic Germans were assigned to the company as well. Gone were the days when units were recruited from the same general area; any sense of regional identity and feelings of shared kinship were gradually disappearing as well, a factor that adversely affected unit cohesion in some of the division's units in the days ahead.

The new company, as with the rest of the *272nd VGD,* had a different sound, too. The days of almost-universal everyday use of *Hochdeutsch* (high German) by the original Hanoverians became a rarity. There were now many regional German accents for the officers and NCOs to adjust to, with the pidgin-German of the *Volksdeutsche* recruits and *Hiwis* further complicating the giving and receiving of orders.

In the training and replacement units whose graduates were destined to fight in the Hürtgen Forest in the Fall of 1944, new recruits were mustered in and received basic training, followed by a few weeks of training in reconnaissance and infantry tactics. Once they had completed their initial training, the replacements were grouped into *March Battalions* (replacement transport battalion), issued rations, placed under the supervision of returning or newly-assigned NCOs or officers, and began their journey to the front.

Once the group arrived in the army rear area of operations, the *March Battalion* commander reported to a *Frontleitstelle* (personnel movement control point) and was given directions to the division. There, the unit was briefly assigned to the division's field replacement battalion, where the men theoretically would undergo additional training and conditioning to front line conditions before being sent onward to their units. Some personnel were kept on for longer periods, such as those chosen to take specialist or leadership courses in *Division Combat School 272*, a component element of the division's *Field Replacement Battalion 272*.

Finally, several months after entry into the *Heer*, the green replacements found themselves assigned to squads and platoons, their "home" for the remainder of the war, if they survived. For the recalled veterans, of course, the route back to their old units took a great deal less time, since they did not have to repeat basic training. They were required, however, to undergo refresher training with their local replacement and training units or with *Field Replacement Battalion 272*.[7]

For replacements from the *Luftwaffe* or *Kriegsmarine,* the records indicate they received even less training before being assigned to the division. After being released by their original branch of service and transferred into the German Army, they were processed into their newly affiliated replacement and training units. There, they were issued field equipment and uniform items, received inoculations, and were then forwarded directly to *Füsilier Company 272* or other units of the *272nd VGD*. Though a few of these men received additional squad leader training at *Division Combat School 272*, most had to learn how to be an infantryman during "on the job training."

The thirty-six *Kriegsmarine* transfers to *Füsilier Company 272* were fortunate that they were assigned to the company on 2 October 1944. This gave the company's leadership about four weeks to teach them basic infantry skills as well as squad and even platoon-level training before these erstwhile sailors experienced their baptism of fire. While even this amount of time was admittedly insufficient, they would be better prepared than later replacements, who received even less training.

Though most of the new replacements were quickly assimilated into their squads and platoons, the *Kriegsmarine* transfers proved troublesome. Most of them were teenagers born in 1926 and 1927, and they deeply resented that they were now destined to be lowly infantrymen instead of *U*-Boat crewmen. All had volunteered for naval service and were angry that they were involuntarily transferred to a branch of service they felt was beneath them. Trouble broke out soon after their arrival in early October, though at first it manifested itself discretely. During road marches to and from training areas, while other members of the company sang standard infantry songs like the *Westerwaldlied* or *Erika*, the *Kriegsmarine* replacement sang naval ditties like *Wir fahren gegen England.*[8]

To make matters worse, the *Kriegsmarine* replacements arrived with two or three changes of clothing, underwear, socks and other items of clothing that the infantrymen had not seen in years. Since they had to conform to what the regulations authorized regarding clothing, the sailors reluctantly had to part with most of their wardrobe, since there was no place to store it anyway once they arrived at the front. Though they all had to part with their blue and white jumpers, pea coats and "Donald Duck" caps, most were allowed to keep wearing their field gray naval ensemble, since clothing of all types was in short supply. With the addition of German Army insignia, their incorporation into the infantry was complete.

After a few incidents of insubordination were reported, *Oberleutnant* Kolb and his sergeant major, *Hauptwebel* Fuhrmeister, cracked down on the unruly sailors. Individuals were separated from their comrades and assigned to different squads. A few were placed in close arrest until they cooled off. To prevent any repeat episodes, Kolb increased the training tempo even further, leaving the young men too busy or too tired to disrupt the unit's constrained time schedule. Reluctantly, the former sailors submitted to their new status and soon became integral parts of the company. By the time the company moved to the Hürtgen Forest, they had become the embodiment of the highly motivated and politically dedicated *Volksgrenadiers* that Heinrich Himmler had envisioned after he assumed command of the *Replacement Army* on 21 July 1944.

While the company and other elements of the division incorporated and trained the new replacements, the German Army High Command or *OKH* was making plans for the future employment of the *272nd VGD*. On 26 October, a secret order was issued by the Chief of the German General Staff, *General der Infanterie* Hans Krebs, that stated that the *272nd VGD*, along with twelve other *Volks-Grenadier* divisions, would begin movement from the zone of the interior to new positions near the Western Front. The *272nd VGD* was scheduled to begin moving to the west no later than 1 November 1944. All thirteen of these divisions were to arrive in their new assembly areas or front line positions no later than 20 November.[9]

Though none of the members of *Füsilier Company 272* were aware of it, their supreme commander, Adolf Hitler, had already decided to strike back at the Western Allies and their division was scheduled to play a part in a massive counteroffensive designed to split the alliance and drive the British and American forces into the English Channel. The plan then being developed would govern their lives for the next three months and led to many of the men's death or injury.

5

Arrival in the Hürtgen Forest

Its six weeks of reorganization and training at Döberitz complete, the main body of the *272nd VGD* began movement from several railheads in the Brandenburg-Magdeburg area to its new area of operations on the Western Front beginning on 2 November 1944. The *Volksgrenadiers* bade their sad farewells to their host families, the barracks at Döberitz were cleaned and handed over to other new units scheduled to begin their own training cycle, and excess belongings were mailed home to their families. Following the route Magdeburg-Kreiensen-Holzminden-Soest-Neuss, the troop trains carrying the division chugged slowly through the war-ravaged industrial and urban areas of the *Reich*.

None of the *Volksgrenadiers* aboard the trains could have failed to notice the level of destruction in the cities or towns they passed through, where nearly every target of significance had been bombed at least once by the American and British air armadas. Despite these constant reminders of danger of air attack, the trains carrying the 10,000 men and the equipment of the *272nd VGD* traveled almost as if it were peacetime, for not a single one was attacked during the entire two-day journey, in stark contrast to the movement the division had to endure when it left the Western Front in September.[1]

By the time the bulk of the division began its movement to the west, the division headquarters had already been in its new command post for nearly two weeks, having arrived at the front on 24 October. Making his temporary headquarters in the millhouse at Pulvermühle, a hamlet three kilometers west of the town of Gemünd, *Oberst* Kossmala and his staff spent the next several days planning the relief in place of the *89th Infantry Division,* whose headquarters was situated in the restaurant "Waldhotel" in nearby Malsbenden. This particular area of the front encompassed the southern boundary of the Hürtgen Forest near Lammersdorf in the north and reaching as far as the lower northern boundary of the Schnee Eifel forest in the south. This area of the front had been chosen for the *272nd* and other new *Volks-Grenadier* divisions because it was deemed to be quiet enough for them to acclimate their troops to frontline conditions prior to being committed to the big offensive scheduled for December. (Refer to Map 1 for the overall situation in early November 1944.)

Besides improving the existing defenses, Kossmala's division was also expected to acquire limited combat experience and continue its training regimen in an area where the threat of an Allied attack was considered negligible. This was essential, since the division had not had sufficient time to carry out collective training above the battalion level while at Döberitz and the commanders and staffs needed more experience. Even though the likelihood of an American attack was deemed to be slim, any training above the company level would be difficult to carry out since all three regiments would be occupying their own defensive sectors and conducting operations.

Once the relief-in-place of the *89th Infantry Division* was completed, Kossmala's headquarters would move into the guesthouse "Waldhotel," which offered better concealment and more space than the millhouse. In addition to the normal planning his staff was expected to carry out, Kossmala's officers were further tasked by its new corps headquarters, *LXXIV Corps,* commanded by *General der Infanterie* Erich Straube, to plan for the evacuation of the remaining civilian population in its future sector, and to devise a plan for the safekeeping of civilian and state property left behind.[2]

On the morning of 3 November the troop trains began to arrive at the division's staging area east of the Roer River valley. The regiments, battalions, and companies offloaded at several railheads twenty or thirty kilometers behind the front, primarily in the area encompassing the towns of Kall, Schleiden, Gemünd, and Mechernich. With this labor-intensive task accomplished under the constant threat of air attack, each unit formed up and began moving toward its forward assembly areas, taking care to avoid attracting the attention of roaming Allied fighter bombers, the dreaded *Jabos*. Whether by truck, horse, bicycle, or on foot, most of the units arrived in their forward areas by 5 November.

Missing, however, was the division's new self-propelled tank destroyer company, *Hauptmann* Denk's *2nd Company, Tank Destroyer Battalion 272*. Equipped with fourteen of the new Jg.Pz. 38(t) *"Hetzers,"* it was still undergoing the final stages of its preparations at the Milowitz training area in Czechoslovakia and would not begin its movement to the west until 16 November.[3] Also lacking was this battalion's *3rd Company*, which contained the division's primary air defense capability, which arrived at the front two weeks later. Due to problems it encountered in obtaining its authorized equipment, this company was not to join the division's order of battle until 11 December. Its nine 37mm antiaircraft guns were sorely missed in the interim period, since the division's other air defense capability consisted only of light machine guns and one unauthorized quadruple 20mm antiaircraft guns in the self-propelled tank destroyer company. Consequently, Allied fighter-bombers were able to operate in the skies above the division's area of operations with near impunity. Good camouflage practices were especially critical.

The division's initial role was envisioned as purely defensive. After relieving the *89th Infantry Division*, the *272nd VGD* was directed to improve its positions and be prepared to ward off any American attacks in its sector. The portion of the German main defense line that the division held stretched from the village of Höfen in the south to the village of Vossenack in the north, a distance of over twenty kilometers. This represented the upper limit of a defensive sector that a *Volks-Grenadier* division could reasonably be expected to hold. Fortunately for the men of the *272nd VGD,* the sector had been relatively quite since Monschau had fallen to the 9th Infantry Division on the night of 15 September and was only lightly held by an American mechanized cavalry group.

Under such conditions, even creating a commander's reserve, one of the German Army's basic tactical concepts, proved to be a challenge. Although neither Kossmala nor any of his officers knew it at the time, the *272nd VGD* had already been earmarked to play a crucial role in the upcoming Ardennes Offensive. Any training in assault tactics would have helped the division's subunits immensely, but the risk of compromising WACHT AM RHEIN (Watch on the Rhine), the German's codename for the Ardennes Offensive, was deemed too great. Due to this need to insure operational security, most division and corps commanders whose troops were slated to participate in the offensive would not learn of their upcoming roles until one week (or less) before the attack was to begin.

One by one, each regiment, guided by an advance party from the division headquarters, moved directly from the railhead into its new frontline positions. The first regiment to arrive, *Grenadier Regiment 981,* quickly left its marshalling areas at Kall and Mechernich and arrived at the front by nightfall on 3 November where it relieved elements of *Grenadier Regiment 1056* of the *89th Infantry Division* by dawn the next morning. Its mission was to hold the southern portion of the line, including the defensive sector that spanned the main defense line from Höfen in the south to the village of Konzen five kilometers to the north. (See Map 2 for initial regimental positions.)

Grenadier Regiment 982 arrived on the same day. Unlike the two other regiments, its troop trains had to be unloaded at the rail yard in the village of Vettweiss, some ten kilometers southeast of the city of Düren. Unloading here meant that the troops would have a quicker and more direct route to their new positions. Had they unloaded in the same area as the other regiments (some fifteen kilometers to the south), the men of *Grenadier Regiment 982* would have had to march at least five to ten kilometers further than their comrades, an unacceptably excessive amount of time given the deadline of relieving the *89th Infantry Division.* After marching from Vettweiss to Nideggen and through the town of Schmidt, *Grenadier Regiment 982* moved into the sector that ran from the area north of Konzen through the large town of Simmerath, ending on the northern outskirts of the village of Rollesbroich.

The bulk of *Grenadier Regiment 982* passed through Schmidt at the same time the 28th Infantry Division began its ill-fated attack against that village from the direction of Vossenack. Though *Grenadier Regiment 982* avoided being committed during this action, some of its trains elements did come under artillery fire while passing through the village and had to be diverted toward the south. After an adventurous detour, they were finally able to join with the rest of the regiment the next day.[4]

Grenadier Regiment 980, the last regiment scheduled to arrive, also was supposed to disembark in Vettweiss, but the tactical situation forced its troop trains to be diverted to the south. Its battalions and companies had to unload at the railroad yards in Mechernich, in the same area where the rest of the division was scheduled to arrive. This regiment had been scheduled to take over the northernmost portion of the division's sector, which ran north of Rollesbroich and through the bunker complex at Raffelsbrand-Ochsenkopf before it turned to the northeast, ending at the southern outskirts of Vossenack. While not found on a map, this hyphenated name is used because the fighting that took place there from October 1944 to January 1945 can only be understood if one visualizes this grouping of nearly two dozen bunkers into one complex entity, not separately. The German veterans with whom the author spoke used this term to differentiate it from the village of Raffelsbrand, which lay nearly 500 meters to the north. The area includes part of the Raffelsbrand forest and the Ochsenkopf, the largest hill in that part of the forest.

The Raffelsbrand and Ochsenkopf area was honeycombed with nearly two-dozen bunkers of various types from the Schill Defensive Line that were located on the northern bank of the Kall one kilometer west of the hamlet of Simonskall. The main hard-surfaced road running from Düren to Lammersdorf passed within 100 meters of these positions. Whoever held the Raffelsbrand-Ochsenkopf positions controlled the road. Both the 9th and 28th Infantry Divisions had made several aborted attempts in October and November to seize this key terrain from the *275th* and *89th Infantry Divisions* and had failed after suffering appalling casualties.

Responsibility for the portion of the division's sector between Rollesbroich and Vossenack was assumed by *Grenadier Regiment 980,* while the neighboring *275th Infantry Division,* which held the key villages of Vossenack and Hürtgen, shifted to the north before it, too, was pulled out of line to be reconstituted. The changing tactical situation, however, dictated that *Grenadier Regiment 980* was sent somewhere where it was needed more.

South of Höfen, the division shared a boundary with the *347th Infantry Division.* Kossmala's orders stated that the relief in place of the *89th Infantry Division* was to be completed by 5 November. In order for Kossmala to carry out this operation, *Grenadier Regiment 1055* was briefly attached to his division on the right flank until all three of his regiments were in the line. *Füsilier Company 272* was initially slated to occupy an assembly area near Mechernich as the division's reserve, but this quickly changed.

While two of the division's three infantry regiments occupied their new defensive positions, *Füsilier Company 272* began its own movement to the west. On the morning of 4 November, *Oberleutnant* Kolb and his men went by truck and bicycle from Falkensee to Magdeburg to begin boarding troop trains along with the rest of the division. Kolb, as a senior company-grade officer, had been placed in control of part of a supply company from *Supply Regiment 272, Ordnance Company 272*, and a company from *Signal Battalion 272.* In all, 325 soldiers were under Kolb's control for the movement.

Arriving at its destination without incident on 5 November, the company and the other units offloaded on a stretch of open railway at the town of Kall, several kilometers southwest of the larger town of Mechernich. Nearly all of Kolb's men and his company's equipment had arrived together, except for nineteen men under the command of *Leutnant* Beyer, who had been temporarily transferred to *Field Replacement Battalion 272*. They returned to the company at a later date after they had completed their specialty training.

The same day that *Füsilier Company 272* began to offload its equipment and horses, *Grenadier Regiment 980* arrived in Mechernich proper and began its own march to the front. The regiment's orders had been changed while it was still en route to Vettweiss. Instead of taking over the division's northern defensive sector (as detailed above), it was directed to move south to the vicinity of Höfen in order to take over *Grenadier Regiment 981*'s sector on the division's left flank. Though it had only arrived the day before, *Grenadier Regiment 981* had been unexpectedly ordered on the night of 4/5 November to shift north to take over the center of the division's defensive sector, which was still held by a regiment from the *89th Infantry Division*.

This division, which had been fighting in the Hürtgen Forest since 12 September, was originally scheduled to be moved to a rest area near Vlatten to undergo reconstitution. Instead it was hurriedly marshaled near Gerstenhof to carry out a counterattack against the US 28th Infantry Division, which had managed a deep penetration in the German main defense line near Vossenack.[5] With half of his division already on the move after giving up their previous positions to the *272nd VGD*, the commander of the *89th Infantry Division*, *Generalmajor* Walter Bruns, was ordered to postpone his division's withdrawal and use both of his regiments to counterattack against the Americans in conjunction with armor from the *116th Panzer Division*.

The change in plans had come about because the 28th Infantry Division had seized the towns of Vossenack on 2 November and Schmidt on 3 November. These initial successes, should the Americans exploit them aggressively, threatened to unhinge the entire German defensive system in the Hürtgen Forest. The ensuing German counterattack against the US 112th Infantry Regiment and its attachments at Schmidt, carried out by both the *89th Infantry Division* and the *116th Panzer Division*, was characterized by some of the heaviest fighting of the war and resulted in a resounding American defeat. While the *272nd VGD* did not directly participate in the fighting, its artillery regiment and mortars provided fire support to the other German units engaged. Its timely arrival in the Hürtgen Forest, therefore, enabled the *89th Infantry Division* to disengage nearly all of its forces from the front line to be hurled with telling effect against the American forces holding Schmidt and Vossenack.

In order to concentrate his dispersed division to launch a coordinated attack, Bruns asked that the relief-in-place of his other regiment, *Grenadier Regiment 1055*, be accelerated. To comply with this request, the *LXXIV Corps* commander (then engaged in a war game with other corps and army commanders being conducted by *Generalfeldmarschall* Walter Model's *Army Group B*), ordered the *272nd VGD* to immediately move one of its own regiments to effect this relief by midnight on 5 November, two days earlier than scheduled.

To carry out these instructions as quickly as possible, Kossmala had to sideslip two of his regiments to the right. In order to perform this complicated movement within the stringent time limit, he decided to shift *Grenadier Regiment 981* from the south, instead of *Grenadier Regiment 982*. Since *Grenadier Regiment 980*, which was then moving up from Mechernich, was much closer to Höfen than it was to Rollesbroich, it could relieve *Grenadier Regiment 981* in the south much more quickly. *Grenadier Regiment 982,* therefore, remained in place, though it was to shorten its left flank slightly to accommodate the movement north of *Grenadier Regiment 981*. Due to an unexpected American attack that had tied down and prevented the regiment from the *275th Infantry Division* from handing over its position, the planned deployment of *Grenadier Regiment 980* to the northern flank no longer made any tactical sense, making it available for commitment elsewhere.

Leaving behind a weak rearguard, the bulk of *Oberstleutnant* Meyer's *Grenadier Regiment 981* began shifting north to the area between Simmerath and Rollesbroich at noon on 5 November, while *Grenadier Regiment 980* hurried to the front and closed the gap before the Americans noticed that it was virtually undefended. Instead of the division's right boundary being demarcated by the village of Vossenack, which now lay in American hands, the boundary had been shifted to Gerstenhof, where it abutted the left flank of the *89th Infantry Division*. So rather than a front line running roughly in a north to south attitude, it now described an inverted "L" with the pivot point located in the Kall River valley at the hamlet of Simonskall.

While the Battle of Schmidt raged from 3 to 8 November, *Füsilier Company 272* had time to get conditioned to own sector of the front in relative peace. After arriving at Mechernich, Kolb and his men bivouacked in an open field while they awaited their first assignment. Finally receiving orders, the company moved by bicycle and truck through Gemünd on the night of 6/7 November to avoid American fighter-bombers. When the company reached the division command post at Malsbenden, Kolb was ordered by the division operations officer to occupy defensive positions west of the village of Rollesbroich along the Kall River due to the change in the overall situation caused by the departure of the *89th Infantry Division*. This move created several dangerous gaps in the front line, forcing Kossmala to commit to battle those forces that he otherwise would have kept in reserve, such as *Füsilier Company 272*.

Here, the company was to relieve the remaining few elements of *89th Infantry Division* by 8 November and take over the bunkers and fighting positions that lay in the vicinity of the village of Rollesbroich. On Kolb's right flank lay elements of *Grenadier Regiment 982*; on his left flank, the men of *Grenadier Regiment 981* were beginning their fourth day in the front lines. Unaware of the larger developments responsible for his company's accelerated commitment to the front, Kolb and his men begin to acquaint themselves with their new positions.

With the company settling into its new positions at Rollesbroich, *Hauptfeldwebel* Fuhrmeister established the company trains in the village of Hergarten, located fifteen kilometers to the east, out of range of American artillery fires. Here in relative safety, the supply section, cooks, mechanics, tailor, shoemaker, armorer, paymaster, clerks, and other personnel went about their business keeping the rest of the company accounted for, supplied, and fed. Their six horse-drawn wagons and half-tracked supply truck were kept hidden from sight, while their twelve draft horses were quartered in local barns.

Although safe from artillery, Fuhrmeister and his rear echelon still had to contend with roving fighter-bombers and stray medium bombers that pounced on any target of opportunity that presented itself. The cooks and other supply personnel who brought up daily rations and ammunition also had to run the gauntlet of interdicting artillery fire in order to reach Kolb and the rest of the company, an assignment which proved on occasion to be extremely dangerous. Still, the chance to sleep in a dry house while their comrades at the front slept in dank foxholes undoubtedly provided some consolation. Despite their relatively cushy assignment, the men of the company trains from time to time knew they might be called upon if needed to serve in *Alarm* (emergency) units, where they would be used to counterattack any Allied penetrations of the front line. Fortunately for them, this eventuality was several months away.

When the company moved into the line at Rollesbroich on 8 November, it had a combat strength of two officers, twenty-one non-commissioned officers, and 123 privates, for a total of 146 men. An additional thirty-five were with the company trains, including runners, the sick, and those detailed to help bring up food and supplies. Nineteen men were still undergoing training with *Field Replacement Battalion 272*, including *Leutnant* Beyer, and soon rejoined the company.

The company's front-line positions were located along the high ground one kilometer west of Rollesbroich, facing the larger village of Lammersdorf, which lay two kilometers to the northwest. Kolb and his men were separated from the Americans by the Kall, a narrow river that ran generally in a northeast direction from its headwaters in the Hohe Venn, an area of high moors, swamps, and patchy forests in neighboring Belgium. To defend his kilometer-wide defensive sector, Kolb was forced to spread his men thinly, with three-man fighting positions spaced every fifty meters. The two heavy-machine-gun teams were intermingled with the frontline positions to provide long-range (up to 1,200 meters) direct supporting fire. Both 80mm mortars and the infantry howitzers were positioned to provide indirect fire support.

These fighting positions had been constructed in September by a Hitler Youth labor battalion during the initial stages of the battle of the Hürtgen Forest and were poorly positioned. Most of the fighting positions lay in open fields, easily observable by the Americans.[6] This forced most movement and re-supply efforts, except for the most urgent, to take place at night. *Oberleutnant* Kolb established his company command post inside a house in Rollesbroich, but made frequent trips at night to the front lines three to five hundred meters away to keep abreast of tactical developments and to keep up his men's spirits.

Füsilier Eduard Zacharuk, an assistant machine gunner with the weapons platoon, who was with the company during this phase of the campaign, later recalled that he could easily see an American observation post with his binoculars from his own three-man fighting position. Naturally, such observation across the lines worked both ways and any movement during the daylight hours drew accurate American fire, so he and his comrades kept their activity outside of their fighting position to a minimum. In addition to his team's MG-42 tripod-mounted heavy machine gun, Zacharuk was armed with a G-43 rifle without a sniper scope and another comrade had a pistol. Every two or three days, he and his fellow *Volks-grenadiers* were allowed to move several hundred meters to the rear, where they could snatch a few hours of uninterrupted sleep in an earthen bunker. Protected by three layers of logs, these bunkers were heated by small stoves whose flue pipes protruded through the top. Wood had to be used sparingly, however, as even small fires generated smoke that immediately drew American artillery fire. Even so, it was better than staying in their cold and damp forward positions, where they had to stand two hours of guard duty for every four hours off. While in the front lines, two of Zacharuk's three-man team were required to stay awake at night for four-hour staggered shifts. It was nearly unbearable, since the stress of staying awake, compounded by the constant artillery fire, tended to wear one's nerves to the breaking point. While in the forward positions, they received no hot food at all; this they got only when they rotated into the relief bunkers.[7] All in all, it was a far cry from the *Kriegsmarine*, which he had left only two months before.

The company's 80mm mortar section was positioned one kilometer to the rear in the courtyard of a farmhouse in Rollesbroich. The section leader, *Unteroffizier* Fritz Fosselmann, remembered that American artillery forward observers were always able to quickly pinpoint their location. Whenever his section fired a mission in support of the troops manning the main defense line, they immediately attracted counter-fire that forced Fosselmann and his men to hastily seek shelter in the cellar of the farmhouse. Even before they moved into the Hürtgen Forest, Fosselmann believed the war was lost, but he put forth his best efforts anyway because his best friend, *Unteroffizier* Heinrich Misskampf, was in an observation post up front with the rest of the company.[8]

Misskampf, like Fosselmann a veteran of the Eastern Front and Normandy, remembered during this period that although the American's artillery fire was very dangerous, one could at least walk about in the open without having to worry much about snipers. This was in stark contrast to the Eastern Front, where even sticking your head out of one's foxhole immediately drew unwanted attention, often with fatal results.

Misskampf had established his observation post in the roof of a half-destroyed house on the western outskirts of Rollesbroich, where he could clearly see the US positions near Lammersdorf. Even so, he was forced to conduct fire support missions only when absolutely necessary, since ammunition was in short supply. One never knew when one might really need it, he related, so each individual round was carefully husbanded until then. Thus, it was somewhat galling when he could see American troops moving about unconcernedly and practicing poor camouflage discipline. This cavalier attitude on the part of the Americans did, however, make his mission much easier when he did call fire down upon them.[9]

A few of the luckier squads, such as *Gefreiter* Hermann Heiermann's, were assigned to defend old bunkers of the *Westwall* that lay scattered throughout their company's defensive sector. When his squad arrived at the front in the early morning hours of 8 November, they were assigned to Bunker 509, which lay directly above the Kall Creek. They found the bunker unoccupied, but equipped with bunks, a stove, and candles.

Heiermann's squad was responsible for observing the American positions and providing covering fire for the movement of German patrols into and out of the barbed wire entanglements emplaced along the creek to their front. He also had the additional dangerous duty of having to repair his platoon's field telephone wire whenever it was severed by artillery or mortar fire. The bunker was cold and dank, but it was impervious to artillery fire and was far preferable to living in an open fighting position.[10]

Opposite *Füsilier Company 272* lay positions held by the US 102nd Cavalry Group (Mechanized). Though lacking organic infantry of its own, this American unit was lavishly equipped with automatic and heavy weapons, and could rely on prompt artillery support should its position be threatened. Since both opponents were ordered to defend their current sectors, most activity was limited to patrolling and improving their positions. For the *Volksgrenadiers* of Kolb's company, this meant laying minefields, stringing barbed wire entanglements, and constructing various obstacles, all at night. Harassing artillery fire was a constant menace and any movement drew a quick response. Periodically, American aircraft made strafing or bombing runs. The *Luftwaffe* was nowhere to be seen.

The first week passed relatively uneventfully for the company. Unaware of the battles raging for Vossenack and Schmidt less than ten kilometers away, Kolb's men went about their daily business, squinting through binoculars; bringing up food and mail; writing letters home; and carrying out frequent patrolling of the American lines. This routine was interrupted abruptly when *Gefreiter* Michael Geier was wounded by artillery fire on 14 November, the company's first casualty. Fortunately, he was only lightly wounded in the right arm and returned to the company after he recovered. American artillery fire would soon claim others, who were not as lucky.

The first to die was *Gefreiter* Otto Göttlicher, a thirty-two-year-old ethnic German from a town near Olmütz in Czechoslovakia. While moving about his fighting position before dawn, he was struck in the chest and stomach by shell fragments and died almost immediately. His remains were evacuated and temporarily interred at the field cemetery in the village of Hechelscheidt, located fifteen kilometers north of Gemünd. He was the first of many of *Füsilier Company 272* to be buried in the *272nd VGD*'s field cemeteries scattered between the east and west banks of the Roer River.

Füsilier Günther Köppe, a radioman, was hit in the stomach by a shell fragment on 21 November while repairing broken field telephone lines outside of one of the company's bunkers. Though medical personnel quickly rescued him, he bled to death on the way to the field dressing station in Rollesbroich. Born October 1926 in Sorau, he had just turned 18 less than two months before his death. He was buried in the field cemetery in Einruhr, a small village on the Roer River eight kilometers west of Gemünd.

Throughout this period of relative calm that lasted until 1 December, the company suffered a total of eleven casualties, including five killed in action and six wounded, all but one from artillery fire (*Gefreiter* Gerhard Klein from Berlin was the sole exception, suffering a gunshot wound to the foot by an American rifleman while on patrol 21 November). *Gefreiter* Heiermann, a twenty-year-old *Volksgrenadier* from Dinslaken, was wounded in the right hand early in the evening of 17 November while bringing up barbed wire. He, too, was evacuated to the rear for treatment. He was eventually discharged from the *Wehrmacht* in March 1945 due to partial paralysis of the hand. The loss of Klein and Heiermann, both veterans of the old *2nd Company, Füsilier Battalion 272* who had fought in Normandy, as well as the loss of other old hands, was a blow that *Oberleutnant* Kolb and the others felt deeply.

There was also one apparent desertion that took place shortly after the company moved into its positions. *Oberfüsilier* Horst Noack, while en route to the rejoin the company along with nine others from the group that had been attached to *Field Replacement Battalion 272,* is believed to have deserted on the night of 9 November. This group, led by *Leutnant* Beyer, was traveling by bicycle from Hergarten and had stopped to rest for the night in the village of Nierfeld, one kilometer south of Gemünd. Throughout the journey, Noack had lagged behind the rest of the group.

The next morning, Noack was nowhere to be found. After a short but fruitless search, the rest of the men continued their journey to the front. Kolb immediately ordered an investigation. Since Noack still had not shown up, he was declared to be a deserter on 20 November and appropriate administrative actions were taken. Noack, a twenty-two-year-old Berliner, was hardly a prime candidate for a soldier. He had been disciplined no less than three times during the last five months, the last incident being a charge of absent without leave on 27 October, an offense that drew him five days of close arrest. Noack had been drafted into the *Wehrmacht* in December 1940 and until August 1944, had served in a supply battalion of the *123rd Infantry Division*, which had been continuously engaged on the Eastern Front until being disbanded in March 1944. Clearly, Noack had had his fill of being a soldier and wanted out. He was never found and his subsequent fate was never discovered.

———◦◦◦◦———

Although the *272nd VGD*'s first month in action in the Hürtgen Forest had been marked by miserably cold and wet weather, as well as by considerable artillery fire, the division had suffered relatively little in comparison to the German units engaged in heavy fighting at Vossenack, Hürtgen, and Schmidt. Just a few kilometers to the north, the *89th* and *275th Infantry Divisions* and the *116th Panzer Division* were losing thousands of men in bitter fighting to hold on to these towns in the face of determined attacks by the 8th and 28th Infantry Divisions, as well as by the 12th Infantry Regiment of the 4th Infantry Division.

The rain and cold weather, made even more miserable by constant artillery fire, had undoubtedly been psychologically more draining on the young recruits from the *Kriegsmarine* and *Luftwaffe*. On the other hand, the division's veterans of the Eastern Front and Normandy could maintain a sense of detachment, for they had seen far worse. The rain and cold could be dealt with, if one knew how to use his shelter quarter and blanket to keep dry and warm. They knew that a snug foxhole with several logs providing overhead cover protected against nearly everything but a direct hit, so there was no point in worrying about something that one had no control over anyway. On 30 November, Kurt Klein wrote "Our present position [near Rollesbroich] is not bad, at least we are safe from bombs."[11]

Even veterans like Klein, however, could not help but comment on the loss of friends and comrades. When his friend, *Obergefreiter* Ernst Schneider, died on 29 November, Klein wrote:

> Too bad that Ernst was killed. Artillery fragments on both sides of his stomach, I myself bandaged him and brought him to the main dressing station. But there was nothing that could be done to save him, too bad—he was such a good lad. So today we had one wounded in the company and two dead— what is one to make of such horror? Everything is going to shit.[12]

Schneider was a Berliner born in 1924 who had survived the horrors of the Eastern Front only to fall victim to American artillery fire while carrying a message for the company commander. Klein later wrote in frustration, "What can one do against this mortar and artillery fire?"

While *Füsilier Company 272* busied itself in its daily routine, the rest of the division's front line continued to shift because of American tactical success elsewhere. On 17 November, the *116th Panzer Division* was pulled out of its defensive sector that lay between the northern outskirts of Vossenack and the southern edge of Hürtgen and sent north to be recommitted elsewhere. To fill the gap, the *89th Infantry Division,* which still could not be spared from combat despite its urgent need for reconstitution, was forced to shift its troop dispositions to the east and north in order to cover this vulnerable area and to lend support to the neighboring *275th Infantry Division,* then being pounded by the 4th and 8th Infantry Divisions and the Combat Command Reserve (CCR) of the 5th Armored Division.

To relieve the leftmost regiment of the *89th Infantry Division* and to assume responsibility for its defensive sector, Kossmala once again had to reposition one of his regiments. This time, he chose *Grenadier Regiment 980,* directing its commander to hand over his defensive positions on the division's left flank between Höfen and Konzen to a regiment from the neighboring *277th Volks-Grenadier Division* and to move out immediately. Consequently, *Oberst* Burian and his men pulled out on the night of 17/18 November and marched along a circuitous route east of the Roer River, which brought them into in their new positions via Gemünd, Heimbach, and Schmidt.

While Bruns' *89th Infantry Division* and the *275th Infantry Division* battled the 8th Infantry Division and CCR, 5th Armored Division between the villages of Grosshau and Vossenack, *Grenadier Regiment 980* settled into the newly-vacated fighting positions and bunkers on the Buhlert hill mass. Here, *Oberst* Burian's regiment was made responsible from 18 November onwards for the defensive sector that stretched from Simonskall on the left to the southwestern outskirts of Schmidt, where it linked up with *Grenadier Regiment 1055* from Bruns' division. Burian's new front line also ran across the northern bank of the Kall to the southern outskirts of Vossenack. Here, his troops maintained a tenuous salient on the hillsides south of that village, all that remained of the German positions there after troops of the *275th Infantry Division* had been driven out of the village on 2 November by the 28th Infantry Division.

To Burian's left, *Oberstleutnant* Rösener's *Grenadier Regiment 982* had to stretch his flank to the right as well. His *2nd Battalion* was repositioned to take over the large bunker complex north of Silberscheidt located in the area known as Raffelsbrand-Ochsenkopf from a battalion from the *275th Infantry Division* that was being pulled out. Here, some of the heaviest fighting ever experienced by either side during the Battle of the Hürtgen Forest had taken place the month before. By no means was the fighting over in this sector, for it raged intermittently until February 1945, when Rösener's regiment was finally forced to withdraw.

The left, or southernmost, portion of the *272nd VGD's* front line, held by *Oberstleutnant* Meyer's *Grenadier Regiment 981,* remained unchanged. Having hurriedly taken over the static sector between Höfen and Rollesbroich on the night of 5/6 November, Meyer had been able to occupy his defensive positions with little interference from the Americans. To his immediate south, the regiment from the *277th Volks-Grenadier Division* found the situation very similar.

Though these shifts of regimental boundaries had no effect whatsoever on *Füsilier Company 272*'s tactical situation, it did mean that by 17 November, *Oberst* Kossmala had been forced to add five more kilometers to the length of his main defense line, dangerously overextending his division. Thus the pattern was set for much of the troubles the division was to experience during the next two months. His division, instead of being allowed a month to complete its training and gain a degree of combat experience in a "quiet" sector, was now fully committed in the front line. Not only was the major German counteroffensive in the Ardennes, in which the division was to play a major role, still over a month away, but the continuation of the American offensive had yet to be felt.

The overall German situation in the Hürtgen Forest began to change for the worse beginning on 16 November, when the US First and Ninth Armies began their long-anticipated offensive, codenamed Operation QUEEN, that was designed to clear the Stolberg corridor and seize crossings along the Roer River. Heralded by an attack by 2,580 Allied bombers and 350 fighter-bombers that pounded German positions in and behind the front lines, American and British forces surged ahead against the *Fifteenth* and *Seventh Armies* on a front that ran in the north from Geilenkirchen, through the Stolberg corridor in the center, and toward Hürtgen in the south. Arrayed against the exhausted troops of *Generalleutnant* Erich Straube's *LXXIV Corps* and *General der Infanterie* Friedrich Köchling's *LXXXI Corps* were the veterans of Major General J. Lawton Collin's VII Corps, including the 1st, 4th, and 104th Infantry Divisions and the 3rd Armored Division, as well as elements of Major General Gerow's V Corps, including the 8th Infantry Division and CCR, 5th Armored Division.[13]

After four days of savage fighting, Collin's and Gerows's corps had advanced only five to six kilometers along a twenty-kilometer front by 20 November. The Germans fought stubbornly everywhere, but the steady pressure exerted by the 8th Infantry Division and CCR, 5th Armored Division had brought the *275th Infantry Division* to the verge of complete collapse. Elements of the *275th Infantry Division* were stubbornly defending west of the town of Hürtgen, but one of its regiments defending west of Grosshau and Kleinhau was virtually destroyed and the division's main line of defense was beginning to unravel. Anticipating that the Americans would attempt to reach Düren, *General der Panzertruppe* Erich Brandenberger, commander of *Seventh Army,* brought in the *344th Infantry Division* to relieve the *275th* on 21 November. Brandenberger, who had been defending in the Hürtgen Forest since mid-September, knew better than anyone did when a unit had reached the breaking point.

As *Seventh Army*'s *LXXIV Corps'* line buckled and was pushed eastwards from 16 to 29 November, the *89th Infantry Division* was forced once again to stretch to the north in order to maintain contact with the neighboring *275th*, then the *344th Infantry Division*. As it lengthened its own front line, it became apparent that unless it was reinforced, Bruns' division would also become perilously overextended. To prevent this from happening, *Generalleutnant* Erich Straube, commander of *LXXIV Corps*, ordered Kossmala on 24 November to detach a battalion from his division to serve as a reserve for Bruns' *89th Infantry Division*. Kossmala chose the rightmost battalion in his division, *2nd Battalion, Grenadier Regiment 980* for this mission. Moving quickly, it took up a reserve position to the rear of *Grenadier Regiment 1055* northwest of the village of Bergstein. Here it sat for nearly ten days before it was committed to action.

To fill the vacancy created by the shift of this battalion, Kossmala was forced to commit the bulk of *Pionier Battalion 272*, less one company that had been detached to secure the Roer River Dam at Heimbach, and subordinate it tactically to Burian's *Grenadier Regiment 980*. Except for this last change, the situation remained stable in the division's sector until the end of November (see Map 3). Although heavy fighting was taking place in the sector of the neighboring divisions to the north, for Kossmala's division most of this period was filled with normal patrol activity, artillery duels, and improving defensive positions. All this was about to change, however, with the fall of Hürtgen village at the end of the month.

The impact of the American offensive in the north began to spill over into the sector held by *2nd Battalion, Grenadier Regiment 982,* when elements of the 8th Infantry Division carried out a raid on 19 November to seize several bunkers in the Raffelsbrand-Ochsenkopf area. The American assault, spearheaded by a battalion from the 13th Infantry Regiment, was intended to tie down and divert German forces while the main attack went forward against the town of Hürtgen with the other two regiments of the division. The Americans quickly broke through the right flank of *Hauptmann* Karl Schneider's *2nd Battalion,* and succeeded in capturing Bunker 111, along with two of its inhabitants, and immediately began preparations to blow it up. Schneider ordered an immediate counterattack, to be proceeded by an artillery barrage.

The men of the 13th Infantry Regiment, who had arrived in the Hürtgen Forest only two days before and were unused to forest fighting, were forced to seek cover as tree bursts sent steel shards and wooden splinters slicing through the undergrowth. Taking advantage of the momentary disorganization caused by the barrage, the counterattack force, consisting of men from *7th Company* led by *Oberleutnant* von Ruden, quickly retook the bunker and captured eighteen of their opponents, who had sought shelter inside. The two captured Germans, one an officer and the other an NCO, took out their pocketknives and severed the demolition fuses to insure that the explosives were rendered inert. Meanwhile, the rest of the American raiding party was forced to withdraw, leaving the front line in the same position as it was when the attack began. Thus began the almost-daily routine that was to characterize *2nd Battalion, Grenadier Regiment 982*'s occupation of Raffelsbrand-Ochsenkopf sector until they were driven out three months later.[14]

———◦◦◦◦◦———

American forces on the opposite side of the front line quickly detected the arrival of the *272nd VGD*. They were able to collect important information using a variety of means, including prisoner interrogations, reconnaissance aircraft, radio intercepts and by tapping into German tactical wire communications. Allied intelligence officers believed the division had been "completely wiped out in Normandy" and were aware that the division had undergone reconstitution at Döberitz. Based on this analysis, the Allies concluded that the division had negligible combat value.

This estimate was to lead them to hold the *272nd VGD* and its sister divisions in low esteem from their inception, a common mindset that had taken hold of a fair percentage of the British and American leadership, most of whom considered that the war would be over by Christmas. Consequently, most of the Allied intelligence and psychological warfare products from this initial period were worded in such a way as to highlight Germany's hopeless military situation.

Based on its assessment of the state of the *272nd VGD*, the US Army developed psychological warfare leaflets that targeted these new recruits to induce them to surrender or to desert. They emphasized the hopelessness of Germany's situation and that like the men of the old *272nd Infantry Division* in Normandy, the new recruits would soon suffer the same fate. In order to separate the new recruits ideologically from their officers and non-commissioned officers and break down unit cohesion, some surrender leaflets depicted in no uncertain terms that their leaders were simply driving them to a certain death. One leaflet proved to be prophetic. On one side, it told each recruit that "You have been inadequately trained and your division is now being thrown into combat. Your national leadership is determined to sacrifice the new division as ruthlessly as it sacrificed the old *272nd*."

To sum up the message of this particular leaflet, "You see, we know you" was printed at the bottom in bold type. It continued, "And you know the fate that awaits you all. When we begin our major attack, and we play all of our trump cards, the fate of the new *272nd VGD* will be the same as the one experienced by the old. Eight survivors out of one company! You can be one of these eight—surrender!"

The leaflet also provided information on how to surrender and promised good treatment if they crossed over the lines voluntarily. For the former *Kriegsmarine* sailors and *Luftwaffe* ground crewmen who made up a large percentage of the infantry and were uncertain of their fate in any case, these leaflets must have been viewed as tickets to survival. No doubt many men hid some of these surrender leaflets should the need ever arise; several of the veterans interviewed by the author still have such leaflets in their possession. Whether they would ever need them or not was a topic that few *Volksgrenadiers* openly discussed, but many soon had an opportunity to decide whether to use them.

In one instance, the Allies received information that *6th Company, Grenadier Regiment 980* had been reduced to a total effective strength of eight men after Normandy. This information was used to create a series of propaganda leaflets that were dropped on the division using air and shell delivery systems that targeted not only the entire division but the new *6th Company* as well. Whether the men believed them or not, many secreted leaflets on their persons, either as insurance should they ever decide to surrender or simply to use as toilet paper during their daily trip to the field latrine.

Certain aspects of the Allied intelligence estimate of the organization of the *272nd VGD* were remarkably accurate, while others were not. According to an American intelligence summary published during the month of November 1944, the division's infantry companies were believed to consist mainly of inexperienced seventeen-year-olds and old men in their fifties. With the exception of a few Eastern Front veterans, the report stated, the new *272nd VGD* consisted primarily of "old men and boys." It also stated that as much as forty percent of the division was composed of naval, *Flak*, and *Luftwaffe* ground personnel who had involuntarily been transferred to the infantry. This estimate was reproduced on surrender leaflets and fired at German troops in order to let them know that the Allies knew more about their own division than they did. Most intelligence officers believed that these hastily slapped-together divisions would collapse when arrayed against battle-tested Allied divisions.

Regarding the division's level of training however, the Allied assessment was fairly accurate, stating that the sum total of the replacements' training consisted of a mere forty days of infantry schooling at Döberitz. To the inexperienced intelligence analyst, or to trained minds that assumed that the war would soon be over, therefore, they wrongly drew the conclusion that because of these shortcomings in personnel, the *272nd VGD* would necessarily perform poorly in combat. While this was accurate in some respects, it proved to be an unreliable prediction of how effectively the division would actually fight when it came in contact with Allied forces for the first time. This last bit of information remained for the American soldiers in the Hürtgen Forest to experience firsthand.

The quiet period of training and rest had finally come to an end and the most violent phase in the division's history was about to begin.

6

The Battle for Bergstein

On 28 November, Hürtgen, the village whose name came to signify more than just a battle, finally fell to troops of the US 8th Infantry Division's 13th and 121st Infantry Regiments. This village had been the long-elusive goal of successive attacks by four American divisions—the 4th, 8th, 9th, and 28th, and their attachments, including CCR of the 5th Armored Division. Its seizure, along with that of the neighboring village of Kleinhau the following day, marked the end of one of the bloodiest chapters of the Battle of the Hürtgen Forest.

While this victory provided a sorely needed morale boost to American forces and the leadership of the First Army, it was also tactically significant. Hürtgen's seizure, after two long months of heavy fighting, cracked the German main defense line and offered tantalizing prospects. A viable avenue of approach ran through Hürtgen to the Roer River along the narrow plateau connecting the village of Kleinhau to the villages of Brandenburg and Bergstein. Beyond Bergstein, the plateau ended like a finger pointing toward the Roer crossings at Obermaubach and Nideggen. Possession of this high ground and the river crossings below, followed by a bold thrust across the Roer, could possibly have thwarted Hitler's future counteroffensive. Tragically, this was a missed opportunity as the Allies were completely unaware of the German leader's ambitious plan. Had the Americans been able to seize a crossing over the Roer in early December 1944, it would have allowed Lieutenant General Courtney H. Hodges's US First Army unimpeded access to the Cologne Plain. Here, units of *SS* General Sepp Dietrich's *Sixth Panzer Army,* constituting the northern attacking wing of the German effort, were making their final preparations for their role in WACHT AM RHEIN. A crossing of the Roer at this point would have detected the Germans in their assembly areas and forced their commitment, spoiling any chances of strategic surprise that Hitler counted on for its success.

At this stage of the battle, however, since the Americans were completely unaware of any German offensive plans, they were more concerned in denying this high ground to the defenders. To this end the US 8th Infantry Division, along with the attached CCR of 5th Armored Division, threw everything available into a drive along the Brandenburg-Bergstein ridge during the following week and a half. It came within a hair's breadth of reaching the river (which would have cut Straube's *LXXIV Corps* in two) and establishing the first American bridgehead over the Roer. A simultaneous series of ferocious attacks to the north of the 8th Infantry Division were launched against the localities of Gey and Strass by the

4th and 83rd Infantry Divisions, with the city of Düren as their ultimate tactical goal.

These attacks nearly unhinged the German defenses by 7 December and consumed the few remaining units available to hold this sector. Once these meager forces were used up, reserves from elsewhere within Brandenberger's *Seventh Army* had to be quickly transferred to bolster the line before it collapsed. As it developed, this fighting eventually rippled in a southerly direction toward the sector held by the *272nd VGD*. This maelstrom soon unavoidably engulfed Kossmala's division, threatening its envisioned role in the upcoming Ardennes Offensive. These events also drew *Füsilier Company 272* into its first major combat action in an area that had already seen some of the fiercest fighting during the Battle of the Hürtgen Forest.

The advance by the 8th Infantry Division and CCR, 5th Armored Division, set in motion a series of events that led the commander of the *Seventh Army* to prematurely commit forces earmarked for WACHT AM RHEIN in a desperate effort to stop the Americans. From 1 to 8 December, Brandenberger directed Straube, commander of *LXXIV Corps,* to focus his main effort (using the bulk of *89th Infantry Division* and major portions of *272nd VGD*) to contain the American drive and regain lost ground. This proved to be easier said than done. The Americans were determined to punch through and seize Brandenberg and Bergstein, and had dedicated a great deal combat power to do so, including two regiments of the 8th Infantry Division and CCR, 5th Armored Division, as well as at least six battalions of corps and division artillery.

Securing these objectives would not only give the Americans a bridgehead over the Roer, but would also secure the high ground that would protect the right flank of "Lighting Joe" Collins' VII Corps' attack against Düren, the US First Army's main objective a dozen kilometers to the north. Thus, the fight for Brandenberg and Bergstein evolved into a German-US race, with the ultimate winner controlling key terrain overlooking the Roer River. The Americans, who possessed the initiative after seizing Hürtgen and the neighboring village of Kleinhau, attacked first. (For the overall US and German situation, see Map 4.)

After a two-day struggle against minefields and a stubborn defense by troops of *Grenadier Regiment 1056* of the battered *89th Infantry Division,* the tanks and infantry of Colonel Glen Anderson's CCR, 5th Armored Division, supported by the 28th and 121st Infantry Regiments of the 8th Infantry Division on Anderson's flanks, took Brandenberg on 3 December. This was followed by the gain of a small foothold in Bergstein later that same day. Despite the fact that the spearhead unit of the American assault was supported by the fire of six field artillery battalions soon to be augmented by twelve more, there was not enough firepower available to hold the ground gained. There was simply insufficient accompanying infantry to protect the armor from roving bands of *Grenadiers,* armed with *Panzerfausts*, who stalked the American tanks with telling effect. Though the initial probe by CCR's 10th Tank Battalion was finally driven off that afternoon, this thrust caused the commander of *89th Infantry Division, Generalmajor* Walter Bruns, to believe that the entire German position between Schmidt and Obermaubach would soon be lost if drastic action was not immediately taken.

By 4 December, all that remained for the 8th Infantry Division and CCR, 5th Armored Division to do was capture Bergstein and the neighboring Hill 400 (called the Burgberg or "Castle Hill" by the Germans); ford the Kall; and continue its attack to the south or to attack to the east and seize the Roer crossing at Obermaubach or Nideggen. Vossenack was still in American hands, though the eastern outskirts were held by newly-arrived elements from *Hauptmann* Schlanstein's *Pionier Battalion 272*. Even by this point in the fighting, the terrain still provided the defenders a few advantages, making them a difficult target for the Americans to defeat except through close combat. After being driven out of Brandenberg on 3 December, the remnants of *89th Infantry Division* were forced to take up positions along the wooded downhill slopes north of the ridgelines occupied by the Americans and in the Tiefenbachtal and Kall valleys, where they continued to make a nuisance of themselves for two more weeks.

By dawn on December 5, the only key terrain remaining in German hands north of the Kall was the southeastern tip of the ridge encompassing the southern and eastern portions of Bergstein and "Castle Hill." As long as the Germans maintained possession of Castle Hill, which overlooked the entire area, they could continue to direct artillery fire with deadly accuracy on any observable movement. If a Roer River crossing was to be successful, the American forces had to seize Bergstein and the hill. At first, it seemed to the German defenders that loss of this terrain was a certainty, because the division originally tasked to hold the town and the village was on its last legs and was hardly in a position to offer any solid resistance.

By 2 December, after the loss of Hürtgen, Kleinau, and Brandenburg, Bruns' burned-out *89th Infantry Division* no longer had the strength to conduct local counterattacks to regain lost ground or even to hold what still remained. Bruns had no recourse and later that day asked Straube for release of the corps reserve, who passed the request up to *Seventh Army*'s commander. Brandenberger quickly concurred.

Though he rightly feared that a premature commitment of elements of the *272nd VGD* would weaken it on the eve of the Ardennes Offensive, Straube reluctantly ordered the commitment of one of Kossmala's infantry battalions, *2nd Battalion, Grenadier Regiment 980*, to reinforce Bergstein on 3 December.[1] This battalion, which arrived in the village shortly after 0940 hours that morning, had been designated the corps reserve on 24 November and had occupied positions northeast of Bergstein. Though a German corps usually maintained a regimental-sized reserve, the continuing US offensive had already forced Straube to commit nearly everything else. Positioned behind Bruns' *Grenadier Regiment 1055*, it could defend the western and northern portions of Bergstein if necessary.

Kossmala must have had strong misgivings upon receipt of this order, since he knew that the commitment of this battalion would further weaken his division. He had already had to detach one-third of his combat strength to another division on 27 November when *Oberstleutnant* Meyer's *Grenadier Regiment 981,* it was sent to reinforce the crumbling sector north of the town of Hürtgen held by *Generalmajor* Eugen König's *344th Infantry Division*

Meyers' regiment arrived in time to prevent a breakthrough of American forces between the villages of Strass and Gey that were aimed toward Düren. Seizure of Düren, according to *Generalmajor* von Gersdorff, Chief of Staff of *Seventh Army,* would have caused the entire German defense along the Roer to collapse. Therefore, desperate measures and improvisations were required to hold the line, a feature that had come to characterize the entire German effort in the Hürtgen Forest as early as September. Though desperate, German tactical countermeasures were repeatedly successful. German reserves, in this instance *Grenadier Regiment 981,* always seemed to show up at the right place at the precisely the right time.

Three days after arriving in its new defensive sector, *Oberstleutnant* Meyer was relieved of command by *Oberstleutnant* Hans Kleinkorres for reasons unknown, though it is believed that he had committed an act of impropriety. Fortunately for the regiment, Kleinkorres was an experienced and battle-hardened commander who had been awarded the German Cross in Gold on 29 January 1942 as an *Oberleutnant* while commanding a company of *Infantry Regiment 431* of the *131st Infantry Division* on the Eastern Front. His rise from *Oberleutnant* to *Oberstleutnant* had taken place in the space of a mere two and a half years, a meteoric rise by German Army standards.

Once it arrived in the *344th Infantry Division*'s sector, *Grenadier Regiment 981* occupied a defensive sector in the vicinity of Gey and held it against repeated attacks by the 4th Infantry Division until the night of 10/11 December, when it was finally pulled out and replaced by a regiment from the *353rd Infantry Division.* Forced to hold a line in mostly open terrain (a rarity in the Hürtgen Forest) for nearly two weeks, *Grenadier Regiment 981* suffered terrible casualties in the process, mainly from American artillery.[2] The *2nd Battalion, Grenadier Regiment 981,* commanded by *Major* Jürgen Fittschen, suffered casualties totaling nearly fifty percent during the see-saw fight for the Hubertus Heights above Gey from 2 to 3 December when it carried out repeated counterattacks against the 22nd Infantry Regiment of the US 4th Infantry Division. At one point on 3 December, twenty-five of Fittschen's men managed to penetrate the front line positions held by the 1st Battalion, 22nd Infantry Regiment before they were rounded up by a counterattack carried out by the headquarters elements of all three rifle companies and the heavy weapons company.[3] Fittschen himself was seriously wounded while leading the attack and was replaced by *Hauptmann* Günther Ragnow. The commander of *7th Company, Leutnant* Vollmer, was killed in action during the same engagement.[4] Bitter house-to-house fighting took place in Gey even while the relief in place was occurring, making it even more difficult for the regiment's new commander to withdraw his weary troops.

After the detachment of this regiment, Kossmala now had only two relatively fresh regiments left to carry out his division's planned mission in the Ardennes, although US intelligence estimates prepared by the 78th Infantry Division in early December missed the fact that his third regiment was engaged further to the north, out of the *272nd VGD's* sector. *Generalmajor* König, whose own battered 344th Infantry Division benefited by the temporary attachment of *Grenadier Regiment 981,* went on to take charge of the *272nd VGD* on 13 December, so he was familiar to some extent with the division's operations in the Hürtgen Forest prior to assuming command.

With the latest crisis unfolding on the Brandenburg-Bergstein Ridge, *Seventh Army,* with the concurrence of *Army Group B,* ordered *Oberst* Kossmala on 1 December to commit a battalion of *Grenadier Regiment 980* to the fighting under the control of yet another division, where it was almost certain to suffer heavy losses. This unwelcome decision, according to the Chief of Staff of *Seventh Army,* seriously degraded the *272nd VGD's* readiness for the upcoming offensive, but there was no other choice.[5]

The decision to commit *2nd Battalion, Grenadier Regiment 980* to the defense of Bergstein was followed shortly thereafter by the detachment of its sister battalion and the regimental antitank company on the night of 5/6 December, leaving the regimental commander, *Oberst* Ewald Burian, without any of his organic infantry battalions. Despite this fact, Burian still had to continue to defend his current regimental sector, which ran along the Buhlert hill mass running southwest from Simonskall to the southern outskirts of Schmidt in the northeast, scene of the terrible battles of early November. North of Schmidt, his regiment linked up with *Grenadier Regiment 1055* of the *89th Infantry Division.* Opposite the Buhlert hill lay the American defenses, which ran along the northern bank of the Kall River valley. Luckily, a network of *Westwall* bunkers contributed to the strength of his thinly-manned defensive line. Burian established his forward command post in one of these bunkers, Bunker 18, constructed near the farm at Gerstenhof.[6]

To make up for the departure of both of his infantry battalions by 5 December, Burian wasted no time in creating an *Alarm* (emergency) company from regimental service troops, which he placed under the command of *Leutnant* Klaus von Below. Burian had been given tactical control of Schlanstein's *Pionier Battalion 272* on 24 November, a unit that had already been involved in heavy fighting on the northern side of the Kall valley and at the base of the Vossenack ridge. Burian was further reinforced by the arrival of *Füsilier Company 272,* which had been ordered out of its defensive positions near Rollesbroich on 2 December. He still had his regimental infantry howitzer company to provide supporting fires, and the regimental engineer and bicycle platoons, but was forced to insert parts of these into the line to serve as infantry. His ace in the hole was

Sturm (Assault) Company 980, an elite unit made up of eighty of the best NCOs and soldiers in his regiment.

Though not specifically authorized as an integral unit by the *Volks-Grenadier* regimental *KstN,* the establishment of this company was officially sanctioned in the order providing detailed instructions for the establishment and training of the new *Volks-Grenadier* regiments. This order, *Hinweise für die Führung des Grenadier-Regiments einer Volks-Grenadier Division,* stated that the regimental commander should first make use of his regimental engineer and bicycle platoons as a reserve force before pulling assets from his line companies. The order further stated that should the commander feel that a larger force was needed at the regimental level, he could comb the infantry platoons of his two battalions to form a leadership and manpower pool. This pool was then formed into a company and kept at the ready, providing that the personnel were constantly rotated among the various companies to ensure that the men maintained their combat skills. Apparently, *Assault Company 980* was created pursuant to this order.[7]

If this were not enough official sanction, another order was issued by *Army Group B* that reinforced the practice, requiring regiments that had been designated to participate in the upcoming Ardennes Offensive (of which the commanders concerned as yet were unaware) to form assault companies at the regimental level and to limit the combat strength of each battalion's three infantry companies to eighty men. This order resulted in the creation of an excess manpower pool at the division and regimental level that could be drawn upon to replace combat losses, thus allowing units to maintain their effectiveness in the coming offensive.[8] The creation of such a company within *Grenadier Regiment 980* and the other two regiments of the *272nd VGD,* combined with the earlier directive, resulted in a unit that was equipped with heavy weapons as well as the usual amount of small arms. It is likely that this order also affected *Füsilier Company 272,* since nineteen of its men were temporarily detached to *Field Replacement Battalion 272* in early November. According to this directive, Instructions for Combat Leaders:

> Assault companies are to be set up, armed, and trained under the command of the best-suited leaders. They are to be reinforced by the addition of mine clearing, tank destruction, and flame-thrower teams, as well as by the addition of artillery forward observers . . . their mission is to overcome, take out, or cut off the enemy's forward outpost line and individual strong points. . . .[9]

Placed under the command of *Leutnant* Josef Stefan, an experienced officer from Vienna known for his daring leadership style during the Normandy Campaign, *Assault Company 980* provided a regimental reserve that allowed Burian a measure of the tactical flexibility needed to conduct a successful defense. As long as the Americans did not press the attack in his sector, he would be able to hold them off long enough until he could secure the return of his two infantry battalions or reinforcements from elsewhere. Burian trusted Stefan completely, especially since the young officer had saved Burian's life near Gomel on the Eastern Front during the summer of 1943.

The attachment of Burian's two infantry battalions to the *89th Infantry Division,* though welcomed by that division, came with strings attached. Once the counterattack against Bergstein had been successfully carried out, both battalions were to revert to the *272nd VGD's* control immediately to replace their losses, bringing the regiment up to strength so it could perform its assigned tasks for the upcoming offensive.[10] *2nd Battalion, Grenadier Regiment 980,* commanded by the capable *Hauptmann* Adolf Thomae, was the first of Burian's battalions to see action, since it had previously been moved to a reserve position immediately behind the front line of the *89th Infantry Division.*

On the morning of 4 December, Thomae was ordered to move part of his force into the village of Bergstein itself, reinforcing the antitank guns of a company from *Antitank Battalion 189* of the *89th Infantry Division,* which had already driven off the first American attempt to take the town the day before. Thomae set up his forward command post in a reinforced *Westwall* bunker, Bunker 320a, 100 meters north of Castle Hill. Here, along with the staff manning the forward command post of *Grenadier Regiment 1055,* he could observe the impending advance by CCR, 5th Armored Division toward Bergstein. From this vantage point he was able to direct artillery fire upon the Americans during their entire approach. His battalion spent most of that day improving its defensive positions, though it must have been a nerve-wracking day for his men. Several German tank destroyers were also situated close by should the need arise for their commitment in support of the defense.

Throughout 4 December, the Germans could clearly hear the sounds of tank engines coming from Brandenberg, where CCR, 5th Armored Division was preparing for its attack along with the rest of the 8th Infantry Division. Besides a tank attack, Thomae's men defending Brandenburg also had to contend with the continuous artillery fire raining down upon them throughout the day. Fortunately, most of his men, occupying foxholes, bunkers, or cellars in the town itself, were protected from the worst of it. Since the assault against Bergstein was to be the main effort of the 8th Infantry Division that day, the bulk of the American's division and corps artillery battalions was dedicated toward providing fire support in this area and appeared to not have suffered from a lack of ammunition.

American tanks and armored infantry, reinforced by riflemen from the 8th Infantry Division, returned in strength to take Bergstein at 1400 hours on 5 December. Initially harassed by a rare appearance of a few strafing ME-109s, they were greeted with heavy German artillery and antitank fire, expertly directed by the forward observation post located in a bunker on top of Castle Hill. Riding on the rear decks of the advancing Shermans, the infantry were forced to dismount under a hail of machine-gun fire to seek cover in the houses on the western edge of the town, while the tanks sought out individual targets. One eye-witness characterized German resistance that day as "extremely severe."[11]

As they advanced, one company from the 10th Tank Battalion swung to the southeast corner of the town and another to the southwest corner to block the roads and prevent the Germans from escaping. To the CCR's left, 1st Battalion, 121st Infantry Regiment, 8th Infantry Division advanced through the woods on the town's northern edge, while 3rd Battalion, 28th Infantry Regiment attacked on the right flank along the southern edge of the ridgeline overlooking the Tiefenbachtal and the Lücasmühle, an old mill located in the valley. Though the Americans outnumbered the Germans at least two to one, Thomae and his men defended stubbornly and skillfully. Two of the remaining three officers of the two leading American companies were immediately killed or severely wounded. Four of the 10th Armored Battalion's tanks were destroyed in the fighting, as well as one German *Jagdpanzer* IV/70 tank destroyer.

Despite heavy casualties, the Americans pressed on and seized most of the town by 1700 hours. CCR, 5th Armored Division claimed to have captured fifty men, later identified as belonging to Thomae's *2nd Battalion, Grenadier Regiment 980,* and to have killed an unknown number. Five German antitank guns from *Antitank Battalion 189* were captured as well. Their work done for the day, the Americans prepared their defensive positions for that night and the inevitable counterattack that they expected the following morning.[12] Teams searched throughout the night for German snipers still holed up in the town who continued to direct harassing fire against the tired Americans. Thomae, temporarily beaten, ordered his remaining men to withdraw to the western slopes of Castle Hill where they dug in and awaited reinforcement.

By this time, both *Seventh Army* and *Army Group B* headquarters had become thoroughly alarmed at the success of the American attack. Bruns quickly completed preparations to carry out a counterattack to drive the Americans out of Bergstein, but needed additional help. As previously mentioned, both Bruns' *Grenadier Regiment 1055* and *1056* were too weak to attack and were hard-pressed to hold what little ground they still controlled. Thomae's battalion could not be committed immediately either, since it had suffered heavy losses during its defense of Bergstein and had become disorganized. The battered survivors of his battalion were directed to hold their current positions on and around Castle Hill to continue denying it to the Americans.

Help was on the way in the form of the newly-arrived *1st Battalion, Grenadier Regiment 980,* under the command of *Hauptmann* Dr. Max Rhein. Bruns lost no time in ordering Rhein to carry out the counterattack. Rhein and his men had departed the vicinity of Schmidt at 2230 hours the night before and had been marching the better part of the night. In addition, the *14th Company* of *Grenadier Regiment 980,* commanded by *Oberleutnant* Kurt Hake, would participate with its *1st* and *3rd Platoons,* adding eighty men to the Rhein's force. Rhein scheduled the operation to begin at 0645 hours 6 December, following an artillery barrage to suppress the American tanks and infantry.

An indicator of how seriously *Seventh Army* took this American incursion was the release to *LXXIV Corps* of the Army's remaining armor reserve to throw the Americans out of Bergstein. This counterattack would be supported by four *Sturmgeschütz* Model III (StuG III) assault guns from *Panzer Battalion 103*, six *Jagdpanzer* IV/70s from *Antitank Battalion 3* (both of these units were from the *3rd Panzer-Grenadier Division*), and several StuG IIIs from *Assault Gun Brigade 667*.* Twelve *Hetzer* tank destroyers of *Antitank Battalions 272* and *277* were also en route to lend support, but do not appear to have been directly committed, being used instead to provide fire support from positions near Kommerscheidt. To approach the objective, the armor would move via the serpentine road that ran from the bottom of the hill at Zerkall to the top at Bergstein after linking up with the infantry.

The assembly area for the infantry was a ravine near the village of Zerkall, 500 meters east of Castle Hill. *Hauptmann* Rhein and *Leutnant* Hake paused here to realign their formations, which had been spread out during movement to minimize the effects of American artillery fire. Once this was accomplished, they began the movement forward at approximately 0500 hours. For Hake's men, this involved moving uphill through the steeply wooded slope south of Castle Hill, where they occupied assault positions on its eastern slope, chosen because it enabled them to avoid American visual detection. Rhein's men formed up south of Hill 358, immediately south of Bergstein, where they linked up with the armor. American harassing fire fell randomly throughout the area, though the Germans suffered few, if any, casualties during their movement into position.

The combined batteries of *Artillery Regiments 189* and *272* began firing the supporting artillery barrage at 0643 hours. They did not spare the ammunition. The *OKW* was so alarmed by this American penetration that it released carefully hoarded 105mm shells from stockpiles amassed for the Ardennes Offensive to the artillery command of *LXXIV Corps*.[13] With the artillery bombardment raining down upon Bergstein, *1st, 2nd,* and *4th Companies* of *1st Battalion, Grenadier Regiment 980*, and *Antitank Company 980*, comprising some 520 men in all, began moving forward. Shortly afterwards, the German barrage lifted and shifted, enabling the gunners to begin engaging targets further to the rear to avoid

---

* The *3rd Panzer-Grenadier Division*, before it was allowed to move to its assembly area prior to the start of the Ardennes Offensive, had been ordered to leave *Kampfgruppe Türke*, consisting of *1st Battalion, Panzer-Grenadier Regiment 29*, reinforced by *Panzer Battalion 103* and *Antitank Battalion 3*, in the vicinity of Nideggen on 4 December to serve as the reserve for *Seventh Army*. It appears that the battle group's commander, *Hauptmann* Gerhard Türke, committed only the armored vehicles to take part in the attack, while his remaining seventy-three *Panzer-Grenadiers* remained in the vicinity of Zerkall protecting the bridge over the Roer River [from Gerhard Dieckhoff, *Die 3. Infanterie-Division* (Podzun Pallas Verlag, Oldenburg, Germany, 1960), 375–76].

killing their own men. The *Volksgrenadiers* began their assault at 0645 hours, advancing out of the woods to the east, south, and southwest of Bergstein. The assault guns and accompanying tank destroyers, which had been in hidden positions on the reverse slope of the hillside, moved out in support by attacking from the south along the road or by firing from overwatch positions (See Map 5).

Part of Rhein's battalion had to cover 300 meters of open ground to reach its objective, most of that uphill. In spite of that, the Germans had some advantages. The *Volksgrenadiers'* approach was aided by the American's poor battlefield visibility, since daylight comes late during December in northern Europe. It was bitter cold, with a light layer of snow helping to muffle the footsteps of the approaching infantry. The only noise to be heard was the impact of the German artillery and the clanking of tank treads, as attested to by American after-action reports.[14]

Alerted by the activity and noise of the approaching armored vehicles, the GIs were ready to meet the attack from their prepared positions. Violent counterattacks were a trademark of German tactics, and the veterans of the 8th Infantry and the 5th Armored Divisions had learned through bitter experience to be ready for them. To the *Volksgrenadiers* in their heavy overcoats and laden with weapons struggling across the open field, the Americans in the darkened village of Bergstein were strangely silent. It must have been unnerving, to say the least.

The defending troops from CCR—consisting of the 47th Armored Infantry Battalion and the 10th Tank Battalion, along with the attached 3rd Battalion, 28th Infantry Regiment of the 8th Infantry Division and Company C, 628th Tank Destroyer Battalion—waited until the Germans, who were approaching across the open field to the south, were twenty-five yards in front of their position before they began firing. What followed can only be described as a slaughter.

The concentrated fire from the village, lighting up the early morning darkness, surprised the *Volksgrenadiers,* causing some of them to panic when their leaders were shot down. Tracers illuminated the formations of the approaching Germans as .30- and .50-caliber machine-gun fire scythed through their ranks. A few tried to retreat the same way they had come. Caught in the open, many of the *Volksgrenadiers* were cut down by artillery or machine-gun fire without having a chance to fire back.[15] Rhein's attack almost failed just as it was beginning.

German assault guns and tank destroyers soon responded in kind. Several of them sped past the western edge of the village and attacked the Americans from the rear. Eight of the eleven remaining Shermans were quickly knocked out. Even though the surviving American armor fought back stubbornly, there were some exceptions. Fear of overhead artillery bursts drove the crews of two newly arrived M-36 tank destroyers to abandon their vehicles and   shelter in a basement during the battle, temporarily depriving the defenders the use of the vehicles' superb 90mm gun. Though the M-36 was a formidable looking tank-like vehicle, its open-topped turret and thin armor made it unpopular with its crews because of its vulnerability to overhead artillery bursts.

Disgusted by the lack of initiative of the tank destroyer crews, infantrymen from the 47th Armored Infantry Battalion volunteered to operate the vehicles and put them to good use. Even though many of the American's shells ricocheted off the front slopes of the advancing panzers, six German tank destroyers and assault guns were quickly knocked out.*

One panzer was knocked out only seventy-five yards from an American tank destroyer that was, in turn, destroyed by another German armored vehicle.[16] Despite the bitter resistance, enough of the attacking German armor and infantry survived to force their way into the town. Stepping over their own dead and wounded, the determined Volksgrenadiers "attacked bitterly," according to one eyewitness from the 47th Armored Infantry Battalion.

Despite the tremendous artillery, tank, and small arms fire being directed at them, a few of Rhein's *Volksgrenadiers* were able to seize several houses on the southern and eastern part of the village before being killed, captured, or forced to withdraw, sometimes after hand-to-hand combat. Fighting raged in the town for nearly two hours before the German tanks and infantry were finally driven back by 0930 hours.[17] One survivor from Company B, 47th Armored Infantry Battalion recalled that had daylight arrived fifteen minutes later, they would not have been able to hold out against another German assault.[18]

It was a near thing. Another survivor wrote that if the Germans had tried again that night, they would have succeeded. Although most of the American forces fought magnificently, one company from the 8th Infantry Division, tasked to support the defense in Bergstein, refused to leave the protection of the town's cellars, forcing the few remaining armored infantrymen and infantrymen from the 28th Infantry Regiment to stretch their already thin line even further.[19]

Two hours later, the battered *1st Battalion, Grenadier Regiment 980*, reinforced by the addition of its *3rd Company*, made another attempt, but this second counterattack was much weaker than the first. The sole armored vehicle supporting them was quickly knocked out and the Germans were driven back downhill into the woods and ravines again. They tried one more time at 1420 hours, but this attack was smashed by artillery fire before it had really begun. With that, Bruns' attempt to retake Bergstein that day came to an end.

Both sides had suffered heavily. When *Hauptmann* Rhein reported to the headquarters of the *89th Infantry Division* at 1240 hours he had only 150 men remaining out of the 520 he had started with six hours before. At least seven German

---

* American reports state that Panzer IV and Panzer V "Panthers" took part in this counterattack, but German records and German eyewitness accounts reveal that only tank destroyers and assault guns were involved. Confusion of tank nomenclatures, especially during the fog of battle, is common even today and reports of Tiger tanks being used in certain actions were frequently shown to have been the relatively more common Panzer IV or assault guns when the dust had settled. The Panzer IV/70 tank destroyer, with its angled armor and long barrel, was often confused with Panthers by inexperienced Americans.

armored vehicles lay smoldering on the field and in the town itself.[20] Because their attempt to retake Bergstein had failed and since it was now too close to the front line, the forward command post of *Grenadier Regiment 1055* was forced to reposition near Zerkall, leaving Thomae in sole possession of the command bunker next to Castle Hill.

One survivor of the doomed counterattack of 6 December was *Unteroffizier* Hans Wegener of *14th Company, Grenadier Regiment 980*. Assigned to the *3rd Platoon* under *Feldwebel* Brockmann, Wegener and the other thirty-nine members of his antitank platoon had marched earlier that morning from the village of Abenden. Crossing the Roer at Zerkall, the antitank gunners, loaded down with *Panzerschreck* and *Panzerfaust antitank rocket launchers,* sweated profusely after climbing the slopes of Castle Hill. As the day slowly dawned, he and the others raced on foot from the wooded slopes of Castle Hill toward Bergstein while the tanks, assault guns, and the bulk of Rhein's battalion advanced in the open field to their left. Wegener remembered the American fire as being harmless at first, but it became more deadly when they reached the eastern edge of the town. "Then came the inferno," he recalled.

> Tank against tank, hand-to-hand combat, tanks burning. . . . *Feldwebel* Brockmann shot at a Sherman with a *Panzerfaust,* but the warhead fell off in mid-air, rendering it useless. He was immediately killed by the tank . . . loud noise of duels between men armed with *Panzerfausts* and tanks . . . burning and exploding tanks, men falling everywhere. . . . My people shot up a Sherman, which started to burn. One of the crewmembers tumbled out and staggered beside his burning tank. I screamed don't shoot! He is defenseless! Then I ordered someone to bring him to safety before the tank explodes. They brought him to me and he appeared unwounded, though he was blinded. Our forces had become too weak to take back the town so we had to retreat. . . .[21]

Of the forty men in Wegener's platoon who started out that morning, only thirteen were still present when they assembled 200 meters to the east of the town in the safety of Castle Hill that afternoon. They were joined that night by one of their machine gunners, who had hidden out during the day in the steeple of the village church, bringing the total number of survivors to fourteen. Their sister platoon had suffered just as badly and its platoon leader, *Leutnant* Kurt Diemichen, was killed in action. By day's end, Rhein's battalion had been reduced to only seventy-nine combat troops, representing a casualty rate of nearly eighty-four percent.[22] Even though he had led each of the counterattacks, Rhein miraculously survived uninjured to supervise the withdrawal of his broken force.

The Americans had not gotten off lightly either. From 4 to 6 December, CCR lost twenty tanks and eleven tank destroyers in Bergstein. Most of the mechanized infantry companies of the 47th Armored Infantry had been reduced in size to platoons, one third of their authorized strength.[23] Company B, 47th Armored Infantry, for example, was reduced in size to forty-three men. Although Bergstein had been held, CCR no longer had the strength to seize the next objective—Hill 400 (Castle Hill). Nor did the 8th Infantry Division have anything left to reinforce it for another attempt. Even their ability to continue the defense of Bergstein was in doubt. According to one American eyewitness:

> Virtually all of the men in CCR were in a state of shock. Their nerves were shot, their physical energy had long since disappeared. They crouched dazedly in their foxholes and basements, loading their guns and waiting for the Germans to come back. They could never hold another counterattack like the last one. There simply were not enough men left. . . . The counter-attack had taken a heavy toll.[24]

In order to seize Hill 400 and maintain of the momentum gained during the past week of heavy fighting, Brigadier General William G. Weaver, the new commander of the 8th Infantry Division, asked V Corps to release its reserve, the elite 2nd Ranger Battalion, for the specific purpose of taking the hill. The V Corps' commander, Major General Gerow, approved his request on 6 December. That night, the battalion was loaded into trucks and began its circuitous journey in the freezing cold to Bergstein, where it would attack the following morning.

Like Weaver, Bruns was faced with a situation that demanded more from his forces than they were capable of giving. On Bruns' left flank, *Grenadier Regiment 1055* repelled an American attack in company strength in the vicinity of Giesenheck, a tree-covered knoll on the far eastern edge of the Vossenack ridge. *Grenadier Regiment 1056* on his division's far right flank, was busy fending off an American advance toward the Roer crossing at Obermaubach from their positions on the Krebsberg and Bovenberg. For once, however, luck was on the side of the commander of the 8th Infantry Division, who had been given the 2nd Ranger Battalion from V Corps. The addition of this reinforcement proved timely indeed and was enough to tip the scales in his favor. Fortunately for Weaver, his German counterpart, General Bruns, was unable to get any additional reinforcements released from *LXXIV Corps* to strengthen his own forces. To make matters worse, Bruns was ordered to retake Bergstein the next day at all costs.

This order was probably too much for Bruns, a quiet professional of the old school, to accept. Since the two battalions from *Grenadier Regiment 980* had suffered heavy casualties totaling nearly seventy percent, Bruns told *General der Infanterie* Straube on the evening of 6 December that without additional troops, it would be impossible to retake the town with the weak forces under his control. His own regiments (the *1055th* and *1056th*) were even weaker. The only other regiment of the *272nd VGD*, *Grenadier Regiment 982,* was tied down defending the main line between Simmerath and the Raffelsbrand-Ochsenkopf bunker complex and could not be withdrawn. Unless reinforcements were brought in quickly, the Americans would soon seize the terrain that would allow them to have a direct view into the Cologne plain, where the forces earmarked for the Ardennes Offensive were beginning their final preparations. He told Straube, in no uncertain terms, that unless this happened, *LXXIV Corps* had to come to grips with the fact that Bergstein was lost for good and that Castle Hill would probably soon be lost as well.

When pressed, Bruns suggested to Straube that since most of the troops in and around Bergstein were now from the *272nd VGD* anyway, it made more sense to assign the responsibility for conducting the counterattack to that division. Straube must have agreed with Bruns' assessment. That evening, the corps commander tasked Kossmala to assume the mission of retaking Bergstein with his division no later than 7 December. Division boundaries were accordingly shifted north to Bergstein, with *272nd VGD* regaining control of both battalions of *Grenadier Regiment 980*, as well as temporary control of *Grenadier Regiment 1055*.[25]

Although *Füsilier Company 272* was not directly involved in the fighting at Bergstein, the transfer of *2nd Battalion, Grenadier Regiment 980* to the *89th Infantry Division* on the evening of 2 December resulted in the company being transferred to fill the hole in the main defense line caused by Thomae's departure. Alerted during the late evening of 1 December, the company moved that night by bicycle from its old positions at Rollesbroich to its new ones located in the vicinity of the former *Reichsarbeitsdienst* (Labor Service) barracks at Gerstenhof, atop the Buhlert hill mass, to cover the now-vacated positions on *Grenadier Regiment 980*'s left flank.

The move, though undisturbed by the enemy, was not without incident. Taking advantage of the darkness and disruption of the usual routine, *Füsiliers* Heinz Weberbauer and Heinrich Wöhl, led by *Obergefreiter* Alfred Plückhahn, separated themselves from the rest of the company. Last seen heading for the American lines, theirs was the second incident of desertion since the company arrived in the Hürtgen Forest. Both Weberbauer and Wöhl had joined the company in October, along with the rest of the draft of sailors from the *Kriegsmarine*. Apparently, the dangerous and uncomfortable duty of a front-line infantryman was not to their liking after all. Plückhahn, though a veteran, had apparently had enough of the war and convinced the two young former sailors to join him. They were not heard from again

Even at this late stage of the war, the charge of desertion still carried a great deal of shame. Family members were stigmatized by their son's or husband's disloyalty and sometimes even suffered at the hands of local Nazi officials. Wöhl's mother refused to believe that her son had "fled the colors" and sought help from her district's party leader, though without success. (Author's note: Though they were still alive and living in Germany at the time of this writing, neither Weberbauer nor Wöhl would respond to letters asking them to tell their side of the story. Regardless, they survived the war; had they remained with the company, the odds of survival were against them).

Though Kolb and his men of *Füsilier Company 272* must have plainly heard the sounds of the heavy fighting taking place at Bergstein from their new fighting positions, their own sector remained relatively peaceful. Kolb established his headquarters in a reinforced dugout several hundred meters northwest of the Gerstenhof farmstead, where he was in close proximity to *Oberst* Burian's own command post. For the next ten days, *Füsilier Company 272* was under Burian's direct command and control, since most of *Grenadier Regiment 980* had been temporarily placed under the control of the *89th Infantry Division*. Though he had been ordered to give up his two infantry battalions, Burian now had enough forces under him to defend his extended front line. In addition to *Füsilier Company 272*, he also controlled *Leutnant* Stefan's *Sturmkompanie 980*, von Below's *Alarm Company 980*, and one company of *Hauptmann* Schlanstein's *Pionier Battalion 272*

Kolb's men did not mind having to give up their old positions near Rollesbroich, where they had been subjected to heavy shelling for over three weeks. Instead of occupying fighting positions and dugouts in plain sight of the Americans, they now moved into a series of log-covered fighting positions and concrete bunkers located within the heavy forest that carpeted the Buhlert hill. According to Kurt Klein, the movement from Rollesbroich to the Buhlert went off without any men being killed or wounded and the company was moved into their new positions without any complications, except for the desertions. Once established in their new location, the company busied itself with a routine reminiscent of what it had endured at Rollesbroich—more patrolling, mine laying, and reinforcing fighting positions. No contact with American forces was reported to have occurred during this time except, of course, the omnipresent artillery fire.

The men used this relatively quiet period to rest and repair their clothing and equipment. It had been wet for most of the month of November, and with the winter having already arrived, the men set to work making their fighting positions as warm and dry as possible. Occasionally, members of the company were allowed to return to the safety of several bunkers behind the Gerstenhof farmstead, where they were allowed to rest undisturbed for short periods and perhaps wash clothing or bathe. Eduard Zacharuk, who had been moved from the *4th Platoon* to the company headquarters to serve as a runner, celebrated his eighteenth birthday on 9 December by opening a package from home that had arrived that day.

To his joy and surprise, his mother had sent him a brand new set of underclothing, which he proceeded to put on immediately. Since there was no changing room to be had, of course, he instead laid out his shelter quarter and disrobed in the open, much to the merriment of his comrades. He shredded and threw away the old underwear that he had worn for over five weeks and which was little more than "stinking rags" by this point.[26]

Zacharuk was not the only one in the company who had a birthday on the Buhlert; for on 3 December, Kurt Klein marked his own twenty-ninth, writing laconically in his diary "Celebrated my birthday today in a bunker position in the Eifel. Outside weather's nasty."

Even though they were now in a relatively secure position, the Hürtgen Forest was still a dangerous place, even in its relatively quiet sectors. It seldom tolerated mistakes. During the ten days the company spent in the Buhlert defensive position, it experienced the loss of four men, including one killed and one seriously wounded in action. *Oberfüsilier* Rudolf Häring was the first, killed on the same day the company moved into its new positions on 2 December. Seeking to fill his canteen, the twenty-one-year-old *Volksgrenadier* left his new fighting position without permission from his platoon sergeant to fetch water from the Kall, which lay only 100 meters beyond the company's front line. Returning in the darkness, he stepped on a mine at 1850 hours. In pain, he screamed for a medic, a cry plainly heard by the rest of the company. As he thrashed about in his agony, he accidentally detonated another mine that killed him outright.

Ten minutes later, a search party led by *Gefreiter* Meinke was assembled to go out and bring back his body, but on the advice of *Feldwebel* Reimann, a combat engineer sergeant attached to the company from *Pionier Battalion 272, Unteroffizier* Matthies, the assistant platoon sergeant, cancelled the order. According to Reimann, so many new mines and wire obstacles had been placed in that sector that it would have been suicidal to search for Häring's body in the darkness. Instead, he proposed to lead the search party at 0700 hours the next morning, armed with a map showing the locations of the minefields in the area. Reimann was recalled sometime during the evening without notifying anyone from *Füsilier Company 272,* however. The search party was not sent out without his expert knowledge of the area, so Häring's body was not recovered until after the war.

An investigation was conducted the following day, but the most Kolb could suggest to *Hauptmann* Witscher, the *Adjutant,* or operations officer, of *Grenadier Regiment 980*, was that *Pionier Battalion 272* should require its personnel to notify other units when they are about to leave the area. Kolb concluded that while Häring's death was tragic, he had been told, after all, that the area was mined and had gone off in search of water anyway.

The next casualty was *Obergefreiter* Otto Chytry, wounded on the left hand 9 December by a piece of shrapnel. After two months of treatment and convalescence, he returned to the company. Two other men were lightly wounded during this period of relative inaction.

Throughout this period, the heavy weapons and infantry howitzer platoons provided supporting fire more or less constantly in support of *Füsilier Company 272* and other units. Most of the fire missions were directed against American patrols attempting to ford the Kall in the vicinity of the hamlet of Simonskall. Though limited in the amount of ammunition they could use, Fosselmann and Misskampf reported that they were still able to achieve the desired effect, mainly through the careful aiming of their 80mm mortars and infantry howitzers, as well as by resorting to frequent use of the "ambush by fire" technique. From 2 to 12 December, the 8th Infantry Division was unable to effect a penetration in this sector, though its 13th Infantry Regiment made several attempts to break through in the vicinity of the Raffelsbrand-Ochsenkopf bunker complex. Here, *Hauptmann* Schmidt's *2nd Battalion, Grenadier Regiment 982* repeatedly fended off a series of company- and battalion-sized attacks.

Kolb's company expected to remain in this position for several more weeks, so it must have been with some surprise that the men received the news on 12 December that they were now to assume an offensive role. Another regiment of the 8th Infantry Division had been able to expand the area under its control along the Kall valley and had even seized the critical Giesenheck bridgehead position east of Vossenack. Finally, after nearly five weeks of static warfare, *Füsilier Company 272* would be given an opportunity to prove the hopes that had been placed in it by its commander. It would prove merely to be a foretaste of the horrors to come.

7

Fight for Control of the Kall River Gorge: The Assault on "Castle Hill"

On the night of 6/7 December, *Generalmajor* Bruns' *Ia*, *Major* Werner Johannes, drove from the *89th Infantry Division*'s forward command post at Nideggen to its main command post in Hasenfeld, where he met with his counterpart from the *272nd VGD, Major* Gerhard Höptner. Both staff officers conferred to plan the transfer of operational control for the attack to regain Bergstein from the *89th Infantry Division* to the *272nd VGD*. According to the corps order, the *272nd VGD*'s attack was to take place the next morning. Along with assuming responsibility for the area encompassed by the boundary shift, Kossmala's division would also assume temporary control of *Grenadier Regiment 1055* from the *89th Infantry Division*.

This regiment, badly weakened after the past two weeks of heavy fighting, was still holding the defensive sector between Schmidt and Zerkall.[1] The two battered infantry battalions from Burian's *Grenadier Regiment 980* were hurriedly reformed for one last attempt to re-take the village. The last remaining armored vehicles, including eleven *Hetzers* from *Tank Destroyer Battalion 272,* were made ready to support the push. Before Kossmala could get any sort of attack off the ground, however, the Americans beat him to the punch.

The Germans' worst fears were realized on the morning of 7 December when Castle Hill fell to the 2nd Ranger Battalion in a pre-dawn attack. Beginning their assault at 0645 hours after a brief mortar barrage, the men of Companies D and F crossed the line of departure along the eastern outskirts of Bergstein and passed through the front line defended by the exhausted troops of CCR, 5th Armored Division and the 8th Infantry Division. Advancing rapidly in a widely-spaced formation while employing marching fire, the Rangers covered the 200 meters of open ground (the same ground that Hans Wegener's company had traversed the day before) and reached the foot of Castle Hill. Amazingly, the Rangers had caught the German defenders from *Hauptmann* Thomae's *2nd Battalion* totally unawares and did not draw any return fire until they were nearly on top of the *Volksgrenadiers'* positions.

When they were virtually within hand-grenade range of the forward positions, the Americans were finally engaged by rifle and machine-gun fire from the few alert defenders who had dug in on the forward slope of the hill. With fixed bayonets, the Americans plunged into the German fighting positions and savagely fought the *Volksgrenadiers* hand to hand. No quarter was asked and none given. The 2nd Ranger Battalion reported the hilltop secure by 0830 hours, but Germans still stubbornly clung to the reverse slopes on the north, east, and south.[2]

With his battalion being overrun and with Rangers milling about on top of his own bunker, Thomae was forced to call artillery fire repeatedly upon his own position, knowing that it would as likely kill his own men as it would the Americans, but he believed that he had no choice. The hill had to be held at all costs. Although Thomae personally led several counterattacks on 7 December to throw the Rangers off of the hill, each time he and his men were beaten back by the Americans, who were just as determined to hold what they had gained. Throughout most of that day, the hill was pummeled by the artillery of both sides. At one point, up to eighteen battalions of artillery again fired in support of the Rangers, while the Germans could call upon the combined artillery battalions of the *89th Infantry Division*, the *272nd VGD,* and *LXXIV Corps*. Concerned that he and his staff might soon be killed or taken prisoner, Thomae was forced to evacuate his command bunker sometime after 0200 hours on 8 December.[3]

Both sides suffered enormously in terms of killed and wounded. By noon on 8 December, only forty-two men remained unwounded of the two Ranger companies that had made the attack, roughly thirty percent of their authorized strength. A portion of the 2nd Ranger Battalion's reserve, a platoon from Company E, was committed to reinforce their beleaguered comrades on the hill. With the aid of the Ranger's forward observer, Lt. Howard K. Kettlehut from the 32nd Field Artillery Brigade, a deadly ring of artillery fire was placed around Castle Hill that made it nearly impossible for the Germans to retake the hill.[4]

Thomae launched two more counterattacks between 1800 hours and midnight that were well supported by artillery and mortar fire, but again both attacks were driven off. The second counterattack got as far as the Ranger's individual fighting positions before the *Volksgrenadiers* were beaten back.[5] Thomae and what was left of his battalion withdrew to the ravine at the eastern face of the hill to rally and to prepare for the following day. The news that Castle Hill had fallen to the Americans was initially not taken seriously by the German High Command. To determine whether the hill had truly been taken by the Americans, *Generalmajor* Bruns, under pressure from his corps headquarters, dispatched a scouting party that night consisting of several officers. After a harrowing night evading American sentries, they duly reported that it was indeed now held by the 2nd Ranger Battalion, after the officers captured two Ranger medics in the act of evacuating a casualty.[6]

With his own attack to retake the village of Bergstein now overcome by events, *Oberst* Kossmala now had to concentrate on retaking the even more important Castle Hill instead. Combining both *1st* and *2nd Battalions* of *Grenadier Regiment 980,* and elements of the attached *Grenadier Regiment 1055*, the *272nd VGD*'s attack resumed the following morning at 0700 hours after an artillery preparation that "was so heavy that it seemed to have a 'drumming' sound," according to an American survivor. This attack failed, and was followed by another one at 0900 hours that was preceded by its own tremendous barrage, but this one also was broken up by the defenders, with the help of overwhelming artillery fire.

At 1700 hours on 8 December, a larger German counterattack involving up to 150 men and assault guns assaulted both Castle Hill and Bergstein from the southeast and north, but it, too, was thwarted by the defender's small arms and artillery fire. The Rangers had augmented their own defensive arsenal with the addition of machine guns that had been removed from several of the disabled tanks and half-tracks abandoned in Bergstein by CCR of the 5th Armored Division, but their defensive line was still quite thin. According to one of the Ranger officers, "Of all the enemy attacks, this final one offered the most dangerous threat as the entire battalion defense system had been weakened through numerous casualties inflicted by enemy fires."[7]

The farthest that Thomae's men got into the town during this last attempt was the church, 100 meters from the town's eastern edge, but they were driven back before they could secure a foothold.[8] Even so, the Americans were at the end of their rope. Survivors later stated that had the Germans attacked one more time with a fresh battalion, they could have taken the town. Fortunately for the Americans, there was no fresh battalion to be had. The attack on 8 December was truly the last gasp. Although he had failed to retake Bergstein or Castle Hill, Thomae was awarded the Knight's Cross afterward in recognition of his heroism and his battalion's performance from 5 to 8 December (Though his name was submitted for the award in December, Thomae did not actually receive it until 24 February 1945.)[9]

Again, losses had been heavy on both sides. The two battalions from *272nd VGD* had been further reduced in strength and sixty-nine of their men were taken prisoner by the 2nd Ranger Battalion.[10] The Rangers had suffered 133 casualties, including twenty-three killed in action. Thanks to the Ranger's achievement, both Bergstein and Castle Hill remained in American hands. It is notable that, up to that point in the war, it was also the farthest penetration into German territory by any American or British unit.[11] The following day, the 2nd Ranger Battalion and CCR, 5th Armored Division were relieved by the 3rd Battalion of the 13th Infantry, 8th Infantry Division, which remained in this position until the end of February 1945.

Generalmajor Bruns, who was already pessimistic about the outcome of any attack to regain Bergstein and Castle Hill, laconically wrote in his diary that evening that the attempt by the *272nd VGD* on 8 December "was not crowned with success."[12] As if to draw a curtain down upon this stage of the campaign, heavy snow began to fall shortly after sunset, covering the shell-wracked and body-strewn battlefield with a white blanket that obscured the harsh outlines and imparted a soft, wintry appearance to the landscape. The soldiers of both sides, in their foxholes and fighting positions, shivered silently, pulling up their collars or another blanket pulled from the body of a dead comrade. To light a fire for warmth invited almost certain death from artillery or mortar shells.

Miraculously, despite the loss of Hürtgen and their decisive defeat on the Brandenburg-Bergstein Ridge, fortune intervened once again in the German's favor. Inexplicably, the 8th Infantry Division halted its eastward drive to the Roer after taking Castle Hill, though the river crossings at the eastern slope of the hill were practically undefended, held by less than 100 infantrymen of *Kampfgruppe Türke*. Only 1,000 meters separated Weaver's exhausted troops from the Roer crossings at Nideggen and Obermaubach. The few remaining German troops were figuratively hanging on by their fingernails on the reverse slopes of the hills overlooking the river. Though this amazing state of affairs left the German leadership dumbfounded, it was not due to any lack of aggressiveness on the part of the 8th Infantry Division that brought about the halt, but rather something far simpler.

After nearly a month of fighting in the Hürtgen Forest, the 8th Infantry Division had suffered nearly 4,000 casualties and was exhausted. Not only that, but its front line was a tangled mess, with German and American units intermingled along the tortured terrain of the Kall River gorge near Simonskall, the slopes south of Vossenack, and along the Brandenberg-Bergstein Ridge. Before any advance could be resumed, the division first had to halt, reconstitute its shattered battalions, and straighten out its front. While this was being carried out, the major focus of the fighting shifted to the north near Düren and the Stolberg corridor, leaving the defenders along the Roer, particularly the men of the *89th Infantry* and the *272nd Volks-Grenadier Divisions,* a few day's time to catch their breath and reorganize their own forces as well. The American's decision not to exploit their hard-won gains later assumed the status of a minor miracle by German veterans of the battle.

Interestingly, observation posts of the 13th Infantry Regiment, 8th Infantry Division, which occupied Castle Hill after relieving the 2nd Ranger Battalion, reported on 13 December that they had seen "considerable moving of troops in [the] enemy's rear." This tantalizing indication of German preparations for the upcoming Ardennes offensive apparently went unnoticed by the chain of command, for it was not even mentioned in the Division's G-2 Summary for that day.[13]

The Fight for the Bridgehead Position at Giesenheck

While the fighting raged along the Brandenberg-Bergstein Ridge from 2 to 9 December, other elements of Weaver's 8th Infantry Division persisted in their attempts to clear the Vossenack Ridge and to exert control of the exits to the Kall River gorge. The German had been using this defile since early November to move troops in and out of the area without being directly observed by the

Americans and to carry out aggressive patrolling with impunity. By 8 December, however, the only German unit controlling terrain north of the Kall valley that still threatened the American's position in Vossenack was the *3rd Company* of *Hauptmann* Schlanstein's *Pionier Battalion 272,* which occupied the southern slope of the Vossenack Ridge

A few German engineers still clung stubbornly to Giesenheck, a small wooded hillock at the eastern tip of the ridge, a point referred to by the Americans as Hill 349. From Giesenheck a serviceable trail led south into the Kall River gorge, past the small iron forge at Zweifallshammer, east into the village of Zerkall on the Roer and uphill to Kommerscheidt. Another trail that led from the Kall valley wound north past Giesenheck into the Tiefenbachtal, where the German field dressing station at Lücasmühle had once been located. Giesenheck, which had been continuously manned by the Germans since the loss of most of Vossenack in early November, also offered excellent observation into Bergstein, which lay only one and a half kilometers to the east roughly at the same elevation.

Although not as prominent as Vossenack or Castle Hill, whoever held Giesenheck still controlled routes leading through the Kall River gorge. German control of this position permitted their observation of American activities in Vossenack, Hürtgen, Brandenburg, and Bergstein. It had assumed such tactical significance by 3 December that it had been designated a *Brückenkopfstellung* (bridgehead position) by *Generalmajor* Bruns' *89th Infantry Division.* As long as the Germans held Giesenheck, its continued possession gave them hope that at some point it could be used as a forward assembly area to launch another attempt to retake Vossenack. Major General Weaver decided that this continued German presence posed a looming threat to the right flank of his division's attack against Brandenburg and Bergstein, and ordered that Giesenheck as well as the entire Vossenack ridge be finally cleared of the enemy. He ordered the 28th Infantry Regiment, still exhausted and understrength from the heavy fighting for Hürtgen the week before, to carry out the mission.

On 7 December, 2nd Battalion, 28th Infantry Regiment, commanded by Major Edward J. Regan, was ordered to take Giesenheck and eliminate the German combat engineers who clung like "beggar lice" to the hilltop. The first attempt failed when heavy automatic weapons fire (some of which were machine guns captured from the US 28th Infantry Division during its abortive attack of the month before) pinned down his Company G, forcing it eventually to retire to Vossenack after losing over a dozen men. The next morning, after a heavy preparatory barrage, Regan's battalion, now, after three weeks of combat, only 366 men strong (authorized strength, 861), conducted a two-pronged attack that surprised the defenders and secured the hilltop by 0815 hours.[14]

During the course of the fighting on 8 December, which saw ground attacks carried out by the *Luftwaffe* against the American's positions, Regan's 2nd Battalion captured or killed over ninety of Schlanstein's combat engineers who were defending Giesenheck. Company E, given the mission of holding the sector, improved the captured German positions and awaited the inevitable response, which came two days later. In response to the loss of Giesenheck, the Germans began aggressive patrolling activities that kept the Americans on edge throughout the day and night.

On the afternoon of 9 December, *Leutnant* Josef Stefans's *Assault Company 980* launched a counterattack that cut off and captured one platoon of 20 men from Company E who were holding Giesenheck and forced the rest of the company back into Vossenack. After retaking the bridgehead position, Stefan handed its defense over to *Oberleutnant* Johann Reineke's emergency company, which had been formed from *Field Replacement Battalion 272* and placed under the tactical control of Schlanstein's battalion.[15] The same day, two Me-109s bombed and strafed Vossenack, though their appearance on that day was due more to happenstance than coordination between ground forces and the *Luftwaffe*.

Despite the setback on 9 December, the Americans continued their advance, so that by nightfall on 11 December, almost the entire Vossenack ridge, except for Giesenheck and a portion of the southern slope bordering the Kall, was in the hands of 2nd Battalion, 28th Infantry. The key to controlling the Kall River gorge appeared to finally be in their grasp. Regan's battalion was not to remain in place long enough to savor its hard-earned victory, however. On 11 December, Major Regan was notified that his battalion was to be relieved by 3rd Battalion of the 311th Infantry Regiment of the newly-arrived 78th Infantry Division. Once that was completed, he was to move his weary men to a rest area near the village of Kall to reconstitute.

The battalion on Regan's right flank was relieved by 1st Battalion of the 311th Infantry Regiment, which would carry out an attack against the Raffelsbrand-Ochsenkopf bunker complex on 13 December. This attack was timed to coincide with a major attack by the main body of the 78th Infantry Division in the vicinity of Lammersdorf that same day. The relief in place of the 2nd Battalion, 28th Infantry was completed by 2100 hours on 13 December. Prior to handing over his sector to the 311th, the portion of his sector on the left flank, including Giesenheck, was handed off to Lieutenant Colonel Edwin M. Smith's 1st Battalion, 28th Infantry Regiment. This shifted the boundary between it and the incoming 311th Infantry to the west so that all of Giesenheck lay in Smith's sector, while the 311th assumed responsibility for Vossenack proper.

While the Americans inserted new divisions into the Hürtgen Forest and shifted division boundaries, the Germans were doing the same. *General der Infanterie* Straube shuffled his *LXXIV Corps'* meager forces to counter the threat posed by the American forces poised at Nideggen. This involved bringing up the *85th Infantry Division* into position to relieve the *89th Infantry Division,* moving a regiment from the battered *47th Volks-Grenadier Division* to hold the Roer Crossings at Obermaubach and Nideggen, and sideslipping the *272nd VGD* to the south five kilometers. On 10 December, the German corps boundaries changed, making Giesenheck and the area south of it, as well as the units holding the ground (including the *272nd VGD*) the responsibility of the *General der Infanterie* Otto Hitzfeld's *LXVII Corps*. Something big was up.

Included in this reshuffling was the relief of Reineke's emergency company from *Field Replacement Battalion 272* holding Giesenheck on the night of 11/12 December by an understrength company from *Battalion Schultrich* of *Grenadier Regiment 1056* (at that time still under the control of the *89th Infantry Division*). The relief of this alarm company enabled Reineke's company to be brought back to Schmidt, where it was combined with other ad hoc units to form a temporary battalion. The withdrawal of Reineke's company and the insertion of the relieving force in its place appear to have been poorly organized. The company from *Battalion Schultrich* apparently failed to show up, leaving only an engineer squad from Schlanstein's battalion to secure Giesenheck. During a probe by Company C, 28th Infantry Regiment on 12 December, most of the hill's few defenders were overcome and captured, with only a few escaping. For the second time, the vital bridgehead position was in American hands.[16]

Oberst Kossmala knew that Giesenheck had to be immediately retaken, but there was little he could do about it. He was in the process of shifting his division to the south and had orders to hand over responsibility for the sector to another unit. Complicating his situation was the orders he received on 12 December that directed him to hand over command of his division the next day to *Generalmajor* Eugen König, who was giving up command of the *344th Infantry Division,* then engaged in heavy fighting to the north at Gey. Kossmala, in turn, was to take command of König's old division and lead it back to Germany, where it was to be rebuilt as a *Volks-Grenadier Division.*

A factor that may explain the loss of Giesenheck on 12 December was the poor level of situational awareness the Germans were experiencing at this time. After taking over responsibility for the *272nd VGD*'s sector that ran from Simonskall to Schmidt on 10 December, the *89th Infantry Division*'s headquarters was pulled out of line on 12 December. It was replaced by the headquarters of the *85th Infantry Division,* which had been engaged in heavy fighting two months before in Arnhem, where it had been nearly wiped out.

Oberst Burian's *Grenadier Regiment 980* (minus its two infantry battalions), which had been defending this sector, was in the process itself of handing over its defensive sector to *Grenadier Regiment 1056*. This regiment from the *89th Infantry Division* had been temporarily subordinated to the *85th Infantry Division* on 12 December after it had been switched from Obermaubach, where it had been defending a bridge over the Roer. Once this handoff had been carried out, Burian's regiment was to move to a rest area, where it prepared for another mission. In accordance with this order, Thomae's shattered *2nd Battalion, Grenadier Regiment 980* had already moved out the night before. In such a situation, a great deal of confusion was bound to occur.

By nightfall on 12 December, the only force from *272nd VGD* still in position on the north side of the Kall valley along the slopes below Vossenack was one company of Schlanstein's *Pionier Battalion 272,* now reduced in size to less than fifty men. As already mentioned, their connection with *Battalion Schultrich* on their right flank was rather tenuous. These engineers were supported south of the Kall by Stefan's remaining thirty men from *Assault Company 980* and *Füsilier Company 272,* both of which were arrayed to the southwest along the Buhlert ridge, with their right flank anchored near Gerstenhof. To the right of Gerstenhof, *Grenadier Regiment 1056* was holding a extended defensive line running from Schmidt to Kommerscheidt and ending at the Roer near Zerkall *Grenadier Regiment 1055,* also of the *89th Infantry Division,* had pulled out of its positions between Schmidt and Zerkall on 12 December, handing them over to *Grenadier Regiment 1056.*

On the night of 12/13 December, *Grenadier Regiment 1056* was reinforced by *3rd Company, Parachute Panzer Training and Replacement Regiment "Hermann Göring." Grenadier Regiment 1056* had suffered so many casualties during the fight for Brandenburg and Bergstein that it was rated as being only suitable for defense. No longer a regiment except in name, its two battalions were only able to field one company-sized battle group each. According to the G-2 of the 8th Infantry Division, *Grenadier Regiment 1055,* its sister regiment, was just as weak, having an effective combat strength of only 200 men as of 11 December.[17] Should the Americans launch a concerted attack, there was little remaining to stop them. Except for *Füsilier Company 272,* the most that these other units could do was to outpost the main defense line with a thin screen of troops.

The *85th Infantry Division* was not in any condition to provide troops to retake Giesenheck either. It had just arrived in the area and was having difficulty in bringing its own subordinate elements units up to the front because of continued Allied air attacks against the German's rail network. Lacking its own infantry, the *85th Infantry Division* consisted primarily of the attached *Parachute Regiment 6,* a battalion of recruits from the *Hermann Göring* replacement regiment, as well as the temporarily attached *Grenadier Regiment 1056.* This agglomeration, commanded by *Generalmajor* Helmut Bechler, was a division in name only and was serving merely as a placeholder until Bruns' division could be sufficiently reconstituted and returned into the line.

For two days, Bechler served as the overall tactical commander for this part of the German main defense line and would have to rely on ad hoc or extremely weak units to man the positions in his area. Because both Kossmala's and Bruns' divisions were preparing for other missions, *General der Infanterie* Hitzfeld, the commander of *LXVII Corps,* made Bechler responsible for retaking Giesenheck. To help Bechler fulfill this mission, on the evening of 12 December Kossmala was ordered to attach *Füsilier Company 272* to the *85th Infantry Division,* since it was the only relatively fresh and well-equipped unit in the area with the strength to take on this mission.

The company received the order for its new mission later that evening. After packing their gear, the main body of the company moved out of its bunkers and fighting positions along the Buhlert Hill and assembled at Gerstenhof before midnight. It handed off its old defensive sector to the battalion from the *Hermann Göring Training and Replacement Regiment*, which held this sector for the next two weeks. *Leutnant* Wegner and the infantry howitzer platoon, as well as the mortar section, remained behind in support of the forces defending the Buhlert and its line of bunkers. Even so, Wegner's platoon near Gerstenhof and the mortar section in Steckenborn would still be able to provide fire support to *Oberleutnant* Kolb and his four other platoons if needed. The distance from Gerstenhof to the designated assembly area near the ruined forge at Zweifallshammer was about six kilometers, three hours away by foot. After a night march from Gerstenhof through Schmidt and Froitscheidt, Kolb and his men arrived at Zweifallshammer after midnight on 13 December.

While en route to their assembly area, *Oberleutnant* Kolb probably stopped briefly in the village of Froitscheidt, to be briefed on the situation by *Hauptmann* Schultrich of *Grenadier Regiment 1056*, the battle group commander responsible for the defensive sector encompassing Zweifallshammer and Giesenheck. Here, Kolb learned that a nine-man engineer platoon from *Combat Engineer Battalion 272*, commanded by *Leutnant* Schöppner, was attached to his company for the assault. Schöppner's help would be essential, because he knew the Giesenheck area well, having defended it until the Americans seized it the day before.

While the men rested, Kolb, Schöppner, and *Leutnant* Bayer made preparations for the impending assault. They planned to attack shortly before sunrise and attempt to infiltrate as closely as possible to the American lines to gain the advantage of surprise. The exact strength of the American unit defending Giesenheck was unknown, but it was believed to be a company. It was a difficult and challenging mission. To reach the objective, Kolb and his *Volksgrenadiers,* about 120 men in all including the attached engineers, had to move silently up the Kall trail and turn off to the right shortly after passing the trail that led north to the ruined mill at Lücasmühle. The men then had to ascend the steep slope, sometimes hand over hand, orienting on a farm path that led directly to the summit where the American positions lay. Artillery support was provided by *Artillery Regiment 189* of the *89th Infantry Division*, as well as by their own heavy weapon platoons. The company's first aid station was set up in the ruins of the smithy at Zweifallshammer.

Kolb and his men set out long before dawn. Moving as quietly as possible, the company, led by *Feldwebel* Hellmonds's *1st Platoon,* reached the base of the hill, and began the ascent in the darkness. About halfway up, Kolb halted the company and deployed his three platoons so that they were abreast of each other. The men moved slowly and cautiously uphill, avoiding any sounds that might give away their presence, yet many could not stop their teeth from chattering due to the cold. Fortunately, it seemed as if the Americans had not bothered to set up a listening post on the hill's southern slope, making it easier to approach undetected.

Nothing stirred from the American positions. Except for the rumble of artillery fire and the sharp report of small arms fire to the southwest in the vicinity of Raffelsbrand where the 311th Infantry of the 78th Infantry Division was beginning its own attack, Giesenheck and neighboring Vossenack were silent. After half an hour, Hellmonds gained the summit and began to deploy his platoon. To his surprise, found himself standing in the midst of American fighting positions. He and his platoon had penetrated the defensive perimeter without being noticed. Hellmonds immediately began firing with his MP-44, shouted "hurrah!" and ordered his men to attack. The startled Americans, many of whom had obviously been sleeping, were quickly overwhelmed and rounded up. With the American defensive line now penetrated, the rest of the company, with Kolb in the lead, quickly began rolling up the startled Americans to the left and to the right.[18]

The Americans, part of Company C, 28th Infantry Regiment, resisted at first, but as the German assault began to build momentum, the shocked survivors either surrendered or fled to the safety of their own lines to the north or into Vossenack, some 500 meters to the west. Some were helped on their way by *Obergefreiter* Karl Piper, who fired rifle grenades with unerring accuracy into position after position, killing and wounding several and forcing others to surrender. Though he was wounded in the arm during the fight, *Feldwebel* Hellmonds stayed with his men until the position was mopped up before he turned over command of his platoon to *Unteroffizier* Heinrich Rave, his deputy platoon leader.

Unteroffizier Kurt Klein of the company headquarters section took it upon himself to check out suspected American positions, throwing grenades into any that posed danger. In this manner, he took several prisoners, being one of the first in the company do to so. While he was delivering a message to a platoon leader, *Füsilier* Harald Nehring, Klein's runner, stumbled upon an American foxhole that someone had overlooked. Thinking quickly, he lobbed a grenade at it, capturing its two occupants, one of whom was wounded. Nehring had only been in the *Wehrmacht* for five months when he saw his first combat in the Eifel.

Feldwebel Dirksen, leader of the heavy weapons platoon (minus the mortar section, which remained in Steckenborn), also distinguished himself by his actions that day. Shortly after Giesenheck was retaken, he ordered both of his heavy machine guns to be quickly set up so that by nightfall they were able to fire and drive off a large American force that was attempting to attack the company's right flank. During this attack, Dirksen himself took up a position in an abandoned foxhole with two MG-42s and poured fire into the attackers. When one of his weapons ran out of ammunition, he switched to the other one until it, too, was empty. When the attack had ended, dead and wounded lay in an arc five meters in front of him. When *Feldwebel* Belder, leader of the *3rd Platoon,* fell wounded during the American attack, Dirksen took over from him and led the platoon for the next two days. According to *Oberleutnant* Kolb, Dirksen's actions, more than anyone else's, were responsible for driving off the American attack. For his bravery and leadership that day, Dirksen was awarded the Iron Cross 1st Class.

Füsilier Karl Seidnader, who at first was believed to have been killed or captured, returned to the company an hour later from the direction of Vossenack. During the initial assault, Seidnader got carried away with enthusiasm, overran the American positions, and kept going, unaware of the fact that he was alone. Sheepishly, he returned with two prisoners in tow who he had captured while trying to make his way back to his own lines at Giesenheck.

Twenty-five Americans from Company C, 28th Infantry Regiment were taken prisoner during the attack and Giesenheck was now back in German hands.

As the sun rose, the rest of 13 December proved to be a beautiful, cloudless day. Temperatures hovered slightly below freezing, enabling Kolb's men to see clearly across the open farmland in all directions. American aircraft uncharacteristically failed to attack them that day. Taking advantage of this slight pause in the action, Kolb's men quickly consolidated their newly-won position, making use of foxholes and log bunkers that the Americans had used a few minutes before. Retaliatory artillery fire was not long in coming and the first few rounds began to fall amongst the trees shortly after the infantry action had ceased. Kolb moved his command post a hundred meters or so down the slope, occupying an abandoned dugout, which also doubled as the forward aid station. Throughout the day, the company was subject to unrelenting artillery fire and three attempts by 1st Battalion, 28th Infantry Regiment to retake the position (See Map 6).

Each of these company-sized attacks was driven off by Kolb and his men with minimum losses. During one, the Americans were stopped only five meters from the German foxholes before they pulled back. Unbeknownst to Kolb and his men, they had also killed the commander of the 1st Battalion, Lieutenant Colonel Edwin Smith, who had taken over the battalion on 7 December after its previous commander became a casualty.

Smith, a 1935 graduate of the US Military Academy at West Point, NY, volunteered for battalion command after serving for six months as a staff officer in the Operations Section of Headquarters, European Theater of Operations. A native of Pocatello, Idaho, he was thirty-four years old at the time of his death and was awarded the Silver Star and Purple Heart posthumously for his actions that day. He was probably the highest ranking American who fell victim to *Füsilier Company 272*.[19] He personally led one of his battalion's counterattacks that day, but was killed by small arms fire.[20] Three wounded Americans were also taken prisoner afterwards, bringing the total number taken that day to twenty-eight. In addition to the dead and captured, the 1st Battalion, 28th Infantry Regiment also reported twenty of its men wounded in action in its morning report the following day.[21]

The true nature of what had happened at Giesenheck that morning seems to have eluded the headquarters of the 28th Infantry Regiment. On the evening of 13/14 December, the duty officer entered into the regimental combat journal an understated account of what had happened, noting that, "C Company reported a slight penetration in its sector . . . no important changes in 1st Battalion's dispositions were noted, except that a part of C Company was driven from its position by a small German counterattack."[22]

The 8th Infantry Division G-2 seems to have noticed that something was amiss in the area when it was reported that evening that there was a "definite increase of [enemy] patrolling in areas southwest of Bergstein and east of Brandenberg." The G-2 also noted in the daily intelligence report that German artillery fire on 13 December was almost twice as heavy than it had been in the last twenty-four hours. He further noted that two newly-formed assault companies of the *272nd VGD* were identified west of the road [at Zweifallshammer].[23]

Clearly, there was only one new company in the area and that was Kolb's, but evidently the robust nature of his counterattack made the Americans believe his force was much larger than it was. No mention was made of the loss of the twenty-eight men from Company C who had been holding the position. The next day, the 8th Infantry Division's G-2 noted that a strong combat patrol was still operating in the Giesenheck area and incorrectly identified it as the "*272nd Alarm Battalion,*" another indicator that the Americans thought that they were dealing with a larger force.

Having successfully seized their objective on 13 December, Kolb and his men were subjected to heavy artillery fire throughout that day and the next. The shells ranged across the position and into the Kall River gorge, killing and injuring *Volksgrenadiers* in their foxholes as well as those moving up and down the trail. Supply parties bringing forward food and ammunition had to face this storm of steel while carrying their burdens up the hill and again going down with the wounded. So bad was the shelling that afterwards survivors referred to the area after the war as the *Teufelsschlucht* (Devil's Gorge). One survivor, *Füsilier* Eduard Zacharuk, assigned to the heavy machine-gun section, later recalled the ordeal. In an interview, he stated:

> The company had no time after taking up this position to dig fighting positions on an open slope. We had no cover at all. Today one cannot imagine how afraid I was when I realized how exposed we were. In the fighting that followed, I thought that my comrades and I fought like programmed machines without thinking much at all. I felt that we accepted this assignment as certain death and a fatalistic attitude set in. There were no heroes that day (13 December); at least, no one set out to become heroes. Sometime during this action, a great deal of firing broke out to the front of my machine-gun position, with mortars and artillery firing blocking fire. There were small arms firing in abundance.[24]

Though the company had been exposed to artillery fire at Rollesbroich and atop the Buhlert Ridge, it was nothing compared to what they now faced. With only hasty field positions, shallow log bunkers, or foxholes for protection, they were subjected to hours of merciless pounding as the Americans attempted to neutralize the defenders before launching another counterattack. Exposed to this unrelenting barrage, Zacharuk recalled that some men lost their nerve.

> During this fighting, I realized just how much of a firepower advantage our opponents possessed. And now they must be launching a counterattack. Everyone from the heavy machine-gun section who could run, including myself, fled from our positions into a ravine to escape the killing artillery fire. After a short while, this horrible fire stopped and I and the two other men from my machine-gun section returned to our positions. From where I stood, I observed the approach of a group of American prisoners who walked past, 30 or so I think, being escorted by several comrades from the company.[25]

That night, Zacharuk was ordered to report to the company command post to replace one of Kolb's runners who had been shot through the stomach and had bled to death earlier that day. Fortunately for the former sailor, he was ordered to carry a message from his commander to the headquarters of *Battalion Schultrich* located across the Kall Valley in Froitscheidt. Dodging artillery fire, he was able to complete his mission, but was unable to return until the late afternoon of 14 December. In this setting, the behavior of *Obergefreiter* Franz Simon, one of the company's medics, was especially noteworthy. Without regard to his personal safety, Simon dashed from foxhole to foxhole, bandaging the wounded, friend and foe alike, dragging several men down the hill toward the forward aid station until he was finally wounded himself. For his bravery, he was nominated by Kolb to receive the Iron Cross 2nd Class.

1st Battalion, 28th Infantry, now temporarily commanded by Major Louis J. Dughi, overcame its initial shock and launched two more unsuccessful counterattacks with Companies B and C on 14 December, one at 0830 and the second at 1430 hours, but both of these attacks were driven off. Kolb's *Volksgrenadiers* took five more prisoners, despite the overwhelming amount of American artillery firing in support of the attack. In all, Dughi's determined 1st Battalion carried out five counterattacks against *Füsilier Company 272* during the two days that Kolb and his men held the position.

During its engagement at Giesenheck *Füsilier Company 272* suffered twenty-eight casualties, including eight killed in action, eighteen wounded, and two missing. Thirteen of these casualties were caused by small arms fire, a rarity in the Hürtgen Forest, since most casualties during the battle were caused by tree bursts or land mines. *Leutnant* Bayer, Kolb's second in command, was seriously wounded by artillery fire during the initial stages of the fight, when his left arm was taken off by a piece of shrapnel that struck his elbow. He was hastily treated by the medics and evacuated to the main dressing station at Gerstenhof that evening. After enduring several operations for this and other injuries, Bayer was finally discharged in April 1945.

Even more serious than Bayer's wounding was the loss of eight non-commissioned officers during the heavy fighting on 13 and 14 December, including two platoon sergeants wounded (Hellmonds and Belder), one sergeant killed (Matthies) and Sergeants Pape, Schroeder, Heyder, Räke, and Mütsch wounded. While Hellmonds was soon back, Belder had been shot through the jaw and needed extensive hospitalization. Fortunately, the veteran *Gefreiters* and *Obergefreiters* were fully prepared to take over these leadership positions until replacements could be provided. Though it had been blooded, the company's efficiency was hardly affected, and as long as this hard core of veterans remained, Kolb was guaranteed a ready supply of capable men who could rise to the occasion when gaps in the ranks appeared.

Nor was the company's sole action between 13 and 14 December confined to Giesenheck. Four kilometers to the southwest, both the mortar section and infantry howitzer platoon saw considerable action firing in support of the rest of the company as well as other units. *Unteroffizier* Kienberger of the *5th Platoon* was nominated for the Iron Cross 1st Class for serving as a forward artillery observer on the western slope of the Buhlert Ridge. When an attack carried out by an element of the 311th Infantry Regiment of the 78th Infantry Division began to exploit a break in the German defensive positions in front of the hamlet of Simonskall, Kienberger was able to direct well-aimed artillery and mortar fire that drove the attackers off, allowing the thin German line to hold until troops could be brought forward to plug the gap.

Though the company had fought well, five weeks in the front line had brought it to the edge of exhaustion. After the action at Giesenheck, the company's effective combat strength (minus the trains) had dwindled to 103 men (from 170 men five weeks before), including the mortar section, which had been temporarily placed under the control of another unit. As usual, the infantry platoons had suffered the heaviest casualties. Hellmonds's *1st Platoon* had been reduced in strength to four NCOs and fifteen men; Reiners's *2nd Platoon* was down to three NCOs and fourteen men; and *3rd Platoon* had only four NCOs and eleven men left standing. *Feldwebel* Dirksen's heavy machine-gun section consisted of only five NCOs and five men, while *Leutnant* Wegner's infantry howitzer platoon still had four NCOs and fourteen men. Seventeen men were still serving with the company trains in Hergarten under *Hauptfeldwebel* Fuhrmeister. With them were twenty-two other men who were either sick or lightly wounded and unable to perform front-line duties until they had recovered. Except for a few men still with *Field Replacement Battalion 272* (which had, in the meantime, been committed to the front line itself) *Oberleutnant* Kolb could not immediately count on receiving any replacements for the men who had fallen.

Giesenheck had been the company's first experience with close combat, but it would not be the last. The company had performed well, routing an enemy unit of comparable strength and holding the position for over thirty-six hours despite five counterattacks and heavy shelling. Overall, Kolb was satisfied with the company's performance and submitted many men for awards. Half a dozen other men were recommended for promotion. To ensure that his men got credit for two close combat days to go toward the award of the coveted Close Combat Badge, Kolb submitted a request to division headquarters asking that 13 and 14 December be so designated. His request was quickly approved.

In addition to dealing with these administrative tasks, Kolb also had to deal with less pleasant ones, including the disposition of the dead and wounded. While the wounded were quickly evacuated to the division's main field hospital located in the Mariawald Abbey, the dead were brought to the collection point at Gerstenhof, where their remains were processed and evacuated further to the temporary soldier's cemetery in Gemünd. Four of the dead could not be located, since their remains had been taken over by the graves registration unit of the *85th Infantry Division* and their identities lost.[26]

Though *Gefreiter* Simon accompanied the remains of these four soldiers, he was wounded yet again by shrapnel and was evacuated to the forward dressing station at Gerstenhof, where he lost track of the bodies. Subsequent inquiries failed to locate where they were buried. Another soldier who died in the fighting at Giesenheck was *Füsilier* Leonhard Werres, who had been one of the young sailors transferred to the company in October. Due to the constant artillery fire, the best his comrades could do was cover him with pine boughs in the hopes that they would be able to return and retrieve his body. That opportunity never came and his remains were not found until after the war.

On the late afternoon of 14 December, Kolb received instructions that placed his company back under the control of the *272nd VGD*. Though he no doubt welcomed this part of the order, it also directed him to hand over the position at Giesenheck to another unit and march his troops that evening to the vicinity of Steckenborn, which probably cheered him even more. What would follow after that the order did not specify; the men hoped that the company would get the long-awaited rest that it had earned.[27]

No doubt feeling a great deal of relief, Kolb's *Volksgrenadiers* waited until the evening when troops from *Kampfgruppe Funke* arrived to take over the position. They then collected their weapons, formed up in a loosely spaced column, and moved out slowly in the darkness. When they neared the ruined smithy at Zweifallshammer, they had to occasionally duck for cover when artillery landed nearby. Their brief ordeal in the Devil's Gorge had mercifully come to an end. What might happen next was anyone's guess.

In addition to retaking the bridgehead position at Giesenheck, another event of significance occurred on 13 December, for on this date, the *272nd VGD* changed commanders. As was previously mentioned, *Oberst* Georg Kossmala had been entrusted with temporary command of the division only until a more senior officer could be appointed. Such an officer finally became available on 12 December, when *Generalmajor* Eugen König was ordered to hand command of his neighboring *344th Infantry Division* to Kossmala. That battered division was then ordered back into the zone of the interior in Germany to be completely rebuilt from the ground up as a *Volks-Grenadier* division before being committed to battle again. The change of command took place the following day at the division headquarters at Malsbenden. König also brought with him his own *Ia, Major* Hans Uhl, who replaced *Major* Gerhard Höptner, who had been the *Ia* since 10 September 1944.*

After the handover of responsibilities, Höptner was transferred to *LXVII Corps*, where he became *General der Infanterie* Hitzfeld's new *Ia*.

In Eugen König, the *272nd VGD* gained a veteran and proven commander. Like Kossmala, he was a veteran of World War One. Born in the city of Trier on 19 September 1896, he enlisted in the Kaiser's army on 19 June 1915 and was commissioned as a *Leutnant* of the Reserves on 12 July 1917. Though he was discharged from the Army as an *Oberleutnant* in 1920, he returned to join the new *Wehrmacht* on 1 May 1937. By 1 September 1940, he had risen to the rank of *Major*.[28]

On 1 September 1939, König was serving as the regimental adjutant of *Infantry Regiment 352* of the *246th Infantry Division* that was committed to border defense duties in the Upper Rhine until April 1940. From that point on, König was given a series of duty assignments that were characterized by increasing levels of authority and responsibility, including battalion commander of *2nd Battalion, Grenadier Regiment 352;* operations officer of the *246th Infantry Division;* Commander, *Grenadier Regiment 352;* Commander, *Grenadier Regiment 451* of the *251st Infantry Division;* and Commander, *Division Group 251* of *Corps Detachment E*. From 22 June 1941 until May 1944, he was continuously engaged in some of the heaviest fighting on the Eastern Front.

König was also highly decorated. In recognition of his leadership and bravery, he had been awarded the Infantry Assault Badge in Silver; the 1939 Bar to both the Iron Cross 1st and 2nd Classes; the Knight's Cross of the Iron Cross awarded 1 August 1942; and the Oak Leaves to the Knight's Cross awarded 4 November 1943. These awards were in addition to those he had already received during World War I, which included the Iron Crosses First and Second Class. Though König was famous for leading his troops from the front, miraculously we was never wounded in action during the war. After surviving three years on the Eastern Front, in May 1944 he was ordered to hand over command of *Division Group 251,* then tied down fighting partisans in the Pripet Marshes, and move to the west, where he was scheduled to attend the division commander's leadership course.

---

* Kossmala returned to Germany with the remnants of the *344th Infantry Division* on 14 December 1944, where, after a short period of reconstitution, it was committed to the Eastern Front by the end of the month. He was promoted to *Generalmajor* on 1 January 1945. The division was quickly embroiled in the Soviet winter offensive that commenced on 12 January 1945 and saw heavy defensive fighting near Cracow and Opeln. On 5 March 1945, he was declared missing in action near Oberglogau and presumed dead.

His first official division command came unexpectedly on 10 June 1944, when he was ordered to assume command of the *91st Air Landing Division,* then engaged in heavy fighting against the Allied invasion in Normandy, after its previous commander, *Generalleutnant* Wilhelm Falley, was killed 6 June by American paratroopers. From 10 June until 10 August 1944, then-*Oberst* König led the division through some of the heaviest fighting he had ever experienced. By 10 August, although the division had suffered such heavy casualties that it had to be disbanded, it had performed well, as had König. According to *General der Panzertruppe* Leo *Freiherr* Geyr von Schweppenburg, Commander-in-Chief of *Panzer Group West,* "The newly organized division, which had not yet been fully trained and equipped, performed well owing to the energetic leadership of [*Oberst*] König."

As the fighting in Normandy reached its climax with the German defeat in the Battle of Falaise Pocket, *Oberst* König and the remnant of his division were transferred to the Eifel region. There it was reconstituted by combining its survivors with *Battlegroup Castorf,* then involved in establishing defensive positions in the *Seventh Army*'s area of operations. On 5 November 1944, the division was re-designated the *344th Infantry Division,* using the number of another division that had been completely destroyed in Normandy and in the retreat through northern France and the Low Countries. Once the reorganization had been completed, König, who had been promoted to *Generalmajor* on 1 September 1944, was ordered by *Seventh Army* to move into the Hürtgen Forest on 19 November to help counter the major American drive against the town of Hürtgen, which was already well underway when it arrived.

König's experienced *Ia, Major i.G.* Hans Uhl, had served alongside him from June 1944 with the *91st Air Landing Division.* Born in Frankfurt am Main on 25 August 1916, Uhl began his wartime service in the *Heer* on 6 August 1939 as a platoon leader in *13th Company, Infantry Regiment 106* of the *15th Infantry Division.* He briefly served as acting commander of the Regiment's *3rd Battalion* from December 1939 to 10 June 1940, when he assumed command of *10th Company, Infantry Replacement Battalion 106.* This brief interlude ended on 12 November 1940 when he was assigned as operations officer of *Infantry Regiment 428* of the *129th Infantry Division.*

Uhl marched into the Soviet Union along with his regiment on 22 June 1941 and soon proved himself as a capable and resourceful staff officer. In recognition of his achievements and demonstrated potential, he was briefly given command 27 August 1942 of the regiment's *3rd Battalion,* then tied down in positional warfare in the Rzhev salient on the Central sector of the Eastern Front. On 23 November 1942, he was assigned as Commander of *2nd Battalion* of sister *Infantry Regiment 430.* Having proven himself in this arduous and demanding position, he was assigned 1 March 1943 to the *OKH Führer Reserve.* Shortly thereafter, he was posted to the staff of the *206th Infantry Division,* which was also manning the Rzhev position.

Promoted to *Major* on 1 April 1943, Uhl was posted on 1 September 1943 from the *OKH Führer Reserve* to the headquarters of *XXXXIII Corps,* where he served as a staff officer until he was assigned as a General Staff candidate to the *Kriegsschule* from 6 December 1943 to 6 May 1944. Having completed his studies, he was assigned provisionally to the General Staff on 7 May 1944 followed by his assignment on 10 June 1944 as the *Ib* (Division Supply Officer or G-4) of the *91st Air-Landing Division,* where he came to work with *Generalmajor* König for the first time.

After surviving two months in this grueling assignment, which saw the division whittled away to battle group size, Uhl was accepted as full member of General Staff on 1 August 1944. On 20 August he was assigned as the *Ib* of the *344th Infantry Division* while it was in the process of being destroyed during the final phases of the Battle for Normandy. While the *91st Air Landing Division* underwent reconstitution near Aachen in early November 1944, it was re-designated as the new *344th Infantry Division* (the old *344th Infantry Division* was disbanded) and Uhl was transferred to the operations staff to become its new *Ia.* From this point, Uhl accompanied König and the division to the Hürtgen Forest in mid-November 1944. Uhl was not merely a qualified staff officer, he had also been awarded the Knight's Cross on 22 January 1943 while commanding *2nd Battalion, Grenadier Regiment 430.* In Hans Uhl, *Generalmajor König* had a superbly qualified General Staff officer who was equally adept as a combat commander. Those traits would stand the division in good stead for the harrowing battles to come.[29]

When König was informed that he would assume command of the *272nd Volks-Grenadier Division* on 12 December, he and Uhl were already very familiar with at least part of it. Since their own division had been holding a defensive sector to the north of the *89th Infantry Division* between Gey and Kreuzau and was assigned to the same corps, he had already gotten to know Kossmala and his staff. In addition, one of Kossmala's regiments, *Grenadier Regiment 981,* had been attached to König's *344th Infantry Division* from the end of November until 11 December, and had been heavily involved in the fighting at Gey. Thus, on 13 December a long association began between König, Uhl, and the *272nd VGD,* which would last well beyond April 1945.[30]

8

Two Divisions Collide at Kesternich

Oberleutnant Kolb's men quickly learned that there were even worse places to be than in the "Devil's Gorge." On the next day after *Füsilier Company 272* retook the bridgehead position at Giesenheck that re-established German control of the Kall River gorge and secured the *272nd VGD*'s right flank, it was ordered to carry out an even more important mission. On this occasion, division headquarters assigned it the even more urgent mission of helping to restore the situation near the town of Kesternich.

It was on the division's opposite flank where the newly-arrived American 78th Infantry Division, in its combat debut, carried out its first attack on 13 December 1944. Its mission was to seize the towns of Simmerath and Kesternich en route to the high ground overlooking the Roer River dams. The previous two American attempts along the northern edge of the forest carried out between early November and early December 1944 were from Vossenack toward Schmidt and from Kleinhau toward Bergstein. This assault instead skirted the southern edge of the forest and attack directly into the defenses of the *272nd VGD*. Fortunately, a few lessons had been learned since then. The attack by the 28th Infantry Division in November had failed disastrously because of overreliance on an insufficient main supply route in the Kall valley. The second attempt to reach the Roer by the 8th Infantry Division via the Hürtgen-Brandenberg-Bergstein avenue of approach had not resulted in the hoped-for breakthrough either. By this third attempt, however, the Allies had finally realized the impact that the Roer River dams would have on future operations aimed at crossing the Roer and had developed a plan that, on paper at least, offered reasonable prospects for success.

Belatedly, Lieutenant General Courtney H. Hodges, commander of the First Army, saw that the best approach to the dams was via the Monschau corridor, following a route that led through the towns of Simmerath, Kesternich, and Rurberg from the north, combined with a supporting attack from the south via Dreiborn, Herhahn, and Gemünd. Here, the terrain appeared better suited for the rapid style of maneuver that the US Army had begun to perfect during the late summer of 1944. Like the other avenues, though, it would be frustrated by a stubborn defense and would eventually stall, but not after some of the heaviest fighting of the Battle of the Hürtgen Forest.

The northern prong of this attack, originating from the Lammersdorf area, would be carried out by two regiments of the 78th Infantry Division. The southern prong of the attack would be launched by the 2nd Infantry Division from the Wahlerscheid area. As written, the plan stated that the 78th Infantry Division would follow a route of advance that led through Simmerath, then through Kesternich, and finally onwards to Rurberg, where the division would seize the commanding heights overlooking the Roer River dams. The intelligence estimate stated that once the division penetrated the German main defense line at Simmerath, the opposing *272nd VGD* would have few forces available to stop the Americans. The 309th Infantry Regiment, reinforced by 2nd Battalion, 310th Infantry, would lead the attack and serve as the division's main effort.

To the immediate north, the 310th Infantry Regiment (minus 2nd Battalion) would conduct a supporting attack on the left to seize Rollesbroich in order to protect the 309th's northern flank. Once that town was secured, the 310th Infantry would continue pushing forward to seize the villages of Strauch and Steckenborn. As mentioned in the previous chapter, the 311th Infantry, temporarily attached to the 8th Infantry Division, would carry out a diversionary attack in the Raffelsbrand-Ochsenkopf area, with the intent of causing the Germans to commit their tactical reserve and divert their attention from the main American effort five kilometers to the southwest. The Americans counted on the element of surprise to help them achieve their objectives during the initial stages of the attack. Providentially, once the 78th Infantry Division's main attack and the supporting operations began, the German initial reaction proved to be uncharacteristically hesitant, even sluggish.

The German's initial surprise and delayed reaction to the American drive could be traced to several changes in command that had taken place at the division, corps, and army levels. These changes left them without leaders whose familiarity with the area had previously proven so vital to their defensive effort in the Hürtgen Forest. German attention at corps level and higher, understandably, was focused on the main effort—that of the impending offensive in the Ardennes, *WACHT AM RHEIN*, scheduled to take place only a few kilometers to the south on the morning of 16 December 1944.

How much these leadership changes affected the overall German effort in the Hürtgen Forest is difficult to measure, but on 10 December, *General der Panzertruppe* Brandenberger and the entire *Seventh Army* headquarters were pulled out and operational control of the forces in the Hürtgen Forest was assumed by *General der Infanterie* Gustav von Zangen's *Fifteenth Army*. This was designed to free Brandenberger and his staff and allow them time to prepare for the coming mission in the Ardennes, where *Seventh Army* would assume control of the southern wing of the offensive.

Von Zangen, whose army already held a defensive sector to the north that reached as far the Netherlands, had to stretch his already overextended front line to the south to encompass the area held by *General der Infanterie* Straube's *LXXIV Corps*, to which the *272nd VGD* was still attached until 10 December. To compound matters, on 10 December, the *272nd* and *277th Volks-Grenadier*

Divisions, as well as the neighboring *89th Infantry Division,* were subordinated to *General der Infanterie* Otto Hitzfeld's *LXVII Corps.* Corps boundaries were shifted the same day, with the border between Straube's and Hitzfeld's corps being drawn along the line Giesenheck-Zerkall-Nideggen.

On 16 December 1944, in the middle of all these developments, to his surprise Straube himself was ordered to hand over command of his corps to *General der Infanterie* Karl Püchler and proceed to the north, where he was to take over command of Püchler's *LXXXVI Corps,* whose headquarters was located in Cleve. Why Straube and Püchler were ordered to swap corps commands at that time can no longer be determined, but in retrospect this made little sense as it gave Püchler precious little time to become acquainted with the plans for the offensive that was to take place on his adjacent flank.*

Although von Zangen, Hitzfeld, and Püchler were all experienced commanders, they needed time to acquaint themselves with their new area of operations before they could function at a peak level of effectiveness. Compounding these modifications to command arrangements was the change of commanders in the *272nd VGD,* which took place 13 December.

In the *WACHT AM RHEIN* corps operations order published 12 December 1944, Hitzfeld's command, designated as *Korps Monschau,* was to be allocated two divisions (*272nd* and *326th Volks-Grenadier Divisions*) to carry out its mission. Hitzfeld's corps would be responsible for securing the far right flank of the overall German attack. Assigned to *SS-Oberstgruppenführer* Sepp Dietrich's *6th Panzer Army,* it was responsible for a zone of operations spanning the area in the vicinity of Simmerath and Lammersdorf in the north to the edge of the Elsenborn Ridge in the vicinity of Kalterherberg to the south.

The primary focus of the corps' effort was the seizure of the town of Monschau and the surrounding key terrain in the Hohe Venn. Once his troops had done this, Hitzfeld was to establish a fixed defensive front along the line Simmerath-Eupen-Limbourg and Liège.[1] Seizing and holding Monschau would provide the Germans the necessary maneuver space for their armored divisions arrayed to the south and block the major north-south highway network that Lieutenant General Courtney Hodges' US First Army needed if it had to reinforce its forces being hit by the main German attack to the south. Once Hitzfeld's corps had established a solid defensive front, it would revert to the control of von Zangen's *Fifteenth Army.*[2]

The *LXVII Corps* order stated that the *272nd VGD* was to be arrayed on the Corps' right flank. The division's role was seen as a vital one if Hitzfeld's mission

---

* *Generalmajor* Carl Wagener, Chief of Staff, *Army Group B,* later reported "This policy of changing commanders in the middle of a major battle as though they were cannon proved to be harmful and dangerous . . . the result was that the right commander was in the wrong place." (MS. A-964, *Summary, Report of the Army Group B Chief of Staff, 25 January—21 March 1945,* 30).

was to succeed, for his corps had been designated to serve as the right pivot point for the entire offensive. With Monschau back in German hands, the lines of operation for the attack would then follow a right wheeling movement that oriented the three attacking armies in a northwesterly direction toward the ultimate objective of Antwerp.

Generalmajor König and his counterparts from the *89th Infantry* and the *277th* and *326th VGDs* learned about their role in the offensive for the first time on the evening of 14 December, when he, *Generalmajor* Bruns, *Generalmajor* Wilhelm Viebig (commander of *277th VGD*), and *Generalmajor* Erwin Kaschner (commander of *326th VGD*), were briefed by Hitzfeld and his staff at *LXVII Corps* headquarters in the village of Dalbenden, ten kilometers southeast of Gemünd. By this time of this orders briefing, however, the American attack on Kesternich had been underway for over thirty-six hours and the role that the *272nd VGD* was slated to play in Wacht am Rhein was already in jeopardy.[3]

The corps order stated that the *272nd VGD* would carry out an attack in a northwesterly direction through the towns of Konzen and Entenpfuhl in order to seize and hold the high ground between Konzen and Bickerath. The division would then advance approximately seven kilometers as far as the Vesdre (Weser) River, a small stream flowing past the southwestern outskirts of the large town of Rötgen on the German border. The division was to anchor its right flank north of Simmerath and its left flank immediately south of Rötgen. Implicit in this task was retaking the town of Lammersdorf. Holding this town and the high ground at Paustenbach would allow the division to control the Allies' only direct high-speed avenue of approach leading through Rötgen to the Ardennes.[4]

To carry out its attack, the corps order directed that the *272nd VGD* was to position what it felt was its strongest regiment on the division's left flank, reinforced by the engineer battalion, the *Füsilier Company,* and several regimental engineer platoons. The second strongest regiment would position itself to the right between Simmerath and Rollesbroich. The weakest regiment would be designated as the division reserve. To make up for the losses suffered during the past two weeks, the division was directed to comb out its supply columns and noncombat units and assign anyone who could be spared to the attacking units.[5]

When the order was written, the German high command apparently assumed that König's division would still be strong enough to carry out its assigned tasks, that is, as long as it was able to conserve its forces or at least rebuild them in time for the attack. To that end, some 1,000 replacement troops from several march battalions were being held in reserve in the vicinity of Mechernich to be brought forward to the various regimental assembly areas on 14 December. These troops would be hastily incorporated into the weakened ranks of König's three regiments in the two days prior to the attack. As it turned out, these troops were withheld from the front lines until about 21 or 22 December, since it was deemed that it would be senseless to incorporate such raw troops into the fighting at Kesternich until the outcome had been decided.

To König's right, Bruns' *89th Infantry Division* would revert to the control of Püchler's neighboring *LXXIV Corps* by 1200 hours on 15 December. Bruns' division was to carry out feint attacks from the Ochsenkopf-Raffelsbrand bunker complex and attempt a push through to the *Totenbruch* (Dead Man's Moor) two kilometers to the northwest. This move was intended to tie up American forces in the area and prevent them from coming to the aid of other units under attack to the south.[6] Attacking to the left of König's division was the *326th VGD,* tasked with the mission of seizing Monschau.

The boundary between *LXXIV* and *LXVII Corps* was to shift to the south on 15 December along the Lammersdorf-Rollesbroich-Schmidt line. The *277th VGD,* currently holding defensive positions between Simmerath and Monschau, would be relieved in place on the night of 14/15 December by the *326th VGD.* This would allow the *277th VGD* to be shifted shift further south to a position opposite Camp Elsenborn, where it would pass under the control of the *I SS-Panzer Corps* in time for the offensive.

While conducting its own parallel planning for its assignment, the *272nd VGD* would have to disengage its two regiments committed in the line near Gey and Schmidt (*Grenadier Regiments 981* and *980*, respectively), move them to several assembly areas located between Gemünd and Mechernich beginning 12 December at the latest, and allow them two days to rest, reconstitute, and absorb new replacements. One of these regiments (the *981st*) would then move into its forward assembly areas by the night of 14/15 December so its battalions could be ready in time to attack by 0540 hours on 16 December.

According to the operations plan, *Oberstleutnant* Rösener's *Grenadier Regiment 982* would constitute the right flank for the attack between Simmerath and Rollesbroich. His *1st Battalion* would shift to the left to an area immediately south of Simmerath, while his *2nd Battalion*, occupying the bunker complex at Raffelsbrand-Ochsenkof, would slip to the south, handing over its position to a battalion of the *89th Infantry Division*. Rösener's regiment would have a relatively easy task to carry out, since it was already manning its jump-off positions for the assault and would only have to carry out limited attacks to its front to tie down American forces.

Oberstleutnant Hans Kleinkorres' *Grenadier Regiment 981,* whose attack König had designated as the division's main offensive effort, would move into position to Rösener's left between Simmerath and Imgenbroich, with a general orientation of attack from Konzen toward the village of Entenfuhl.[7] Kleinkorres' defensive positions near Gey would be handed over to the *353rd Infantry Division,* while *Oberst* Burian would hand over his sector near Schmidt to the *89th Infantry Division.*

Burian's *Grenadier Regiment 980* was to be the division's reserve, but would have to remain on standby until called forward to join in the attack. It was directed to occupy an assembly area in the vicinity of Roggendorf near Gemünd, except for Thomae's *2nd Battalion,* which was directed to proceed directly to

Strauch, where it would occupy a forward assembly area. The order stated that all units were to have completed their reorganization by 14 December. Most members of the division still had no idea of the role their division was supposed to play in the upcoming offensive.

To complicate the preparations, Kleinkorres' regiment had been heavily engaged some ten kilometers to the north (out of the division's sector) in the Gey-Strass area, where it had been committed to support the crumbling defense of *344th Infantry Division* since 28 November. During its ten days in the line, *Grenadier Regiment 981* had suffered casualties approaching nearly fifty percent against determined attacks by the 4th Infantry Division. After only one week in action, its *2nd Battalion* had suffered 194 casualties and had only 164 combat troops remaining when it was finally pulled out of the line on the night of 10/11 December, when the Americans began a major attack by the 83rd Infantry Division.[8] To make up the shortfall of combat troops, Kleinkorres ordered that supply and service personnel be transferred to fill the depleted ranks, though many veterans questioned the wisdom of transferring these older and less experienced men to the infantry, but orders were orders.

Burian's *Grenadier Regiment 980* was not pulled out of its defensive positions between Bergstein and Gerstenhof until 12 December. His regiment was in even worse shape than Kleinkorres's. The savage fighting in and around Bergstein, as well as the disastrous counterattacks that failed to retake Castle Hill, had reduced both of his grenadier battalions' combined *Kampfstärke* (fighting strength) to a total of 319 men, a loss rate approaching seventy percent.[9] Though his regimental infantry howitzer company was in relatively good shape, his regiment was badly in need of infantry replacements.

The Lightning Division Attacks

While *Generalmajor* König and his staff began the complex series of maneuvers designed to get the bulk of *272nd VGD* into position for its attack on 16 December, the unexpected advance of the US 78th Infantry Division against Simmerath and Rollesbroich completely upset their plans. Though the presence of the 78th Infantry Division had been detected on 12 December, the Germans must have assumed that, as a new division, it had been moved into the front line to gain combat experience before being given an attacking role, which appears to have been the German's assessment of other American units committed to the "sleeping front" in the Eifel.

Adding to the shock and surprise of this unexpected American assault from Lammersdorf was the change in German leadership, which forced the new commanders to come to grips with a crisis before they were even familiar with the troops under their command. It was to be the Germans' saving grace that their troops were already on the move to their new assembly areas when the blow struck, thereby allowing *Generalmajor* König to lay his hands on reserves that were not been available two days before. It was a race for time as to who would ultimately control Kesternich, but having moved first, the Americans had the initial advantage.

Simmerath itself was defended by troops of *Hauptmann* Leykauf's *1st Battalion, Grenadier Regiment 982*. This battalion had been reinforced earlier by the nine 75mm antitank guns of *Leutnant* Teich's *1st Company, Antitank Battalion 272*, which was tasked with providing antitank coverage in depth in the vicinity of the hamlet of Witzerath, one kilometer northeast of Simmerath. While Leykauf's men were experienced and had been in the area for almost six weeks, they were spread thinly on the ground. He also had a outpost line of troops posted atop Paustenbach Hill, key terrain that overlooked both Lammersdorf and Simmerath. On a hill crowned by several *Westwall* bunkers, any observer there should have been able to see any developing American attack and break it up with artillery fire, should anyone be foolish enough to attack during the day.

The town of Simmerath itself was held by his *3rd Company,* reinforced by heavy weapons teams of the *4th Company*. To their south, near the *Am Gericht* crossroads, *1st Battalion* of *277th Volks-Grenadier Division's Grenadier Regiment 939,* was arrayed along the *Westwall*. Oriented to the northwest, this battalion occupied a series of bunkers that *Füsilier Company 272* would become intimately familiar with three weeks later. *First Battalion, Grenadier Regiment 939* was preparing to move to the south in order to conduct an attack of its own as part of the offensive after handing off its positions to the incoming *326th VGD*. Except for a very few casualties, the *277th Volks-Grenadier Division* was not greatly influenced by the attack since the American drive took place to its north in the *272nd VGD's* sector. Consequently, it was able to disengage and move to its new assembly areas without being disturbed. (For an overview of the situation, refer to Map 7.)

Although the Germans had been aware that the 78th Infantry Division was moving into position to relieve portions of the 102nd Cavalry Group (Mechanized) and the 8th Infantry Division, they were caught off guard by the attack. The area around Lammersdorf and Simmerath had been quiet for over two weeks and even though Leykauf had been sending out foot patrols at night, there appeared to be no indication that the newly arrived American division was preparing to attack. A German intelligence estimate issued on the morning of 13 December stated, "The *LXVII Corps* sector at this time can be characterized as quiet, with the exception of the area around Vossenack." The report did lay out the possibility that the Americans might make a push in the direction of Lammersdorf, but saw any movement coming from that direction as being flank protection for the units engaged to the north near Vossenack, and not as a harbinger of an offensive in its own right.[10]

Consequently, Leykauf and his men were completely unprepared for the size and scope of the 78th Infantry Division's attack, which burst forth at first light, heralded by a powerful artillery barrage from eight division and corps-level artillery battalions. The powerful fire forced the defenders to seek cover in their bunkers, cellars, and foxholes. Caught off guard and expecting more salvoes to come, they were still under cover when they belatedly discovered that the men of the 309th Infantry Regiment, making their combat debut, were already in their positions. Soldiers in the German outpost line, occupying a group of bunkers in the vicinity of Paustenbach Hill, were completely surprised and quickly overcome by the American assault. Taking advantage of their initial success, the men of the 309th Infantry kept driving forward as quickly as they could. Shortly afterwards, house-to-house fighting was taking place in Simmerath itself. A lone German forward observer who had somehow remained undetected in one of the bunkers directed sporadic mortar fire against the advancing American columns before he was located and dispatched.

By noon, several dozen prisoners had been rounded up in Simmerath and sent to temporary prisoner of war enclosures in the US First Army rear area. Except for some snipers and isolated pockets of resistance on the southern edge of town, Simmerath was in American hands. The survivors of *3rd Company, Grenadier Regiment 982,* as well those of *2nd Company* to their immediate north, were forced to fall back to the east toward Kesternich and Strauch as quickly as they could. They had little time to establish a new defensive line that could slow or halt the American's advance, however. Fortunately for the Germans, the neighboring battalion from the *277th Volks-Grenadier Division* retained control of the bunkers southwest of Simmerath and Bickerath, which meant that there was at least a strong shoulder on their left flank with which to tie in should the Germans launch a counterattack to restore the main defense line.

By late afternoon, troops of 2nd Battalion, 309th Infantry, supported by a company of tanks from the 709th Tank Battalion, had routed the German defenders in Simmerath, then prepared to move on to their next objective on the western edge of Kesternich. The *272nd VGD* was caught completely off guard by this attack, so preoccupied it had been with repositioning its regiments for its intended attack three days hence. American surrender leaflets were dropped on German positions later that day and for the next several days, urging members of the *272nd* and *277th Volks-Grenadier Divisions* to surrender (see Figure 1). Though surprised, König insured that Rundstedt's headquarters at *Oberbefehlshaber West* was made aware of the situation by noon on 13 December.[11]

After its battalions had reached the eastern outskirts of Simmerath and advanced through the neighboring village of Witzerath, the 309th Infantry, with its attached elements, continued its push eastwards toward Kesternich, moving carefully across the snow-covered open fields between the towns. To the north, 310th Infantry (minus its 2nd Battalion) quickly took Rollesbroich from Leykauf's *2nd Company* and pushed on toward Strauch and Steckenborn. This attack—though it encountered stubborn pockets of resistance in the village and north of it—moved so quickly that the left flank of the neighboring *2nd Battalion,*

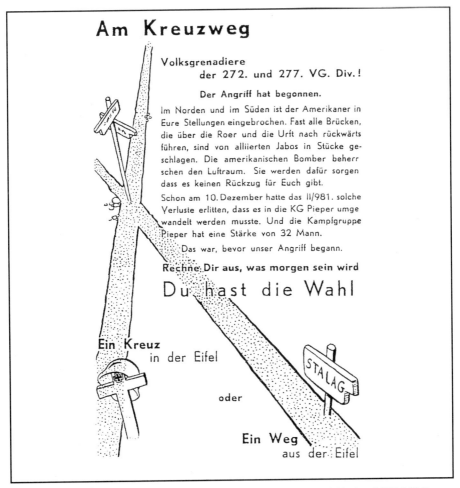

Figure 1. This leaflet reads "At the Crossroads—Grenadiers of the *272nd* and *277th Volks-Grenadier Divisions*! The attack has begun. In the north and south the Americans have broken into your positions. Nearly every bridge across the Roer and Urft that lead to the rear have been destroyed. American bombers rule the air. They will insure that there will be no retreat for you. As of 10 December the *2nd Battalion, Grenadier Regiment 981* had already suffered such losses that the battalion had to be regrouped as *Kampfgruppe Pieper*. And *Kampfgruppe Pieper* had a combat strength of only 32 men. That was before our assault began. Consider what will happen tomorrow! The choice is yours—a cross in the Eifel or a way out of the Eifel!"

Grenadier Regiment 982, commanded by *Hauptmann* Karl Schneider, was completely exposed. Fortunately for the Germans, the 310th Infantry did not take advantage of this success, enabling Schneider and his troops to repulse the attack by the 1st Battalion, 311th Infantry against the Raffelsbrand-Ochsenkopf area, though with heavy casualties.[12]

As they pushed forward using the sparse hedgerows common to this area as cover from the defender's sporadic machine-gun and mortar fire, the troops of the 309th Infantry were briefly halted at the western edge of Kesternich by minefields and a large concrete troop shelter (this was Bunker 47, manned by newly-arrived troops from *8th Company (Heavy Weapons)* of Thomae's *2nd Battalion, Grenadier Regiment 980*). The bunker's defenders succeeded in pinning down the American's forward elements with withering machine-gun fire that brought the advance to a standstill. A single German antitank gun emplaced within the bunker succeeded in keeping the accompanying tanks at bay, forcing the infantry to attempt to neutralize it with small arms fire, grenades, and bazookas, but to no avail.

Following the news of the unfolding attack from his division's headquarters at the Pulvermühle in Malsbenden, *Generalmajor* König must have viewed these initial reports with alarm. Just as *Oberst* Kossmala had been forced to do two weeks earlier at Brandenberg and Bergstein, König also had to prematurely commit substantial elements of his division to prevent WACHT AM RHEIN from being compromised. At least there was something he could do to affect the situation, however, for two of his three regiments were in motion or had already arrived at their new assembly areas close by.

Unfortunately for the Germans, the *272nd VGD*'s role in the offensive, its attack to secure the northern shoulder for *LXVII Corps,* now finally had to be shelved for good. Its mission was now changed from attacking Lammersdorf and Rötgen to that of defending Kesternich and blocking the approaches to the dams. Holding Kesternich was not König's only worry, for he had another significant concern of his own—should the American attack succeed, his division would be cut in half.

Kesternich's tactical and operational significance soon figured prominently in the course of events of the Battle of the Bulge (though the battle for Kesternich itself took place within the historical context of the Siegfried Line Campaign). Located as it was on the eastern edge of a plateau that dropped sharply off to the east and southeast, Kesternich commanded the avenues of approach to the Roer River dams from the north, west, and south. Several important roads ran through the town, connecting Kesternich with Simmerath, Rurberg, Strauch, and Steckenborn. The main highway and supply artery for the *272nd VGD* ran through Kesternich to the southeast, where it dipped steeply into the Roer River valley at Einruhr. Like the town of Bastogne, soon to be made famous by events during the Battle of the Bulge, the control of Kesternich was vital to the success of both sides' offensive plans.

If the Americans were able to seize Kesternich and continue their drive into Einruhr, at least half of the *272nd VGD*'s units would be cut off and stranded on the western side of the Schwammenauel and Urft Reservoirs, where they could be destroyed piecemeal. Though the leaders of *272nd VGD* were keenly aware of this possibility, few of their men seemed to know just how dire their situation truly was. Upon first glance, though, Kesternich appeared insignificant. Like the town of Schmidt to the north, Kesternich before the war had been a small rural village of less than 1,000 inhabitants. Luckily, most of the civilians had been evacuated in September so they would not have to experience the inferno to come A few of Kesternich's civilian inhabitants braved out the fighting by hiding in holes carved along the sides of the steep Tiefenbach ravine, fewer than 500 meters south of the town.[13] The soldiers did know, however, that whoever controlled Kesternich controlled access to the dams. It was for that reason—access to the dams—that fighting was to rage in and around the town for the next two months, with Kesternich changing hands several times.

Until 12 December, Kesternich was still virtually undefended, since the German main defense line lay three kilometers to the west along the western outskirts of Simmerath. Though there were some supply elements from the trains of *1st Battalion, Grenadier Regiment 982* in Kesternich, they were of little combat value. Fortunately for the Germans, *Hauptmann* Thomae and the remnants of his *2nd Battalion, Grenadier Regiment 980* had begun to arrive in the area that same day, after having moved out of their old defensive positions to the west of Schmidt that they had handed over to three *Kampfgruppen* from *Grenadier Regiment 1056* of the *89th Infantry Division*.

Leaving one company positioned between Kesternich and the village of Strauch, Thomae set up his command post in Kesternich near the triangle area in the eastern portion of the town. Shortly after the American attack began, his battalion's *8th Company* took up positions in and around Bunker 47, located along the road from Simmerath approximately one kilometer west of Kesternich. His *7th Company,* commanded by *Oberleutnant* Simmersk, apparently took up hasty defensive positions across the open fields southwest of town, where they tied in with the right flank of the *277th Volks-Grenadier Division*. His heavy weapons company positioned its mortars and howitzers several hundred meters to the northeast of Kesternich on the outskirts of Rurberg, while the company commander, *Leutnant* August Englbrecht, set up his command post in Bunker 47. By all accounts, they arrived just as the defenders of Simmerath and Rollesbroich were being forced from those towns. By sheer luck, they were ideally positioned to blunt the first American probes toward Kesternich.

As the American attack began to develop momentum, another German force was beginning to move into positions that later provided valuable support to Thomae's defensive efforts. This unit, an ad-hoc emergency or *Alarm* battalion, had been brought up during the night of 12/13 December from the vicinity of Schmidt. This makeshift battalion, briefly known as *Alarm Battalion 272,* was composed of two company-sized elements that had previously operated independently. The first was an *Alarm* company that had just marched from its position at Giesenheck, where it had held the bridgehead position east of Vossenack after *Leutnant* Stefan's *Assault Company 980* had retaken it from 2nd Battalion, 28th Infantry of the 8th Infantry Division on 10 December. This was the same position that *Füsilier Company 272* had to retake on 13 December. In fact, it was the withdrawal of this *Alarm* company that gave the US 8th Infantry Division the opportunity to retake the position after hardly firing a shot on 12 December (see previous chapter).

Originally a force of about eighty soldiers from *2nd Company, Field Replacement Battalion 272, Alarm Battalion 272* was formed on the night of 12 December by combining this *2nd Company* with a similar unit, *Alarm Company 980* (a force composed of seventy cooks, bakers, clerks, and drivers gleaned from the regimental trains of Burian's *Grenadier Regiment 980* as well as a few other men from *Field Replacement Battalion 272*). Before receiving the order to form a makeshift battalion, this company had served as Burian's emergency stopgap, occupying positions to the right of *Leutnant* Stefan's *Assault Company 980* along the Buhlert ridge. Unlike Stefan's unit, *Alarm Company 980* was equipped only with rifles and one light machine gun. To strengthen *Alarm Battalion 272, Oberst* Burian stripped Stefan's assault company of most of its men and transferred them to the new battalion, leaving Stefan with only a skeleton force to guard Burian's command post.[14]

Both of these emergency units were commanded by lieutenants—the first one by *Oberleutnant* Johann Reineke and *Alarm Company 980* by *Leutnant* Klaus von Below. Reineke, an officer from the division officer's reserve originally from *Grenadier Regiment 982,* was ordered to lead this miniature battalion.[15] He entrusted the immediate leadership of his company to a junior officer, a *Leutnant* Günther Schmidt, and kept von Below in place as leader of the other. Though Reineke was not from Thomae's regiment, he and Thomae would soon work closely together during the heavy fighting that was to come.

Despite its best efforts at maintaining security as it moved into position, Thomae's unit appeared on the 78th Infantry Division G-2's order of battle on 13 December. One of Thomae's men had deserted to the Americans near Strauch the night before and had divulged this important piece of information to his interrogators. Fortunately for Thomae, the man knew little about the battalion's plans. Had he been better informed, the Americans undoubtedly would have strengthened the force that was to seize Kesternich. All told, the troops available to Thomae, including the anticipated addition of Reineke's, were not much in terms of fighting power, perhaps 300 men in all. It was large enough, though, to delay the Americans a few hours or perhaps a day or two until a larger force could be moved into position (of the total force, only about 163 men were from Thomae's battalion).[16]

As previously mentioned, the American breakthrough came much earlier than anyone had anticipated, forcing Thomae to act quickly. He and his men soon found themselves in the front line as the American assault drew rapidly near. By midday on 13 December, remnants of Leykauf's battalion and *1st Company, Antitank Battalion 272* were falling back under pressure toward Kesternich and Strauch, with the men of the 309th Infantry following closely behind. Although these retreating elements were quickly intercepted by Thomae's companies and incorporated into their ranks (many continued fleeing to the rear, despite Thomae's efforts), *2nd Battalion, Grenadier Regiment 980* scarcely had any time to prepare its defense before the American assault on Kesternich proper began.

Generalmajor König, knowing full well that the forces holding Kesternich were insufficient to hold against a concerted attack, cast about for more troops to send to bolster the defenses. While the division commander sought more men and guns to retake the sector lost by Leykauf's battalion, Thomae's battalion, along with Leykauf's force and the antitank company, put up a stiff fight west of the town, forcing the men of the Lightning Division to fight for every inch of ground. When the commander of the supporting company from the 709th Tank Battalion adamantly refused to advance into the town due to his fear of mines and *Panzerfausts,* the infantrymen had no option but to proceed without them. Despite the lack of armor support, the men of Companies E and F, 309th Infantry Regiment, were able to seize several houses along the town's western edge by nightfall of 13 December.*

Throughout that day and the next, the troops of 2nd Battalion, 309th Infantry, joined by 2nd Battalion, 310th Infantry, solidified their hold on the northern, western, and southern edge of Kesternich, driving most of the defenders out of their positions toward the central and eastern part of town. They captured twenty-nine Germans that first day and sixty-six more by 1800 hours the next (including twenty-four men from Thomae's battalion).[17] An unknown number of Germans lay dead in the fields west of the town and in the town itself. To the Americans, it must have appeared that the worst was over and that the division's baptism of fire had not been so bad after all. To the Germans, the situation must have seemed catastrophic.

That evening, weakened by its recent fight for Bergstein and battered even further by this new American advance, Thomae's battalion had little strength left to throw the Americans out. Even its ability to continue holding the town throughout the night was in doubt. For the time being, there was little else that König could do to help Thomae until the division could be reinforced. The division's other infantry regiments, *Grenadier Regiment 981* and *982,* were for the most part already committed or on the move and would be unavailable for the first two days. Ultimately, every major unit in the *272nd VGD* was involved in the struggle for Kesternich to some degree.

Oberstleutnant Rösener's *Grenadier Regiment 982* had already had one of its battalions smashed in Simmerath (Leykauf's) and his *2nd Battalion* was tied

---

* The failure of the tanks to advance into Kesternich was the subject of an Inspector General investigation and a subsequent court hearing. This failed to determine the root cause of the tank company commander's refusal to enter the town and led to bitter feelings by the supported infantrymen that still persist today. Source: Letter, T/4 William H. Baker, Historian, 78th Infantry Division, to MAJ Ferris, HQ ETO US Army, 1 July 1945.

down to the north of Rollesbroich defending positions in the vicinity of Raffels-brand and Ochsenkopf threatened by the diversionary attack by 1st Battalion, 311th Infantry. Kleinkorres' *Grenadier Regiment 981* was just arriving in its assembly area in the vicinity of Gemünd after marching a circuitous route from Gey and Strass. It was scheduled to undergo two days of hasty reconstitution and was in no shape to be committed immediately.

Oberst Burian had already moved Thomae's battalion of *Grenadier Regiment 980* into Kesternich. His *1st Battalion*, which was supposed to pull back to Roggendorf for two days of rest, was diverted instead through Gerstenhof to cover the left flank of *2nd Battalion, Grenadier Regiment 982* and to secure the gap that the US 310th Infantry had torn between Steckenborn and Silberscheidt. The only elements of Burian's regiment that reached Roggendorf were his headquarters and his two regimental support companies.

The arrival of Reineke's *Alarm* battalion was the only bright spot in the *272nd VGD*'s situation that first day. Arriving after midnight on 13/14 December, Reineke reported to Thomae at the latter's command post in the eastern portion of Kesternich and was ordered to defend what was left of the town. Reineke placed half of his force under *Leutnant* Schmidt along the northern edge of town and the other half under his control along the southern edge. The main road that ran through the town from Einruhr to Simmerath served as the boundary between the two companies.[18] *Leutnant* von Below served as his second in command.

Except for encountering a German squad on the southern edge of town, Reineke saw no sign of any other defenders, though Thomae's men in Bunker 47, led by *Leutnant* Englbrecht, commander of the *8th Company, Grenadier Regiment 980,* still held out defiantly By this point, only a small portion of southeastern Kesternich was still in German hands. A *Feldwebel* from the unit he was replacing (most likely from Leykauf's battalion), when asked where the front line was, told Reineke that "There is no frontline here anymore. The front is exactly where you are standing. It's a cat and mouse game!" When asked where the Americans were, the man could only shrug his shoulders. With that, the sergeant gathered up his remaining men and headed to the rear. Reineke and his battle group were virtually on their own and the battle was only beginning.

The American push into Kesternich continued the following day until most of the center and the northern and southern outskirts were in their hands by that evening. Although the fight for Kesternich had so far been very tough indeed, the situation must have appeared well in hand at the headquarters of the 78th Infantry Division by nightfall on 14 December. Losses during the past two days, though heavy in some infantry companies, had been lighter than expected. Mopping up of the occupied portion of Kesternich by the 2nd Battalion, 310th Infantry seemed to be nearly complete. Company E of 2nd Battalion, 310th Infantry had even penetrated to the far eastern outskirts of the town, where it occupied a cluster of houses.

The final assault by 2nd Battalion, 309th Infantry and 2nd Battalion, 310th Infantry was planned for the morning of 15 December. This was intended to bring the entire town under 78th Infantry Division control and secure the line of departure for the next phase of the operation. One more push, and the men of the Lightning Division hoped to gain the high ground overlooking the Roer River dams. Just as the American drive to Brandenberg and Bergstein had been similarly threatening, however, this new attack in turn provoked another violent reaction from their enemy. On this occasion, the Germans had no choice but to stop the Americans at all costs and throw them back. Once more, at the eleventh hour, the strategic surprise that was a precondition for the success of WACHT AM RHEIN was in jeopardy.

The American success at Kesternich quickly drew the attention of *Generalfeldmarschall* Rundstedt's headquarters (*OB West*), where the true nature of the situation was far from clear. Several conflicting reports obscured what had really happened, and at one point on 14 December, it seemed as if the *272nd VGD* had restored the situation and had sealed off the American's penetration. By the evening though, *OB West* had concluded that the attack by the 78th Infantry Division would probably continue until it reached the dams. It had also realized that the *272nd VGD* was probably not strong enough to clean up the breakthrough without assistance.[19]

König had few resources left of his own to keep the Americans at bay other than what he had already gleaned from his own division. He certainly lacked the forces needed to carry out an immediate counterattack to retake the town. *The 89th Infantry Division* was in no situation to offer help, since its nearest unit was twelve kilometers away and *Generalmajor* Bruns would have to denude a portion of his own front in order to get there in time, an unacceptable solution since he was already tied up in defensive fighting. The bulk of Bruns' forces were holding defensive positions between the Buhlert Hill and Zerkall. He was still awaiting the arrival of the rest of the *85th Infantry Division* so his own division could be relieved and go into reserve. König's former corps headquarters, Straube's *LXXIV Corps* to the north, had nothing to offer either since it was focused on fighting its own major defensive action in the Gey-Strass area. Any help had to come from other units of *General der Infanterie* Hitzfeld's *LXVII Corps*.

Hitzfeld was greatly concerned by this crisis involving one of his spearhead units. Initially moved into the *Westwall* in November to serve as a leading unit for the WACHT AM RHEIN, the *272nd VGD* was now so seriously weakened that Hitzfeld concluded on 14 December that it was no longer fit for offensive operations.[20] In little over one month of combat, losses suffered by its three grenadier regiments had been greater than fifty percent, with Burian's *Grenadier Regiment 980* having suffered the most during its fruitless counterattacks at Brandenberg and Bergstein during the first and second weeks of December. The only element of the division's combat power that was relatively untouched was the artillery regiment. Even the division's sole armored unit, *2nd Company, Antitank Battalion 272*, had lost six of its fourteen *Hetzers* during the fighting near Brandenberg and Bergstein. (Incidentally, Adrario's *2nd Company, Antitank Battalion 272* had initially been designated as *Tank Destroyer Company 1272*. Raised as a separate unit, it was incorporated into Adrario's battalion immediately upon arrival in the Hürtgen on 16 November 1944.[21])

If the Americans were going to be pushed out of Kesternich, Hitzfeld would have to provide König the necessary forces to give him the combat power he needed to launch a successful counterattack as well as to protect his Corps' right flank. Hitzfeld dutifully notified *6th Panzer Army* headquarters of the situation on the afternoon of 14 December, which relayed the news to *Generalfeldmarschall* Model's *Army Group B* headquarters at Fichtenhain near Krefeld. Model spoke shortly thereafter with von Rundstedt at *OB West*, telling him that the surprisingly strong American breakthrough at Simmerath and seizure of Kesternich could possibly tie up forces designated to form the offensive's pivot point at Monschau.[22]

This development forced *SS-Oberst-Gruppenführer* Sepp Dietrich to direct Hitzfeld to restore the situation in Kesternich before the offensive began, even if he had to temporarily detach elements from within his own corps to do so. Since the *89th Infantry Division* was in no position to help and the *277th Volks-Grenadier Division* was in the process of moving to the south where it would join the *I SS-Panzer Corps* for the coming offensive, the only available infantry unit in *LXVII Corps* was the *326th VGD*. Even that division, though, was scheduled to play a critical role in the offensive. If it was used, it could not afford to become bogged down in heavy fighting on the eve of the offensive. The operational plan envisioned that this newly reconstituted division would serve as *LXVII Corps'* main effort, charged with seizing Monschau and establishing a defense line that protected the northern shoulder of the offensive in conjunction with *272nd VGD*

Hitzfeld pinned his hopes of the arrival of this division, which had only completed its organization as a new division. The original *326th Infantry Division* was virtually destroyed in Normandy the previous August. Its successor, the *326th Volks-Grenadier Division*, was created in September 1944 at the Galanta Training Area in Hungary from the still-forming *579th VGD* along with remnants of the old division and was shifted to the *Westfront* on 21 November 1944 for its impending role in the Ardennes Offensive. Its commitment in the *272nd VGD's* sector would have to be a short one in order to maintain its timetable.[23]

Nevertheless, Hitzfeld had no choice but to order *Generalmajor* Kaschner, commander of the *326th VGD*, to temporarily detach one of his battalions to the *272nd VGD* to help retake Kesternich, under the proviso that it had to be withdrawn within twenty-four hours of accomplishing the mission. A quickly executed counterattack, it was thought, would allow Kaschner to pull the battalion out and replace its losses before moving it to its assembly area east of Monschau in time to rejoin the rest of *326th VGD* for the attack. After notifying *Sixth Panzer*

Army, Hitzfeld promptly ordered König to plan and carry out the counterattack by midday of 15 December. This action was *LXVII Corps'* main effort until the following day, when the Ardennes Offensive began, whether Kesternich had been retaken or not.

In addition to the battalion coming from the *326th VGD*, König still had Thomae's Battalion, reinforced by the remaining elements of Leykauf's battalion, with both units continuing to hold the part of the town still in German hands. Since Thomae's battalion was tied down defending its current positions along the town's eastern outskirts, another battalion had to be brought up to provide the necessary weight to carry through with the attack. Even the battalion from *326th VGD* designated to make the main effort, *1st Battalion, Grenadier Regiment 753*, commanded by *Hauptmann* Otto Schmidt, was weaker than expected, though. It had been occupying a bivouac area in the vicinity of Gemünd when it was inadvertently bombed several days before by the Royal Air Force in another unsuccessful attempt to destroy the Urft Dam.

Since many of Schmidt's men had been killed and wounded during the bombing, his battalion was reinforced by transferring some individual replacements from *2nd Battalion, Grenadier Regiment 753*. After marching from Gemünd, Schmidt's battalion arrived at its forward assembly area, located in a stone quarry east of Kesternich near the hotel Schöne Aussicht, during the early morning hours of 15 December.[24]

To round out the counterattacking force, Kleinkorres' *Grenadier Regiment 981* was alerted and ordered to move forward in support of Schmidt's battalion. His regiment had been decimated during the fight to defend Gey, and since leaving the town on 11 December there had been little opportunity to replace missing personnel or destroyed equipment. Kleinkorres temporarily combined both of his battalions into a single force, with each battalion forming a company-sized unit. Kleinkorres' regimental howitzer and antitank companies would follow behind the main body of troops and provide supporting fire.

This force (perhaps 300 men in all) was then ordered on the morning of 15 December to move from its rest area near Gemünd to a forward assembly area at the Ölmühle, located in the Tiefenbach ravine between Huppenbroich and Kesternich. The men were exhausted after ten days of being in the line where they had been subjected to relentless artillery fire and determined attacks by the 4th Infantry Division. Regardless of its condition, this makeshift battalion would have to suffice. Though *Grenadier Regiment 981* consisted of less than half of its original strength, it was enough to tilt the balance in the German's favor.[25]

To give the attack the needed offensive punch, it was reinforced by three *Hetzers,* a self-propelled *Vierlingsflak* (four 20mm *Flak* 38 cannons mounted on the big *Sonder-Kraftfahrzeuge* [Sd.Kfz.] Model 7/2 halftrack) and three self-propelled 37mm antiaircraft guns from *Hauptmann* Friedrich Adrario's *2nd* and *3rd Companies* of *Antitank Battalion 272*.[26] Adrario, a veteran officer from Vienna, was placed in overall command of the counterattack and would follow closely behind his tank destroyers in his radio command vehicle (a Sd.Kfz. 251/3 Type D). All told, the counterattack force consisted of approximately 900 to 1,000 *Volksgrenadiers* and supporting troops.

Close liaison was established with *Hauptmann* Weber's *2nd Battalion, Artillery Regiment 272,* which would provide fire direction and control of the division and corps artillery allocated to support the attack. In order to exercise direct divisional oversight of the attack, the newly-assigned division *Ia, Major* Hans Uhl (who had accompanied König when the general departed the *344th Infantry Division*), was directed to establish the division's forward command post, co-located with that of Weber's, in the town of Einruhr. Uhl's predecessor, *Major* Gerhard Höptner, had already begun planning the counterattack the day before and had been kept with the division an additional day after Kossmala had departed to ensure that that the transition was carried out seamlessly. Once this had been done to König's satisfaction, Höptner left the evening of 14 December for his new assignment as the *Ia* of *LXVII Corps.*[27]

A telephone cable was run from the forward CP to the outskirts of Kesternich and a staff NCO was sent forward with a field telephone to keep *Major* Uhl abreast of the developing situation.[28] Uhl issued the orders to the assembled commanders at 1100 hours on 15 December. *Generalmajor* König had planned to begin his counterattack at 1500 hours on the same day, but this action was nearly spoiled when when another unit acting independently (probably a company from the neighboring *277th VGD*), attacked from the area southeast of Simmerath. This uncoordinated attempt by a unit not scheduled to take part in the operation was easily beaten back by the troops of 2nd Battalion, 310th Infantry Regiment, supported by the entire 78th Division artillery.[29] (For an overview of the German attack, see Map 8.)

While the Germans completed their preparations to retake the town, the Americans continued with their own attack, reaching the vicinity of the church by noon on 15 December. By 1500 hours, they had seized both the southern and most of the eastern edges of the town and it seemed as if Kesternich was finally theirs, except for a few holdouts in the rubble. The 78th Infantry Division had already smashed one German counterattack and Major General Edwin P. Parker, Jr., the 78th commander, probably thought that the *272nd VGD* had little capability left to carry out another one.[30] Most likely Parker thought that he had the situation well in hand.

If he held such an optimistic assessment, however, it proved to be premature. Had Parker known that the troops in Kesternich that afternoon had failed to "organize the ground" (for example, to set up proper defensive positions or observation posts in the town's outskirts, as it was revealed afterwards) or that they had failed to coordinate artillery defensive fires, he would not have felt so sure of himself.[31] This was later borne out by evidence that showed that instead of carrying out these onerous but fundamental tasks—involving digging fighting positions in the partially frozen soil, filling sandbags, and establishing forward observation posts—the inexperienced GIs instead had remained inside the relatively warm and dry basements in the town itself, dramatically limiting their observation and ability to react. This combination of inexperience, fatigue, and inattentive leadership set the conditions for the stunningly successful German counterattack that was about to be unleashed.

By 1500 hours, the German troops had arrived in their assault positions in the Tiefenbach valley 500 meters south of Kesternich and in the Ahornhof manor east of Kesternich where they formed up for what was to be the decisive action of the day. The sky was overcast and a light snow was falling, perfect weather that denied the Americans their strongest support asset, the dreaded fighter-bombers. At 1530 hours, taking advantage of a particularly accurate and well-timed five-minute barrage fired by 100 barrels from division and corps artillery batteries, the two-pronged German counterattack began. Spearheaded by troops from *1st Battalion, Grenadier Regiment 753* and the amalgamated battalion from *Grenadier Regiment 981,* along with the accompanying *Jagdpanzer 38(t)* tank destroyers, *Vierlingsflak* and self-propelled 37mm *Flak,* the German attack poured out of the western exit of the Tiefenbach ravine and from the Ahornhof along the main road to Einruhr.[32]

On the left, the consolidated battle group from Kleinkorres' *Grenadier Regiment 981* attacked in a northerly direction along a farm track that led out of the steep Tiefenbach ravine. Deploying quickly on line, this force covered the several hundred meters of open ground separating them from the Americans in a few minutes, swept past the frightened outposts and rolled into the town from the south, hitting the American defensive positions arrayed along the town's central and western approaches before the GIs knew what had happened.[33] This unexpected assault, coming as it did in the late afternoon from an unlikely direction, caught the startled American troops of Company F, 310th Infantry Regiment completely by surprise. The defenders had failed to set up forward observation posts or minefields along this avenue of approach, since they had decided that an enemy attack out of such a steep ravine was all but impossible.[34]

On the right, the attack by Schmidt's *1st Battalion, Grenadier Regiment 753,* spearheaded by the three *Hetzers* and supported by the self-propelled *Flak,* conducted a forward passage of lines through Thomae's and Reineke's positions and kept going. It, too, made good progress, though the advance along a 500-meter wide front and across an open field left them exposed to American artillery and machine-gun fire during the last several hundred meters and the battalion suffered many casualties. Once this force reached the eastern edge of the town, they quickly isolated Company E, 310th Infantry, which was still defending the town's eastern outskirts, and pushed onward into the town proper, down the main road running through the center of the town. Schmidt's battalion was aided by the *Flak* wagons, whose devastating fire blew apart the houses held by the Americans.[35]

As the German artillery barrage shifted to the town's western approaches, all communications wires leading to the 309th Infantry Regiment's headquarters were severed and from that point the regimental commander had no clear idea what was happening to the attached 2nd Battalion, 310th Infantry in the town itself. Adding to this battalion's inability to adequately respond to the German attack, the regimental artillery liaison officer from the 309th Infantry had positioned himself in Kesternich's town square (why he had not installed an observation post in the steeple of the church remains a mystery). This error made it impossible for him to see what was happening on the southeastern and southern edges of the town, where the German attack was rapidly developing momentum.

American survivors later remarked that they saw the *Volksgrenadiers* "surging out of the woods" from the ravine south of the town that had prevented observation of their approach and protected them from artillery fire. Cloaked by rapidly approaching darkness and backed by Adrario's *Hetzers* and the self-propelled *Flak,* the Germans swept into Kesternich from south and east and quickly overwhelmed Lieutenant Colonel Byron W. Ladd's 2nd Battalion, 310th Infantry. Caught off guard and completely outgunned, the American defense line quickly collapsed.

According to another participant from the 78th Infantry Division, "Gray figures were all about, firing burp guns and throwing grenades. . . . The Germans wanted Kesternich and they had sent an overwhelming force to take it."[36] Fighting house to house in small, isolated groups, most of the men from Companies E and F were forced to retreat into cellars where they were quickly rounded up. The Germans scattered the men of Ladd's Company G while the GIs attempted to reestablish contact with the other two companies that had been trapped inside the buildings. The 78th Infantry Division's headquarters was not informed that the counterattack had even begun until 1620 hours.

Inexplicably, the attached tank platoon from the 709th Tank Battalion failed to engage Adrario's tank destroyers and withdrew instead through the town back toward Witzerath after losing one tank.[37] Even without observed artillery fire, German losses from the American guns were still substantial (especially in *1st Battalion, Grenadier Regiment 753*), though most German units reported taking few casualties once they entered the town. Even these dead and wounded were too many, since they could not be replaced in time for the offensive. Typically, German small unit leadership suffered heavily. *Hauptmann* Schmidt, commander of *1st Battalion, Grenadier Regiment 753* of the *326th VGD,* fell during the initial stage of the attack, leaving his battalion in the hands of his senior lieutenant. More fell during the next three days.

Most of the town was back in German hands by midnight, though fighting continued until 0300 hours the next morning, when the leading companies of Kleinkorres' and Schmidt's battalions reached the western edge of the town and linked up. The 309th Infantry, reinforced by an ad hoc force that included cooks, supply personnel, and drivers, attempted to rescue their entrapped comrades in a hastily-conceived counterattack the following morning, but were initially prevented from entering the town from the west by heavy fire from the defenders of Bunker 47, who were still holding out doggedly. The Americans were able to knock it out of commission and capture most of the defenders, including *Leutnant* Englbrecht, later that afternoon after a tank placed direct fire on its observation slits. Although the bunker was finally eliminated, the 309th Infantry's attack had lost momentum and died out after losing two tanks and recovering only a portion of the town's westernmost outskirts.

Over 300 Americans, mostly from 2nd Battalion, 310th Infantry, were taken prisoner that evening and were quickly marched off to the POW camp at Stalag 12A near Limburg. The battalion commander, Lieutenant Colonel Ladd, was among the captured. The commander of 2nd Battalion, 309th Infantry, Lieutenant Colonel Wilson L. Burley, was killed in action when he went into town to see for himself what was going on. His body was not recovered until Kesternich was finally recaptured nearly two months later. German troops quickly helped themselves to K-Rations, winter clothing, boots, watches, and the rest of the booty left behind when the Americans surrendered. *Hauptmann* Thomae later commented on the quality of the abandoned American radio equipment, with which he was able to clearly hear messages still being transmitted even though there were no longer any US troops left alive to receive them.[38] These radios were later used to intercept American communications and issue bogus orders to other units.

Once the town was back in German hands by the early morning hours of 16 December, *Grenadier Regiment 981* was withdrawn from Kesternich and quickly moved to the southwest, where it occupied a new defensive line stretching from the area southwest of Kesternich to the area south of Simmerath. Here, *Oberstleutnant* Kleinkorres' regiment would link up with a newly arrived battalion from *Grenadier Regiment 752* of the *326th VGD* in the vicinity of Bunker 94. He established his new regimental forward command post in the village of Huppenbroich and insured that his regimental supporting weapons were quickly emplaced and made ready to help repel another American attack from the area south of Simmerath. The defenses of the western edge of Kesternich for the next few hours became the sole responsibility of *1st Battalion, Grenadier Regiment 753,* until it was relieved during the morning or afternoon of 16 December.

The Americans were stunned by this major setback, after their early morning continuation of the attack on 15 December had gone so well. Only fifty-two men from Company F, 310th Infantry were able to infiltrate back to American lines that day, though a few others managed to make it back a few days later. Companies E and G were almost totally wiped out. For the 78th Infantry Division, its first major combat action, which had seemed so promising at its outset, had turned into an unmitigated disaster.

American casualties incurred during the fighting for the Monschau Corridor were considerable. Between 13 and 19 December, the 78th Infantry Division suffered approximately 1,515 dead, wounded, missing, and injured, including the battalion virtually wiped out in Kesternich. So astonished had the Americans been by the German's counterattack on the evening of 15 December, that many of the survivors later reported that they been attacked by an entire *SS-Panzer Division*, rather than by a few dozen "lowly" *Volksgrenadiers!*[39] Some eyewitnesses swore the attackers were accompanied by Tiger tanks, but that can be attributed to their relative greenness and poor visual conditions, since the nearest *Waffen-SS* units, or Tiger tanks for that matter, were arrayed several dozen kilometers to the southeast and were being held back to make the rapid penetration necessary for the success of the upcoming Ardennes Offensive.

Now that Kesternich had been retaken and the danger from the Americans momentarily averted, *1st Battalion, Grenadier Regiment 753* had to be pulled out quickly, by the early afternoon of 16 December at the latest. This move allowed the battalion enough time, if it conducted a forced march, to reach its assault positions near Monschau and join up with the main body of the *326th VGD,* which had already begun its own attack that morning. Fully engaged in the fight for Monschau, Hitzfeld could no longer afford to be distracted by Kesternich. He needed everything he had at his disposal to conduct his corps' main effort, where the attack by *326th VGD* against the American defenses in Monschau was running into difficulty. The Ardennes Offensive was now in full swing and quickly eclipsed the Battle for Kesternich.[40]

9

The Defense of Kesternich

When dawn broke on Saturday, 16 December 1944, most of the Western Front between Luxembourg City and Monschau became enveloped in turmoil, as thousands of guns began firing preparatory barrages upon what had previously been considered a "Ghost Front." Shortly before daylight, Field Marshal Rundstedt initiated WACHT AM RHEIN, Germany's last attempt to create a more favorable strategic situation in the West. Hundreds of thousands of men and nearly a thousand tanks and assault guns—the Third Reich's last strategic reserve—were flung at American forces spread out across the Ardennes. Thirteen *Volks-Grenadier Divisions,* which had been assembled for this very purpose, would play a key role in the offensive, but not the *272nd.*

Due to the need to hold Kesternich, the *272nd VGD* would not officially be involved in WACHT AM RHEIN at all. Its place in Hitzfeld's *LXVII Corps* was soon taken by *277th Volks-Grenadier Division* and other divisions, which were heavily involved in attacks to the south along the Elsenborn Ridge against the US 2nd and 99th Infantry Divisions. To hold Kesternich, *Generalmajor* König had no recourse but to scrape together whatever forces he could lay his hands on to relieve the battalion of the *326th VGD.* He was now on his own, except for what little help Hitzfeld's corps could provide, which was not much, since after 16 December the corps commander was totally occupied with his effort to get past Monschau.

To make matters worse, *General der Infanterie* Hitzfeld's headquarters in Dalbenden, identified via Ultra intercepts, was hit by thirty Allied bombers on the morning of 18 December, a raid that killed and wounded many key members of his staff. As a result, command and control of both the *272nd* and *326th VGDs* was temporarily passed to the *I SS-Panzer Corps* until *LXVII Corps'* headquarters could be reconstituted. This additional command and control burden proved too much for *I SS-Panzer Corps'* staff to manage, forcing *Army Group B* to place the *272nd VGD* once again under the control of the neighboring *LXXIV Corps,* led by *General der Infanterie* Karl Püchler, effective 1200 hours on 19 December.[1]

In order to carry out his new orders directing him to hold Kesternich at all costs, the *272nd VGD*'s commander had to act quickly. To do this by the deadline of the evening of 16 December, König had to free up and move enough of his own troops into the town to relieve the battalion from *Generalmajor* Kaschner's division, before it withdrew too precipitately. Should this occur, his division would inadvertently hand a major portion of the town back to the Americans without them having to fire a shot to retake it.

Initially, Thomae's *2nd Battalion, Grenadier Regiment 980* was given the mission to replace *1st Battalion, Grenadier Regiment 753* on the morning of 16 December, but since his battalion's actual effective strength was now probably less than one hundred men, this mission was tasked to another unit instead. This assignment befell *Hauptmann* Schneider's *2nd Battalion, Grenadier Regiment 982*, requiring that it be temporarily relieved by a battalion from the *85th Infantry Division* and brought to Kesternich by forced march, following the road snaking from Hechelscheidt to Rurberg.[2] In addition to ordering Adrario to leave his three *Hetzers* where they were (his *3rd Company* with the 37mm *Flak* having been withdrawn to Einruhr), König instructed the remnants of Leykauf's battalion to remain in the line as well.

Hauptmann Schneider's battalion in turn would then be relieved by the early morning of 17 December at the latest by a grouping consisting of *Füsilier Company 272*, artillerymen from *1st Battalion, Artillery Regiment 272*, and one company from *Pionier Battalion 272*. These units were ordered to disengage and move immediately to Kesternich from their present locations and relieve the *2nd Battalion, Grenadier Regiment 982*, taking up defensive positions in the town before the surprised Americans could recover.[3]

Fortunately, except for the aforementioned attempt by 309th Infantry to retake Kesternich, nothing of tactical significance took place throughout the rest of the 78th Infantry Division's sector on 16 December, allowing both sides to catch their breath and prepare for a showdown the following day.

The drive by the 310th Infantry against Strauch and Steckenborn had sputtered to a halt the day before in the face of several determined German counterattacks carried out by *1st Battalion, Grenadier Regiment 980* and remnants of *1st Battalion, Grenadier Regiment 982*. The attack by the 311th Infantry Regiment against the Raffelsbrand and Ochsenkopf bunker complex had also failed to make any measurable progress against the determined defenses of *2nd Battalion, Grenadier Regiment 982*, allowing that battalion to pull out and hand over its positions to another unit on the evening of 15/16 December without difficulty. The struggle for Kesternich, therefore, would prove to be a fight by the 309th Infantry Regiment against almost the entire *272nd VGD*.

Oberleutnant Kolb probably received the order to move to Kesternich late in the evening of 14/15 December. That night, his weary men turned over the position at Giesenheck they had just retaken at great cost to *Kampfgruppe Funke* from *Grenadier Regiment 1056, 89th Infantry Division* and began moving south.[4] Forming up in the valley near the Zweifallshammer forge, they made the long, slow ascent toward Schmidt and Kommerscheidt, arriving there around daybreak. Here, they probably rested during most of the day to avoid American fighter-bombers, and began the final leg of their journey the night of 15/16 December.

Most likely, Kolb's men reached the town of Steckenborn, located approximately two kilometers northeast of Kesternich, during the early evening of 16 December. They must have arrived shortly after the first American attempt to retake Kesternich had failed, though the situation in Steckenborn itself was calm. Kolb established his command post in the village and coordinated his plans with those of *Hauptmann* Rhein's *1st Battalion, Grenadier Regiment 980,* which was responsible for this defensive sector. Ironically, shortly after Kolb and his men departed Giesenheck, Company K, 311th Infantry Regiment of the 78th Infantry Division launched an audacious daylight attack on the morning of 15 December and retook the hillock after a short but sharp fight. During the fight, Company K killed a number of the defenders from *Kampfgruppe Funke* and captured twelve more.[5] The Americans actually overran the position, going as far as the Kall River trail before they realized their error and turned back, but not   the company commander, Captain Robert A. McChord, and eight of his men had been surrounded and captured.[6]

By then, however, Kolb and his men were long gone. Whether *Füsilier Company 272* could have held the bridgehead position at Giesenheck against the determined American assault is an open question, but it probably would have put up a far more spirited defense than did *Kampfgruppe Funke*. Several attempts were made over the next few days to recapture Giesenheck in order to maintain German control of the Kall gorge exits at Zweifallshammer and Lücasmühle. Indeed, the bridgehead position changed hands several times more before the Americans finally retained control just before the end of the month.

Upon reaching Steckenborn, Kolb ordered his men to seek temporary shelter in cellars while he awaited further orders. At some point during the night of 16/17 December, he was notified by division headquarters that he was to form two of his platoons into an emergency unit and place them under *Hauptmann* Thomae's control. Their mission was to occupy the crossroads in the center of Kesternich and defend it against an American counterattack, which was expected shortly. That was all that Kolb was told.

Since his *2nd Platoon* had suffered the most casualties at Giesenheck two days before, Kolb decided to send his *1st* and *3rd Platoons* to Kesternich. These he placed under the command of a *Leutnant* Schneider, who was apparently assigned to *Füsilier Company 272* that same day as a replacement for *Leutnant* Beyer, who had been seriously wounded three days earlier at Giesenheck. The *2nd* and *4th Platoons,* as well as Kolb himself, remained in Steckenborn to defend that locality in cooperation with *Hauptmann* Rhein's *1st Battalion, Grenadier Regiment 980,* which held the town with some of the remnant of Leykauf's battalion, while Wegner and the *5th Platoon* remained in their previous position in the Gerstenhof area. Little is known of *Leutnant* Schneider except that he came out of the division's officer's reserve and was captured the following day. He had not even been entered in the Company's records before he was taken prisoner.

Füsilier Company 272, after retaking the crossroads in front of the church in the town square, was supposed to defend this crucial intersection with the two remaining *Hetzers* (one had been knocked out in the previous days' fighting) backed up with artillery support.[7] Before he could move his men into position, 1st and 3rd Battalion of the 309th Infantry Regiment, along with supporting armor, initiated their own attack in the early morning of 17 December. The Americans quickly punched a hole through the defensive line held by troops from the newly-arrived *2nd Battalion, Grenadier Regiment 982* and pushed them back toward the town's center. This battalion had been assigned the mission of holding the town's western outskirts and had been occupying its new positions since 0500 hours 16 December, after having relieved the outgoing *1st Battalion, Grenadier Regiment 753.*[8]

In retrospect, it appears that the battle handoff between *1st Battalion, Grenadier Regiment 753* and *2nd Battalion, Grenadier Regiment 982* was poorly carried out. Coordination between the two forces seems to have been haphazard at best and it is doubtful that anything approaching a man-for-man relief in place occurred. More likely, the *Leutnant* serving as the acting commander of *1st Battalion, Grenadier Regiment 753* began moving his men out of their positions on the town's western edge in order to rejoin the rest of the *326th VGD* shortly before dawn on 16 December without waiting for all *2nd Battalion, Grenadier Regiment 982* to arrive on the scene. This undoubtedly contributed to the relative ease with which the force from the 309th Infantry Regiment was able to retake the town's western outskirts. Had it not been for the defiant last stand by *Leutnant* Englbrecht and his men still manning Bunker 47, the Americans might well have retaken most of Kesternich on 16 December 1944.

The 309th Infantry then advanced rapidly through the town toward the eastern district where *Leutnant* Schneider and his two platoons from *Füsilier Company 272* were busy preparing to take up their new defensive positions at the crossroads. In the few hours since he had been assigned to the company, Schneider probably had little time or opportunity to become acquainted with any of the men he was leading. This, combined with the fact that he had little chance to become familiar with the town and the environment, undoubtedly contributed to the disaster that followed.

With the Americans now forcing their way into the heart of the town, Schneider's mission was quickly changed. Instead of occupying defensive positions near the church, *Hauptmann* Thomae ordered him to lead his two platoons in an immediate counterattack to retake the crossroads from the Americans. Preceded by a fierce artillery barrage that laid 800 rounds on the American positions, the two platoons from *Füsilier Company 272* and elements from *2nd Battalion, Grenadier Regiment 982* rushed forward to retake the ground lost earlier that day. Almost immediately, Schneider and his men collided with troops of 1st Battalion, 309th Infantry, who had begun their own coordinated attack, supported by the firepower of several accompanying Shermans.

The hastily planned German advance was quickly overpowered by the onrushing Americans. In the confusion that ensued from this meeting engagement, the *3rd Platoon* was cut off and all but one of its men were killed, wounded, or captured before *Leutnant* Schneider ordered the rest to retreat. *1st Platoon* also suffered heavily. Only a well-timed artillery barrage directed by *Oberleutnant* Reineke prevented the Americans from advancing any further.[9]

Another man who fought in Kesternich that day was *Füsilier* Eduard Zacharuk, the former leader of a heavy machine-gun section and now one of the company runners with *3rd Platoon*. As Zacharuk crouched behind a building near the intersection, a tank approaching from the right unloaded a barrage of heavy machine-gun fire on him and several others. Caught between enemy coming from the front and right the *Unteroffizier,* serving as platoon leader, ordered his men to fall back to the crossroads in front of the church along with the *1st Platoon*. In the rush to pull back to safety, Zacharuk and most of the *3rd Platoon* was left behind. He also lost his helmet as he and the others dove for cover when the tank began firing at them again. It was now approximately 1200 hours.

While huddled in a doorway in order to avoid the artillery fire, the now helmetless Zacharuk was struck in the forehead by a small piece of shrapnel, which left an 8-centimeter gash that bled profusely and rendered him unconscious. Had it not been for the extreme cold, he believed, he would have bled to death, but the blood quickly froze about the wound and luckily stanched the flow. Drifting in and out of consciousness, he remembered being picked up by a large soldier and carried into a cellar, where he was laid down and had his wound treated. The first words he heard when he regained his senses were "Let's go, boy!" It was at that point that he realized that he was now a prisoner of the Americans. For him, at least, the war was over.[10]

Interestingly, an account of the action involving Schneider and *Füsilier Company 272* was provided by Johann Reineke, who was an eyewitness to the failed counterattack. Reineke was sitting in his command post near the "Triangle"(where the roads from Einruhr and Rurberg intersected) in eastern Kesternich late that morning when he observed the *Hetzers* and infantrymen roar by him without providing him the opportunity to carry out any coordination or exchange of information with *Leutnant* Schneider.

Reineke spotted a *Leutnant* leading the attack, whom he later referred to as "Rohrbach" (clearly a pseudonym for Schneider), who shouted to him, "I'm supposed to take Kesternich!"

Reineke shouted back, "Be careful beyond the church!" as the *Leutnant* moved out with his men and the *Hetzers*. Shortly after they passed by, Reineke and his men heard a tremendous outburst of machine-gun and tank fire. Schneider and his counterattacking forces had walked directly into the advancing US force without bothering to deploy properly in anticipation of enemy contact. Reineke later remarked, "I have never before had such a clear view of an attack going into the trash bin so quickly!"[11]

Shortly thereafter, Reineke observed individual infantrymen running past him to the rear. Not long after that, the two remaining *Hetzers* roared past him heading in the same direction. It quickly became apparent that the Americans, having stopped the German attack, were launching another counterattack of their own. As he watched, an artillery shell landed in the midst of a group of retreating soldiers, seriously wounding four of them. Reineke's own medic had a leg blown off, just when his skills were needed most. As mentioned above, only Reineke's timely call for artillery *Sperrfeuer* (blocking fire) brought the American assault to a halt and enabled him to reestablish a German defense line.

A rattled *Leutnant* Schneider, separated from his men and accompanied by a solitary messenger, reported to Reineke in the latter's cellar command post. After Reineke handed the *Leutnant* a cigarette and a shot of schnapps to calm his nerves, Schneider told him what had happened. As recounted by Reineke, Schneider told him that:

> Early this morning I received an order to take over and lead an alarm unit toward Strauch and await further instructions. The orders arrived and directed me to retake Kesternich with the help of three assault guns. I did not know anyone in this unit, nor did I know the leader of the assault guns. I knew nothing of Kesternich or anything of the military situation there. There was no time for a briefing nor any time to prepare for the attack. But I am a soldier and asked no questions. I marched as ordered. 'What do I do now?' He asked.[12]

After a spirited exchange over the field telephone with *Hauptmann* Thomae, who was under orders to retake Kesternich at all costs and apparently had already reported that the town was back in German hands, Thomae and Reineke decided that Schneider should gather up his remaining forces and wait until darkness to conduct a reconnaissance toward the American positions as far as the situation permitted. In this way, it could still be honestly reported that German forces were in the western portion of the town, though the fact that they were only patrolling the area was conveniently omitted.

In all, nineteen men from both platoons were made prisoners of war that day, including *Leutnant* Schneider. While leading his patrol that night on the northern outskirts of Kesternich, Schneider and two others were captured, though the rest of *Füsilier Company 272* that he was leading made it safely back to the German lines. The *Leutnant* must have proven to be an ideal prisoner. Not only did he report all the details of his mission, but Schneider also told his captors about the company's organization; number and types of weapons it had; names of company commander and executive officer; and its total strength of about 170 men.[13]

For the remainder of that day and into the early morning hours of the next, *Füsilier Company 272* and the other defenders held their ground behind hastily improvised defensive positions near the triangle in the town's eastern district.

Later, after action reports from the US 78th Infantry Division revealed that German forces in Kesternich carried out at least four counterattacks on 17 December. Losses on both sides were heavy, though the Germans were finally able to push the Americans back to the town's western district, where the front line was to remain for the next six weeks. Both sides were exhausted after a week of heavy fighting. From the beginning of the American attack on 13 December until midnight on 18 December, the Germans had probably lost over 770 men in and around Kesternich and Simmerath, including 358 men taken prisoner.[14]

On 18 December, due to a combination of bad weather, heavy casualties, and the overriding need to support the main battle raging in the Ardennes, the 78th Infantry Division was ordered to go over to the defensive. That afternoon, the division was detached from US V Corps and attached to US VII Corps and was instructed to hold its present positions and secure the road network in the vicinity of Konzen. The Paustenbach knoll, which providing an excellent artillery observation point, was also to be held at all costs.[15] As a reserve, CCR, 5th Armored Division and the 102nd Cavalry Group (Mechanized) were attached to the division that same day, though CCR reverted to control of 5th Armored Division three days later. For the time being, the "Lightning" Division conserved its forces and licked its wounds. It would soon be back after absorbing replacements to fill the ranks of the two battalions battered in Kesternich.

Although the remnants of the two *Füsilier* platoons had held their positions after their failed counterattack and had helped to prevent the Americans from retaking the town, they had suffered twenty-seven casualties in the process, including one dead, three wounded, and twenty-three missing in action. Of these, nineteen were later confirmed captured by the 309th Infantry Regiment, including three men captured on the night of 17 December already mentioned before the surviving *Füsiliers* were pulled out.[16]

On the evening of 17 December, when the tempo of fighting in Kesternich finally began to taper off, Kolb received new orders. He was directed to withdraw his remaining forces from Kesternich during the morning of 18 December and march them, together with the rest of the company, to the company trains area in Hergarten. Even with his *1st* and *3rd Platoons* having returned from Kesternich, the company was now down to an effective strength of 101 men. In less than one week, the *Füsilier Company 272* had suffered fifty-five casualties in heavy fighting at both Giesenheck and Kesternich, the majority of them from the *1st, 2nd, and 3rd Platoons*. It had been a bloody baptism of fire. Since arriving at the front in early November, the company had suffered seventy-five casualties in all, a loss rate of forty percent.

Shortly after the *Füsiliers* departed, *Hauptmann* Thomae and the rest of his decimated force from *2nd Battalion, Grenadier Regiment 980* were relieved of their defensive duties early on the morning of 18 December by *2nd Battalion, Grenadier Regiment 982*. This latter unit, roughly at about sixty to seventy-five percent of strength, was still in relatively good shape after helping defend portions of Kesternich since 16 December. It still had enough combat power to take over from the battered troops who had been fighting in and around Kesternich for the past week.

After 18 December, when it became clear that the men of the US 78th Infantry Division had assumed a defensive posture, the *272nd VGD* took advantage of the relative calm that descended upon this section of the front to take a breathing spell of its own. Many of its subunits had been intermingled and nearly all of them had suffered heavy losses. *Grenadier Regiment 981* had been forced to combine all of its remaining combat troops into an emergency battalion because of losses it had suffered even before it was committed to battle in Kesternich. *Grenadier Regiment 980* was not in much better shape. Half of *Grenadier Regiment 982* had been smashed and needed to be rebuilt. *Pionier Battalion 272* had sustained heavy casualties, too. Only the division's artillery regiment was near full strength, and even its effectiveness was impaired because of a shortage of ammunition, which had been diverted to support the offensive unfolding in the Ardennes.

On 19 December, *Generalmajor* König was ordered to hand over his defensive sector, including the town of Kesternich, to the *246th Volks-Grenadier Division* beginning that evening, with all units scheduled to be relieved by the next morning (like the *272nd,* it had been redesignated as a *VGD* the previous September). The *246th VGD* had been positioned to the rear of König's force in the vicinity of Gemünd and was slated to conduct a relief-in-place to allow the *272nd VGD* a few days to recover from the heavy fighting it had just experienced. Following four days of rest and reconstitution, König's division was in turn to relieve the *246th.*[17] The latter division sideslipped to the left in order to take over the defensive sector being held by the *326th VGD,* whose own attack against Monschau had been cancelled on 18 December because of heavy losses and its inability to get beyond the American's defenses.

For the next few days, König directed his energies toward rebuilding as much of his division as he could. The large number of replacements that *LXVII Corps* had held back to reconstitute his division in order for it to assume its role in the offensive were now released. These troops, some 1,000 in all from several *March Battalions,* according to American intelligence reports, were allocated beginning on 21 December, with each regiment receiving between 300 to 350 men each.[18] All of the division's subordinate elements were not pulled out of line simultaneously, however. Due to the staggered arrival of the various battalions and regiments of the *246th VGD,* some of König's units had to hold their positions until 23 or 24 December before it was their turn to be relieved. Despite the defeat that the 78th Infantry Division had suffered at Kesternich, the US Army's psychological warfare troops kept up a steady barrage of surrender leaflets, instructing König's men when and how to give themselves up. More and more of his men began to secret these leaflets on their persons, and not just for use in the nearest field latrine.

In order to reconstitute the regiments, König had each of them move sequentially to rest areas between Gemünd and Schleiden. To free up manpower and to distribute desperately needed experienced non-commissioned officers, he ordered that *Field Replacement Battalion 272* be temporarily disbanded. Due to this action and other expedients, the division was able to field an effective combat strength of approximately 4,500 men by the end of the month.[19] Training within the units commenced immediately upon arrival in their rest areas to ensure that the division would be as combat ready as possible in the shortest amount of time.[20] By the end of December, all of the *272nd VGD* was back in the line. By this point, the main defense line stretched to Schmidt in the north to the Am Gericht crossroads to the south, nearly identical to its front line position that it held when it arrived in the Hürtgen Forest in early November.

In line with König's directive, *Oberleutnant* Kolb and his men were to undergo two weeks of badly needed rest and reconstitution in order to restore the company's capability as the division's *Feuerwehr*. This honorific, which meant that they were now considered the division's "fire fighters," made the survivors feel very proud. They felt at the time that *Füsilier Company 272* certainly had earned the title, since they had been rushed into action at critical points on two separate occasions.

This title had come at a cost, however; after enduring heavy artillery fire and infantry combat during these two engagements, the company's effective combat strength (not counting the combat trains) had sharply declined. It was reported that *1st Platoon* had twenty-four men remaining, *2nd* had the same, *3rd* had only one survivor, *4th* had twenty-eight, and *5th* (soon returned to company control) counted twenty-four men. To make matters worse, many of the casualties were experienced NCOs and senior corporals who were, at this point of the war, nearly irreplaceable. Included in the number of men killed and wounded were two sergeants who were listed as missing in action at Kesternich, *Unteroffiziere* Wilhelm Pfalzgraf and Johann Dahmen, both from the *3rd Platoon*.

With clouds hanging heavily above them and temperatures hovering in the low teens, *Füsilier Company 272* made it way slowly back to Hergarten on 18 December. The twenty-two-kilometer-long march via the serpentine route through Einruhr, Sauermühle, and Gemünd probably took a good eight hours, but at least the men did not have to worry about the dreaded *Jabos* for a change. As they marched toward the east, off to their right they could hear the sounds of the fierce fighting then raging near Monschau, where the *326th VGD* was conducting its futile attack, as well as the noise from the even bigger fight going on along the Elsenborn Ridge, where elements of *I SS-Panzer Corps* was trying to break through the American defenses. The men arrived in the village shortly after nightfall. With the Battle of the Bulge raging a few miles away, *Füsilier Company 272* began its first rest period since arriving at the front over a month before.

After living in damp bunkers or wet foxholes for nearly six weeks, the barns, sheds, and outbuildings of Hergarten must have seemed like paradise. Besides having a roof over their heads, the men also did not have to worry about being killed in their sleep by artillery or mortar fire, nor did they have to go out on patrol. Except for the occasional fighter-bomber sortie (by this point, most Allied aircraft were grounded by the weather or committed to repulsing the German offensive), life in the rest area was almost serene. After delousing, they were sorted out and assigned to different quarters where they would stay for the next two weeks. After living without them for weeks on end, the men were finally permitted to retrieve their knapsacks from their supply wagons and change underwear and socks. They were finally able to bathe, get their hair trimmed, and have their uniforms mended and boots repaired.

Oberleutnant Kolb and *Oberfeldwebel* Fuhrmeister also used this period to catch up on administrative matters—there were letters to next of kin to write on behalf of killed or missing soldiers, promotions to authorize, and awards to be handed out. Thirteen men were promoted to *Gefreiter* on 24 December alone, a sign that these men who had been raw recruits at Falkensee were now experienced veterans. Kolb also requested permission to award close combat credit for the two days the Company was engaged on Giesenheck.

Kolb and Fuhrmeister also tracked down the status of the wounded who had been evacuated, including eight of the men wounded at Giesenheck and cared for by *Pioneer Battalion 272*'s aid station so they could reassure their families that they were in safe hands. On a sadder note, Kolb also had to verify the deaths of the four men killed at Giesenheck whose remains had been evacuated to the graves registration collection point, as well as to answer a division inquiry regarding the whereabouts of the remains of two soldiers that had been misplaced.* In addition to these mundane but important matters, Kolb also conducted the mandatory security and loyalty classes mandated by Himmler, including one he gave on the evils of desertion on New Year's Eve.

Mail also arrived from loved ones at home with news that could hardly have been very cheerful, given Germany's critical situation during this stage of the war and the reality of constant air raids on population centers. The advance of the Red Army was also a concern, particularly to those soldiers whose families lived in East Prussia, Pomerania, and Silesia.

Letters from soldiers who had been assigned to the Company previously or who were recovering in hospitals also arrived. *Gefreiter* Georg Wierbitzsky, for

---

* The two men killed in action were *Füsilier* Leonhard Werres, who fell at Zweifallshammer, and *Obergefreiter* Hermann Vogt, who fell in Kesternich. Werres' body could not be recovered due to enemy fire and when *Füsilier Company 272* pulled out on 15 January, it was hastily covered with pine boughs. A search party sent out a week later failed to locate his remains. Vogt's body could not be recovered since the place where he fell lay under American fire. An inquiry sent to *Oberst* Burian of *Grenadier Regiment 980* failed to achieve any results. This illustrates that German units did exercise due concern about the disposition of soldier's remains, despite the stereotypical view of the *Wehrmacht*'s disdain of human life and suffering.

example, wrote a letter from his hospital bed in Wernigerode on 23 December wishing everyone in the company a Merry Christmas and a Happy New Year. He had been wounded in the thigh by a shell splinter on 13 December at Giesenheck. Another soldier, *Gefreiter* Otto Rohde, wounded the same day as Wierbitzsky, wrote a letter from his hospital bed in Quedlinburg on 21 December, wishing everyone well and thanking *Oberfeldwebel* Fuhrmeister for saving his life by ensuring that he was quickly evacuated. Such were the bonds of loyalty former members of the Company felt for their *Kameraden* still in harm's way.

An unpleasant duty that Kolb had to carry out was the investigation and prosecution of one of his own NCOs, *Unteroffizier* Gerhard Pleger, who was accused of gross dereliction of duty while in combat. Although the exact circumstances of the incident are unknown, the offense must have been rather serious. Pleger was tried by a court marshal convened by the judge advocate of the *272nd VGD* on 30 December and was condemned to one year, three months in confinement and loss of all rank and privileges. Due to the overall military situation and manpower shortage, the punishment was commuted to only three months, but had to be carried out in a penal unit where he would be given a chance to redeem his honor. Pleger was placed under arrest in the company area until his transfer to the Division's punishment platoon could be arranged for 14 January 1945.

This breathing space from the front lines was not only dedicated toward rest, relaxation, and administrative matters. While these functions were important, this time was also used to absorb new replacements and begin refresher training for the next mission. During its rest period in Hergarten from 19 December 1944 to 4 January 1945, the company received sixty-seven replacements (twenty-nine on 21 December from *Grenadier Replacement Battalion 440* and thirty-eight the next day from *Grenadier Replacement Battalion 167*), enough to bring the company back up to nearly full strength by 28 December. It also had received four replacements earlier that month, for a total of seventy-one replacements for the month of December 1944.

By the time of the Ardennes Offensive, the German manpower situation had become truly desperate and even more extreme measures were being taken to make up the shortfall. Thousands of men from the *Luftwaffe* and *Kriegsmarine* were being transferred directly to the *Heer* without any infantry training whatsoever and often without even receiving a set of army clothing. American intelligence reports from this period are replete with accounts of German prisoners being taken wearing field gray army overcoats over blue *Luftwaffe* uniforms. Naval personnel were being transferred to the army without even receiving army pay books. If a soldier received a week of training before joining his unit, he could count himself lucky. Many of the new recruits were seventeen-year-old youths or men over fifty.

The replacements that *Füsilier Company 272* received during this time were an exception. Perhaps in the recognition of their elite status, the new men assigned were a cut above average. Nearly all of them came from infantry assignments, though most of the veterans had been wounded and had just come off of convalescent status. Of these seventy-one men, most of the them were married and in their twenties or early thirties, though twenty-three were in the 1925 and 1926 year groups. The youngest replacement, born 18 December 1926, was *Füsilier* Fritz Sebald of Castrop, who was assigned four days after his eighteenth birthday. The oldest was *Gefreiter* Ernst Branch, born 23 April 1906 in Dortmund.

Replacement non-commissioned officers also arrived in the drafts to take the place of those who had fallen or had been wounded. *Feldwebel* Alois Mizioch was assigned to replace the platoon leader of *3rd Platoon, Feldwebel* Belder, whose jaw had been smashed by a bullet at Giesenheck and whose deputy, *Unteroffizier* Wilhelm Pfalzgraf, was posted as missing in action in Kesternich. Mizioch, born 14 May 1914 in Ratibor, was an Eastern Front veteran, who had been awarded the Iron Cross 1st and 2nd Classes, Infantry Assault Badge, Eastern Front Medal, and the Black Wound Badge while serving in *Grenadier Regiment 452* of the *252nd Infantry Division.*

Feldwebel Hellmonds of the *1st Platoon* had only been lightly wounded at Giesenheck and rejoined the Company during this period. *Feldwebeln* Reiners, Dirksen, and Etzmannsdorfer continued to serve as the platoon sergeants of *2nd, 4th,* and *5th Platoons,* respectively. To replace NCOs killed or wounded in action, *Unteroffiziere* Bartl, Groh, Groner, Jagielski, Kullmann, Nitschke, Pape, Prang, Sommerschuh, Sroka, and Walther were assigned from a variety of infantry and reconnaissance training and replacement units. Nearly all were veterans. All in all, the *Füsilier Company 272* received probably the best non-commissioned officers that were still available, but they still needed training and familiarization with their new squads and platoons before they could be committed to battle.

With his unit nearly at full strength again, *Oberleutnant* Kolb urged the men to make the most of the time available to rest and to prepare for future missions. Fortunately, the heavy fighting in the Ardennes had brought relative quiet to the *272nd VGD*'s sector and the men were able to celebrate Christmas in peace. The men cherished these few quiet moments, for they knew that it would not last long. They scrounged the snow-covered countryside for something to drink or for food to supplement their rations. In his diary for 31 December, Kurt Klein wrote, "Tomorrow is New Year's. We've got ourselves a goose!" After a small celebration with Kolb and the other senior noncoms, he wrote the following day that "A new year has begun. We are back with the company trains. I wish I could have gone to church. How nice it would be if there were no war."

During this idyllic pause in the fighting, training continued, for the replacements had but little time to familiarize themselves with their weapons, new comrades, and leaders. From 28 December until 3 January, the Company conducted squad- and platoon-level field exercises, concentrating on offensive operations and shock troop tactics. Throughout this period, the heavy rumble of artillery fire echoed from the scenes of heavy fighting far off to the southwest. Though the grenadier regiments carried out constant patrolling actions between Kesternich and Raffelsbrand that frequently involved exchanges of fire with American patrols, *Füsilier Company 272* was able to enjoy the Christmas holiday in peace. Few doubted that their section of the front would soon spring to life again, however. When it did, their relatively pleasant situation in Hergarten would come to an end.[21]

Generalfeldmarschall Walter Model, Commander of *Army Group B* from 17 August 1944 until 21 April 1945. *(NA)*

General der Panzertruppe Erich Brandenberger who led *Seventh Army* 28 August 1944 to 19 February 1945. *(Scherzer)*

General der Infanterie Gustav von Zangen, Commander, *Fifteenth Army* from 23 August 1944 to 17 April 1945. (*Scherzer*)

General der Panzertruppe Hasso von Manteuffel, who led *Fifth Panzer Army* the 10 September 1944 to 9 March 1945. *(NA)*

General der Infanterie Erich Straube, Commander of *LXXIV Corps* from 22 July to 16 December 1944. *(NA)*

General der Infanterie Carl Püchler, Straube's successor as Commander, *LXXIV Corps* from 16 December 1944 to 16 April 1945. (*Trees*)

General der Infanterie Otto Hitzfeld, who led *LXVII Corps* 12 December 1944 to 19 April 1945. *272nd VGD* served in his Corps between December 1944 and April 1945.

Oberst Georg Kossmala, the *272nd Volks-Grenadier Division*'s first commander from 30 September to 12 December 1944. (*NA*)

Generalmajor Eugen König succeeded Kossmala in command of the *272nd VGD* from 13 December 1945 until its end in the Ruhr Pocket on 18 April 1945. *(NA)*

One of the *272nd Volks-Grenadier Division*'s best-known officers was *Oberst* Ewald Burian, commander of *Grenadier Regiment 980*. *(Gehle)*

Hauptmann Adolf Thomae, commander, *2nd Battalion, Grenadier Regiment 980* (shown as a *Leutnant* prior to the war). *(Scherzer)*

Hauptmann Karl Schneider, Commander of *2nd Battalion, Grenadier Regiment 982*. He wept when his staff was sacrificed during a ill-advised counterattack. *(Schmidt)*

Oberleutnant Heinz Kolb, the first commander of *Füsilier Company 272* until his death 5 January 1945, pictured at the Döberitz Training Area, October 1944. (*Klein*)

Oberleutnant Helmut Aretz, commander of *Füsilier Company 272* during the counterattack at Herhahn 4 February 1945. *(Aretz)*

Oberleutnant Walter Ableiter, last leader of *Füsilier Company 272*, whose command ended on 25 March 1945 at the Bonefeld Forest Lodge. *(Wolfram)*

Leutnant Günther Schmidt, adjutant of *2nd Battalion Grenadier Regiment 982,* watched the 78th Infantry Division overrun his battalion near Silberscheidt, February 1945. *(Schmidt)*

Top Row (left to right):

Major Fritz Adrario, Commander, *Antitank Battalion 272* (shown here as a *Hauptmann*) in January 1945 shortly after being awarded the Knight's Cross. *(Adrario)*

Major Hans Uhl of the General Staff was König's *Ia,* or Operations Officer, from 13 December 1944 until the Division was disbanded in April 1945. A bright, capable officer, he served as König's right-hand man during some of the Division's most demanding assignments. Courtesy of Alex Moore.

Leutnant Josef Stefan, an Austrian and commander of *Assault Company 980,* was a brave officer who specialized in conducting raids through the American lines. *(Stefan)*

Bottom Row (left to right):

Leutnant Ernst Wegner, who served as *Füsilier Company 272*'s infantry howitzer platoon leader (shown here as a *Feldwebel*).

Hauptfeldwebel Hermann Fuhrmeister, the tough sergeant major of *Füsilier Company 272* from its inception until the end of the war. *(Fuhrmeister)*

Feldwebel Ludwig Hellmonds, platoon sergeant, 1st Platoon, *Füsilier Company 272.* Considered a daredevil by his fellow NCOs, he embodied the offensive mindset Hitler thought necessary for the success of the new *Volks-Grenadier Divisions*. He served as the right-hand man for the company's second-in-command, *Leutnant* Helmut Beyer, who doubled as the platoon leader.

Top Row (left to right):

Feldwebel Heinz Reiners, platoon leader of the 2nd Platoon, wears in the Reich Labor Service uniform he was wearing when he was drafted.

Feldwebel Kurt Belder, platoon leader of the 3rd Platoon, pictured here in a pre-war photograph.

Unteroffizier Fritz Fosselmann, leader of *Füsilier Company 272*'s mortar section. An *Afrikakorps* veteran and wounded several times in Russia, he knew that Germany had lost the war by the summer of 1944, but continued to soldier on out of patriotism and a sense of sheer professionalism. *(Fosselmann)*

Bottom Row (left to right):

Unteroffizier Heinrich Misskampf, forward observer for the company's mortar section and a close friend of Fritz Fosselmann. A professional like Fosselmann, he continued to serve although he knew the war was lost after the Normandy invasion.

Unteroffizier Ludwig Groh, leader of the heavy machine-gun section of the *4th Platoon*. A veteran of the Russian Front and Normandy, he was seriously wounded in action during the unsuccessful counterattack at Herhahn 5 February 1945.

Feldwebel Karl Etzmannsdorfer, platoon sergeant of the 5th Platoon. Formerly a *Luftwaffe Flak* gunner, was transferred to *Füsilier Company 272* in October 1944 where, according to his official evaluation, he performed his duties with "great efficiency."

Top Row (left to right):

Feldwebel Heinrich Dietz, the armorer of *Füsilier Company 272,* who was killed by an artillery shell fragment 27 February 1945 while serving with the company's trains in the village of Sinzenich.

Unteroffizier Kurt Klein, *Füsilier Company 272'*s Headquarters Troop leader, who accompanied the company commander into the field and supervised the company's radiomen, runners, medical personnel, and sniper section. *(Klein)*

Unteroffizier Fritz Johns (pictured here in Russia in 1943) *Füsilier Company 272'*s Company Supply Sergeant, was one of the few veterans of the old *216th Infantry Division.* (*Johns*)

Bottom Row (left to right):

Gefreiter Johann Anderka, mail clerk of *Füsilier Company 272.* Along with Ulrich Lorenz, he helped maintain the company's records including those for all outgoing and incoming mail.

Gefreiter Ulrich Lorenz served as the company clerk of *Füsilier Company 272* until the end of the war. He left the company's astonishingly detailed and well kept records in a farmhouse in the Harz Mountains at the end of the war.

Gefreiter Peter Moog, company headquarters runner for *Oberleutnant* Kolb. He was one of the few who survived the disastrous engagement near Simmerath on 5 January 1945, paradoxically because he had been assigned a suicide mission. (*Moog*)

Above (left to right):

Gefreiter Erwin Buchwalder, a gunner with 5th Platoon, *Füsilier Company 272,* who escaped from the disaster at Vlatten on 2 March 1945 only to be taken prisoner during the fighting in Hönningen on the Rhine two weeks later. Previously, he had served with the *Luftwaffe* as an aircraft ground crewman and had been transferred to the *Füsilier* Company in January 1945.

Gefreiter Otto Gunkel, *Grenadier Regiment 981,* a survivor of the horrific fighting around Gey in early December 1944 against the 4th Infantry Division and the fighting in Kesternich against the 78th Infantry Division one week later.

Grenadier Eduard Zacharuk, former sailor and ethnic German from Rumania on the steps of the Berlin Olympic Stadium, October 1944. In this photo, he still wears his field-gray *Kriegsmarine* uniform, which he continued to wear when he first saw combat in the Hürtgen Forest. *(Zacharuk)*

Oberst Ewald Burian, commander of *Grenadier Regiment 980;* his *Adjutant, Hauptmann* Hans Witscher (center); and his *aide-de-camp, Leutnant* Hermann Gehle (right) discuss their regiment's operations in Normandy, July 1944. *(Gehle)*

160

Feldwebel Kurt Dirksen, platoon leader of the *4th Schwere* (heavy weapons) Platoon, pictured on the right. This photograph was taken in October 1944 at a sidewalk café near Berlin-Falkensee along with his friend *Feldwebel* Hellmonds (second from right).

Hauptfeldwebel Hermann Fuhrmeister, seen here in his back yard in the city of Hildesheim with his wife while taking his last home leave in October 1944. *(Fuhrmeister)*

Gefreiter Hermann Heiermann, a platoon signalman and veteran of the Battle of Normandy, severely wounded within the first two weeks of the company's arrival near Rollesbroich by American artillery fire. Pictured here with his sibling. *(Heiermann)*

Grenadier with horse at the Schleiden rail yards. *Volks-Grenadier Divisions* relied upon horsepower for most of their transportation needs. Care and feeding of the thousands of horses each division was authorized consumed a large amount of attention from farriers, veterinarians, and drovers. *(Haslob)*

Unit clerks filling out *Wehrpasses* in log bunker somewhere on the Western Front, fall 1944.

Generalfeldmarschall Walter Model, commander of *Army Group B* (third from left), during a visit to the forward headquarters of the *246th Volks-Grenadier Division,* commanded by *Oberst* Gerhard Wilck (second from left). Model frequently made trips to the front line to ascertain conditions that his troops faced. *(NA)*

Photo of an unnamed young *Luftwaffe* airman who was transferred to *Füsilier Company 272* in October 1944. Upon joining the company, he had to turn in his *Luftwaffe* blue uniform for the field gray of the army.

Photo of an unnamed young *Kriegsmarine* sailor who was transferred to *Füsilier Company 272* in October 1944.

General der Infanterie Erich Straube (right), Commander, *LXXIV Corps* from 22 July to 16 December 1944 during a meeting with *Generalfeldmarschall* Model near Vossenack, mid-November 1944. *(Haslob)*

Shown above is a group shot of *Grenadier* Wilhelm Frey and others from the headquarters company of *Field Replacement Battalion 272* taken outside of a destroyed *Westwall* bunker in early November 1944, shortly after the battalion's arrival in the Hürtgen Forest. Frey stands in the center with the pipe. Within a month, Frey was assigned as a replacement to *Füsilier Company 272*. *(Frey)*

The Pulvermühle (powder mill) at Malsbenden, which served as main headquarters of the *272nd Volks-Grenadier Division* from mid-November 1944 until early February 1945, when the division was forced to move its headquarters to Vlatten. *(eifelmaler.info)*

Elements of the *272nd Volks-Grenadier Division* unloading their horse-drawn equipment from open rail cars at the rail yard in Schleiden after their two-day journey from Döberitz during the first week of November 1944. *(Haslob*

The "Waldhotel" in the hamlet of Malsbenden, which served as the temporary headquarters of the *272nd Volks-Grenadier Division* from early to mid-November 1944. It shared this headquarters with the *89th Infantry Division* during the relief in place of the latter division. This *Gasthaus* was later destroyed during Allied bombing raids that targeted the town of Gemünd. *(Haslob*

Volksgrenadiers manhandle horse-drawn wagons off of railcars after their arrival in Schleiden. Movements like these were carried out under constant threat of attack by the dreaded Allied fighter-bombers. The Germans were fortunate during the first half of November 1944, since low-lying clouds and poor flying weather frequently kept the *Jabos* grounded. *(Haslob*

Shown here is one of the bunkers in the vicinity of Rollesbroich occupied by *Füsilier Company 272* during its defense of the area from early November until the end of the month. Facing west, this bunker covered approaches to the Kall and American positions in Lammersdorf. *(CMH)*

Once they had arrived at their various railheads in Schleiden, Kall, and Mechernich, the regiments had to march on foot to their forward positions, since the fuel-starved *Wehrmacht* could not afford to use trucks for routine movements. Here, a group of camouflaged *Volksgrenadiers* march along the serpentine road above Gemünd towards their new positions along the *Westwall*. *(Haslob)*

A group of young *Volksgrenadiers* adjust their chinstraps as they prepare to move out for a mission on their bicycles. Two combat elements in the *272nd Volks-Grenadier Division* were equipped with these, *First Battalion, Grenadier Regiment 980* (with over 400 bicycles) and *Füsilier Company 272* (with 166). Although bicycle-equipped troops could not move nearly as quickly as those equipped with half-tracks or trucks, they still had more tactical mobility compared to foot-mobile infantry.

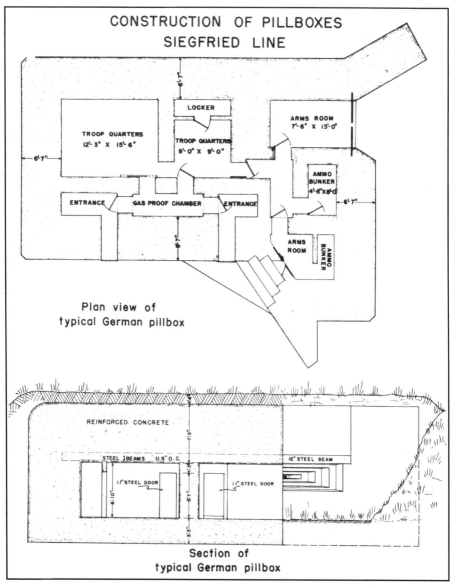

CONSTRUCTION OF PILLBOXES
SIEGFRIED LINE

LOCKER

ARMS ROOM
7'-6" X 13'-0"

TROOP QUARTERS
12'-3" X 15'-6"

TROOP QUARTERS
9'-0" X 9'-0"

AMMO BUNKER
4'-6"X8'-0"

ENTRANCE   GAS PROOF CHAMBER   ENTRANCE

ARMS ROOM

AMMO BUNKER

Plan view of
typical German pillbox

REINFORCED CONCRETE

STEEL I BEAMS 11.8" O.C.

12" STEEL BEAM

1.1" STEEL DOOR

1.1" STEEL DOOR

Section of
typical German pillbox

Floor plan of a typical late-1930s *Regelbau* bunker of the *Limes* Program found in large number in the Hürtgen Forest. Thousands of these bunkers from over two-dozen types comprised the German *Westwall* fortification zone that ran hundreds of miles from the Dutch border in the northwest to the Swiss border in the southeast. The men of *Füsilier Company 272* occupied several bunkers similar to the type shown here when they first arrived in the vicinity of Rollesbroich and when they moved to the Buhlert Hill in early December 1944. *(US Army)*

Hauptmann Adolf Thomae with his staff from *2nd Battalion, Grenadier Regiment 980,* taken late-November 1944 when his battalion was occupying a reserve position east of the village of Bergstein. From left to right, *Oberleutnant* Kurt Hake, commander, *14th Company; Leutnant* August Englbrecht, German Cross in Gold recipient; *Hauptmann* Thomae; *Feldwebel* Katheder; *Leutnant* Beilstein; *Leutnant* Klaus von Below; and *Feldwebel* Hardt. *(Hake)*

The main dressing station in the farmyard at Gerstenhof, used by both the *89th Infantry Division* and the *272nd Volks-Grenadier Division* between November 1944 and February 1945. One of the outbuildings shown here concealed a *Westwall* bunker that was not discovered by the Allies until the station was occupied by American troops in February 1945. *(Haslob)*

Shortly after arrival in the Hürtgen Forest, the division commander, *Oberst* Georg Kossmala, made it a point to visit each regiment's frontline positions. In this picture, Kossmala (2nd from right) visits the command post of *Grenadier Regiment 982* in the Tiefenbachtal, established in Bunker 125. From the right, *Oberstleutnant* Paul Rösener, regimental commander; Kossmala, *Hauptmann* Karl Schneider, commander of the *2nd Battalion;* and *Oberleutnant* von der Malsberg, Kossmala's aide-de-camp. *(Schmidt)*

General der Panzertruppe Erich Brandenberger (left), Commander, *Seventh Army* from 28 August 1944 to 19 February 1945, seen here in mid-November 1944 with *Generalmajor* Walter Bruns, commander, *89th Infantry Division* near Vossenack. *(Haslob)*

Leutnant Josef Stefan in the command bunker of *Oberst* Ewald Burian's *Grenadier Regiment 980* on the Buhlert Hill getting a light from a lantern, December 1944. *(Stefan)*

Leutnant Klaus von Below, a friend of Stefan's, inside the command bunker of *Grenadier Regiment 980*. *(Stefan)*

Ordinary German infantryman photographed walking through town of Schmidt to the front lines, late November 1944. It was upon men such as these that the German defense in the Hürtgen Forest relied for nearly six months. *(Haslob)*

A leader of a foot patrol observes American frontline positions in the Hürtgen Forest, November 1944. He is armed with an MP-44 assault rifle, one of the most advanced weapons introduced during the war. *(Haslob)*

Crew of 120mm mortar from *Heavy Mortar Battalion 628* in an apple orchard located on the outskirts of Schmidt, mid-November 1944. This battalion supported both the *89th Infantry Division* (which lacked its own heavy mortars at the time) and later, the *272nd Volks-Grenadier Division* until it was withdrawn in mid-December 1944 to participate in the Ardennes Offensive. Note the extreme youth of the crew, an indicator of the increasingly younger year groups being called up for service in the *Wehrmacht* during 1944. *(Haslob)*

German soldiers receiving supplies on the shell-blasted slopes of the Teufelsley, northern tip of the Buhlert Hill, late November 1944. *(Haslob)*

A knocked-out *Jagd-panzer IV/70* of the *3rd Panzer-Grenadier Division,* abandoned near the base of Castle Hill at Bergstein, December 1944. *(Signal Corps)*

Another *Jagdpanzer IV/70* of *3rd Panzer-Grenadier Division* captured inside the town of Bergstein by troops of CCR, 5th Armored Division after the unsuccessful German attack of 6 December 1944. *(Signal Corps)*

Weapons of the *Volks-grenadier.* Here, a soldier on the Western Front awaits the next Allied assault, March 1945. Arrayed alongside him are an MP-44 assault rife, G-43 semi-automatic rifle, and the devastatingly effective *Panzerfaust* antitank rocket.

174

Der Buhlert Hill

Raffelsbrand-Ochsenkopf

Simonskall

Kall River

View from the Vossenack ridge looking southwest towards the Kall Valley, where the hamlet of Simonskall can be seen in the middle background. On the horizon to the left can be seen the hill mass known to the locals as *"Der Buhlert."* *Füsilier Company 272* occupied defensive positions along this hill during the first two weeks of December 1944. On the horizon to the right looms the forested hillside known as the Raffelsbrand-Ochsenkopf, where fighting raged for possession of the formidable *Westwall* bunker complex.

The rebuilt smithy at Zweifallshammer, location of *Füsilier Company 272*'s forward dressing station during its attack of 13–14 December 1944. To the right looms the eastern tip of Giesenheck. In the foreground flows the Kall River.

The castle at Nideggen after its destruction by American bombing and artillery fire during the struggle for Bergstein and Castle Hill in early December 1944. It briefly served as the forward division headquarters of the *89th Infantry Division*. It has since been restored. *(Haslob)*

Major Fritz Adrario, fourth from the left, with his staff aboard his half-tracked command vehicle, a *Sonderkraftfahrzeuge 251/ 3* Model D in Kesternich, December 1944. Adrario's communications section leader, *Unteroffizier* Paul Seitz, is second from the left. On the far right in the foreground stands *Leutnant* Beer, his communications platoon leader. Adrario personally led the counterattack on 15 December 1944 that retook Kesternich. *(Ips)*

Two damaged *Jagdpanzer 39(t) Hetzers* of *Antitank Battalion 272* abandoned in Kesternich after its fall to troops of the 311th Infantry Regiment, 78th Infantry Division, January 1945. *(Signal Corps)*

With the onset of the Ardennes Offensive, the Hürtgen Forest became relatively dormant after the Battle of Kesternich. Heavy snowfall during this period further compounded the inactivity. In this picture, a young *Volksgrenadier* mans a forward observation post on the edge of the forest south of Simmerath. The hills in the background mark the edge of the German-Belgian border. Clad in a camouflaged winter combat suit, with a "potato masher" hand grenade Model 24 lying nearby, he awaits the US Army's next move. *(NA)*

A dead *Volksgrenadier* and his horse, killed by American interdiction shelling while bringing up food and mail to front line positions, early February 1944. The insulated food containers have been wrapped in straw to reduce any metallic sounds, but apparently this measure did not help. The light wagon to which this horse had been harnessed was the standard model *Infanteriekarren If.8* (light infantry cart). *(Hohenstein/Schulz)*

Men of a *Volks-Artillery Corps* near the Roer Dams carrying 150mm shells towards firing position, outskirts of Neuenhof. While the Allied forces were able to rely upon trucks to move ammunition to artillery firing positions, in contrast the Germans had to resort to manpower to bring the shells forward. *(Haslob)*

178

Soldiers of the 311th Infantry Regiment, 78th Infantry Division stand next to a dead *Volks-grenadier* from *2nd Battalion, Grenadier Regiment 980* in newly retaken Kesternich, 31 January 1945. *(Signal Corps)*

The Schwammenauel Dam after its penstocks had been damaged by demolition teams from *Combat Engineer Battalion 272,* rendering them inoperable and unable to stem the flow of water from the reservoir. The waters of the Roer River that were released created a flood that gave the Germans a three-week reprieve from the Allied Offensive. *(Haslob)*

Bedraggled prisoners from the *272nd Volksgrenadier Division* shortly after being captured by the US 78th Infantry Division during the second battle of Kesternich. *(Signal Corps)*

An aerial view of the town of Hönningen on the eastern bank of the Rhine burning after it fell to the troops of the 99th "Checkerboard" Infantry Division, 18 March 1945. The cluster of smokestacks on the right of the picture (marked with a circle) shows the areas where *Hauptmann* Thomae's battalion made its last stand before being taken prisoner. *(Signal Corps)*

The final levy. *Volksgrenadiers* from an unnamed *March Battalion* fresh from a Training and Replacement unit in the heart of Germany, march towards the Rhine Front and an uncertain future, mid-March 1945. Equipped with small arms and *Panzerfausts*, they proved no match for the modern, highly mechanized Allied forces.

German Volksgrenadiers taken prisoner during the fighting for the Remagen bridgehead being marched away by troops of the 78th Infantry Division. *(Signal Corps)*

The Mariawald Abbey, which served at times as the main dressing station of the *272nd Volks-Grenadier Division* as well as a regimental headquarters for one of its regiments during the last days of February 1945. Heavily bombed by the Allies despite the Red Cross markings, both *Volksgrenadiers* and Trappist Monks sought shelter in its cellars, used in peacetime as the monastery's beer cellars. Photo taken April 2001.

View of the Schwammenauel Reservoir looking southeast from the Eschauler Hill, one kilometer south of the town of Schmidt. Troops from the 78th Infantry Division finally wrested this area from the *272nd Volks-Grenadier Division* on 8 February 1945. The Schwammenauel Dam can be seen in the distance.

The primary school in the village of Hergarten, which served as the rear area headquarters of the *272nd Volks-Grenadier Division*. The company trains of *Füsilier Company 272,* as well as those of the Grenadier Regiments at one time or another, were located in this village, which served as a rest area for the division's soldiers despite the attention paid to it by Allied fighter bombers. Photo taken April 2001.

The *Falkenhagener* School in the town of Falkensee, which served as *Füsilier Company 272*'s enlisted man's barracks between 18 September and 5 November 1944 while it trained at the nearby Döberitz Training Area. It has since been restored to its original purpose. Officers and NCOs were billeted with families living in the town. Photo taken Summer 2003. *(Heckner)*

The German Wargraves Cemetery in Vossenack, where hundreds of members of the *272nd Volks-Grenadier Division* who fell in the Hürtgen Forest between November 1944 and February 1945 are buried. *Generalfeldmarschall* Model also lies buried here alongside his men.

The German Wargraves Cemetery in the Mariawald Forest. In distance lies the Mariawald Abbey, site of the *272nd Volks-Grenadier Division*'s main field hospital. Hundreds of soldiers who were killed in action or who died as a result of wounds, including dozens of members of *Füsilier Company 272,* lie buried here in this beautiful and well-maintained cemetery.

10

The Interlude
of January 1945

Although the Battle of Bulge raged unabated a few dozen kilometers to the south, at the beginning of January 1945 relative quiet had settled upon the troops on both sides occupying positions in the Hürtgen Forest. During this lull in the action, most of the activity that took place on both sides was limited to the firing of artillery concentrations, improving defensive positions and aggressive patrolling. As US First Army continued to adjust to the German's rapid initial gains in the Ardennes, corps headquarters were shuffled about in order to control the forces being massed to conduct a counterstrike.

One result of this was that the VII Corps was ordered to assume responsibility for the area encompassing Kesternich from V Corps effective 2200 hours on 18 December. Shortly thereafter, VII Corps' commander, Major General Lawton Collins, ordered the 8th and 78th Infantry Divisions to carry out a series of small-scale raids on the bunkers still held by the Germans along this section of the *Westwall* in order to tie down enemy reserves and to distract German attention from the Ardennes. Facing the Americans, the *85th Infantry Division* and *272nd VGD* of *General der Infanterie* Karl Püchler's *LXXIV Corps* were ordered to defend their positions and not to yield so much as an inch of ground, including all of the *Westwall* bunkers still in their possession. (For an overview of the general situation at the beginning of January 1945, refer to Map 9.)

A heavy snowfall in early January added up to two feet of snow throughout most of the battlefield occupied by the *272nd VGD* and the 78th Infantry Division. This, combined with below freezing temperatures, contributed to the difficulties faced by both sides when they conducted any sort of operation. Frostbite, trench foot, and hypothermia were a constant threat, particularly to the soldiers occupying front line fighting positions, where shelter was inadequate and warming fires unerringly attracted the attention of the other side's artillery and mortars.

To replace the heavy casualties suffered at Kesternich and Simmerath, the American and German divisions both absorbed thousands of new replacements during the month of January, though König's division was only able to build his three *Volks-Grenadier* regiments up to about fifty percent strength. While the combatants dedicated considerable effort to the reconstitution and training of their regiments, battalions, and companies, neither side could afford to allow their troops to remain idle.

The missions of both divisions were remarkably similar—tie down as much of the enemy as possible in order to prevent him from reinforcing the main battle being fought in the Ardennes. With this in mind, both sides put considerable effort into improving and expanding their defensive positions, while at the same time maintaining a high level of vigilance. This translated into a proliferation of patrols and raiding parties being sent out, wherein each side sought to harass and to tie down the other while learning as much as possible about their opponent's order of battle and future intentions from prisoners taken during such operations. Navigating the shattered woods in the Hürtgen Forest was a hazardous undertaking even in the best of circumstances. It was even riskier in the dead of winter when sound carried great distances and when movement was easily detected. Nevertheless, both sides, most notably the 78th Infantry Division, undertook a considerable number of infantry raids and aggressive company-sized patrols.

Few prisoners were actually taken by either side and even fewer positions were lost, but these activities served the purpose of keeping the men sufficiently alert and managed to inculcate a certain level of aggressiveness that was needed when large-scale operations resumed.

Both sides made tactical innovations to conserve manpower and deny their opponent the information they sought. The Germans used command detonated mines and explosives. American patrols noted that on several occasions, forward observation posts of the *272nd VGD* electrically detonated these devices when approached, serving the dual purposes of alerting their comrades to the approaching Americans and inflicting casualties, an interesting early (and apparently successful) use of improvised explosive devices. Records of the 78th Infantry Division also state that their own raids met stiff resistance whenever they encountered German front line positions, which had been heavily mined and laced with concertina wire.[1] The Germans, for their part, also reported having little success in infiltrating the American front lines.

Artillery and mortar fire remained a constant danger, although it was less intense than it had been the previous month due to limits placed on ammunition resupply by both sides because of the fighting still raging in the Ardennes. Any careless movement observed in the immediate area of the front lines on either side, however, was certain to draw fire. American spotter planes continued to plague the Germans, forcing them to conduct nearly all troop movements and resupply operations at night.

The penalties for carelessness were harsh. On one occasion, an artillery observer in a spotter plane saw German troops in Strauch standing in line at a field kitchen and called fire upon them "with excellent effect."[2] Both sides also preferred the use of indirect fires against infantry patrols, since neither wanted to expose their men to capture and interrogation any more than absolutely necessary. American harassment fire was the order of the day, with certain well-known crossroads, assembly areas, and highway intersections in towns and villages being hit repeatedly with artillery.

On the German side, because of the continuing artillery ammunition shortage, similar targets on the American side could not be engaged nearly as often, much to the frustration of the forward observers. At one point near the end of January, the forward observer of *3nd Battalion, Artillery Regiment 272* in Strauch could clearly see with his naked eye a long column of American supply trucks moving unconcernedly along the road between Rollesbroich and Lammersdorf. Such a movement in daylight by the Germans would have resulted in almost immediate attack by the opponent's artillery or fighter-bombers.

Officially, regimental headquarters denied the supporting battery permission to fire by because of ammunition rationing that limited expenditures to only two rounds for each gun per day. Fortunately for the forward observer, the supporting battery in question had surreptitiously accumulated a number of extra shells, "off the books" so to speak, and was able to engage the trucks with good effect without incurring the wrath of regimental headquarters. The artillerymen thought it was the least they could do to support the infantrymen, who were located in front line fighting positions enduring the awful cold and primitive living conditions.[3]

By this point in the campaign, chances for Germany's ultimate victory appeared bleak to just about everyone. Not only had the Western Allies closed up to—and in many cases crossed over—Germany's frontiers, but the Red Army was rampaging across East Prussia, Pomerania, and Silesia. What then, did the average German soldier think of all of this? How did he manage to find the strength to continue to fight so effectively while living in deplorable circumstances? One indication of the mind of the average *Landser* in the *272nd VGD* can be discerned in the following passage written by an officer of *Grenadier Regiment 980* in a letter home:

The icy cold creeps through the boots and into the feet of the soldier standing watch behind the machine gun, through his bones and underneath his overcoat. If only his feet had not gotten wet! A feeling of defeat comes over him. He reproaches himself because he knows that his feet always freeze whenever his socks are damp. But in spite of this he know that he still has to keep standing for another half an hour. Then his comrade will arrive to relieve him and he will be able to crawl back into his foxhole and get some sleep. It will then be his comrade's turn to be alert, because the enemy has already reached the nearest hedgerow over there. Tomorrow afternoon it is the grenadier's turn to pick up hot food for his squad at the company command post, located in a basement where there is a warm stove. All of his thoughts revolve around the cold and the longing for warmth. But until then, he has to stand here and hold out. For nearly four weeks his company has been in these positions. He will have to bear it a little longer. The company must continue to hold its position, so his company commander had said to him again the night before, as he crawled from position to position encouraging his men. The position must be held at all cost, he said, and the men must not go soft on him. One night not long ago *Oberst* Burian had also come by, since it was impossible to move during the day, and had asked each man if he could rely on him to do his duty. *"Jawohl, Herr Oberst!"* each of them had said. Then he passed out cigarettes, so that each man got at least a couple. After he had been relieved that night, the grenadier crawled into the bottom of his hole and smoked one, since if he stood up, the enemy would notice the cigarette's glowing ember. If it wasn't for this icy wind! he thought. But in Russia things were much worse. That was the only consolation. There, you had to pay more attention, so that you didn't immediately get frostbite. Yes, the *Oberst* could rely on him, just as he had in Russia and in Normandy at Caen. His other comrades thought the same thoughts and silently carried out their duty. The only ones who understood what it was like in the front line were those who shared the same foxholes for days and weeks with the Grenadiers. There are no songs to sing and no words to describe the quiet, hard, and taciturn life of the infantryman in combat.[4]

During early January 1945, one area in particular that drew American attention was a small German salient comprising a line of bunkers and troop shelters a few kilometers deep that stabbed in a westerly direction deep into the sector of the 78th Infantry Division immediately south of the towns of Simmerath and Bickerath. This salient, one of the few that still encompassed parts of the original *Westwall,* threatened the flanks of the American salient to the north that reached eastwards as far as the western edge of Kesternich, the scene of the heavy fighting that had taken place two weeks earlier.

To reduce the threat of a possible German attack against the Kesternich salient, the 78th Infantry Division issued orders on 2 January 1945 that directed its 311th Infantry Regiment to carry out "small demonstrations" on the morning of 3 January. American patrol activity was stepped up that night and Major Edwin C. Gatz' 1st Battalion, 311th Infantry Regiment developed plans for blowing up any remaining bunkers and troop shelters in its defensive sector. The patrols netted only three prisoners that night, who confirmed the presence of *2nd Battalion, Grenadier Regiment 981.*[5]

On the morning of 3 January, dense fog impaired visibility for the impending attack against Bunker 27, a so-called troop shelter that had been designated as one of the objectives for Company B, 1st Battalion, 311th Infantry. Bunker 27 was located about 500 meters south of the village of Bickerath (see Map 10) and had been erected in 1938 during the initial *Westwall* construction program using 380 cubic meters of concrete. Built according to the *Regelbau* (general construction plan) as a Type 11 bunker, it housed up to twenty-seven soldiers and had a single machine-gun embrasure.[6] With walls and ceiling to up 1.5 meters thick, it would be difficult to overcome with infantry weapons. Bunker 27 was vulnerable to attack from the rear, however, where its defenses were minimal and where its occupants had a limited field of vision. Fortunately for the troops of Company B, Bunker 27's sole machine-gun port faced to the west. Due to the nature of the

American's salient, which ran from an east to west direction relative to the bunker's orientation, they would be approaching the bunker's northeast side, away from the firing ports, and would not be exposed to the direct fire of the defenders until they were practically on top of their objective.

During the previous evening, the German defenders had been on high alert, firing automatic weapons and a large number of flares throughout the night. Firing had quieted down by the morning of 3 January, leading the Americans to assume that the Germans were unaware of the impending attack. To ensure that the attackers were able to get as close as possible to the bunker before being seen and engaged by its defenders, Second Lieutenant Gus Hank, platoon leader of the 2nd Platoon of Company B, decided to have his men follow or "hug" the creeping artillery preparatory fire on the bunker as closely as possible while the Germans had their heads down. At 1030 hours, Hank's Platoon and the Weapons Platoon from Captain Paul Foran's Company B, 311th Infantry, supported by a squad of engineers from Company C, 303rd Combat Engineer Battalion, advanced rapidly across 500 meters of open snow-covered ground.

Once they reached the bunker undetected, the 2nd Platoon, supported by men of Second Lieutenant John Robinson's Weapons Platoon, employed satchel charges and other demolitions to blow off the entrance doors. With its inhabitant immobilized by the blast as well as by several hand grenades thrown into its embrasures, Hank and his men quickly seized Bunker 27. Nearly twenty inhabitants of the bunker were killed outright and two captured. Sixteen *Volksgrenadiers*, including men from *1st Battalion, 689th Grenadier Regiment* from the *246th VGD*, a unit that had not been previously identified in the sector, as well as several men of the regimental engineer platoon from *Grenadier Regiment 981* were taken prisoner that day by Company B.

The GIs of Company B were not only interested in conducting the raid, but wanted the bunkers themselves for their own comfort and protection. While bunkers were usually dark and damp, they were infinitely preferable to a soggy foxhole and were a reliable shield against incoming artillery fire. According to the official history of the 311th Infantry:

> Patrolling was Joe's main occupation with assaults on pillboxes for diversion. The 1st Battalion found one pillbox known as number 27 that looked inviting and which might have furnished a little cover from the weather if they could take it and if Company C of the 303rd Engineers would refrain from blowing it before we could get the prisoners out.[7]

After the war, veterans of Company B failed to appreciate this attempt at humor, since assaulting pillboxes was one of the most harrowing and danger-prone assignments an infantryman could possibly be given. The action that took place between 3 and 5 January was no exception and proved to be the Company's bloodiest of the war.

Their objective for the day secured, the men of Company B's 2nd and 4th Platoons settled in for the night and prepared to ward off the inevitable German counterattack. Communications wire was laid to the rear and artillery fire was registered so that it could be quickly and accurately be called upon in an emergency. The Americans could hear sounds of battle a few kilometers to the south, where the neighboring 9th Infantry Division was carrying out similar small-scale attacks of its own.

Although they were prepared for the usual German response, no counterattack came that night, which must have struck the men of Company B as odd. Its men, who after three weeks of combat in the Hürtgen Forest could now count themselves as veterans, knew how the Germans reacted whenever bunkers or troop shelters were lost. No enemy counterattack came during the day either, though German artillery and mortar fire was heavy. According to the regimental after action report, some 530 rounds of artillery and 600 rounds of mortar fire fell in the 311th Infantry sector on 4 January alone.

Taking advantage of the absence of any German counterattacks, the assault troops from the two platoons from Company B experimented on 4 January with various methods of knocking out bunkers in order to determine the most effective technique to deal with them. Though the neighboring German-occupied Bunker 24 was only 300 meters away, it remained silent, even though its occupants had a direct line of sight to Bunker 27 from the machine-gun turret on its roof. It snowed heavily throughout the day, providing some concealment for the Americans who freely moved in and around Bunker 27. A team from Company C, 303rd Engineer Battalion provided instruction in the use of the new shaped charge explosives (called "beehive" charges by the troops), which promised to be especially effective against bunkers and other fortifications.

The men of *Füsilier Company 272* were unaware of any of these events. They spent 3 January in Hergarten, where they continued training and preparing for future action. Other elements within the division had suffered such heavy losses during the past several weeks, especially in specialists personnel such as medics, artillerymen, and radio operators, that apparently an order went out to evenly distribute soldiers with critical specialties to insure that every unit had a least the minimum number of such personnel needed to operate effectively. Since *Füsilier Company 272* still had its full complement, it was ordered to transfer some of its men to other units that lacked their skills. A large number of specialist personnel, thirteen in all, were transferred out of the company that day to other units in the division, bringing its total strength down to 170 men.

Late that afternoon, the operations officer of the *272nd VGD* contacted *Oberleutnant* Kolb and informed him to prepare the company for an important mission, though he did not say what it was. All Kolb was told was that he was to move his men immediately to the village of Dedenborn, on the division's far left flank, where Kolb would receive a situation briefing from the commander of *Grenadier Regiment 981, Oberstleutnant* Kleinkorres. It seemed that *Füsilier*

Company 272 would once again be employed as the division's *Feuerwehr* to retrieve the situation, whatever it was. Packing hurriedly, the men loaded their field equipment on their bicycles and finally set out for Dedenborn at 2200 hours.

The company arrived at Dedenborn in the early morning hours of 4 January and the men took advantage of a few hours' of rest. In the meantime, *Oberleutnant* Kolb was briefed by Kleinkorres on the mission, which was short and succinct: Retake Bunker 27 one kilometer southwest of Simmerath. Peter Moog, who was there with Kolb, recalled later that he thought that they were supposed to rescue some combat engineers who had been trapped in the bunker (evidently these men were from the engineer platoon of *Grenadier Regiment 981*).[8]

The attack was to begin at 1730 hours that afternoon. After being briefed, Kolb moved up to Bunker 94, located 800 meters southwest of Simmerath, where he linked up with *Hauptmann* Günther Ragnow, the commander of the supported unit, *2nd Battalion, Grenadier Regiment 981*. Taking advantage of the remaining daylight, the main body of the company had meanwhile departed Dedenborn at 1430 hours. Leaving their bicycles behind, they marched northwest along the bottom of the steep ravine that ran from Dedenborn to Huppenbroich, arriving on the outskirts of the latter village by 1530 hours. The tracked *RSO*s towing the two infantry howitzers followed.

The company then moved several hundred meters to its forward assembly area located near the destroyed mill in the Tiefenbach gorge, where it was directed to await the arrival of two guides from *2nd Battalion, Grenadier Regiment 981* who were supposed to lead them to their attack positions. The guides failed to show up, however. After waiting an hour, *Feldwebeln* Hellmonds and Dirksen, not wanting to leave the company exposed at the mill much longer, set out to find *Oberleutnant* Kolb, who had gone forward previously to coordinate the attack and to conduct a quick personal reconnaissance.

Finally linking up with their commander, they sent a runner to fetch the rest of the company, which finally arrived in its designated attack position near Bunker 94 by 1730 hours. At 1830 hours, Kolb assembled *Leutnant* Wegner, his five platoon leaders, and his squad leaders, and briefed them on their upcoming mission. Their scheduled attack was already an hour late and platoon leaders had only ten or fifteen minutes at the most to orient their own men. One survivor, *Unteroffizier* Josef Sommerschuh of *3rd Platoon,* stated afterwards that neither *Oberleutnant* Kolb nor any of the men had been provided even the slightest useful information about the terrain and enemy defenses in the vicinity of Bunker 27. Nor had there been any time to make a thorough inspection of the area in daylight.

Essentially, the company had to conduct a night attack across several hundred meters of open terrain before they reached their objective, Bunker 27, and the positions occupied by Company B, 311th Infantry immediately to the east of the bunker. Their line of departure was a hedgerow approximately 200 meters to the south. Over a foot of snow blanketed the area. About 300 meters to the left or west of the company's line of departure lay Bunkers 24 and 25, held by troops of *1st Battalion, Grenadier Regiment 689* of the *246th Volks-Grenadier Division.*

The company's line of departure was held by *7th Company, Grenadier Regiment 981,* commanded by *Leutnant* Martin, through whose defensive positions Kolb's men had to pass en route to their objective. *Füsilier Company 272* had to advance directly along the boundary between two divisions, never a favorable location in which to conduct an attack. As in any war since the dawn of the modern era, coordination errors tend to multiply along a seam whenever two large formations share boundaries with one another and this day proved no different. Unless an exchange of information or communications measures had been arranged in advance, any coordination between the units once the fighting started would be difficult, if not impossible. *Second Battalion, Grenadier Regiment 981* was responsible for insuring this coordination was carried out, but evidence indicates that this was done poorly, if at all.

Oberleutnant Kolb briefed the plan as follows: *Feldwebel* Hellmonds's *1st Platoon* was placed on the left and was designated as the company's main effort for the upcoming attack. Two of his squads, the 2nd and 3rd, would approach Bunker 27 from the right and roll up any American defensive positions located in front of the bunker. Once that was carried out, they would attack the bunker frontally. The 1st Squad would attack to the left of the bunker and encircle it from the rear, where it would kill or capture any of its occupants who tried to escape.

On Hellmonds's right, *Feldwebel* Reiners's *2nd Platoon* would keep abreast of Hellmonds's platoon, protecting its right flank. Once the bunker was taken, Reiners and his men would roll up American positions to the right and set up a hasty defense to ward off any counterattack. The company's reserve consisted of *Feldwebel* Mizioch's *3rd Platoon,* which would follow *1st Platoon* and cover its left flank. Once Bunker 27 had been taken, Mizioch and his men would fan out to the left of Hellmonds's platoon. *Oberleutnant* Kolb and the company's command group would accompany *Feldwebel* Hellmonds's platoon in the attack, keeping a few meters to the rear.

Feldwebel Dirksen's heavy machine gun section, consisting of two MG-42s, would take up an overwatch position in the hedgerow immediately behind *2nd Platoon* and provide covering fire for both *1st* and *2nd Platoons* as they advanced. The medium mortar section, with its two 80mm mortars, co-located in the village of Huppenbroich with the mortar platoon of *8th Company, Grenadier Regiment 981,* where it would coordinate its fires with those of its *2nd Battalion.*[9]

The infantry howitzer platoon, under *Leutnant* Wegner, would fire in support from its positions in Eicherscheid, where it was co-located with the guns of *13th Company, Grenadier Regiment 981.* Fire support plans were coordinated with *Grenadier Regiment 981* and the company's forward observer section was located close to the front to direct supporting fire.

Ultimately, *Füsilier Company 272* committed 133 men to this attack (out of 170 assigned). Operations began when the company crossed its line of departure at 1910 hours, nearly two hours late, with *1st Platoon* on the left, *2nd Platoon* on the right, and *3rd Platoon* behind *1st Platoon*. Kolb's *Volksgrenadiers* crawled silently through the deep snow, almost invisible in their white winter combat suits. Snow continued to fall, a factor that should have aided the attackers. For the first few minutes, everything went according to plan and the attack went unde-tected by the Americans. Things began to go wrong shortly thereafter, though.

As planned, the supporting artillery and mortars began to fire in order to pin the Americans in their foxholes. Rounds began to land short, however, exploding among Kolb's men and inflicting considerable damage, indicating that the fire direction center of *Grenadier Regiment 981* had made a serious miscalculation. Squad leaders shouted orders and the wounded cried out *Sani!* (short for *Sanitäter*, or medic). Working feverishly, the medics heroically crawled back and forth at great personal risk through the fire to the wounded, providing first aid where they could and bringing back as many as possible to the aid station at Bunker 34.

To make matters worse, the forward screening elements in front of Bunker 24 from the neighboring *246th VGD,* mistaking the noise and movement to their front for an American attack, began to fire on Hellmonds's *1st Platoon,* wound-ing one of his squad leaders and pinning down the rest of his platoon. Evidently, they had not been notified of the impending attack by their own unit. *Feldwebel* Dirksen, hurrying forward with his heavy machine gun section, positioned his guns about 150 meters south of the American positions forward of Bunker 27 and began firing short bursts in support at 2030 hours.

The resulting noise and tracer fire roused the troops of the two platoons from Company B, 311th Infantry Regiment to their feet and they began to fire in return. The Americans quickly called in their own artillery on the attackers who had, in the meantime, managed to have their own supporting fire lifted. American 105mm and 155mm shells soon began to fall across the open field south of Simmerath, showering the Germans with metal fragments and rock-hard frozen clumps of earth. Hellmonds and the rest of his platoon were now completely pinned down in the open field between Bunkers 24 and 27, directly to the south-east of the latter bunker. Trapped immediately in front of the forward American positions, Hellmonds and his men had no choice but to hug the earth and wait for the artillery fire to lift before they could go anywhere. Only the darkness seemed to work in their favor.

To Hellmonds's right, *Feldwebel* Reiners and his platoon had found the going easier and had managed to reach the forward area of the American-held trench-line that lay east of the bunker, but could advance no farther without *1st Platoon* closing up on their left to protect their open flank. Some of Reiners's men engaged in hand-to-hand combat with the defenders, but failed to take the trench line, and after losing several men killed or captured, were driven back. To Hellmonds's rear, *Feldwebel* Miziock and his men were also pinned down and began to suffer casualties. With his entire attack stalled, Kolb decided at 0050 hours to order the company to remain where it was. They would try again a little later after he had sorted things out. Through the use of runners like Peter Moog, Kolb was able to notify *Feldwebeln* Reiners and Dirksen that he was going to renew the attack at 0100 hours.

The two platoons from Company B, 311th Infantry Regiment, secure behind their curtain of supporting artillery fire, had no idea of the size of Kolb's assault force and estimated that it had been attacked by nothing greater in strength than a platoon. The German advance had been halted so completely that not a single *Volksgrenadier* had successfully penetrated into Company B's position. Six Germans lay dead in and around the American's foxholes where they had fallen. The company's thorough preparations to defend itself against a counterattack were now paying off. Several wounded Germans, clad in white overgarments, lay crying out in pain immediately forward of the American's positions.[10]

The confusion, compounded by the darkness and American fire, prevented Kolb from continuing his attack until 0200. Even then this renewed attack was brought to an immediate halt, again with heavy losses. Reiners's platoon was now pinned down in the open and could neither advance nor retreat. To the left, contact had been lost with Hellmonds's platoon and the overall situation must have seemed unclear to Kolb or anyone else.

In the hedgerow to Kolb's rear, Dirksen also had no idea of what was occurring to his immediate front or to his left. He had sent runners to Bunker 24 to see what was going on, but none of them were able to get through the murderous fire or communicate with *Oberleutnant* Kolb. At midnight, Dirksen and a runner, *Gefreiter* Helmut Wilke, walked back to Bunker 94 to see if anyone there knew what was happening on the left flank. Here, Dirksen and Wilke were told by *Leutnant* Otterns of *3rd Company, Grenadier Regiment 689,* that "everything was going according to plan." Dirksen had no choice but to return to his position and keep fighting in hopes that the situation improved.

Meanwhile, *Feldwebel* Reiners had managed to crawl back to Dirksen's position to inquire about the situation, since he, too, had not heard from Kolb or Hellmonds. While both sergeants were trying to reach a decision, two runners from the headquarters of *1st Battalion, Grenadier Regiment 689* on the left flank, arrived at their location at 0330 hours and informed Reiners and Dirksen that Hellmonds's platoon had been driven back to Bunker 24.

While Dirksen and Reiners were trying to determine what to do in light of this new information, a runner from the company's tactical headquarters arrived with an order from *Oberleutnant* Kolb that Reiners was to disengage immediately and move with his men to Bunker 24, where they would link up with the remnants of Hellmonds's platoon. Dirksen was ordered to take over *2nd Platoon's* sector once Reiners and his men withdrew and then to support (with his machine-gun section) a relieving attack to be carried out by *Leutnant* Martin's *7th Company, Grenadier Regiment 981.* Mizioch's platoon had already pulled back on Kolb's command and had taken up positions in a trench line that ran to the right of Bunker 24.

By this point, the attack had been underway for nearly nine hours and most of the men of *Füsilier Company 272* had been lying in the open since the attack began. Although they were wearing adequate protective winter clothing, the temperature had been below freezing the entire night and many men began to develop frostbite as they lay in the deep snow. Wounded men lying in the open air were in danger of freezing to death and, in fact, several did.

Kolb planned to make a third attempt at Bunker 27 beginning at 0700 hours, using the remaining men of both *1st* and *2nd Platoons,* some twenty-two men in all. Miziochs's *3rd Platoon,* since it was composed of nearly all new personnel, was ordered to hold its positions in the trench line and support the attack with fire. Kolb's last assault fared the same as the first two, and he and his men were quickly driven back into Bunker 24. By this point, the company had suffered perhaps forty or fifty casualties.

With daylight quickly approaching, Kolb decided to halt the attack, since it would be suicide to continue when the full force of the American firepower could be brought to bear. What his intentions were remain unknown. He could have withdrawn or consolidated his remaining troops and made another attempt that evening. The last report the company received from Kolb arrived at 0900 hours, when *Gefreiter* Peter Moog of the company command group was dispatched to deliver a message while he brought back a seriously wounded soldier to *7th Company, Grenadier Regiment 981*'s first aid station. Moog reported to *Feldwebel* Dirksen that there were about thirty men inside Bunker 24. In addition to the twenty survivors from *Füsilier Company 272,* there were also ten men from *Leutnant* Ottern's company, the bunker's original inhabitants and the same men who had mistakenly fired on Hellmonds's platoon earlier that evening.

Bunker 24, known as a "silo bunker" by the Americans, was a fighting bunker of the general construction plan Type SK/6a or *Kampfbunker.* Built in 1938, the same year as Bunker 27, it was slightly smaller than the troop shelter, but boasted an armored machine-gun turret on the roof. Protected by walls two meters thick, it could accommodate a crew of nine, though more could fit inside if the situation warranted.[11] Impregnable to even direct hits from the largest shells then in use, it suffered from the same weakness as Bunker 27, in that its northwestern orientation also left it vulnerable to an attack from the sides and rear, where its main entrance lay.

When Moog left the bunker to deliver a message from *Oberleutnant* Kolb and evacuate a wounded soldier to Bunker 94, he was reluctant to obey, even though he greatly respected Kolb. Moog considered this mission a virtual death sentence, since American artillery was already falling heavily outside of the bunker and small arms fire was increasing as dawn approached. He slipped out of the bunker and half crawled, half ran to the rear, dragging the wounded man with him.

Somehow, Moog and the wounded soldier were able to make it out without incident. It was to be the first in a long series of events that saw Moog safely through the war's end.[12]

As the morning wore on, the Americans began to mount their response. Determined to rid themselves in one blow of the threat against their newly-won Bunker 27 and to take Bunker 24 as well, the two platoons of Company B, 311th Infantry Regiment, now supported by four tanks from 2nd Platoon, Company A, 709th Tank Battalion, initiated their own attack at 1030 hours 5 January.

Riding atop the tanks in order to avoid "bouncing betty" antipersonnel mines, the Americans quickly reached Bunker 24 and Bunker 25, a smaller troop shelter 100 meters to the southwest, and began to methodically assault both structures. One of the tanks was equipped with a bulldozer blade, which it used to push dirt over Bunker 24's firing embrasures and exits, while infantrymen placed shaped charges on top. After several of these charges were detonated, two Germans rushed out of the exit and surrendered.[13]

Several hundred meters to the right, *Feldwebel* Dirksen vainly tried to determine what was happening at Bunker 24, but his view of the American attack was blocked by intervening terrain. Although he could not see the tanks, he could hear the clanking of their treads and roar of their engines as they drove back and forth around the bunkers. In addition to the noise made by the Shermans and incessant artillery fire from both sides, Dirksen also heard someone shouting unintelligibly and a loud explosion at 1130 hours. Clearly, a lot of fighting was going on, but no one on the German side, except perhaps those in the immediate vicinity of Bunker 24, knew what was happening.

The American attack began to bog down at the same time. Although Bunker 25 fell quickly to a team of infantrymen and combat engineers supported by one of the tanks, Bunker 24 proved to be a more difficult challenge. While engaged in placing shaped charges on Bunker 24, heavy German artillery and mortar fire, as well as small arms fire (probably from the positions of the nearby *3rd Platoon*), forced the men of Company B to withdraw to their line of departure at Bunker 27 to seek shelter after they had suffered heavy losses. As he was directing the fire of the tanks, Lieutenant Hank was fired upon by a German machine gunner, whose rounds pierced his right sleeve and ignited a book of matches in the breast pocket of his field jacket. His coat on fire, Hank jumped off the tank he was riding and rolled around in the snow to extinguish the flames.[14]

While the infantry pulled back to safety, the four tanks from Company A, 709th Tank Battalion continued the attack against Bunker 24, and its adjacent trenchline with cannon and machine-gun fire. One Sherman was soon knocked out by a direct hit caused by the intense German artillery fire. The bulldozer tank attempted to use its blade to bury the occupants of the bunker alive, but it slipped over the edge of the ice-covered embankment at the rear exit and became wedged against the door.

The crew's frantic efforts to place the engine in reverse and back out of their predicament proved unsuccessful. Undeterred, the GIs inside the dozer tank decided to do as much damage to the bunker as possible and fired all of their ammunition, about seventy rounds of 75mm high explosive and white phosphorus, against the armored door, scarcely ten feet away. While they were eventually forced to abandon their tank, the crew at least could boast that "We didn't get in, but the Krauts didn't get out."[15]

What the conditions were like for the men trapped in the bunker can hardly be imagined. The combination of noise, overpressure from the detonation of the shaped charges, and choking smoke must have made it hellish inside the cramped space where nearly thirty men were desperately trying to survive. Outside, that afternoon and early evening the survivors of *Füsilier Company 272,* assisted by elements of *7th Company, Grenadier Regiment 981* and *3rd Company, Grenadier Regiment 689,* carried out several unsuccessful counterattacks to push the Americans back and rescue the men inside.

These constant attacks forced the two platoons from Company B and the two remaining tanks to withdraw to their original line of departure by late afternoon on 5 January, leaving Bunker 24 and much of the surrounding battlefield by default in German hands. Before pulling back, Lieutenant Robinson, responsible for providing covering fire while Lieutenant Hank withdrew what was left of his platoon, personally evacuated several wounded men who still lay in the snow where they had fallen, as Germans took potshots at him.[16]

It was no German victory, however; in fact, it was just the opposite. Nearly every man in the bunker, including Kolb, was a casualty, and the surrounding fields were littered with dead and wounded men. The survivors of Mizioch's *3rd Platoon,* who had been occupying the trench line a few meters to the right of the bunker, were the first to reach the scene. Soon joined by soldiers from *7th Company, Grenadier Regiment 981,* at dusk they began recovering the dead and wounded.

Leutnant Wegner, who had been with the infantry howitzer platoon in Eicherscheid during the entire affair, was ordered forward by *Oberstleutnant* Kleinkorres to take charge of what was left of the company and supervise the recovery of dead and wounded. When Wegner arrived at Bunker 94 at 1700 hours, he encountered *Feldwebel* Mizioch of *3rd Platoon* and a runner. Mizioch was described by Wegner as being "extremely agitated" and reported that his platoon had been nearly wiped out in and around the bunker during the American attack. Wegner got little else out of him, since Mizioch went immediately back into action with the remnant of his platoon to carry out another counterattack.

When Wegner arrived at Bunker 24 at 2000 hours, he noticed that there were ten sacks of American high explosives and shaped charges stacked along the entrance side of the bunker. He couldn't help but notice the dozer tank partially blocking the right entrance door and saw that the outer walls of the bunker were heavily damaged. On the steps by the left entrance lay rubble and he noticed metal reinforcing rods sticking out of the concrete at the corner that completely blocked the entrance. Near the right entrance lay two seriously wounded soldiers who had just been brought out of the bunker. A step or two inside the entrance he stumbled on two bodies that had just been laid near the door.

Inside the right side of the bunker, Wegner saw a dim light burning and noticed several soldiers engaged in caring for the wounded and clearing out the interior. In his words, the interior of the bunker presented a "tragic sight." From the roof hung steel reinforcing rods and metal strips. The interior walls of the bunker were also cracked and shattered, evidence of the American's use of the new "beehive" shaped charges Bits of concrete and equipment lay upon the dead and wounded.

Wegner found the body of *Oberleutnant* Kolb underneath that of another dead *Volksgrenadier*. When he lifted Kolb's body, the smell of phosphorus filled the air, already chokingly thick with the smell of gunpowder and concrete dust. Except for skin abrasions and bruises, none of the dead or wounded had any marks on them; evidently they were killed or injured by blast overpressure and concussion. Wegner helped move two of the more seriously wounded soldiers, who were unconscious, back to Bunker 94, where medics awaited them. A few of the stunned and deafened survivors, including *Unteroffizier* Kurt Klein, who had miraculously survived, made their way back to the aid station on their own power.

Wegner estimated that there were twenty to twenty-five dead and wounded inside the bunker, including several from other units. The casualties lying in the positions outside the bunker had already been brought back to friendly lines. Heavy snowfall, which continued throughout the day, limited American observation and aided in the recovery effort. By this point, what remained of the company lay in positions near their previous line of departure or in the immediate vicinity of Bunker 24.

Except for constant artillery and mortar fire, the Americans made no effort to continue their attack that evening. Company B, 311th Infantry was relieved by Company A of the same regiment at 0825 hours the following morning on 6 January and placed in regimental reserve. After laying mines and trip wires, Company A also pulled back 600 meters the next day to previously prepared positions; the regimental commander evidently thought their position was too exposed to enemy counterattack to justify keeping it.[17] Thus, *Füsilier Company 272* had at least accomplished its original mission of forcing the Americans back, even though it had paid a very high price doing so. American losses were also high; of the fifty-four men who participated in the assault from the 2nd and 4th Platoons of Company B and their attachments, at least four were killed and between thirty-two and thirty-five were wounded from 3 to 6 January.

Of the 133 men engaged from *Füsilier Company 272*, sixteen had been killed outright and thirty-four had been wounded, twenty-one seriously. A further thirty-two were missing in action, scattered across the battlefield in and around the American positions. Sixteen of these were later found dead and brought back. At least ten men were taken prisoner by the Americans. The company's losses in leadership were high—in addition to *Oberleutnant* Kolb, sixteen out of twenty-two NCOs were killed, wounded, or missing. In all, the company suffered eighty-two casualties from 4 to 6 January, sixty-one percent of the men who took part in the attack.

Among those listed as missing in action was *Unteroffizier* Gerhard Pleger, who the previous month had been found guilty of a serious disciplinary infraction by a division court-martial. Though he had been sentenced to serve in the Division's disciplinary platoon, his punishment had yet to be carried out when the attack on 4 January was ordered. Originally the leader of a gun crew in the infantry how-itzer platoon, Pleger had been reduced in rank to *Füsilier* and assigned to one of the infantry squads until the time came for him to join the disciplinary company. At first, it was believed that he had been killed in action, though his body could not be found. Subsequently, he was reported to have been taken prisoner. If he had allowed himself to be captured rather than serve in a disciplinary unit can only be surmised, though perhaps becoming a prisoner was at least a more hon-orable way out of the war compared to desertion.

One of the wounded men recovered from inside the bunker was *Füsilier* Heinrich Horstkotte, who had been hit by shrapnel earlier that morning. When the American tanks began their attack, he said, panic broke out among the wounded men who had been moved inside the bunker to relative safety. As the men fought for air, the Americans detonated explosive charges atop the bunker, showering all those inside with debris. Horstkotte thought that everyone inside except himself had been killed before he was knocked unconscious.

An hour later, he found himself outside the bunker, where he had been laid in a trench along with another wounded soldier. He had no idea how he got there or who had rescued him. His steel helmet was gone, although the leather and metal liner was still on his head, held there by his chinstrap. Evidently the blast had sheared the pins that secured the helmet to the liner! Aside from the concussion, he also suffered serious phosphorus burns that kept him in the hospital until the end of the war.[18]

Another survivor of Bunker 24 was *Unteroffizier* Kurt Klein, who had accom-panied Kolb as NCO in charge of the company's command group. Klein was found covered in blood and babbling incoherently, evidently having suffered a mental breakdown from the strain of being trapped in the bunker while artillery, shaped charges, and tank shells were detonated within feet of him and the others. It was Klein who had found the body of his best friend, Heinz Kolb and though wounded himself, had tried to shield the body from further harm. In addition to his psychiatric injuries, Klein also suffered from phosphorous burns on his face and neck that required extensive treatment.

After receiving first aid, Klein was evacuated to a military hospital in Plauen, where he was beset by nightmares and crying fits. Shortly thereafter, he was moved to an Army mental hospital in Rodewisch, where one doctor wanted to apply shock therapy to cure his depression. A kindly staff doctor, who also had a son in the *Wehrmacht* who was Klein's age, took a liking to him and had him put to work in the hospital telephone exchange as part of his therapy. Here, he worked as an operator until the end of the war, when he was taken prisoner. Classified as a combatant, Klein was forced to walk to the nearest POW camp while still dressed in his hospital pajamas. Fortunately, he was held as a prisoner of the Americans for only four weeks. He was eventually released on humanitarian grounds to join his wife, Else, in Gera, Thuringia. His wife had followed him throughout his journeys as a patient and as a POW, had repeatedly implored the camp commander to let him go until he finally relented.[19]

The body of *Oberleutnant* Kolb was recovered and placed in a *Wehrmacht*-issued coffin and buried in the division's temporary military cemetery at Gemünd. As with his men, his personnel effects, including his wallet and paybook, were collected and sent to his family.[20] Kolb's family heard on an Allied radio broadcast that their son was a POW of the Americans. While still in the hospital, Klein broke the news to them, telling them that he had been killed instead. Though they found this news hard to believe, Kolb's parents finally yielded to the sad reality. After the war Klein helped Kolb's parents have their son's body disinterred from the cemetery in Gemünd and moved to the municipal cemetery in Cologne for reburial. Kolb was posthumously promoted to *Hauptmann*.

The following day two more of Kolb's men were killed and two wounded by artillery fire while engaged in removing bodies from no-man's land, ratcheting up the total casualty figure still more. Only fifty-one men were left from the combat element of the company and most of these were concentrated in the heavy weapons and howitzer platoons. Since being committed in the Hürtgen Forest, the company had suffered 157 casualties in two months, or about seventy-six percent of its authorized strength. *1st Platoon* had been virtually wiped out and its platoon leader, *Feldwebel* Hellmonds, killed in action. *Feldwebel* Reiners's *2nd Platoon* had suffered casualties nearly as severe. Reiners himself was moderately burned by white phosphorus and was evacuated. Eight lightly wounded men, who had been evacuated to the company trains, were soon back in action, though it took several days for their wounds to heal.

Generalmajor König seized upon this incident as an example of the folly of attempting to use such *Westwall* bunkers in forward positions where they were vulnerable to attack. Now that the Americans had perfected bunker-busting techniques, they had become little more than concrete deathtraps for anyone caught inside. Accordingly, König used this as an opportunity to issue a divisional order that directed all units using such frontline bunkers abandon them at once and set up defensive positions outside, even if it meant that new trenches had to be dug. Soldiers were ordered not to use them under any circumstance, even for shelter lest they be trapped and killed as had the men in Bunkers 27 and 24. This order clashed with Hitler's long-standing order not to allow any *Westwall* bunker to fall into enemy hands, lest commanders on the spot be held personally responsible, but there was little else that König could do. Exceptions were made for bunkers used as command posts and shelters, so long as they were not located in the immediate front line. This order seems to have selectively obeyed, since numerous American reports later confirmed that many of them were still manned when attacked.[21]

Kolb's death necessitated the appointment of a new commander. It was determined that Wegner was too junior and too inexperienced for such an important command, so König appointed *Hauptmann* Kurt Heldt from the Division's officer reserve. Born 14 September 1918 in Bremen-Farge, Heldt was an experienced veteran who had fought on the Eastern Front in a variety of units, most recently *with 3rd Company, Corps Signal Battalion 430 (motorized),* where he had been awarded both the Iron Cross 1st and 2nd Classes as well as the Russian Front Medal and Black Wound Badge.

While Wegner was forward in the vicinity of Simmerath on the evening of 5 January, Heldt arrived in Dedenborn at 2100 hours and linked up with *Hauptfeldwebel* Fuhrmeister in the company trains area. The following day he busied himself with the task of supervising the recovery of the dead and wounded, which must have seemed a rather bitter introduction to his new command. By 7 January, most of the job was complete, allowing the company to finally return to its quarters in Hergarten that night The recovery of the last of the dead took place on 12 January Most of the men killed as a result of this engagement were buried in the temporary division cemeteries at Gemünd or Sauermühle, but all were disinterred after the war and finally laid to rest permanently in several cemeteries maintained by the German War Graves Commission. Once in Hergarten, *Füsilier Company 272* began a three-week period of reconstitution.

A few soldiers from the company volunteered to remain behind to finish the recovery and identification of the bodies from Bunker 24 and the surrounding area. This was a dangerous assignment, since the men of the 311th Infantry Regiment opposite them neither granted a cease-fire nor allowed the bodies to be recovered in daylight without dispatching indirect fire. One man, *Gefreiter* Schäfer, was killed and two men, *Füsiliers* Tengen and Gerlach, were seriously wounded during this hazardous operation.

Despite the danger, the men worked throughout the long nights to retrieve their comrades' bodies. One man in particular, *Gefreiter* Rudolf Schniesko of the company trains, was cited for his dedication to duty. He volunteered for the work despite the fact that he had a duty position safely in the rear area and did not have to face the hazards of front-line combat. He did not stop until all of the casualties were brought back, even though he was lightly wounded in the effort. For his steadfastness in a particularly difficult and gruesome mission, he was awarded the War Service Cross, 2nd Class with Swords by *Hauptmann* Heldt.

The company's positions were handed over to *Hauptmann* Ragnow's *2nd Battalion, Grenadier Regiment 981.* These men had not fared much better in the fighting around Simmerath and Bickerath than had *Füsilier Company 272;* shortly thereafter Ragnow was ordered to hand over his positions to the regiment's *1st Battalion* and was pulled out of the line. Ragnow's battalion had now been designated as *LXXIV Corps'* reserve, so his battalion, like *Füsilier Company 272,* was reconstituted as well.[22] *Major* Gerhard Thürmer's *1st Battalion, Grenadier Regiment 981,* which had not been engaged by the Americans during this period, now had to extend its own front line to assume responsibility for the sector that

2nd Battalion vacated. Thürmer's men, who had not enjoyed a rest period since 22 December, now inherited additional bunkers and fighting positions to defend.

After four days of living in the open and enduring freezing temperatures as well as heavy shelling, the men of *Füsilier Company 272* looked forward to moving back to Hergarten, where they slept, for a few days at least, in relatively warm and dry outbuildings. They and the men of the *2nd Battalion, Grenadier Regiment 981,* were the fortunate ones, since the rest of their division had no choice but to remain in the line in daily contact with their American opponents.

While the company paused to honor its dead and prepare for its next battle, the war continued. On 9 January, the light infantry howitzer platoon, along with *Leutnant* Wegner, was temporarily detached from the company and sent to support *General der Infanterie* von Zangen's *Fifteenth Army Heeres-Stosstruppschule* (Assault School) at Simmelerhof located in the Dahlemer Forest, some forty kilometers south of Hergarten. Even though the company itself had to be reconstituted, the howitzer platoon had suffered no losses at Simmerath, so it was sent where its firepower was badly needed.

The *Fifteenth Army Assault School* was initially established in December 1943 in northern France as *Sturmbataillon der Armeewaffenschule AOK 15,* consisting of three companies, by converting *Grenadier Battalion LXXXIX* of the *LXXXIX Corps.* Its mission was to train NCO candidates in realistic field conditions and could, if called upon, be utilized as a special army reserve strike force.[23] Lacking its own organic heavy weapons section, the addition of Wegner's two howitzers added the offensive punch to partially fulfill the fire support needs of the battalion. Once he arrived with the platoon in Simmerlerhof, *Leutnant* Wegner was made acting adjutant to its battalion commander, *Hauptmann* Ulrich Bork, while the howitzer platoon was left in the capable hands of *Feldwebel* Etzmannsdorfer. Wegner and his platoon passed most of January uneventfully, occupied mainly by their duties with the assault school.

Two other noteworthy events occurred during the month of January in addition to the action at Simmerath, for which both sides claimed tactical success. The first took place on 10 January, when the 309th Infantry of the 78th Infantry Division launched an operation to clear the Raffelsbrand-Ochsenkopf bunker complex once and for all. The second involved a German raid on an American-held bunker.

This Raffelsbrand-Ochsenkopf salient west of Simonskall had bedeviled the Americans since the previous October. Hundreds of men had been killed, wounded, or reported missing after unsuccessful attacks launched by the 4th, 8th, 9th, 28th, and 78th Infantry Divisions. Held by the *982nd Grenadier Regiment* on and off since late November, this segment of the *Westwall* was the only area in the Hürtgen Forest west of the Kall still held by the Germans. As long as it remained in their hands, it constituted a threat to the flanks of any attacking force that sought to advance east toward the dams either to the north or south of the salient.

At this particular moment, the *272nd VGD* was arrayed as follows: in the north between the Raffelsbrand-Ochsenkopf area to the northern edge of Strauch lay the two battalions of the *982nd Grenadier Regiments;* arrayed in the center was the *980th Grenadier Regiment,* whose lines ran from Strauch to the southern outskirts of Kesternich, which it still occupied; and to the south lay the *981st Grenadier Regiment,* which held the area between the eastern outskirts of Simmerath to the southwest where the division shared a boundary with the *246th VGD* at the Am Gericht crossroads. *Second Battalion, 981st Grenadier Regiment* lay in *LXXIV Corps* reserve. On the division's right, or northern, flank lay the *85th Infantry Division,* brought back into the line when the *89th Infantry Division* was sent to the Ardennes shortly after Christmas.

The objective of the American attack, to be carried out by the 1st Battalion, 309th Infantry Regiment, was the capture of several bunkers and troop shelters, including Bunkers 22, JG3, and P2 (see Map 11). These bunkers, with their surrounding trenchlines and fighting positions (since they were forbidden by expressed order to actually fight from within them), controlled the approaches to the Ochsenkopf, which encompassed two hills (Hills 485 and 486) that overlook the Kall gorge at Simonskall. The area was defended by the *5th* and *6th Companies* of *2nd Battalion, Grenadier Regiment 982.* Though at only fifty percent strength, these companies were intimately familiar with the terrain and had successfully withstood every American attempt to seize them.[24]

The Americans commenced their attack from the southwest of the objective at 0700 hours on 10 January with raiding parties from Companies A, B, and C spread out along a 500-meter wide front. Surprise was lost when several of the raiding parties encountered anti-personnel mines. Now alerted, the defenders located in positions surrounding two of the bunkers directed lethally accurate mortar and machine-gun fire against the Americans, who were forced to withdraw their assault elements after losing nearly half of their men.

Though hampered by deep snow, fallen branches, and poor visibility, the 144 men of the 1st Battalion, 309th Infantry Regiment comprising the raiding parties resumed their attack. Working their way forward slowly, the men crawled laboriously through wire entanglements, minefields, and machine-gun fire. It was dangerous and difficult work. The leader of one platoon (a second lieutenant) and eight men decided that they had enough and refused to move forward. The battalion commander sent them all to the rear under arrest and continued his attack. Though Bunkers 22 and JG3 were taken, the Germans resisted skillfully and American casualties were heavy.[25] The German battalion commander, *Hauptmann* Schneider, was satisfied with his men's defensive efforts that day and wrongfully assumed that the worst was over.[26]

The next morning, the American battalion commander, Lieutenant Colonel Robert H. Schellman, USMA Class of 1939, initiated a general attack against the Ochsenkopf with all three of his line infantry companies taking part. Since both sides wore white snow capes, it was difficult to tell friend from foe. The fighting frequently took place at close quarters, with hand grenades and flamethrowers often providing the decisive advantage. Hand-to-hand combat in the zig-zag trenches supporting the bunkers was also reported. One American combatant, Private First Class Volonino of Company C, 1st Battalion, surprised an German soldier armed only with a potato masher grenade coming up the trench line toward him. Both men lunged at one another and fought for a few moments in the trench before Volonino stunned his assailant with a blow to the head with the German's own hand grenade and captured him.[27]

By that evening, the Americans had seized the high ground, as well as Bunker P2. Possession of the area now allowed Schellman and his men to observe all German movement in the vicinity of Simonskall and made it somewhat easier to take the remaining bunkers the following day. They were also able to break up *Hauptmann* Schneider's attempts to move reinforcements into his position, since they had to move uphill in the face of American artillery and small arms fire. Schneider's battalion launched two counterattacks that day, though neither were successful, and all the Germans had to show for their efforts were several dozen dead and wounded soldiers. Over twenty-five of his men were taken prisoner as well when Bunker P2, a company command post, was captured.

Evacuation of the wounded proved to be an especially difficult task. In addition to the normal difficulties encountered when carrying a casualty across such torturous terrain, incoming artillery, mortar, and small arms fire made this essentially humanitarian task a very risky one for medical personnel as well as the wounded. According to an eyewitness, *Gefreiter* Heinrich Müller of *2nd Battalion Grenadier Regiment 982,* who was called in to help,

The worst was the steep and rocky slopes of the Tiefenbach and Kall Valleys, which lay under constant heavy fire of the Americans . . . at times, we lost our orientation in the [snow-covered] desolate beech forests, where everything was shot-up and splintered and where trees lay everywhere broken and intermingled. Of course, this affected the Americans, too. Sometimes our people would blunder into captivity; sometimes the Americans would do the same. The worst thing about it was evacuating the wounded from this hopelessly confused situation. Our *Feldwebel* found a seriously wounded *Landser* with artillery fragments sticking out of his back. We had to get him out, despite the danger of [enemy] fire. We were able to load him onto a shelter quarter after stumbling over the bodies of several dead Americans. The steep slope demanded all of our strength! We would take two steps forward and one back. Enemy fire fell constantly and we could hear the cries of other wounded as we passed them. We could not see them, though, since the completely devastated forest blocked our view. Finally we were able to reach a dressing station in a *Westwall* bunker. I myself was captured on 15 January.[28]

The attack continued on 12 January, with Schneider having to throw not only the last of his own reserves into the battle to hold the Ochsenkopf, but also the regimental reserve, *1st Company, Combat Engineer Battalion 272,* and an alarm company from *1st Battalion, Grenadier Regiment 982.*[29] Even the corps reserve was moved forward to Strauch, but ultimately was not committed.

Though the men of 1st Battalion, 309th Infantry Regiment (joined later that day by 2nd Battalion) suffered numerous casualties from German mortar and artillery fire, they were able to take the rest of the Ochsenkopf position by nightfall. Consolidating on the objective, the Americans improved their defensive positions and destroyed several captured bunkers over the next three days.[30]

The American attack on the final objective, Bunker 115, was carried out on 17 January by two specially trained teams from Companies E and F of 2nd Battalion, 309th Infantry Regiment. Preceded by a heavy artillery and mortar barrage that impacted directly on and around the bunker, the assault teams commenced their attack at 0200 hours. One of the teams was delayed when an observant sentry pinned them down with fire from his machine pistol, but he was quickly silenced by fire from the platoon leader, Second Lieutenant Donald P. Jamison.

With the Germans trapped inside the bunker, the team quickly placed a shaped charged on the bunker door and blew it wide open, the terrific blast immobilizing the occupants. After clearing the bunker, the demolitions team placed 400 pounds of TNT inside and at 0325 hours set the primer. The explosion was so powerful that the bunker was blown apart, the concussion and falling concrete killed Lieutenant Jamison and blew the clothing off some of the men.[31] With Bunker 115 destroyed, the core of the German defensive line in the Raffelsbrand-Ochsenkopf area was finally broken.

German counterattacks were conducted throughout the day on 17 January to retake the position, but with little success. Left with no other recourse, the Germans were forced to advance up the steep hill under the observant eyes of the Americans, and were driven off with heavy losses. Schneider himself is reported to have refused at one point to carry out another counterattack, since he knew that any attempt to do so in broad daylight would be suicidal. Though his regimental commander agreed with him, Schneider was overruled by the division commander. The counterattack was carried out with predictable results. Launched by ten men from his headquarters company, it was a bloody failure; all of the men who took part were killed. According to his operations officer, *Leutnant* Günther Schmidt, Schneider broke down and wept when he received the report.[32]

Though *2nd Battalion, Grenadier Regiment 982* continued to hold several lesser bunkers in the area for two more weeks, Schneider's command was shattered, having been reduced to an effective strength of only twenty to twenty five percent.[33] During the week's fighting, German losses amounted to an estimated 300 killed, wounded, and missing. Lieutenant Colonel Schellman's losses during this period had also been considerable.

Yet, the 78th Infantry Division did not hold a monopoly on offensive spirit during this lull in the fighting. The *272nd VGD* still possessed enough veterans with the skill and dedication to challenge the Americans, and time and time again proved that the military skills of the *Volksgrenadiers* were not to be taken lightly.

They gave the Americans an impressive display of their capabilities on 17 January when a large German combat patrol surrounded an artillery observation post that had been established in a partially destroyed pillbox. Severing communications wires just before dawn, the German patrol, demonstrating "excellent technique," captured all of the pillbox's occupants. According to the 78th Infantry Division after action report, the Germans' "all-around security was well-placed and his mission appeared to have been successfully accomplished."[34]

Still, these two actions were exceptions rather than the rule. Most of the rest of the month of January passed relatively uneventfully. Replacements continued to arrive from the interior of Germany, though the quality of the men and amount of training they had received was far below the accepted standard. By the end of January, the effective combat strength of the *272nd VGD* was estimated to be between 3,500 and 4,500 men.[35] While the regiments continued to rebuild and train their units as much as the situation permitted, *Generalmajor* König and his staff conducted elaborate command post exercises designed to prepare the defense against the American attack that they knew would soon come.

Since *Füsilier Company 272* had suffered the highest casualties of any of its subordinate units, the *272nd VGD* singled it out for special attention, taking the steps needed to bring the company back to fighting strength. On 11 January, the first group of replacements, seventeen enlisted men including three NCOs, arrived in Hergarten after enduring a long train ride from Ludwigslust, where they had been assigned directly to the company from *Reconnaissance Replacement and Training Battalion 14.*

Two days later, thirty-one fully equipped replacement troops, including four NCOs, were assigned to the company from *Field Replacement Battalion 272,* where they had undergone the usual combat indoctrination. With this influx of forty-nine new men, the new company commander on 14 January was able to reestablish *1st* and *2nd Platoons. 3rd Platoon* received only one or two new men; its losses had been much lighter at Simmerath because, like the *4th Platoon,* had remained in support during the worst of the fighting. To add to the total, six additional men were assigned by the end of the month.

One result of the disaster at Simmerath had been the loss of two of the company's three senior platoon sergeants—*Feldwebel* Hellmonds, killed in action, and *Feldwebel* Reiners, wounded in action. That left only *Oberfeldwebel* Mizioch as the surviving senior NCO in charge of an infantry platoon, aside from *Feldwebel* Dirksen of heavy weapons platoon and *Feldwebel* Etzmannsdorfer of the infantry howitzer platoon. This left a serious gap in the company's noncommissioned leadership. Numerous junior leaders had also been lost, but for the most part had been replaced, though the new men lacked experience and, more importantly, were not yet a part of the company' "family."

The shortage of senior NCOs was made up, in outward appearances at least, by the assignment of *Feldwebel* Heinrich Bechstein to command the *1st Platoon* on 11 January and *Oberfeldwebel* Herold Pamin to command the *2nd Platoon* on 13 January. While each outwardly appeared adequate, upon closer examination, however, both lacked the credentials to carry out the duties of an infantry platoon sergeant in combat, a sign of the rot that was rapidly setting in German small unit leadership. Like nearly everything else in the Third Reich by this stage of the war, experienced NCOs were in short supply and expedients had to be found somehow, even if it meant forcing unqualified or unsuited men into positions of responsibility.

Bechstein, born 1912 in Offenbach, had served primarily in administrative positions since the beginning of the war. Though he had attended a cursory course of instruction in the division's combat school, he was woefully unprepared to exercise his new responsibilities. Pamin, born 1914 in Isabellow, Poland, had gained his rank in the *Luftwaffe* before being transferred to the *Heer* just a few months before. They simply had not sufficient time to become capable combat leaders before their first battle. They and their men soon paid for this lack of experience, much as the rest of the division's grenadier regiments had already done.

The *272nd VGD*'s personnel administrative staff had not ignored the officer replacement situation either. *Leutnant* Bayer, whose arm had been amputated as a result of the wounds suffered at Giesenheck, was replaced by *Leutnant* Herbert Gomm in mid-January. Gomm originally joined the company as an *Oberfeldwebel* on 2 October 1944 when he and the rest of the *March Company* of 108 replacements from *Reconnaissance Replacement and Training Battalion 9* arrived in Falkensee.

Though his service record is not available, the company consolidated personnel roster shows that he joined the *Heer* in November 1935 and had already been awarded the Iron Cross 2nd Class and Wound Badge in Black. Shortly after being assigned to the company, Gomm volunteered to become an officer and was sent to an officer's candidate school. By mid-January 1945, he was back with *Füsilier Company 272* and was assigned to serve as the company's junior *Leutnant* and platoon leader of the *1st Platoon*. Though he found a few of the old faces still with the company, he was probably saddened to hear of Kolb's and Hellmonds's death and the wounding of the other men.

To incorporate the influx of new personnel into the company, *Hauptmann* Heldt used the period between 15 and 22 January to focus on basic tasks, including individual and collective training, as well as anti-tank tactics. He chose to concentrate his main efforts to training the company in the conduct of deliberate attacks as assault troops to carry out special missions. Extensive rehearsals and practice assaults were carried out in the local area. The weather cooperated, remaining overcast throughout most of the period, preventing American aerial observation and fighter-bomber attacks.

On 23 January, *Generalmajor* König himself observed the company's field training along with his *Ia*, *Major i.G.* Uhl. To demonstrate his company's proficiency, Heldt carried out a simulated ground attack against the old Labor Service barracks in Hergarten. Apparently, the division commander approved of what he saw, since he granted Heldt and his men a day of rest for the following day. Ominously, the weather cleared later that afternoon.

The men of *Füsilier Company 272* spent 24 January improving their quarters in Hergarten and catching up on missed sleep. The clear weather continued to hold, but there was little that the company could do about it, since the presence of German forces in Hergarten was well known to the US Army Air Force. In the afternoon, fighter-bombers bombed and strafed Hergarten repeatedly. Only one man was injured, *Gefreiter* Liemann, who was severely wounded in the head by machine-gun fire.

All that the men of the *272nd VGD* could do was wait for the impending Allied offensive. Many of *Generalmajor* König's men were worried about their families who lived in the eastern parts of Germany that lay in the path of the Soviet onslaught. On 12 January, the Red Army launched a massive offensive from its Vistula bridgeheads, rampaging across most of Poland and forcing the *Wehrmacht* to retreat as far west as the Oder River. All that was known was that the Soviets had shown great cruelty toward the German citizens in newly-occupied towns. Many men did not learn the fate of their families for weeks, if not months.

News of these events adversely affected morale, but the only solution to this problem was to tighten discipline even further, including the screening of mail for any defeatist tendencies. One man in *Füsilier Company 272, Gefreiter* Helmut Lürkens, was given three days of close arrest by *Hauptmann* Heldt on 19 January for making sarcastic remarks about the conduct of the war in a letter to his wife, Lena. The net effect of such actions, of course, was to lower morale even further. Therefore, it was with little enthusiasm that the men of the *272nd VGD* faced the end of January 1945, for they knew it was their turn next to feel the weight of the Allied attack.

One soldier from another unit in the *272nd VGD, Gefreiter* Hans Gunkel, a company runner in *Grenadier Regiment 981,* wrote in January 1945 that "the opponent has increased his level of activity, including the use of artillery fire, now that they have stopped our Ardennes Offensive. The complete German defeat in the West is now only a matter of time."[36] The American buildup could only be hidden so much. *Leutnant* Günther Schmidt of *Grenadier Regiment 982* noted on 10 January that "This quiet period seemed to be lasting too long and we began worrying about it. We could observe that the enemy was organizing large scale artillery concentrations behind their front at Rötgen. Every day we could see an increasing number of vehicles . . . our own artillery fire didn't trouble the enemy very much."[37] Martin Jenner, commander of one of the division's artillery battalions, stated, "The low strength of the companies in the wide [defensive] sectors of the division left little room for doubt, that with a renewal of the enemy attack, large sections of the front line would be forced back . . . if only the Allies could get to Berlin before the Russians do!"[38]

11

The Americans
Drive for the Dams

The six-week lull that had settled in the Hürtgen Forest and along the Roer River front finally came to an end when the Americans began their long-anticipated attack on 30 January 1945. With the costly German offensive in the Ardennes defeated and forced back to its original line of departure during the last week of the month, the Allies were once again in the position to reassert the operational initiative. Germany's strategic and operational reserves were now virtually exhausted and General Dwight Eisenhower, with his armies' and air forces' over-whelming numerical superiority, now renewed the Western Allies' drive toward the Rhine, while Stalin's Red Army continued its relentless drive toward Berlin.

In order for the Western Allies to reach the Rhine, Eisenhower directed Field Marshall Bernard Montgomery's 21st Army Group to cross the lower Rhine once the rest of the American, British, and Canadian forces had closed up to that river along a broad front. But before this attack could take place, Montgomery first had to wait until the Roer River dams at Urft and Schwammenauel were taken. This salient fact, which had overshadowed the fighting in the Hürtgen Forest since September 1944, still held true in January 1945. Whichever side held the dams controlled the level of the Roer; any Allied force that crossed the Roer to reach the Rhine could easily be cut off from its logistical tail by the simple expedient of blowing the dams or opening their floodgates.

General Simpson's US Ninth Army of the 21st Army Group was given the assignment of taking the dams with its southernmost unit, Major General Parker's 78th Infantry Division, at the time assigned to the US VII Corps. Though a rela-tive newcomer to the Hürtgen Forest compared to the other divisions that had pre-ceded it, nearly two months of combat against the *272nd VGD* and other German units had transformed the men of the "Lightning Division" into hardened veter-ans. The Americans had been bogged down in the Hürtgen Forest for nearly five months and there was a strong belief within the Allied leadership and within the division itself that this final assault had to succeed.

Much depended upon a successful conclusion to an episode that had already claimed thousands of American casualties for an advance of a mere twenty-five miles. With this in mind, the command and staff of the 78th Infantry Division had been occupied throughout much of January in drafting and perfecting their con-cept of operations. The fighting in the Hürtgen Forest came to an end and the Roer was crossed in less than two weeks, which is a tribute to the skill and abilities of the leaders and the men they led. It was to be hard fighting all the way, however.

Essentially, the fight for the Roer dams would unfold in three distinct phases—clearing the corridor in the south as far as the Urft Dam, then occupying the Schmidt plateau (key terrain overlooking the Schwammenauel Reservoir), and finally the seizure of the larger Schwammenauel Dam to the north. The first phase, planned to begin on 30 January, envisioned a two-division attack along parallel lines to clear the southern approaches to the dams along the Monschau corridor. The 78th Infantry Division would be reinforced for this operation by Combat Command A (CCA), 5th Armored Division; the 736th Tank Battalion and the 893rd Tank Destroyer Battalion (both independent units, the latter of which had fought at Schmidt during the first week of November 1944); and a company of British flame-throwing Crocodile tanks. This would constitute the - far-right flank division of the US Ninth Army and would protect the left flank of the neighboring US First Army arrayed to its south.

The 78th Infantry Division would attack on the left, or northern, axis of advance of the two-division attack. It would clear a zone between Monschau in the west and Einruhr in the east, with its right flank anchored on the Roer itself, which flowed in an easterly direction in this region. Following the seizure of these objectives, the division would once again revert to control of Hodges' US First Army (from US VII Corps to V Corps). In order to accomplish this mission during this first phase of the operation, the division would also have to seize and clear the localities of Imgenbroich, Eicherscheid, Huppenbroich, and Kesternich.

On the right, or southern, axis of advance, the 9th Infantry Division, then the leftmost division of the US First Army, would clear the zone along the Roer between Höfen in the west and Gemünd in the east, a task made more difficult by the large expanse of the Monschau Forest that lay between these localities. Along the way, the men of the "Old Reliables" would have to clear the towns of Rohren, Schöneseiffen, Dreiborn, and Herhahn, as well as the crossroads at Wahlerscheid; this town was the scene of ferocious fighting in December when the veteran 2nd Infantry Division's assault was thrown back to its line of departure in the initial stages of the German Ardennes Offensive.

The 9th Infantry Division was also tasked to seize the town of Einruhr after its other objectives had been taken in order to free up the bulk of the 78th Infantry Division so it could pivot to the north in time for the next phase of the operation. The seizure of Einruhr would also cut off the German defenders west of the Roer from their lines of communication to Gemünd, forcing them to either retreat to the north or surrender. Once this phase was complete, the Urft Reservoir and its dam would be in the American's possession and the stage would be set for the next phase of the operation.

With the Monschau corridor and the Urft Dam in American hands, control of the second phase of the operation would be assumed by Hodges' US First Army of the 12th Army Group. US First Army would shift its left boundary with the

Ninth Army northward to a line drawn along the Kall valley between Vossenack and Schmidt. This phase of the attack would essentially clear the Germans from the west bank of the Roer, from Rurberg in the south to Nideggen in the north. In accomplishing this task, the main effort once again fell to the 78th Infantry Division, which would then be under the control of Major General C. Ralph Huebner's US V Corps. The 78th Infantry Division would then seize the Schmidt plateau, encompassing the towns of Strauch, Steckenborn, Kommerscheidt, and Schmidt. This move would effectively place the Americans in a dominating position overlooking the Schwammenauel Dam and Reservoir before they began the third, and final, phase.

For the seizure of Schmidt and the other localities along the Schmidt plateau, the division would be reinforced by a regimental combat team from the 82nd Airborne Division and Combat Command R, 7th Armored Division, giving it a considerable amount of combat power. Since the 78th Infantry Division would constitute V Corps' main effort, it would receive priority in the allocation of artillery supporting fires as well. The other independent armor units that had been attached during the first phase would remain under the task organization. Flame-throwing Crocodiles, a specially modified version of the venerable Churchill main battle tank, would be used primarily to neutralize German bunkers and then would revert to British control. To further decrease the Germans' already low morale, especially in the salient that jutted west between Simmerath and Imgenbroich, thousands of surrender leaflets targeting the *272nd VGD* were fired into the area in the days leading up to the assault (see Figure 2).

The seizure of Schmidt and the high ground overlooking the reservoir would signal the third, and final, phase of the operation, the actual capture of the Schwammenauel Dam and the villages of Heimbach and Hasenfeld. This would be the most risky phase of the operation, since nearly everyone on Hodges' staff and the staff of the 78th Infantry Division expected the Germans to blow it up before it fell into American hands. Its destruction had to prevented if possible, since this would release millions of cubic feet of water into the Roer downstream and delay Allied river crossings planned to occur simultaneously to the north in the vicinity of Düren. Its seizure, despite the risks, therefore, was essential for the success of the entire Allied operational concept for the drive to the Rhine.

That this would involve heavy fighting was a given. The Germans had defended most of these areas for months and were known to have heavily fortified their approaches. Wire entanglements, minefields, bunkers, and communications trenches dotted the shell-torn and snow-covered landscape, more reminiscent of a First World War battlefield rather than one of the Second. A mitigating factor arguing toward continuing the attack was that all three of the German divisions occupying the main line of resistance in the Hürtgen Forest and west of the Roer were believed to be exhausted after months of fighting and significantly under authorized strength.

The southernmost area between Konzen and Monschau was defended by the fought-out *62nd Volks-Grenadier Division,* which had been decimated in the

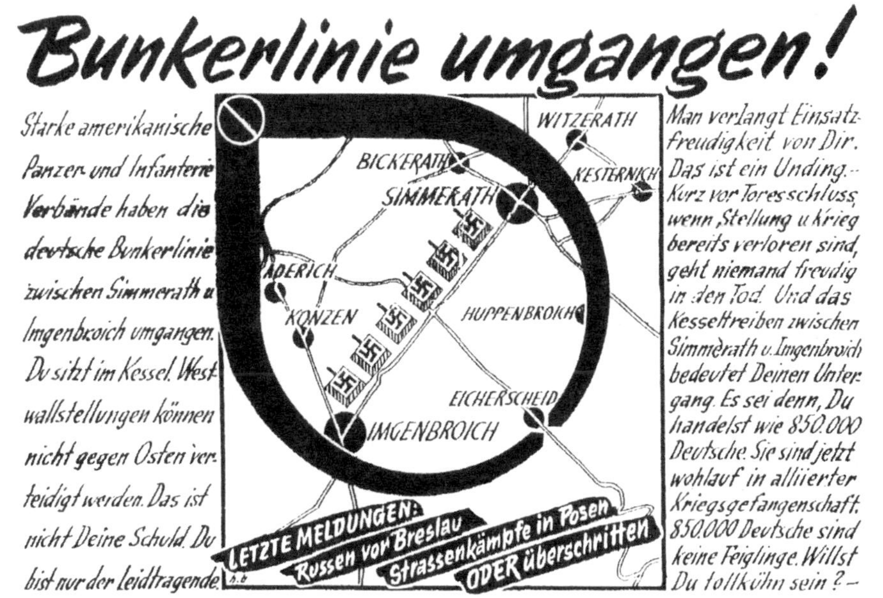

Figure 2. Bunkerline Encircled! This surrender leaflet was dropped on German troops holding the last remaining portion of the *Westwall* in the Hürtgen Forest during the last week of January 1945. Targeted specifically towards the men of the *62nd* and *272nd Volks-Grenadier Divisions* holding the line between Simmerath and Imgenbroich, it advises them that they will soon be encircled by strong tank and infantry formations. It tells them that they will soon be faced with the choice of surrender or death. Will you be wise, the leaflet asks, like the other 850,000 German troops who have surrendered so far, or will you choose to fight and die in the pocket rapidly forming? It emphasizes the hopelessness of the German soldier's cause by flashing headlines announcing the Russians arriving before the gates of Breslau, street fighting in Posen, and the Oder River crossed, areas that until January 1945 had been sacrosanct.

Ardennes and had been transferred to the north to rest and absorb replacements. This division had relieved the *246th Volks-Grenadier Division* on 23 January so it had not yet completely arrived with all of its components before the American attack began. Its new division commander, *Generalmajor* Friedrich Kittel, did not arrive to take command of the *62nd* until the night of 27 January 1945.[1]

During the fighting in the Ardennes, the *62nd VGD* had been virtually smashed and its infantry regiments had been reduced to little more than mere cadres. As such, it was not capable of withstanding any kind of determined attack, nor had there been time to reconstitute it despite the best efforts of the corps commander, *General der Infanterie* Püchler, to do so.[2] All three of its regiments—*Grenadier Regiments 164, 183,* and *190*—had been reformed as emergency units of battalion size even after an influx of 800 replacements, most of whom were former *Luftwaffe* and *Kriegsmarine* personnel with no infantry training whatsoever. The only bright spot was that there were sufficient weapons on hand to equip them.[3]

To its north, occupying a defensive sector between Konzen and Silberscheidt, lay the *272nd VGD* with perhaps 5,000 to 6,000 men, with an average of fifty to sixty men per infantry company. Though it had suffered heavy losses in December, it was still prepared to repel the impending attack. Its northern neighbor, the *85th Infantry Division,* was a division in name only, consisting of a hodgepodge of various units that occupied a defensive sector that ran from Schmidt to Nideggen. Its most capable sub-element, *Parachute Regiment 6,* consisted mainly of young recruits, though they were well armed and fanatically determined to resist. Of *LXXIV Corps'* three divisions, only the *272nd* was rated by *Fifteenth Army* as being "fully suitable" for defense; the other two as "conditionally suitable" for defense.[4]

General der Infanterie Karl Püchler's *LXXIV Corps,* under the control of *General der Infanterie* von Zangen's *Fifteenth Army,* had overall responsibility for the German defensive sector in the Hürtgen. The *272nd VGD* had reverted to Püchler's corps' control from *General der Infanterie* Hitzfeld's corps on 19 December after it had become apparent that *LXVII Corps'* attempt to seize Monschau had failed. Püchler faced the challenge of defending an overextended corps front held by three weak divisions with a river and two reservoirs behind his back, an unenviable tactical situation even for a such an experienced commander.

To make his situation more difficult, many of his corps troops—especially artillery, engineer, and tank destroyer units—had been siphoned off to support the fighting in the Ardennes. He had no tanks and his only reserve was one weak battalion of the *272nd VGD* ＊ Other supporting arms were in hardly better shape. The *407th Volks-Artillery Corps,* tasked to support *LXXIV Corps,* had only returned from its commitment in the Ardennes a few days before the American attack. In supporting the German offensive, the artillery command had suffered high losses in men and equipment, and was evaluated by *Fifteenth Army* as having a low combat capability. Ammunition stocks were low and fuel reserves for prime movers were at their lowest levels. Firing an artillery concentration of more than four rounds per gun required a division commander's permission.[5] The possibility of air support by the *Luftwaffe* was now merely wishful thinking.

While these factors by themselves were enough to give any commander reasons to doubt the final outcome of the coming battle, another problem surfaced, one that had not been encountered before. Morale of the troops had reached a low point after the failure of the Ardennes Offensive and the proven ineffectiveness of the highly-touted wonder weapons. Troops in the combat elements, usually the most reliable, began to display a battle weariness that manifested itself in worsening discipline, desertions, and rude behavior toward their officers.

＊ At this point, *Antitank Battalion 272* had only eight *Jagdpanzer* 38(t) *Hetzer* tank destroyers of its original fourteen; of these eight, only three were operational. It is unknown whether *62nd Volks-Grenadier Division* or the *85th Infantry Division* had any operational armor at all; each might have had two or three at the most.

This attitude, which had remained hidden at first, was to come to the forefront once the American counteroffensive began and units that had previously been considered rock-solid disintegrated rapidly once they were faced with their opponents' overwhelming combat power.[6] Tasks that normally were supervised by NCOs, such as construction of field positions and the laying of minefields, had to be closely watched by officers lest the work be done improperly. But by all existing accounts, the *272nd VGD* was still considered to be efficient and well led, at least compared to the other two divisions in the corps.

The attack by the US 78th and 9th Infantry Divisions began at 0530 hours on 30 January after a five-minute artillery preparation that caught the Germans, accustomed to much longer barrages, completely by surprise (see Map 12). German employment of their own artillery was hampered by a lack of communications when telephone lines were severed by American fire and by the capture of artillery forward observation positions. In the vicinity of Konzen, troops from the *62nd VGD* waited too long to leave their bunkers located behind the front line to reoccupy their forward fighting positions after the barrage lifted. As a result, they were quickly overrun by troops from the 3rd Battalion, 310th Infantry of the 78th Infantry Division.[7]

That was not the only American success that morning. To the left, 2nd Battalion, 310th Infantry, supported by the British flame-throwing Crocodiles of the Fife and Forfar Yeomanry, seized thirty-two bunkers in the vicinity of Bickerath and the crossroads at Am Gericht in only three hours while suffering negligible losses.[8] Dozens of dazed prisoners from *Grenadier Regiment 164* of the *62nd VGD* were taken, the first of hundreds to be rounded up that day. Further south, troops of the 39th Infantry Regiment of the 9th Infantry Division reported similar successes near Höfen, Alzen, and Rohren.

The tank-led assault by CCA, 5th Armored Division, supported by 1st Battalion, 311th Infantry Regiment, did not initially fare as well as those conducted by its neighbors on its right flank. The goal of seizing Eicherscheid and the surrounding area initially proved elusive, as the village was stoutly defended by *Major* Gerhard Thürmer's *1st Battalion, Grenadier Regiment 981* of the *272nd VGD*. The attack became bogged down short of the village due to a combination of deep snowdrifts, wire entanglements, minefields, and stubborn resistance. Soon the tanks were separated from the infantry by the minefields, and the latter had to forge ahead without tank support until a route through the mines was cleared.

At 1600 hours, the Americans were ready to try again. Supported by a barrage fired from 120 guns of divisional and corps artillery, CCA, 5th Armored Division and 1st Battalion, 311th Infantry surged into Eicherscheid. House-to-house fighting quickly ensued and by nightfall the village had fallen, though a few German strongpoints held out until the next morning.

Directly to the north of CCA, 5th Armored Division, the 3rd Battalion, 311th Infantry Regiment entered Huppenbroich by noon on 30 January. Fighting was intense at first. Troops had to advance uphill through deep snowdrifts, all the while under intense mortar and machine-gun fire. Even the weather seemed to conspire against them by maintaining a steady east wind that blew snow into their eyes. Many men were evacuated with frostbite due to a shortage of adequate winter clothing. German resistance was soon overcome after the battalion commander, Lieutenant Colonel Andy A. Lipscomb, ordered his antitank guns to knock out individual German fighting positions. By the time it was over the next morning, Lipscomb's 3rd Battalion had suffered over 125 casualties.[9]

By the morning of 31 January, a total of 230 demoralized German prisoners, including three women, were taken and most of Thürmer's *1st Battalion, Grenadier Regiment 981* had been wiped out.[10] For the first time, an entire battalion of the *272nd VGD* had to be stricken from the order of battle. The battalion would be re-constituted by 13 February, but with new personnel and a new cadre of leaders whose efficiency would never again rival that of the old battalion's officers and NCOs. It was a harbinger of things to come.*

Overall, the initial attack had gone well. By nightfall of 30 January, the southern wing of the 78th Infantry Division's assault had reached the outskirts of Imgenbroich and the defending *Grenadier Regiment 981* was reeling. After the elimination of his *1st Battalion* (the *2nd Battalion* was still serving as corps reserve to the north and was not engaged on this date), all that *Oberstleutnant* Kleinkorres had available to delay the advance of the Lightning Division in *Grenadier Regiment 981*'s sector was a variety of hastily formed emergency units made up of elements of his own regiment, as well as several others sent to help by divisional headquarters.

Since these emergency units were thrown together from soldiers from battalion and regimental trains completely lacking in combat experience or from stragglers from other units lacking any sort of heavy weapons, their combat effectiveness was markedly low and their introduction into the fighting west of the Roer only served to swell the overall number of prisoners taken during the next several days.

The big fight of the day, however, proved to be the second American attempt to retake the village of Kesternich, this time once and for all. Although it had meticulously prepared for the attack in detail, the attack by Lieutenant Colonel Richard W. Keyes's 2nd Battalion, 311th Infantry Regiment quickly bogged down in house-to-house fighting. Supporting armor from Company A, 736th Tank Battalion (this was their first combat action) and a platoon from the 893rd Tank Destroyer Battalion were not effectively used and the defending troops from

---

* Included in those captured was a "fine specimen of a German officer," who stated that even he and his own officers were becoming discouraged by the news of the Soviet offensive and that he "sincerely regretted that the attempt (on Hitler) on July 20th was not successful." He also bemoaned the fact that he had been forced to lead his men to slaughter out of necessity. Source: Headquarters, 78th Infantry Division, G-2 Monthly Report for January 1945, 1.

Hauptmann Thomae's *2nd Battalion, Grenadier Regiment 980* accounted for four M4 Shermans knocked out by Hetzers and mines on the first day alone.[11]

The German's frequent and accurate use of mortar concentrations to break up attacking American formations caused numerous delays and casualties, which slowed the momentum of the attack as medical personnel had to be brought forward to evacuate the wounded.[12] The Germans used *Panzerfausts* as indirect fire weapons to create tree bursts that had a devastating effect on troops moving through the orchards on the town's western outskirts. Another German tactical innovation that made the fighting even more difficult involved the remote firing of machine guns using a system of wires and pulleys operated by *Volksgrenadiers* from cover several meters away.[13]

Fires, caused by heavy shelling, burned out of control in many of the ruined houses, and the resulting smoke limited observation and prevented effective command and control of the operation. Deep snow obscured navigational landmarks and many of the German antitank obstacles and minefields. These impediments further compounded by problems the Americans were then experiencing with radio and field telephone communications, caused the attack to lose momentum. To make the fighting even more confusing, the soldiers from both sides were again wearing white snow coveralls, hindering visual recognition of friend and foe. German artillery and mortar fire was intense and accurate.

Keyes, in order to keep the operation from bogging down, was forced to commit his reserve company by 1030 hours. By nightfall, his battalion had advanced only a few hundred yards. Although over half of the town was in American hands, the attack was called off, to resume in the morning, once the tanks and tank destroyers had been replenished. German resistance had been far more determined than anticipated, but would have to be broken the following day if the 311th Infantry Regiment was to achieve all of its objectives on schedule.

Knowing that he had to hold Kesternich as long as possible, *Generalmajor* König granted *Oberst* Burian the tactical flexibility to do whatever was necessary to hold the town, since the entire defensive scheme of the *272nd VGD* depended on it. Should it fall, the division's positions west of the Roer would become untenable and it would have to retreat or become entrapped. To bolster *2nd Battalion, Grenadier Regiment 980*, *Leutnant* Stefan, then acting as Burian's orderly officer or *O1*, who served as an assistant operations officer, was ordered once again to form an *alarm* company from regimental trains, perhaps fifty or sixty men in all, and march toward Kesternich from Strauch. His orders were to hold at all costs. Arriving at 0230 hours the next morning, Stefan and his men, joined by two fortress infantry companies, were a welcome addition to Thomae's beleaguered force. The two *Hetzers* from Adrario's *Tank Destroyer Battalion 272* were ordered to remain in town under Thomae's control.

Luckily for Keyes and his men, though, Thomae did not counterattack on the night of 30/31 January. Keyes' interpreted this as a sign that Thomae's forces were weakening, since local counterattack was a hallmark of German doctrine.[14]

One American participant noted that if an aggressive counterattack had been launched that morning, especially if preceded by a heavy mortar or artillery barrage, it would have been "not hard to visualize the success" it would have had at that particular time.[15] Why Thomae chose not to do so is still a mystery, since he had previously demonstrated a penchant for carrying out such attacks, as he had done at Castle Hill (Hill 400) and during the first battle for Kesternich. Perhaps he did not wish to sacrifice any more of his men than absolutely necessary.

The 2nd Battalion, 311th Infantry's attack resumed at 0830 hours the next day after a short artillery preparation. Fighting room to room, the men of the 2nd Battalion moved forward inexorably against bitter opposition. It was noted later that the defenders gave up no more ground "than was absolutely necessary."[16] One man, Staff Sergeant Jonah E. Kelly of Company E, single-handedly cleared several houses of German defenders, killing and wounding over a dozen. Despite his wounds, he continued fighting until he was mortally wounded as he ran across an open space to another building, though he managed to kill the *Volksgrenadier* who shot him. Kelly was posthumously awarded the Medal of Honor, the only soldier in the 78th Infantry Division to receive the United States Armed Forces' highest medal for valor.[17]

By nightfall on 31 January, fewer than a dozen German-occupied buildings on the northern edge of town and twenty building on the eastern edge remained to be taken, a task left for the following morning. After working out procedures to ensure better cooperation between the tanks and infantrymen, the attack was finally able to push all the way through Kesternich. Tanks effectively placed direct fire on German strong points, which were then cleared of stunned survivors by the infantry. At one point, Lieutenant Colonel Keyes himself mounted a Sherman to direct its fire against a position. By nightfall on 1 February, virtually all of Kesternich was finally in American hands, more than six weeks after the first abortive attack.

The attack, though successful, had been costly for the 2nd Battalion, 311th Infantry Regiment. Of the 224 front-line infantrymen (excluding heavy weapons, headquarters, and service troops) of the 2nd Battalion who fought for Kesternich, losses between 30 and 31 January totaled 190 killed, wounded, missing, or medically evacuated for exposure.[18] Only eight of the fifteen tanks that began the attack were still operational. The town itself was completely destroyed; not a single house was left standing. Even the church had been reduced to rubble. The fighting had been so heavy and the damage so extensive, that even Cedric Foster of *The Star and Stripes*, the American Forces' newspaper, declared Kesternich a "Little Aachen."[19]

The loss of German life and equipment was even greater. Both *Hetzers* were damaged and had to be abandoned by their crews. Over 400 German bodies were recovered afterward by American graves registration teams. Though many of these dead were a result of the fighting that took place in Kesternich during the December fighting, the Americans estimated that as many as 260 of the bodies were those of *Volksgrenadiers* killed during the second battle, though this figure was probably exaggerated.[20] Whatever the actual number of casualties, the Germans had forever lost this key town with its commanding view of the plateau and the Roer valley below.

Thomae, with fewer than one hundred survivors of his battalion, was forced to withdraw east of Kesternich, where he was ordered to occupy hasty defensive positions along some hedgerows and in the forests and ravines southwest of Rurberg. Here, he and his men awaited the next phase of the assault, which was not long in coming. Though Thomae and his men had fought exceptionally well, in the end they had been outnumbered by a margin of three to one and had but two *Hetzers* and *Panzerfausts* to fight against twenty tanks and tank destroyers. The only achievement that he could point to is that he and his battalion had delayed the fall of Kesternich, thus enabling what was left of *Grenadier Regiment 981* to withdraw safely across the Roer. Although Thomae did not know it, his battalion had slowed the American advance for three critical days, foiling Lieutenant Colonel Keyes' plan to take Kesternich by 30 January. (See Map 13)

The honor of being the last *Volksgrenadier* to pull out of Kesternich belonged to *Grenadier* Gerd Hörner, an eighteen-year-old conscript from Wuppertal. He and the others in his *Marsch* (replacement) Battalion, including his friend, Willi Pispers, had been scheduled originally to be assigned to the *344th Infantry Division* on 13 December 1944, but had been diverted to the *272nd VGD* instead. After a two-day march to Herhahn, where *Grenadier Regiment 980* had its regimental trains, Hörner and the others were finally issued weapons, told to drop off their rucksacks, and ordered to be prepared to move to the front lines with only their assault packs.

Upon arrival in Kesternich on 22 December, Hörner and Pispers were assigned to *Leutnant* Helmers's *8th Company, Grenadier Regiment 980*. The two replacements and several other new arrivals were greeted in person by *Hauptmann* Thomae, who welcomed them to his battalion and ensured that they were quickly integrated into their new company. Hörner and Pispers were both assigned to a heavy machine-gun team under the command of *Unteroffizier* "Maco" Malkowski. From 22 December until 30 January, Malkowski's team secured the battalion's left flank along the northern edge of the Tiefenbachtal, where it shared a boundary with the neighboring *Grenadier Regiment 981*.

Hörner and Malkowski, along with the rest of their machine-gun team barely escaped capture on 1 February when they were forced to hastily evacuate a cellar in Kesternich only a few seconds ahead of their American pursuers, who were using Shermans to spearhead their attack. After fighting for several days on the town's southern edge, Malkowski and his group found themselves in danger of being cut off from the rest of the battalion and captured. His friend Willi Pispers, shot through the ear by a sniper, had been taken into the cellar for treatment by a company medic. With the Americans now within feet of the house they were occupying, Hörner was ordered to cover the retreat of the rest of his company.

As Hörner lay in the snow with his MG-42, he watched as Pispers and several other wounded soldiers who had been left behind in the cellar were marched away into captivity. Feeling quite uncomfortable in the knowledge that he was the last German soldier fighting in Kesternich, Hörner was relieved when Malkowski shouted at him from behind a wall to pick up his machine gun and get out of there. Joining his sergeant, both men ran across the open field fronting the eastern side of town, dodging American bullets and exposed landmines the whole way.

Malkowski, who was much larger than Hörner, carried the machine gun for the younger man so they could run faster. After a few hundred meters, they reached the rest of the company, which was then busily engaged in digging new foxholes under *Leutnant* Helmer's direction. Once again, Hörner and Malkowski placed their machine gun into position and waited for the next attack. Four days later, Hörner was severely wounded in the leg by shell fragments during an artillery barrage and evacuated to a hospital near Münster, where he remained until the end of the war when he was captured laying in his hospital bed.[21]

While the fighting raged in Kesternich, the attack toward the south continued to build momentum. Between 31 January and 1 February, the 1st Battalion, 310th Infantry Regiment drove remnants of *Grenadier Regiments 981* and *164* from their outpost line between Eicherscheid and Imgenbroich. During the same period, the 2nd Battalion of the 310th Infantry captured the village of Hammer against light opposition and earned the distinction of becoming the first battalion in the 78th Infantry Division to reach the Roer River.

German attempts to stem the tide can be characterized as being too little, too late. Called forward to plug the gap near the village of Huppenbroich that was developing between *Grenadier Regiment 980* in Kesternich and *Grenadier Regiment 981* in the vicinity of Eicherscheid, the *2nd Battalion* of the latter regiment, after a forced march from its reserve position near Strauch and a harrowing crossing of the Roer bridge at Einruhr, arrived on the outskirts of Huppenbroich too late to reoccupy it and was quickly driven toward the southeast by the American force that had taken the village the day before.

Finally coming to a halt on the southeast edge of the village next to the Tiefenbach Ravine, *Hauptmann* Günther Ragnow's *2nd Battalion, Grenadier Regiment 981* was forced to take up hasty positions along the hedges and fences outlying Huppenbroich. According to one participant, *Gefreiter* Otto Gunkel, the ground was too frozen to dig foxholes, and he and his comrades were rotated in and out of the few remaining outbuildings to keep from freezing to death. The following day, several American tanks supported by infantry chased the German survivors away after a brief stand, forcing them to take up new positions on the northern outskirts of Dedenborn, approximately two kilometers southeast of Huppenbroich.[22]

Ragnow's *2nd Battalion, Grenadier Regiment 981* was able to hold out for three more days at Dedenborn before being forced to withdraw eastward to the resort area at Schöne Aussicht. Though the *Volksgrenadiers* tried to make a stand from the heights encircling Dedenborn, the attacking 1st Battalion, 311th Infantry quickly overwhelmed the defenders after men from Company C forded the Roer and scaled the near-vertical cliffs. Fighting house to house, the attackers seized the town by nightfall on 3 February, after capturing forty-three Germans and killing twenty others.[23] By that date, a five-kilometer-wide wedge had been driven between the *272nd* and *62nd Volks-Grenadier Divisions.* Both had been forced back to the Roer and the Monschau forest further acted to separate the two divisions. To make matters worse, the *272nd VGD* was being pushed toward the northeast, while the *62nd* was being forced back to the southeast.

One grenadier regiment of the *62nd Volks-Grenadier Division*, the *164th* under *Oberst* Jüttner, was completely separated from the rest of the division and temporarily attached to the *272nd VGD.* Placed in a defensive position along the heights overlooking the Roer in the vicinity of Finkenauel, the most that Jüttner and his men could do was report on American movement and direct artillery fire. The drive of the US 9th Infantry Division toward Gemünd had also proved unstoppable, with nearly all of its objectives being taken on schedule. Therefore, with the initial stages of the American operation having succeeded in clearing the Monschau corridor and the right flank of the 78th Infantry Division, the way was now clear to launch the second phase, which would focus primarily on the assault against the town of Schmidt.

⟞⟩∘∘∘⟨⟝

Unaware of the American offensive preparations, *Füsilier Company 272* continued weapons training and unit-level field exercises at Hergarten with the new replacements and leadership until 30 January. At 0615 hours that morning, *Hauptmann* Heldt received an order from the *Ia* of 272nd VGD, *Major i.G.* Uhl, directing that Heldt prepare his company for a new mission. In addition, he was instructed that he and his company were to be ready to move by 1000 hours.

After receiving the warning order from their company commander, the *Unteroffiziere* swung into action, instilling a sense of urgency in the men, who hastily packed their kit onto their bicycles, cleaned their weapons, and discarded any unnecessary items, such as letters, magazines or newspapers. It would be the company's first action in over three weeks, since the bloody disaster at Simmerath.

Their new objective would be the town of Einruhr, some twenty kilometers away by road. Here, at the southern tip of the Roer Reservoir, *Hauptmann* Heldt was to report to the commander of *Grenadier Regiment 981, Oberstleutnant* Kleinkorres, whose regiment was responsible for protecting the division's left flank where it tied in with the right flank of the neighboring *62nd Volks-Grenadier Division.* No more information was provided.

Heldt probably reasoned that the Americans were finally mounting their long-anticipated final drive from the direction of Monschau toward the dams. He did not know that the *62nd Volks-Grenadier Division* was in the process of being rapidly overrun by the 9th Infantry Division. With no idea of what lay in store ahead, the men formed up with their bicycles in a column of platoons as they had been trained to do and waited. While they stood there, the rumble of artillery could be heard in the west and southwest.

Ten o'clock came and went, but the order to move had not arrived. Nearly everyone was aware that the longer they remained in the open street, the greater the chances were that they would be spotted by *Jabos* or the omnipresent artillery spotter aircraft and attacked, just as had happened six days earlier. A few nervously smoked their cigarettes or made jokes, but most of the men simply stood there stoically and waited. Finally, at 1130 hours, they received the order to move out, leaving the company trains behind in Hergarten under the watchful eyes of *Hauptfeldwebel* Fuhrmeister.

Their route took them initially south through the flat countryside south of Hergarten, where they took a right turn in the village of Düttling. Here, they entered the forest once again and for a little while at least were safe from air attack. The ground rose sharply, however, forcing many of the men to dismount their bicycles and push them up the hill. When they reached the summit overlooking the town of Gemünd from the north, they breathed a sigh of relief, for they would be able to coast downhill for the next kilometer or so until they reached the center of town.

Quickly passing through shell-torn Gemünd, the column continued pedaling southwest, where they soon encountered another hill northeast of the crossroads village of Herhahn. After a short rest, they continued on their way for the remaining eight kilometers, coasting most of the way, before finally reaching Einruhr by late afternoon on 30 January. Here, the men bedded down, spending a cold, wet night in ruined houses on the outskirts of Einruhr. Artillery fire fell intermittently. The next morning *Hauptmann* Heldt, accompanied by *Leutnant* Gomm, was able to locate the headquarters of *Grenadier Regiment 981*, where Heldt was told by Kleinkorres that *Füsilier Company 272* was to serve as the division reserve, but would be under the tactical control of his regiment.

This was the second time in a month that the company had been subordinated to Kleinkorres and, as before, it had come at an hour of dire need. *Grenadier Regiment 981* had just lost its *1st Battalion* in and around Eicherscheid and the *2nd Battalion* was being hastily moved forward from its reserve position to shore up the regiment's crumbling front. Until *2nd Battalion* was in place, emergency units and *Füsilier Company 272* would have to hold the line.

Heldt and Gomm were then issued orders that directed the company to be prepared to occupy screening positions southwest of Einruhr in order to cover the road leading toward Erkensruhr, some three kilometers away. Gomm, accompanied by a guide from *Grenadier Regiment 981*, then returned to the company and briefed the platoon leaders on their new assignment, while Heldt remained with Kleinkorres The commitment of the company toward Erkensruhr can probably be explained as a precautionary move to counter the successful American seizure of Hammer on 1 February and the possible continuation of the attack across the Roer. As it turned out, the 311th Infantry Regiment of the 78th Infantry Division attacked Dedenborn instead.

An hour or so later, Gomm, leading *1st, 2nd, 3rd,* and *4th Platoons* (the Infantry Howitzer Platoon had still not returned from its mission in support of the *Fifteenth Army Assault School*), guided them into their new positions at Einruhr where they remained that day and the next. It remained relatively quiet, save for the continuing sounds of fighting from the west and northwest, that now sounded relatively close, which, in fact, it was, since the 311th Infantry Regiment of the 78th Infantry Division was nearing the village of Hammer on the Roer, fewer than three kilometers away as the crow flies.

Heldt soon had cause to wish that he still had control of his infantry howitzers because their added firepower would have proven useful. As it was, *Leutnant* Wegner and his platoon were at that very moment experiencing heavy fighting with the *Fifteenth Army's Assault School* (or "AOK 15" as described in US intelligence reports), which was attempting to stem the advance of the 9th Infantry Division in the vicinity of Höfen. This special unit had been committed under the direct order of *General der Infanterie* von Zangen, *Fifteenth Army's* commander, in order to "temporarily alleviate the situation" by delaying the American advance until more forces could be made available.[24]

With Wegner and his infantry howitzers firing in support, the 400 troops composing the bulk of the *Fifteenth Army Assault School* collided at 2055 hours 31 January with the advance guard of the approaching 39th Infantry Regiment of the US 9th Infantry Division. This unit had halted for the evening in preparation for an attack against the Wahlerscheid crossroads and was awaiting the arrival of the main body of the division. Heavy fighting soon broke out up and down the line of the 1st and 2nd Battalions of the 39th Infantry as the German NCO candidates charged determinedly out of the woods.[25]

During the first stages of this counterthrust, the Germans, according to one American eyewitness, came on "shouting, screaming, and yelling in a Banzai manner" as the fighting degenerated at times to hand-to-hand combat.[26] The attack was supported by Wegner's two howitzers, located in the forest on the western edge of Schöneseifen, as well as by the artillery of both *62nd* and *272nd VGDs*. The fighting raged back and forth until 0300 hours 1 February, when the Americans finally gained the upper hand and forced the Germans to withdraw.

When the 2nd Battalion, 39th Infantry Regiment renewed the advance at 0430 hours, it was greeted by "considerable [enemy] artillery fire," some of which no doubt was delivered by *Füsilier Company 272*'s infantry howitzer platoon. This was not enough, however, as the determined "Old Reliables" of the 9th Infantry

Division soon forced the *Fifteenth Army Assault School* to hurriedly withdraw toward the direction of Schöneseifen, leaving dozens of dead and wounded behind. Though they had been thrown back, they had delayed the American attack and were able to buy time for others to set up defenses further to the rear.

During its support of the *Fifteenth Army's Assault School* from 9 January to 4 February, the infantry howitzer platoon suffered only two casualties, *Gefreiter* Max Fröschl and Konrad Brill, both injured by US artillery fire. While Fröschl's wounds were serious, Brill was to return to duty with his platoon a few weeks later after a short stay in the division field hospital at the Mariawald Abbey. *Leutnant* Wegner spent little, if any, time with his guns during this period, as he was involved in the fighting while serving as the battalion adjutant to the *Fifteenth Army Assault School's* commander.

Unaware of the howitzer platoon's fight at Wahlerschied, the main body of *Füsilier Company 272* arrayed in their screening position near Einruhr did not know how far the Americans had advanced or even which German unit was on their left flank. In fact, they were alone and virtually unsupported, had their opponents taken advantage of this opportunity and elected to attack. German units passing through Einruhr to the east were in total disarray and the situation at the sole remaining bridge over the Roer was chaotic. Doughboys from the 9th Infantry Division were in close pursuit, placing additional unwelcome pressure on the German leadership.

Unbeknownst to Heldt's *Volksgrenadiers,* the 310th and 311th Regiments of the 78th Infantry Division and the 9th Infantry Division had quickly smashed through the *272nd* and *62nd Volks-Grenadier Divisions'* defenses by 1 February and had reached the Roer at several points. This latest advance placed the American vanguard only a few kilometers from Einruhr, where the road to the east, leading to the *272nd VGD* headquarters in Gemünd, lay wide open.

By 2 February, the situation on the *272nd VGD's* left flank was deteriorating so rapidly that Heldt and his company were ordered to move out and take up its previously described screening mission in the vicinity of Erkensruhr. There they would link up with elements of *Grenadier Regiment 164* holding positions near Finkenauel. Leaving the *3rd* and part of *4th Platoons* behind to cover the approaches to Einruhr, Heldt and the remainder of the company set out at once on foot toward Erkensruhr, which lay two kilometers away. Einruhr had been under harassing artillery fire since that morning and Heldt was keenly aware that he had to move quickly before his column was spotted by American observation aircraft and shelled. They had been lucky so far, with the weather keeping the spotter aircraft grounded because of low ceilings. While crossing the bridge five hundred meters south of Einruhr, however, Heldt's luck ran out.

As the head of the column approached the far end of the bridge, American artillery began to fall. Shell bursts compelled both *1st* and *2nd Platoons,* as well as the company headquarters section, to seek cover. *Hauptmann* Heldt was killed immediately by fragments to the chest, as was the unit's senior medical NCO,

Sanitäts-Feldwebel Paul Bajohr and a runner, *Obergefreiter* Paul Radek. *Leutnant* Gomm was also severely wounded, with fragment wounds to the leg and foot. Again, the company was deprived of its leadership. Rather than continuing toward Erkensruhr, the company, now thoroughly demoralized, dug in a few hundred meters south of the bridge and tended to its casualties.

The company, probably the only sizeable reserve that *272nd VGD* possessed at the moment, needed to be placed in the hands of a competent commander as soon as possible. Since *Leutnant* Wegner was still fighting with the *Fifteenth Army Assault School* at Schöneseiffen, he could not be recalled immediately to assume command. Instead, *Generalmajor* König selected an officer from his own division's combat school, *Oberleutnant* Helmut Aretz, as Heldt's replacement. Aretz, who had recently been assigned to the division, arrived that evening in Einruhr to take command of the company.

Oberleutnant Aretz was an experienced officer who had been fighting continuously along the *Westwall* since the previous November, serving as a company commander and as battalion adjutant of *1st Battalion, Grenadier Regiment 77* of the *26th Volks-Grenadier Division.* Born 13 May 1921 in Krefeld, Aretz had fought on the Eastern Front, where he had been severely wounded during the summer of 1944. After convalescence, Aretz was placed in the pool of available though unassigned officers to be used as replacements wherever the need dictated.[27] With his experience, he was probably the ideal man for the assignment, though he had hardly any time to get the company back on its feet again and to help it recover from the shock of losing two of its three officers.

On 3 February, one day after the death of *Hauptmann* Heldt, division headquarters ordered the company to withdraw immediately from its defensive position in the vicinity of Einruhr and move to the southeast to block the rapid American advance from the direction of Dreiborn. Aretz's orders instructed him to set up a *Gefechtsvorpostenkette* (screen of outposts) facing to the southwest so his company could guard the road that ran from the village of Herhahn southeast to the larger town of Schleiden, four kilometers away.

The move had become an urgent necessity because the 1st Battalion, 60th Infantry of the 9th Infantry Division had punched through the feeble defenses of *Grenadier Regiment 183* of the exhausted *62nd Volks-Grenadier Division* in Dreiborn the previous day. The Americans had also scattered the remnants of the *Fifteenth Army Assault School* and a battalion of the *12th Volks-Grenadier Division* that had attempted to bar the American advance near the forked crossroads west of Schöneseifen. The road to Schleiden now lay wide open, had the Americans only known of the advantage that this opportunity gave them, they could have inflicted an even greater defeat upon the Germans. As it was, what soon followed was nearly as decisive.

At Dreiborn, a bitter house-to-house fight took place 3 February that threatened to widen the gap between *Generalmajor* König's division and his neighbor to the south. This American attack, if pursued vigorously, would also trap *Füsilier*

Company 272 and other units of the division in the vicinity of Einruhr, which lay only four kilometers northwest of Dreiborn. Unless something was done immediately, the Americans might also continue their attack along the division boundary between König's and *Generalmajor* Kittel's divisions and seize Gemünd, thus threatening to collapse the entire German defense between Düren and Schleiden. As it had before at Zweifallshammer and Simmerath, *Füsilier Company 272* was again hastily committed to protect the division's threatened flank.

Before having a chance to become familiar with his new command, *Oberleutnant* Aretz found himself saddled with great responsibility but with little knowledge about the actual military situation that he would soon have to face. As snow began to fall on the afternoon of 3 February, he got his men moving out to their new assignment. After proceeding northeast for two kilometers, he and his men turned right at the intersection 500 meters south of Einruhr, only an hour or two ahead of an American force, and then continued marching southeast for another six kilometers along the serpentine road that wound uphill through what is nowadays the Vogelsang training area.

Herhahn, a small crossroads town of less than 500 people, lay astride the main road from Gemünd west toward Monschau. Only two kilometers to the southwest lay Dreiborn, which had fallen to the Americans earlier in the day on 3 February. The village was situated on a plateau that permitted excellent observations and fields of fire in all directions; whoever held Herhahn controlled access to Schleiden, Gemünd, and the crossings over the Urft River, as well as the vital dam regulating the Urft Reservoir. Huebner's US V Corps had designated the dam as a key objective for the 9th Infantry Division's attack. Its seizure was a prerequisite for the continuation of the American offensive against Schmidt and the Roer dam at Schwammenauel that lay only a few kilometers to the north.

While *Oberleutnant* Aretz and his *Volksgrenadiers* were marching toward Herhahn, troops of the 3rd Battalion, 60th Infantry Regiment supported by several attached tanks and tank destroyers were also en route to the same objective, arriving there at approximately 2000 hours, slightly ahead of *Füsilier Company 272*. The Americans quickly succeeded in routing the disorganized elements from the *62nd Volks-Grenadier Division* that was holding the crossroads on the western edge of the town and began to dig in.

With this important road junction now in the hands of the Americans, the main supply route of the *272nd VGD* along the Roer was cut and a significant portion of the divisional artillery of *62nd* and *272nd VGD* as well as the main body of *Grenadier Regiment 164* were trapped in the vicinity of the Vogelsang training area near the village of Wollseifen. The loss even of a few artillery pieces would have a decisive effect at this late stage in the campaign, since every single gun was needed to support the rapidly fading German infantry. The left flank of *272nd VGD* was also now completely open and vulnerable to attack, and the southernmost dam at Urft was virtually undefended. Something had to be done quickly before the tottering German defenses collapsed completely. (See Map 14)

Unaware of the approach of *Füsilier Company 272* on their own left flank, the Americans quickly went about setting up a hasty defensive line facing southeast at the northwestern outskirts of Herhahn. There the men of 3rd Battalion, 60th Infantry Regiment waited for their sister 39th Infantry Regiment, still mopping up after the fight in Dreiborn, to catch up with them so they could continue the attack. A few kilometers to the northwest, the third regiment of the 9th Infantry Division, the 47th Infantry, had taken Einruhr after a brief but sharp fight, shortly after *Füsilier Company 272* had departed.

1st Battalion of the 39th Infantry Regiment arrived at the western outskirts of Herhahn and began passing through the lines of the 3rd Battalion, 60th Infantry Regiment shortly after midnight on 3/4 February. There were at least three Shermans from the 746th Tank Battalion and two M-10 tank destroyers from the 899th Tank Destroyer Battalion accompanying the infantry, but most of these were covering the approaches to the northwest, which seemed to the Americans to be the likely enemy avenue of approach. It was at this moment that the Germans struck from the northeast.

The news of American's arrival at Herhahn and the collapse of the *62nd Volks-Grenadier Division* had generated a crisis in *Generalmajor* König's headquarters that reverberated as high as *Fifteenth Army*. To restore the situation, *General der Infanterie* von Zangen ordered an immediate counterattack. Should this town and its commanding position fall to the Americans, a continued defense of the dams and approaches to the Urft and Roer Rivers from the south would become impossible. It would also isolate the bulk of the *272nd VGD* on the west bank of the Roer, with the only escape route passing around the north of the Schwammenauel Reservoir near Schmidt, a town that now figured prominently in the Allies' offensive plan.

The loss of the eastern tip of the Monschau corridor would further contribute to the widening gap between the *62nd and 272nd VGDs*; it had become nearly impossible for the Germans to do anything about this development unless *Fifteenth Army* could carry out a substantial counterattack. Of course, von Zangen lacked the means to do much of anything about it. His army's last remaining reserve, *Fifteenth Army Assault School,* had been nearly wiped out in the attack at Wahlerscheid crossroads and the retreat to Dreiborn two days before. To make the situation even more difficult, *Generalfeldmarschall* Model at *Army Group B* had not yet authorized the commitment of any of the armor that he still held in reserve, though the *3rd Panzer-Grenadier Division* lay nearby in a tactical assembly area.

While von Zangen begged for reinforcement, Aretz halted his company just outside of town at dusk. Here, he linked up with the survivors of the *62nd Volks-Grenadier Division* who had been thrown out of Herhahn earlier. They told him that Herhahn was occupied by a tank-supported American force of unknown size. To avoid being caught on the open plateau northwest of the town, Aretz moved his troops quickly into the neighboring village of Morsbach, less than 500 meters away from the Americans, and contacted division headquarters for further instructions.

He was informed that in order to restore the situation or at least clear a withdrawal route for the artillery at Wollseifen, Aretz was to launch an attack to retake Herhahn immediately. In a letter to the author, Aretz recalled that he was supposed to attack in order to open a route for German artillery and heavy equipment retreating from the third battle of Aachen, an illustration of the type of misunderstanding even a supposedly well-placed German officer could have of the overall military situation at this stage of the war, since Aachen had fallen to the Allies four months previously (as yet the Germans had not given a name to the fighting in the Hürtgen Forest—that would come after the war).

Aretz recalls that the *272nd VGD* operations officer promised him that the attack would be supported by a few tanks from *3rd Panzer-Grenadier Division,* sent from their assembly area near Brunfeld, and two assault guns, all of which were to arrive shortly. Besides the one hundred or so men he had brought from his own company, he also had a few dozen men of *Grenadier Regiment 164, 62nd VGD* and some artillerymen and tank destroyer crews without cannon subordinated to him from his own division with which to carry out his counterattack.[28]

These troops had been forcibly ejected from the crossroads on the western edge of town earlier that evening during the initial American advance. Although a few self-propelled 37mm *Flak* cannon from *Major* Adrario's *Antitank Battalion 272* had been positioned in the town earlier that day, they were recalled to reoccupy their old fighting positions one kilometer away at Huhnerbush shortly before the Americans attacked.[29] They would now be ordered return and support Aretz's counterattack in the ground combat role, just as they had at Kesternich on 15 December.

Even with this augmentation, retaking Herhahn would be a difficult mission to carry out. Because radio or wire communication with the cut-off artillery battalions near Wollseifen was lacking, Aretz's men would have to fight without indirect fire support, except for what the *3rd Panzer-Grenadier Division,* which had been place in reserve by *Army Group B* between Gemünd and Schleiden, could provide. It was pitch dark, he had only a sketchy knowledge of the terrain, and knew none of the leaders in the other units subordinated to him.

According to Aretz, his attacking force numbered "300–350 men of mixed origins, consisting of former pilots, *Flak* troops, artillerymen, and infantry."[30] He planned to retake the town later that same night, when American superiority in the air and in artillery would not be as telling, but first he had to know where the Americans were located. Shortly after 2100 hours on the evening of 3 February, as the Americans began to establish defensive positions at the crossroads at the western edge of Herhahn, Aretz sent out a reconnaissance team led by *Unteroffizier* Franz Sichler to feel out the American dispositions. Meanwhile, he and the rest of his force moved into an assembly area in the large ravine between Herhahn and Morsbach to prepare for their attack.

Stripped down to the bare essentials, leaving behind any equipment that might make noise, Sichler and his men crept silently across several hundred meters of snow-covered fields and disappeared into the night. A couple of hours later, he and his men returned from their reconnaissance patrol, having suffered no casualties. Sichler then positioned his men and went to the company command post to brief *Oberleutnant* Aretz on what he had seen. As soon as he had finished, he turned to rejoin his platoon, but never made it. An American shell burst nearby that sent fragments into Sichler's skull, killing him instantly. It was to prove a bad omen for the pending attack.

Shortly after midnight, as on 4 February, as troops of the 39th Infantry Regiment began to pass through the lines of the 60th Infantry Regiment, they were hit by Aretz' counterattack from the north and east, which "struck in spurts at first" according to an American eyewitness. While moving into their foxholes, they were "subjected to a peppering of small-arms fire" from German troops.[31] At 0200 hours on 4 February, two tanks and two self-propelled *Flak* cannon came up from the south to reinforce Aretz's battle group. These vehicles, augmented by a portion of Aretz's force, threatened to cut the Americans off from the rest of their division.

According to an eyewitness, Willy Nissel, a *Flak* gunner assigned to *3rd Company, Antitank Battalion 272,*

After a short artillery barrage on Herhahn, we rattled up the road. . . . Shortly before the village's entrance, we fired the first high explosive shells from our cannon. The German infantry pushed into the town, firing their assault rifles as they went. The enemy defended himself vigorously on this occasion. Our talk about the enemy being "too afraid to fight" was unmasked this night as a bloody fairy tale. The call "medic medic" resounded again and again throughout the night. *"Hände Hoch!"* and "Hands up!" were heard back and forth all night long.[32]

The tanks and self-propelled *Flak* soon lent their weight to the assault, clanking up and down the streets firing directly into foxholes and houses where American had established their hasty defensive positions. Shortly afterwards, these tanks and Aretz's infantry were joined by two assault guns and the German counterattack rolled forward through the town.

Interrupted in the middle of conducting a passage of lines in the dark, the American troops were initially caught off guard, since the commander of the 1st Battalion, 39th Infantry had been told by some anonymous staff officer at division headquarters that the town had been "completely secured" earlier that evening.[33] Though the Germans entered the town in force, they failed to thoroughly search the houses as they advanced.

Nissel observed with some dismay that the *Volksgrenadiers* appeared to have contented themselves with a grenade through a window or door as sufficient to suppress or discourage the Americans. They would soon have cause to regret this oversight. Nissel remarked that "I couldn't really say that houses 'cleared' in this manner were actually free of the enemy."[34] Still, Aretz's battle group continued its advance, reaching the front of the American positions near the crossroads on the western edge of town before his men were finally stopped by the combined efforts of the two American infantry battalions. In some instances, fighting was so intense that hand-to-hand combat was reported in forward positions.

Ironically, the *Volksgrenadiers* appeared to believe that they had captured the town and began to let down their guard just as the Americans had a few hours earlier. Rather than consolidate their positions and prepare for an American counterattack, the Germans seemed to have decided that the fighting was over that evening, secure in the adage that the "*Amis* never attack at night." Its mission accomplished, Nissel's *Flak* platoon was pulled out and sent back down the hill toward Huhnerbusch, along with the tanks and assault guns from the *3rd Panzer-Grenadier Division.*

The Germans could not have been more wrong. Fortunately for the Americans, plenty of divisional and V Corps artillery support was at hand. This devastating fire, consisting of over nine battalions of 105mm and 155mm artillery, was quickly brought to bear by the US 9th Infantry Division. The barrages first scattered the German pickets on the western outskirts of town, then shifted to pound the town's northern and eastern approaches, where it sealed off the area from any further German reinforcements with a continuous ring of fire. Hundreds of illumination shells were fired that night, lighting up the area for miles and making easy targets for the Americans, who had remained in their foxholes or who had found shelter in many of the houses the *Volksgrenadiers* had failed to search.

Using bazookas, captured *Panzerfausts*, antitank guns, and their own devastating artillery, the Americans then began their own counterattack. With the aid of three additional tanks and three more tank destroyers, the American push to retake the town began at 0415 hours. One infantry company, accompanied by one tank and one tank destroyer, began clearing the northern half of the town, while another, also accompanied by one tank and one tank destroyer, cleared the southern half. The third company was to remain in Herhahn to serve as a reserve. By dawn, they had scattered the final German counterattack, at which point the 1st Battalion, 39th Infantry Regiment resumed its effort to take the rest of Herhahn and continue the advance north toward Morsbach.[35]

Just as the German tanks had done four hours earlier, the American tanks and tank destroyers, closely followed by the infantry and backed by ample artillery support, clanked down the narrow streets of the town, firing into windows and likely centers of resistance with both cannon and machine guns, "thoroughly eradicating" all German resistance in Herhahn by 0700 hours. The survivors, completely overwhelmed by the American firepower, had a choice of surrendering or beating a hasty retreat toward Morsbach or south toward Hühnerbusch.[36]

Those who avoided capture began pulling back as the sun rose over the cold landscape. The German retreat quickly turned into a rout. The 3rd Battalion, 39th Infantry Regiment, moving up to the left of the 1st Battalion, soon joined in the fray, and swept through the northern edge of Herhahn toward Morsbach. After overcoming initial resistance at the town's edge, the 3rd Battalion quickly thrust through the town, capturing a German aid station in the process, and chased the survivors toward the cliffs overlooking the Urft River.

After a sharp but brief fight for the heights, the Germans gave up all pretense of defense and fled for the river. Many made good their escape, but Company L, 39th Infantry Regiment, occupying the high ground, had a field day shooting at the fleeing enemy. Literally firing "everything in the book at the retreating Germans, caution, cover and concealment were thrown to the winds as footsloggers [sic] had a field day" as the *Volksgrenadiers* attempted to cross the river.[37]

German losses in men and materiel were heavy. With the road severed between Einruhr and Herhahn, the gunners of *2nd Battalion, Artillery Regiment 272* and *8th Battery, Artillery Regiment 272,* as well as a battery from *62nd Volks-Grenadier Division* had no way to pull their guns out of Wollseifen. They had no choice but to blow up all twenty-five of them, a loss that severely degraded the combat power of both divisions. *Generalmajor* Jüttner reported that he and the survivors of his regiment, *Grenadier Regiment 164*, had to escape via the damaged spillway of the Urft Dam.[38] The 39th Infantry Regiment reported capturing over 321 Germans during this period, many of whom were taken in Herhahn.[39]

While the losses of the attached troops from *62nd Volks-Grenadier Division* cannot be determined with any accuracy, *Füsilier Company 272* alone lost thirty-eight men including one killed in action (*Unteroffizier* Sichler), eleven wounded in action, and twenty-six missing. As it was admitted later, the German High Command had little hope that the action to retake Herhahn had any chance for success. According to *General der Infanterie* Karl Püchler, the desperate attack to free the road through Herhahn, using "troops hastily scraped together" had been nothing more than a forlorn attempt and a failure.[40] Loss of the entire west bank of the Roer was now simply a matter of time.

One of those casualties of the fighting at Herhahn was *Oberleutnant* Aretz himself, who was wounded early in the action, his sixth combat wound since the beginning of the war. Shot through the upper thigh and lower arm in the initial assault, he was no longer capable of exercising command and was forced to turn it over to the senior surviving *Feldwebel* until a new commander could be designated. His loss early in the fighting deprived the motley German force of the leadership it sorely needed and probably contributed to its rapid disintegration when the battle started going against them. The men of *Füsilier Company 272* who survived this action limped back to the company's old troop billets in Hergarten, where it had gone to lick its wounds after the disaster at Simmerath almost one month before.

The only good news that the company received on 4 February was that its infantry howitzer platoon had finally come back. The records indicate that it had been ordered to rejoin the company after it was forced to withdraw from its positions near Schöneseiffen, overrun by the US 9th Infantry Division's attack on 3 February. After suffering heavy casualties near the Wahlerschied crossroads and in front of Dreiborn, the battle group from the *Fifteenth Army Assault School,* to which the howitzer platoon had been attached, was hastily withdrawn in order to establish new defensive positions in the vicinity of Schleiden.

Here, the *Assault School's* battle group and the remnants of *62nd Volks-Grenadier Division* were placed under the control of *Generalmajor* Walter Denkert's hurriedly brought-up *3rd Panzer-Grenadier Division,* which was released from *Army Group B* reserve in order to plug the hole in the German lines between Gemünd and Schleiden. Curiously (to the Germans, at least), the Americans stopped just short of both towns and did not advance any further for the next two weeks. No longer needed, *Füsilier Company 272's* howitzer platoon was released.[41] While the guns and their crews quickly found their way back to Hergarten as ordered, *Leutnant* Wegner, however, had to remain behind with the *Fifteenth Army Assault School,* where he continued to serve as the unit's adjutant for the next several days.[42]

While *Füsilier Company 272* and the rest of its parent division hurriedly reorganized in order to regain some semblance of effectiveness, the Americans opposite them did the same, only they would be able to draw on a immense stock of munitions, fuel, food, and more importantly, trained replacements. With the Monschau corridor now cleared of Germans as far as Gemünd, the 78th Infantry Division could proceed with the next phase of the operation without having to worry about its southern flank, now firmly secured by the 9th Infantry Division.

The second phase would entail seizing the town of Schmidt and the area northwest of the Schwammenauel Reservoir. Only then could the attack across the Roer and the seizure of the dams go forward. The momentum was irresistibly swinging in the American's favor and the defeat of the *272nd VGD* west of the Roer was now a foregone conclusion. Unlike the fighting that had taken place in the Monschau corridor, where losses were relatively light (with the exception of the fight to seize Kesternich), however, the fight for Schmidt would be much more complex and costly.

12

Withdrawal Beyond the Roer

By 4 February, the collapse of *Generalmajor* König's *272nd VGD's* and the *LXXIV Corps'* defensive effort west of the Roer was only a matter of time. To the south, the Americans had cleared the Roer as far as the Urft Dam and the 9th and 2nd Infantry Divisions were within striking distance of Gemünd and Schleiden. Einruhr had fallen, cutting off the German line of retreat south of the dams. Kesternich had finally been seized as well, making any coherent defense west of the dams all but impossible.

The neighboring *62nd Volks-Grenadier Division* to the south had been thoroughly defeated, its regiments scattered, and only the timely release of the *3rd Panzer-Grenadier Division* from *Army Group B* reserve had prevented the Allied drive from continuing.[1] *Grenadier Regiment 981* had lost an entire battalion and *Oberstleutnant* Kleinkorres had been forced to withdraw what was left of his regiment, including the attached *Füsilier Company 272*, to positions in an area of the peninsula jutting out between the Schwammenauel and Urft Reservoirs known as *der Kermeter*.

Although *Artillery Regiment 272* had been forced to blow up and abandon a battalion's worth of guns at Wollseifen when its withdrawal route was severed at Herhahn by the 9th Infantry Division on 4 February, the rest of the regiment was intact. The *272nd VGD* had been bloodied and some of its subordinate elements scattered, but overall it was still capable of effective resistance. It also held strongly developed defensive positions between Steckenborn and Schmidt that blocked Allied access to the Schmidt plateau and the Schwammenauel Dam. König, however, needed time to rebuild his shattered southern flank, after *Grenadier Regiment 981* and *2nd Battalion, Grenadier Regiment 980* were forced out of their positions west of the Roer and after nearly one third of his division artillery was lost. The Allies, though, had no intention of allowing him the opportunity.

No sooner had Kesternich and Einruhr fallen on 3 February than the 78th Infantry Division began the next phase of its attack, which focused on the seizure of the Schmidt plateau overlooking the biggest prize of them all—the Schwammenauel Dam. König had precious little left under his direct control to stop Parker's 78th Infantry Division and the attached CCR, 7th Armored Division and 814th Tank Destroyer Battalion. With Kleinkorres's regiment smashed, König had only *Grenadier Regiments 980* and *982* left to oppose the attack and neither one of them was in very good shape.

In Burian's *Grenadier Regiment 980, Hauptmann* Thomae's *2nd Battalion* had suffered heavy losses in the unsuccessful defense of Kesternich and had been forced to withdraw across the Roer at Rurberg where, along with *Grenadier Regiment 981,* it would for the time being help ward off any American incursion across the river on the Kermeter Peninsula.[2] *Hauptmann* Rhein's *1st Battalion* was still holding a line that stretched from Strauch to Steckenborn, where the open fields approached Schmidt like a tapered funnel until they ran up against the forest along the western edge of the Schmidt plateau.

Rhein's battalion drew the assignment of barring the most likely American high-speed avenue of approach to Schmidt because it was now the stronger of the two in the regiment, with perhaps 250 men. In a last-minute boundary change, Rhein was ordered to shift his battalion to the south and east on 3 February, following the repositioning of *Grenadier Regiment 982* (described below), so that Rhein's left flank would be anchored in the village of Woffelsbach on the edge of the Schwammenauel Reservoir and his right on the northern edge of Steckenborn. Strauch would have to be given up without a fight to enable the repositioning to take place. With this tactical adjustment, *Oberst* Burian was ordered to displace his regimental headquarters from Steckenborn across the Roer to the Kermeter peninsula to a temporary site at the Paulushof forester's lodge.[3]

A shortage of antitank weapons complicated *Grenadier Regiment 980's* already unenviable situation. This was partly due to the loss of most of the regiment's *14th* (Antitank) *Company,* which was wiped out when Burian threw it into the fight at Kesternich in the infantry role.[4] Divisional antitank assets were also stretched thin. The *2nd Company* of Adrario's *Antitank Battalion 272* had no operational *Hetzer* tank destroyers remaining at the beginning of the impending American attack (two were destroyed in Kesternich though eight were in various stages of repair) and fewer than half a dozen of his *1st Company's* 75mm towed antitank guns were still in service.[5] Adrario's *3rd (Flak) Company* was still committed in the Gemünd area and so was unable to contribute to the defensive effort near Schmidt at all.

Rösener's *Grenadier Regiment 982* still held the area between Silberscheidt and the area south of Vossenack with two weak battalions, a total of perhaps 550 combat troops but their left flank was vulnerable should Burian's regiment fail to successfully hold the southwestern end of the Strauch-Schmidt ridge at Steckenborn.[6] A repositioning of Rösener's regiment was long overdue, especially since the 309th Infantry of the 78th Infantry Division had been exerting pressure on Rösener's regiment in the Tiefenbach valley for several days. If they succeeded in taking Kallbrück and pushing on to Silberscheidt, *Grenadier Regiment 982* would be cut off from the rest of the division.

As a precautionary move, on 3 February König ordered Rösener to withdraw his *2nd Battalion,* commanded by *Hauptmann* Karl Schneider, from its exposed position west of the Kall near Kallbrück and pull back several hundred meters to the southeast. Bunkers 122 through 125, defended at great cost for the past three months, were to be evacuated and destroyed with explosives to prevent them from being used by the Americans. Logically, these bunkers should have been evacuated in the middle of January, after the Americans successfully took most of the Raffelsbrand-Ochsenkopf bunker complex, but a standing order from Hitler that required that no *Westwall* bunkers be given up without a fight prevented such a logical move. With Hitler's attention focused on heavy fighting then taking place on the Eastern Front, König made the risky decision to abandon them without seeking permission. A month earlier, this same action would have earned him a courts marshall.

Following completion of this task by that evening, Schneider's battalion were in their new positions ranging between Silberscheidt and the northern edge of Steckenborn, where his leftmost *5th Company* linked up with the right flank of Rhein's battalion from *Grenadier Regiment 980.* Though Schneider's battalion was shelled continuously throughout this maneuver, the withdrawal went according to plan.[7] *Hauptmann* Leykhauf's *1st Battalion* remained in place and continue to defend its positions arrayed along the Buhlert hill mass facing the Kall valley. The battalion of about 150 men occupied positions between Silberscheidt and the bend of the Kall near Simonskall, where it tied in with the left flank of *Kampfgruppe Dreyer* of the *85th Infantry Division.*

Fortunately for the Germans, most of the division's surviving artillery and heavy weapons had been moved into the Roer valley or had taken up positions in the forest east of Schmidt and could still provide continuous fire support, as long as ammunition supplies held out. To direct the upcoming battle, König relocated his forward command post to a position north of the village of Klaus, protected only by his headquarters' security platoon. Thomae's *2nd Battalion, Grenadier Regiment 980,* having withdrawn across the Roer at Rurberg, became the division reserve.

The withdrawal of Thomae's battalion was accelerated by a pre-dawn attack carried out 4 February 1945 by 2nd Battalion, 311th Infantry Regiment, whose Company G overwhelmed one of Thomae's strongpoints barring the exits east of Kesternich. This attack forced his decimated *2nd Battalion* and other elements of the *272nd VGD,* including what was left of *Grenadier Regiment 981,* to withdraw through Rurberg, which fell to the rapidly pursuing Americans by 1335 hours that same day. This attack also interrupted the planned movement of Burian and his regimental headquarters across the Roer, though he and fifty or so of his men were able to reach safety at Paulushof by fleeing to *Westwall* bunkers on the eastern bank along with Thomae's *2nd Battalion.*[8]

To König's north, the weak *85th Infantry Division,* under the command of *Generalmajor* Helmut Bechler, still held a strong defensive line stretching from the bend of the Kall at Simonskall through Kommerscheidt and Schmidt before it connected at Nideggen with the left flank of the *353rd Infantry Division* of the neighboring *LXXXI Corps.* The major portion of its defenses faced the northwest, however, which was the least likely American avenue of approach.

Several dozen *Westwall* bunkers studded the area between Steckenborn and Kommerscheidt, but with the exception of a few minefields, there was no indepth antitank defense covering the southwest approaches to Schmidt. Many of the bunkers could not be manned because of a shortage of troops, thereby undermining any remaining tactical value these positions might have had, since they were designed to be mutually supporting. With so many gaps in the defense, the only remaining purpose of these bunkers was to serve as shelters from artillery fire or for the treatment of casualties. Most of the fighting would be done outside them, using trenches and individual fighting positions, conclusive evidence that the vaunted pre-war *Westwall* was tactically irrelevant 5 years after it was built.

Should the Americans succeed in breaching the main line of resistance between Steckenborn and Silberscheidt, König would be faced with the alternatives of having his division pinned up against the west bank of the Schwammenauel Reservoir and annihilated if he remained in place or withdrawing through Schmidt and around the northern edge of the reservoir as quickly as possible. Here, König could try to set up a new main defense line north of the Schwammenauel Dam, provided that the *85th Infantry Division* could hold open an escape corridor. Neither alternative was tactically appealing, but any decision could only be made by *Army Group B*, not by him or even *LXXIV Corps*. Again, no operational reserve was immediately available should the Americans break through, since the *3rd Panzer-Grenadier Division* was still positioned at Gemünd to ward off any continued American attack in that direction.

Thus, the only realistic course of action left to the German high command was to instruct König to fight a delaying action with some of his forces while allowing him to withdraw the rest across the dam and blowing it up before the Americans could seize it. Whether the Germans or Americans would get there first or whether *Army Group B* would approve such a decision in time was an open question. To confuse matters even more, a command and control change occurred on 4 February that took Püchler's *LXXIV Corps*, including *272nd VGD*, out from under *General der Infanterie* von Zangen's *Fifteenth Army* and placed it under *General der Panzertruppe* Hasso von Manteuffel's *Fifth Panzer Army*.[9]

The *Fifteenth Army* was far more concerned about Operation GRENADE, the code name for the impending Allied attack across the lower Roer, scheduled to commence on or about 8 February. Though holding Schmidt was important in its own right, keeping the Allies from crossing the Roer to the north, where the Cologne Plain was far more conducive to their mobile operations and was even more vital. Von Zangen sought and received permission to detach *LXXIV Corps* to *Fifth Panzer Army*, allowing him to focus on the area to the north and leave the defensive fighting at Schmidt to the supervision of the neighboring army to the south. The change in higher command relationships would have very little effect on König's division, as it turned out, however.[10]

As noted in the previous chapter, the 78th Infantry Division's attack against Schmidt and the seizure of the Schwammenauel Dam during Phase III of the operation would be carried out using all three of its regiments, as well as with the newly-attached CCR, 7th Armored Division and a regimental combat team from the 82nd Airborne Division. (For overall plan of attack, refer to Map 15.)

On the left flank, the 309th Infantry Regiment would attack across the Kall with one battalion from the Rollesbroich area toward the former *Reichsarbeitsdienst* camp 500 meters west of Gerstenhof, followed by another battalion that was prepared to assume the lead should the lead battalion falter. One company would attack Silberscheidt and cross the Kall to the north, while the third battalion would remain in reserve.

In the center, the 310th Infantry, making the division main effort, would attack between Strauch and Steckenborn along with the attached CCR, 7th Armored Division toward the Schmidt-Harscheidt area, once the 309th Infantry had created a penetration in the German defenses in the vicinity of Gerstenhof.

On the right flank, the 311th Infantry would attack in a northerly direction along the west bank of the Schwammenauel Reservoir, oriented on the line Woffelsbach-Hechelscheidt-Klaus, and attack Schmidt from the south. The 505th Regimental Combat Team of the 82nd Airborne Division would conduct a supporting attack across the Kall valley from the direction of Vossenack in a southerly direction to seize Kommerscheidt and threaten Schmidt from the north.

Once Schmidt had fallen (within two days at the most, according to the plan), the drive would continue toward the villages of Hasenfeld and Heimbach, ending with the seizure of the Schwammenauel Dam by 8 February. To prevent the German defenders from escaping, the 517th Regimental Combat Team, a separate unit attached at that time to the 82nd Airborne Division, attacking from the direction of Bergstein, would cross the Kall northeast of Vossenack and strike south, cutting off the German withdrawal route and blocking the way for any counterattack.

While the 82nd Airborne Division (whose command post was in the process of being transferred to the Hürtgen Forest from the Ardennes mopped up in Schmidt, the 78th Infantry Division would continue its attack until it had seized the dam and pushed a bridgehead across the Roer, providing that the dam had not been destroyed. To the south, the 9th Infantry Division would conduct a supporting attack at Rurberg with its 47th Infantry Regiment. One of its battalions would cross the Roer via the Urft Dam spillway at Paulushof in order to tie up German forces defending the Kermeter Peninsula.

Expectations were high and it was obvious to Major General Parker and his staff that both US V Corps and First Army were keenly interested in the outcome of the 78th Infantry Division's attack. Though planning had been extremely thorough and sufficient forces had been assembled for the attack, the successful outcome depended to a large degree on whether the division could get to the dam before the Germans could blow it up. Should the dam be destroyed, Operation GRENADE would have to be postponed for several weeks until water levels in the Roer had returned to normal.

The staff of the division's 303rd Combat Engineer Battalion, commanded by Lieutenant Colonel John J. Closner, Jr., already had been briefed so they had a good idea of the dam's layout, using copies of blueprints of similar structures, so they knew which installations the men from their battalion's Company C would have to reach first in order to prevent its demolition Regardless, this would prove to be a difficult task. The only avenue of approach to the dam was exposed to enemy observation and direct and indirect fires, so a night attack would be necessary. Nevertheless, the division had to go through with its mission in the knowledge that the success of the entire Allied offensive across the Roer depended on it. This was a heavy burden indeed for a division that was still considered unproven by its chain of command, despite its solid performance since its commitment to combat the previous December.

The attack began on schedule at 0300 hours 5 February. In a steady rain, the men of the 309th, 310th, and 311th Infantry Regiments and CCR, 7th Armored Division, along with their attachments, crossed their lines of departure without the usual artillery preparation. Company E, 309th Infantry, attacking on the division's far left, rapidly forded the Kall and swept up the steep slopes of Buhlert Hill, catching the defenders at Silberscheidt asleep in their fighting positions and bunkers. To its right, Lieutenant Colonel Floyd Call's 3rd Battalion, 309th Infantry quickly gained ground as well, reaching the *Reichsarbeitsdienst* barracks area west of Gerstenhof by mid-morning.

The tactical surprise of the American's attack was complete. Though it had been expected for several days, the men of *Grenadier Regiment 982* were completely overwhelmed and unable to mount any serious opposition to the initial assault. The 309th Infantry did not report any German small arms fire at all until it reached the area southwest of Gerstenhof. Even more amazingly, at least thirty-five *Westwall* bunkers on the Buhlert Ridge, in the Silberscheidt area and east of Rollesbroich were seized, mostly without a fight. Over 135 prisoners from *2nd Battalion, Grenadier Regiment 982* were taken, many of whom had just begun eating breakfast and had no idea an attack was taking place.[11]

Leutnant Günther Schmidt, the operations officer for the *2nd Battalion,* was one of those captured that morning. After having moved the battalion command post from the Silberscheidt area to a new one northeast of Strauch the previous day, Schmidt, his battalion commander, and the rest of the staff were surprised to receive reports that American troops had appeared at the *Reichsarbeitsdienst* barracks area to their rear unannounced, capturing most of the battalion's *4th Company* and its heavy weapons without firing a shot.

From their position in command Bunker 220/221, Schmidt and the others could see American troops moving south from the barracks area and engaging the many *Westwall* bunkers dotting the fields one by one from the rear, where the bunkers were most vulnerable. Another group attacked to the east of their position, cutting off the *2nd Battalion* from the rest of the regiment. The battalion's communications bunker, Number 717a, fell shortly thereafter, as well as Bunker

P11 only 100 meters to the north, which housed the only antitank gun in the battalion's defensive sector. Schmidt was ordered to lead a four-man counterattack to regain this bunker, but Schmidt and the men with him were trapped within and captured shortly after retaking it. Within moments, *Hauptmann* Schneider and the rest of the staff were taken prisoner when their bunker was surrounded as well.[12]

The survivors were assembled at the prisoner collection point located near the barracks area and marched to the POW holding area in Roetgen. Within the span of six hours, the *2nd Battalion* had been wiped out. To its right, *1st Battalion* had been cut off from the rest of the regiment during the attack and only a few dozen men were able to fight their way back to Schmidt over the Buhlert Ridge. For all practical purposes, Rösener's *Grenadier Regiment 982* had ceased to exist. *Generalmajor* König ordered him to gather what was left of his regiment into one company-sized battle group and told him to withdraw through Schmidt and across the Roer.

The attack on the American's right flank by the 311th Infantry did not fare as well initially as the one carried out by the 309th Infantry on the left, but eventually managed to achieve its objectives for the day. Approaching the town of Woffelsbach along the shore of the Schwammenauel Reservoir, the leading 2nd Battalion encountered several steep ravines studded with *Westwall* bunkers and fighting positions manned by troops from Rhein's *1st Battalion, Grenadier Regiment 980*, who contested every step. But by 1630, Company F had been able to overcome the last ridgeline and was able to flank the German defenders from the west, forcing them to fall back toward Hechelscheidt.

In the center, the attack to seize Strauch and Steckenborn initially began favorably. Preceded by a rocket barrage that shook both villages, the troops of 3rd Battalion, 310th Infantry, attached to CCR of the 7th Armored Division, crossed the line of departure at 0630. Surprisingly, Strauch fell without a struggle and was reported cleared by 1100 hours, evidence that the defenders had already pulled out, leaving behind only a few snipers to harass the approaching Americans.

The main body of CCR, 7th Armored Division began its own attack at 0800, reaching Steckenborn two hours later after overcoming the weak defenses of *1st Battalion, Grenadier Regiment 980*'s right flank. What little resistance the American task force encountered in Steckenborn amounted to a few snipers and poorly directed artillery fire, due to the capture of *Oberleutnant* Bieler, the commander of *7th Battery, Artillery Regiment 272* in his battery's forward observation post, along with his gun chief, *Leutnant* Kropf. Both men were beaten severely by their captors, but were fortunate considering artillery forward observers were often shot out of hand by troops who had to advance through their terrifying barrages.[13] While elements of the 310th Infantry were left to mop up the few remaining men of Rhein's battalion still holding out, CCR 7th Armored Division quickly bypassed Steckenborn. The town itself was reported completely cleared of Germans by nightfall.

Though Parker's men had done extremely well during the first part of the morning's attack, seizing all of their initial objectives, the attack in the center began to lose its momentum around 0900 hours when indecisiveness and unnecessary command interference began to plague the 78th Infantry Division. The defenders, who had initially been caught completely off guard by the pre-dawn attack, were quick to take advantage of this delay and used the breathing space to reorganize their forces and reestablish an intermediate defensive line that would soon slow the advance of the 78th Infantry Division to a crawl and completely disrupt its timetable.

Originally, the plan envisioned that the 310th Infantry would pass through the lines of the 309th Infantry in the vicinity of the *Reichsarbeitsdienst* camp and continue the push through Gerstenhof toward Schmidt. Before this could occur, however, a large minefield was discovered that had to be cleared by the 303rd Engineer Battalion. This task took longer than expected, forcing the men of both the 309th and 310th Infantry to wait while the rain poured down incessantly.

Fearing that his attack was in danger of losing steam, Major General Parker briefly considered ordering the 309th Infantry to continue its attack but was overruled by Major General Huebner, his corps commander, who instructed him to press forward with both regiments, a decision which created confusion at a critical point in the operation. To make matters worse, German resistance began to stiffen, as *Generalmajor* König and his operations officer, *Major* Uhl, personally intervened in the repositioning of forces and the commitment of emergency units to carry out hasty counterattacks.[14]

Huebner also ordered Parker to have the 311th Infantry use its 1st Battalion to launch an attack that same morning across the Urft Dam at Paulushof via the spillway and seize a bridgehead on the Kermeter Peninsula. While forming up for its assault in the village of Rurberg, the battalion came under heavy German mortar fire. A lucky hit took out nearly the entire command group, wounding three men (including the battalion commander) and killing six others. It quickly became apparent that the Germans (most likely men from Kleinkorres' *Grenadier Regiment 981*) defended the crossing site in strength and any attempt to cross the long, narrow spillway would be suicidal. The attack was called off.[15]

Near Gerstenhof, artillery and mortar fire began to impact in the American's assembly areas, causing numerous casualties. When it became apparent that it was going to take longer than usual to clear the minefield, a frustrated Huebner drove to the 78th Infantry Division's forward headquarters and began personally to direct Parker how to deploy his individual battalions, instructing him to send the 3rd Battalion, 309th Infantry onward to Schmidt without worrying about its flanks. This proved easier said than done.

By mid-afternoon, due to a series of conflicting orders and misunderstandings, Parker's drive on Schmidt had completely stalled. So intermingled had the 309th and 310th Infantry become, primarily due to Huebner's meddling, that it was to take the division all night to sort them out and get their men back into their attack positions by the next morning. The infantry companies, thoroughly soaked and exhausted from being on their feet for nearly twenty-four hours, dug in and tried to get some sleep before continuing their attack.

Surveying the events of the day, *Generalmajor* König undoubtedly had little reason to believe that his battered division could hold out much longer. Another of his regiments had been smashed and *Grenadier Regiment 980,* his last intact regiment, was rapidly dwindling in strength. Positioned near the front line, he had to watch helplessly as the early morning American attack rapidly rolled up one position after another. After the war he remarked that

> Our positions were overrun without a sound hardly being heard. The first complete telephonic reports about the unfolding events did not come in until the attack had already reached the mortar and infantry howitzer positions [near the *Reichsarbeitsdienst* barracks] . . . the enemy literally seemed to appear out of thin air in the hundreds . . . it even came down to hand-to-hand combat. For a long time, we did not get any reports at all. . . . Systematically the opponent rolled through the first point of breakthrough along the antitank obstacles and occupied all of the bunkers on the right and even some of those on the left were taken by midday. In the afternoon, the rest of the bunkers were taken one after the other . . . the only thing left that we could do was to try to organize a defense line to the left and right of the road [to Schmidt]. . . .[16]

If he were to have any chance of saving his division and bringing enough of it back across the Roer to continue an effective defense, König needed to start issuing the necessary orders to begin falling back in phases. Those units in contact would have to delay as long as possible in order for another intermediate defense line to be set up to their rear. Each delay, even if successful, would still mean more men and equipment lost.

It was a high-stakes gamble and only the timely intervention of a mobile reserve by corps or army headquarters would enable the *272nd VGD* to successfully disengage and withdraw to safety. To bolster the remnants of the two regiments barring the way to Schmidt, König ordered that they be reinforced by emergency units, created by ruthlessly combing through of division and regimental trains, as well as by bringing up the recently reconstituted *Field Replacement Battalion 272,* including the division's combat school.[17]

Parker resumed his attack toward Gerstenhof at 0300 hours 6 February using two battalions of the 310th Infantry, but after seven hours they had advanced barely 500 meters, due to confusion (one battalion got lost in the dark near the *Reichsarbeitsdienst* barracks) and other factors. Resistance began to increase steadily. At 1055 hours, the first German counterattack was reported, when a force estimated to consist of two platoons hit Company E, inflicting heavy casualties before they were driven off.[18]

From that point until evening on 7 February when they finally reached the outskirts of Schmidt, both the 309th and 310th Infantry had to fight every step of the way against determined German resistance, particularly in the open area east of Gerstenhof. General Huebner again expressed his displeasure at the slow pace of the advance, telling Parker that he had expected far greater gains than what had been achieved. Casualties in the attacking infantry companies had been far heavier than anticipated and at least one company had to be withdrawn to be reconstituted with new personnel.[19]

The fighting intensified. The Germans had set up a series of mutually supporting machine-gun nests that raked the open fields between Gerstenhof and Schmidt with lethally accurate fire and each one had to be overcome before the attack could resume. German artillery and mortar fire was heavy and becoming more accurate. To the surprise of Parker's troops, German paratroops were beginning to make their appearance felt in an area where none had so far been reported.

On the right flank, however, things were going much better for elements of the 310th and 311th Infantry. By the evening of 6 February, most of *Hauptmann* Rhein's *1st Battalion* had been surrounded in Steckenborn and Hechelscheidt and wiped out. Rhein and his operations officer, *Oberleutnant* Ebert, along with twenty-seven men, were taken prisoner at their command post between Steckenborn and Hechelscheidt.[20] Continuing its attack the next morning, the lead battalion of the 311th Infantry pushed onward toward Schmidt, overrunning the defensive line south of Klaus and forcing *Generalmajor* König to finally shift his forward division command post to a point east of Schmidt.

During the first interrogation by his captors, *Hauptmann* Rhein at first was described as being non-committal and arrogant, opining that Germany could not possibly lose the war, which would most likely last many more months before its outcome was decided. In a session later that day with his interrogators from the 78th Infantry Division, however, Rhein stated that he had actually countermanded orders from higher headquarters to fight to the last man, and had instructed his company commanders that it was up to them to decide when to surrender their units. Asked why he had disobeyed his orders, Rhein said that upon reflection, the end of the war was clearly in sight and he did not want to senselessly sacrifice the lives of his men, a fact that would weigh heavily upon his conscience. Significantly, Rhein said that "a soldier's loyalty to his oath ceases to apply when the individual realizes that the pledge is based on falsehoods and the personal ambitions of a villainous few." Though he came to this realization somewhat belatedly, at least most of his men survived the fighting, albeit as prisoners.[21]

In order to reinforce the defenders of Schmidt, König ordered *Hauptmann* Thomae on 6 February to move his *2nd Battalion, Grenadier Regiment 980* from reserve positions on the Kermeter Peninsula to a location southeast of the village of Kommerscheidt, where he was to set up an intermediate position as elements of the *85th Infantry Division* began their own withdrawal. Though Thomae still had most of his own *8th (heavy weapons) Company*, the other battalion in

Grenadier Regiment 980 had not fared very well. Not only had the *1st Battalion* lost its commander near Hechelscheidt, but fifty men from its *4th (heavy weapons) Company,* with all of their remaining 80mm mortars and 75mm light infantry howitzers were captured by Company G, 311th Infantry Regiment.[22] Not content with this small victory, the 311th Infantry continuing its advance and reached the southern edge of Schmidt by the evening of 7 February after negotiating a series of steep ravines and sporadic resistance.

The final catastrophe was averted, however, when Thomae was ordered to withdraw what was left of his battalion (less than 100 men) along with the rest of the division on the morning of 7 February after skirmishing with advanced elements of the 3rd Battalion, 309th Infantry Regiment at Kommerscheidt. Handing over his positions to a platoon of newly arrived paratroopers of the *8th Fallschirmjäger Regiment*, *3rd Fallschirmjäger Division,* Thomae and his decimated battalion made good their escape before that village was taken by 3rd Battalion, 309th Infantry that afternoon. After escaping through Schmidt's eastern outskirts, Thomae and his remaining men were then ordered to establish defensive positions on the bluffs overlooking the northern end of the Schwammenauel Dam.

Orders had finally been issued by *LXXIV Corps* for the *272nd VGD* to extract itself from the fighting (withdrawing after the *85th Infantry Division* had made good its escape), cross the Roer, and set up new positions on the east bank. Thus, König and his men would be spared the final battle for Schmidt. As the remnants of the division fell back across the Roer from 7 to 8 February, *Oberst* Burian was ordered to defend the key villages of Hasenfeld and Heimbach as well as the approaches to the dam with what was left of his regiment, perhaps 200 men in all, while combat engineers of *Hauptmann* Schlanstein's *Pionier Battalion 272* prepared the structure for demolition.[23]

It now appeared even to *Generalfeldmarschall* Model that there was no longer any point in holding on to this tiny bridgehead on the west bank of the Roer Though there is no longer any record of this decision, Hitler must have given permission for Model to issue this order, since even an army group commander could not do such a thing on his own authority. Since Kesternich had fallen and the Americans now occupied the west bank of the Roer as far north as Schmidt, it was only a matter of time before any German forces remaining west of the river would be cut off and destroyed. The only important task remaining to be carried out was the destruction of the Schwammenauel Dam. This would bring about the flooding that would affect the Roer through Düren and Jülich as far north as the Dutch frontier.

The orderly destruction of the dam would require time, however, so the remnants of both the *85th Infantry Division* and *272nd VGD* were to fight a delaying action, then give up control of Schmidt and withdraw under the protection of a counterattack by a battle group composed of element of the *Panzer-Grenadier Regiments 8* and *29* from the *3rd Panzer-Grenadier Division,* brought up from

Gemünd area and placed under König's tactical control for this purpose.[24] The *85th Infantry Division*, which would soon be pulled out for reconstitution, had already passed under the control of the neighboring *LXXXI Corps* on 6 February, and was in the process of being relieved by the *3rd Fallschirmjäger Division*, whose own forces would also help cover the withdrawal of the other two divisions.[25]

Once it had managed to withdraw across the river, the *272nd VGD* was directed by *LXXIV Corps* to establish the "Richthofen Position," a new defensive position that ran in an arc from the Hasenfeld-Heimbach area in the north around the western tip of the Kermeter Peninsula and to the south near Pulvermühle. The new division command post would be set up in a group of bunkers near the village of Vlatten, six kilometers east of the Schwammenauel Dam.[26]

With the area between Sildberscheidt and Woffelsbach in hand by the evening of 6 February, the 78th Infantry Division was able to continue its advance without having to worry about its flanks. The Americans intensified their attack against Schmidt on 7 February in the face of desperate German resistance. With all three of its regiments attacking abreast and ably supported by the tanks and armored infantry of CCR, 7th Armored Division, the assault on Schmidt, Kommerscheidt, and Harscheidt began in earnest. (See Map 16)

Heavy fighting took place throughout the day of 7 February. The 774th Tank Battalion, a separate unit attached to the division, lost several tanks to antitank fire before the 78th Infantry Division was able to crack the German defense line west of the town. Despite determined resistance by rear guard elements of the *85th Infantry Division* and the newly brought up *3rd Fallschirmjäger Division*, the town's western outskirts were penetrated by nightfall. The fighting was house-to-house and American success seemed to be only a matter of days, if not hours, away.

To Major General Huebner, commander of US V Corps, however, that was still too long for his taste. Believing that the 78th Infantry Division was not carrying out its attack on Schmidt aggressively or quickly enough, on the early afternoon of 8 February Huebner attached two of Parker's regiments, the 309th and 311th Infantry, to Major General Louis A. Craig's 9th Infantry Division, which was operating to the south in the vicinity of Einruhr. This move generated considerable controversy at the time and is still discussed with bitterness today by members of the Lighting Division, who felt their corps commander had slighted them. While Huebner was no doubt feeling considerable pressure from Hodges at First Army and Bradley at Twelfth Army Group to get through with Schmidt and seize the dam, his interference did little to actually speed up the pace of operations.

By this point, fatigue had set in among the attacking infantry battalions and it had begun to affect their efficiency, an unavoidable characteristic of continuous warfare. Most of the men had been fighting for over forty-eight hours and had not had any warm food or shelter from the cold and rainy weather. Fortunately, the staffs of both the 9th and 78th Infantry Divisions willingly cooperated and seemed to have carried out their tasks in a professional manner, despite the fact that the 9th Infantry Division now controlled more of the 78th Infantry Division that it did itself.

By nightfall on 8 February, most of Schmidt and the surrounding villages were in the hands of the men of the 78th Infantry Division. Several hundred prisoners were taken, primarily from the *85th Infantry Division* and for the most part the fight for the town, which had resisted several American attempts to seize it since the previous October, was over. As they continued their push through the town, the 505th Regimental Combat Team of the 82nd Airborne Division mopped up pockets of resistance that had been bypassed.

An attempt by the 82nd Airborne Division's attached 517th Regimental Combat Team to cut off the withdrawing enemy forces miscarried when, after crossing the Kall north of Kommerscheidt, the paratroopers accidentally fired into the left flank of the 1st Battalion, 310th Infantry, which was clearing German stragglers from several ravines north of the village. After straightening out this misunderstanding, the 517th relived the 310th Infantry in Kommerscheidt. Claims advanced by the 82nd Airborne Division that it had captured Schmidt were laughingly dismissed by the troops of the Lightning Division, who knew better. To prove their point, members of the division erected a sign at the town's western approaches stating that "You are now entering the town of Schmidt through the courtesy of the 78th Division."[27]

The American advance to the Schwammenauel continued through the town's eastern outskirts on the morning of the 9th, pushing the defenders through Harscheidt and beyond. The battle group from the *3rd Panzer-Grenadier Division* finally made its appearance, attempting a counterattack consisting of a battalion's worth of infantry, five tanks, and supporting artillery. American artillery fire and fighter-bombers hit them hard throughout the day, destroying at least two Panzer IVs and scattering the escorting *Panzer-Grenadiers* before they could press home their attack. While the German counterattack had failed to achieve the desired success, it at least enabled the rear guards of the *85th Infantry* and *272nd VGDs* to make good their escape.

The recently arrived paratroops of the *3rd Fallschirmjäger Division* had little time to get settled into their new defensive positions before they were also driven back to the Roer with heavy losses. Many of its men, paratroopers in name only, had been transferred from aviation or *Flak* units only a short time before and surrendered in Schmidt without firing a shot. Still, there were enough old hands in that division to make a good showing of themselves, particularly machine-gun and heavy weapons crews, who continued to inflict casualties on the advancing Americans, especially once they entered the forest on Schmidt's eastern outskirts. Slowed by the infusion of additional German forces, the 9th and 78th Infantry Divisions nonetheless continued moving forward doggedly.

By the evening of 9 February, the 9th and 78th Infantry and 82nd Airborne Divisions had driven virtually all of the Germans back across the Roer, with the exception of those defending the bluffs overlooking the dam itself. The village of Hasenfeld fell to a battalion of the 60th Infantry Regiment of the 9th Infantry Division after the men drove remnants of *Grenadier Regiment 980* and the battle group from *Panzer-Grenadier Regiment 8* out of virtually every house and shed.[28] The Germans made a final attempt to throw the Americans out of Hasenfeld that evening with a force supported by three tanks, but it was driven off and the tanks were destroyed by Company G, 60th Infantry. Hasenfeld itself was declared secure by 0430 hours 10 February.[29] From that point the only other German soldiers west of the Roer, with the exception of a few bypassed elements, were those who were marching   west as prisoners. But the last act of the drama had yet to be played out—the seizure of the dam itself.

The 9th Infantry Division's Major General Craig selected the attached 1st Battalion, 309th Infantry, commanded by Lieutenant Colonel Robert H. Schellman, to carry out the last phase of the operation. Moving out from Schmidt at 1800 hours on 9 February, the battalion passed through the lines of the 310th Infantry, which were approximately one-and-a-half miles east of Schmidt. Because of the confusing fighting that had taken place that afternoon, Schellman and his men found to their surprise that their forward assembly area was occupied by German troops! The Americans attacked on the move, dispersed the German troops, then quickly reorganized to begin their own attack.[30]

This completed, 1st Battalion, 309th Infantry began its approach to the dam at 1830 hours, but by then it had become completely dark. Nevertheless, Schellman ordered his men to continue. With its right flank protected by the 60th Infantry Regiment of the 9th Infantry Division, after a nightmarish march through pitch black forest and steep ravines punctuated by American and German artillery and mortar fire, the 1st Battalion reached the bluffs overlooking the Schwammenauel by 2115 hours. Before they realized what had happened, some of the men of Company B, the battalion's lead element, stumbled into the forward defensive positions of *Grenadier Regiment 980,* catching their inhabitants completely by surprise. Hand-to-hand combat with the frantic defenders immediately broke out, a fight that lasted for nearly forty-five minutes before the last German was subdued.[31] Some of the Germans who had surrendered were killed in the wild shooting, as it was difficult in the darkness to tell friend from foe and the men of Company B were not taking any chances.

While the fighting on the bluffs continued above them, specially trained assault teams from Company A approached the building housing the control valves for the dam, but found that German engineers had already destroyed them. Since there was nothing more they could do, the assault teams then pressed on over the rubble to the dam itself, their next objective. Relieved that it had not yet been blown up, the infantrymen and the attached demolitions experts from the 303rd Combat Engineer Battalion quickly searched the dam and the inspection tunnels for explosives, all the while hoping to find them before the Germans set them off. To their amazement, there were none.

Another element of the battalion that had moved around the German's flank to seize the lower portion of the dam faced stiff resistance near the power generation station. After a brief stand, the defenders pulled back across the base of the dam or surrendered. By 2300 hours, most of the Schwammenauel Dam was now in the hands of the 78th Infantry Division. An attempt to cross the dam and seize the opposite side via the road running along the top of the spillway was driven away by heavy fire from a bunker manned by troops of *Grenadier Regiment 980,* preventing a more thorough inspection.

To silence the German guns on the opposite bank, thirty artillery battalions fired a barrage that "turned the night into day," according to one eyewitness.* The Americans' elation was soon tempered, however, when they discovered that the Germans had destroyed the penstock gates and the valves controlling the water flow to the power station, creating a column of water thirteen feet in diameter that rushed out of the dam.[32] In fact, the floodgates of both the Schwammenauel and Urft Dams had been open since 6 February. The demolitions had also been carried out in such a manner that the Americans were unable to close the floodgates even after the dams were seized.[33]

While 1st Battalion, 309th Infantry subdued the remaining *Volksgrenadiers* and cleared the area around the north side of the dam, the combat engineers assessed the situation. Though the dam had not been blown up after all, what the Germans had done was far worse from a tactical perspective. A steady flow of water from the Roer Reservoir, averaging a speed of eighty meters per minute, had been created that would last for weeks.[34] While a complete demolition of the Schwammenauel would have been more catastrophic, the twenty-two billion gallons of water pent up behind it would have passed through the Roer valley more quickly. Property damage and loss of life downstream would have been high had this occurred, but Operation GRENADE would have been delayed only a few days.

It was soon reported that the Germans upstream had also inflicted the same sort of damage to the Urft Dam at Paulushof, thus insuring that the flow of water would continue even after the Roer Reservoir would normally have emptied. That both dams had been placed out of operation in such a manner was not due to any expressed order from Hitler; in fact, he had ordered that the dams be completely destroyed. Rather, the commander of *Fifth Panzer Army, General der Panzertruppe* Hasso von Manteuffel, had forbidden this, ordering *Generalmajor* König instead to render them inoperable not only to increase the time it would take for the waters to recede, but to spare the inhabitants of the area the immense destruction a complete demolition would have brought about.[35]

The American's failure to prevent the Germans from flooding the Roer kept Operation GRENADE from beginning on schedule and brought about a two-week

---

* At one point, up to forty battalions of artillery were available to support the attack toward the dam, enough, as General Hodges said, to "blast a road from our present front line positions straight to the dam," (Source: Charles B. MacDonald, *The Last Offensive*, CMH, 1973, 80).

lull in the fighting. Until the water held back by the Schwammenauel completely drained away, neither side could do much but stare across the flooded river and
fire artillery and mortars at each other. Though patrols from both sides frequently crossed the river to conduct reconnaissance, overall there was little that the
272nd VGD had to fear, since the Americans had no boats or landing craft to cross
with. Unknown to the Germans at the time, was that virtually all of the Allies'
river assault craft were still being held in marshalling areas, in readiness for the
big Allied attack across the Roer to the north.

As the water level in the Roer continued to drop, the Americans spied a mud-
covered stone bridge that had lain unseen under the river since the construction
of the dam. An attempt was made to seize it on the night of 24 February, but this
was forestalled when a strong German patrol drove off the troops of 1st Battalion,
309th Infantry and blew it up to prevent it from falling into Americans hands.[36]

Throughout most of the second battle for Schmidt, the men of *Füsilier Company 272* had done little but watch from the sidelines while they held defensive
positions on the Kermeter Peninsula under the control of *Grenadier Regiment
981*. Without a commanding officer since the loss of *Oberleutnant* Aretz, the
company was gladdened while still in Hergarten to hear that *Leutnant* Wegner
was coming back to take command. He had been ordered by the division headquarters to return by 6 February, since no other suitable senior lieutenant or captain had yet been found to exercise permanent command of the company.

One of his first orders was to reorganize the company. Losses in the two
machine pistol platoons and the rifle platoon had been so high—there were only
five to ten men left per platoon—they could no longer be tactically employed as
platoons. Wegner, therefore, ordered that the remnants be grouped into a single
twenty-two-man platoon until more replacements could be assigned. At least in
this manner, the company would be able to field one strong platoon with enough
machine pistols and machine guns to constitute a balanced force.

After recuperating for four days in Hergarten after the disaster at Herhahn, the
company received orders on 8 February to move west to take up a screening position along hill 317.3 in a "quiet" sector in the state forest overlooking the
Schwammenauel Reservoir, six kilometers northwest of the Mariawald Abbey
near the northwest tip of the Kermeter Peninsula. At the time, in addition to the
one combined infantry platoon, the company still had one heavy machine gun,
one 80mm mortar, and both 75mm infantry howitzers available for this mission.
Meanwhile, *Hauptfeldwebel* Fuhrmeister and the company trains were ordered to
displace to the town of Schwerfen, eight kilometers to the northeast of Hergarten.
The distance between the combat elements of the company and the trains occa-
sioned by this move indicated that a big withdrawal was scheduled to occur soon.

Over the next several days, the company was subjected to intense American
artillery fire by the 78th Infantry Division, which was at the time concluding its
successful seizure of Schmidt and envelopment of the dams from the north. Safe
in their positions on the Kermeter Peninsula, Wegner's *Volksgrenadiers* did not

know that, of course; they knew only that they had been granted a short breathing spell to recover from the devastating losses suffered at Herhahn while the rest of their division was being mauled by the Americans. From 8 to 10 February, the company suffered four casualties from artillery fire, including one man killed in action and three wounded, proving that this was not a very quiet sector after all.

While the company was holding its positions west of the abbey at Mariawald, on 10 February the company trains was ordered to hand over its three tracked *RSO*s in exchange for horse teams and gun limbers for the light infantry howitzers and supply section. With the company so reduced, evidently the division's transportation officer felt that the few remaining *RSO*s needed to be reallocated within the division where they were most badly needed. The *RSO*s were finally turned in on 17 February, with two going to *Antitank Battalion 272* and one to *Artillery Regiment 272*. Three new MG-42s were delivered to the company trains in Schwerfen the following day. *Leutnant* Wegner ordered that the former drivers be trained as machine gunners—quite a switch from their former duties—and be assigned to the remaining rifle platoon.

In the meantime, on 12 February the company was ordered to withdraw to the forest in the vicinity of the convent with orders to set up a security line facing north toward Hasenfeld, overlooking the Schwannemauel Dam, which the Americans had taken on 10 February. Except for sporadic artillery fire, it remained fairly quiet, though a runner, *Füsilier* Töpfer, was killed by artillery fire the next day. On 17 February, *Unteroffizier* Misskampf, the mortar section forward observer, was wounded at 0530 hours in the section firing position one kilometer southeast of Heimbach by artillery fire while sitting in his dugout. Caught unawares, he had little time to seek cover before a hot shell splinter shot in through the dugout entrance and embedded itself in his lower right leg.

The severe wound that resulted, which sizzled and smoked from the hot piece of metal sticking out of his leg, led to Misskampf's immediate evacuation, leaving the mortar section without an experienced forward observer. Although an infection in the wound forced doctors to amputate his right leg below the knee, Misskampf survived the war.

During the next week, the company suffered no losses at all. The weather remained overcast and it rained more often than not, keeping American fighter-bomber activity to a comfortably low level. The infantry howitzer platoon set up firing positions in a few sheds on the grounds of the convent and fired sporadic missions in support of units to the north, where fighting was still taking place. On the morning of 20 February, the company was given an alert order to be prepared to move at a moment's notice, but nothing came of it.

On 21 February, *Oberleutnant* Wilhelm Krüssmann took command of the company, replacing *Leutnant* Wegner yet again. Krüssmann, born 3 March 1922 in Kervendonk, was another experienced officer from the division's reserve, though little is known about him. His first command was to order the mortar platoon and infantry howitzer platoon out of their positions and to return to

Schwerfen, to co-locate with the company trains. The first sergeant was ordered to conduct a reconnaissance in the neighboring town of Sinzenich to find suitable lodging for the troops and horses. Something big was brewing, though it is clear from studying the company's journal that no one had any idea what that was.

It rained heavily over the next two days. The ground grew so waterlogged that foxholes and trenches frequently collapsed. On one occasion, the canvas-covered foxhole occupied by the company runner, *Gefreiter* Peter Moog, and another soldier caved in on them while they slept, nearly burying them alive. The experience shook Moog so badly that he was temporarily evacuated to the company trains, where he would recover, though in truth he probably needed a great deal more care than that, since nearly all of the men could have been characterized as psychiatric casualties by this point.[37]

The mortar section and infantry howitzer platoon, upon arriving in Schwerfen, were directed toward Sinzenich, where the men bedded down for a couple days of rest. Luckily, they made it by the evening of 22 February, for American fighter-bomber activity was high the following day, and the horse-drawn guns would have been easy prey. With the heavy weapons and the company trains thus occupied, the remaining twenty-two men of the consolidated rifle platoon and the sole remaining heavy machine gun were detached 23 February to reinforce the reconstituted *Field Replacement Battalion 272,* which had been subordinated to *Grenadier Regiment 981* for a few days.

From 24 to 26 February, the situation remained fairly quiet, though to the north the US 8th Infantry Division had succeeded in crossing the Roer at several points in order to establish bridgeheads for the coming offensive. The company suffered only one casualty during this period, *Obergefreiter* Josef Wiche, who was killed 25 February near the Mariawald Abbey by artillery fire. Wiche, who had been transferred to the company for disciplinary purposes in January after conviction for a petty crime while serving in a cushy job with a replacement battalion in Germany, was buried in the nearby soldier's cemetery.

Things began to heat up again for the company on 27 February, when enemy artillery sought out and pounded Sinzenich. *Feldwebel* Dietz, the unit's armorer, was killed when he was hit in the neck by a shell fragment; he was buried the following day. Since Sinzenich was obviously no longer safe, the company trains and the heavy weapons were ordered to return to Schwerfen. Fortunately for the Germans, the hazy weather again kept American airpower at bay, allowing the company to reach its destination without loss. The next day, however, the company was ordered to prepare quarters in the vicinity of the town of Firmenich, a few kilometers east of Schwerfen and out of range of enemy artillery.

Also on 27 February, the company received another draft of replacements, twenty-four in all, including three NCOs. This time, however, most of the new men had not been associated with *Füsilier Company 272* or any other unit affiliated with *272nd VGD.* Fourteen were assigned to the division directly from the now-defunct *85th Infantry Division,* three were from the *Kriegsmarine,* and one had been assigned from a *Luftwaffe* unit in the hinterland. Only six had served previously with *272nd VGD,* but none with the *Füsilier* company. This latest addition brought the company's strength back up to 107 men, including the twenty-two in the infantry platoon that had been detached and were still fighting elsewhere.

One of these new replacements, *Gefreiter* Günter Ecker, was not new to combat or to fighting in the Hürtgen Forest. A seventeen-year-old Rhinelander from Herschweiler, Ecker had volunteered to become a *Fallschirmjäger* in 1944 after serving on a *Luftwaffe* antiaircraft-gun crew during his six-month stint in the labor service. After completing his basic and advanced training, he was assigned to *Oberst* von der Heydte's *Fallschirmjäger Regiment 6* and fought with that unit during the Normandy Campaign.[38]

In late November 1944, when his decimated regiment was pulled out for reconstitution in Holland, Ecker and other survivors of his company were formed into a battle group and attached to *Grenadier Regiment 1053* of the *85th Infantry Division.* This division, as previously related, was ordered to move to the southeast sector of the front on 13 December 1944 west of the town of Nideggen. Here, it took up positions in the Raffelsbrand area in order to buttress German defenses in the Hürtgen in order to free up the *89th Infantry Division,* which was designated take part in the great German counteroffensive scheduled to begin in the Ardennes later that month. (For additional information about the employment of the *85th Infantry Division*, refer to Chapter 8.) By 15 December, Ecker and his few remaining paratrooper comrades found themselves occupying a bunker on the outskirts of the town of Schmidt, scene of the epic battle of November 1944.

During the second battle of Schmidt, the *85th Infantry Division* had absorbed so much punishment that it was pulled out of the line. Rebuilt in March 1945 from the ground up under the new *Infantry Division 45* table of organization, it was renamed *Infantry Division Potsdam.*[39] Before it left the Hürtgen, however, it was ordered to immediately transfer most of its combat troops to serve as badly needed infantry replacements to shore up the crumbling ranks of *272nd VGD.* So, on 27 February, fourteen survivors of *Grenadier Regiment 1053,* including Günter Ecker (still wearing his *Luftwaffe* paratrooper smock and carrying his MP-44), found themselves immediately assigned to *Füsilier Company 272* upon arrival in Hergarten.

Another replacement assigned from the same draft that day was *Obergefreiter* Wilfried Wilts, born 20 April 1922 in Emden. Wilts had formerly been with the *Kriegsmarine,* where he had been a crewmember on a minesweeper stationed in a French port. After his ship was sunk by a torpedo off the coast of Normandy in June 1944, he was transferred to the *Volksgrenadiers.* Though a decorated veteran, who had been awarded the Iron Cross 2nd Class, Minesweeper Badge, and the Black Wound Badge, he was no infantryman, but at this stage of the war, that did not matter. Instead of a sturdy ship beneath his feet, he found himself armed with a rifle and assigned to a ground combat unit in the Eifel.[40]

Ecker and Wilts hardly knew anyone and didn't even know the names of their squad leaders or platoon sergeant. They only knew that they were in the vicinity of the Roer River dams when they joined the company. Neither got much of a chance to get very acquainted with any of their comrades, at least not outside of captivity, nor did they have much time to train for what was to come. *Oberleutnant* Krüssmann probably sympathized with them, for he was no better off. Still, he did the best he could and supervised what limited training could be done while at the same time ensuring that the company manned its defensive positions. Like *Oberleutnant* Aretz before him, he had precious little time to learn his men's strengths and weaknesses or to get to know the company's area of operations. With the protective barrier of the Hürtgen Forest lost for good, what concerned him and his men was that as soon as the Roer reservoirs drained away, the Americans would attack and that the only thing that would stop them this time was the Rhine River. Whether they could reach it before the Americans did was a question that no one could answer.

The seizure of the Schwammenauel Dam finally brought the Battle of the Hürtgen Forest to a close, nearly five months after it began. Except for a lull between 18 December 1944 and 29 January 1945, the fighting had raged continuously throughout this part of the Western Front in what the Allies would later call the Siegfried Line Campaign. In the period that began when the 47th Infantry Regiment of the 9th Infantry Division penetrated the Schill Defensive Line near Schevenhütte on 16 September 1944 and ended with the capture of the Roer dams on 10 February 1945, nearly 120,000 Allied and as many as 80,000 German soldiers had fought here and many thousand had been killed in action or died of wounds.[41]

All told, all or part of eight American infantry divisions—the 1st, 2nd, 4th, 8th, 9th, 28th, 78th, and 83rd—the 82nd Airborne Division and combat commands from both the 5th and 7th Armored Divisions, as well as numerous separate units, had fought at one time or another in the forests with Hodges' US First and Simpson's US Ninth Armies. In addition, four corps headquarters—V, VII, XIX, and XVIII Airborne Corps—had been engaged in command and control of the fighting. Casualties had been high, with at least 33,000 killed, missing, captured, or evacuated for non-combat injuries and disease by 13 December 1944 alone, representing a casualty rate approaching twenty-five percent. Additionally, Hodges' US First Army lost an additional 14,000 men from all causes from that point until the battle ended on 10 February 1945.[42]

On the German side, all or part of the following seventeen divisions were engaged—the *85th, 89th, 275th, 344th, 347th,* and *353rd Infantry Divisions;* the *12th, 47th, 62nd, 246th, 272nd, 277th,* and *326th VGDs*; the *9th* and *116th Panzer Divisions;* the *3rd Panzer-Grenadier Division;* and the *3rd Parachute Division.* At one time or another, three German armies—the *Seventh, Fifteenth,* and *Fifth Panzer*—had been engaged in the attempt to stop the Allied move through the forest, as well as three corps headquarters—*LXVII, LXXIV,* and *LXXXI Corps.*

German losses had been at least as high as those suffered by the Allies, representing a higher loss in relation to the overall percentage of the forces engaged, but the exact number will never be known with precision because of the destruction or loss of the relevant records. The number of Germans taken prisoner during the entire Siegfried Line Campaign exceeded 90,000, of which the Battle of the Hürtgen Forest contributed a significant number.[43]

During its commitment to the Hürtgen Forest between 5 November 1944 and 10 February 1945, the *272nd VGD* suffered losses of approximately sixty to seventy-five percent. Each of the three *Grenadier* regiments had been reduced in strength to that of a rifle company by the end of the fighting, a loss rate exceeding ninety percent. *Füsilier Company 272*'s loss rate of seventy-five percent during the period was not uncommon and in comparison to the grenadier regiments, the number of casualties it actually suffered was lower.

Though the division would laboriously be built back up to nearly fifty percent in strength by the end of the February, it would never again be the same. Not only had many of its men and much of its equipment been lost, but even more consequential had been the high loss rates among junior and mid-level leaders—the sergeants, lieutenants, and captains upon whom any modern western military organization relies in order to function effectively. These men could no longer be replaced and those assigned to fill the gaps would prove to be unable to stand up to the Allied onslaught that was only a few days away.[44]

13

The Retreat to the Rhine

With the Roer River dams now in the hands of the Americans and Allied Forces standing along the entire length of the western bank of the Roer, the German defenders feverishly worked to strengthen their defenses to prepare for upcoming general offensive, but there was precious little left with which to do so. Now that the Roer floodwaters had subsided, Lieutenant General Simpson's US Ninth Army, still a part of Montgomery's 21st Army Group, was free on 23 February finally to launch its long-anticipated Operation GRENADE with its VII, XIII, and XIX Corps, while the First Canadian Army, to Simpson's north, continued with their own operation east of the Maas, codenamed Operation VERITABLE, which had begun two weeks earlier.* Once both armies had cleared their respective areas, they were to conduct a pincer movement to trap all German armies between the Rhine and the Roer-Maas defensive line. Nearly everywhere, German attempts to stem the tide were unsuccessful and by 24 February, the Ninth Army had seized eight bridgeheads along the Roer's eastern bank.

On the eastern edges of the Stolberg corridor, troops from the 8th and 104th Infantry Divisions of Major General Lawton Collins' US VII Corps, composing US Ninth Army's right flank, succeeded in establishing several bridgeheads along the Roer north and south of Düren, despite difficulties mainly caused by the current and inexperience in handling assault craft. Neither the opposing *12th Volks-Grenadier Division,* now a shadow of its former self, nor the *353rd Infantry Division* of *LVIII Panzer Corps* (which had taken over responsibility for the sector from *LXXXI Corps*) had managed to offer effective resistance and many of their troops were reported to have surrendered at the first sight of American forces. By the end of 27 February, elements of six of Simpson's divisions had firmly established themselves on the river's eastern bank at little cost. American casualties during the five-day operation totaled just 1,066, of which 92 were killed in action. VII Corps suffered 381 total casualties, including 66 killed, many

---

* Operation VERITABLE began 8 February when General Crerar's Canadian First Army attacked in a southeasterly direction between the Maas and the Rhine. Despite a promising start, the offensive bogged down quickly due to a combination of bitter German resistance, water-soaked terrain and poor flying weather that denied effective use of Allied tactical air power. Eventually, the pincers of Canadian First Army and Simpson's Ninth Army met at Geldern on 3 March, resulting in the total collapse of the German defensive effort west of the Rhine in the north. The last German bridgehead on the Lower Rhine west of Wesel was eliminated by 10 March. Source: Depuy and Depuy, *The Encyclopedia of Military History, From 3,500 B.C. to the Present,* Revised Edition (New York: Harper and Row, 1977), 1119.

of whom had drowned when their assault boats capsized on the still swiftly-moving Roer.[1]

By 27 February, Collins' VII Corps had advanced as far as ten and a half miles east of the Roer and had reached the Erft River Canal, halfway to the Rhine. With this task accomplished, Operation GRENADE was declared completed. Ninth Army would now serve as the anvil and the First Canadian Army to the north as the hammer, with the objective of crushing both *Fifteenth* and *First Parachute Armies* between the Roer and Rhine before either could withdraw across Germany's last great defensive barrier. With German forces thus occupied, the way was now clear for the First Army to begin its own dash to the Rhine, part of an overall operation codenamed Operation LUMBERJACK.

Operation LUMBERJACK was designed to clear all remaining German forces on the western bank of the Rhine and to bring all of General Omar Bradley's 12th Army Group, composed of the US First and Third Armies, to the western bank of the river (Lieutenant General Jacob M. Devers' 6th Army Group had already cleared the Upper Rhine from Karlsruhe to the Swiss Border by 9 February). Bradley's plan envisioned that any German forces that had managed to escape the initial American assault would be trapped by both armies in a pocket encompassing the area between the northern edge of the Eifel Mountains and the Ahr River and then destroyed before they got across the Rhine to safety.[2]

Lieutenant General Hodges' First Army, consisting of US VII (which would revert to First Army control), III, and V Corps, would constitute the northern arm of the pincer, while Lieutenant General Patton's US Third Army, constituting the southern arm, would attack from the vicinity of Bitburg and Trier with its US VIII, XII, and XX Corps. Bradley's intelligence staff estimated that American forces would possess a numerical advantage of at least five to one, a figure seconded by von Rundstedt himself.

According to German estimates, each of their infantry battalions employed along the Roer on 12 February 1945 faced off against two-thirds of an Allied division. In all, Allied intelligence estimated that the Germans had only 53,500 men, supported by 180 assault guns and tanks and thirty battalions of artillery (roughly 360 guns), to defend along the Roer, compared to the 303,243 men, 1,394 tanks, and more than 2,000 pieces of artillery fielded by the US Ninth Army alone. German air power was no longer a factor, and Ninth Army could count on the dedicated support of XXIX Tactical Air Command with 375 aircraft, not to mention heavy bombers that could be called upon if needed.[3]

Before Operation LUMBERJACK could begin, however, Major General John Millikin's III Corps would first have to secure First Army's left flank by establishing a bridgehead over the Roer between Nideggen and Heimbach. Though VII Corps, which was still attached to the US Ninth Army, had established its own bridgehead across the Roer, it could not proceed very far beyond the Erft Canal unless its own flank was protected. Once VII Corps had carried out its mission, it would revert to the command and control of US First Army. Consequently, III

Corps, consisting of the US 1st, 9th, and 78th Infantry Divisions and the 9th Armored Division, launched its own operation beginning 25 February when the 16th Infantry Regiment of the 1st Infantry Division crossed the Roer using the bridges erected at Düren by the 8th Infantry Division two days before.

Attacking upstream along the eastern bank of the Roer, the men of the 1st Infantry Division dispersed feeble German efforts to slow their advance until the lead battalion reached the vicinity of Kreuzau, where it ran up against scattered resistance offered by the *353rd Infantry Division*. Once the lead battalion had cleared the town of the its defenders, the remainder of the regiment assisted the main body of the division to secure a crossing site at that location. By that evening, 1st Infantry Division engineers had managed to erect a temporary bridge that was used to pass the 39th Infantry Regiment of the 9th Infantry Division across the Roer the next morning. The 39th Infantry then turned to the right and executed the same type of maneuver that the regiments of the 1st Infantry Division had just done earlier that day.

Using this bridgehead as a springboard, the 9th Infantry Division continued to attack upstream in a southerly direction toward Nideggen that day and the next, overcoming determined resistance offered by the *3rd Parachute Division,* arrayed on the *272nd VGD*'s right flank. Despite the young *Fallschirmjägers* best efforts, they were slowly forced to withdraw eastward toward Wollersheim and Vlatten, where they quickly dug in to prepare for the next round.

By the evening of 27 February, the 311th Infantry Regiment of the 78th Infantry Division had moved to a point opposite Nideggen, where it would cross the Roer the next morning and initiate its own attack against the *272nd VGD* from the north at Blens and Heimbach. The 78th Infantry Division, fresh from its recent experience in seizing Schmidt and the Schwammenauel Dam and having undergone two weeks of rest and replenishment, was now poised to complete the destruction of the German division that it had faced off against since 13 December 1944.

In the meantime, *Generalmajor* König had not been idle in his defensive sector either. Using the two weeks of breathing space available to him while waiting for the water to recede, he put this time to good use and did what he could to put his shattered division back together again before the 78th Infantry Division resumed it attack. This time, however, there was very little material for him to work with. Not only were there shortages of heavy weapons and other equipment, but the manpower needed to defend the newly named "Richthofen Position" along the Roer's eastern bank was lacking as well, for the 78th Infantry Division alone had captured 2,303 men between 30 January and 10 February (most of whom most likely from the *272nd Volks- Grenadier Division)*, and claimed to have killed and wounded 5,000 to 6,000 more.[4]

To partially make up for the shortage of manpower, combat troops from the *85th Infantry Division* were transferred to König's control in mid-February before that division was shipped out to Döberitz to be reconstituted. Once again battalion, regimental, and division trains were raided for suitable manpower. Even this infusion of several thousand replacements was not enough. After the beating they took at Eicherscheid, Kesternich, Steckenborn, and Schmidt, each of König's three regiments had dwindled to 200 combat troops or less, forcing them to be reorganized as battalion-sized battle groups.

Since sufficient troops to defend a continuous front line were no longer available, König had to make do by ordering each regiment to set up a series of mutually supporting "hedgehog" positions or strongpoints. Bolstered by the addition of the few remaining heavy weapons that each regiment still possessed, these strongpoints, laid out on a pattern of two or three per kilometer, were a mere tactical improvisation designed to buy time until a counterattack could be carried out to cover a withdrawal to an intermediate defensive position. Easily bypassed should one strongpoint fall and susceptible to being attacked from the rear, these widely-spaced strongpoints were a clear indication that the *272nd VGD* was now fighting a "poor man's war."

Oberstleutnant Rösener's *Grenadier Regiment 982,* with its headquarters at the Mariawald Abbey, was positioned on the division's right flank, sharing a boundary with the *3rd Parachute Division.* Rösener and his regiment were responsible for the defensive position that ran from Abenden along the Roer, through Heimbach and to the south side of the Schwammenauel Dam opposite Hasenfeld. Rösener's regiment, now temporarily renamed *Kampfgruppe 982,* had been reinforced by the remnants of *Combat Engineer Battalion 272* and *Field Replacement Battalion 272.*

On the division's left flank defending the Kermeter Peninsula lay *Kampfgruppe 981.* Reinforced by the addition of the men from *Grenadier Regiment 1053* of the *85th Infantry Division,* it was now the largest battle group in the division, with six companies (including the regimental infantry howitzer and antitank companies and a platoon from *Füsilier Company 272*). The commander of the *1053rd, Oberst* Meyer, whose men had been incorporated into *Battle Group 981,* was placed in temporary command and *Oberstleutnant* Kleinkorres was made his deputy.[5] The battle group's headquarters was located in the Mariawald forester's lodge. On its left, *Kampfgruppe 981* tied in with the weak *62nd Volks-Grenadier Division,* which was centered on Gemünd and constituted *LXXIV Corps'* southern boundary with neighboring *LXVII Corps.*

Burian's *Kampfgruppe 980,* the weakest of the three, was designated the division reserve and placed in the vicinity of the Mariawald forester's lodge. All of its remaining personnel were placed in the now-reformed *1st Battalion* with the exception of *Hauptmann* Thomae, who was ordered to move to the vicinity of Hergarten to reform his battalion with only a skeleton cadre. Since *Hauptmann* Rhein had been captured, *Hauptmann* Hans Witscher was chosen to command the newly-reconstituted *1st Battalion;* moved from his previous position as *Oberst* Burian's operations officer, he was replaced by *Oberleutnant* Hans Gehle, the former deputy operations officer of the regiment.

Artillery Regiment 272 was reorganized into two firing battalions and its excess manpower, brought about by the loss of the batteries that had been abandoned earlier at Wollseifen, was parceled out among the infantry companies. Even with this infusion, the combat strength of each of the infantry companies rarely exceeded twenty to thirty men.[6] To reinforce the scattered defensive positions, mines and barbed wire entanglements were laid as much as the supply situation permitted, but there was never enough to cover the gaps.

Three *Hetzers* from *Tank Destroyer Battalion 272* were also available to bolster the defense and five more were in the division's repair shop awaiting parts. Aside from these vehicles, the only other assets the division had that could keep American tanks at bay were *Panzerfausts,* a few *Ofenrohr* bazookas, and two or three antitank guns. Snipers kept down the heads of American patrols on the other side of the near-empty Schwammenauel Reservoir, though a few small raiding parties from both sides slipped over occasionally at night. The few *Westwall* bunkers dotting the area were used strictly as protection from artillery fire or as command posts. Division headquarters remained in the air raid bunkers at Vlatten, close enough for König to make daily visits to the front, but far enough to the rear to avoid most of the American's artillery fire.

Relative quiet reigned on the division's front between 11 and 27 February, allowing the division to get on with the business of completing the Richthofen Position, as well as continuing the training and reorganization of the battle groups. Nearly everyone in the division could see that this welcome pause would not last forever, though, simply by looking at the steadily receding waters of the Roer. Surely, by the end of February at the latest, the Americans would attack. The amount of vehicular traffic observed or heard on the opposite bank indicated that their buildup continued to increase, as did the American artillery fire and attacks by fighter-bombers. As a precautionary move, König ordered Burian on 25 February to move his battle group from Mariawald to the vicinity of Hergarten to be in a better position to serve as the division reserve, since the American Roer crossings at Jülich and Düren had already been reported. An attack in the direction of the *272nd VGD* could be expected in a matter of days if not hours.

König had no intention of defending the Kermeter Peninsula and allowing part of his division to become entrapped once more. He identified a shorter, easier-to-defend line that stretched across the base of the Kermeter between Heimbach and Pulvermühle. The same day that Burian received the order to move to Hergarten, scouts informed König that the levels of the Roer and the Schwammenauel Reservoir had equalized and could be crossed easily on foot. The American attack could now be expected momentarily. In fact, the sound of artillery fire could clearly be heard a few miles to the north, where US III Corps had begun its bombardment of German defenses in the Nideggen area.

Consequently, König ordered the division to withdraw to the shortened Richthofen Intermediate Position beginning on 27 February, after gaining consent from *Generalleutnant* Püchler at *LXXIV Corps* to do so. A few observation posts were left on the Kermeter Peninsula to provide early warning with orders that they were to withdraw as soon as they confronted advancing American forces. The division's right flank was protected by an intermediate defensive position manned by elements of the *3rd Parachute Division* in the vicinity of the village of Vlatten. The left flank was anchored tenuously at the northern outskirts of Gemünd, held by the *62nd VGD*, a unit of questionable defensive value. König had done everything that was in his power—now all he could do was wait.[7]

The first contact between the *272nd VGD* and the 78th Infantry Division took place on the evening of 28 February, after the 311th Infantry had advanced from Nideggen to the eastern outskirts of Abenden. After pushing through the defenses of the *3rd Parachute Division* at 0615 hours, 1st Battalion, 311th Infantry Regiment found itself facing troops of Rösener's *Kampfgruppe 982* north of the village of Blens. Although Rösener's men fought well, utilizing automatic weapons and mortars with good effect, they were pushed back toward Heimbach by the inexorable American advance. In one instance, an entire company of thirty-eight *Volksgrenadiers* surrendered, including its commanding officer, after they had been surrounded in the hills a few hundred meters north of the village.[9]

By that afternoon, two battalions of the 311th Infantry had seized the high ground northeast of the village of Hausen and immediately prepared to the assault the town itself. German resistance in the form of artillery, mortar, and machine-gun fire was fierce at first, compelling the Americans to advance slowly and methodically, although they still suffered several casualties while covering the last several hundred meters of open space remaining between the woods and the village's outskirts. Fighting house to house and even room to room, the men of 3rd Battalion, 311 Infantry finally routed Rösener's remaining men from the village by 1700 hours and established advanced positions on the high ground toward the village's eastern outskirts in order to prepare for their attack the following day against Heimbach.

Once he was informed of the loss of Hausen on the evening of 28 February and of Rösener's inability to prevent the Americans from attacking into the division's now-open right flank, *Generalmajor* König ordered *Oberst* Burian's *Kampfgruppe 980* toward Heimbach to stop or at least delay the advance of the 78th Infantry Division. At the same time, it was reported that Americans forces were preparing an attack on his division's left flank in the vicinity of Gemünd, held at the time by a much weakened *62nd Volks-Grenadier Division,* which was in even worse shape the *272nd.*

Logically, the best course of action remaining to König was to order an immediate withdrawal from the Richthofen Position toward the Rhine, but his request to do so was denied by *LXXIV Corps.* His corps commander, *Generalleutnant* Püchler, was well aware of the seriousness of the situation, but was forbidden by

General der Infanterie von Zangen's *Fifteenth Army* to allow his divisions to withdraw one foot unless *Generalfeldmarschall* Model at *Army Group B* had personally granted permission. Model's Chief of Staff, *Generalleutnant* Karl Wegener, had already been seeking permission from Hitler to withdraw *Fifteenth Army* before it was too late, but the dictator, whose headquarters had been moved into the *Führerbunker* underneath the Reich Chancellery in Berlin, refused to even consider it.[10] The best that Püchler could do, since his only reserve, the *3rd Panzer-Grenadier Division,* had been taken away and allocated to the neighboring corps on his right, was to shift as much of his corps artillery as he could to the north to support the defense being conducted there, but in the final equation this was no substitute for infantry.

The 311th Infantry Regiment's attack to seize Heimbach began at 0300 hours on 1 March, when its 2nd Battalion moved to seize the high ground east of the town. Heimbach, which lay along the eastern bank of the Roer two kilometers north of the Schwammenauel Dam, was attacked at the same time by 1st Battalion, which moved south directly from Hausen along the main road with the support of Company C, 774th Tank Battalion. Delayed by a series of minefields overwatched by one or two *Hetzers* of *Antitank Battalion 272,* 1st Battalion's Company B was able to secure a foothold on the town's western edge by 0700 hours. At the same time, despite stubborn resistance offered by Burian's *Kampfgruppe 980* and fire support provided by *3rd Battalion, Artillery Regiment 272,* the Germans were unable to prevent Company A from penetrating Heimbach's northern outskirts.

Facing encirclement, Burian ordered his troops out of the town, leaving only a small rear guard behind to delay the Americans until he and his men could withdraw. By 1330 hours, the town was declared secure by 1st Battalion, 311th Infantry after most of the German rear guard surrendered after firing a few token shots at their pursuers. Earlier that day, 1st Battalion had sent its Company C two thousand yards to the east to gain control of the main road running from Heimbach to Vlatten, where it linked up with troops of the regiment's 3rd Battalion by 1500 hours.[11]

With Heimbach now in American hands on the division's right flank and the *62nd Volks-Grenadier Division* forced to withdraw from Gemünd on the left by the 2nd Infantry Division, the entire defensive scheme of the *272nd VGD* began to collapse by the afternoon of 1 March. *Generalmajor* König ordered the division to begin pulling back immediately from the Richthofen Position, and not a moment too soon. The 310th Infantry Regiment had crossed the Roer along the top of the Schwammenauel Dam and its forward elements had already pushed deeply into the woods of the Kermeter Peninsula, scattering the weak German outposts that stood in their way. There was little that Püchler's *LXXIV Corps* could offer to König in support, since the few reserves had already been committed to the fight near Wollersheim against the bulk of the American armor arrayed there.

Not limited by its seizure of the Roer between Nideggen and Heimbach, the 78th Infantry Division aggressively pressed forward its attack toward its next objective. To its immediate left, Combat Command A of the 9th Armored Division, attached to the 1st Infantry Division, had already reached the northern outskirts of Wollersheim late that afternoon, but was stopped in its tracks by a skillfully-led battle group from the *3rd Parachute Division,* reinforced by a few tanks and assault guns from the *9th Panzer Division.* After having secured Heimbach, the main effort of the 78th Infantry Division was switched to the attack that day by the 309th Infantry Regiment, which crossed the Roer near the town of Blens in the wake of the 311th Infantry. After assembling on the eastern bank that evening, the regiment then attacked eastwards through the lines of the 311th toward Wollersheim and Vlatten in the early morning hours of 2 March, plunging along the boundary between the *3rd Parachute* and the *272nd VGDs.*

The official history of the 78th Infantry Division reported that there was little light that morning and the temperature was very cold with scattered snow showers, difficult conditions in which to begin an attack, though they would benefit the attackers more than the Germans. At dawn, 2nd Battalion of the 309th Infantry left its assembly area in the Wollersheimer Forest east of Blens and moved undetected across the three kilometers of rolling countryside toward Vlatten and began its attack. To its left, the 3rd Battalion began its own attack against Wollersheim, reinforcing Combat Command A of the 9th Armored Division.

One of the units defending the intermediate position at Vlatten was *Füsilier Company 272.* It had been reunited as a company once again on 28 February, with the return of its detached infantry platoon, but after this had been effected it was immediately ordered by *272nd VGD* to move from its reserve position in Schwerfen to a new location eight kilometers toward the east, where it would help cover the withdrawal of the rest of the division. *Oberleutnant* Krüssmann was instructed to position the company on the southern edge of the town of Vlatten, whose westward approaches would be covered by the battered *Fallschirmjäger Regiments 5* and *8* of *Generalleutnant* Schimpf's *3rd Parachute Division.*[12]

Luckily, 28 February proved to be a cloudy day, limiting the activity of American fighter-bombers and artillery, allowing the company to move to Vlatten without loss. Meanwhile, *Hauptfeldwebel* Fuhrmeister was directed to move the company trains to the town of Firmenich to keep them out of range of the American guns. The headquarters of *272nd VGD,* which had been occupying a group of bunkers in Vlatten since 5 February, had been forced to displace to a new location east of Mechernich near Iversheim the same night that the company arrived, departing only hours before the American attack began. The Company's combat element, now about seventy to eighty men, began to dig entrenchments in anticipation of the imminent American assault. It would not be long in coming.

The terrain immediately west of Vlatten was relatively open, offering little in the way of cover or concealment for the attackers. Several hundred troops from the *3rd Parachute Division* had constructed an in-depth defensive position, complete with trenches, fighting positions, and hasty field fortifications in the hopes that this would substitute for numbers and firepower. There was no time to dig antitank ditches and no antitank weapons were available except bazookas, *Panzerfausts* and at least one 20mm *Flak* gun.

The German forces in the Vlatten area, including *Füsilier Company 272,* were tasked with the mission of holding the Americans as long as possible until the bulk of *LXXIV Corps,* consisting of the *3rd Parachute Division* and the *272nd VGD,* located north and south of Vlatten respectively, could begin an orderly withdrawal to the Rhine. This would soon prove to be a task beyond the capability of this small force to carry out. *Füsilier Company 272* had been sent to Vlatten as the division's right flank unit, tasked with maintaining contact with the elements of *3rd Parachute Division* that were primarily responsible for holding Vlatten. Again, and not for the last time, *Füsilier Company 272* would be employed on one of the *272nd VGD*'s most exposed flanks.

The burden of the attack that day was borne by the 2nd Battalion of the 309th Infantry, commanded by Major Jesse Moorefield (see Map 17). His battalion would be amply supported by division and corps artillery as well as by a company of Shermans from the 774th Tank Battalion. Advancing in the early morning darkness, the Americans initially met a heavy volume of automatic weapons fire from the paratroopers dug in on the low ridge one kilometer west of the town. While two of Moorefield's infantry companies pinned the defenders down by fire, his third company, positioned on the right, maneuvered around the German left flank, forcing the Germans to either surrender or pull back. Once it became evident that the *Fallschirmjäger* were attempting to reposition their defense to meet this threat, Moorefield ordered his other two companies, now joined by the tanks, to attack on line toward the town, but were momentarily stopped at the town's edge by the heavy fire of the stubborn defenders.

In order to soften up the unexpectedly tough German defense in Vlatten, the Americans began a forty-five minute artillery barrage that commenced at 0830 hours. Now completely closed up to form a solid attacking line, the entire 2nd Battalion with its supporting tanks closed the distance and began clearing Vlatten house by house. At 1000 hours, it was reported that the southeast portion of the town had been overrun. Fighting ceased by 1200 hours, though bypassed pockets of German defenders, including snipers, continued to resist and had to be cleared out one by one. By 1500 hours, the town was completely in the hands of the Americans, who quickly consolidated their position in preparation to continue the advance eastward.

The few surviving Germans beat a hasty retreat toward the neighboring towns of Eppernich and Burvenich, where they again began to set up a series of blocking positions designed to slow the American advance, but to little avail. According to the official history of the 78th Division, "Walking along, the men appraised the now-empty system of trenches which ran along for miles. . . . They noted the sprawling bodies lying in the ditches—in the fields. The country they traversed had been held by the Germans only a few hours earlier. . . ."[13] Moorefield's battalion reported having captured 200 prisoners, many of whom undoubtedly from *Füsilier Company 272.*

While it is difficult to determine the exact course of the battle from the standpoint of *Füsilier Company 272,* it seems clear is that it was positioned in a defensive line on the town's southern outskirts and suffered heavy losses. According to the brief report written shortly afterward, "The Company was engaged at Vlatten, when the enemy carried out an attack with tank support upon this location. Heavy fighting soon developed, during the course of which the enemy was able to approach our forward positions. Suddenly, the enemy pushed into the company's flank and was able to take a portion of the company prisoner."

One participant in the fighting, *Gefreiter* Wilfried Wilts, was part of a five-man machine-gun team, commanded by a sergeant, who set up their fighting position in a haystack several hundred meters forward of Krüssmann's command post the night before. Here, they constructed a snug machine-gun nest and lined it with straw, providing a little insulation from the cold, wet weather. The next morning, Wilts and the others heard the sound of enemy tanks approaching the village and he was ordered by his NCO to notify the commander, who told him to go back to his foxhole and prepare to fight from "hedgehog" all-around defensive positions.

Wilts and the others were soon forced to abandon their positions, however, when the tanks broke through the thin defensive perimeter set up by the paratroopers, threatening to overrun their machine-gun section. As he and the others retreated, they were pursued by American artillery fire that seemingly chased them from haystack to haystack across the wide-open fields east of the village. They passed a 20mm *Flak* gun crew firing determinedly from a small hilltop directly at the advancing tanks, but with little effect. Wilts and the others never saw what happened to it or its brave crew, since they kept going, bending over at the waist and running as fast as possible.

At one point, an American tank approached to within one hundred meters of their position, forcing them to duck behind a stack of corn stalks. Luckily, due to the approaching darkness, the five men remained undetected and the tank moved on. Wilts and the others realized, however, that they were now behind enemy lines and would have to march all night if they were to have any chance of reaching their company again. The NCO decided that they should hide behind a haystack while they waited for it to become completely dark.

Their NCO, one of the few remaining old timers who knew the area well, was able to successfully navigate across the fields that moonless night. After several detours to avoid American patrols, they reached the town of Schwerfen in the early morning hours of 3 March, where he led them to the company trains, which provided them with some hot soup and coffee. Here, they reported to *Hauptfeldwebel* Fuhrmeister, who crossed their names off of the missing in action list and declared them present and accounted for.[14] They were among fifteen of the men who made it back to the Company that night.

Vlatten proved to be an even bigger disaster for the Company than either Simmerath or Herhahn had been. For all intents and purposes this battle marked the end of the original *Füsilier Company 272* that had arrived in the Hürtgen Forest the previous November. Of the 107 men assigned to the company on 2 March, including the company trains, fifty-five men were lost that day. Only one man was recorded killed in action, *Oberleutnant* Krüssmann, the new company commander, who was struck by multiple shell fragments in the chest and legs. He had commanded the company for only ten days.

Others were undoubtedly killed as well, but their deaths were not recorded until after the war. The only man recorded as being wounded was *Obergefreiter* Reinhold Klein, who was evacuated to the nearest field hospital. Most of the rest were listed as missing in action and believed captured. One member of the infantry howitzer platoon, *Gefreiter* Erwin Buchwalder, struck out to the east with his friend Walter van der Geest and reached the safety of the company trains later than night. With the combat elements wiped out or scattered, the Company had, for the moment, virtually ceased to exist as a fighting organization.

Those who escaped from Vlatten, like Wilfried Wilts and Erwin Buchwalder, were exceptions. While some men were forced by the Americans to surrender, many others undoubtedly were fed up with fighting and only wanted to get it over with as soon as possible in order to increase their chances of survival. The driving motivation behind those few who kept going that night, according to one survivor, was to do everything possible to rejoin the Company, his substitute family, even though the situation looked hopeless. What made the difference was leadership. The few remaining NCOs and officers who still expressed confidence and a sense of duty were the ones the stragglers rallied around and the ones who convinced even the faintest of heart to keep soldiering on.

Good leaders, however, were becoming increasingly scarce. Among the list of those missing were men who had been with the Company since its inception, including *Leutnant* Wegner, *Feldwebel* Dirksen, *Unteroffizier* Albrecht, and *Unteroffizier* Kienberger, as well as ten other NCOs who had been assigned since January. Most of these men were later determined to have been captured in Vlatten when the tanks surrounded the town. After this disaster, there were only fifty-two men left in the Company, nearly half of whom were assigned to the company trains. Losses in equipment had been heavy, too. In addition to losing thirty-three rifles, MP 44s and pistols, the company also lost three MG 42s.

As disturbing as the loss of the Company's precious remaining manpower was, the loss of its remaining heavy weapons was nearly as bad. The horse-drawn heavy weapons and infantry howitzer platoons could not displace quickly enough while attempting to cross the fields east of Vlatten, and promptly got stuck in the mud. Under heavy American fire, they were forced to abandon their last heavy machine gun, 80mm mortar, and 75mm light infantry howitzer, though the crew had been able to remove the breechblock and optics of the howitzer before leaving it behind.

The first men who made it back during the daylight hours on 2 March, some eight men in all, were hastily reorganized into a squad that afternoon by a *Leutnant* Günzel, the leader of a emergency company from the *272nd VGD*. Günzel, an officer from the division's leader reserve, led them back to Schwerfen, where they were lumped into his ad-hoc unit with many others from various units. Before the withdrawal began in earnest the next morning 3 March, survivors from *Füsilier Company 272* continued to filter into Schwerfen from Vlatten; by evening on 3 March, twenty-four combat troops had returned to the Company, bringing its fighting strength back up to about thirty-two soldiers. This fighting remnant would remain with Günzel's emergency company for at least a week. This emergency company was a hodge-podge, in the main consisting of service and supply soldiers, including troops from not only the *272nd VGD,* but from other divisions as well. Its fighting value must have been pretty low.

Not everyone in the company remembers having experienced heavy fighting at Vlatten, however. At least one platoon apparently had been bypassed during the American attack and only realized it until after the fact. During the early morning hours of 2 March 1944, *Gefreiter* Günther Ecker was awakened by a senior NCO (probably *Oberfeldwebel* Volckner) and was told that they were now behind the American lines. Before Ecker and the others could mount any kind of offensive action or attempt a breakout, they were soon spotted and ordered to surrender by American infantry supported by tanks. Realizing that resistance was hopeless, Ecker and others in his platoon reluctantly surrendered.

Ecker could not recall hearing a single shot fired by anyone on either side, though due to fatigue and exhaustion he possibly could have slept through the entire battle. After being searched for weapons or other material of intelligence value, he and the others then began their long march into captivity, which was to culminate in a one-year stay in a French prisoner of war camp. Less than one year later he was home again, released early due to his age. He had only served four days with the company.[15]

The defeat at Vlatten on 2 March was only one of many futile German attempts to stem the resurgent Allied offensive. The weakened divisions of *Army Group B,* including the *272nd VGD,* began to fall back to the Rhine River in earnest during the first week of March 1945. Now that the US First and Ninth Armies had created numerous bridgeheads across the Roer at multiple points along a fifty-kilometer wide swath between Heimbach and Linnich, there was little that *Generalfeldmarschall* Model could do to stop them. The force ratio had now passed overwhelmingly and permanently to the Allies' favor, with a battalion's equivalent of Germans defending a fifteen-kilometer wide front line, now facing the equivalent of an Allied division. *Army Group B* now had to contend with over 1,000 Allied tanks with fewer than 115 of its own.[16]

The Allied forces (particularly those of the Americans) were nearly at full strength, well equipped and enjoyed a level of motorization that the Germans could only envy. As the tattered and exhausted remnants of once-proud regiments and divisions withdrew their horse-drawn equipment to the Rhine, it now become a race to see who would reach the river first—the German forces, who hoped to establish a new defensive line that would hold, or the Allies, who were eagerly seeking an intact bridge in order to establish a foothold on the eastern bank of the river and begin their drive into the heart of Germany. In most instances, the Germans arrived first, though barely.

The *272nd VGD* was one division that made it. With his division's front line pierced at Heimbach, his right flank turned at Vlatten and both divisions on its flanks withdrawing hastily, *Generalmajor* König had no choice but to order a withdrawal as well. Gathering his remaining forces, König conducted a series of delaying actions to impede the American's advance while the bulk of the division made good its escape. The situation was similar to the hurried retreat across northern France, Belgium, and Holland the previous autumn, only this time under even worse circumstances. On 3 March, König was forced to move his command post from Iversheim to the village of Wachendorf, ten kilometers east of Mechernich.

The pursuing Americans from the 78th Infantry Division and 9th Armored Division followed inexorably, threatening to completely unhinge the German withdrawal and scatter their troops in all directions. According to the *272nd VGD*'s official history,

> The Americans punched through the flanks of the divisional front and com-
> pelled the division to conduct a fighting withdrawal in order to avoid
> becoming encircled. A continuous front line no longer existed. Battle
> groups from the regiments defended by conducting hard-hitting rear guard
> actions along the roads and highways.[17]

To deal with the division's open northern flank, König ordered *Oberst* Burian's *Kampfgruppe 980* to ward off attacks from that direction while the rest of the division rapidly moved toward the designated Rhine crossing points at Nieder-Breisig and Brohl. *Kampfgruppen 981* and *982* were directed to disengage as quickly as possible and join the rest of the division, with one regiment screening toward the south in an attempt to maintain contact with the unit on the division's left flank. This proved to be nearly impossible, since the unit to the south, the *62nd Volks-Grenadier Division,* was disintegrating as it withdrew from its defens-es near Gemünd, with the US 2nd Infantry Division in hot pursuit, and all con-tact with it had been lost. (See Map 18)

Over the next several days, *Oberst* Burian's *Kampfgruppe 980,* reinforced by *3rd Battalion, Artillery Regiment 272,* fought skillful delaying actions at Schwerfen, Enzen, Rheder-Kreuzweingarten, Schweinheim, Totenfeld, and Bad Neuenahr, slowing the pursuing American forces and buying time. At some point during the withdrawal, *Leutnant* Günzel's emergency company with the survivors from *Füsilier Company 272* was apparently tactically subordinated to Burian.

Burian had now been tasked with covering the withdrawal of the entire division down the Ahr River valley. The *272nd VGD* was being hard pressed by the Americans attacking from both the north and the south and was in real danger of being cut off from the Rhine. On 4 March, an attack by Combat Command A of the 9th Armored Division, supported by 3rd Battalion of the 310th Infantry Regiment of the 78th Infantry Division, caught up with Burian and his men between Schwerfen and Enzen, resulting in a brief, but sharp, fight. By nightfall, American troops had seized control of those towns, though *Kampfgruppe 980* managed to slip away in the darkness.

Although *Leutnant* Günzel was able to withdraw his troops in good order before these towns fell, ten members of *Füsilier Company 272* were declared missing in action that evening, presumed captured. Two of the men lost between Schwerfen and Enzen, *Stabsgefreiter* Konzak and *Gefreiter* Ortloff, had been wounded and presumed captured, since there was no means to evacuate them. Harald Ortloff was indeed captured by the Americans, who treated his wounds and administered a shot of penicillin to stave off a raging tetanus infection that would have resulted in an amputation, to say the least. For that kindness, Ortloff was grateful. After being released from a POW camp in June 1945, he went back to his home in Rudolstadt, where he died in 1991.

By this point in the campaign, the company had suffered 257 casualties (out of 200 men authorized!) since 5 November 1944 and the war still had two months left to go.[18]

While these rear guard actions were being bitterly fought, *Hauptfeldwebel* Fuhrmeister was ordered to move on the evening of 3 March with the twenty or so men assigned to the company trains a distance of fourteen kilometers from Firmenich through Mechernich to Hohn, which they reached by midnight. Located some twenty-five kilometers behind the front lines, the horse-drawn trains of the company would be safe here for a few days. Snow fell throughout the day, sparing Fuhrmeister and his men the ordeal of further Allied fighter-bomber attacks.

Meanwhile, with no time left to wait for stragglers and harried by the Americans, *Oberst* Burian continued to conduct his fighting withdrawal to the southeast. During this maneuver, Günzel's emergency company took up a delaying position in the Billigen Forest four kilometers southwest of Euskirchen near the village of Satzvey. The rain and snow which had plagued the men the past several days finally let up, though the sky remained overcast, a godsend. Here, Burian, with Günzel's attached troops and other rearguard elements, sharply checked the advance of 1st Battalion, 311th Infantry, though the regiment's 3rd Battalion slipped around the German right flank in neighboring Obergarten later that afternoon.[19] Under a heavy covering artillery barrage fired by all twelve guns of *3rd Battalion, Artillery Regiment 272* during the evening of 5 March, the Germans counterattacked and succeeded in immobilizing the battalion headquarters of 1st Battalion, 311th Infantry in Satzvey. With the Americans temporarily stunned, Burian took advantage of this short breathing space and withdrew again, this time east through Euskirchen.

As it withdrew, the *272nd VGD* was most vulnerable along its right flank (to the north), where advancing US forces threatened to cut off its route of retreat to the Rhine and sever contact with neighboring *3rd Parachute* and *353rd Infantry Divisions*. This soon happened anyway, despite the *Volksgrenadiers'* best efforts to maintain contact. Under intense pressure, the division was soon forced to change its original easterly withdrawal route to one angled further toward the southeast, away from Bonn and toward the town of Ahrweiler. The increasing distance between König's division and *3rd Parachute Division* made it increasingly difficult for *General der Infanterie* Püchler's *LXXIV Corps,* which was being forced into Bonn, to exercise effective command and control of this formation. To correct this problem, *General der Infanterie* von Zangen placed the *272nd VGD* once again under the control of *General der Infanterie* Hitzfeld's *LXVII Corps* on the evening of 6 March 1945 and shifted corps boundaries accordingly.[20]

As the corps and divisions of *Fifteenth Army* were being rapidly pushed back to the Rhine, *Army Group B* informed von Zangen that he would be given the *11th Panzer Division* on 7 March to carry out a counterattack from the direction of Bonn toward Rheinbach that would enable him to reestablish contact between his *LXXIV* and *LXVII Corps,* thereby enabling a defense line to be built up once again west of the Rhine. This attack was to be supported by a drive from the south launched simultaneously by *LXVII Corps* using both the *272nd* and *277th Volks-Grenadier Divisions* from the direction of Münstereifel.[21]

This major traffic center had to be held not only as a springboard for *LXVII Corps'* attack, but also to ensure the Americans did not reach Remagen ahead of the Germans. *Army Group B* was still using the Ludendorff Bridge at Remagen to pass retreating units to the east bank of the Rhine. A key assumption in order for this plan to succeed was the belief by the *Fifteenth Army* staff that Münstereifel was still controlled on 6 March by the *272nd VGD*. It is doubtful, however, whether *Generalmajor* König ever received this order, since he was out of radio contact with both his old and new corps headquarters during most of the fateful period between the afternoon of 6 March and the early morning hours of 7 March and had most likely abandoned the town by that point.

For his part, Hitzfeld, who had been charged by von Zangen with carrying out this attack, believed that it should not be attempted under the circumstances.

Hitzfeld did not believe that there was time to plan an attack, nor did he even know where the *272nd VGD* was on 6 March, except for a vague sense that its headquarters lay somewhere to the north of Bad Neuenahr. He did not believe that an attack by only one weak division would stand any chance of success. He tried to get the order repealed, but to no avail.[22] To complicate matters, *Fifteenth Army* gave Hitzfeld responsibility for defending the Ludendorff Bridge at 0100 hours on 7 March, in addition to his existing orders to counterattack.[23] At this point, the American spearhead was closer to the Rhine than most of Hitzfeld's forces.

While the *11th Panzer Division* struggled to get enough fuel for its tanks to begin the attack on 7 March (fuel would not be available until 9 March), the whereabouts of the *272nd VGD* remained a mystery. Hitzfeld even sent his chief of staff, *Oberstleutnant* Elmar Warning, to find König's headquarters so he could relay the order in person, but he was unable to locate it until the next morning. In truth, the *272nd VGD* was fighting for its life as it struggled down the Ahr valley, keeping the pursuing tanks and combat teams from the 78th Infantry and 9th Armored Divisions at bay long enough to reach the Rhine, so it would have been unable to contribute much to the attack, even had its commander wished to do so.

By 1400 hours on 7 March, it finally became apparent to the *LXVII Corps* staff that the *272nd VGD* would not be able to carry out its scheduled attack. Even worse was the realization that the division had no units defending Münstereifel either.[24] In fact, it was not until 1600 hours when Hitzfeld was finally able to speak face to face with König about the situation at a forester's hut near Königsfeld, but by then it was too late. Without the *272nd*, any hopes of *LXVII Corps* carrying out a successful attack were dashed. Even more disconcerting, the only force available to prevent the spearhead of the 9th Armored Division from reaching the bridge at Remagen was a local defense company of thirty-six men commanded by *Hauptmann* Willi Bratge and three batteries of light *Flak*.

As a result, troops from Company A, 27th Armored Infantry Battalion of the 9th Armored Division were able to seize both sides of the bridge by 1520 hours when the demolition charges failed to properly explode, shortly after the last German unit, a straggling battalion from *Artillery Regiment 272* (most likely elements of the *4th Battalion*), made it safely across at approximately 1300 hours. Besides the aforementioned artillery battalion, several other elements of the *272nd VGD,* including one of its veterinarians and his staff, had crossed the Rhine at Remagen only hours earlier and eventually linked up with the main body of the division a few days later.

The US 9th Armored Division's unbelievable stroke of luck came about because the German artillery battalion's commander (most likely *Hauptmann* Lieser), had convinced the local battle commander, *Major* Hans Scheller, to remove the mines blocking access to the bridge so his battalion could cross with its guns and vehicles unimpeded.[25] Apparently, before Scheller (who a few hours earlier had been Hitzfeld's aide-de-camp) could have the mines re-emplaced, the

Americans began their attack and caught him and the other defenders by surprise Though the German engineers desperately tried to blow up the bridge before the Americans could seize it, the charges were only partially successful and the defenders were overwhelmed before they could make a second attempt. Thus the 9th Armored Division had achieved one of the most significant tactical successes of the entire war and now had a foothold on the eastern bank of the mighty Rhine.

Upon hearing the news of the bridge's capture, Hitler flew into a rage and demanded that those responsible be put to death. In Model's hunt for scapegoats that soon followed, *Major* Scheller and three other officers were found guilty by a Nazi kangaroo court and executed shortly thereafter. No one from *272nd VGD* was charged or apparently even considered suspect, a remarkable omission given that the *272nd VGD* was supposed to have defended the bridge.

It only became apparent after the war what had happened to the *272nd*. The last orders it had received from *LXVII Corps* on 6 March directed it to prevent the American advance toward the southeast along the route Fritzdorf to Gelsdorf and to attempt to secure assistance if needed from the garrison at Remagen. Neither *Generalmajor* König nor his *Ia, Major* Uhl, learned that their division had been ordered by *Fifteenth Army* to carry out an attack in conjunction with the *11th Panzer Division* or even to hold Münstereifel. Rather, the division had proceeded instead to withdraw slowly along the Ahr River toward Sinzig on the west bank of the Rhine.

Alone, the battle group from *277th Volks-Grenadier Division* initiated its attack toward Rheinbach on the morning of 7 March as ordered, encountering forces of the 102nd Cavalry Group (Mechanized) and 78th Infantry Division as it advanced. Though it reached as far as its intermediate objective of Kalenborn, the battle group was brought to a halt short of its goal of Gelsdorf, though its commander claimed to have destroyed nine armored vehicles.[26] After a promising beginning this small force, consisting of a grenadier battalion and eight assault guns, was driven back south of the Ahr by both the 38th Cavalry Reconnaissance Squadron and 2nd Battalion, 309th Infantry Regiment, 78th Infantry Division by nightfall. All the German counterattack had to show for its efforts were a number of killed, wounded, and missing as well as the loss of several of the precious assault guns. The attack made so little of an impression that the Americans had barely noticed that the counterattack had even taken place![27]

The anticipated main effort by the *11th Panzer Division* never materialized and any hope of restoring a defensive line west of the Rhine between Bonn and Koblenz quickly evaporated, especially when the news circulated that the Americans had seized a bridgehead at Remagen. In his postwar report, von Zangen bitterly remarked that "If the [*272nd*] Division had at least fulfilled the order of the Corps in barring the way to the enemy, [the enemy's] drive to the Remagen bridge would have been rendered much more difficult."[28] Von Zangen's assessment of the Division's ability to carry out this critical mission, seen in retrospect, was far too optimistic and reflected how little he knew about the uncertain situation.

When *Oberstleutnant* Warning finally located the headquarters of the *272nd VGD* near the village of Scheuren on the morning of 7 March, he reported to *General der Infanterie* Hitzfeld upon his return that the state of the division was "appalling," that it was "no longer fit for defense" and its ability to execute any order given to it should be considered a dubious proposition.[29] Events would soon prove Warning assessment to have been overly pessimistic, but at the time the temporary disappearance of König's division inadvertently played a crucial role in helping the Allies cross the Rhine.

It is interesting to speculate how the course of the war might have differed had any of the *272nd VGD*'s radios received the crucial orders from *Fifteenth Army* or *LXVII Corps* during the afternoon of 6 March 1945, for even an infantry company with one or two antitank guns, properly emplaced, may well have held up the American advance long enough for the engineers to complete their demolition of the bridge.

Though fateful, the dramatic events of 6 to 7 March 1945 that were to hasten the end of the war in northwest Europe were played out without the knowledge of most of the combat troops involved in the retreat to the Rhine. Most *Volksgrenadiers* by that point were probably just concerned about getting across the river to safety. The combat element of *Füsilier Company 272,* now reduced to twenty-two men, lost only one man as it withdrew through Euskirchen on 6 March and that was *Obergefreiter* Josef Lautensack, who had simply disappeared. Evidently, Lautensack had been killed in action near Euskirchen on 6 March and his body was not recovered until after the war. He lies buried in the German War Cemetary in Lommel, Belgium.

Meanwhile in Hohn, the company trains were now threatened by the advance of the 311th Infantry Regiment, attacking from the direction of Obergarten. To prevent the company's remaining wagons and trucks from falling into the hands of the enemy, Fuhrmeister was ordered by the local area commander, *Leutnant* Schneeganz, to withdraw the trains through Münstereifel. By the evening of 6 March, the company trains had reached Altenahr, a few kilometers west of Ahrweiler on the Ahr River, the last obstacle to cross before reaching the Rhine.

On 7 March, the company trains and several stragglers from the company's combat element linked up again in Bad Neuenahr and continued the withdrawal to the Rhine under the supervision of *Hauptfeldwebel* Fuhrmeister, while the combat element continued to fight rearguard actions along with the rest of Burian's troops.

Only one man from the company was reported missing that day, *Obergefreiter* Peter Moog of Bad Godesberg, who was still convalescing with the company trains. While the company was waiting its turn to cross the Rhine, Moog had received permission from Fuhrmeister on the evening of 6 March to visit his cousin and his family in nearby Nierendorf. He was also granted permission to spend the night there, providing that he linked up again early the next morning with the company as it continued its withdrawal.

Moog, a veteran of the Eastern Front and *Füsilier Battalion 272* since Normandy, never reported back and in fact was captured the next day.[30] As Moog retold his story, he overslept while at his cousin's house and the company had departed without him. As he wandered the streets of Nierendorf, he rounded a corner and walked into a German straggler collection unit, which quickly rounded him up and incorporated him into a rear guard unit, tasked with delaying the movement of the Americans into the town.

Not wanting to be part of a *Himmelfahrtskommando* (or "forlorn hope") and be killed or captured, Moog slipped away at the first possible opportunity and made his way back to his cousin's house. Just when his goal was in sight, a jeep full of American soldiers drove up. Ignoring his entreaties to let him join his family, the Americans took him prisoner anyway and drove him to the nearest POW cage on the jeep's front fender. He was now out of the war for good.

The company now consisted of only forty men, though a few stragglers would catch up with the main body during the next several days. Due to the order from *General der Infanterie* Hitzfeld to withdraw all divisional supply elements to the east bank of the Rhine, Fuhrmeister and the others became separated in Nieder-Breisig from the company's remaining combat element. Instead, he, *Unteroffizier* Johns, *Gefreiter* Lorenz, and the rest were directed by the local traffic control unit to move the company trains that afternoon toward the southeast, moving along the left bank of the Rhine passing through Sinzig and Andernach toward Koblenz. In a heavy rain shower, the company trains finally crossed the Rhine before midnight on 7 March via the railroad bridge at Engers. Once across, Fuhrmeister and his men proceeded north again toward the town of Isenburg via Sayn, where they were supposed to link up with the rest of the division.

Meanwhile, *Füsilier Company 272*'s remaining combat element, along with the rest of *272nd VGD,* was busy establishing new defensive positions on the west bank of the Rhine. *Generalmajor* König, following instructions from *LXVII Corps,* had managed to form an enclave on the west bank of the Rhine along the heights that encompassed Nieder-Breisig and Brohl with a depth of approximately five kilometers and width of eight. There was no contact with any German units on its right flank, where the 9th Armored and 78th Infantry Divisions were hurriedly establishing their bridgehead across the Rhine at Remagen. The *277th Volks-Grenadier Division* was positioned to its left, though it was little more than a division headquarters with several thousand mixed personnel and few heavy weapons.

At one point during the withdrawal to the Rhine, the Company was assigned a new acting commander, *Leutnant* Mrusek, who was to serve until a more senior officer assigned from the Division's officer reserve replaced him. Little is known about Mrusek, but it can be safely assumed that he was assigned temporarily from the one of the infantry regiments of the division, since his name was never entered into the Company's personnel roster. During the crossing of the Rhine, Mrusek and the rest of the company's few remaining combat troops would remain attached to Burian's *Kampfgruppe 980* and would fight as part of his command for the next ten days.

The front was relatively quiet on 8 March, primarily due to the General Millikin's desire to get as many troops of his US III Corps across the bridge at Remagen as quickly as possible, diverting the attention of US First Army, his higher headquarters, for the time being. While the Americans redirected the bulk of the 9th Armored Division and the 78th and 99th Infantry Divisions across the Rhine at Remagen from 7 to 12 March, a few kilometers to the south the *272nd VGD* was absorbing hundreds of stragglers, guns, and vehicles from a myriad of retreating units and was attempting to reestablish some sort of coherent defense before the Americans turned their way again.[31]

It did not take the Americans long. On the night of 8/9 March, US forces renewed their drive against the Germans on the west bank of the Rhine south of Remagen, probably in the belief that the Germans, if they made a concerted effort, could threaten the American bridgehead from the rear and trap their troops fighting on the eastern bank.

That evening, the 11th Armored Division of US Third Army's VIII Corps attacked with tanks and mechanized infantry from the south toward Nieder and Ober-Zissen, ten kilometers southwest of König's division headquarters at Brohl, but were prevented from breaking through German defenses at the last moment by well-directed artillery fire from *Artillery Regiment 272* under *Oberstleutnant* Wilbrandt, who had somehow managed to salvage two battalion's worth of his guns during the pell-mell retreat from the Roer.

To the south of *272nd VGD,* however, things were beginning to look grim. Divisions of the US V and VIII Corps had ripped through the *277th VGD*'s defenses, scattering its troops, capturing the division commander and his entire staff, and nearly reaching the bank of the Rhine River near Koblenz before they were stopped by a combined attack from two other divisions of Hitzfeld's corps. Straggling was becoming an epidemic and many of the *272nd VGD*'s neighboring units simply melted away, as men sought to remove themselves and hide until an opportune moment to surrender to the Americans presented itself. Columns of refugees only added to the congestion, making it difficult for units still in control of their leaders to carry out orderly withdrawals or to launch counterattacks. Vehicles that had been abandoned for lack of fuel contributed to the delays.

Even local Nazi Party officials had given up and were heading for the Rhine. At one point near Mechernich, a withdrawing column from *Artillery Regiment 272* encountered a group of Nazi officials pulling a handcart filled with loot. Hard to miss in their brown Party uniforms, the "Golden Pheasants" demands for transport were ignored by the *Landsers,* who yelled out catcalls and other disrespectful remarks. If these Nazis made it to the Rhine crossings at all, it was on foot and without their baggage train.[32]

With the advance of US VIII Corps with its 4th Infantry and 11th Armored Divisions temporarily stalled to his south, König then ordered his troops to build up a new main line of defense from Waldorf, through the hills south of Gönnersdorf as far as the southern edge of Brohl, while at the same time to begin ferrying troops and material across the Rhine. Stragglers from the fighting in the Eifel continued to arrive, many without weapons and most all of them demoralized or apathetic. Between 8 and 10 March for example, some 300 men, including two general officers, were received in the *272nd VGD's* Brohl bridgehead. While the generals were allowed to cross, the stragglers, regardless to which division they had previously belonged, were quickly incorporated into the ranks of the division.

In the meantime, the division's chief engineer, *Major* Arne Rasmussen, had already begun collecting boats and other materials in order to ferry troops and equipment across the river several days before the division arrived in Nieder Breisig. The ferrying operation began 8 March, using a steamer that had been confiscated near Bingen and a Dutch ferryboat taken at gunpoint from its crew by *Leutnants* Mewes and Köhler from *Artillery Regiment 272*.

With these two vessels and a variety of barges, the division was able to transport most of what was left of its units and equipment across the river, despite continuous artillery fire.[33] Had the Americans not been preoccupied with strengthening their own bridgehead over the Rhine at Remagen, it is doubtful whether they would have allowed the German pocket to survive as long as it did. As it was, König and his men had a difficult time holding their defensive line while the ferry operation continued.

The indefatigable *Major* Rasmussen, who worked for nearly seventy-two hours straight without sleep, was even able to ferry the three remaining *Hetzer* tank destroyers of *Antitank Battalion 272* to the east bank of the Rhine. Platoons, companies, and battalions waited patiently until it was their turn to cross, leaving their positions only when they had been directed to do so. As the number of troops left to hold the line continued to dwindle, König was forced to adjust his rapidly shrinking perimeter constantly, all the while shuttling forces here and there to keep the Americans at bay.

Finally, nearly everyone had been ferried across. The commander of *3rd Battalion, Artillery Regiment 272, Major* Martin Jenner, was one of the last to leave the Brohl Pocket on the west bank, crossing the river on the afternoon of 12 March in a canoe with two of his men and his beloved mare, Pia, swimming behind them. *Leutnant* Josef Stefan, having survived both the Hürtgen Forest and the retreat to the Rhine, crossed the river with several of his comrades in a bullet-riddled Volkswagen *Schwimmwagen* with its many holes plugged with pieces of bread. Shortly after reaching the opposite shore, Stefan was sent to a military hospital for treatment of exhaustion.[34]

The evacuation of the main body of the division continued day and night until 11 March, when American artillery fire destroyed the last operational ferry. The only remaining vessels still afloat were several rubber assault boats of *Pioneer Battalion 272,* which continued shuttling men across until the afternoon of 12 March. The few remaining men of the rearguard left on the west bank that evening had no choice but to swim or surrender. Several officers and NCOs, adamantly refusing to give up, followed the bank of the river toward the south and crossed near Neuwied in fishing boats.[35]

While the ferry operation continued unabated from 8 to 12 March, American forces kept up their efforts to split up the German pocket. On 8 March, four tanks attacking from the south surrounded the forward observation post of *Leutnant* Milbratz of *4th Battalion, Artillery Regiment 272,* demanding his surrender. Before his capture, he telephoned his command post and notified his commander, *Hauptmann* Lieser that he was signing off, since he could do no more.

On 9 March, an American foray was launched from the west through Burg-brohl. This attack, consisting of ten to fifteen tanks and infantry, was thoroughly shelled by *3rd Battalion, Artillery Regiment 272,* enabling the remaining infantry of *Kampfgruppe 980* to withdraw to a more tenable defensive line. On 11 March, a larger American attack from the direction of Koblenz cut off *Hauptmann* Lieser and most of his *4th Battalion* before they could be evacuated. Lieser and most of his men, including their guns, were captured.[36]

Since the division's higher headquarters, Hitzfeld's *LXVII Corps,* had lost all of its signal equipment during the American thrust toward Ober-Zissen on 9 March, the task of controlling the crossing of the Corps and its remaining subordinate units was assigned to König and his staff. The *272nd VGD* was now the only one that still possessed the required communications means and was also the only division left in the corps with any significant degree of combat power. As the division and other attached units crossed the Rhine, the Brohl bridgehead was evacuated systematically until the König's headquarters was practically the last element to cross to the other side, leaving the left bank of the Rhine north of Koblenz entirely in American hands.

Leutnant Mrusek and the remnant of *Füsilier Company 272*'s combat element crossed the Rhine along with the *Oberst* Burian and the rest of *Kampfgruppe 980* during the early morning hours of 10 March. Those few who were unable to link up with the division in the Brohl Pocket and cross the Rhine at Nieder Breisig were directed by radio to keep moving south toward Koblenz. Here, they would be able to cross the river on the still-standing bridge at Engers, which the company trains of *Füsilier Company 272* had crossed a few days earlier. No rest areas awaited the *Volksgrenadiers* after crossing the river. Instead, they were directed to new defensive positions north of Rheinbrohl in and around the town of Hönningen as quickly as they were offloaded. Here, they would form a new defensive line, where they would do their utmost to prevent the Americans from sweeping south down the right bank of the Rhine.

Throughout this chaotic period in the division's history stands the figure of *Generalmajor* Eugen König. Seemingly everywhere, the commander often provided the encouragement and leadership his men needed to overcome the significant tactical disadvantages they found themselves facing. Frequently found in the front lines, König rallied the men at one critical position after another or moved a gun or *Hetzer* to where it was needed the most, often in the nick of time to stop or delay an American attack. In action continuously since he arrived in the Hürtgen Forest in November 1944, he deserves most of the credit for holding his battered division together during a hopeless situation and even managed to carry most of it to safety. How much longer the division would be able to count on his leadership to stave off disaster was an open question.

While what was left of the *272nd VGD* had been able to escape across the Rhine relatively intact, the rest of Hitzfeld's corps was not so lucky. Most of his other units, such as the *26th* and *277th Volks-Grenadier* and the *89th Infantry Divisions*, were in total disarray and lacking any claim to unit integrity. The only other unit that could claim to be a viable military organization was the *12th Volks-Grenadier Division* under *Generalmajor* Engel. Many of the other units were hopelessly intermingled and any semblance of military order had seemingly disappeared.

A further indication of the *Wehrmacht*'s increasing lack of cohesion during the retreat to the Rhine was an order issued by *Generalfeldmarschall* Model on 9 March. In an attempt to reverse the increasing incidents of straggling and desertion, Model issued the following order:

THE SUPREME COMMANDER OF THE ARMY GROUP B
                                        Headquarters, 9 March 1945
Soldiers of the Army Group!
Fighters on the Rhine River and in the Eifel!
In the tremendous battle on which the fate of Germany and of every single German depends, the German soldier is fulfilling his difficult duty courageously and faithfully. But there are a few individuals who betray their own people in these grave days of emergency by shirking their duty. They loaf around behind the front line and present themselves as stragglers.
Therefore the following will be announced to all troops with the greatest possible speed:

BASIC ORDER
In the future, stragglers or men lost from their units do not exist any more!
If anyone shall have lost contact with his unit in the course of action, he will attach himself within 24 hours to the nearest unit committed in the front line. This unit can always be easily found by the noise of battle. The soldier that fails to do so is an evil traitor to the community of the German people and will be treated as a state criminal. Excuses that he has lost his unit and is now looking for it will not be accepted any more.

For the period of transition I order:

Until the 16th of March all stragglers will report to the nearest unit in or behind front lines. These units will put them into their ranks regardless of the arm or branch to which they belong. There will be ample time for their return to the original units and this will be taken care of at a later date.

Signed,
MODEL
Generalfeldmarschall

As one American observer commented after reading this order, "To what a sorry state the vaunted *Wehrmacht* had fallen![37]

As a testimony to the problem Model was trying to address as well as the speed of the American advance, two division commanders and a corps commander had been captured during the retreat to the Rhine in a neighboring sector These generals, *Generalleutnant* Richard Schimpf of *3rd Parachute Division* and *Generalmajor* Ludwig Heilmann of *5th Parachute Division,* were both veteran commanders of divisions with illustrious combat records and their capture denied their men of the leadership when they needed it the most. The commander of *LIII Corps, General* Rothkirch, was captured a few days earlier.[38]

As a further sign of disintegration, veritable mountains of equipment, supplies, vehicles, and ammunition had been left behind. In one case, 2,000 tons of badly needed artillery and small arms ammunition had been abandoned in a huge dump in the forest southeast of Rheinbach, directly in the path of the advancing 78th Infantry Division. The trucks that the Germans had sent to recover as much of the ammunition as possible ran out of gas while en route and the 78th Reconnaissance Troop of the 78th Infantry Division captured the entire complex.[39]

That ammunition would be sorely needed for the upcoming battles on the east bank of the Rhine. Even though *Artillery Regiment 272* had managed to evacuate a battalion's worth of its guns, without a steady supply of 105mm and 150mm shells, there was little chance of holding a defensive line on the opposite bank. Now that the Americans had seized the bridge over the Rhine at Remagen, it would only be a matter of time before they began to expand their bridgehead and strike out into the heart of Germany. Without fuel for *RSO* prime movers or teams of horses to pull them, the division's cannon would sit idle or be quickly overrun.

Germany's fate would soon hinge on whether the Rhine could be held. With the Americans already across at Remagen and Montgomery's forces poised to cross further downstream, *Generalfeldmarschall* Model had little time to consolidate his scattered and disorganized armies, corps, and divisions. Many men and much of his army group's equipment had been abandoned on the west bank of the mighty river. Those units that had made it across would need several days, if not weeks, to reorganize, absorb stragglers, and repair as many of their weapons as possible.

Time was rapidly running out, however, and the Americans showed little sign of sitting still. Lieutenant General Hodges' First Army was now showing a degree of initiative that it had never displayed before when it had fought its way slowly through the Hürtgen Forest that previous autumn. One of the first and decisive clashes fought in a town on the east bank of the Rhine to stem the American advance would soon involve the *272nd VGD*. That town was named Hönningen, and in that place the division, and *Füsilier Company 272,* would soon find itself once again facing hopeless odds.

14

The Battle for Hönningen

While the *272nd VGD* struggled to maintain a tenuous bridgehead on the west bank of the Rhine long enough for its men and remaining equipment to be ferried to the opposite bank, support elements, including the trains of *Füsilier Company 272,* marched northeast from Isenburg toward Brückrachdorf after crossing the river. Under cloudy skies, the supply regiment and the trains elements from each of the grenadier regiments, as well as thousands of stragglers from dozens of units, had already crossed the Rhine to the south in the vicinity of Koblenz and had reached the safety of the hills on the river's eastern bank. Weary *Volksgrenadiers* sought to link up with their companies, even while many others thought only of surrendering at the first opportunity.

Several additional stragglers from *Füsilier Company 272* managed to catch up with the company trains on 9 March near the village of Dierdorf. The next day, *Hauptfeldwebel* Fuhrmeister and the others were directed by the division's military police platoon to move toward the town of Walrod; there they finally reestablished contact with elements of *Supply Regiment 272,* which controlled the division's remaining service and support elements and from which they drew their meager supplies. Fuhrmeister and the rest of his men remained in Walrod for two days before they were ordered to move toward Niederbreitbach, where they finally reestablished contact with *Leutnant* Mrusek and the company's combat element. There, the reunited *Füsilier Company 272* would participate in a desperate attempt to prevent the Americans from breaking out of the Remagen bridgehead.

On 10 March, the *272nd VGD,* still reorganizing while it continued to conduct its Rhine crossing, was ordered by *LXVII Corps* to establish a new main line of resistance northeast of the town of Hönningen facing the rapidly expanding American bridgehead. To the immediate north of the division's new defensive sector, other German units carried out poorly coordinated and ineffective counterattacks against the Remagen bridgehead. These attacks, launched by a succession of hastily organized emergency units, had nothing to show for their efforts during the four days that had passed since the American's bold seizure of the Ludendorff Bridge.

Oberst Burian's *Kampfgruppe 980* was again given a difficult mission, this time that of defending the area north and east of Hönningen with his two depleted battalions and *Füsilier Company 272,* in all less than three hundred men. *Kampfgruppe 980* was reinforced by the three remaining *Hetzers* of Adrario's *Antitank Battalion 272* and a battery from *Artillery Regiment 272.* The division's two other regiments were also re-designated as battle groups. *Kampfgruppe 981* was initially arrayed to Burian's right, while *Kampfgruppe 982* was positioned to his left. König established his new division command post in Rheinbrohl that same day and prepared to do what he could to stop the American advance. While the *272nd VGD* had managed to cross the Rhine with most of its remaining personnel and equipment, of those troops still under *Generalmajor* König's command, "[actual] members of the division were in the minority."[1]

To König's dismay, the division had been prevented from bringing all of its artillery across the Rhine; unbelievably, a *Führerbefehl* (a direct order from Hitler) had been issued from Berlin a few days before stating unequivocally that no heavy weapons could be evacuated across the river without Hitler's express permission. While this order forced the artillery regiment to blow up many of its precious remaining guns to prevent capture, *Oberstleutnant* Wilbrandt, the regiment's commander, had evacuated nearly an entire battalion's establishment of guns to the opposite bank several days before the order was received.

These guns were the so-called "spares" maintained by the regiment using the two extra guns culled from each of the four light artillery (105mm) batteries. The regiment's commander, with knowledge of the division staff, had ignored the orders stipulating that each battery in a *Volks-Artillery Regiment* shall consist of six guns rather than four, which is the number that each battery in the *2nd* and *3rd Battalions* had been accustomed to using. This decision, made while the division was reorganizing into a *Volks-Grenadier Division* at Döberitz the previous October, proved to be a wise one.

In addition, the commander of *3rd Battalion, Artillery Regiment 272, Major* Jenner, chose to ignore the order prohibiting evacuating of guns and surreptitiously brought most of the guns from his 7th and 8th Batteries across the river to safety on 11 March. So, unlike other divisions that followed this senseless order to the letter, *272nd VGD* was still capable of offering effective resistance against the advancing US forces as it filed into its new defensive sector with two nearly full-strength artillery battalions.[2]

The biggest threat the Germans faced along the Rhine during the second week of March was the possibility that the American forces in the Remagen bridgehead, now consisting of the 9th Armored and the 78th and 99th Infantry Divisions, would fan out in all directions, but especially toward the south along the eastern bank of the river. Field Marshal Montgomery, it was believed, would soon begin his long-awaited crossing of the Rhine to the north near Wesel, where the main assault by his 21st Army Group was expected. In the meantime, it was vital that the American bridgehead be hemmed in as long as possible, if it could not be eliminated entirely. Terrain still worked in favor of the defenders, but should the Americans break out, they would soon reach the Frankfurt-Düsseldorf autobahn that ran in a north-south direction. Should this occur, the highly mobile Americans could move rapidly in either direction and bring about the collapse of the entire Rhine front in short order.

General der Infanterie Hitzfeld, commander of *LXVI Corps,* "deeply anxious" about the threat the Americans posed to his corps' right wing, ordered *272nd VGD* and the remnants of other divisions to set up a new line immediately, comprising four division-sized defensive sectors. The corps front faced both to the north and to the west, with the northern sector being the most seriously threatened by the American forces in the Remagen bridgehead. Hitzfeld's right flank was anchored at Leubsdorf, where it tied in with *Generalleutnant* Fritz Bayerlein's hastily assembled *LIII Corps,* which had up to that point carried out most of the hasty counterattacks against the bridgehead. Hitzfeld's left flank lay at Vallendar, a town along the Rhine two kilometers northeast of Koblenz. The bulk of Hitzfeld's corps was arrayed along the eastern bank of the Rhine facing west. He located his new corps command post at Altwied, which soon came under heavy American harassing fire from the opposite bank, especially at night.[3]

Hitzfeld, at this time, had four "divisions" under his control, most of which were fragments reinforced by hundreds of stragglers from other units. His most capable division, the *272nd VGD,* with *Kampfgruppe Bremm* from *277th Volks-Grenadier Division,* held the northern portion of the corps sector facing the American bridgehead. To its left, remnants of the *26th Volks-Grenadier Division* (only a few hundred men), organized as a battle group, held a defensive sector that ran along the Rhine facing to the west, with its right flank anchored at Hönningen.

To the left of the battle group from *26th Volks-Grenadier Division* lay a hodge-podge of units holding the third divisional sector, comprised of elements from the *326th* and *167th Volks-Grenadier Divisions*, the *89th Infantry Division*, and *5th Parachute Division*, as well as other smaller elements of *272nd* and *277th Volks-Grenadier Divisions*. The fourth and least vulnerable sector was held by another conglomeration of units, consisting mainly of replacement battalions and engineer units of the *Replacement Army*.

Of these units, Hitzfeld considered the *272nd VGD* to be the only one organized enough to be considered as a division. Even so, he rated the fighting capabilities of all of the units to be poor, since they had little in the way of artillery, ammunition, and supplies of every category. A far more serious problem, as he saw it, was the shortage of manpower. There simply were not enough men to adequately man the new defensive line. Even worse, many of the troops who had made it across the river had been badly shaken and were not prepared, from a psychological point of view, to offer effective resistance.

According to Hitzfeld, "Such a Rhine crossing could not remain without a detrimental influence on the frame of mind and the fighting qualities of the troops."[4] Lack of communications equipment hampered the effective transmission of orders and reports as well, resulting in slow and haphazard operations by subordinate units.

The defense of Hönningen was initially assigned to the remnant of *26th Volks-Grenadier Division* that had managed to cross the Rhine in the vicinity of Bonn a week earlier. To its immediate front, in direct contact with the advancing 394th Infantry Regiment of the US 99th Infantry Division, the *403rd Combat Engineer Training Regiment* had set up hasty defensive positions, but was being rapidly forced back southward toward the town. The possession of Hönningen was vital, since it controlled access to the highway that ran along the east bank of the Rhine toward Neuwied, where terrain more favorable to a rapid advance opened up in the direction of Frankfurt, a key objective of the Americans. It also was selected to serve as the jumping-off point for demolitions teams that were being assembled to swim downriver and destroy the Ludendorff Bridge at Remagen.

Initially, as previously mentioned, the approaches to Hönningen and the town itself were defended by a small battle group composed of forty to fifty men from the *26th Volks-Grenadier Division*. This small battle group was reinforced by six or seven 20mm and 37mm *Flak* guns of *2nd Battery, Light Flak Battalion 764,* commanded by *Oberleutnant* Hans Fluhrer, that were positioned along the hills immediately north of the town. When the attack by the US 394th Infantry across a wide front began at 0830 hours on 11 March, the *403rd Combat Engineer Training Regiment* and other subordinated units were quickly pushed aside and the Americans were able to easily gain the heights north of the town by 13 March.[5] Though Fluhrer and five of his men were killed, the *Flak* battery remained in action under his successor, *Leutnant* Joachim Hertha.

In fact, the Americans reported only light resistance initially and it appeared that taking Hönningen would pose no serious tactical challenge at all, with the rugged terrain north and east of the town being their most serious concern. A poorly executed German counterattack carried out on the afternoon of 13 March, which failed miserably, only reinforced the American's perception.[6] Two hundred German troops of *272nd VGD* carried out another counterattack that evening against the 3rd Battalion of the 394th Infantry that was larger than the first It, too, was easily repulsed with the help of an American artillery concentration.

The first German commander in Hönningen, a *Leutnant* from the *26th Volks-Grenadier Division,* was no doubt keenly aware of the impending American attack. It appears that he came to the conclusion that holding the town was an impossible task. Evidently, he had been influenced by the mayor of the town and the chief of police that any resistance would only result in the complete destruction of the town and the death of many of its 4,500 inhabitants who had not been evacuated. The *Leutnant* consented to allowing the mayor and others to hang white bed sheets and pillowcases out of windows and doorways to announce to the Americans the following morning that Hönningen was undefended.[7]

According to the town's archives, the *Leutnant* planned to surrender his men and allow the town to be taken by the Americans without any fighting.[8] Unaware of the German plans to surrender, 1st Battalion, 394th Infantry sent a patrol into the northern end of the town on the afternoon of 14 March to feel out the German defenses. Shortly afterwards, the patrol returned and reported that there were only forty or so defenders to be seen and that "there did not seem to be evidence of serious preparation for the defense of the town." Taking Hönningen, it seemed, would be a "walkover" for the soldiers of the 99th Division.[9]

The news that American forces had reached the outskirts of Hönningen rocketed up the German chain of command and created a sense of alarm within von Zangen's *Fifteenth Army* and Field Marshal Model's *Army Group B*. To prevent the town from falling into American hands and thereby foil its use as a springboard for attempts to blow the bridge at Remagen, Hitler instructed Model to designate Hönningen on 14 March as a *Festung* (fortress). This meant that the town was to be defended to the last bullet, even after the town and its garrison become surrounded. Permission to evacuate a fortress town could be granted only by Model himself. The order also stated that if a commander surrendered the fortress, he would be tried by a Court of Honor after the war, a process that would inevitably lead to imprisonment or summary execution. Fortress commanders were furthermore required to sign an oath agreeing to carry out their duties "at all costs."[10]

Hitzfeld had no choice but to comply with the directive. Accordingly, he gave the mission of defending the fortress of Hönningen to *272nd VGD,* the only unit he had that was capable of carrying out the assignment. König thought it was a senseless order and said as much to Hitzfeld, but ordered it to be carried out anyway. Since Burian's *Kampfgruppe 980* was defending the area immediately to the northeast, König assigned him the mission. He knew that designating any locality a fortress almost always resulted not only in the loss of the town, but of all its defenders, too.

Burian received the order during the late afternoon of 14 March at his command post located in a farm near the village of Arienheller, one kilometer southeast of Hönningen. He reluctantly ordered *Hauptmann* Adolf Thomae's *2nd Battalion* (with eighty men) of *Kampfgruppe 980* and *Hauptmann* Hans Witscher's *1st Battalion* (with 110 men) into the town proper, while he left the defense of the high ground east of the town to the *2nd Battery, Light Flak Battalion 764,* which was already in position under the command of *Leutnant* Hertha.

To the east were few or no defenses, save a thin screen connecting *Kampfgruppe 980* to the neighboring *Kampfgruppen 981* and *982*. As required, Burian sent one of his staff officers, *Leutnant* Karl Bolzmann, with a document for both Thomae and Witscher to sign, acknowledging that they had received and understood the order that declared Hönningen a fortress. Witscher, being the more senior of the two, was declared *Festung* commander.[11]

Since he felt that the limited number of troops available for the defense of the fortress could be easily controlled by one battalion staff, Burian requested permission from *Generalmajor* König to be allowed to withdraw *Hauptmann* Thomae and his staff before they were trapped. Burian believed this would allow him to salvage at least one of his subordinate staffs around which he could form a new battalion, but his request was denied. König's hands were tied, and no one would be allowed to withdraw without *Army Group B*'s permission. *Oberst* Burian, as well as *Leutnant* Hermann Gehle, Burian's adjutant, both knew at that moment that Thomae's and Witscher's battalions were doomed.[12]

That evening, the surrender plans of the mayor of Hönningen and the chief of police were spoiled when Thomae and Witscher arrived with their battalions.[13] Witscher established his command post in a tunnel that ran underneath the train station on the western side of Hönningen. Thomae placed his inside the Hubertus Mineral Water bottling plant on the town's eastern side, which was primarily an industrial area. The rail line that split the town in two was used to delineate each battalion's defensive sector.[14] After including into their battle group the hapless *Leutnant* and his troops who were planning to surrender, Witscher and Thomae immediately had their men begin work to fortify the town as quickly as possible, for the American attack was expected momentarily.

Thomae's attention was initially diverted by the presence of two *Kriegsmarine* officers, *Oberleutnant* Mitbauer and *Oberleutnant zur See* Dörpinghaus, who had been rousted out of a cellar in one of the houses and brought to him for interrogation. Thomae initially thought these two men were Allied agents or saboteurs, and placed them under arrest. After two hours, he had these men sent to see *Oberst* Burian at the latter's command post. An hour later, Burian was finally able to determine their true identities after making several telephone calls. The men stated that they had been sent by *OKW* to lay the groundwork for the employment of frogmen against the Ludendorff Bridge at Remagen, who were to blow up the span and cut off American forces on the eastern bank of the Rhine. Burian reportedly stated that he wanted nothing to do with the operation and set them free. Because the necessary explosives failed to arrive from Rotterdam, the *Kriegsmarine*'s role in the demolition of the Remagen Bridge came to nothing.[15]

The *Volksgrenadiers* quickly established positions in buildings, cellars, and in the steeple of the town's church. Mines and barricades were put into position, though there was no time to properly bury and conceal the former. *Major* Jenner's *3rd Battalion, Artillery Regiment 272* was dedicated to fire in support, though his batteries lacked sufficient ammunition for the job. Moreover, the Germans had no armored vehicles of their own, save one ancient *Panzer IV* with a short-barreled 75mm gun. Several batteries of light *Flak* emplaced in and about the town were apparently all the heavy weapons support his battle group could count on.[16]

The defense of Hönningen was buttressed by the attachment of the remaining combat troops of *Füsilier Company 272*, who lent their badly needed manpower to his force. By 14 March, built up by the return of stragglers, the company's combat element now consisted of a twenty-three man platoon commanded by *Leutnant* Mrusek, assisted by *Feldwebel* Etzmannsdorfer, the former infantry howitzer platoon sergeant. The company trains, with twenty-seven men (including sick and walking wounded) was located in Niederbreitbach several kilometers to the southeast.

According to one surviving participant, this platoon was placed under the command of *Hauptmann* Thomae and positioned on the southern side of the town along the Rhine River. *Gefreiter* Wilfried Wilts, who had been assigned to the company only two weeks before, was now one of the last survivors. He and a few other *Füsiliers* occupied a house on the riverbank and prepared to put up a stiff fight. Wilts and another soldier set up their machine gun in an upper story window hoping to put it to good use.

The Americans were not long in coming. 1st Battalion, 394th Infantry Regiment of the 99th Infantry Division, commanded by Lieutenant Colonel Robert H. Douglas, initiated the expected attack the following morning, 15 March, with the aim of seizing Hönningen and continuing its drive to sweep the eastern bank of the Rhine free of Germans and to reach the Wied River before the defenders could establish a continuous line. The Americans still held the initiative in this area and intended to make the most of it before the Germans could recover.

To initiate the assault, Company B would drive along the low hills bordering the town to the north, with the mission of cutting the town off from the east. Company A, supported by Company C on the right flank, would take the town itself. To the north, the 3rd Battalion of the 394th would attack to seize the high ground held by *Kampfgruppe 981* of the *272nd VGD*. Douglas' battalion was reinforced by the addition of Company B, 786th Tank Battalion and one platoon of tank destroyers. (See Map 19). Douglas and his men did not expect much in the way of resistance and felt the town would be theirs by nightfall.

To the north and northeast, fighting raged near the villages of Laubsdorf and Rothe Kreuz. Here, *Generalmajor* König, using several battle groups gleaned from *Grenadier Regiment 981* and *982,* along with the last *Hetzer* tank destroyers from Adrario's *Antitank Battalion 272* (which he had taken back from *Oberst* Burian's *Kampfgruppe 980*), attempted to stop the 99th Infantry Division from pushing the *272nd VGD* off a series of ridges that ringed the eastern and southeastern perimeter of the Remagen Bridgehead. At Ginsterhahn, a series of determined armor-supported counterattacks by the *11th Panzer Division* crashed against the defenses of the 393rd Infantry Regiment, temporarily slowing the American's progress.

During these engagements, König's hard-pressed troops were supported by the remaining guns of *Artillery Regiment 272,* firing with good effect from positions near Frohrath, ten kilometers east of Sinzig.[17] Shortages of ammunition and radio equipment for artillery forward observers were more of a problem than the lack of artillery pieces, since much of the division's stocks had been left on the west bank of the Rhine the week before. König would simply have to do the best he could, even if this meant trading away his precious few remaining men for time. Yet the truly decisive fight would be that for Hönningen. If this town fell, the Germans would have to conduct a speedy withdrawal to the Wied, the next defensible line.

The American attack began at 0630 hours on 15 March. All three attacking companies ran into trouble immediately. As it moved along low hills north of the town, one platoon from Company B was fired upon by a 20mm *Flak* gun dug in near an intersection on the northern outskirts of the town. Firing uphill, the gun inflicted eight casualties before the Company B commander succeeded in silencing it with artillery and mortar fire, some of which fell into his own position, wounding one soldier. The attack then continued, throwing elements of Thomae's battalion off of the second hill, capturing twenty *Volksgrenadiers* and killing eight or nine in the process.

Meanwhile, in the town itself, Company A's lead platoon had run into trouble. Surprised by such a stout German defense, this platoon encountered a "hornet's nest of resistance" from snipers, infantrymen armed with machine pistols fighting from houses along the town's main street, and from several light machine guns dug in at a road intersection.[18] To make matters worse, some German defenders who had not been spotted by Company B fired downhill at the Americans from their positions on the slopes north and south of the town. In the middle of the afternoon, the attack in the town stalled when the platoon leader was killed.

Realizing that his attack was in danger of falling apart, Lieutenant Colonel Douglas committed all of Company A to the attack, ordering it to shift its axis of advance toward the east instead of the south, but this attack was also stopped by heavy German fire. To make matters worse, Company B was unable to tie its right flank in with Company C, which had been committed along the riverbank along with the bulk of the tanks. By nightfall, Company A had lost twenty men and was ordered to stop and reorganize. Company B, attacking to the north, was ordered to delay its advance until the situation in the town was sorted out.

Company C's attack that day had not gone well either. Jumping off at 1000 hours after a ten-minute artillery barrage, it encountered "stiff, unexpected resistance" when its men were lashed by fire from 20mm *Flak* guns, snipers, and machine guns.[19] It took the company the rest of the day just to reach its intermediate objective. Poor flying weather had denied the GIs the customary air support they had come to rely upon as a matter of course; the "Battle Babies" of the 99th Infantry Division had to fight for the town the old-fashioned way, man against man. In doing so, Company C suffered heavy casualties, losing forty-two men, including two officers. Thomae's and Witscher's troops fought stubbornly for every house. One American platoon was reduced to fifteen men, commanded by a sergeant.[20] *Major* Jenner's battalion fired 315 rounds in support of Hönningen's defenders that day, belying the American's claims that they encountered no German artillery fire during their assault.[21]

The Americans were forced to completely revise their plan, since it was now obvious that taking Hönningen would not be easy. Despite his initial success, however, Witscher's situation was basically unchanged. He was still required to hold out to the bitter end, when it made far more sense by this point to delay the

Americans as long as possible and then pull out. The attack of Company C severed contact between his battalion and Thomae's, and he was all but cut off by this point. He and his men, including the twenty-three *Füsiliers,* would have to fight where they were until their ammunition ran out. *Oberst* Burian, at his command post near Arienheller, could only monitor the radio and offer encouragement.

In order to continue the attack, Lieutenant Colonel Douglas contacted his regimental commander and requested that a company from the neighboring battalion be attached to his to buttress the strength of his attack force. Shortly thereafter, Company K, 394th Infantry arrived, with one platoon reporting to Douglas at 1800 hours on the evening of the 15 March. The company was quickly inserted between Company A and Company C, which adjusted their own attack zones accordingly. To beef them up, Douglas also ordered that each company be reinforced with a section of tanks and tank destroyers. Company B, once the two other companies had come on line, would renew its successful attack of the previous day and seize the hills commanding the northerly approaches to the town. The attack would resume the next morning at 0700 hours.

That morning, working from building to building, the Americans advanced inexorably. Each platoon, supported by two to three tanks or tank destroyers, attacked the houses individually, then searching them to round up prisoners or merely lobbing in hand grenades to keep snipers' heads down. In this manner, by 1000 hours half of the town had been taken and seventy-seven prisoners had been rounded up. There were many reports of civilian snipers and one female sniper was shot and killed by a soldier from the Negro platoon attached to Company K.*

By late afternoon, nearly the entire town had been taken, although not completely cleared. Only the industrial quarter to the east, where Thomae had his command post, remained in German hands. Witscher, though cut off, still held out with a small group of defenders at the train station. At this point, Douglas called for a halt to reorganize and prepare for the continuation of the assault the following morning. During the past two days, his battalion had taken 101 German prisoners and twelve civilian snipers. To the northeast and east, Company B and the adjacent 3rd Battalion had all but wiped out the *Luftwaffe* units holding the hills.

As the tank-supported American infantry swept past the town and continued their attack, they approached to within several hundred meters of Burian's command post near Arienheller, forcing him and his staff to hurriedly withdraw, leaving a small rear guard behind in the village itself. Prior to attacking, the Company

---

* According to the 99th Infantry Division, a company of African-American soldiers had been attached to the 394th Infantry to serve as reinforcements. All of these men were volunteers, some having accepted demotions in rank for the chance to fight as equals alongside their Caucasian countrymen. By all accounts, they performed admirably in combat and quickly earned the respect of the "Battle Babies" of the 99th Division. The report of the female sniper is found in Walter Lauer's *Battle Babies: The Story of the 99th Infantry Division in World War II (Nashville: Battery Press),* 210.

B commander called for a heavy artillery concentration upon Arienheller to enable his troops to get close to its outskirts before being fired upon by the defenders. Even so, four of his men were wounded by machine-gun fire from a house and only the point-blank fire of high-explosive rounds by tank destroyers into the windows finally forced *Kampfgruppe 980*'s rear guard to surrender. Company B continued on to its last objective, a hill that overlooked the road leading into Hönningen, and captured one officer and eight soldiers. Witscher and Thomae were now completely isolated. Shortage of artillery ammunition meant that Jenner's battalion was only able to fire 170 rounds that day, not nearly enough to hold back the American assault. With Hönningen lost, *3rd Battalion, Artillery Regiment 272* withdrew across the Wied in order to set up new firing positions for the next round of fighting.[22]

Unlike the experience of some units that fought under Thomae and Witscher in Hönningen, *Füsilier Company 272*'s role appears to have been anticlimactic. Until 17 March, their defense sector along the riverbank had been relatively quiet. During the late morning hours, however, an M4 Sherman was seen approaching their position from the west. A *Leutnant* (perhaps Mrusek) fired a *Panzerfaust* at the tank from a staircase window, but missed. Seeing this unfold before their eyes, Wilts and the others quickly ran down the stairs into the cellar while the tank above shot the building to bits. Wilts later wrote, "I have never gone down a set of stairs so fast in my life."

The American's advance continued the next morning, but it was almost over. The industrial area was cleared by 1400 hours after "desultory" fire and little determined resistance. Thomae himself was wounded and captured at approximately 1700 hours when his command post was overrun. While attempting to surrender, he was shot in the leg and arm by an American with a submachine gun before he was captured

Before his radio communications were abruptly cut off, Thomae's last message was "We are surrounded by twenty-one tanks and American infantry. We are out of ammunition and have fought to the last man. I have carried out my orders. Long live Germany!"[23] The same fate befell the fortress commander, *Hauptmann* Witscher, who had been forced to surrender two hours previously.

Thomae's wounds were hastily dressed and he was taken out to a waiting jeep on a door that had been removed to serve as a stretcher. Taken to an American field hospital in Linz, he was given a transfusion and a shot of penicillin, a drug not yet available to German medical personnel. While being treated, his awards and personal papers were stolen, prompting him to complain to a high ranking American officer. All of his awards and personal effects were immediately returned, except for his German Cross in Gold, which his captors thought was a Nazi Party badge.[24]

In the early afternoon of 17 March, before Thomae was captured, the assistant operations officer of *272nd VGD, Oberleutnant* von der Malsberg, arrived at Burian's new regimental command post with orders from *Generalmajor* König that *Kampfgruppe 980* was to launch an immediate counterattack to relieve the two surrounded battalions. Burian, who had only his headquarters personnel and a few men from *13th* and *14th Companies* at his disposal, reluctantly agreed. With less than one hundred men, he knew there were little if any chance of breaking through to Hönningen and even less of continuing to hold it. Nevertheless, Burian radioed Thomae and Witscher "Hang on, we're coming to get you out" and began his counterattack.[25]

His tiny force, backed by small arms and mortar fire, had progressed only two kilometers when it encountered the defensive positions of 1st Battalion, 394th Infantry on the town's southeastern outskirts. The German assault, consisting of sixty to seventy men (according to the American after-action report), made no further progress at all and was forced to turn back to prevent being overrun. One of Burian's officers was captured and a quick search revealed that he was carrying a map that detailed the new line of resistance being constructed in front of the Wied River. This information would be used against the Germans shortly.[26]

The Battle for Hönningen was over. It had not been a completely bloodless affair for the Americans, who lost ninety men killed and wounded during the three days of fighting. The Germans claimed to have knocked out nine tanks with heavy *Flak* mines, and antitank weapons. A total of 63 Germans died in the fighting and were buried in a mass grave at the foot of the Arenfels castle.[27] The battle also saw the ever-shrinking combat element of *Füsilier Company 272* again whittled down; nineteen men were lost by the time the town finally fell into American hands Another soldier, *Obergefreiter* Richard Geyer, was wounded by artillery fire 13 March while serving with the company trains. Of the combat troops, three were wounded and evacuated to the division main dressing station, while sixteen others were declared missing when the German defenses caved in under the pressure of the American tank-led assault.

Included in this number was one of the last old-timers in the company, *Feldwebel* Etzmannsdorfer, who was declared missing in action. Another veteran, *Gefreiter* Erwin Buchwalder, the former *Luftwaffe* mechanic and light infantry howitzer gunner, was taken captive that day along with his best friend, Walter van der Geest. In order to escape the deadly artillery fire, Buchwalder, von der Geest, and a few others opted for the safety of a cellar in one of the houses inside the town. As American tanks rumbled on the street above shooting through windows, the *Füsiliers* awaited the opportunity to make their escape, but it never came. An American patrol found them in their hiding place, rousted them outside, and marched Buchwalder and the others off into captivity. He and the others were soon shipped to a POW camp at Sillery near Reims, where they sat out the rest of the war.

Wiltfried Wilts and several others were captured later that same day. Flushed out of their cellar by a tank, just as Buchwalder had been, Wilts and his companions were quickly searched and placed into a wine cellar under guard, where they spent the night. The next morning, they were transferred to Namur in Belgium, then on to Attichy in France the following day. Then Wilts, like Buchwalder, was shipped on to the POW camp in Sillery, where he was released from captivity in October 1946.[28]

As Burian's shattered *Kampfgruppe 980* fell back, four survivors from *Füsilier Company 272* were somehow able break through American lines and make their way back to the company trains in Niederbreitbach—*Leutnant* Mruzek, *Unteroffizier* Karl Nagel, *Gefreiter* Konrad Brill, and *Füsilier* Willi Walz. In the meantime, five other men, *Unteroffizier* Fritz Fosselmann; *Füsiliers* Heinz Klenke and Wolfgang Klünner; and *Gefreiters* Paul Schönherr and Josef Fereberger had also made their way back to the company trains where they had been fighting with other ad hoc units. Now there were only twenty-nine men left, hardly a company at all except in name. Broken, the remnant of the company moved to its new location in Hanroth during the evening of 17 March to await further orders, while unbeknownst to them, a large draft of reinforcements was already being incorporated into the company in one last-ditch attempt at reconstitution. The American forces would also take advantage of the lull in the fighting to prepare for their final assault on the German Rhine defensive line.

15

Last Stand on the Wied Defense Line

The defeat at Hönningen should have marked the end of *Füsilier Company 272* for all intents and purposes. Had it been an American or British unit, it probably would have been stricken from the rolls or, at the very least, completely reconstituted far to the rear, where it would then have undergone months of reorganization, reequipping, and training. Despite the seemingly hopeless situation, however, the headquarters of the *272nd VGD* decided to keep the company in the field. Incredibly, the German personnel replacement system was still functioning, despite the ongoing turmoil Eleven new personnel from *Grenadier Replacement Battalion 398,* for example, had been assigned to the company, even as it was being sent to Hönningen, where they were promptly listed as missing in action with the others.

After the loss of the key position at Hönningen on 17 March, the defensive positions of the *26th, 272nd,* and *326th Volks-Grenadier Divisions* along the Rhine had become untenable. Fighting as they withdrew, the remnants of these divisions moved some ten kilometers east and southeastward toward a new German defensive position drawn up along the eastern bank of the Wied, a small river that flowed from north to south toward Neuwied, where its waters mingled with the Rhine. The *272nd VGD* was assigned an eight-kilometer-wide defensive sector that ran from Rossbach in the north to Niederbreitbach in the south. The neighboring *26th Volks-Grenadier Division* to its left, now somewhat reorganized, held the Wied defensive sector south of Niederbreitbach that ended on the Rhine in the vicinity of Neuwied.

On 18 March *Generalmajor* König temporarily established his new division command post in Niederbreitbach, a town that had been recently evacuated by the company trains of *Füsilier Company 272.* A battalion-sized rear guard (which included the reconstituted *Füsilier Company 272*) was left on the west of the bank of the Wied River along the heights running from Solscheid to Hönningen to delay temporarily the American advance until the new defense line could be established.[1]

König shared his new command post, located in a village inn, with his staff and the family of Johann Hermann, the inn's owner. No evacuation orders for the civilian population had been issued, so Hermann and his family were to experience several artillery barrages directed against their house, precipitated by Allied radio direction finding that had detected radio signals emanating from König's

289

headquarters.[2] Since the Americans had pinpointed his command post's location and would soon be subjecting it to even heavier barrages, he was forced to move to Kurtscheid, where he and his headquarters would remain undetected, at least for several days.

According to the division history, the *272nd Volks-Grenadier Division* "no longer consisted of any organized units. Small battle groups, which had organized themselves under proven, inspired leaders, were the soul of resistance."[3] These few cohesive battle groups were aided considerably by the few remaining guns of the artillery regiment, whose employment in the antitank role forced the pursuing Americans to advance cautiously, allowing the bulk of the division sufficient time to slip behind the relative security of the Wied.

Here, due to what was thought to be American hesitation, the division was able to take advantage of five days of relative quiet to catch its breath and set up its new defensive line oriented along the high ground overlooking the river. Actually, American attention was diverted elsewhere within the Remagen bridgehead, while the 99th Infantry Division, located on the western side of the Wied, was only directed to secure favorable jump-off positions for a subsequent attack.[4] Several dozen kilometers to the north, however, the situation had grown dire.

Here, north and east of Remagen, several counterattacks mounted by the *Panzer Lehr* and *11th Panzer Divisions,* as well as the *106th Panzer Brigade* and *340th Volks-Grenadier Division* of *Generalleutnant* Beyerlein's *LIII Corps,* had been shattered with little to show for their efforts. Collins' VII and Van Fleet's III Corps of Hodges' US First Army had been able not only to thwart Bayerlein's desperate efforts to eliminate the American bridgehead, but had been able to expand steadily the Remagen bridgehead toward the Sieg River.[5] Should the Americans be able to cross the Sieg in the vicinity of the town of Siegburg, the road to the Ruhr, Germany's industrial heartland, would be wide open. With no natural obstacles or noteworthy German forces available to block a determined advance to the Ruhr, the Allies had been handed a great opportunity to bring the war in the West to an end once and for all.

Not only was *General der Infanterie* von Zangen concerned about the northern sector of his army's defensive line, he had to worry about his center and southern flank as well. In the south, after clearing Hönningen, Van Fleet's III Corps shifted to the center of First Army's front, after handing off the far right portion of its sector to Major General Huebner's incoming V Corps. Van Fleet and his men were busily engaged in preparing to continue offensive operations against part of both *General der Infanterie* Hitzfeld's *LXVII* and *General der Infanterie* Püchler's *LXXIV Corps.*

Both German corps were hurriedly establishing defensive positions in anticipation of the continuation of the American offensive. Though *LXVII* and *LXXIV Corps* both occupied terrain that was highly conducive to the defense, they lacked enough men to establish coherent main lines of resistance and were forced to resort to manning a series of strong points, rather than a solid line.

Had he chosen to do so, Hodges could have advanced at will, but he was directed to delay his seven-division attack until Field Marshal Montgomery's 21st Army Group began his own crossing of the Rhine further to the north near Wesel, scheduled to occur on 23 March. Instead of racing to the northeast as the Germans anticipated, Hodges was to initiate his attack on 23 March toward the southeast in the direction of the Lahn River, in an effort that was to completely unhinge the German defensive scheme.[6] Rather than focus on seizing only the Ruhr industrial district, Bradley had instead decided to trap the entire German Army holding the northern Rhine Front, along with the Ruhr.

So alarming had been the advance of Collins' VII Corps toward the Sieg that the German high command, including both *Fifteenth Army* and *Army Group B,* became absolutely convinced that the American breakout, when it came, would occur in a north or northeasterly direction.[7] What few reserves von Zangen still had, therefore, were concentrated in this area to stop or slow the Americans. As a consequence of Model's and von Zangen's miscalculation, Hitzfeld's *LXVII Corps,* on the southern perimeter of the front, was practically denuded of corps-level armor and artillery reinforcement, making it particularly vulnerable to what was to come. Not even the Allies would know how weak Hitzfeld's corps actually was until they began their attack on 23 March.[8]

Even had *Fifteenth Army* been ready for the impending attack, by 22 March, von Zangen's army could field only fifty tanks against the northern flank of the Remagen bridgehead. By this point, the *272nd VGD* had but three *Hetzer* tank destroyers left, and only one of these was in operational condition. While the *Heavy Tank Battalion 506* (equipped with Panzer VIb "King Tiger" tanks) was attached to Hitzfeld's corps, by 22 March it had lost all of its vehicles and due to lack of fuel and mechanical breakdown, and the battalion's personnel had been placed under Hitzfeld's administrative control while they awaited delivery of a new complement of tanks.[9] In every aspect, then, the *272nd VGD* would find itself fighting at a severe disadvantage and in retrospect it is clear that neither it nor its higher headquarters had any reasonable chance at any time to thwart the Allies' plans.

While the last of the old *Füsilier Company 272*'s fighting troops were being killed or captured in Hönningen, the company itself came in for a good share of attention by the division's leadership. Virtually wiped out during the last two weeks' of fighting, the division headquarters took steps to restore some semblance of fighting capability to this shattered unit. Since the company trains was still intact under its old leadership and possessed nearly a full complement of support personnel, the decision was made to assign to it a large draft of replacements. After a few days of training and organizing, the division personnel officer must have been thought, the company would soon be back in fighting trim and would be able to serve once again as the division's *Feuerwehr.*

Shortly after the company trains arrived in Hanroth, where it had set up shop in a small camp in the forest, *Hauptfeldwebel* Fuhrmeister was told on 15 March that the company would soon be receiving new replacements that day or early the next. Imagine his surprise when eighty-two men assigned from *March Company XI/272/4* showed up literally on his doorstep on the night of 15/16 March while the battle for Hönningen was still underway. This unit had been forming since the end of February at Kaiser Bleeck Barracks in Goslar, home of *Grenadier Training and Replacement Battalion 398,* long affiliated with the division.

Like most draft replacement companies at this stage of the war, it consisted chiefly of recovered convalescing wounded men from a wide variety of units, including several returning veterans of the company, such as *Gefreiter* Johann Heitzer, who had been wounded three months before. Now, since their wounds had healed, the men had been perfunctorily pronounced fit for combat duty and returned to their parent units in order to be fed back into the field replacement system. The company also included twenty-one new recruits from the 1926 and 1927 year groups, including the youngest soldier in the company, seventeen-year-old *Grenadier* Günter Küster, born 12 July 1927 in Duisburg. None of these young men had seen any combat at all.

Surprisingly enough, there were few, if any, former *Luftwaffe* or *Kriegsmarine* personnel in this *March Company,* making it somewhat of an anomaly at this stage of the war. Other elements of the *272nd VGD* also received an infusion of motley replacements, though these were not sufficient to bring the companies and battalions back even to fifty percent strength. Worse still was the near-total lack of replacement heavy weapons. Had the artillery regiment not taken steps to ferry their guns across the Rhine in direct contravention of orders, the division would have had no heavy weapons at all, except for the few *Hetzer* tank destroyers that had been brought over.

In addition to returning convalescents, *March Company XI/272/4* also included six soldiers who had been assigned to the front line for "rehabilitative purposes." Some of them had been caught engaged in profiteering or outright theft. A year earlier, these men would have been assigned to a penal unit, but by March 1945 the manpower situation was so dire that normal disciplinary procedures were held in abeyance. So instead of being punished, these miscreants were shipped out to the front where it was hoped that they would be motivated to perform creditably enough to regain their honor and full military standing. Events would soon prove whether this was a rosy assumption or merely a cynical way to justify feeding the virtual meat grinder that was consuming men faster than they could be replaced.

By this stage of the war, any distinction between a *Volks-Grenadier Division,* a standard infantry division, or the new *Infantry Division 45* was meaningless. Lack of men, material, and time to organize or reconstitute new or proven formations meant that virtually every unit in the German Army had begun to look the same—that is, all looked like *Alarm* units that were devoid of structure, supporting weapons, leadership, and most of all, the vital cohesion needed to bond these formations together in combat. Even old, established, and proven divisions such as the *272nd VGD* or the supposedly more elite panzer divisions were a shadow of their former selves and not capable of standing up very long against their Allied counterparts. *Füsilier Company 272* was thus a microcosm of what the rest of the German Army looked like in mid-March 1945.

Regarding leadership, the reconstituted company looked promising, at least on paper. *Oberleutnant* Walter Ableiter, the *March Company*'s commander, immediately was appointed as the new commander of *Füsilier Company 272,* taking over from *Leutnant* Mrusek, the acting commander. Ableiter was to be the company's seventh and last. A veteran of the old *216th Infantry Division,* he had served on the Eastern Front with *2nd Company, Grenadier Regiment 396.* Born 22 January 1922 in Ludwigsburg, Ableiter left the university and enlisted in the Army on 20 June 1940 with *Infantry Replacement Battalion 59,* then located in Olmütz in the "Reichs Protectorate of Bohemia-Moravia," the Third Reich's term for the Czechoslovak Republic, which had been dismembered at the Munich Conference in 1938.

Ableiter's first field assignment was that of an infantryman serving with *5th Company, Infantry Regiment 460* of the *260th Infantry Division,* which was assigned occupation duties in France until it was shipped to the Eastern Front in July 1941. Ableiter, however, did not accompany it, as he had instead been posted to the Infantry School in Döberitz the previous May as an officer candidate, where he was commissioned as a *Leutnant* 8 August 1941.

Shortly thereafter, he was posted to the Eastern Front, where officer casualties had been extremely high as a result of the heavy fighting during the fall of 1941. His first assignment as an officer was as a platoon leader in *3rd Company, Infantry Regiment 413* of the *206th Infantry Division,* a unit consisting chiefly of East Prussians from the Insterburg area. Here, his division was committed to the defense of the key town of Rzhev, located on the Volga River north of Moscow, and suffered terribly from both the Soviet Winter counteroffensive and the brutal weather. The survivors, including Ableiter, were awarded the infamous Russian Front Medal, struck to commemorate those that made it though one of the worst winter campaigns in living memory

The *206th Infantry Division* defended its positions at Rzhev for the next year, finally withdrawing with the rest of the German forces when the Rzhev salient was evacuated in March 1943. During the time with his regiment, Ableiter distinguished himself for bravery and leadership. For his actions during one particular engagement at Rzhev, while serving as the acting company commander, he was awarded both the Iron Cross 1st and 2nd classes on 5 March 1942 by the division commander.

Such conspicuous gallantry had its price, however. Wounded twice in one month, he was sent back to Germany after his second wound on 13 March 1942. His wound was serious enough to require a month's convalescence, but he was finally discharged from the reserve hospital in Bunzlau on 4 April 1942. After enjoying two more weeks of convalescent leave at home, he was back at the front

by the end of April. On 15 June, he was sent back to Germany to attend an officer's course with *Infantry Replacement Battalion 151* to prepare him for company command.

Upon completion of this course, instead of being transferred back to his old
regiment that autumn, Ableiter was assigned to *Infantry Regiment 396* of the
216th Infantry Division, where he immediately assumed command of *2nd Company,* which was holding defensive positions in the same Rzhev salient where he
had fought with his old regiment nearly a year before. Here, Walter Ableiter made
his first acquaintance with the Hanoverians of the *216th Infantry Division.* As a
Swabian, known for their joviality, he must have stood out in stark contrast to the
more taciturn north Germans. Promoted to *Oberleutnant* on 1 January 1943,
Ableiter gained further experience while successfully leading his troops and had
somehow managed to survive.

For fourteen continuous months, he was to lead his unit in nearly every
engagement, ranging from the withdrawal of the Rzhev salient to the Battle of
Kursk to the withdrawal to the Dnepr River, where he was again seriously
wounded on 14 October 1943 by a gunshot wound to the chest. His bravery and
leadership prior to his injury had been so noteworthy in a division where such
conduct was commonplace, that it drew the attention of the division commander,
Generalleutnant Friedrich August Schack, who submitted his name for the award
of the German Cross in Gold while Ableiter was still in the hospital, though he
was not presented the actual award until 10 January 1944 after he had returned to
his unit. The award certificate, signed in person by *Generalfeldmarschall* Keitel,
is still in the possession of Ableiter's family.

Discharged from the hospital on 10 December 1943, he was soon in back in
action in the East with his company again, which in his absence had been
assigned to *Divisional Group 216.* This was a cover name assigned to the remnant of the *216th Infantry Division,* which had been disbanded and its remnant
shipped to France to form the newly-reactivated *272nd Infantry Division.*
Ableiter fought with *Divisional Group 216* for four more months until he was
finally medically evacuated on 10 April 1944 for vision problems caused by a
concussion he suffered from an exploding shell. After being discharged on 6 July
1944, he was assigned to his replacement unit, *Grenadier Replacement Battalion
396* in Northeim, passing the time attending various officers' instructional courses while recovering from the lingering effects of his wound.

Deemed to be fit for only limited combat duty due to his many and varied
wounds, Ableiter was transferred on 14 January 1945 to *Grenadier Replacement
and Training Battalion 398* in Goslar, where he was assigned as the battalion's
training and operations officer. When the *272nd VGD's* last reinforcement levy
from Goslar was being formed into *March Company XI/272/4,* he was chosen as
its acting commander on 28 February. The school would be closed down soon
anyway and officers with his skill and experience were urgently needed at the
front, which now lay only two hundred kilometers to the west. The fact that he

was still suffering from the lingering effects of his wounds does not appear to have disqualified him from combat, nor does it seem to have disqualified many of his men, either.

Ableiter brought with him several experienced non-commissioned officers, including *Oberfeldwebel* Gerhard Hoke, *Stabsfeldwebel* Wilhelm Berlin, and *Feldwebeln* Werner Matthies, Karl Köster, and Gustav Duckstein. All, except Berlin, had just completed lengthy periods of convalescence, having been wounded in action during the past several months. Berlin, on the other hand, had been assigned to the front for rehabilitative purposes, having been convicted of a petty offense by a divisional courts marshal of the *Replacement Army*. While serving at the front, he would redeem his honor and, if he survived, all charges were to be expunged from his record. It takes little imagination to picture Berlin's professional enthusiasm when he arrived at the crumbling Rhine front in mid-March 1945.

During the second week of March 1945 while the battle of the Remagen bridgehead was raging, Ableiter led his one hundred man-strong replacement company of convalescents, raw recruits, and jailbirds across northwestern Germany. They traveled mostly by foot, since the railways had been virtually knocked out of operation by incessant Allied air attacks. After arriving in the *272nd VGD*'s area of operations, Ableiter and the others were assigned to *Field Replacement Battalion 272,* where eighteen of his men were distributed to other units in the division. He and the rest were assigned to *Füsilier Company 272* on 15 March, while the remnant of the old company was still fighting in Hönningen.

With the loss in Hönningen and most of the old company, *Füsilier Company 272* at that time consisted of the company trains and little else. The arrival of Ableiter and his group was timely indeed, for with the infusion of eighty-two men, the company's combat strength increased to ninety-one, not counting the trains By 18 March, the only members of the "old" company still present for duty with the combat element was *Feldwebel* Klose; *Unteroffizier* Fosselmann; *Obergefreiters* Fereberger, Hein, Geschwandtner, and Hauser; *Gefreiter* Langer; and *Füsiliers* Wertenbach and Klünner.

Though they had brought no heavy weapons with them, the replacements at least carried their own weapons, a departure from the usual procedure. The group also included six newly-trained snipers, who brought with them their G-43 sniper rifles, equipped with scopes. What Ableiter thought or knew about the generally hopeless military situation is unknown, although he probably hoped to get a few days to know his men and to prepare his company for battle. The newly reconstituted *Füsilier Company 272,* however, was to be committed almost immediately.

Few records remain from this period of the division's history to adequately document what occurred along the Wied defense line, because the events there happened too quickly for most survivors to remember clearly. In the general chaos and confusion of an already hopeless situation, hardly anyone believed that the line could be held for very long. It is known that *Oberst* Burian's *Kampf-gruppe 980,* augmented with a few stragglers to a combat strength of about 150 men, was assigned a defensive sector that would have required two full-strength regiments to hold. This sector, which protected the division's left flank, ran along the Wied in the vicinity of the town of Waldbreitbach. Burian made his new head-quarters in the Wolfenacker Mühle three kilometers south of the town.[10]

The other two regimental battle groups, *981* and *982,* were arrayed to Burian's right along the Wied. Positioned on Burian's left was a motley battle group con-sisting of remnants of several divisions. At this time, both *Oberstleutnant* Rösener and *Oberst* Kleinkorres were still in command of their grenadier regi-ments, though neither one would have recognized many of the men, since nearly all of the veterans of the Hürtgen Forest fighting were gone. Like Burian's regi-ment, theirs were also fleshed out with stragglers who had been rounded up at collecting points and assembled into ad hoc battle groups with few, if any, heavy weapons. There were many instances reported where retreating *Luftwaffe* airmen, army administrative personnel, and even elderly men of the *Volkssturm* were pressed into service in these units.

By this time, the division probably had only 200 to 300 infantrymen, exclud-ing the newly-assigned men of *Füsilier Company 272.* It also still possessed sev-eral anti-tank guns, one or two antiaircraft guns, three tank destroyers, and eight to ten artillery pieces, all that was available to withstand an assault by the nearly full-strength 99th Infantry Division supported by tanks and air power.[11] The only way that König and the shattered remnant of his division could delay the American advance in this sector (there was no longer any belief that they could be effectively stopped) would be by conducting a series of ambushes, well-exe-cuted local counterattacks, and clever use of terrain. There was no other recourse. The troops that would be needed to hold the ground simply were not available, nor was there sufficient communications equipment to carry out effective com-mand and control—that, too, had been left on the west bank of the Rhine Even the division commander began to openly express his views on the hopelessness of the situation. On the night of 18 March, *Generalmajor* König was overheard to say via telephone to the *LXVII Corps* staff that "It is insanity to keep fighting on now. We do not have anything left to even defend ourselves with. It is time to end it, you idiots!"[12]

Hitzfeld's corps, though large on paper, was little more that a collection of weak battle groups. All told, nine different divisions were under his command. For command and control purposes, he regrouped them under three divisional headquarters. As before, the only division worthy of the name was the *272nd VGD* that, at least in theory, still fielded its three infantry regiments. The Corps also controlled *Kampfgruppe Hudel* of the *Panzer Lehr Division* (with no tanks) and a battle group of the *5th Parachute Division.* Both of these were arrayed to the right of the *272nd VGD* between Obersteinbach in the north, where Hitzfeld's corps shared a boundary with Püchler's neighboring *LXXIV Corps,* to

Hümmerich in the south, where the battle group from the *5th Parachute Division* shared a boundary with the right-most regiment of the *272nd VGD*.

To König's left lay the *26th Volks-Grenadier Division*, under the command of *Generalmajor* Hans Kokott, with his headquarters in Jahrsfeld. On the far left flank or southeast corner of Hitzfeld's corps with its front facing the Rhine River lay Kaschner's worn-out *326th Volks-Grenadier Division*, with his headquarters in Monrepos. These two division headquarters controlled a collection of battle groups from the *18th, 26th, 277th,* and *326th Volks-Grenadier Divisions*, the *89th Infantry Division*, and another battle group from the *5th Parachute Division*.[13]

While Hitzfeld, König, and the other two division commanders thought they could at least delay the Americans along the Wied, the commander of *Fifteenth Army*, General von Zangen, was not so sanguine. Noting that *LXVII Corps* had the "least [amount of] steadfastness in its forces," he felt that the defensive line along the Wied "will be . . . penetrated within a short time, especially inasmuch as the Corps has still not brought the enemy to a halt in the forested terrain on its left wing."[14] To make matters worse for von Zangen's Army, only one day's supply of artillery ammunition was available at the firing positions, far too little to fight an effective defensive battle.[15]

Von Zangen, for his part, was proposing a withdrawal further to the east along the line Honnef-Krautscheid, but was turned down by Model at *Army Group B*. The part of that proposal that would have helped the *272nd VGD* the most was the suggested move to a new defensive line that lay to the east of the autobahn. Had this suggestion been approved, the division would have been spared the worst of what was to come. As it was, von Zangen rated the division as no longer being capable of fighting effectively, days before the American attack had even begun.[16] Though the post-war division history takes issue with their former army commander, emphasizing that the men fought well and tenaciously considering the situation, von Zangen's assessment was proven to be correct.

The overall condition of the German forces along the Remagen Bridgehead on 21 March 1945, two days prior to the American attack, could best be summed up by *Generalmajor* Carl Wegener, Chief of Staff of *Army Group B*, who wrote after the war:

The German Army in the West stood in a fairly continuous front along the Rhine. But what a front! Divisions were no more than weak battle groups, composed, in part, of untrained replacements and *Volkssturm*. Every unit was inadequately equipped, not only with artillery, but even with light infantry weapons. Mobility was limited. The supply situation was very grave, aggravated by the loss of numerous dumps and depots west of the Rhine. The state of troop morale varied from suspicion to callous resignation. It had an officer corps that lacked confidence and wondered just what were the demands of duty. Even were this shadow of an army still willing to battle decisively, it could only pretend to resist. It would be an almost

helpless victim to any attacker, even one considerably weaker than the powerful enemy ready to thrust across the Rhine and into the heart of Germany
in a final race with its ally approaching from the east.[17]

Immediately after Hönningen fell, the *272nd VGD* found itself being pressured
even as it withdrew across the Wied. Determined to give the Germans no rest,
Lieutenant General Walter E. Lauer, the commander of the 99th Infantry
Division, ordered his regiments to stay close on the heels of their retreating foe
and use the enemy's confusion to score tactical advantages that would come in
handy later. Though the main body of König's division was able to make its way
to safety, the division's rearguard suffered heavily against the aggressively pursuing Americans while carrying out its mission.

From 17 to 20 March, Lauer's 393rd and 394th Infantry Regiments pushed
through and seized the villages of Hesseln, Frorath, Hausen, Langscheid, and
Solschied. Indeed, the greatest impediment to the American's advance was the
difficult terrain, which for the most part, consisted of heavily wooded hilltops and
draws, steep defiles, and streams. The resistance of the German rearguard was
sporadic and poorly organized, though isolated detachments occasionally fought
ferociously to defend key hilltop positions or road junctions.

The attached battle group of 223 men from the *326th VGD* defending Hausen
surrendered to the 3rd Battalion of Colonel Woolnough's 393rd Infantry Regiment after only token resistance.[18] Though most of these men were stragglers
who had been hastily incorporated into this battle group to defend the town, it
was still a significant loss, placing the Americans on the Wied for the first time.

Another reason for the American's success was the often-overlooked fact that
they had simply become extremely proficient at waging war. Gone were the days
of Kasserine Pass, when the *Amis* could be dealt with easily. Since then, the average American infantry or armored division had become a deadly and efficient
fighting organization, aided by control of the air and a superbly functioning logistical system. Man for man, the GI, long derided by the Germans as being poorly
suited for combat, had surpassed his German counterpart by this stage of the war.
Younger, fitter, better trained, better fed, and secure in the knowledge that the war
was almost won, the American soldier now almost always bested his German
opponent, even when the odds were even.

German defensive preparations were dealt another setback when *Major* von
Koehler, commander of the *403rd Combat Engineer Training Regiment,* was captured by troops of the 99th Infantry Division on 20 March. On his person were
found complete maps detailing all of *LXVII Corps'* unit locations; division and
regimental boundaries; as well as locations of artillery and antitank defenses.
This information was quickly disseminated throughout the V Corps, and the 99th
Infantry Division was to use this knowledge to great effect in its assault along the
Wied against the *272nd VGD.*[19] There is no evidence that the Germans even knew
that their plan was compromised, since no effective countermeasures appear to
have been taken.

Oberleutnant Ableiter, who had hoped to have time to prepare his new company for battle, instead found himself and his men thrown almost immediately into the fray. With the bulk of the division withdrawing hastily to the eastern bank of the Wied, Ableiter was assigned the mission of holding the village of Solscheid, approximately one kilometer southwest of Niederbreitbach. Solscheid, a small village of less than 200 inhabitants, occupied a hilltop at the southeastern end of a two-kilometer long ridgeline that provided a dominating position overlooking the Wied and Niederbreitbach. It had to be held as long as possible to allow as many men of the *272nd VGD* as possible to get safely across the river. Now assigned a critical mission only a couple of days after taking over his new command, early on 17 March, Ableiter marched his company from Hanroth to Solscheid, a distance of over fifteen kilometers.

On that day, Solscheid was in the sights of the 1st Battalion of the 393rd Infantry Regiment, which had orders to seize the high ground overlooking the river by the end of the day. Before Ableiter and his company had time to prepare their defensive positions, at 1345 hours the Americans commenced their attack against the village and neighboring Langscheid. Despite "light" German artillery and small arms fire, both towns were taken by 1740 hours.[20] After putting up heavy initial resistance, the defenders withdrew eastward down the hill, where they were then forced to wade across the Wied in order to escape.

Ableiter's first engagement as the new commander of *Füsilier Company 272* had not gone well. Not only had he been unable to hold the town for more than a few hours, he had also lost twenty-four men out of the eighty-two he had led into the village that morning. Of these, one was killed in action (*Unteroffizier* Kotrba), three were wounded, and the rest declared missing in action, including *Feldwebel* Matthies, one of Ableiter's few remaining senior non-commissioned officers. It was an inauspicious beginning.

Over the next several days, the 99th Infantry Division and the 2nd Infantry Division on its right fought their way to the Wied, eliminating remaining German forces west of the river in the process. Neuwied, which was supposed to have anchored the German left flank along the Rhine, fell to the Americans on 22 March, when its garrison of 150 to 200 men of the *26th VGD* were surrounded by a tank-supported regiment of the 2nd Infantry Division and quickly annihilated. Only four men succeeded in breaking out and returning to their division.[21] In preparation for the coming attack, the 9th Armored Division was inserted to the right of the 2nd Infantry Division, with its right flank resting on the Rhine itself, and the 99th Infantry Division shifted its boundary to the north. (For overall Allied and German dispositions, refer to Map 20.)

Füsilier Company 272 was directed to occupy new defensive positions on the western outskirts of the town of Ehlscheid, which commanded the high ground overlooking the crossing sites along the Wied. This sector was held by a battle group of the *277th Volks-Grenadier Division,* commanded by *Oberstleutnant* Josef Bremm, which was attached at the time to the *26th Volks-Grenadier Division*. Here, Ableiter was assigned a wide sector, forcing him to place most of his company in widely separated strong points. They worked from 18 to 22 March in preparation for the next American attack, which could be expected in a matter of days, if not hours.

It was during this same period before the front collapsed when a peculiar incident took place that illustrates that even in the midst of a terrible war, enemies could show simple humanity toward one another. Knowing that the American offensive was imminent, the commander of the *272nd VGD* sent a parliamentary across the river on the night of 21 March to negotiate a cease fire to enable the evacuation of a considerable number of refugees, mainly women, children, and elderly citizens, from a church-operated hospital and an asylum in the town of Waldbreitbach, where they had taken shelter after being driven from their homes on the western side of the Wied. These two facilities, the Mariawald Abbey and the Antoniushaus, lay directly in the path of the American assault.[22]

König sent *Hauptmann* Massberg, his own division intelligence (*Ic*) officer and a fluent English speaker, to negotiate a twelve-hour truce in order to conduct an evacuation of these innocents through the German lines to safety. König had received permission from the commander of *Fifteenth Army* to negotiate with the Americans for the safe passage of the refugees. Now all Massberg had to do was to pass between the lines with a white flag and a bugler without being shot by a trigger-happy sentry.

After crossing the ruined bridge that lay across the Wied at Waldbreitbach, Massberg and his *Unteroffizier* were escorted to the headquarters of Company L, 393rd Infantry Regiment of the 99th Infantry Division. Here, he sat in conversation with his American counterpart, 1st Lt. Rolland L. Neudecker, while word was passed to his battalion then regimental headquarters. Finally, after spending the night in the American command post, Massberg received word that General Lauer, commander of the 99th, had granted permission for a six-hour truce.[23]

While waiting for the decision, Massberg and Neudecker, who were both the same age, spent the night smoking and talking about the war. Neudecker thought that the war was as good as finished and that the prospects for the Third Reich looked grim. Massberg agreed and admitted that he had known for a long time that Germany had lost the war, but when queried by Neudecker as to why he kept fighting, he replied that as a professional soldier, he was duty bound to serve until a final decision was reached. When the American asked him to just stay with him instead of returning to his division, Massberg said that he had not survived five and a half years of war just to desert at the final hour.[24]

When dawn came and word of Lauer's decision arrived, Neudecker had Massberg and his sergeant blindfolded. Leading his German counterparts by the hand, he brought them both safely through the American lines and to the bridge at Waldbreitbach, where they were released. Massberg and Neudecker shook hands and wished each other good luck. Before departing, Massberg received assurances that the refugee convoys would not be fired upon. In fact, Lauer had gone so far as to have his artillery spotter planes fly above the convoys to ensure that they were able to pass in safety (and possibly to insure that the Germans were not using the evacuation as a subterfuge to withdraw their own troops!).[25]

The evacuation of the refugees from Waldbreitbach began immediately upon Massberg's return. The women, children and elderly were loaded into trucks and driven to the southeast, where they were dropped off at a more safe and secure location. Though some errant artillery fire fell close by during the evacuation, there were no injuries. The next day, when the 99th Infantry Division crossed the Wied, Captain Neudecker found the body of Massberg's sergeant, which was laying alongside those of several other *Volksgrenadiers* in one of the outposts overlooking the river

A postwar claim by the 99th Infantry Division that the Germans had threatened to shoot 200 of their own citizens in Waldbreitbach if the Americans did not immediately stop firing white phosphorous into the town must be discounted.[26] It is inconceivable that König would order this done to his own countrymen, especially in light of the extraordinary effort he made at about the same time to evacuate the two refugee centers discussed above.

Only hours after Massberg returned to division headquarters on the afternoon of 22 March, Hodges' First Army began its three-corps attack. To the north, Collins' VII Corps would drive toward the northeast in the direction of Altenkirchen with its two infantry and one armored division. In the center, Van Fleet's III Corps would push in an easterly direction with one armored and two infantry divisions in support of V Corps on its right. Huebner's newly deployed V Corps, with one infantry and one armored division, would initially attack down the eastern bank of the Rhine before it turned to the southeast in the direction of Limburg on the Lahn River.

The Americans began their attack at 0001 hours, achieving complete tactical surprise. In the *272nd VGD's* sector, the 393rd and 395th Infantry Regiments of the 99th Infantry Division attacked along a five-kilometer-wide front and quickly penetrated nearly four kilometers. German resistance was initially very light. The troops of the 395th Infantry Regiment, attacking on the left, quickly crossed the Wied and had seized the towns of Rossbach and Breitscheid by 0800 hours.

On the right, the 393rd Infantry Regiment experienced considerably more difficulty as its battalions attacked uphill into the face of tough resistance offered by Burian's newly-reconstituted *Kampfgruppe 980*. Fighting from hilltop strong points, Burian's men, supported by the remaining divisional artillery, contested the crossing of the Wied with small arms and machine-gun fire. They succeeded in forcing the Americans to advance slowly, giving ground only when it appeared that they would be bypassed or surrounded. Outnumbered three to one, the best that Burian could hope for was to delay as long as possible. Despite his men's best efforts, Kurtscheid, Waldbreitbach, and Niederbrietbach fell to the Americans by 2100 hours that evening.

On Burian's left, the 2nd Infantry Division attacked that same day in support of the 99th. Having crossed the Wied the day before when it succeeded in seizing

Neuwied, the 38th Infantry Regiment of the 2nd Infantry Division attacked to the north, striking *Kampfgruppe Bremm* of the *26th Volks-Grenadier Division* in its left flank. Cooperating with the 393rd Infantry Regiment, the 38th Infantry was able to seize Datzeroth, Rengsdorf, and Ehlscheid by nightfall. Supported by tanks from the 9th Armored Division, the men of the 2nd Infantry Division quickly routed the defenders, including *Füsilier Company 272.*

During this short, violent battle, *Oberleutnant* Ableiter lost thirty-eight men, nearly half of his remaining force. With the exception of *Obergefreiter* Kollar, who was wounded by artillery fire, the rest were all posted as missing in action, presumed captured. Apparently, few men had decided to fight to the last, since all American units reported large numbers of POWs taken that day, 571 in the 99th Infantry Division's area alone. Some indication of the morale of the company was illustrated by an event that took place that evening, when two men took the opportunity to desert.

While bringing hot food from the company trains in Hanroth to the new positions near the town of Bonefeld during the night of 23 March, *Feldwebel* Hans Klose and *Füsilier* Wolfgang Klünner disappeared while passing through the town of Strassenhaus. Taking advantage of the nearby impact of American harassing artillery fire, both men ducked into a building, leaving their rifles hanging on the wagon carrying the food.

After calling their names and waiting forty-five minutes for them to reappear, the rest of the food carrying party, led by *Gefreiter* Schönherr, searched the village but Klose and Klünner could not be found. Field police on the scene quickly determined that they had fled. Charges were filed against the two and both were found guilty in absentia, but the sentences were never carried out. Klose, an old Eastern Front veteran from Berlin, obviously had had his fill of war and had convinced the younger man to desert with him. Neither was caught and both successfully made their way home after the war.

By nightfall, it was obvious that the German defense along the Wied had crumbled and the only recourse was to fall back to the autobahn, where Hitzfeld would try to set up another delaying position. His rightmost division, the *272nd Volks-Grenadier,* was withdrawing in an orderly fashion, but in the center and left, Kokott's *26th* and Kaschner's *326th Volks-Grenadier Divisions* had been smashed and were in retreating in complete disarray. Many of their ad hoc battle groups, recruited from stragglers from over seventy-five different units, simply melted away or surrendered at the first opportunity. The 9th Armored Division sliced several miles down the eastern bank of the Rhine and rolled up *Generalmajor* Kaschner's entire division, sending it reeling before the American tanks finally halted at Engers on the Rhine that night.

Generalmajor König was forced to displace his headquarters five kilometers from Kurtscheid to Ellingen during the morning of 23 March, keeping one step ahead of the advance of the Americans of the 99th Infantry Division. To cover the division's withdrawal and to delay their advance, the two remaining batteries of *3rd Battalion, Artillery Regiment 272* fired 680 rounds before they were forced to displace to new firing positions.[27] After a commander's conference convened at the *272nd VGD*'s temporary command post that afternoon, Hitzfeld told König that *Panzer Brigade 106 "Feldherrenhalle,"* under the command of *Oberstleutnant* Wilhelm Drewes, would be made available the following day for a counterattack in the vicinity of Bonefeld. Problems encountered in securing fuel for Drewes' tanks and other vehicles, however, forced a delay of twenty-four hours.[28]

The following day, the Americans continued their advance, though most of the action on 24 March was limited to aggressive patrolling. Still, modest gains of up to a kilometer were made throughout the 99th Infantry Division's zone of attack. German resistance was characterized as "light to moderate," and only sixty-three POWs were taken. What was left of *Füsilier Company 272*'s combat element, some forty-three men in all, managed to withdraw to Bonefeld, where it reverted to division control and was ordered to dig in and defend the village. König and his staff did their best to have ammunition and food brought up to replenish the decimated regiments, but American fighter-bombers and artillery interdiction fire made the task difficult. König and his staff hoped the attack the next day by the *106th Panzer Brigade "Feldherrenhalle"* would relieve some of the pressure and allow the division to hold the Americans short of the autobahn.

On 25 March, the US III and V Corps continued their attack to clear the approaches to the autobahn, once again choosing a night attack to catch the Germans by surprise. The entire staff of *Grenadier Regiment 981* was taken prisoner that morning by the 2nd Battalion, 393rd Infantry Regiment near the town of Strassenhaus, including *Oberstleutnant* Kleinkorres. Kleinkorres, whose headquarters had been captured while he and most of his staff were asleep, remarked during his interrogation later that day that he thought the American night attack had been "faultlessly executed," which was, in his opinion, "an art for which the American Army is not generally noted."[29]

The 3rd Battalion, 393rd Infantry Regiment, to the right of the 2nd Battalion, initiated its attack at 0315 hours and had seized Bonefeld by 0820 hours on 25 March. After mopping up in Bonefeld, the 3rd Battalion continued its advance to the northeast, seizing the towns of Hardet and Anhauser by 1730 hours. *Füsilier Company 272* was involved in the initial defense of Bonefeld before it was forced to withdraw to the north after suffering nine casualties, who were posted as missing in action that evening by *Hauptfeldwebel* Fuhrmeister.

Later that day, in an attempt to delay the American advance, the *272nd VGD* launched its long-overdue counterattack against the GIs advancing north of Bonefeld, with the support of several tanks and two self-propelled guns as well as *Panzergrenadiers* from the *106th Panzer Brigade*. *Oberleutnant* Ableiter and his remaining men were incorporated into this force, along with remnants of *Grenadier Regiment 981*. *"Feldherrenhalle"* would relieve some of the pressure and allow the division to hold the Americans short of the autobahn. Despite causing the Americans some initial consternation and bringing the attack of the 393rd Infantry Regiment to a temporarily standstill, the *272nd VGD*'s counterattack got nowhere and was followed up by an immediate American counterattack. The *106th Panzer Brigade* was soon called away to deal with a threatened American breakthrough near Willroth, leaving the *272nd VGD*'s meager forces to deal with the resurgent Americans.[30] In the ensuing confusion, Ableiter and his remaining men were cut off in the vicinity of the Wilhelmsruh Forester's Lodge, 300 meters southeast of Bonefeld

Isolated in the woods, they were subjected to a brief artillery barrage that convinced Ableiter that the only reasonable course of action left for him was to surrender what was left of his command. That afternoon, he, *Leutnant* Mruzek, and his remaining thirty-three men surrendered to troops from 3rd Battalion, 393rd Infantry Regiment. *Hauptfeldwebel* Fuhrmeister again posted them all as missing in action that evening when a survivor filtered back to the company trains. For the last time, the company was without a company commander.

The disastrous counterattack at Bonefeld on 25 March 1945 was the final nail in the coffin of *Füsilier Company 272*. With the exception of the six survivors of the original company who had remained with the trains after the arrival of Ableiter with his men, the company now consisted solely of support personnel. There would be no additional replacements to rebuild the company. Incredibly, a weakened shadow of their division would continue to resist for three more weeks. The last chapter now remained for the survivors, who would see the remnant of the once-proud *272nd VGD* finally stricken from the *Wehrmacht*'s order of battle.

Despite German hopes, the Americans did not stop at the Wied. Inserting the 7th Armored Division into the III Corps area of operations, General Van Fleet ordered its commander to pass quickly through the 99th Infantry Division in order to begin the breakthrough phase of Hodge's operation. Timed to coincide with the push of the 3rd Armored Division in VII Corps zone of attack near Siegburg to the north and the 9th Armored Division's zone at Neuwied in the south, the 7th Armored Division plunged through the tattered defensive sector of the *272nd VGD* on 26 March 1945.[31] To the north of *LXVII Corps*, Püchler's *LXXIV Corps*, with *62nd* and *363rd Volks-Grenadier Divisions* and the *3rd Panzer-Grenadier Division*, had been nearly annihilated by the combined attacks of VII and III Corps. Only the *9th Panzer Division* seemed to be capable of offering any effective resistance, but it was to no avail.[32]

To Hitzfeld's left (where his corps shared a common boundary with *Army Group G*), there lay absolutely nothing at all. Here, *Defense District XII* had been holding a weak defensive sector along the Rhine and was quickly shattered by the rampaging 9th Armored Division. It was no longer a defensive battle for the Germans—it had now become a race for survival.

16

From the Hürtgen Forest to the Heart of the Reich

Once they had smashed through the Wied defense line by 25 March, the divisions of US First Army's VII, III, and V Corps found themselves astride the Frankfurt-Düsseldorf Autobahn and encountered nothing to seriously impede their push into the heart of the Reich. The Allies now held the initiative along the entire Rhine front. The Germans could no longer even slow them down, much less wrest the initiative away from them. To Model's dismay, *Army Group B* lacked even the power to form a coherent defense line, as most of his army, as well as two corps from *Generaloberst* Johannes Blaskowitz's *Army Group H* in Holland, now found themselves facing the imminent threat of encirclement.

Two days before, Field Marshall Montgomery's 21st Army Group had finally launched its own Rhine crossing operation at Wesel and by 26 March had succeeded in breaking through the last German defensive line along the Lippe River at Haltern. In the *Fifteenth Army* sector, Hodges' First Army quickly began sending spearheads that night to the north and south to trap as many of the retreating German units as they could and to link up with other elements of Ninth and Third Armies that had crossed the Rhine on either flank.

The next day, as the American advance became unstoppable, the *272nd VGD* was cut in two by the attack of Major General Robert W. Hasbrouk's 7th Armored Division, supported by a regimental combat team from the 99th Infantry Division. Burian's already decimated *Kampfgruppe 980*, part of *Artillery Regiment 272* and other odds and ends of the division, including the remnant of *Füsilier Company 272*, were cut off from the rest of the Division. The division itself, along with *Kampfgruppen 981* and *982*, was being rapidly shoved to the northeast into an area that was to become known as the Ruhr Pocket.[1]

The events of 26 to 28 March can best be charitably characterized as a military disaster, as myriad elements of *LXXIV* and *LXVII Corps*, including the *272nd VGD*, rapidly withdrew to the east and northeast, while others attempted to form a new front line to stop or delay the American advance, all to no avail. What happened next to the divided elements of the division can best be told separately, since both groups met decidedly different fates.

The End of *272nd VGD* in the Ruhr Pocket

Compared to *Kampfgruppe 980*, which had at least managed to escape to the east, the division itself had little hope for staging any kind of successful delaying action or even escape once the Americans broke through the Wied defense line. The division's disintegration, which had already begun at Hönningen, only accelerated in the weeks to come until there was nothing left for *Generalmajor* König to command. Unlike most of the other divisions soon to be trapped in the Ruhr industrial basin, however, at least the *272nd VGD* would be able to maintain its unit integrity to the end of the battle.

The Americans renewed their drive on 26 March after breaking through the Wied defense line the day before. The division headquarters narrowly avoided capture near Hachenburg when a task force of the 3rd Armored Division entered the town unexpectedly and lunged at the surprised German defenders. During this fight, the headquarters of *Grenadier Regiment 982* was surrounded by a number of tanks and overrun. Forty-five-year-old *Oberstleutnant* Paul Rösener, who had led the regiment since its inception in December 1943, was killed in action, along with several of his staff. Thus fell another one of the division's regimental commanders, renowned for his bravery and concern for his troops.

The division lost another of its veteran commanders at about the same time, when *Major* Adrario, the highly decorated commander of *Antitank Battalion 272,* was wounded in action. Shot in the right hand and right calf while leading a counterattack, he was captured shortly afterwards by American forces who treated his wounds before taking him to a prisoner of war camp. Lost also was the last of his battalion's Jg.Pz. 38(t) *Hetzers,* abandoned due to lack of fuel. His other two companies, which had lost most of their antitank and antiaircraft guns, were either scattered or pressed into service as infantry, where they were quickly killed or captured. Some of his men, such as radioman *Gefreiter* Rudolf Ips, who had served aboard a *Hetzer* during the first battle of Kesternich, simply walked away and struck out for home rather than be taken prisoner.[2] Adrario himself would be released from captivity by the end of 1945 due to his wounds and the fact that he was the head of a family and an Austrian, but most of his men would not be released until 1946.

As for the now-trapped division headquarters, rather than surrendering (a decision that would have deprived the division of the command and control that it so badly needed at this critical juncture), König instead ordered the staff and staff company to break out to the north immediately. After several anxious hours, his staff and most of its remaining vehicles were able to slip through the American lines and link up again with the rest of the division near the town of Haiger, where they rested a short while before resuming their withdrawal to the northeast.

Although the division headquarters made it through to safety, the attacks by the US III and V Corps had cut the division in two. While Burian's group and the divisional trains escaped to the east, König was forced to retreat to the northeast with what was left of the division. By this point, he had only about two hundred infantrymen left under his command and only one or two antitank guns and artillery pieces. König employed these meager forces as best he could in order to delay the American's advance north into the Ruhr area, the heart of Germany's heavy industrial infrastructure. The division was even able to shoot up several American tanks, forcing its opponent to follow more warily as the division slowly withdrew from the Rhine to the vicinity of the town of Erndtebrück (which it reached on 30 March 1945), covering a distance of about 110 kilometers in three days.[3] (See Map 21)

While the division retreated toward the Ruhr, it passed from control of Hitzfeld's *LXVII Corps* for the last time to Püchler's *LXXIV Corps* on 27 March. After the war, Püchler wrote that he did not consider the *272nd VGD* at the time "a great reinforcement of the corps . . . however, it was most welcome as every rifle counted in this situation."[4] Once they arrived in the Ruhr, Püchler assigned König the mission of holding a defensive sector along the Lichenbach-Heinsberg defense line. The division had few resources remaining with which to carry out its task. It no longer had any logistical capability, which was lost when the Americans attacked at Hachenburg and cut it off from its supply services, so it had to improvise nearly everything, including appropriation of local stocks of food as well as horse-drawn carts to carry it. Most of the forces under his command were now amalgams of different units, including *Volkssturm* and *Luftwaffe*. Yet the companies, battalions, and regiments somehow still received orders from division headquarters and amazingly attempted to carry them out as best they could.

The looming threat of encirclement became a reality for *Army Group B* on 1 April 1945 when the armored spearheads of Simpson's Ninth and Hodges' First Armies linked up near the city of Paderborn. Trapped within a 4,000-square-mile territory that comprised the Ruhr industrial basin lay virtually all of Model's army group. Instead of immediately ordering Model to break out, which was the only possible course of action from a military perspective, Hitler characteristically ordered his most trusted field marshal to stand fast and hold out until relieved by the reorganized *Eleventh SS Army*. It was vital, Hitler informed him, to hold on to Germany's last remaining industrial heartland as long as possible in order to continue the war. Model knew that this order was nonsense and that no relief was forthcoming. Practically speaking, *Army Group B* and its armies, corps, and divisions had been written off. Loyal soldier to the end, though, Model kept his thoughts to himself and threw all of his energies into organizing an all-round defense of the Ruhr, a task that he pursued with his legendary ruthlessness and skill, although this was one battle from which he would not escape. On 14 April, Hitler changed his mind and ordered Model to fight his way out. It was too late, however, as by that point American attacks from both the north and south of the pocket had split it into two.

At one point during the Battle of the Ruhr Pocket, a local Nazi Party leader assigned König 600 *Volkssturm* for use as infantry, all of whom had shortly before been employed as miners. Not wanting to see these middle-aged men slaughtered, and since none of them arrived with any armaments or uniforms, he ordered his aide-de-camp, *Oberleutnant* von der Malsberg, to discharge them and send them home. Besides being a totally inhumane act, using these men as combat troops would have further burdened the division with a large number of untrained men suited to serve as nothing more than mere cannon fodder by this stage of the battle.

Everything was in short supply by this point. Since telephone wire was lacking and there were few serviceable radio sets remaining, the division's signal battalion improvised a communications system by tapping directly into the local telephone system and even successfully used electrical high-power lines to send signals back and forth.

From 30 March to 12 April, the division was slowly used up in a series of hopeless delaying actions and counterattacks, which saw the final capture of the remnants of *Kampfgruppen 981* and *982,* as well as the rest of *Artillery Regiment 272.* Nearly all of the guns were now horse-drawn due to the lack of fuel that had forced the abandonment of their towing vehicles. Although there were still stocks of fuel to be had, to the frustration of *Oberstleutnant* Wilbrandt and his men, these were blown up in their faces "on orders" by local supply officers to prevent them from falling into hands of the pursuing Americans.[5]

On 6 April, the division came under the control of *LVIII Panzer Corps,* commanded by *Generalleutnant* Walter Botsch when the *LXXIV Corps* and its remaining units were switched to the northern sector of the pocket to assume command of other units. This change of higher headquarters did not mark an improvement in the overall tactical situation for the division, whose strength had been slowly ground away by the relentless American attacks being carried out by the 8th and 9th Infantry Divisions and the 7th Armored Division.[6]

That same day the *272nd VGD* came under attack near Allenbach and was only able to restore the front line after *Combat Engineer Battalion 12* of the *12th VGD* was temporarily attached to carry out a counterattack, since König's division by now had no units of its own strong enough to carry out the mission. By 9 April, the *272nd VGD* had lost contact with units on both its flanks and was forced to retreat once more in the direction of Olpe. By that point all it was capable of was to serve as a blocking force along the road that ran in a westerly direction from Berg-Neustadt to Olpe.[7] The last surviving battery of *Artillery Regiment 272,* after losing several men in Lützel in an Allied air attack the night before, established firing positions in a railroad cut between Olpe and Altena, but were forced again to displace quickly because of rumors of approaching American tanks.[8]

Realizing that his division effectively no longer existed, König gave the order on 12 April for the *272nd VGD* to be disbanded, an act which formally took place in the vicinity of the town of Olpe. König's staff, virtually all that remained of the division, was grouped as an emergency unit near Wuppertal under the direct command of *Generalfeldmarschall* Model himself, though it saw no further action. König was assigned command of the *12th Volks-Grenadier Division* that same day, though this division was disbanded four days later when Model offered his capitulation to the Allies on 16 April.[9] Due to a breakdown in communications, the artillery regiment was not informed of the surrender until two American military policemen arrived at its headquarters in the village of Östrich the following day. Having been informed of their new status as prisoners of war, the regiment (by now less than a battalion in size) was marched away into captivity.[10]

The few hundred men of the *272nd VGD* who had not yet been killed, wounded, or scattered, formally surrendered along with the remaining 317,000 men of Model's *Army Group B* on 18 April 1945. Rather than face surrender himself, Model committed suicide on 21 April, after stating, "I would never have thought that I would ever be so disappointed. My only aim was to serve Germany."[11] When his staff officers begged him not to take his life, he characteristically said, "It is unthinkable for a field marshal to allow himself to be captured."[12] After the war, Model's remains, which had been secretly buried, were removed to the military cemetery at Vossenack, where he now lies among the men he led during the Battle of the Hürtgen Forest.

Kampfgruppe Burian and the Retreat to the Harz Mountains

While the main body of the division was pushed into the Ruhr Pocket, *Oberst* Burian and his *Kampfgruppe 980,* as well as other remnants, did their best to stage an orderly withdrawal in the face of overwhelming American pressure. One of the survivors of *Füsilier Company 272, Unteroffizier* Fritz Fosselmann, recalls that he soon found himself and a few others from the company being rounded up and put into yet another ad hoc unit. His last recollection of the fighting after the American breakthrough at the Wied involved himself and five other men from the company, who, along with fourteen other strangers, were hastily formed into a platoon commanded by a *Leutnant.*

Fosselmann's squad was evidently attached to a larger body of survivors from Burian's regimental battle group, which was attempting to withdraw deeper into the heart of Germany by a series of forced marches in order to find a new main defense line rumored to lie in the vicinity of the Marburg-Fritzlar area. The company trains—along with *Hauptfeldwebel* Fuhrmeister; *Unteroffizier* Johns; *Obergefreitern* Lorenz and Bernutz; as well as a dozen or so other men—had linked up with this group earlier, but had gone somewhere ahead of Fosselmann's group to avoid being trapped in the rapidly forming pocket.[13] The four *Hiwis* attached to the company had long since deserted, having left before the withdrawal over the Rhine. Their fates remain unknown, though one thing is certain— if their American captors handed them back over to the Soviet Union after the war, they most likely were executed by their countrymen for treason, the same fate that would have befallen them had the Germans apprehended them for desertion.

By this point, *Kampfgruppe 980* had been reduced to about thirty or forty combat troops with no heavy weapons. The regimental trains had another sixty to seventy men ahead of them along the line of march, having pulled out earlier with the other support troops from the *272nd VGD* who had also avoided capture. After pausing to hastily reorganize, Burian and his men then began a rapid withdrawal to the northeast, staying just ahead of the pursuing Americans. During their retreat, they had managed to save one Volkswagen *Schwimmwagen* and a Steyr light truck, as well as two motorcycles with sidecars, but little else.

Later that day, Burian and his men reached the town of Harschbach. That night, near the village of Erbsen, Fosselmann and his five fellow *Volksgrenadiers* were ordered by a *Hauptmann* to dig a defensive position overlooking the village to prevent the Americans from breaking through. He recalls that no one wanted to be the last ones to die in a hopeless war, so their enthusiasm for fighting was pretty low. Nevertheless, they quickly set about digging fighting positions just as they always had, so ingrained was their discipline.

In the early morning hours of 27 March, while laid up in the darkened woods near Harschbach, Burian and his men observed about forty American tanks enter the town, cutting off their withdrawal route. Quickly assessing the situation, Burian ordered the group to take a detour in the darkness through the Niederdreiser Forest. To their dismay, however, the Americans were inexplicably waiting for them, evidently having heard them as they detoured around Harschbach.

Now trapped, Burian had to decide whether to give up then and there and march with his men into captivity, or to try to break out so they could make it back to their homes. He had given up any idea of senselessly sacrificing his men to a war that he knew had long been lost. His troops, by this point, were ready to surrender. So Burian decided to break out before daylight while they still had a chance; his gamble paid off. All but a few were able to make it out safely in the darkness. Evidently the Americans had either gone to sleep or were confident that the Germans would march in that morning and surrender.

Not everyone got the word to break out. Left behind in the darkness and confusion, Fosselmann and the others watched as the American tanks passed through the town a few hundred meters away in the early morning light. They slowly realized that they had been overlooked when the main body of Burian's troops had departed a few hours before. With little else to consider, they waited a few hours until an opportune moment to surrender appeared. Then, Fosselmann marched his men down to the town to surrender. Here, the Americans casually disarmed them and ordered them to climb on one of the tanks, which soon brought them to a POW collecting point.

Meanwhile, the rest of Burian's tiny battle group continued its march to the northeast.

On the afternoon of 27 March, near the town of Herborn, Burian and his men ran into thirty-four men from his regiment who were riding in a truck that had broken down. Thus reinforced, they pressed on, reaching the Hachenburg-Langenbach area that night, where they ran into the regimental trains, as well as the company trains from *Füsilier Company 272,* which had evidently linked up with the larger regimental trains several days earlier. Counting the few vehicles they had brought with them and those from the regiment's maintenance platoon, there were now enough vehicles to guarantee everyone a seat. *Kampfgruppe 980,* or what was left of it, was now fully motorized. Ominously, there had still been no contact from the division for two days, and they could only assume the worst.

Around midnight, the column, now numbering over 150 men, reached Marburg, where they narrowly avoiding having to report in to the local defense headquarters, where Burian and his men would have been seized by a *Heldenklaukommando* and marched back to the front for a last-ditch stand. Burian's method, proven again time after time, was to tell anyone they met along the roads or in towns that the Americans were immediately behind them and that they were the last force between the local townspeople and the approaching enemy (which indeed they frequently were). Burian repeatedly urged local *Volkssturm* units to stay home whenever the Americans arrived in order to keep the fighting and destruction to an absolute minimum.[14]

Early on the morning of 28 March, the pursuing Americans reached Marburg, forcing Burian and his men to pull out of the town before they were overtaken. No one, least of all Ewald Burian, was pleased to have to adopt such cautious tactics, but he and his men were faced with a choice of either being taken prisoner or being hauled before a People's Court or the military police to be tried and hanged as *Vaterlandverräter* (Betrayer of the Fatherland, or traitor) or as cowards. No one believed in wonder weapons any longer and no one desired a hero's death, but none wanted to be seen as a traitor, either. Even at the war's end, most German soldiers still felt that this was unthinkable.

Burian and the rest of his men reached the town of Werkel near the city of Fritzlar on the afternoon of 29 March. There, he was informed that Americans were reported to be moving to the north through Braunau toward Kassel, thus thwarting any attempt to reach Hannover, his next destination. Here he had planned to disband his regiment, since most of the survivors came from the Hannover area. A rumor that German military authorities were rounding up stray units into several emergency units in the Kassel area was enough to persuade him to keep pushing his tired men northeast.

Traveling separately again, the regiment's trains, including that from *Füsilier Company 272,* reached the town of Udenhausen on the Weser the next day and crossed the river that evening. At about this point, Burian's forces linked up with *3rd Battalion, Artillery Regiment 272,* which had also escaped encirclement. It had managed to bring along several guns, a major accomplishment at the time due to the Allies' complete control of the air that made any attempt at movement during the day a questionable proposition at best.[15] Despite the continuing collapse of the Third Reich, German field formations and the *Wehrmacht's* military administration continued to function right up to the end. Even in an atmosphere of impending chaos, order somehow seemed to be able to reassert itself. Burian and his little band expected to be rounded up at any moment, pressed into some sort of emergency formation and senselessly sacrificed to buy time until another equally ineffective emergency unit could be formed.

Burian and his remaining troops crossed the Weser River on 31 March 1945 at the village of Vernavahlshausen near the town of Uslar on the edge of the Harz Mountains. Here, they celebrated their last Easter of the war and were informed by local military authorities that they were now officially incorporated into the *Eleventh SS Army,* which had been transferred to the Harz from Neustrelitz after its defeat in Pomerania the previous month.*

This new army, which was to be placed under the command of *General der Artillerie* Walther Lucht, had been assigned on 1 April 1945 the rather ambitious mission of carrying out the rescue of Model's *Army Group B* in the Ruhr Pocket. Upon arrival in the Harz, the army was given control of *LXVI* and *LXVII Corps* and the *VI* and *IX Military Defense Districts,* including all troops that fell within the area, as well as the thousands of stragglers from dispersed units passing through the area.[16]

This new command arrangement immediately affected Burian's battle group, which was given orders take up new defensive positions until all of the other units earmarked to take part in the relief operation could assemble. Arriving in an assembly area near the castle at Bodenstein-Wörbis, Burian discharged several men from among the ranks who were farmers in civilian life and allowed them to leave the column with a couple of horses so they could begin plowing that spring. By this point, Burian had only two vehicles left, since fuel was scarce. He hoped that the Americans would bypass the Harz and leave them alone, giving them the opportunity to infiltrate back to their homes and don civilian garb, thus avoiding the ignominy of being taken prisoner. His hopes were in vain, for the Americans, fearing that the *Eleventh SS Army* might launch an attack against their extended flanks, quickly began efforts to encircle and reduce the Harz defensive position.

Now redesignated *Kampfgruppe Burian,* the survivors of *Grenadier Regiment 980,* numbering less than 100 men, took up new defensive positions on 6 April in the vicinity of the town of Heiligenstadt. Four days later, Burian learned that his men had been incorporated into a scratch unit, *Division Sturm,* composed of stragglers from a variety of organizations. This division-sized battle group, named after its newly appointed commander, *Generalleutnant* Alfred Sturm of the *Luftwaffe,* was composed of two other small regimental-sized ad hoc organizations, *Kampfgruppen Marx* and *Janta.*[17] To bolster Burian's available combat

---

* This was now an SS Army in name only. It had previously been commanded by *SS-Ober-gruppenführer* Felix Steiner until 5 March 1945. Steiner, a commander of some renown, had led the army during the abortive *Sonnenwende* Offensive in Pomerania during the previous February. By the time the army arrived to carry out its new assignment in the Harz, it no longer had any *Waffen-SS* units subordinated to it at all and was little more than a headquarters without troops. However, upon arrival in the Harz, its *LXVI Corps* was given control of *SS-Replacement Brigade "Westfalen,"* which had a strength of perhaps 3,000 to 4,000 men.

strength, hundreds of stragglers were hastily assigned from every branch of the *Wehrmacht.*

Division Sturm itself was subordinated initially to the *LXVII Corps,* under temporary command of *General der Infanterie* Otto Fretter-Pico, who had to contend with organizing some semblance of a corps from remnants of five different divisions (*26th, 272nd,* and *326th Volks-Grenadier Divisions,* as well as the *89th Infantry Division* and *5th Parachute Division*) and a multitude of various local replacement units from the *VI* and *IX Military Defense Districts,* the Panzer School for NCOs at Eisenach, and an engineer brigade consisting of four weak battalions. The corps lacked nearly everything, but was particularly short of artillery, signal equipment, antitank weapons, and ammunition.*

LXVII Corps' situation was not unique, however; the *Eleventh SS Army* chief of staff, *Oberst* Fritz Estor, later wrote that the shortage of experienced NCOs and junior officers was particularly acute. In Estor's assessment, the *Eleventh SS Army* did "not have a single complete unit with any real fighting power, no artillery worth mentioning, no reserves, and no air support." In his opinion, *Eleventh SS Army* did not even qualify for the designation of an army at all, and amounted to little more than a "blocking unit" capable of only delaying, not stopping, the American's advance.[18]

Eleventh SS Army's situation from the outset was desperate, a fact clearly recognized by its commander, *General der Artillerie* Lucht. Lucht, a realist, had quickly sized up the situation and felt that the most he could hope for was to keep his army together in order to prevent its complete disintegration and to keep its men from becoming marauders, since he felt that the populace within his area of operations had suffered enough already. Having to endure the incessant bombing and artillery fire was more than enough without having to deal with armed mobs of German soldiers roaming about the Harz without any leadership or discipline. He seems to never have seriously entertained the thought of carrying out an attack to relieve Model's army group, despite his orders. He simply lacked the wherewithal to conduct such an operation, much less to conduct any kind of effective defense with the hopelessly inadequate forces he had available. In fact, *Generalfeldmarschall* Kesselring cancelled the planned relief attack on 4 April when it became apparent that it had no chance whatsoever of success. This sealed the fate of *Army Group B.* Instead, Lucht's orders were changed to reflect a new defensive posture, with the mission of holding the Harz region at all costs.

---

* *Generalleutnant* Maximilian Fretter-Pico took command of *LXVII Corps* from *General der Infanterie* Hitzfeld on 2 April 1945, when Hitzfeld assumed temporary command of the *Eleventh SS Army.* Hitzfeld resumed command of his corps on 8 April when the officially designated commander, *General der Artillerie* Walther Lucht, arrived on the night of 7 April to assume leadership of the *Eleventh SS Army.* Fretter-Pico then took command of the *IX Military District,* now re-christened *IX Corps.*

Accordingly, Lucht tried to hold his patchwork command together as long as he could until he could arrange an orderly surrender. Not only did he succeed in keeping his troops under control, but he also refused to carry out the scorched earth orders issued to him and other army commanders by Hitler's headquarters in Berlin. By limiting most fighting to delaying actions, Lucht was certain that he could keep destruction to a minimum; on this point, at least, he succeeded.[19] Lucht was informed by *OB West* that *General der Panzertruppe* Walter Wenck's newly-raised *Twelfth Army* would conduct a relief attempt in his direction beginning on 17 April, but Wenck's army was shortly thereafter redirected toward the east to relieve Berlin instead and Lucht was left to his own devices.

The men of *Kampfgruppe Burian* did not know this, of course, and looked at each day as yet another unwanted chance to be the last man to "die for the Fatherland." Many were having no part of it. Burian and *General* Sturm witnessed this firsthand, as the division grew from 2,000 to between 6,000 and 7,000 men on 10 April, only to dwindle to less than thirty men two weeks later, as desertion and straggling quickly took their toll.[20] By 10 April, the day they were incorporated into *Division Sturm,* American pressure had forced Burian and his remaining men (now only thirty-five, not counting the trains elements) to withdraw to Ellrich on the southern edge of the Harz. (For the overall withdrawal route of *Kampfgruppe Burian,* refer to Map 22.)

To defend its sector along the Nordhausen-Sangerhausen-Hettstedt defensive line, *Division Sturm* had the aforementioned three infantry battle groups. Artillery support was limited to one 170mm gun and a few medium and heavy mortars. The guns that *3rd Battalion, Artillery Regiment 272* had so painstakingly salvaged from the Wied defense line were lost the day before to an Allied fighter bomber attack near the town of Walkenried that killed all of the battalions horses. The battalion would no longer be able to contribute its support to the defensive effort and its men were quickly incorporated into another ad hoc unit as infantrymen.[21]

Generalleutnant Sturm's biggest concern at this point was that the American forces (primarily the 1st Infantry Division) might work their way behind his right flank, resulting in the loss of contact with the neighboring *LXVI Corps.* To prevent that from happening, he was forced continually to refuse his right flank, though this did not prevent the Americans from finally bypassing his division by 14 April and cutting him off from the main body of *Eleventh SS Army.*

Meanwhile on 11 April, Burian and his men, reinforced by the addition of several hundred stragglers to replace those that had already melted away, arrived in town of Tanne to set up blocking positions, but were forced to withdraw under American pressure toward Lindenberg later that afternoon. By 13 April, the line had temporarily stabilized. Burian was able to establish his battle command post at Haus Dombachtal after positioning his men in defensive positions in the vicinity of the village of Steinbrücken.

Here, the survivor's of Burian's regiment and the other ad hoc units of *Division Sturm* were able to catch their breath, as their American pursuers took the time to bring up additional supplies and to tighten the net around the Harz. By this time, *Obergefreiter* Josef Bernutz remembers that there were only seven or eight men left in *Füsilier Company 272,* including himself, Fuhrmeister, *Gefreiter* Lorenz, a couple of cooks, and two or three drivers.[22]

This relatively quiet period was shattered on 15 April, when the pursuing US 1st and 83rd Infantry Divisions renewed their advance against the center of the *Eleventh SS Army.* In *Division Sturm*'s sector, three American tanks were reported that day conducting a reconnaissance in the vicinity of Neudorf, but were driven off by the 170mm gun. Toward evening, they returned, forcing *General* Sturm to bring up reinforcements to hold the town, which had become the hinge of his now-exposed right flank. A *Panzerschreck* knocked out one M-4 Sherman and a second one was damaged, forcing the Americans to withdraw. The following day the Americans resumed their attack, pouring artillery fire into the town, which killed the local commander and inflicted heavy casualties on the defenders.

That same day, Burian ordered that the remaining personnel assigned to the trains (including the men from *Füsilier Company 272*) be discharged near the village of Rübeland south of the town of Wernigerode. Bernutz remembers that morning they had been ordered to dig a defensive line for a last stand near Thale, but to his surprise he and the others were allowed by an officer or perhaps the sergeant major to take off and try to make their way home the best way they could before they were captured. While the men from the regimental and company trains began their trek home, Burian's remaining combat troops prepared to carry on the fight.

Burian directed that all remaining equipment be destroyed, including all records contained in the unit orderly rooms, but for some inexplicable reason, *Gefreiter* Lorenz stashed the suitcase containing all of *Füsilier Company 272*'s files instead. According to Bernutz, how the papers, files, and identity documents ended up in the cellar of a farmhouse in Wernigerode nearly thirty years later was a complete mystery. Discharged from the *Wehrmacht* and now considered by their own army as civilians, Bernutz and two other comrades from the local area struck out for their homes on horseback, having unharnessed the remaining horses from the last of the company's wagons.

By 17 April, the German defense in the Harz was finally broken after bitter resistance. On that day alone, the 1st Infantry Division recorded over 1,300 prisoners taken, though not   after they had experienced the "severest artillery fire yet received in the Harz area."[23] The now inappropriately-named *Kampfgruppe Burian,* reduced in strength to seventy men, defended itself against a determined attack by 3rd Battalion, 16th Infantry of the US 1st Infantry Division in a forest near the village of Königshütte.[24] Burian and his men were able to drive off the leading American company, buying themselves enough time to stage an orderly withdrawal and to bury the dead from this engagement, including *Oberleutnant* Bolzmann, the last officer of the regiment to fall during the war.

By 18 April, the German retreat further into the Harz had become a rout, and even the newly-raised *Infantry Division Potsdam,* which had been sent to provide some relief to Lucht's army, was quickly crushed before it could even fully deploy its regiments, though one regiment reportedly put up a good fight before it too was rounded up.* *Division Sturm* was cut off from the rest of *LXVII Corps* and reported that some of its subordinate elements had been captured. Unknown to Burian, this was the same day that the survivors of the *272nd VGD*, who were trapped far to the west in the Ruhr Pocket, were forced to capitulate with rest of Model's *Army Group B.*

On 19 April, Sturm and his rapidly dissolving division were completely surrounded. *General der Infanterie* Otto Hitzfeld personally disbanded his *LXVII Corps* later that day and surrendered along with his staff. During interrogation, Hitzfeld, described as a "tight-lipped, brisk and hard young man," told his captors that though the war was over militarily, Germany still had a few political cards left to play (though what these cards were, he failed to explain). Hitzfeld impressed the G-2 of the 1st Infantry Division with his love of his profession and asked the Americans to "Give me one of your corps with your personnel and immense supplies and I could go anywhere in Europe I cared to go."[25] The only place he was to go as a guest of the Americans was a POW camp.

Meanwhile, with the non-combat personnel effectively out of the way, Burian's troops improved their positions near Thale and prepared to conduct their last defensive battle as part of *Division Sturm,* but to no avail. By the evening of 20 April, attacks by the US 1st, 83rd, and 104th Infantry Divisions forced the surviving German units out of their positions and put them to flight. During the ensuing pursuit, *Kampfgruppe Burian* was completely dispersed, its men scattered to the four winds, killed, or taken prisoner. Burian and the dozen or so who remained with him evaded capture and reached Bad Suderode, a military hospital town, where they were able to stay one day.

The last fighting remnant of the *272nd VGD* was to follow *Division Sturm* into captivity soon thereafter. On 20 April, Burian, *Oberleutnant* Stefan, *Oberleutnant* Gehle, and the last nine enlisted men of *Grenadier Regiment 980* slipped through the American encircling ring and arrived at Neuwerk in the Harz. *Gefreiter* Schaller, a veteran from the local area, convinced Burian and the others to hide in some caves until the war was over, when they could try to return to their homes

---

* *Infantry Division Potsdam* was formed 29 March 1945 from the remnants of the *85th Infantry Division* using troops from schools and replacement units of all branches of the German Army to fill out its regiments. Only one weak regiment survived the Division's brief commitment to the Harz defense and escaped; this regiment was shortly thereafter assigned to *Infantry Division Scharnhorst* as its Füsilier Battalion. (Source: Tessin, Vol. 14, 199–200.)

and evade capture. Here, they hid themselves until the afternoon of 21 April, when they taken prisoner by a squad of American soldiers laying telephone wire. They were quickly searched, stripped of their decorations, and herded into one of dozens of hastily-establish prisoner of war enclosures where they awaited processing by their captors.

More fortunate than Burian's tiny group was *3rd Battalion, Artillery Regiment 272,* which successfully escaped from the Harz Pocket. Its commander, *Major* Martin Jenner, chose to strike out east toward Torgau on the Elbe. When he and his men encountered advancing Soviet troops, they made a detour to the south instead and reached Ludwigslust, where the commander surrendered his men to American forces. After nearly one year of hard fighting in the West and after only sixteen months in existence, the career of the *272nd VGD* finally came to an end.

As for *General* Sturm, after attempting to continue resisting the Americans, he was forced to give himself up on 23 April with his thirty remaining men. Out of food and ammunition, he established his final command post in a woodsman's hut and sent out a capitulation note to the 1st Infantry Division, which sent a patrol the next morning to pick him up. Upon interrogation, Sturm said that he realized that the war was over immediately upon assuming command of his division when he looked at the men he was supposed to lead. Every one of them, in his words, was "a straggler, and hardly ten of them came from the same unit originally."[26]

In all, some 73,490 German soldiers and seventeen generals were captured in the Harz, leading the G-2 of the 1st Infantry Division to comment on 20 April that

> When Julius Caesar overran the pelted and fur-bearing Germans centuries ago, his own POW [cage] could have been no more flushed and crowded than was the 1st Infantry Division cage today, nor more filled with strange and guttural tribesmen. Today in the Division cage there were Hungarians, German sailors, *Wehrmacht* infants, ancient and spavined *Flak* men, *SS* men, women auxiliaries, RAD workers—anything that the German *Reich* could turn out in a uniform. . . . Interrogators who had leaped avidly on second lieutenants for information early in the day merely grunted at anything less than full colonel in the afternoon, and by night even generals had trouble making themselves heard in the Babel. It was a lovely sight. . . ."[27]

While Burian was attempting to evade capture, that same day Josef Bernutz reached his hometown of Hettstedt, where he was reunited with his wife. Unfortunately for him, he was rounded up shortly thereafter by American troops looking for German soldiers disguised in civilian clothes, and was placed in a POW camp. To his amazement, he was discharged less than a month later and allowed to go home because he was the sole surviving son in the family. He soon resumed his life as a farmer, though soon had to submit to Soviet occupation once American forces withdrew in accordance with agreements previously drawn up at Potsdam. He was not to taste true freedom again until the Communist East German regime collapsed some forty-five years later.

The last member of the *272nd VGD* to be captured in the Harz, according to American records, was a twenty-eight-year-old *Unteroffizier* from *Antitank Battalion 272* (probably a fugitive from *Kampfgruppe Burian*), who was taken prisoner by the 1st Infantry Division on 23 April near the village of Hüttenrode. He had been captured twice before—once during the retreat from northern France the previous summer and again near Hönningen, but had escaped on both occasions. This sergeant had fought both in the Eifel and in the Rhineland from November 1944 to March 1945.

He also had the dubious distinction of being the one-hundred-thousandth prisoner taken by the "Big Red One" in the Second World War. He had dug himself a hiding spot in the forest and intended to wait out the end of the war or join up with another unit still fighting. He was captured only when he had left his hiding spot to get water. So even when all hope was lost, there were still professional soldiers left in the division who had not admitted defeat—a fitting epitaph to the *272nd VGD* and *Füsilier Company 272*.[28]

Epilogue

Füsilier Company 272 did not survive to see the end of the war. Its role in the conflict ended on 15 April 1945 in the Harz Mountains, after suffering losses of its entire complement several times over. Despite its repeated destruction, the commander of the *272nd VGD* chose to prolong the company's life by over four months, each time reconstituting it with dozens of replacements so it could once more be sent back into combat. Finally, the *Wehrmacht* simply ran out of men to replace those who had been lost. With no more men to replenish its ranks, the company died out slowly, but did not officially cease to exist until *Oberst* Burian issued the order for the company trains to be disbanded. Virtually every member of the *272nd VGD* had been captured, killed, or wounded. Most had been lost in the Hürtgen Forest, but quite a few fell during the fight to hold the Roer, the battles along the Rhine, and the Wied.

The fate of *Füsilier Company 272* was no different than that of any other unit in the division. Six months of steady combat had ground it away to nothing, leaving the remnant no choice but ignominious surrender or death.

What became of its men? Of the 482 *Volksgrenadiers* who had been assigned to the company at one time or another during its seven months in existence, records indicate that 405 of them became casualties, of which fifty-one were confirmed killed in action or died of wounds, eighty-three were wounded, and over 271 were listed simply as missing in action. Most of these were probably captured by the Allies, though a few are still unaccounted for, sixty years after the fact. Some forty-eight men were transferred out of the company to other units for one reason or another. Fewer than a dozen were known to have deserted. It had seven different commanders assigned, with three of them being killed in action. The last official report indicates that only twenty-two men were still present for duty on 27 March 1945, out of 200 men authorized. Surely, *Füsilier Company 272* had more than paid its dues. Its men had given the last full measure of devotion. And all for a cause that was not worthy of that sacrifice.

In some respects, the men of the *272nd VGD* who survived the war were fortunate. After they surrendered, whether in the Hürtgen Forest, along the Rhine, in the Ruhr Pocket or in the Harz, at least they were not handed over to the Soviet Union like millions of their comrades and marched off to die in a Siberian POW camp. Instead, they were sent to various American, British, or French prisoner of war camps scattered throughout Western Europe. In comparison to those run by the Soviet Union, even French-administered camps seemed humane. By 1948, nearly all of the German soldiers, airmen, sailors, and even most of the members of the *Waffen-SS* had been released by their Western captors. Many of those held by the Soviet Union did not return home until 1956.

After enduring months or even years in Allied prisoner of war camps, most of the survivors of the *272nd VGD* made their way back to their homes, or what was left of them. A few men, such as those who had homes in Silesia, Pomerania or East Prussia, had no home to go back to, since the Soviet Union had either claimed these German territories as their own in retribution or had awarded them to Poland to compensate for huge swaths of land taken when Stalin moved the border of the USSR hundreds of kilometers westwards at the end of the war. Many men spent weeks or months trying to find their families, only to be told that they, too, were missing or feared dead. The ethnic Germans from the Balkans or other regions of eastern Europe faced a similar situation, made all the more difficult by the forced expulsion of most of the remaining ethnic German communities by their new Communist overlords.

Even those lying wounded in hospitals were not spared prisoner of war status or internment. Some, such as *Unteroffizier* Kurt Klein, were marched out of the hospital in pajamas and forced to move into a British POW camp. Here he stayed until the end of August 1945, when his wife was finally able to convince his captors to release him because of his wounds. Many men from the division were reported to have died in French camps such as the one at Attichy, where malnutrition and sickness were rampant. Most of the veterans interviewed agreed that while in French custody, their treatment was harsh, food was poor, living conditions were primitive, and abuse by their captors was the norm, not the exception. Most had to carry out forced labor, such as repairing France's damaged infrastructure, mining coal, or clearing minefields, actions now banned under the 1949 Geneva Convention.

For Germany, it was truly the "Zero Hour," or *der Stunde null* in Germany's history. The Thousand-Year Reich had lasted slightly over twelve years and many of Germany's victims demanded a harsh retribution for the damage that Hitler's legions had done. With their country thoroughly beaten and ravaged by Allied bombing and ground fighting, the survivors of the *Wehrmacht* and their fellow citizens began to rebuild. And rebuild they did, transforming a shattered country into a model western democracy in the short span of ten years. The surviving members of *Füsilier Company 272* were no exception to their countrymen and quickly melted back into German society.

In comparison to their fellow countrymen living in the new eastern zone of Germany, many of the survivors of the company enjoyed relatively good fortune, since the state of Lower Saxony, which most of them called home, had been assigned to the Occupation Zone controlled by the British military government. Strict but fair, the British ensured that men were put back to work and that a functioning local provisional government was quickly put in place to handle most of the day-to-day administrative duties.

Home, of course, was not what they had remembered when they had marched off to join the *Wehrmacht*. Extensive Allied bombing, the effects of ground combat, famine, and the dislocation of thousands of people had transformed the face of Germany. Most of the survivors, if they could, went back to their old professions, such as farming, manufacturing, or business. Those who had lost their private businesses during the war would have to start over. The younger men, who had never known a profession because they had been drafted before they had begun a career, found that they had a relative amount of freedom to start over. Though most of the jobs immediately after the war involved manual labor, as more and more businesses got up and running, millions of men moved back into their old professions and their former laborer jobs were taken up by a wave of so-called guest workers—Yugoslavs, Italians, and Turks.

Kurt Klein, burned so badly at Simmerath, resumed his prewar job as a metalworker at one of the large foundries in Solingen. Reunited with his wife and children, he rebuilt his life and retired as a master tradesman, passing away in October 2000.

Oberleutnant Helmut Aretz, who briefly commanded the company at Herhahn, spent most of the rest of the war in the hospital recuperating from his wounds. After his release, he went back to his family's construction business in Krefeld, building it up to a major corporation that he still operates today. *Leutnant* Helmut Bayer, minus the arm he lost at Giesenheck, received his law degree from the University at Göttingen and still practices law.

The company's last commander, *Oberleutnant* Walter Ableiter, went back to his Black Forest home in the town of Wildbad after being released from captivity, and eventually rose to become owner of one of the largest hotels in the area. Active in the regional Chamber of Commerce and local politics, he was awarded the Federal Service Cross 1st Class for decades of community service by German President Richard von Weizsäcker upon his retirement in 1989. After a long and eventful life, he passed away in June 1993.

Peter Moog resumed work at his family's farm near Bonn after rebuilding his parents' home, destroyed during an air raid in March 1945, and made many friends over the years among the staff of the newly established US Embassy in neighboring Bonn.

Friedrich Fosselmann went back to work for the German Federal Railway, after having searched the length and breadth of Germany for his wife, who had fled Silesia in January 1945. They were finally reunited in August 1945, after he had nearly given up hope. His close friend, Heinrich Misskampf, despite the loss of his leg on the Kermeter Peninsula, became a respected local official in a municipality near Frankfurt am Main, married, and raised a family.

The *Spiess*, *Hauptfeldwebel* Hermann Fuhrmeister, made his way home to Hildesheim and quickly resumed the threads of his life. He became an accountant for a large housewares manufacturing company, raised two sons and daughter with his adoring wife, and joined a well-known German men's choir that toured throughout Europe. Fuhrmeister died suddenly of a heart attack on 17 April 1976 one day after performing a solo from the *Matthäus Passion* during a performance in the northern Italian city of Merano.

...acharuk, the "booty German" from Rumania, eventually settled near ...ter being released from the POW camp and became a full German cit-...hout having to die to earn that privilege. His son helped design the city ...kfurt's modern convention center.

The division's senior leadership also found their way home, though usually after longer stays in POW camps. *Generalmajor* Eugen König was kept in Special Camp 11 at Bridgend in Britain, along with hundreds of other former general officers of the *Wehrmacht* and was not released until 1947. After the war, he settled in the Bitburg area, remaining active in veterans' affairs until his death on 8 April 1985. *Oberst* Ewald Burian, after his release from captivity, settled in Cologne, where he worked with an engineering firm until he died on 3 November 1981. *Major* Friedrich Adrario returned to his native Vienna, where he initially worked in his family's lumber business. In 1956, he joined the postwar *Bundesheer*, the federal army of Austria, rising to the rank of *Generalmajor* before he retired from active duty in 1983. He lives today in Vienna and still remains in contact with the men of his battalion. *Hauptmann* Dr. Adolf Thomae, after recovering from his wounds, was released in late 1945 and went back to his home to near Düsseldorf to work in a large business concern, culminating in his appointment as the firm's general manager. He died in Munich on 2 December 2002 at the age of eighty-seven after a lengthy illness.

Most of the returning veterans fit back into society with relative ease and hastened to forget the war and everything that happened to them. Few seem to still harbor any hate toward the Americans, and some veterans, such as Hans Wegener, Kurt Hake, Hans Below and Gerd Hörner, have even taken part in German-American friendship tours in the Hürtgen Forest with fellow veterans "from the opposite *Feldpostnummer*," the famous 78th "Lightning" Division. Many more became active after the war in the veteran's association of the *272nd VGD*, which conducted annual reunions in Hannover until 2004. Many of its veterans still meet every November to decorate the division's monument in the city park with wreaths on *Volkstrauertag*, the annual day set aside by the German government to honor and commemorate the victims of war. The division's official history, authored by former artilleryman Martin Jenner, was published by the Veteran's Association in 1964 and was recently republished in 2005.

Though most of the men who served in the *272nd VGD* have since passed away, the survivors still vividly remember the months they spent in the Hürtgen Forest—in places such as Rollesbroich, Giesenheck, Strauch, Kesternich, and Simmerath, as well as other battlefields, such as those of Herhahn, Vlatten, and Hönningen. These places and the memories associated with them were burned indelibly into their memory; try as they might to forget. Perhaps the best evocation of what it was like fighting and a fitting conclusion to this story was written in 1945 by one of their comrades who did not survive the war, *Oberleutnant* Karl Bolzmann of *Grenadier Regiment 980,* who was killed in action near Wernigerode on 11 April 1945:

Night at the Front
In the Eifel, Winter of 1944/45

The pine trees tower gloomily in the clear night.
The stars stand helpless in the heaven's tent.
Shredded clouds move hither as if in wild chase,
through which the light of the moon falls like silver.
Ghostly glides its shadows through the grass,
and the wind blows through the wide meadows.
The air is cool and the trees and bushes glisten with moisture.
The sentries listen in the night with alert wariness.
Icy death crawls through the white wall of fog,
shrouding him as he moves into the valley where lies both friend and foe.
He whets his scythe in his bony hand,
to begin mowing when the first rays of the sun begin to stir.
Though the Fatherland reigns over life and death,
behind the stars awaits God in his might.
We grip our fates in our own hand,
and prepare for the morning like we do each night.

The everyday existence of a *Volksgrenadier* from 31 August 1944 until 8 May 1945 could be described best, paraphrasing British philosopher John Locke, as "nasty, brutish, and short." In sharp contrast to Germany's deteriorating military situation, at this point in the war the Anglo-Americans possessed not only the means to manufacture sufficient tanks, artillery, and close air support, but their commanders and soldiers alike grew increasingly more proficient in the use of those weapons as they gained more combat experience. Heavy casualties thus became commonplace during the eleven months of bitter fighting separating the Allied landings in Normandy from the final German surrender at Reims as *Wehrmacht* commanders were often forced to rely on manpower, rather than firepower.

Paradoxically, while the German soldier began to be issued some of the most modern weapons in the world, he found that ammunition for these weapons was becoming increasingly scarce. Though the introduction of the V-1 flying bomb and V-2 ballistic missile gained much of the world's attention, shortages of fuel kept many of Germany's more mundane tanks and aircraft from ever reaching the field. Uniforms and equipment, though practical and economically made, appeared shabby and wore out much more quickly than those issued earlier in the war. Food, though sufficient, became increasingly bland and laced with substitutes such as saccharine and soybean meal. Still, the young Volksgrenadiers of late 1944 fought on in hopes that his personal sacrifices would ensure that these new wonder weapons would arrive in enough quantities to turn the tide at the eleventh hour.

Ironically, the development of the *Volks-Grenadier Division* resulted in an organization that was poorly suited to conduct offensive operations, almost in spite of German infantry doctrine, which stressed the primacy of the offense. Though infantry doctrine had remained virtually unchanged since the publication of the German Army's basic tactical manual, *Truppenführung*, in 1933, the last significant evolution in German infantry structure resulted in a division that lacked the necessary organizational depth, striking range, and mobility to do anything except defend a static front line.

An increased allotment of more powerful and effective weapons meant nothing if such divisions did not possess the means to keep them supplied with ammunition once it had begun its attack. Yet it was in these very divisions that Adolf Hitler had placed his hopes for the success of one of the most daring offensive operations carried out during World War Two—*WACHT AM RHEIN*.

As a concept, the *Volks-Grenadier Division* represented the culmination of the evolution of the German infantry division. Had there been sufficient time, personnel, and material to commit fifty or sixty of them at once, they might have made a difference, but would only have delayed the end of the war and could not reverse the Third Reich's declining fortunes.

Despite the initial promise they offered, they never lived up to expectations. In the final analysis, the scarce resources committed to create them probably would have been put to better use had they been instead sent to reinforce the veteran divisions that had been starved of the very same men and material they needed in order to maintain their own dwindling ranks. Like most of the Hitler's last-ditch efforts, the *Volks-Grenadier* division was too little, too late.

Endnotes

Prologue

1. Charles B. MacDonald, *The Siegfried Line Campaign* [US Army Office of the Chief of Military History (CMH), 1984], 3.

2. Ibid, 617.

3. Charles B. MacDonald, *The Battle of the Hürtgen Forest* (New York: J. B. Lippincott, 1963), 195–96.

4. MacDonald, *Siegfried Line Campaign*.

5. *Three Battles: Arnaville, Altuzzo, and Schmidt (Washington, D.C.: US Army),1993.*

6. Adolf Hohenstein and Wolfgang Trees, *Hölle im Hürtgenwald* (Hell in the Hürtgen Forest) Aachen: Triangel Verlag, 1981.

7. Letter from Gevert Haslob, former Adjutant to General Bruns, Commander of the *89th Infantry Division,* and post-war military historian with the *Bundeswehr.*

Chapter 2

1. Hugh M. Cole, *The Lorraine Campaign* (Washington, D.C.: Historical Division, US Army, 1950), 33.

2. Some have credited Stauffenberg with the design of the *Volks-Grenadier Division* concept, but this is patently false. The historical record indicates that as the Chief of Staff of the *Ersatzheer,* he was the designer the so-called *Sperr* (blocking) divisions, subsequently renamed as *Grenadier Divisions.* These divisions were activated as "emergency" formations, established in the wake of the destruction of *Army Group Center,* to serve as stopgaps to help stitch the crumbling Eastern Front back together.

3. Heinz Guderian, *Panzer Leader* (New York: Ballantine, 1957), 289.

4. Article from 3 August 1944 issue of *Völkischer Beobachter* as quoted in Heinz Höhne, *The Order of the Death's Head: The Story of Hitler's SS* (New York: Ballantine, 1971), 612.

A recently-discovered comment that Heinrich Himmler made in a public speech to assembled Nazi Party District Chiefs in Posen, 3 August 1944, provides even greater depth as to his thoughts on where the new *VGD*s should fit into the *Wehrmacht*:

"However, I must say this [to you] once again: do not expect any magic from me alone. This [task] will require months. I fear it will need years until the last part is completed. It has become clear [to me] that the new army can be grown from [the current one] only gradually. I have likewise indicated the name of this army in my order of the day: the National Socialist People's Army. I have asked the *Führer*—and the *Führer* has approved—that the new divisions that are now being created should receive the name 'People's Grenadier Divisions.' Therefore, we have to do away with the old term *'Reichswehr'* and everything associated with it. Yes, we had to find a suitable name for it . . . I believe that the war that we are now waging is what I call the people's holy war, and that the only army that can win this war must be the National Socialists People's Army . . . it must be clear to everyone, that this army must be imbued with a uniformly National Socialist worldview." Source: *Vierteljahrsheft fuer Zeitgeschichte* (Quarterly Publication for Contemporary History), 1, no. 4 (1953): 357.

5. Helmuth Reinhardt, MS. P-065b, "The Volks-Grenadier Division and the Volkssturm," "Volks"—Organizations in German Military Establishment [US Army Europe Historical Series (USAREUR Series), 1950, National Archives, Washington, D.C.], 7.

6. The term "wave," beginning with the first mobilization of wartime divisions in 1939, served to designate a group of divisions activated at the same time and having roughly the same characteristics in structure, composition of personnel and equipment. A total of thirty-five waves were mobilized before war's end. From Reinhardt, MS. P-065a, "The Volks-Grenadier Division and the Volkssturm" (USAREUR Series), 1950, 7.

7. George Tessin, *Verbände und Truppen der deutschen Wehrmacht und Waffen-SS 1939–1945* (Formations and troops of the German armed forces and Waffen-SS), vol. 8 (Osnabrück, Germany: Biblio Verlag, 1979), 90.

8. Kurt Mehner, *Die Deutsche Wehrmacht 1939–1945: Führung und Truppe* (Norderstedt, Germany: Militair-Verlag Klaus Patzwall, 1993), 110–13.

9. Tessin, 90.

10. Further details about the administrative measures taken by Himmler to track the assignment and professional development of officers posted to *Volks-Grenadier* divisions can be found in Wolf Keilig's *Das Deutsche Heer 1939–1945*, vol. 3, section 209/9, *"Bearbeitung von Offizierspersonalien aller dem Reichsfuehrer SS unterstellten Truppenteile des Heeres"* (The handling of all army officer personnel subordinated to the Reich Leader of the SS), H.M. 1944 S. 356 Nr. 675. (Bad Nauheim: Podzun Verlag, 1956).

11. Reinhardt, MS. P-065b, 9.

12. Ibid.

13. Wolfgang Fleischer, *Das letzte Jahr des deutschen Heeres 1944–1945* (The last year of the German Army (Wolfersheim, Germany: Podzun-Pallas Verlag, 1997), 125.

14. Edward A. Shils and Morris Janowitz, "Cohesion and Disintegration in the *Wehrmacht* in World War II." *Public Opinion Quarterly*, 12 (summer 1948): 288.

15. Ibid, 285.

16. Ibid, 288.

17. Mehner, 8.

18. Guderian, *Panzer Leader,* 271.

19. Ibid, 307–308.

20. Martin Jenner, *Die Niedersächsische 216./272.Infanterie-Division 1939–1945* (The Lower Saxony 216th/272nd Infantry Division) (Bad Nauheim, Germany: Podzun-Pallas Verlag, 1964), 180.

21. Raymond A. Velasco, *German Wool Fabric and Manufacturing of World War Two,* article posted at www.lostbattalions.com/Resources/RayonArticle.html.

22. US intelligence report on German Fortress Battalions intended to man the *Westwall* and other German defenses from "Fortress Battalions and How They Are Used," US Army, *Intelligence Bulletin*, February 1945.

23. Jenner, *Niedersächsische,* 177.

24. Cormack, AJR. *German Small Arms*. (London: Exeter Books, 1979), 76 and 80.

25. Ibid, 84.

26. Fleischer, 134–35.

27. Conversation with Klaus Schulz, Kesternich, Germany, 5 September 2000.

28. Fleischer, 137.

29. US War Department, *Handbook on German Military Forces*, TM-E 30-451 (15 March 1945), VII-4.

30. In this regard, the US Army's weapons evaluators displayed the same kind of bias that led them in the early 1930s to elevate the Model 1903 A3 Springfield bolt-action rifle over the M1 Garand, probably the finest infantry weapon ever made. American World War One veterans and traditionalists resisted the weapon's introduction, claiming that the M1 was inaccurate, too complicated, and wasteful of ammunition. Despite this resistance, the US Army Ordnance Department adopted it as the standard infantry weapon in 1936. Source: Harry C. Thomson and Lida Mayo, Center of Military History Pub. 10-10, "Ordnance Department: Procurement and Supply" (Washington, D.C.: Historical Division, US Army, 1960), 160–68.

The MP-44 was truly a revolutionary weapon, many of whose features were copied by the Soviet Union in its stupendously successful AK-47, but perhaps due to its all-metal construction and crude appearance, the American evaluators turned their noses up at it rather than evaluate it without their preconceived ideas as to what weapons should look like. Source: U.S. War Department, "Machine Carbine Promoted," *Tactical and Technical Trends,* 57, April 1945.

31. Cormack, 66–67.

32. Ibid, 74.

33. Ibid, 93–94.

34. US War Department, "The New German Machine Gun—M.G. 42," *Technical and Tactical Trends*, 20 (11 March 1943): 28.

35. Cormack, 114.

36. Ibid, 116.

37. For example, during the Battle of Pomerania between 22 February and 9 March 1945, of the 580 Soviet tanks destroyed by elements of *Third Panzer Army*, 380 were destroyed by individual infantrymen using the *Panzerfaust*. Source: Steven H. Newton, *Panzer Operations: The Eastern Front Memoir of Generaloberst Erhard Raus* (Cambridge, Mass.: Da Capo, 2003), 340.

38. Reinhardt, MS. P-065b, vol. 2, 10.

39. Samuel Lewis. *Forgotten Legions: German Army Infantry Policy, 1918–1941* (New York: Praeger, 1985), 48.

40. US War Department, Military Intelligence Service, *The German Squad in Combat* (translation of the German manual), special series no. 9 (25 January 1943): 32.

41. Reinhardt, MS. P-065b, vol. 2, 10.

42. Report: *Stellungsnahme des OB.West zu den Zustandberichten,* by Gerd von Rundstedt to Karl Jodl, 1 December 1944 (reprinted in Edgar Christoffel, *Krieg am Westwall 1944/45* (Trier, Germany: Verlag der Akademischen Buchhandlung Interbook, 1989), 242.

43. *Leaders Pocket Guide,* April 1944. Author's collection.

44. Fleischer, 129.

45. Charles B. MacDonald, *Company Commander* (New York: Bantam, 1978), 123–24.

46. Headquarters, 5th Panzer Army, *Directive on Tactics*, 30 November 1944.

47. Shils and Janowitz, 297.

48. Höhne, *Order of the Death's Head:* 611.

49. Christoph Jahr, *Gewöhnliche Soldaten. Desertion und Deserteure im deutschen und britischen Heer 1914–1918.* (Ordinary soldiers: Desertion and deserters in the German and British Army 1914–1918) (Göttingen, Germany: Vandenhoeck & Ruprecht, 1998), 123.

50. Shils and Janowitz, 291.

51. *"Verpflegung des Soldaten"* in *Lexicon der Wehrmacht,* www.lexicon-der-Wehrmacht.de/inhaltsverzeichnis1.htm.

52. *Handbook on German Military Forces,* VI-18 to VI-19.

53. From *Heeres-Dienstvorschrift* (H.Dv.) 86/1 *"Vorschrift für die Verpflegung der Wehrmacht in besonderem Einsatz."* (Instructions for the supply of the armed forces in special circumstances), (Berlin: Oberkommando des Heeres, 20 June 1940).

54. Bill Mauldin, *Up Front* (New York: Henry Holt, 1945), 172.

55. Dr. Günther Höhne, *Der Feldverpflegungsbeamte* (Berlin: Verlag Bernhard und Graefe, 1939), 262.

56. George Forty, *The Armies of Rommel* (London: Arms & Armour, 1998), 76.

57. *Handbook on German Military Forces,* VI-19.

58. The Quartermaster Food and Container Institute of the Armed Forces, *German Rations and Subsistence Items* (Chicago: Quartermaster Food and Container Institute, May 1947), 10.

Chapter 3

1. Source for the *Grenadier Regiment 398* and the *216th Infantry Division's* history, as well as its conversion into the *272nd Infantry Division* and its participation in the Normandy Campaign can be found in Jenner, *Niedersächsische 216./272.Infanterie-Division.*

2. Füsilier Battalion 272, Strength Report, 23 July 1944.

3. *Mitteilungsblatt der Niedersächsischen 216./272. Infanterie-Division* (Newsletter of the Veterans Association of the Lower Saxony 216th/272nd Infantry Division) 5, (July 1967): 8.

4. Letter from Hans-Gerhard Sandmann, son of Gerhard Sandmann, Hannover, Germany, to the author, 8 January 2007.

5. Jenner, *Niedersächsische,* 174.

6. Conversations with Eduard Zacharuk, Taufkirchen, Germany, 19 August and 7 November 2000.

7. Jenner, *Niedersächsische,* 227.

8. Ibid, 170.

9. Ibid, 175.

10. Christian Zentner and Wolfgang Fischer *"Artillerie von A biz Z"* (Artillery from A to Z) in *Soldaten im Einsatz: Tapferkeit und Pflichterfülung in Angriff und Verteidigung* (Soldiers in action: Bravery and fulfillment of duty in attack and defense) (Hamburg: Jahr Verlag, 1983), 239.

11. Fleischer, 167–68.

12. Ibid, 169–70.

13. *Handbook on German Military Forces,* II-36 and II-40.

14. Oberkommando des Heeres (OKH), *Hinweise für die Führung des Grenadier-Regiments einer Volks-Grenadier Division* (Instructions for the leadership of the grenadier regiment of a volks-grenadier

division) (Generalstab des Heeres, 1a Nr. 313844, 5 September 1944).

15. OKH/GenStdH/Org.Abt. Nr. I/19200/ 44 g.Kdos. v. 18.9.44 (NARA Microfilm Roll T78 R398, frame 6367895).

16. Tessin, vol. 15, 13.

17. *Handbook on German Military Forces*, II-85.

18. Fleischer, 137.

19. Ibid.

20. Ibid, 160.

21. Jenner, *Niedersächsische,* 177.

22. Mehner, 111.

23. Ibid, 166–67.

24. Wolf Keilig, vol. 3, sect. 211, 176.

25. Ibid, 110.

26. Ibid, 111.

27. An excellent German division-level General Staff description and composition written by Jason Pipes can be found at the Feldgrau Historical Research website www.feldgrau.com/articles.php?ID=24.

28. Günter Wegmann, *Die Dienstlaufbahnen der Offiziere des Generalstabes des deutschen Heeres, 1935–1945,* vol. 1 (Osnabrück, Germany: Biblio Verlag, 1995).

Chapter 4

1. The Infantry Assault Badge was instated on 20 December 1939 and was issued in two grades—silver for infantry and bronze for mechanized (*Panzer-Grenadier*) infantry. In order to be eligible, a soldier had to have taken part in at least three infantry assaults on three different days. Source: John R. Angolia, *For Führer and Fatherland: Military Awards of the Third Reich* (San Jose: R. James Bender, 1976), 80.

2. The Close Combat Badge was authorized on 25 November 1942 by Hitler himself in order to recognize those men who had engaged in hand-to-hand combat when unsupported by armor. It came in three grades—bronze for five close-combat days within an eight-month period, silver for ten close-combat days in a twelve-month period, and gold for fifteen or more close-combat days within a fifteen-month period of service. Source: Angolia, 99.

3. Conversation with Else Klein, 2 January 2001.

4. Letter from Helmut Beyer, Göttingen, Germany, to author, 22 December 2000.

5. Interview with Peter Moog, Bad Godesberg, Germany, 19 March 2001.

6. Kurt Klein diary entry, 9 October 1944.

7. A extremely thorough overview of the German Army's training and replacement system appears in the *Handbook on German Military Forces,* I-58 to I-74.

8. Interview with Heinrich Misskampf, Nauheim, Germany, 2 June 2001.

9. *Oberbefehlshaber (OB) West,* message no. 9625/44, dated 26 October 1944. Subject: Transfer of *Volks-Grenadier* divisions to *Army Group B* for the defensive battle of *OB West.* Facsimile of original reproduced in Christoffel, 172.

Chapter 5

1. Jenner, *Niedersächsische,* 177.

2. Ibid. A few weeks later, the Division staff was forced to move back to its initial location at the Pulvermühle, after Allied air attacks destroyed the Waldhotel.

3. Bundesarchive-Militärarchiv (BA-MA), RH 10/106, *Übersicht der in Umgliederung und Auffrischung befindlichen Pz.Jg.Abt.* (Overview of the reorganization and reconstitution of existing antitank battalions), 6.

4. Günther Schmidt, *"Die 272.Volks-Grenadier Division in Eifeleinsatz, 1944/45"* (The 272nd VGD in action in the Eifel, 1944/45) (Hameln, Germany, 2 February 1996), 3. Translation by Ron van Rijt.

5. Gevert Haslob, *Ein Blick zurück in die Eifel, Schicksalweg der 89. Infanterie-Division* (A look back to the Eifel: The fateful path of the 89th Infantry Division) (Emmelshausen, Germany: Condo Verlag, 2000), 81–82.

6. Ibid, 45.

7. Letter from Eduard Zacharuk, Taufkirchen, Germany, 17 January 2001.

8. Interview with Misskampf.

9. Interview with Friedrich Fosselmann, Berg, Germany, 6 May 2001.

10. Letter from Hermann Heiermann, Dinslaken, Germany, 27 July 2000.

11. Kurt Klein diary entry, 30 November 1944.

12. Ibid.

13. An excellent survey of the battle of the Hürtgen Forest in general and the Allied Offensive of 16 November 1944 in particular can be found in a variety of sources, most notably Charles B. MacDonald's *The Siegfried Line Campaign* and *The Battle of the Hürtgen Forest;* Edward G. Miller's *A Dark and Bloody Ground* (College Station: Texas A&M University Press, 1994); and Adolf Hohenstein and Wolfgang Trees' *Hölle im Hürtgenwald.*

14. Gunther Schmidt, "The Counterattack at Bunker 111, 19 November 1944," from *The Flash* (October 2001): 100.

Chapter 6

1. Erich Straube, MS. C-016, *"LXXIV. Armeekorps* from September to December 1944" (USAREUR Series, 4 November 1948), 14.

2. Letter from Otto Gunkel, *8th Company, Grenadier Regiment 981* to *The Flash* (December 1986).

3. Combat Journal, 22nd Infantry Regiment, 4th Infantry Division, entry dated 3 December 1944.

4. The information about losses and the names of the German commanders came from the IPW Report of the daily G-2 Periodic Report, 4th Infantry Division, entry dated 1800 hours 3 December 1944).

5. Rudolf von Gersdorf, MS. A-891, "The Battle of the Hürtgen Forest, November to Early December 1944" (USAREUR Series, November 1945), 26.

6. For a more detailed survey of the history of the *Westwall,* including maps depicting the locations of all of the bunkers emplaced in the Hürtgen Forest, a good source is *Landschaftsverband Rheinland* (Rhineland Outdoors Association), *Der Westwall: Vom Denkmalwert des Unerfreulichen,* vol. 2 (Cologne: Rheinland-Verlag, 1997).

7. OKH, *Hinweise für die Führung des Grenadier-Regiments einer Volks-Grenadier Division,* 4–5.

8. *Heeresgruppe B* Order Number 2691/44, further enunciated in *Weisungen für die Kampfführung* (Letters of instruction for battle leadership), *Anlage* 3, order 0100/44

issued by *5th Panzer Army* under its codename of Military Police Command z.b.V. It was believed that eighty was the largest number of combat troops that could be efficiently led by relatively inexperienced company commanders. Placing the excess troops in *Field Replacement Battalions* would guarantee that the losses suffered in initial contact with the enemy could be quickly replaced, enabling infantry companies to maintain a relatively adequate combat strength throughout the offensive. Source: Heinz Günther Guderian, *Das letzte Kriegsjahr im Westen: die Geschichte der 116.Panzer Division 1944–1945* (Sankt Augustin, Germany: SZ Offsetdruck-Verlag, 1997), 579–85.

9. Ibid, 581.

10. Walter Bruns, *"Gefechtstätigkeit der 89.Infanterie-Division in der Zeit vom 1. Dezember 1944 bis 4. März 1945"* (Combat engagements of the 89th Infantry Division in the time frrom 1 December 1944 until 4 March 1945), MS. P-032a. (USAREUR Series, August 1949), 18–19.

11. 5th Armored Division, After Action Report for December 1944, 5 January 1945, 4.

12. Richard S. Gardner, *Paths of Armor: The Fifth Armored Division in World War II* (5th Armored Division Association, 1950), 167.

13. Percy E. Schramm, Ed. *Kriegstagebuch des Oberkommando der Wehrmacht 1944–1945, Teilband I.* (Bonn: Bernard und Gräfe Verlag, 2002), 428.

14. Battle of the Hürtgen Forest combat interviews with officers from Task Force Boyer (Company B, 10th Tank Battalion, and Company B, 47th Armored Infantry Battalion), Eupen, Belgium, 30 December 1944, interviewed by Forrest C. Pogue and J. M. Topete, 42.

15. Marc F. Griesbach, *Combat History of the 8th Infantry Division in World War Two.* (Divisional Historical Association, Germany, 1945), 12.

16. Miller, 167. These tanks had been previously reported to have been Panzer V "Panthers," though the German records do not support this assertion since none of the units participating in this action were equipped with this particular vehicle.

17. 5th Armored Division, After Action Report, 4.

18. Combat interviews with three officers from Task Force Boyer, 43.

19. Ibid, 46.

20. Bruns, 18.

21. Letter from Hans Wegener to author, 24 July 2004.

22. POW interrogation report, Annex 1, p. 2 of G-2 Periodic Report 151, 8th Infantry Division, 11 December 1944.

23. Miller, 167.

24. Gardner, 168.

25. Bruns, 19.

26. Zacharuk Letter, 2.

Chapter 7

1. Bruns, 19–20.

2. Frank U. Roquemore, *The Operations of the 2nd Ranger Battalion in the Huertgen Forest, 6–8 December 1944 (Rhineland Campaign), Personal experience of a platoon leader.* (Ft. Benning, GA: Advanced Infantry Officer Course, 1948–1949), 17.

3. *Landschaftsverband Rheinland,* 238. The last German telephone contact from the bunker was 0200 hours, though it may have been evacuated even later than that.

4. Miller, 171,

5. Roquemore, 19.

6. *Landschaftsverband Rheinland,* 239.

7. Roquemore, 22.

8. Ibid, 172.

9. Walter Fellgiebel, *Die Ritterkreuz-traeger des Eisernes Kreuzes 1939–1945,* (Wolfersheim, Germany: Podzun Pallas Verlag, 1996), 422.

10. CCR After Action Report, 1–31 December 1944, 5.

11. Excerpted from Alfred E. Baer, *D for Dog: The Story of a Ranger Company* (Privately published, 1946), 9.

12. Bruns, 21.

13. Headquarters, 13th Infantry, Report of Enemy Action, 1–31 December 1944, 4.

14. *Battle Journal,* 2nd Battalion, 28th Infantry, 8th Infantry Division, 1–31 December 1944, 4; and letter from Merrill B. Westhoff, 2nd Battalion, 28th Infantry, 8th Infantry Division.

15. Jenner, *Niedersächsische,* 181.

16. After Action Report 1–31 December 1944, 28th Infantry Regiment, 8th Infantry Division, 5 January 1945, entry dated 13 December 1944.

17. G-2 Report, 8th Infantry Division, 1–31 December 1944, 3.

18. After Action Report for 13 December, *Füsilier Company 272,* 20 December 1944.

19. *Assembly* magazine, October 1946, 22–23 (Journal of the Association of Graduates, US Military Academy, West Point, NY.)

20. Millard Ireland, *Unofficial Combat History of the First Battalion, 28th Infantry Regiment, 8th Infantry Division* (Germany: 28th Infantry Regiment, 1945), 21–22.

21. Morning Reports for 1st Battalion, 28th Infantry Regiment, 8th Infantry Division for 13–15 December 1944.

22. G-3 Combat Journal, 1–31 December 1944, 8th Infantry Division, entry dated 14 December 1944.

23. G-2 Report, 8th Infantry Division, 1–31 December 1944, 4.

24. Zacharuk interview, 3.

25. Ibid.

26. *Füsilier Company 272,* Report to *272nd VGD* Graves Registration Officer, 5 January 1945.

27. Interviews with Fritz Fosselmann and Heinrich Misskampf; and the diary of Kurt Klein.

28. Keilig, vol. 3, sect. 211, 172.

29. Wegmann, vol. 2.

30. The complete König biography can be found online at www.islandfarm.fsnet.co.uk.

Chapter 8

1. Jean Paul Pallud, *Battle of the Bulge, Then and Now* (London: Battle of Britain Prints International, 1984), 70.

2. Fritz Kraemer, "Operations of Sixth Panzer Army 1944–45" in Danny Parker's *Hitler's Ardennes Offensive: The German View of the Battle of the Bulge* (London: Greenhill, 1997), 41.

3. Erwin Kaschner, MS. B-092, *"326th Volksgrenadier Division (Ardennen)"* (USAREUR Series, 1946), 2; and Bruns, 24.

4. LXVII Corps, *Abt. 1a Nr. 80/44, Korpsbefehl Nummer 1 fuer den Angriff beiderseits Monschau* (Corps order number 1 for

the assault on both sides of Monschau), Korps Gefechtstand, 12 December 1944, 1, para. 5.a.

5. LXVII. Corps, *Abt. 1a Nr. 89/44, Bereitstellung der Infanterie-Verbände* (Assembly areas for the infantry formations), Korps Gefechtstand, 12 December 1944, 1, paragraph III. 1) a; and Bruns, 24.

6. Bruns, 24.

7. Jenner, *Niedersächsische,* 183–84; and LXVII. Corps, *Abt. 1a Nr. 94/44, Nachstehender Angriffsplan,* Korps Gefechtsstand, 13 December 1944, 1.

8. Otto Gunkel, *"Tod und Vernichtung: Winterkrieg 1944/45"* in *Monschauer Land* (Monschau: Das Monschauer Land Jahrbuch, 1990), 110.

9. Bruns, 22.

10. *Feindnachrichtenblatt Nr. 2, 326th VGD, Abt. Ic, Nr. 757/44 geheim, Divisions-Gefechtstand,* 13 December 1944, 2.

11. *OB West Meldungen und Befehle, Mittagsmeldung,* 13 December 1944.

12. Schmidt, *"Die 272.Volks-Grenadier Division in Eifeleinsatz, 1944/45,"* 7.

13. Letter from Hans Wegener, 14 September 2004.

14. Letter from Josef Stefan, Baden, Austria, to author, 10 May 2005.

15. Jenner, *Niedersächsische,* 181; and Johann Reineke, *"Verteidigung in Kesternich, Herbst und Winter 1944 Auszug aus meinen Kriegsnotizen,"* letter, 11 August 1954 to citizens of Kesternich, 1.

16. Bruns, 22.

17. Annex 2 to G-2, 78th Infantry Division Periodic Report Number 5, "IPW Report No. 2," 14 December 1944, 1.

18. Reineke, 1–2.

19. *OB West, Meldungen und Befehle, Tagesmeldung,* 14 December 1944.

20. Otto Hitzfeld, MS. A-937 *"Ardennen-Offensive Dezember 1944 am rechten Flügel"* (USAREUR Series, February 1946), 3.

21. BA-MA, RH 10/106, 6.

22. BA-MA, WF03-4694, *Kriegstagebuch Oberbefehlshaber West,* Para. 4, 12 (footnote).

23. Tessin, vol. 9, 159–60.

24. Arnulf Wöstmann, *"Erinnerungen an Kesternich/Eifel Dezember 1944,"* published in *OSS Hemet* (27 November 1992), 9 (The Association of the Local History Kesternich, Germany).

25. Otto Gunkel, *Lebenserinnerungen 1943–1946: Reichsarbeitsdienst, Kriegsdienst, und Kriegsgefangenschaft* (Bad Nauheim, German: Privately published, 1987), 47–49.

26. Willy Nissel, *"Als unbekannte Soldat in der Eifelschlacht."* quoted in Arntz, *Kriegsende 1944/45 im Altkreis Schleiden* (Schleiden, Germany: Kreisarchiv Schleiden, 1984), 174. Nissel had been a 37mm *Flak* gunner assigned to *3rd Company, Panzer Jäger Abteilung 272* and directly took part in the counterattack from the east along with *1st Battalion, Grenadier Regiment 753, 326th VGD.* This self-propelled system consisted of the 37 mm Model 36 *Flak* gun mounted on a Sd.Kfz.7/2 half-track. Often, the crews up-armored their vehicles and gun mounts, providing a modicum of armored protection that enabled these systems to be used in direct ground combat. The gun had a maximum effective horizontal range of approximately 7,000 meters and was able to fire up to eighty rounds per minute with a muzzle velocity of 2,690 feet per second.

27. Hans Uhl, typewritten account of the battle presented to Eugen König, Bitburg, Germany, 1962 (quoted in Hohenstein and Trees, 220–21).

28. Jenner, *Niedersächsische,* 182. Later, this NCO would be awarded the Iron Cross 1st Class for his actions.

29. After Action Report, 78th Infantry Division, 1–31 December 1944, 14.

30. Ibid, 15.

31. Interview with William E. Brubeck, S-3, 2nd Battalion, 310th Infantry, 78th Infantry Division, Korbach, Germany, 18 May 1945 by Robert E. Maxwell, 2nd Information and Historical Services Unit.

32. Uhl, quoted in Hohenstein and Trees, 220–21.

33. Ibid.

34. Letter from Hans Wegener, 6 October 2004.

35. Nissel, 175.

36. 78th Infantry Division Historical Association, *Lightning: The History of the*

78th Infantry Division (Washington, D.C.: Infantry Journal Press, 1947). 55.

37. Interview with William E. Brubeck, 6.

38. Hohenstein and Trees, 223.

39. *Lightning,* and consolidated casualty reports from 309th, 310th, and 311th Infantry Regiments. These totals do not include divisional troops. The division history and other accounts purport that the division was attacked by the *10th Panzer Division,* although that division had officially disbanded in May 1943. There were also rumors that *SS* troops had taken part in the action, but these proved unfounded. Source: *Lightning,* 55.

40. As it turned out, *1st Battalion, Grenadier Regiment 753* suffered heavy casualties during its short commitment in Kesternich. The return march to its parent division took longer than anticipated and it arrived almost twenty-four hours late, too late to carry out its original mission. As a result of this and other related factors, the attack by the *326th VGD* against Monschau was too weak to overpower the defenders from the US 99th Infantry Division and 38th Mechanized Cavalry Squadron. This failure along northern shoulder of the offensive allowed the Americans to immediately exert pressure on *I SS Panzer Corps.* This in turn contributed to the inability of Sepp Dietrich's *Sixth Panzer Army* to break out to the open ground beyond the Elsenborn Ridge.

Chapter 9

1. *OB West, Meldungen und Befehle, Abendmeldung vom 19 December 1944,* 1.

2. Schmidt, *"Die 272.Volks-Grenadier Division in Eifeleinsatz, 1944/45,"* 6.

3. Postwar statement by Eugen König, in Hohenstein and Trees, 235.

4. *Kampfgruppe Funke* was a hastily assembled mishmash of survivors of *Grenadier Regiment 1056's 2nd Battalion,* as well as stragglers, replacements, and returning convalescents. With little cohesion and no time to prepare their defense, they were caught off guard by the American's attack. See IPW Report number 155, G-2 Periodic Report, 8th Infantry Division, 15 December 1944, 2.

5. After Action Report, 311th Infantry Regiment, 78th Infantry Division, 1–31 December 1944, entry for 15 December 1944.

6. Daily Morning Report, 3rd Battalion, 311th Infantry Regiment, 15 December 1944; and telephonic interview with Robert A. McChord, July 2001.

7. Schneider interrogation in Headquarters, 78th Infantry Division, Annex 2 (Consolidated IPW Report) to G-2 Periodic Report Number 5, 1800 hours 16 December to 1800 hours 17 December 1944, 2.

8. Schmidt, *"Die 272.Volks-Grenadier Division in Eifeleinsatz, 1944/45,"* 7. Schmidt's battalion, *2nd Battalion, Grenadier Regiment 982,* was also required to link up on its left flank with the battle group from *Grenadier Regiment 981,* which was defending the area south of Simmerath after taking the western approaches to Kesternich the previous evening. The deployment of three separate battalions in the darkness during the early morning hours of 16 December seems to have contributed to the overall level of confusion after the successful counterattack of 15 December, leaving one with the impression that the defense of the western outskirts of Kesternich was an unimportant task. Nothing could have been farther from the truth.

9. Reineke, 10.

10. Zacharuk interview, 3.

11. Reineke, 10–11.

12. Ibid.

13. Consolidated IPW Report to G-2 Periodic Report, 78th Infantry Division, 17 December 1944, 2.

14. Ibid., 13–18 December 1944.

15. After Action Report, 78th Infantry Division, 1–31 December 1944, 18.

16. Ibid.

17. *OB West, Meldungen und Befehle, Abendmeldung,* entries from 19 and 23 December 1944.

18. After Action Report, 78th Infantry Division for Period 1–31 January 1945, 1700 hours 5 February 1945, 24.

19. Ibid.

20. This was the division's estimated combat strength or *Kampfstärke,* not total strength. In actuality, the division probably had between 7,000 to 8,000 men assigned,

including its combat support and combat service support elements, such as the division's medical company, maintenance company, and the various logistical elements in the regimental and battalion trains.

21. Even *Generalmajor* König, who had been in action continuously since the Normandy Invasion, took a little time off for himself at the beginning of January 1945. During the week or so he was on leave, command of the division was temporarily placed in the hands of *Oberst* Hinrich Warrelmann, a Knight's Cross with Oak Leaves holder who had previously commanded *Grenadier Regiment 502* of the *290th Infantry Division* on the Eastern Front. Warrelmann ended the war as a *Generalmajor* in command of the *183rd VGD.* (Wolf Keilig, vol. 3, *"Die Generalität des Heeres im 2. Weltkrieg,"* 211, 356.)

Chapter 10

1. After Action Report, 78th Infantry Division for 1–31 January 1945, 5 February 1945, 17.

2. Ibid, 18.

3. Peukert, Günther. *"Der Einsatz in der Eifel im Winter 1944/45"* in *Alte Kameraden,* 3 (1995): 13.

4. "In der HKL" by *Oberleutnant* Karl Bolzmann, *Grenadier Regiment 980,* letter dated 9 January 1945, *Mitteilungsblatt* 5 (July 1967): 24.

5. After Action Report, 311th Infantry, 1 to 31 January 1945, 6.

6. Neil Short, *Germany's West Wall: The Siegfried Line* (Oxford, UK: Osprey, 2004), 16–17; and 7Grad.org, *Regelbau 11 Gruppenunterstand mit angehängtem Kampfraum,* description found at www.7grad.org/Exkursionen/Westwall/Der_Buhlert/Bunker_139_40/bunker_139_40.html.

7. *Combat Journal: The Story of the Timberwolf Regiment of the 78th Lightning Division in World War II, 1944–1945* (Privately Published, 311th Infantry Association, September 1945), 24.

8. Interview with Peter Moog, Bonn, Germany, 19 March 2001.

9. The official account of events from the perspective of *Füsilier Company 272,* except where otherwise noted, are found in the

collection of documents from that company: The two official after-action reports written by *Leutnant* Wegner and *Hauptmann* Heldt, sworn statements from *Feldwebeln* Mizioch and Dirksen, the *Kriegstagebuch* of *Füsilier Company 272* for the period 3 to 11 January 1945 as well as casualty reports for the same period.

10. Statement by John Robinson, 24 April 2001.

11. For a detailed description of this type of bunker, refer to the 7grad.org website, at http://www.7grad.org/Exkursionen/Westwall/Stadtwald_AC/stadtwald_ac.html. The text is in German, but the photos and diagrams are useful even for the non-German reader.

12. Interview with Peter Moog, Bonn, Germany, 19 March 2001.

13. After Action Report, 311th Infantry Regiment, 1 to 31 January 1945, 7.

14. Statement from Gus E. Hank, 26 April 2001.

15. *Combat Journal,* 24.

16. Statement from Ed Malouf, Dallas Texas, 8 June 2001.

17. After Action Report, 311th Infantry, 1–31 January, 7.

18. Letter from Maria Horstkotte, wife of Heinrich Horstkotte, Kirchlengern Germany, 6 January 2001.

19. Telephonic interview with Else Klein, 2 January 2001.

20. Since the war, all of those killed or missing during the battle between 4 and 6 January 1945 have been accounted for.

21. Jenner, *Niedersächsische,* 187.

22. Ibid.

23. Tessin, vol. 4, 4.

24. Schmidt, *"Die 272.Volks-Grenadier Division in Eifeleinsatz, 1944/45,"* 8.

25. Jacob Goldman, Ninth Army Historical Officer, "Raids on the West Bank of the Kall River: A Preliminary Operations to the Taking of the Roer River Dams 8–17 January 1945." Headquarters, 78th Infantry Division, 22 January 1945, 11–12.

26. Schmidt, *"Die 272.Volks-Grenadier Division in Eifeleinsatz, 1944/45,"* 9.

27. Goldman, 27.

28. Heinrich Mueller, quoted in Hohenstein and Trees, 254.

29. Schmidt, *"Die 272.Volks-Grenadier Division in Eifeleinsatz, 1944/45,"* 11.

30. Ibid, 10.

31. Goldman, 33.

32. Schmidt, *"Die 272.Volks-Grenadier Division in Eifeleinsatz, 1944/45,"* 11.

33. Ibid, 12.

34. After Action Report, 78th Infantry Division, January 1945, 17.

35. Ibid, 24.

36. Gunkel, *"Lebenserrinerungen,"* 51.

37. Schmidt, *"Die 272.Volks-Grenadier Division in Eifeleinsatz, 1944/45,"* 9.

38. Jenner, *Niedersächsische*, 188.

Chapter 11

1. Püchler, Karl, MS. B-118, "The Rhineland—LXXIV Armeekorps—the Periods from 2 to 27 October 1944 and 16 December to 23 March 1945" (USAREUR Series, 28 July 1946), 6.

2. Gustav von Zangen, MS. B-811, "Fifteenth Army: Defense of the Roer and Rhine 22 November 1944 to 9 March 1945," part 4 (USAREUR Series, 15 November 1947), 48.

3. Arthur Jüttner, *Retreat of the 62nd Volks-Grenadier Division from the Ardennes and Defense of the Westwall, 27 December 1944 to 30 January 1945* (Morsbach, Germany), 1.

4. Von Zangen, MS. B-811, part 4, 58.

5. Ibid, 59.

6. Assessment of German morale in von Zangen, MS. B-811, part 4, 60.

7. Charles B. MacDonald, *The Last Offensive* (CMH, 1973), 72.

8. Miller, 191.

9. Ibid.

10. *Lightning*, 81.

11. Miller, 192.

12. Burner, John W., Operations of the 2nd Battalion, 311th Infantry in the Attack on Kesternich, Germany, 30 January to 1 February 1945 (Fort Benning, Georgia: Advanced Infantry Officer's Class, The Infantry School, 1949), 45.

13. Ibid, 29.

14. Ibid, 30–31.

15. Ibid, 45.

16. Ibid.

17. MacDonald, *Last Offensive*, 73.

18. Burner, 39.

19. *Lightning*, 88; and Burner, 39.

20. Burner, 39.

21. Gerd Hörner, Face to Face: Kesternich, Germany, January 29–31, 1945 (Hannover, Germany: unpublished manuscript).

22. Gunkel, 53.

23. *Lighting*, 90–91.

24. Von Zangen, MS. B-811, part 4, 49.

25. Combat interview, 39th Infantry Regiment, 9th Infantry Division, *The Fight to the Roer, 9th Infantry Division 30 January to 10 February 1945*, "Walherscheid, Dreiborn, Herhan and Morsbach," 18 February 1945. Interviewed by A. J. Webber, V Corps. (Carlisle, PA: US Army Military History Institute), 3–4.

26. Ibid, 4.

27. Letter from Hellmund Aretz, Krefeld, Germany, 21 March 2001.

28. Hohenstein and Trees, 278.

29. Nissel, 178.

30. Letter from Helmut Aretz, Krefeld, Germany, 8 December 1994.

31. Joseph B. Mittelman, *Eight Stars to Victory: A History of the Veteran Ninth US Infantry Division* (Columbus, OH: The Ninth Infantry Division Association, 1948), 305–6.

32. Nissel, 178.

33. Combat interviews, 1st Battalion, 39th Infantry, 3.

34. Nissel, 178.

35. Mittelman, 306.

36. Combat interview, 1st Battalion, 39th Infantry, 4.

37. Mittelman, 307.

38. Jüttner, 2.

39. Combat interview, 1st Battalion, 39th Infantry, 8.

40. Püchler, MS. B-118, 9.

41. Ibid.

42. Entry for 6 February 1945, Combat Journal, *Füsilier Company 272*.

Chapter 12

1. Wagener, Carl. MS. A-964, "Army Group B: Report of the Chief of Staff. Results of the Ardennes Offensive, 25 January–21 March 1945" (USAREUR Series, 4 February 1946), 22. Apparently, the German high

command was unaware that the Allies had no plans to advance beyond Gemünd, deciding to wait until Schmidt was taken before resuming the advance. The Germans puzzlement is understandable, however, in light of the fact that it was virtually open for the taking.

2. Gerd Hörner, letter to *The Flash*, 2006, no. 2 (April 2006): 29. (Translated by Merle Hill).

3. Written postwar report by Eugen König, as quoted in Hohenstein and Trees, 282.

4. Letter from Hans Wegener to author, 17 September 2004.

5. BA-MA, RW 4 von 636, *Meldung einsatzbereite Panzer bei OB West am 5 Februar 1945* (Report of combat ready tanks, 5 February 1945).

6. After-Action Report, G-2, 78th Infantry Division, for the month of February 1945, 27.

7. König quoted in Hohenstein and Trees, 282.

8. *Attack for Schmidt and the Schwammenauel Dam 30 January to 10 February 1945.* Combat interviews, compiled by Forrest C. Pogue, Historian, V Corps, 34–35

9. Von Zangen, MS. B-811, part 4, 50.

10. Ibid.

11. MacDonald, *Last Offensive,* 75.

12. Schmidt, *"Die 272.Volks-Grenadier Division in Eifeleinsatz, 1944/45,"* 12–13.

13. Jenner, *Niedersächsische,* 190.

14. König quoted in Hohenstein and Trees, 282.

15. Miller, 196.

16. König quoted in Hohenstein and Trees, 282.

17. Jenner, *Niedersächsische,* 190.

18. *Attack for Schmidt and the Schwammenauel Dam,* 46.

19. Ibid.

20. König quoted in Hohenstein and Trees, 282.

21. Prisoner of War Interrogation Report, V Corps, 8 February 1945, as copied in the 82nd Airborne Division Annex No. 2 to the G-2 Situation Report Summary No. 17, 8 February 1945, 1.

22. *Attack for Schmidt and the Schwammenauel Dam,* 60.

23. Hohenstein and Trees, 284.

24. Püchler, MS. B-118, 11. The G-2 of the 78th Infantry Division reported later that elements of the *9th Panzer Division* were also committed to the delaying operation, but the German records do not support this assertion, nor does the 78th Infantry Division's POW interrogation report.

25. Von Zangen, MS. B-811, part 4, 50.

26. Jenner, *Niedersächsische,* 190.

27. *Lightning,* 115.

28. Hohenstein and Trees, 284.

29. Mittelman, 311–12.

30. Thomas P. Lockhart Jr., *Diehard: History of the 309th Infantry Regiment.* (Durham, NC: 78th Infantry Division Veterans Association, June 1990), 17.

31. *Lightning,* 117–18; and Lockhart, 17.

32. *Lightning,* 119–20.

33. Von Zangen, MS. B-811, part 4, 50.

34. Hohenstein and Trees, 285.

35. Manteuffel quoted in *The Last Offensive,* 82.

36. *Lightning,* 128.

37. Interview with Peter Moog, Bonn, Germany, 19 March 2001.

38. Interview with Günter Ecker, Herschweiler, Germany, 17 September 2000.

39. Tessin, vol. 14, 199.

40. Letter from Wilfried Wilts, Emden, Germany, 13 June 2001.

41. MacDonald, *Battle of the Hürtgen Forest,* 195–96.

42. MacDonald, *Siegfried Line Campaign,* 617.

43. Ibid.

44. In order to learn more about the Battle of the Hürtgen Forest, there are several excellent works that approach the subject from perspectives ranging from that of individual participants to those that view the battle from the top down. Two of the more substantive works on the topic are Miller's *A Dark and Bloody Ground* and MacDonald's *The Battle of the Hürtgen Forest.* The battle still elicits considerable controversy in the United States and the United Kingdom, though there is surprisingly little sentiment about the event in modern Germany, except by a limited number of military historians such as Klaus Schulz, Gevert Haslob, Adolf Trees, and the late Adolf Hohenstein. Most German veterans

and their offspring see the battle merely as yet another tragedy in a war filled with tragedy and suffering. If they remark on it at all, they often view it in the overall context of the Battle of Aachen.

Chapter 13

1. MacDonald, *Last Offensive*, 162.
2. Ibid, 185.
3. Ibid, 137 and 139–40.
4. *Attack for Schmidt and the Schwammenauel Dam*, 91.
5. Jenner, *Niedersächsische*, 190–91.
6. Ibid, 190.
7. Ibid, 191.
8. Ibid, 135.
9. *Lightning*, 133.
10. Wegener, MS. A-964, 32.
11. *Lightning*, 134.
12. Ibid, 135.
13. Ibid, 139.
14. Wilfried Wilts letter.
15. Ecker interview, 17 September 2000.
16. Schramm, vol. 4/7.
17. Jenner, *Niedersächsische*, 192.
18. Company casualty reports, *Füsilier Company 272*.
19. *Lightning*, 150.
20. Hitzfeld, MS. B-101, "Battles in the Neighborhood on the West Wall 26 January–6 March 1945," part 1 (USAREUR Series, undated), 25.
21. Gustav von Zangen. MS. B-828, "Fifteenth Army Defensive Actions at the Roer and the Rhine from 22 November 1944 to 22 March 1945," part 6: British-American Large-scale Attack across the Roer and the Rhine (USAREUR Series, 23 February 1948), 26; and Hitzfeld, MS. B-101, 24.
22. Von Zangen. MS. B-828, part 6, 27.
23. Hitzfeld, MS. B-101, part 1, 29.
24. Von Zangen, MS. B-828, part 6, 28.
25. Ibid, 32.
26. Hitzfeld, MS. B-101, part 1, 37. Incidentally, the 38th Cavalry Reconnaissance Squadron, which lay in the path of the *277th VGD*'s counterattack, lost only two or three vehicles and less than a dozen men, but inflicted thirty or forty casualties and captured over 100 prisoners on 7 March 1945

(After Action Report, 1–31 March 1945, 38th Cavalry Reconnaissance Squadron, 7–9). Clearly, *General der Infanterie* Hitzfeld had been given a highly optimistic, but inaccurate situation report from the 277th VGD!
27. After Action Report, 38th Cavalry Reconnaissance Squadron, 102nd Cavalry Group, Mechanized, 1–31 March 1945, 10–11.
28. Von Zangen, MS. B-828, part 6, 35.
29. Hitzfeld, MS. B-101, Part 1, 31.
30. Interview with Peter Moog, Bonn, Germany, 19 March 2001.
31. Jenner, *Niedersächsische*, 192.
32. Günther Peukert, "Von der Eifel in den Ruhrkessel" in *Alte Kameraden* 8 (1995): 28.
33. Jenner in *Mitteilungsblatt*, 13–18.
34. Josef Stefan, Baden, Austria, letter to author, 24 January 2005.
35. Jenner, *Niedersächsische*, 193.
36. Jenner in *Mitteilungsblatt*, 16–17.
37. Walter E. Lauer, *Battle Babies: The Story of the 99th Infantry Division* (Nashville, Battery Press, 1985), 217–18.
38. MacDonald, *Last Offensive*, 223.
39. *Lightning*, 157.

Chapter 14

1. Jenner, *Niedersächsische*, 193.
2. Jenner, in *Mitteilungsblatt*, 16–17.
3. Otto von Hitzfeld, MS. B-101, part 2, Battles in the Region of the Rhine from 6 to 21 March 1945, 52.
4. Ibid, 52–53
5. Interview with Thomas S. Bishop, Asst. G-3, 99th Infantry Division, 20 March 1945, "The Remagen Bridgehead 7–21 March 1945," as interviewed by John S. Howe, III US Corps Historical Section (Carlisle, PA: US Army Military History Institute), 6.
6. Combat interviews, ibid, 4.
7. From the chronicle of Pastor Peter Hellbach, *Chronik der Pfarrei Hönningen* (Chronicles of the Hönningen Parish), (Hönningen, Germany), as quoted in Jakob Weiler's *Tagebuch* (daily journal) (Unpublished manuscript), 34
8. Combat interviews, 1st Battalion, 394th Infantry Regiment, 99th Infantry Division, "The Battle for Hönningen, 15–17 March

1945," conducted by John S. Howe, III US Corps Historical Section, 3 April 1945. (Carlisle, PA: US Army Military History Institute), 5.

9. Ibid, 2.

10. Hitzfeld, MS. B-101, Part 2, 53–54.

11. Interview with Hermann Gehle, Heilbronn, Germany, 17 February 2001, 1.

12. Ibid.

13. Combat interview, 1st Battalion, 394th Infantry, 99th Infantry Division, The Battle for Hönningen, 15–17 March 1945, 5.

14. Interview with Jakob Weiler, Hönningen, Germany, 19 March 2001.

15. Bericht *"Lederstrumpf" an Kommando "Strandkoppel," nach Generalkommodos Fernschreiben von Oberleutnant Mitbauer, den 11 März 1945*. From the papers of Alexander Mitbauer, in the possession of Jakob Weiler of Bad Hönningen

16. The oral interviews conducted with key leaders from 1st Battalion, 394th Infantry make no mention at all of any supporting German artillery, except for *Flak*, during the battle. The presence of the German tank was also confirmed in a radio message by *Oberleutnant* Mitbauer to *Fifteenth Army*, who was assigned to serve as the liaison officer for the *Kriegsmarine* demolitions team being sent to Hönningen. (Source: *Bericht "Lederstrumpf"*). The parent unit of this lone tank unfortunately can no longer be ascertained.

17. Jenner, *Niedersächsische*, 194.

18. William C. C. Cavanaugh, *Dauntless: A History of the 99th Infantry Division* (Dallas: Taylor, 1994), 299.

19. Ibid.

20. Combat interview, 1st Battalion, 394th Infantry, The Battle for Hönningen, 4–5.

21. Martin Jenner, *Gefechtsbericht der III. Bataillon, Artillerie-Regiment 272,* entry for 14 March 1945.

22. Jenner, *Gefechtsbericht,* entry 15 March 1945.

23. Jenner, *Niedersächsische*, 194.

24. Jenner, in *Mitteilungsblatt,* 14–15.

25. Gehle interview, 2.

26. Combat interview, 1st Battalion, 394th Infantry, The Battle for Hönningen, 6.

27. Weiler interview.

28. Wilts letter.

Chapter 15

1. Jenner, *Niedersächsische*, 194.

2. From *"Kurtscheid—Frontübergang im zweiten Weltkrieg,"* (Kurtscheid—When the frontline passed through in World War Two) from http://www.astro.uni-bonn.de/~wittlich/kurtscheid/dunkel.html.

3. Jenner, *Niedersächsische*, 194.

4. Combat interview, 1st Battalion, 394th Infantry, The Battle for Hönningen, 4–5.

5. General Millikin, though he had successfully exploited the seizure of the Ludendorff Bridge at Remagen, incurred the wrath of General Hodges for III Corps' "steady but unspectacular" progress in expanding the bridgehead. After informing General Omar Bradley that the "troops have had bad leadership in this bridgehead battle," Hodges relieved Millikin of command on 17 March and replaced him with Major General James A. Van Fleet, former commander of the 90th Infantry Division (see MacDonald's *The Last Offensive,* 229).

6. MacDonald, *Last Offensive,* 344–45.

7. Von Zangen, MS. B-848, part 6, 3.

8. MacDonald, *Last Offensive,* 345.

9. Jakob Weiler, *Tagebuch* (daily journal) (Unpublished manuscript), entry for 21 March 1945.

10. Interview with Gehle, 2.

11. Jenner, *Niedersächsische*, 198.

12. From *"Kurtscheid—Frontübergang im zweiten Weltkrieg,"* at www.astro.uni-bonn.de, 1.

13. Weiler daily journal, entry for 21 March 1945.

14. Von Zangen, MS. B-829, "Fifteenth Army: Defensive Engagements along the Roer and the Rhine 22 Nov 1944 to 22 March 1945, part 7: Battles of the Remagen Bridgehead (9–22 March 1945)," 15.

15. Von Zangen, MS B-848, 4.

16. Ibid, 6.

17. Wegener, MS. A-964, 51.

18. After Action Report, 99th Infantry Division, March 1945, 13.

19. Combat interview with Howard B. St. Clair, G-2, 99th Infantry Division, Breakout at Remagen Bridgehead, 23–26 March 1945, 2. Interview by A. J. Webber.

20. Ibid.

21. Hitzfeld, MS. B-101, "Part 2: Battles in the Region of the Rhine 6–21 March 1945," 54.

22. Jenner, *Niedersächsische,* 194–95.

23. Lauer, 220.

24. Jenner, *Niedersächsische,* 196–97.

25. Lauer, 220.

26. Ibid, 219.

27. Jenner, *Gefechtsbericht,* entry dated 23 March 1945.

28. From personal diary of *Oberleutnant* Wilhelm Engel, aide-de-camp of *General der Infanterie* Hitzfeld, entry dated 23 March 1945. Engel had also been assigned as the Corps' *NSFO,* with orders to report on Hitzfeld's activities.

29. After Action Report, 99th Infantry Division, for the period 23–26 March 1945, entry 26 March 1945.

30. War Diary, 106th Panzer Brigade, 1–31 March 1945, entry 25 March 1945.

31. MacDonald, *Last Offensive,* 347.

32. Ibid.

Chapter 16

1. Gehle interview, 6.

2. Letter from Rudolf Ips to author, 12 July 2004 and interview with Friedrich Adrario, 5 October 2005.

3. Jenner, *Niedersächsische,* 199.

4. Püchler, MS. B-549, *Battles of the LXXIV Army Corps from 25 March to 16 April 1945: East of the Rhine and in the Ruhr Pocket* (USAREUR Series, 12 May 1947), 6.

5. Peukert, *"Von der Eifel in den Ruhrkessel"* in *Alte Kameraden,* 8, (1995): 28.

6. Ibid, 11.

7. Engel in *Alte Kameraden,* vol. 20/72, 28.

8. Peukert in *Alte Kameraden* 8, 28.

9. König, MS. B-171, *"Kämpfe in Rheinland"* (Engagements in the Rhineland) (USAREUR Series, June 1948), 8.

10. Peukert in *Alte Kameraden* 8, 28.

11. Corelli Barnett, *Hitler's Generals: Authoritative Portraits of the Men Who Waged Hitler's War* (New York: Quill/William Morrow, 1989), 330.

12. Max Hastings, *Armageddon: The Battle for Germany, 1944–1945.* (New York: Vintage/Random House, 2005), 490.

13. Fosselmann interview, 3.

14. Gehle interview, 7.

15. Jenner, *Niedersächsische,* 202.

16. Estor, Fritz, MS. B-581, "Eleventh Army 1–23 April 1945" (USAREUR Series, 9 June 1947), 1–2.

17. Selected Intelligence Reports, Office of the Assistant Chief of Staff, G-2, US 1st Infantry Division December 1944—May 1945, 99.

18. Estor in MS. B-581, 3–4.

19. Lucht in MS. B-151, 48–49.

20. Alfred Sturm, MS. B-318, "Combat Sector Southeast Harz Mountains, 12–23 April 1945" (USAREUR Series, 1947), 1.

21. Jenner, *Niedersächsische,* 202.

22. Erich Bernutz interview, Wernigerode, Germany, 12 May 2001.

23. Reports, 1st Infantry Division, 82.

24. Ulrich Saft. *Krieg in der Heimat: bis zum bitteren Ende im Harz* (War in the homeland: To the bitter end in the Harz) (Walsrode, Germany: Militaerbuchverlag Saft, 1996), 311.

25. Reports, 1st Infantry Division, 93.

26. Ibid, 99.

27. Ibid, 92.

28. Ibid, 98.

Appendix A
Command and Staff,
272nd Volks-Grenadier Division*

Division Commander:
  Oberst Friedrich Kittel, acting commander 14–30 September 1944
  Oberst Georg Kossmala, 30 September–13 December 1944
  Generalmajor Eugen König, 13 December 1944–14 April 1945
General's Aides-de-Camp:
  Oberleutnant von der Malsberg
  Oberleutnant Mehler
  Leutnant Most
Ia (Chief Operations Officer):
  Oberstleutnant in Generalstabsdienst (i.G.) Hubert Werner, until
      10 September 1944
  Major i.G. Gerhard Höptner, 10 September–13 December 1944
  Major i.G. Hans Uhl, 13 December 1944–14 April 1945
Ib (Division Supply Officer): *Oberstleutnant* Vetzberger
  Assistant *Ib*: *Hauptmann* Colshorn
Ib/Kfz (Division Engineer): *Major* Arne Rasmussen
Ic (Division Intelligence Officer): *Oberleutnant* Petri;
  replaced by *Hauptmann* Heinz Massberg
IIa (Division Officer Personnel Officer [Acting]): *Major* Arne Rasmussen
IIb (Division Enlisted Personnel Officer): *Hauptmann* Schmidt
III (Division Staff Judge Advocate): *Kriegsgerichtsrat* Dr. Twehl
IVa (Division Administrative Officer): *Oberstabsintendant* Bettenhäuser
IVb (Divisional Surgeon): *Oberfeldartzt* Dr. Mestwerdt
IVc (Divisional Veterinarian): *Oberstveterinär* Dr. Michel
Headquarters Company Commander: *Hauptmann* Hermann
Divisional Signal Officer: *Leutnant* Janz
Division Band: *Stabsmusikmeister* Kanngiesser

Volks-Grenadier Regiment 980
Commander: *Oberst* Ewald Burian
Adjutant: *Hauptmann* Hans Witscher, *Oberleutnant* Hermann Gehle
  Headquarters Company: *Leutnant* Josef Stefan
  1st Battalion (1st–4th Companies)
    Commander: *Hauptmann der Reserve* Max Rhein,
        succeeded February 1945 by *Hauptmann* Hans Witscher
    Adjutant: *Leutnant* Ebert

---

* As of 1 October 1944, except where otherwise noted.

2nd Battalion (5th–8th Companies)
   Commander: *Major* Ernst Werner, succeeded November 1944 by
      Hauptmann Adolf Thomae
   Adjutant: *Leutnant* Klaus von Below
13th Company (Infantry Howitzer): not known
14th Company (Anti-tank) Commander: *Oberleutnant* Kurt Hake

Volks-Grenadier Regiment 981
Commander: *Oberstleutnant* Meyer, succeeded by *Oberstleutnant* Hans
   Kleinkorres 1 December 1944
Adjutant: *Hauptmann* Heinz Massberg
   Headquarters Company: *Leutnant* Meier
   1st Battalion (1st–4th Companies)
      Commander: *Major* Gerhard Thürmer
   2nd Battalion (5th–8th Companies)
      Commander: *Major* Jürgen Fittschen, succeeded by *Hauptmann*
         Günther Ragnow on 4 December 1944
   13th Company (Infantry Howitzer) Commander: *Oberleutnant* Knigge
   14th Company (Anti-tank) Commander: *Leutnant* Pieper

Volks-Grenadier Regiment 982
Commander: *Oberstleutnant* Paul Rösener
Adjutant: *Hauptmann* Jung
   Headquarters Company: *Oberleutnant* Lorenz
   1st Battalion (1st–4th Companies)
      Commander: *Hauptmann* Leykauf
      Adjutant: *Leutnant* Petzhold
   2nd Battalion (5th–8th Companies)
      Commander: *Hauptmann* Karl Schneider
      Adjutant: *Leutnant* Günther Schmidt
   13th Company (Infantry Howitzer): not known
   14th Company (Anti-tank): *Hauptmann* Tauschmann

Artillery Regiment 272
Commander: *Oberstleutnant* August Wilbrandt
Adjutant: *Oberleutnant* Gustl Laubach
   Headquarters Battery: *Leutnant* Franke
   1st Battalion (7.5 cm leFK): (1st–3rd Batteries)
      Commander: *Hauptmann* Riedel
      Adjutant: *Leutnant* Weber
   2nd Battalion (10.5 cm leFH): (4th–5th Batteries)
      Commander: *Hauptmann* Weber
      Adjutant: *Leutnant* Simon

3rd Battalion (10.5 cm leFH): (7th–8th Batteries)
Commander: *Major* Martin Jenner
Adjutant: *Leutnant* Strümpler, *Leutnant* Prautsch
4th Battalion (15 cm sFH): (10th–11th Batteries)
Commander: *Hauptmann* Lieser
Adjutant: *Leutnant* Hausmann

Nachschub (Supply) Regiment 272
Commander: *Major* Ritter
Adjutant: *Oberleutnant* Weiss
    Feldzeug (Ordnance) Company 272: *Oberleutnant* Bolzmann
    Instandsetzung (Maintenance) Company 272: *Oberleutnant* Wicke
    Nachschub (Administration and Logistics) Battalion 272:
        Oberstabsintendant Bettenhäuser, *Hauptmann* Hugo Böhm
    Sanitäts (Medical) Company 272: *Oberfeldartzt Dr. med.* Fiedler
    Veterinär (Veterinary) Company 272:
        Oberstabsveterinär Dr. med. vet. Meyer
    Feldpostdienste (Field Post Office) 272: *Fieldpostmeister* Schreiner

Nachrichten (Signal) Battalion 272
Commander: *Major* Schossig
Adjutant: *Oberleutnant* Klaus Lohmann

Pionier (Combat Engineer) Battalion 272
Commander: *Hauptmann* Schlanstein
Adjutant: *Leutnant* Jentsch

Panzerjäger (Anti-Tank) Battalion 272
Commander: *Hauptmann* (later *Major)* Friedrich Adrario
Adjutant: *Oberleutnant* Kynast

Feldersatz (Field Replacement) Battalion 272 and *Kampfschule* (Division Combat School) 272
Commander: *Major* Schütz

Füsilier Company 272
Commander: *Oberleutnant* Heinz Kolb

Appendix B
Volks-Grenadier Division Crew-Served Weapons

Indirect Fire Weapons

Description	Caliber (mm)	Total Weight (lbs.)	Max. Range (meters)	Shell Weight (lbs.)	Qty per Regt./ Div.
Medium Mortar (*Schwerer Granatenwerfer 34*)	80	124	2,400	7.7	12/36
Heavy Mortar (*Granatenwerfer 42*)	120	616	6,035	35	8/24
Light Infantry Gun (*leichte Infanterie Geschutz 18*)	75	880	3,566	13.2	12/38 (incl. 2 w/ Füs. Co.)
Light Howitzer (*leichte Feld Haubitze 18/40*)	105	4,320	12,326	32.75	24/24
Medium Howitzer (*schwere Feld Haubitze 18*)	150	6.05 tons	13,377	95.7	12/12
Field Cannon (*Feldkanone FK 40*)	75	1.57 tons	12,300	12.85	18/18

Antitank Weapons

Description	Caliber (mm)	Total Weight (tons)	Muzzle Velocity (m/sec)	Shell Weight (lbs.)	Speed (km/hr)	Qty per Div.
Medium Antitank Gun (*Panzerabwehr Kanone 40*)	75	1.57	990.5	12.5 (AP)	N/A	9
Tank Destroyer 38 (*Jagdpanzer 38(t) L/48 "Hetzer"*)	75	16.65	989	9 (AP)	37	14

Antiaircraft Weapons

Description	Caliber (mm)	Total Weight (tons)	Muzzle Velocity (m/sec)	Rate of Fire (rds/min)	Range (m)	Qty per Div.
Self-propelled Anti-aircraft gun (*Flak 36 auf Sd.Kfz. 7/2*)	37	11.4	820	120	4,800	9

Source: US War Department Technical Manual TM-E 30-451, *Handbook on German Military Forces,* 15 March 1945; and Uwe Feist, *German Halftracks in Action* (Warren, Mich.: Squadron Signal, 1972).

Appendix C
Standard Organization of a Volks-Grenadier Division and Füsilier Company, September 1944

Volks-Grenadier Division

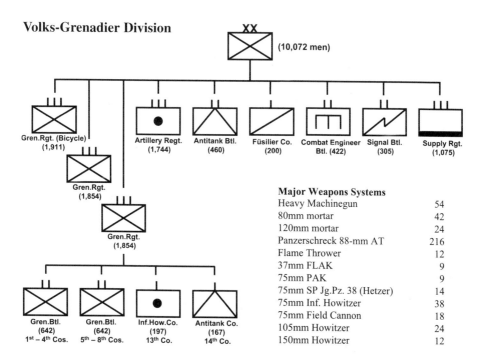

Major Weapons Systems

Heavy Machinegun	54
80mm mortar	42
120mm mortar	24
Panzerschreck 88-mm AT	216
Flame Thrower	12
37mm FLAK	9
75mm PAK	9
75mm SP Jg.Pz. 38 (Hetzer)	14
75mm Inf. Howitzer	38
75mm Field Cannon	18
105mm Howitzer	24
150mm Howitzer	12

Füsilier Company

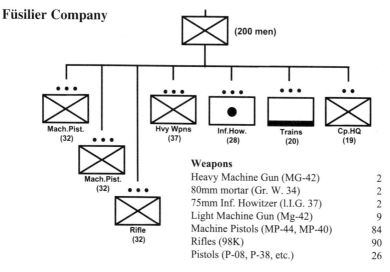

Weapons

Heavy Machine Gun (MG-42)	2
80mm mortar (Gr. W. 34)	2
75mm Inf. Howitzer (l.I.G. 37)	2
Light Machine Gun (Mg-42)	9
Machine Pistols (MP-44, MP-40)	84
Rifles (98K)	90
Pistols (P-08, P-38, etc.)	26

Source: *Kriegsstärkenachweisung (KStN)* 149 V, 1 September 1944.

Organization of a Division Füsilier Company

Element	Officers	Noncommissioned Officers	Enlisted Men	Rifles	Machine Pistol	Pistols	Light Machine Guns	Heavy Machine Guns	Mortars	Infantry Howitzers	RSO*	Horses	Wagons	Bicycles
Co. HQ Plt	1	2	16	10	8	1	0	0	0	0	0	0	0	19
SMG Plt	1	3	28	4	26	2	1	0	0	0	0	0	0	32
SMG Plt	0	4	28	4	26	2	1	0	0	0	0	0	0	32
Rifle Plt	0	4	28	19	9	4	3	0	0	0	0	0	0	32
Hv Wpns Plt	0	7	30	16	9	12	0	2	2	0	1	0	0	35
Inf How Sec	1	4	23	20	5	3	1	0	0	2	2	0	0	12
Co. Trains (Tross)	0	5	15	17	1	2	3	0	0	0	1**	12	6	4
Total	3	29	168	90	84	26	9	2	2	2	4	12	6	166

Source: *Kriegsstärkenachweisung (KStN)* 149 V, 1 September 1944

* RSO: *Raupenschlepper Ost* (Eastern Front Mover)

** The company trains was authorized 1 half-tracked cargo truck (Maultier).

Note: In addition to the 200 men authorized by the *KStN,* companies often carried Russian auxiliaries, or 4 *Hiwis,* on their rolls.

Appendix D
Volks-Grenadier Division Numbering

During the last nine months of the war, a total of forty-nine *Volks-Grenadier Divisions* were activated and organized as such under its unique table of organization and equipment (known in German as the *Kriegsstärkenacherweisung* or *KStN*). The nineteen divisions originally designed specifically to be *Volks-Grenadier Divisions* were formed out of the 32nd Mobilization Wave beginning 31 August 1944. All were to be organized using a standard *KStN* and were to comprise the series numbering *564th* through the *582nd Volks-Grenadier Divisions*. These divisions were to be formed either out of four existing *Schatten* ("shadow") divisions or raised completely from scratch. ("Shadow" divisions were formed primarily from personnel assigned from the *Replacement Army's* manpower pool and organized along the lines of a regular division, though in most cases without appreciable amounts of equipment or experienced leadership. Not assigned a division number, they were used to augment or rebuild existing divisions through their wholesale transfer to form new companies, battalions, and regiments. Under this system, a division that had been shattered in battle and had lost the bulk of its combat troops could quickly and efficiently be reconstituted in a remarkably short period of time, often in two weeks or less.)

Shortly after they had begun their establishment, they were ordered to assume the numbers of nineteen older infantry divisions that had been either wiped out during the summer or to merge with those that had suffered such heavy casualties that they had been pulled out and sent into the interior of Germany to be completely rebuilt. As a result, the following numerical re-designations occurred:

Original Division	Redesignated Division
564th VGD	183rd VGD
565th VGD	246th VGD
566th VGD	363rd VGD
567th VGD	349th VGD
568th VGD	256th VGD
569th VGD	361st VGD
570th VGD	337th VGD
571st VGD	18th VGD
572nd VGD	340th VGD
573rd VGD	708th VGD
574th VGD	277th VGD
575th VGD	272nd VGD
576th VGD	271st VGD
577th VGD	47th VGD

578th VGD	212th VGD
579th VGD	326th VGD
580th VGD	276th VGD
581st VGD	352nd VGD
582nd VGD	26th VGD

Another *Volks-Grenadier Division* was formed from a 31st Mobilization Wave division, *Infantry Division Breslau* on 28 August 1944, actually making it the first *Volks-Grenadier Division,* since it was designated three days before the rest. Intended to serve as a "Shadow" division to replenish the ranks of the *357th Infantry Division* (under the "Division New Type 1944" *KStN*), *Infantry Division Breslau* was instead converted to a *Volks-Grenadier* organizational structure and became the *357th Volks-Grenadier Division.*

A second group of six additional *Volks-Grenadier Divisions* were formed from the 32nd Mobilization Wave on 16 September 1944. Like the first group, they were used to rebuild shattered and destroyed infantry divisions that had been withdrawn to the zone of the interior. Like the nineteen divisions that preceded them, their original 500-series numbers were expunged and replaced by the numbers of the divisions they were used to rebuild. Units so re-designated included the following:

Original Division	Redesignated Division
583rd VGD	62nd VGD
584th VGD	9th VGD
585th VGD	167th VGD
586th VGD	79th VGD
587th VGD	257th VGD
588th VGD	320th VGD

A third group of six *Volks-Grenadier Divisions* were created during the last week of August 1944 out of the 30th Mobilization Wave as grenadier divisions. Again, like the *357th Volks-Grenadier Division,* most of these were built from "shadow" grenadier divisions. Using these as a base, the decimated *16th, 19th,* and *36th Infantry Divisions* were rebuilt as grenadier divisions. Two more, the *560th* and *563rd Grenadier Divisions,* were formed from scratch. Since so many of its NCOs and enlisted men had escaped the destruction of *Army Group Center* in July 1944, the *12th Infantry Division* was rebuilt without being augmented by a "shadow" division, but with a normal intake of new recruits. All six were re-designated as *Volks-Grenadier Divisions* on 9 October 1944. The *12th Volks-Grenadier Division* was a noteworthy exception because it kept the old New Type 1944 Infantry Division organization although it had been officially designated as a *Volks-Grenadier Division.* By December 1944, it had converted to the *Volks-Grenadier Division KStN* as well.

The fourth group that was designated *Volks-Grenadier Divisions* were actually created during the 29th Mobilization Wave, which was called up after 13 July 1944. These were formed originally as "grenadier" divisions using the "Division New Type 1944" *KStN*. These seventeen divisions were supposed to replace many of the infantry divisions that had been lost in June and July 1944 during the destruction of *Army Groups Center* and *North Ukraine*. The first thirteen divisions of this Wave so designated carried the numbers *541, 542, 544, 545, 547, 548, 549, 551, 553, 558, 559, 561,* and *562*. Four other grenadier divisions (*543, 546, 550,* and *552*) were re-designated with the numbers of divisions that had been totally wiped out that summer (the *78th, 45th, 31st,* and *6th Infantry Divisions*, respectively), after Hitler had personally intervened to ensure that their traditions would be maintained. These seventeen divisions were re-designated *Volks-Grenadier Divisions* on 9 October 1944 and reorganized according to the *KStN* developed that summer. Some of these grenadier division's organizational structures remained unchanged, such as the maintaining of a full *Füsilier Battalion*, which under the new *Volks-Grenadier KStN* was supposed to have been reduced to a company.

Several other existing infantry divisions were re-designated as *Volks-Grenadier Divisions* during the last several months of the war, though the evidence indicates that no structural changes were made. This leaves one with the impression that the title was little more than an honorific, since commanders were authorized to request that their divisions be so designated based on their performance in battle. The infantry divisions so renamed were the *211th, 278th, 334th, 347th,* and *462nd Volks-Grenadier Divisions*. The last-named division was the most curious of all, because it was formed from *Division Number 462*. This division was a purely administrative headquarters that was employed as an ad hoc division headquarters during the Battle of Metz from September to October 1944 to control various home defense units and replacement battalions. Though it was renamed as a *Volks-Grenadier Division* on 23 October 1944 in recognition of the tenacious defense of that city, it was destroyed by 17 November and was not reformed. Any resemblance to a true *Volks-Grenadier Division* in the case of the *462nd* was purely coincidental. Although all of these late additions carried the designation, they were *Volks-Grenadier Divisions* in name only and are not considered such for the purposes of this study.

Sources: Gerber, Kurt MS. B-632, Numerical Designations Allotted to the Divisions of the German Army (USAREUR Series, 29 July 1947); Mehner, 110–113; and Tessin, vol. 1, 87–93.

Appendix E
Higher Headquarters of 272nd Volks-Grenadier Division from 2 November 1944 to 12 April 1945

Corps Headquarters

2 November– 10 December 1944	*LXXIV Corps* (*General der Infanterie* Erich Straube)
10–19 December 1944	*LXVII Corps* (*General der Infanterie* Otto Hitzfeld)
19 December 1944– 6 March 1945	*LXXIV Corps* (*General der Infanterie* Karl Püchler)
6–26 March 1945	*LXVII Corps* (*General der Infanterie* Otto Hitzfeld)
26 March–4 April 1945	*LXXIV Corps* (*General der Infanterie* Karl Püchler)
5–12 April 1945	*LVII Panzer Corps* (*Generalleutnant* Walter Botsch)

Army Headquarters

2 November– 10 December 1944	*Seventh Army* (*General der Panzertruppe* Erich Brandenberger)
10–19 December 1944	*Sixth Panzer Army* (*SS-Oberstgruppenführer* Sepp Dietrich)
19 December 1944– 19 February 1945	*Fifteenth Army* (*General der Infanterie* Gustav von Zangen)
19 February– 1 March 1945	*Fifth Panzer Army* (*General der Panzertruppe* Hasso von Manteuffel)
1 March–12 April 1945	*Fifteenth Army* (*General der Infanterie* Gustav von Zangen)

Appendix F
Table of German Rank Equivalents

German Rank	Abbreviation	US Equivalent
Generalfeldmarschall	*G.F.M.*	General of the Army
Generaloberst	*Gen.O.*	General
General der Infantrie, Kavalerie, etc.	*Gen.d.Inf.*	Lieutenant General
Generalleutnant	*Gen.Lt.*	Major General
Generalmajor	*Gen.Maj.*	Brigadier General
Oberst	*O.*	Colonel
Oberstleutnant	*Oberstlt.*	Lieutenant Colonel
Major	*Maj.*	Major
Hauptmann or *Rittmeister*	*Hptm.* *Rittm.*	Captain Captain (of cavalry)
Oberleutnant	*Oberlt.*	First Lieutenant
Leutnant	*Lt.*	Second Lieutenant
Hauptfeldwebel	*Hfw.*	Sergeant Major
Oberfeldwebel	*Ofw.*	Master Sergeant
Feldwebel	*Fw.*	Sergeant First Class
Unterfeldwebel	*Ufw.*	Staff Sergeant
Unteroffizier	*Uffz.*	Sergeant
Obergefreiter	*Ogefr.*	Corporal/Specialist
Gefreiter	*Gef.*	Private First Class
Obergrenadier Oberkannonier, etc.	none	Private Second Class
Grenadier, Kanonier, Funker, etc.	*Gren., Kan.,* etc.	Private

Appendix G
Knight's Cross and German Cross in Gold Holders,
272nd Volks-Grenadier Division

Knight's Cross Holders

Name	Rank	Date	Unit
Adrario, Friedrich	*Major*	26 Dec. 1944	*Antitank Battalion 272*
Burian, Ewald	*Oberst*	4 Oct. 1944	*Grenadier Regiment 980*
König, Eugen	*Generalmajor*	1 Aug. 1942	Division Commander
			Oakleaves 4 Nov. 1943
Kossmala, Georg	*Oberst*	13 Mar. 1942	Division Commander
			Oakleaves 26 Mar. 1944
Thomae, Adolf	*Hauptmann*	24 Feb. 1945	*2nd Battalion, GR 980*
Uhl, Hans	*Major*	22 Jan. 1943	Division *Ia*
Werner, Ernst	*Oberstleutnant*	19 Aug. 1944	*2nd Battalion, GR 980*

German Cross in Gold Holders

Name	Rank	Date	Unit
Ableiter, Walter	*Oberleutnant*	10 Jan. 1944	*Füsilier Company 272*
Adrario, Friedrich	*Major*	6 May 1942	*Antitank Battalion 272*
Burian, Ewald	*Oberst*	21 Oct. 1943	*Grenadier Regiment 980*
Englbrecht, August	*Leutnant*	22 Sep. 1944	*8th Company, GR 980*
Fittschen, Jürgen	*Major*	20 Jun. 1944	*2nd Battalion, GR 981*
Honisch, Johann	*Oberfeldwebel*	14 May 1944	*6th Company, GR 980*
Kleinkorres, Hans	*Oberstleutnant*	29 Jan. 1942	*Grenadier Regiment 981*
Lohrberg, Erich	*Feldwebel*	15 Jun. 1944	*1st Company, GR 980*
Ondrazek, Willi	*Oberfeldwebel*	28 Aug. 1944	*Grenadier Regiment 980*
Ragnow, Günther	*Hauptmann*	25 Mar. 1944	*2nd Battalion, GR 981*
Rasmussen, Arne	*Major*	11 Sep. 1944	*Ib/Kfz* (Div. Engineer)
Rhein, Dr. Max	*Hauptmann*	29 Mar. 1943	*1st Battalion, GR 980*
Rösener, Paul	*Oberstleutnant*	24 Dec. 1941	*Grenadier Regiment 982*
Schneider, Karl	*Hauptmann*	8 Jan. 1943	*2nd Battalion, GR 982*
Thomae, Adolf	*Hauptmann*	20 Jan. 1945	*2nd Battalion, GR 980*
Thürmer, Gerhard	*Major*	30 Sep. 1944	*1st Battalion, GR 981*
Werner, Ernst	*Major*	26 Sep. 1943	*2nd Battalion, GR 980*
Werner, Hubert	*Oberstleutnant*	29 Feb. 1944	*Division Ia*

Appendix H
Füsilier Company 272
Casualties and Replacements
September 1944–March 1945

Monthly Rollup

Month	Assigned	Casualties	Additions	Departed	End of Month Strength
Sept 44	50	0	50 (cadre)	0	50
Oct 44	50	0	157	12	195
Nov 44	195	13	1	4	179
Dec 44	179	62	68	1	184
Jan 45	184	78	52	20	138
Feb 45	138	51	33	9	111
Mar 45	111	201	101	0	22

Total number of personnel serving from 15 September 1944
     to 27 March 1945: 479

Initially assigned to company on 31 October 1944: 207

Total number of known casualties from 15 September 1944
     to 27 March 1945: 405

Total number of replacement from November 1944 to Mar 1945: 255

Total number of personnel transferred out from 15 September 1944
     to 27 March 1945: 48

Total number of personnel present for duty on 27 March 1945: 22

Total number of wounded personnel returned to duty: 11

Casualty rate November 1944 to March 1945: 195 percent

Bibliography

Books and Journal Articles

78th Infantry Division Historical Association, *Lightning: The History of the 78th Infantry Division.* Washington, D.C.: Infantry Journal Press, 1947.

311th Infantry Association, *Combat Journal: The Story of the Timber Wolf Regiment of the 78th Lightning Division in World War II 1944–1945.* Privately published: 311th Infantry Association, 1945.

After the Battle Magazine, 71. "Battle of the Hürtgen Forest." London: Battle of Britain Prints International, 1991

Angolia, John R. *For Führer and Fatherland: Military Awards of the Third Reich.* San Jose: R. James Bender, 1976.

Arntz, Hans-Dieter. *Kriegsende 1944/1945 im Altkreis Schleiden.* Schleiden, Germany: Kreisarchiv Schleiden, 1984.

Assembly magazine, October 1946.

Astor, Gerald. *The Bloody Forest.* New York: Presidio, 2000.

Barnett, Corelli. *Hitler's Generals: Authoritative Portraits of the Men Who Waged Hitler's War.* New York: Quill/William Morrow, 1989.

Baumann, Martin J. *History of the 303rd Engineer (Combat) Battalion.* Berlin: Druckhaus Tempelhof, 1945.

Baer, Alfred E. *D for Dog: The Story of a Ranger Company.* Privately published, 1946.

Brückner, Paul. "The Battle of the Hürtgen Forest." *Truppenpraxis* 3 (1970). Translated by Joseph Whitehorne.

Cavanaugh, William C. C., *Dauntless: A History of the 99th Infantry Division* (Dallas: Taylor, 1994).

Christoffel, Edgar. *Krieg am Westwall 1944/45.* Trier, Germany: Verlag der Akademischen Buchhandlung Interbook, 1989.

Cole, Hugh M. *The Lorraine Campaign.* Washington, D.C.: Historical Division, US Army, 1950.

Cormack, AJR. *German Small Arms.* London: Exeter, 1979.

Currey, Cecil B. *Follow Me and Die.* New York: Stein and Day, 1984.

Fellgiebel, Walter. *Die Ritterkreuztraeger des Eisernes Kreuzes 1939–1945,* Wölfersheim-Berstadt, Germany: Podzun Pallas Verlag, 1996.

Fleischer, Wolfgang. *Das letzte Jahr des deutschen Heeres 1944–1945* (The last year of the German Army, 1944–1945). Wölfersheim-Berstadt, Germany: Podzun-Pallas Verlag, 1997.

Forty, George. *The Armies of Rommel.* London: Arms & Armour, 1998.

Gardner, Richard S. *Paths of Armor: The Fifth Armored Division in World War Two.* Divisional Historical Association, 1950; Nashville: Battery, 1993.

Griesbach, Marc F. *Combat History of the Eighth Infantry Division in World War II*. Divisional Historical Association, 1945.

Guderian, Heinz Günther. *Das letzte Kriegsjahr im Westen: die Geschichte der 116.Panzer Division 1944–1945*. Sankt Augustin, Germany: SZ Offsetdruck-Verlag, 1997.

Guderian, Heinz. *Panzer Leader*. New York: Ballantine, 1957.

Gunkel, Otto. *Lebenserinnerungen 1943–1946: Reichsarbeitsdienst, Kriegsdienst, und Kriegsgefangenschaft*. Bad Sooden-Allendorf, Germany: Privately published, 1987.

————. Letter to *The Flash* (December 1986). (Journal of the 78th Infantry Division Veterans Association, Pittsburgh, Pa.).

————. "Tod und Vernichtung: Winterkrieg 1944/45" in *Monschauer Land* Monschau: Das Monschauer Land Jahrbuch, 1990.

Haslob, Gevert. *Ein Blick zuruck in die Eife–Schicksalweg der 89. Infanterie-Division*. Emmelshausen, Germany: Condor Verlag, 2000.

Hastings, Max. *Armageddon: The Battle for Germany, 1944–1945*. New York: Vintage/Random House, 2005.

Heichler, Lucian. *The Germans Opposite VII Corps in September 1944*. Washington, D.C.: US Army Chief of Military History, December 1952.

Hellbach, Peter. *Chronik der Pfarrei Hönningen* (Chronicles of the Hönningen Parish), (Hönningen, Germany).

Höhne, Heinz. *The Order of the Death's Head: The Story of Hitler's SS*. New York: Ballantine, 1971.

Höhne, Dr. Günther, *Der Feldverpflegungsbeamte*. Berlin, Verlag Bernhard und Graefe, 1939.

Hogg, Ian, Ed. *German Army Order of Battle, 1944*. London: Greenhill, 1994.

Hohenstein, Adolf, and Wolfgang Trees. *Die Hölle in Hürtgenwald*. Aachen: Triangel Verlag, 1981.

Hörner, Gerd. "Face to Face: Kesternich, Germany January 29–31, 1945." *The Flash*, 2003, no. 1 (January 2003) (Journal of the 78th Infantry Division Veterans Association, Pittsburgh, Pa.).

———— *Life and Death in the Hürtgen Forest with the German 272nd Volks-Grenadier Division*. Hannover, Germany: Unpublished personal manuscript.

Ireland, Millard. *Unofficial Combat History of the First Battalion, 28th Infantry Regiment, 8th Infantry Division*. Germany: 28th Infantry Regiment, 1945.

Jahr, Dr. Christoph. *Gewöhnliche Soldaten. Desertion und Deserteure im deutschen und britischen Heer 1914–1918."* Göttingen, Germany: Vandenhoeck & Ruprecht, 1998.

Janta, Leonhard. *Kreis Ahrweiler unter dem Hakenkreuz, II. Band: Studien zu Vergangenheit und Gegenwart*. Bad Neuenahr-Ahrweiler, Germany: Privately published, 1989.

Jenner, Martin. *"Der Rhein-Übergang der 272.I.D. im März 1945 aus der Sicht des verantwortlichen Generals und von der Truppe aus gesehen,"* in

Mitteilungsblatt der Niedersachsichen 216./272. Infanterie-Division, 5 (July 1967).

―――. *Die Niedersächsische 216./272.Infanterie-Division 1939–1945*. Bad Nauheim, Germany: Podzun-Pallas Verlag, 1964.

Jüttner, Arthur. *Retreat of the 62nd Volksgrenadier Division from the Ardennes and Defense of the Westwall, 27 December 1944 to 30 January 1945*. Morsbach, Germany: unpublished manuscript.

Kaeres, Kurt. *Das verstummte Hurra: Hürtgenwald 1944/45*. Aachen, Germany: Helios Publishing, 2002.

Keilig, Wolf. *Das Deutsche Heer 1939–1945*, Vols. 1–3. Bad Nauheim: Podzun Verlag, 1956.

Klein, Kurt, diary.

Landschaftsverband Rheinland. *Der Westwall: Vom Denkmalwert des Unerfreulichen*, vol. II. Cologne: Rheinland-Verlag, 1997.

Lauer, Walter. *Battle Babies: The Story of the 99th Infantry Division in World War II*. Nashville: Battery, 1985.

Lavender, Donald. *Nudge Blue: A Rifleman's Chronicle of World War II*. Bennington, Vt.: Merriam, 2001.

Lewis, Samuel. *Forgotten Legions: German Army Infantry Policy 1918–1941*. New York: Praeger, 1985.

Lockhart, Thomas P. Jr. *Diehard: History of the 309th Infantry Regiment*. Durham, NC: 78th Infantry Division Veterans Association, June 1990.

Mauldin, Bill. *Up Front*. New York: Henry Holt, 1945.

MacDonald, Charles B., *The Battle of the Hürtgen Forest*. New York: J.B. Lippincott, 1963.

―――. *Company Commander*. New York: Bantam, 1978.

―――. *The Last Offensive*. Washington, D.C.: US Army Office of the Chief of Military History, 1973.

―――. *The Siegfried Line Campaign*. Washington, D.C.: US Army Center of Military History, 1984.

―――. *Three Battles: Arnaville, Altuzzo, and Schmidt*. Washington, D.C.: US Army, 1993.

Mehner, Kurt. *Die Deutsche Wehrmacht 1939–1945: Führung und Truppe*. Norderstedt, Germany: Militair-Verlag Klaus Patzwall, 1993.

Miller, Edward G. *A Dark and Bloody Ground*. College Station: Texas A & M University Press, 1994.

Mittelman, Joseph B. *Eight Stars to Victory: A History of the Veteran Ninth US Infantry Division*. Columbus, Ohio: The Ninth Infantry Division Association, 1948.

Newton, Steven H. *Panzer Operations: The Eastern Front Memoir of General-oberst Erhard Raus*. Cambridge, Mass.: Da Capo, 2003.

Ostien, Georg. "In the Hürtgen Forest with 3rd Battery, Artillery Regiment 272." *The Flash*, 2001, no. 2 (April 2001).

Pallud, Jean Paul. *Battle of the Bulge, Then and Now*. London: Battle of Britain Prints International, 1984.

Parker, Danny. *Hitler's Ardennes Offensive: The German View of the Battle of the Bulge*. London: Greenhill, 1997.

Peukert, Günther. *"Der Einsatz in der Eifel im Winter 1944/45"* in *Alte Kameraden*, 3 (1995).

———. *"Von der Eifel in den Ruhrkessel"* in *Alte Kameraden*, 8 (1995).

Raus, Erhard, Translated by Newton, Steven H. *Panzer Operations: The Eastern Front Memoir of Generaloberst Erhard Raus*. Cambridge, Mass.: Da Capo, 2003.

Reichelt, Walter E. *Phantom Nine: The 9th Armored (Remagen) Division, 1942–1945*. (Austin, Tex.: Presidial Press, 1987.)

Rhineland Outdoors Association. *Der Westwall: Vom Denkmalwert des Unerfreulichen*, Vols. I and II, Cologne: Rheinland-Verlag GmbH, 1997.

Saft, Ulrich. *Krieg in der Heimat: bis zum bitteren Ende im Harz*. Walsrode, Germany: Militaerbuchverlag Saft, 1996.

Schmidt, Günther. *"Die 272.Volks-Grenadier Division in Eifeleinsatz, 1944/45"* (Unpublished manuscript, Hameln, Germany: 2 February 1996).

———. "The Counterattack at Bunker 111, 19 November 1944." *The Flash*, 2001, no. 4 (October 2001).

Schramm, Percy. *Kriegstagebuch des Oberkommandos der Wehrmacht*, vol. 4/7. Bernard und Gräfe Verlag, 1982.

Shils, Edward A., and Morris Janowitz. "Cohesion and Disintegration in the Wehrmacht in World War II." *Public Opinion Quarterly* (Summer 1948).

Short, Neil. *Germany's West Wall: The Siegfried Line*. Oxford, UK: Osprey, 2004.

Tessin, George. *Verbände und Truppen der deutschen Wehrmacht und Waffen-SS 1939-1945*, (Formations and troops of the German armed forces and Waffen-SS) vols. 1–17. Osnabrück, Germany: Biblio Verlag, 1979.

Traditionsverband der Niedersächsichen 216./272. Infanterie-Division. Mitteilungsblatt 4 (August 1964), 5 (July 1967), and 6 (April 1971).

Vierteljahrsheft fuer Zeitgeschichte (Quarterly Publication for Contemporary History), 1, no. 4 (1953).

Wegmann, Günter. *Die Dienstlaufbahnen der Offiziere des Generalstabes des deutschen Heeres 1935–1945*, Vols. I and II. Osnabrück, Germany: Biblio Verlag, 1995.

Wöstmann, Arnulf. *"Erinnerungen an Kesternich/Eifel Dezember 1944,"* edited version published in *OSS Hemet*, periodical of the Association of the Local History of Kesternich, Germany, 27 November 1992. The full, original version was provided to the author by Hans Wegener.

Zentner, Christian, and Wolfgang Fischer, Eds, *Soldaten im Einsatz: Tapferkeit und Pflichterfülung in Angriff und Verteidigung*. (Hamburg: Jahr Verlag, 1983).

US Operational Documents

12th Army Group, Assistant Chief of Staff, G-2. Weekly Intelligence Summaries 18 and 19 (Weeks ending 9 December and 16 December 1944, respectively).

1st Infantry Division, G-2 Reports, December 1944–May 1945.

4th Infantry Division, IPW Report of the daily G-2 Periodic Report, December 1944.

22nd Infantry Regiment, 4th Infantry Division, After Action Report, 1–31 December 1944.

22nd Infantry Regiment, 4th Infantry Division, Combat Journal, December 1944.

8th Infantry Division, After Action Report, 1–31 December 1944.

8th Infantry Division, Daily Assistant Chief of Staff G-2 Periodic Reports 1–31 December 1944.

8th Infantry Division. G-2 Daily Reports, 1–31 December 1944.

8th Infantry Division, IPW Reports, G-2 Periodic Report, 1–31 December 1944.

8th Infantry Division. G-3 Combat Journal, 1–31 December 1944.

13th Infantry Regiment, 8th Infantry Division, Report of Enemy Action, 1–31 December 1944.

28th Infantry Regiment, 8th Infantry Division, After Action Report 1–31 December 1944, entry dated 13 December 1944.

1st Battalion, 28th Infantry Regiment, 8th Infantry Division, Morning Reports, 12–16 December 1944.

2nd Battalion, 28th Infantry Regiment, 8th Infantry Division, Combat Journal, 1–18 December 1944.

78th Infantry Division, After Action Reports, December 1944–April 1945.

78th Infantry Division, Annex 2 to G-2, Periodic Report no.5, Consolidated Enemy Prisoner of War Report, 1–31 December 1944.

309th Infantry Regiment, 78th Infantry Division, After Action Report, 1–31 December 1944.

310th Infantry Regiment, 78th Infantry Division, After Action Report, 1–31 December 1944.

311th Infantry Regiment, 78th Infantry Division, After Action Reports, December 1944–May 1945.

311th Infantry Regiment, 78th Infantry Division, Morning Reports, December 1944.

99th Infantry Division, After Action Report, March 1945.

5th Armored Division, After Action Report, 1–31 December 1944.

102nd Cavalry Group (Mechanized), After Action Report, 1–31 December 1944.

102nd Cavalry Group (Mechanized), Annex No. 1 to 20 February 1945 Historical Report, Defense of the Monschau Sector by 38th Cavalry Reconnaissance Squadron.

BIBLIOGRAPHY   357

V Corps, Prisoner of War Interrogation Report, 8 February 1945, as copied in
the 82nd Airborne Division Annex No. 2 to the G-2 Situation Report
Summary no. 17, 8 February 1945, 309th Infantry Regiment, 78th Infantry
Division, After Action Report, 1–31 December 1944.

US Official Reports and Studies

Baker, William M. "Operations of the 78th Infantry Division 30 January to 4
February 1945." (Headquarters, 78th Infantry Division, July 1945).
Burner, John W. "Operations of the 2nd Battalion, 311th Infantry in the Attack
on Kesternich, Germany 30 January to 1 February 1945." Fort Benning,
Georgia: Advanced Infantry Officer's Class, The Infantry School, 1949.
Goldman, Jacob. Ninth Army Historical Officer, "Raids on the West Bank of
the Kall River: A Preliminary Operations to the Taking of the Roer River
Dams 8–17 January 1945." HQ, 78th Infantry Division, 22 January 1945.
The Quartermaster Food and Container Institute of the Armed Forces, German
Rations and Subsistence Items. Chicago, IL: The Quartermaster Food and
Container Institute, May 1947.
Roquemore, Frank U., Operations of the 2nd Ranger Battalion in the Huertgen
Forest, 6–8 December 1944 (Rhineland Campaign), Personal experience of a
platoon leader. Ft. Benning, Ga.: Advanced Infantry Officer Course,
1948–49.
US Army. "Fortress Battalions and How They Are Used." *Intelligence Bulletin*,
February 1945.
War Department, Military Intelligence Service, *The German Squad in Combat*
(translation of the German manual), Special Series No. 9, January 25 1943.

German Operational Documents

Feindnachrichtenblatt Nr. 2, 326th VGD, Abt. Ic, Nr. 757/44 geheim, Divisions-
Gefechtstand, 13 December 1944.
Generalkommando LXVII Armee-Korps. *Abt. 1a Nr. 89/44, Bereitstellung der
Infanterie-Verbände* (Assembly areas for the infantry formations), Korps
Gefechtstand, 12 December 1944.
Generalkommando LXVII Armee-Korps. *Abt. 1a Nr. 94/44, Nachstehender
Angriffsplan,* Korps Gefechtsstand, 13 December 1944.
Generalkommando LXVII Armee-Korps. *Korpsbefehl Nr. 1 für den Angriff bei-
derseits Monschau*, Corps Headquarters, 12 December 1944.

German Official Reports and Studies

Bundesarchiv-Militärarchiv (BA-MA) WF03-4694, *Kriegstagebuch OKW*, Para.
4, p. 12 (footnote).

BA-MA RW 4 von 636, *Meldung einsatzbereite Panzer bei OB West am 5 Februar 1945.*

BA-MA RH 10/106 *Übersicht der in Umgliederung und Auffrischung befindlichen Pz.Jg.Abt.*

Füsilier Battalion 272, Strength Report, 23 July 1944.

Füsilier Company 272, After Action Report, 13 December 1944.

Füsilier Company 272, Casualty Reports, 5 November 1944–28 March 1945.

Füsilier Company 272, Report to *272nd VGD* Graves Registration Officer, 5 January 1945.

Grenadier Regiment 981, Stellungsbesetzung am 13 Januar und 13 Februar 1945, Regimental Headquarters, *Grenadier Regiment 981.* Aachen: Bundesarchiv Zentralnachweisstelle Kornelimuenster.

Haslob, Gevert. Kriegsgeschichtliche Arbeitsgruppe Heeresamt–Abteilung I1, *Die Kämpfe im Hürtgenwald und Rur-Stausee.* (Cologne: Ministry of Defense, 18 February 1983).

Fifth Panzer Army. Directive on Tactics, 30 November 1944.

Heeres-Dienstvorschrift (H.Dv) Einsatz-Wehrmachtsverpflegungvorschrift 86/1: *Vorschrift für die Verpflegung der Wehrmacht in besonderem Einsatz.* (Berlin: Oberkommando des Heeres, 20 June 1940).

Heldt, Kurt. *Einsatz der Füsilier Company 272 am 4. und 5. Januar 1945.*

Jenner, Martin. *"Gefechtsbericht der III. Bataillon, Artillerie-Regiment 272."*

Kolb, Heinz. *Einsatz der Füsilier Company 272 am 13. und 14. Dezember 1944, Sturm-und Nahkampftage.*

Kriegstagebuch, 106th Panzer Brigade, 1–31 March 1945.

Kriegstagebuch, Füsilier Company 272, 28 December 1944–17 March 1945.

Leaders Pocket Guide, April 1944.

Oberbefehlshaber West, Message Number 9625/44 dated 26 October 1944, Subject: Transfer of *Volks-Grenadier* divisions to *Army Group B* for the defensive battle of *OB West.*

Oberbefehlshaber West Kriegstagebuch. *Meldungen und Befehle, Tagesmeldungen, 1 November to 31 December 1944 (US National Archives, Records of German Field Commands: Army Groups. Microfilm Publication T-311.*

Oberkommando des Heeres (OKH). *Hinweise für die Führung des Grenadier-Regiments einer Volks-Grenadier Division.* (Generalstab des Heeres, 1a Nr. 313844, 5 September 1944).

OKH/GenStdH/Org.Abt. Nr. I/19200/44 g.Kdos. v. 18.9.44 (NARA Microfilm Roll T78 R398, frame 6367895).

Schramm, Percy E. Ed. *Kriegstagebuch des Oberkommando der Wehrmacht 1944–1945, Teilband I.* Bonn: Bernard und Gräfe Verlag, 2002 edition.

Warrelmann, Hinrich. *Zuteilung von Eisernes Kreuz 1. und 2. Klasse für Verdienste zu Verleihungster in 30. Januar 1945 der Füsilier Kompanie 272.* Division Gefechtstand, *272. Volks-Grenadier Division,* 5 Januar 1945.

Wegner, Hans. After Action Report, *Füsilier Company 272,* 3–5 January 1945.

Manuscript Collections

The following papers are part of the US Army Europe Series, available in the Captured German Documents Section, National Archives, Washington, D.C.:

Bruns, Walter. *"Gefechtstätigkeit der 89.Infanterie-Division in der Zeit vom 1. Dezember 1944 bis 4. März 1945,* Project *22 (Ardennen Offensive)."* MS. P-032a, 1949.

Estor, Fritz. "Eleventh Army 1–23 April 1945." MS. B-581, 9 June 1947.

Gerber, Kurt. "Numerical Designations Allotted to the Divisions of the German Army." MS. B-632, 29 July 1947.

von Gersdorff, Rudolf. "The Battle of the Hürtgen Forest November to Early December 1944." MS. A-891, A-892, November 1945.

———. "Defense of the Siegfried Line." Ethint # 53, November 1945.

Hitzfeld, Otto. *"Ardennen-Offensive Dezember 1944 am rechten Flügel."* MS. A-937, February 1946.

———. "LXVII Corps," part 1: Battles in the Neighborhood of the Westwall (Subsequent to the Ardennes Offensive 26 January–6 March 1945)" MS. B-101, undated.

———. "LXVII Corps," part 2: "Battles in the Region of the Rhine 6 March–21 March 1945." MS. B-101, undated.

———. "LXVII Corps 22 March–19 April 1945." MS. B-309, undated.

Kaschner, Erwin. *"326th Volksgrenadier Division (Ardennen)."* MS. B-092, 1946.

König, Eugen. "Engagements in the Rhineland." MS. B-171, June 1948.

Müller-Hillebrand, Burkhart. "Personnel and Administration." MS. P-005, 30 August 1948.

Püchler, Karl, "The Rhineland—LXXIV Armeekorps—the Periods from 2 to 27 October 1944 and 16 December to 23 March 1945." MS. B-118, 28 July 1946.

———. "Battles of the LXXIV Armeekorps from 25 March to 16 April 1945 East of the Rhine and in the Ruhrpocket." MS. B-549, 12 May 1947.

Reinhardt, Hellmuth. "Voluntary Service in the German Army and in the Armies Allied with Germany in World War II." MS. P-063, 24 January 1951.

———. "The Volksgrenadier Division and the Volksturm," Part I. MS. P-065a, 22 September 1950.

———. "The Volksgrenadier Division and the Volksturm," Part II. MS. P-065b, 7 November 1950.

Straube, Erich. "LXXIV Corps from September to December 1944. MS. C-016, 4 November 1948.

Staudinger, Walter. "Artillery Leadership and Artillery Assignment during the Course of the Ardennes Offensive." MS. B-759, January 1948.

Sturm, Alfred. "Combat Sector Southeast Harz Mountains 12 April to 23 April 1945." MS. B-318, 1947.

Wagener, Carl. "Army Group B: Report of the Chief of Staff. Results of the Ardennes Offensive, 25 January–21 March 1945." MS. A-964, 4 February 1946.

von Zangen, Gustav. "Fifteenth Army: Defense of the Roer and Rhine 22 November 1944 to 9 March 1945, Volumes 1–7." MS. B-811, 812, 828, 829, and 848, 15 November 1947.

US Government Documents

Department of the Army. "The Volksgrenadiers: Germans Whittle Down Division Strength." *Tactical and Technical Trends,* 51 (October 1944).

Handbook on German Military Forces, U.S. War Department, TM-E 30-451, 15 March 1945.

Thomson, Harry C., and Lida Mayo, Center of Military History Pub. 10-10, "Ordnance Department: Procurement and Supply" Washington, D.C.: Historical Division, US Army, 1960.

US War Department, Military Intelligence Service, *The German Squad in Combat* (translation of the German manual), special series no. 9 (25 January 1943): 32.

US War Department, "Machine Carbine Promoted" from *Tactical and Technical Trends,* 57 (April 1945).

US War Department, "The New German Machine Gun—M.G. 42," *Technical and Tactical Trends,* 20 (11 March 1943).

Combat Interviews

Combat interviews were conducted by Army officers immediately after combat action. They are found in the US Army Military History Institute, Carlisle, Pa.

8th Infantry Division:
Task Force Boyer (Company B, 10th Tank Battalion; and Company B, 47th Armored Infantry Battalion), *Battle of the Hürtgen Forest*, Eupen, Belgium, 30 December 1944, conducted by Forrest C. Pogue and J. M. Topete.

9th Infantry Division:
39th Infantry Regiment, 9th Infantry Division, 18 February 1945, The Fight to the Roer, 9th Infantry Division 30 January to 10 February 1945, "Walherscheid, Dreiborn, Herhan and Morsbach," conducted by A. J. Webber, V Corps.

1st Battalion, 39th Infantry, 9th Infantry Division, The Fight to the Roer, 9th Infantry Division 30 January to 10 February 1945, "Wahlerscheid, Dreiborn,

Herhahn and Morsbach," 30 January to 10 February 1945, conducted by A. J. Webber, V Corps, 19 February 1945.

9th Armored Division:

From the Roer to the Rhine, CCA, 9th Armored Division, 28 February–8 March 1945, conducted by Robert E. Maxwell, III U.S. Corps 2nd Information and History Services, 12 March 1945.

78th Infantry Division:

The Battle of Hurtgen Forest (Action at Kesternich) 78th Infantry Division 13–16 December 1944, conducted by Robert E. Maxwell, 2nd Information and Services Section, III U.S. Corps.

Oral Interview with William E. Brubeck, S-3, 2nd Battalion, 310th Infantry, 78th Infantry Division, conducted at Korbach, Germany 18 May 1945 by Robert E. Maxwell, 2nd Information and Historical Services Unit.

Raids on the West Bank of the Kall River: A Preliminary Operation to the Taking of the Dams, 8–17 January 1945, 309th Infantry, 78th Infantry Division, conducted by Jacob Goldman, Ninth Army Historical Officer.

Remagen Bridgehead 8–20 March 1945, 78th Infantry Division, conducted by Fred L. Hadsel and George E. Moise, 2nd Information and Historical Service, VII Corps Team, 31 May 1945.

Story of the Attack on Schmidt and the Schwammenauel Dam 30 January–10 February 1945, conducted by Forrest J. Pogue, V Corps Historian. Includes combat interviews with: Floyd Call, Commander, 3rd Battalion, 309th Infantry; Frank C. Camm, 303rd Engineer Battalion; John Herzig, S-3, 1st Battalion, 310th Infantry; Charles A. Jenkins, S-2, 78th Infantry Division Artillery; I. W. Keyes, Commander, 2nd Battalion, 311th Infantry; Henry Lutz, Commander, 3rd Battalion, 310th Infantry; Robert L. McKinney, G-3, 78th Infantry Division; Peter J. Newton, Executive Officer, 3rd Battalion, 311th Infantry; John G. Ondrick, Commander, 310th Infantry; Robert H. Schellman, Commander, 1st Battalion, 309th Infantry; C. M. Willingham, Commander, 311th Infantry; Robert C. Wilson, G-2, 78th Infantry Division

99th Infantry Division:

394th Infantry Regiment, 99th Infantry Division; The Remagen Bridgehead and Breakthrough, 9–21 March and 25–28 March 1945, conducted by John S. Howe, III U.S. Corps Historical Section, 3 April 1945.

1st Battalion, 394th Infantry Regiment, 99th Infantry Division, The Battle for Hönningen, 15–17 March 1945, conducted by John S. Howe, III U.S. Corps Historical Section, 3 April 1945. Individuals interviewed Robert H.

Douglas, Battalion Commander; John S. Sandiland, Battalion Executive Officer; Willard W. Clark, Commander, Company B; and Victor Palumbo, Platoon Leader, 2nd Platoon, Company B, 786th Tank Battalion.

Thomas S. Bishop, Asst. G-3, 99th Infantry Division, 20 March 1945, The Remagen Bridgehead 7–21 March 1945, conducted by John S. Howe, III U.S. Corps Historical Section.

Walter Lauer, The Remagen Bridgehead 11–31 March 1945, 99th Division, 19 April 1945, conducted by Kenneth W. Hechler, III U.S. Corps Historical Section.

Howard B. St. Clair, G-2, 99th Infantry Division, 19 April 1945, Breakout at Remagen Bridgehead 23–26 March 1945, conducted by A. J. Webber, III U.S. Corps Historical Section.

US Veterans Interviews and Correspondence
Except as noted, all veterans below are members of the 78th Infantry Division.

Irving Berg, 2nd Battalion, 310th Infantry Regiment
Francis W. Berry, 3rd Battalion, 309th Infantry Regiment
Robert D. Burgess, 3rd Battalion, 311th Infantry Regiment
Frank Camm, 303rd Combat Engineer Battalion
Albert H. Clayton, 1st Battalion, 28th Infantry Regiment,
    8th Infantry Division
James L. Cooper, 3rd Battalion, 311th Infantry Regiment
Melvie Gilbert, 3rd Battalion, 311th Infantry Regiment
Hermann Gonzalez, 3rd Battalion, 311th Infantry Regiment
John W. Granath, 2nd Battalion, 311th Infantry Regiment
Robert L. Greivell, 1st Battalion, 311th Infantry Regiment
Gus E. Hank, 1st Battalion, 311th Infantry Regiment, 26 April 2001.
B. C. Henderson, 1st Battalion, 394th Infantry Regiment, 99th Infantry Division
W. Merle Hill, 1st Battalion, 311th Infantry Regiment
Walt Landry, 28th Infantry Regiment, 8th Infantry Division
Don Lavender, 39th Infantry Regiment, 9th Infantry Division
George F. Lockwood, 2nd Battalion, 311th Infantry Regiment
Edward Malouf, 1st Battalion, 311th Infantry Regiment, Dallas, Tex.,
    8 June 2001.
Robert A. McChord, 3rd Battalion, 311th Infantry Regiment, July 2001.
William Parsons, 1st Battalion, 311th Infantry Regiment
Stan Polny, 1st Battalion, 311th Infantry Regiment
John Robinson, 1st Battalion, 311th Infantry Regiment, 24 April 2001.
John K. Rains, 3rd Battalion, 311th Infantry Regiment
Merrill B. Westhoff, 2nd Battalion, 28th Infantry Regiment,
    8th Infantry Division

German Participant Interviews and Correspondence

Friedrich Adrario, *Antitank Battalion 272*, Vienna, Austria.

Helmut Aretz, *Füsilier Company 272*, Krefeld, Germany.

Erich Bernutz, *Füsilier Company 272*, Wernigerode, Germany. Interview 12 May 2001.

Helmut Beyer, *Füsilier Company 272,* Göttingen, Germany.

Erwin Buchwalder, *Füsilier Company 272,* Storkow, Germany.

Günter Ecker, *Füsilier Company 272,* Herschweiler, Germany. Interview 17 September 2000.

Friedrich Fosselmann, *Füsilier Company 272*, Berg, Germany. Interview 6 May 2001.

Adolf Fuhrmeister, brother of Hermann Fuhrmeister, *Füsilier Company 272,* Süpplingen, Germany.

Ernst Fuhrmeister, son of Hermann Fuhrmeister, *Füsilier Company 272*, Bremen, Germany.

Hubert Gees, *Füsilier Company 275, 275th Infantry Division,* Scharmede, Germany.

Hermann Gehle, *Grenadier Regiment 980*, Heilbronn, Germany. Interviews 6 January and 17 February 2001.

Erwin Gläsig, *Füsilier Company 272,* Berlin, Germany.

Otto Gunkel, *Grenadier Regiment 981.* Interview 28 December 2000 and correspondence.

Kurt Hake, *Grenadier Regiment 980*, Düsseldorf, Germany.

Haslob, Gevert, *89th Infantry Division.* Interview 14 December 2000, Vossenack, Germany.

Heiermann, Hermann, *Füsilier Company 272,* Dinslaken, Germany.

Hörner, Gerd, *Grenadier Regiment 980,* Wuppertal, Germany.

Horstkotte, Maria, widow of Heinrich Horstkotte, *Füsilier Company 272,* Kirchlengern, Germany.

Ips, Rudolf, *2nd Company, Anti-Tank Battalion 272*, Gifhorn, Germany.

Johns, Fritz, *Füsilier Company 272,* Stendahl, Germany.

Kaiser, Herbert, *Heavy Mortar Battalion 628,* Schwanebeck, Germany.

Klein, Else, widow of Kurt Klein, *Füsilier Company 272,* Solingen, Germany. Interview 2 January 2001.

Misskampf, Heinrich, *Füsilier Company 272,* Nauheim, Germany. Interview 2 June 2001.

Möckel, Erich, *Füsilier Company 272,* Mannichswalde, Germany.

Moog, Peter, *Füsilier Company 272,* Bonn, Germany. Interviews 19 February and 19 March 2001.

Ortloff, Erna, widow of Harald Ortloff, *Füsilier Company 272,* Rudolstadt, Germany.

Peukert, Günther, *Artillery Regiment 272*, Gera, Germany.

Post, Ferdinand, *Füsilier Company 272,* Hamm, Germany.

Reineke, Johann, *"Verteidigung in Kesternich, Herbst und Winter 1944 Auszug aus meinen Kriegsnotizen"* (letter to citizens of Kesternich). Bremerhaven, Germany, 11 August 1954.

Sandmann, Hans-Gerhard, son of Gerhard Sandmann, Germany.

Schmidt, Günther, *2nd Battalion, Grenadier Regiment 982,* Hameln, Germany.

Stefan, Josef, *Grenadier Regiment 980*, Baden, Austria.

Thiele, Irene, widow of Friedrich Thiele, *Füsilier Company 272,* Zeimendorf, Germany.

Thomae, Adolf, *Grenadier Regiment 980*, Münich, Germany.

Wegener, Hans, *Grenadier Regiment 980*, Hilden, Germany. Interview 14 December 2000, Vossenack, Germany.

Weiler, Jakob, *Tagebuch* (daily journal) (Unpublished manuscript); and interview.

Winkler, Anna, widow of Karl Winkler, *Füsilier Company 272,* Trippstadt, Germany.

Wilts, Wilfried, *Füsilier Company 272,* Emden, Germany.

Wolfram, Annegret, daughter of Walter Ableiter, *Füsilier Company 272,* Stuttgart, Germany.

Zacharuk, Eduard, *Füsilier Company 272,* Taufkirchen, Germany.

Online Sources

Axis history factbook: www.axishistory.com.

Island Farm prisoner of war camp 198/Special Camp XI, Bridgend, South Wales: www.islandfarm.fsnet.co.uk.

Feldgrau research forum on the German armed forces, 1918-1945: www.feldgrau.net/phpBB2/index.php.

German wool fabric and manufacturing of World War Two: www.lostbattalions.com/Resources/RayonArticle.html.

German World War Two bunkers and fortifications: www.7grad.org.

History of the 62nd Volks-Grenadier Division: http://62vgd.de.

Lexicon der Wehrmacht: www.lexikon-der-wehrmacht.de/ inhaltsverzeichnis1.htm.

Niehorster's World War II armed forces orders of battle and organizations: www.orbat.com/site/ww2/drleo.

Volksbund Deutsche Kriegsgräberfürsorge, e.V: www.volksbund.de/kontakt_links.

Wehrmacht awards: www.wehrmacht-awards.com/.

World War Two day by day: www.wwiidaybyday.com.

Index

About the Author

Douglas E. Nash, son of an Air Force senior master sergeant, grew up on a variety of different military bases across the United States. Interested in military history as long as he could remember, his enthusiasm for the service led him to volunteer for the US Army in June 1974, days after his high school graduation. After serving a tour of duty with the 1st Squadron, 2nd Armored Cavalry Regiment in Bindlach, Germany, he applied for and was accepted to the U.S. Military Academy Preparatory School in 1975. Graduating from the U.S. Military Academy with the Class of 1980, Doug then served as an Armor officer in various armor and cavalry units in the United States and Germany. As his interest in military history deepened, he was awarded a Master of Military Arts and Sciences from the

Author taken in front of the Remagen Bridge ruins. *(Klodt)*

Army's Command and General Staff College in 1995. After penning several articles about civil affairs in the Gulf War of 1990–91, where he served as a Civil Affairs officer, he then wrote articles for publication on *The Forgotten Soldier* by Guy Sajer, Eastern Front subjects, and several book reviews for *Military History,* the official publication of the U.S. Army's Center for Military History. His first book, *Hell's Gate: The Battle of the Cherkassy Pocket, January to February 1944* was published by RZM Publishing in 2002. Since his retirement from the Army in July 2006, he has continued to work in the military history field and lives with his family in northern Virginia.

Vossenack, April 2001. Here, from left to right, *Hauptmann* Volker Loessner of the *Bundeswehr,* the author, Klaus Schulz (veteran of the 353rd Infantry Division), Hans Wegener, and Raymond Fleig examine photographs taken during the battle.

Other Titles by The Aberjona Press

Victims, Victors: From Nazi Occupation to the Conquest of Germany as Seen by a Red Army Soldier
by Roman Kravchenko-Berezhnoy; foreword by David M. Glantz
  "A remarkable document, casting light on events little understood. It should be required reading for any student of World War II and modern Russian history."
  —Walter S. Dunn, *Journal of Military History*
310 pages. 6 Maps. 22 Photos.
Paperbound. ISBN 13: 978-0-9777563-2-2.
$19.95; plus $4.00 U.S. shipping

Sledgehammers: Strengths and Flaws of Tiger Tank Battalions in World War II
by Christopher Wilbeck
  "This detailed, yet readable study, enhanced by fascinating photographs and superb maps deserves to be on every tank warfare devotee's bookshelf."—*WWII History* magazine
272 pages. 35 Original Maps. 42 Photos.
Paperbound. ISBN 13: 978-0-9717650-2-3.
$19.95; plus $4.00 U.S. shipping

Slaughterhouse: The Handbook of the Eastern Front *David Glantz et al.*
  "A virtual treasure trove of information and lore for all those who can't get enough of the personalities, equipment, unit histories and orders of battle related to the war in which Hitler fought Stalin. . . . *Slaughterhouse* is a 'must have'."
  —*Armchair General* magazine
520 pages. 9 Maps. 88 Photos. Extensive 16-page bibliography. Paperbound. ISBN 13: 978-0-9717650-9-2.
$29.95 plus $4.50 U.S. shipping

Waffen-SS Encyclopedia:
by Marc J. Rikmenspoel
  "Few units arouse such intense interest as the Waffen-SS: love them or hate them, the Waffen-SS has had more books printed about them then probably any other unit. Unfortunately, some of them are more about the 'SS cult fetish' then tangible information. Thankfully, Marc Rikmenspoel has supplied us with a one-stop reference tool worth its spot on the bookshelf."— *Broadsword Military Magazine*
300 pages. 82 Photos. Extensive 20-page bilbiography.
Paperbound. ISBN 13: 978-0-9717650-8-5.
$19.95 plus $4.00 U.S. shipping

Odyssey of a Philippine Scout: Fighting, Escaping, and Evading the Japanese, 1941–1944
by Arthur Kendal Whitehead
304 pages. Maps. Photos.
Paperbound. ISBN 13: 978-0-9717650-4-7.
$19.95 plus $4.00 U.S. shipping

Black Edelweiss: A Memoir of Combat and Conscience by a Soldier of the Waffen-SS
by Johann Voss
  "A fascinating and unique contribution to our knowledge of the motivations of the men who comprised not only the Waffen-SS, but much of the rest of the German armed forces in the Second World War. . . . It is highly recommended."—*The Journal of Military History*
224 pages. Maps. Photos.
Paperbound. ISBN 13: 978-0-9666389-8-1.
$19.95 plus $4.00 U.S. shipping

Into the Mountains Dark: A WWII Odyssey from Harvard Crimson to Infantry Blue *by Frank Gurley*
  "Yet another Aberjona Press classic. . . . A profound coming of age story of a young man's transition to manhood. Emotionally charged, meticulously edited, and expertly packaged, *Into the Mountains Dark* is a wonderful WWII memoir."
  —*Military Heritage* magazine
256 pages. Maps. Photos.
Paperbound. ISBN 13: 978-0-9666389-4-3.
$14.95 plus $4.00 U.S. shipping

Five Years, Four Fronts: The War Years of Georg Grossjohann, Major, German Army (Retired)
by Georg Grossjohann
  "This is not an *All Quiet on the Western Front* or another *The Forgotten Soldier*. In my opinion, it is a better book."
  —*The Journal of Military History*
218 pages. Maps. Photos. Index.
Paperbound. ISBN 13: 978-0-9666389-3-6.
$14.95 plus $4.00 U.S. shipping